Order additional c

2003 AL

D1258910

SAVEUPTO50%

Celebrating Fifty Years in Publication

Complete, up-to-date information about your pay, benefits, retirement, and workplace policies!

No. of Copies	Price per Copy	Shipping/Handling	
1	$14.95	$3.95	
2-5	$14.20	$5.95	
6-20	$13.46	$9.95	
21-49	$12.71	$19.95	
50-99	$11.96	$39.95	
100-249	$10.47	$~~79.95~~	FREE
250-499	$8.97	$~~184.95~~	FREE
500+	$7.48 - SAVE 50%	$~~184.95~~	FREE

To order, call 1-800-989-3363 - visit www.FederalDaily.com or complete the order form on the reverse side of this card, send to: FEND, Inc., P.O. Box 8550, Reston, VA 20195-2450; FAX: 703-648-0265

2003 FEDERAL EMPLOYEES ALMANAC

ORDER FORM

send to: FEND, Inc., P.O. Box 8550, Reston, VA 20195-2450; or FAX: 703-648-0265

See reverse side of card for pricing

Please send me _____ copy(ies) of 2003 Almanac at $ _____ per copy $_____

I would like _____ copy(ies) of my order to be SPIRAL BOUND for $3.00 additional per copy $_____

I would like _____ copy(ies) of my order to include the Federal Employees Resource CD for
$6.00 additional per copy $_____

SHIPPING & HANDLING $_____
Please enter correct total shipping amount from grid on back of card

TOTAL $_____

SHIP TO

First Name	MI	Last Name

Agency/Organization | Bldg. No./Room No./Suite/Mail Stop

Address | City | State | Zip

PAYMENT INFORMATION

☐ Check Enclosed   Check # _____
(payable to Federal Employees News Digest)

☐ Purchase Order   P.O. # _____

☐ Charge to my Credit Card

eMail Address

☐ Visa ☐ Mastercard ☐ AMEX ☐ Discover

Name on Card

			–				–				–				–		

Credit Card Number

Expiration Date

Signature (Required)

Daytime Phone

PRIORITY: A00272

2003 FEDERAL EMPLOYEES ALMANAC

ORDER FORM

send to: FEND, Inc., P.O. Box 8550, Reston, VA 20195-2450; or FAX: 703-648-0265

See reverse side of card for pricing

Please send me _____ copy(ies) of 2003 Almanac at $ _____ per copy $_____

I would like _____ copy(ies) of my order to be **SPIRAL BOUND** for $3.00 additional per copy $_____

I would like _____ copy(ies) of my order to include the Federal Employees Resource CD for
$6.00 additional per copy $_____

SHIPPING & HANDLING $_____
Please enter correct total shipping amount from grid on back of card

SHIP TO

TOTAL $_____

First Name | MI | Last Name

Agency/Organization | Bldg. No./Room No./Suite/Mail Stop

Address | City | State | Zip

PAYMENT INFORMATION

☐ Check Enclosed   Check # _____   eMail Address _____
(payable to Federal Employees News Digest)

☐ Purchase Order   P.O. # _____   ☐ Visa   ☐ Mastercard   ☐ AMEX   ☐ Discover

☐ Charge to my Credit Card
Name on Card _____

Credit Card Number | Expiration Date

Signature (Required) | Daytime Phone | **PRIORITY: A00272**

Order additional copies of the

2003 ALMANAC

SAVE UPTO 50%

Complete, up-to-date information about your pay, benefits, retirement, and workplace policies!

Celebrating Fifty Years in Publication

No. of Copies	Price per Copy	Shipping/Handling	
1	$14.95	$3.95	
2-5	$14.20	$5.95	
6-20	$13.46	$9.95	
21-49	$12.71	$19.95	
50-99	$11.96	$39.95	
100-249	$10.47	$~~$79.95~~	FREE
250-499	$8.97	~~$184.95~~	FREE
500+	$7.48 - SAVE 50%	~~$184.95~~	FREE

To order, call 1-800-989-3363 - visit www.FederalDaily.com or complete the order form on the reverse side of this card,
send to: FEND, Inc., P.O. Box 8550, Reston, VA 20195-2450; FAX: 703-648-0265

ORDER NOW FOR 2004
2004 Federal Employees Almanac

SAVE UP TO 50%

when you order the **2004 Almanac** for everyone in your office!

No. of Copies	Price per Copy	Shipping/Handling	
1	$14.95	$3.95	
2-5	$14.20	$5.95	
6-20	$13.46	$9.95	
21-49	$12.71	$19.95	
50-99	$11.96	$39.95	
100-249	$10.47	~~$79.95~~	FREE
250-499	$8.97	~~$184.95~~	FREE
500+	$7.48 - SAVE 50%	~~$184.95~~	FREE

HURRY! These prices good through 8/31/03

Complete, up-to-date information about your pay, benefits, retirement, and workplace policies!

To order, call 1-800-989-3363 - visit www.FederalDaily.com or complete the order form on the reverse side of this card, send to: FEND, Inc., P.O. Box 8550, Reston, VA 20195-2450; FAX: 703-648-0265

2004 FEDERAL EMPLOYEES ALMANAC
ORDER FORM

send to: FEND, Inc., P.O. Box 8550, Reston, VA 20195-2450; or FAX: **703-648-0265**
See reverse side of card for pricing

Please send me _____ copy(ies) of 2004 Almanac at $ _____ per copy $_____

I would like _____ copy(ies) of my order to be SPIRAL BOUND for $3.00 additional per copy $_____

SHIPPING & HANDLING $_____
Please enter correct total shipping amount from grid on back of card

TOTAL $_____

SHIP TO

First Name	MI	Last Name

Agency/Organization	Bldg. No./Room No./Suite/Mail Stop

Address	City	State	Zip

PAYMENT INFORMATION

☐ Check Enclosed   Check # _____
  (payable to Federal Employees News Digest)

☐ Purchase Order   P.O. # _____

☐ Charge to my Credit Card

eMail Address _____

☐ Visa ☐ Mastercard ☐ AMEX ☐ Discover

Name on Card _____

Credit Card Number [ ][ ][ ][ ] - [ ][ ][ ][ ] - [ ][ ][ ][ ] - [ ][ ][ ][ ] - [ ][ ][ ][ ]   Expiration Date [ ][ ]

Signature (Required) _____

Daytime Phone _____

PRIORITY: A00280

2004 FEDERAL EMPLOYEES ALMANAC

ORDER FORM

send to: FEND, Inc., P.O. Box 8550, Reston, VA 20195-2450; or FAX: **703-648-0265**

See reverse side of card for pricing

Please send me _____ copy(ies) of 2004 Almanac at $ _____ per copy $_____

I would like _____ copy(ies) of my order to be SPIRAL BOUND for $3.00 additional per copy $_____

SHIPPING & HANDLING $_____

Please enter correct total shipping amount from grid on back of card

TOTAL $_____

SHIP TO

First Name   MI   Last Name

Agency/Organization   Bldg. No./Room No./Suite/Mail Stop

Address   City   State   Zip

PAYMENT INFORMATION

☐ Check Enclosed   Check # _____
(payable to Federal Employees News Digest)

☐ Purchase Order   P.O. # _____

☐ Charge to my Credit Card

eMail Address _____

☐ Visa   ☐ Mastercard   ☐ AMEX   ☐ Discover

Name on Card _____

Credit Card Number   Expiration Date

Signature (Required)   Daytime Phone   **PRIORITY: A00280**

ORDER NOW FOR 2004
2004 Federal Employees Almanac

SAVE UPTO 50%

when you order the **2004 Almanac** for everyone in your office!

No. of Copies	Price per Copy	Shipping/Handling
1	$14.95	$3.95
2-5	$14.20	$5.95
6-20	$13.46	$9.95
21-49	$12.71	$19.95
50-99	$11.96	$39.95
100-249	$10.47	~~$79.95~~ FREE
250-499	$8.97	~~$184.95~~ FREE
500+	$7.48 - SAVE 50%	~~$184.95~~ FREE

HURRY! These prices good through 8/31/03

Complete, up-to-date information about your pay, benefits, retirement, and workplace policies!

50th Annual Edition

Federal Employees Almanac 2003

Published annually by
FEDERAL EMPLOYEES NEWS DIGEST, INC.

1850 Centennial Park Drive • Suite 520 • Reston, VA 20191-1517
Phone: (703) 648-9551 • Fax: (703) 648-0265
E-mail: *info@FederalDaily.com* • Internet: *www.FederalDaily.com*

Publisher of:
Federal Employees News Digest
Federal Workers' Compensation Update
Federal Job Dispute Procedures
Federal Workers' Compensation Guide
Increase Your CSRS Retirement Income
Insuring Your Future
Understanding Survivor Benefits
Whistleblowing
Your Financial Guide
Your Retirement
Your Thrift Savings Plan
Divorce & Your Federal Benefits
A Guide to Long Term Care Benefits
Civil Service Handbook for Ex-Military Personnel

Cover Design: Brian Moore (www.Utilimedia.com)

Printed in U.S.A. • ISBN 0-910582-66-1

Preface

This year marks the golden anniversary of the *Federal Employees Almanac*. Over the past half-century we have published and sold more than six million almanacs to America's civil servants, helping them navigate an increasingly complex maze of federal protocols, regulations, and opportunities. The volume's success continues to demand consistent, reliable news reporting to help federal workers understand government regulations, recognize their rights and obligations, keep abreast of the major and minor changes affecting their jobs, and get all the benefits due them.

The *Federal Employees Almanac* has been a family business from the beginning, and is now published and managed by Linda Young Gsell, the daughter of founder Joe Young. In the early days, friends and family would process subscriptions and insert the newsletter or books into envelopes for mailing. While we don't stuff every envelope and box by hand, and while the volume and variety of our publications has grown, our mission remains the same as ever: to write "solid, fair, objective and pertinent news for federal employees, beholden to no special interest," in Joe's words.

Today at age 84, Joe Young continues to contribute articles and insights to both the annual *Almanac* and its weekly sister publication, *Federal Employees News Digest*, which the company has published without break for 52 years on paper and more recently online at *FederalDaily.com*.

In 1953, the federal government was growing rapidly in the aftermath of World War II and the Korean War, with the return of many heroic GIs to the federal workforce. As author of *The Washington Evening Star's* "Federal Spotlight"—a syndicated column for federal employees in the District of Columbia and throughout the country—Joe recognized that our nation's civil servants were not receiving important job-related news from their own personnel representatives, and were missing out on vital information affecting their careers and benefits. Heretofore, personnel regulations were contained in massive loose-leaf notebooks—loose-leaf to accommodate the frequent updates—that sometimes didn't even make it to federal field offices. The rules were complex, wordy, and rife with jargon, written (or so it seemed) so people could not understand them without a translator.

Joe and two partners decided to be that translator. They created the *News Digest* and two years later the *Almanac*, which was the first comprehensive reference book for federal employees. Rank and file workers, managers, personnel officers and federal contractors could keep the *Federal Employees Almanac* on their desks and use it to answer basic questions. It was also their ready road map to the many authorities they might need to consult for further elaboration in complex cases.

More recent editions have contained an increasingly detailed collection of pertinent tables and other information on pay, retirement, health and life insurance, estate planning, savings and investment plans, tax information and bargaining rights for unions and individuals. Over the years, we've also broadened and personalized our services, and now sponsor seminars on topics of interest to federal employees.

The first *Almanac* was lean at 62 pages, nearly half of which were pay tables for the General Schedule, Wage Board, Postal and Rural Carriers. The 2003 edition reflects not only routine changes to pay and benefits earned by federal workers, but also a plethora of regulations and major transformations affecting the United States and the federal workers who support it. This volume weighs in at about 400 pages.

Says Joe Young, "Our philosophy and intent in publishing the *Almanac* has been to give federal workers—in one clear and concise book—the information they need about their benefits and job rights, guidance on how to pursue their claims in cases of unjust firings, demotions, discrimination and other litigious matters. Changes occur every year due to legislation and executive orders, and we do our best to keep the *Almanac* up to date. When changes occur after we go to press, we share updates online. We strive every year to make our product better than the year before."

For each of the last 50 years, the *Almanac* has reduced the voluminous Federal Personnel Manual and other relevant data to concise, readable copy. It is the bestseller by far among books on this subject, thanks to loyal readers and a staff dedicated to accurate reporting and delivery of the finished product. It continues to be written by professionals and distributed by a conscientious staff. And we have an expanding list of specialized publications answering questions about retirement, financial planning, insurance and how government reorganization affects the individual.

The past half-century has seen periods of near paralysis and of rapid change.

Lately, quick change has been the order of the day for our country, for our government and for our federal workforce. The writers and publishers of *Federal Employees News Digest*, the *Federal Employees Almanac* and *FederalDaily.com* strive to keep you, our customers, up to date and fully informed on the events and actions that matter to you. We are grateful to you, our readers, for your continued patronage. We welcome your suggestions on how we can continue to serve you better, how we can remain the premier source of federal news for federal workers. We thank you for your business and will continue to do all we can to merit the trust the federal employee puts in us and in our products.

Our very best to you,

Linda Young Gsell, Publisher

Joe Young, Founder

Contents

Chapter 8—
Employment Procedures and Policies 233

Federal Workplace in 2002:
The Year in Review

During a year in which homeland security concerns topped the national agenda, civil service issues took on an unaccustomed prominence. That provided an education to the public in the workplace rules applying to federal employees and made federal employee unions and other organizations major players on the national policy stage.

The issue of federal employee pay became linked to homeland security as well, with supporters of higher salaries using the opportunity to point out that it is federal employees who for the most part actually provide homeland security and to argue that they should be better paid. Also, new attention was brought to the federal pay-setting process and proposals to reform it. The homeland security bill also became the vehicle for several previously proposed government-wide civil service reform proposals, notably including new buyout and early retirement authorities.

Federal benefits in general enjoyed a year of exemption from the kind of budgetary scrutiny they suffered so many times in the past, and several improvements occurred. The long-planned Federal Long-Term Care Insurance Program was launched, and the government announced that starting in 2003 it would allow employees to use tax-favored flexible spending accounts to fund certain out-of-pocket expenses for dependent care and medical and dental care.

However, premiums in the Federal Employees Health Benefits program continued their steady upward rise, and premium increases affecting many older Federal Employees Group Life Insurance enrollees were announced for 2003 and beyond. And employee and retiree groups once again failed to win passage of several high-priority benefit improvements relating to retirement benefits.

In the November elections Republicans maintained control of the House and gained control of the Senate, setting off a reshuffling of leadership on civil service issues for the 2003-2004 meeting of Congress. The changes were expected to give the administration a freer hand in pursing initiatives such as privatization and further civil service reforms.

Homeland Security Department

One of the most visible and most contentious of national issues in 2002 was the concept of creating a Department of Homeland Security out of some 22 agencies and sub-agencies employing some 170,000 employees, about a tenth of the executive branch work force. While there was relatively little disagreement over which agencies to include and the responsibilities the new agency would have, issues involving the employment rights of affected employees quickly moved to the forefront and stayed there.

The Bush administration proposed a "flexible and contemporary" personnel system for the new agency, although officials did not define exactly what such a system would look like. It was generally assumed, though, that the agency would have more freedoms in hiring, firing and other discipline, performance evaluation, compensation and labor relations—while there would be no changes in basic insurance or retirement benefits or in policies involving merit principles, discrimination law, whistleblower protection, veterans preference, overtime, and leave.

The House relatively quickly approved a bill essentially giving the administration what it wanted. But the measure bogged down in the Senate, where the version under consideration would not have granted those new powers. Especially at issue were the union rights of the new department's employees. The Senate split down the middle on the question of whether to restrict the President's ability to revoke union rights to situations where jobs were significantly changed and the new duties involved investigation of terrorism, as Democrats generally wanted, or to allow the President to revoke union rights where there would be a substantial adverse impact on the department's ability to protect homeland security, as Republicans generally wanted. The administration threatened to veto any bill that did not grant personnel flexibilities and that restricted the President's authority to revoke or prevent union rights.

After numerous attempts to find compromise language, the Senate shelved the measure until after the November elections when Congress returned for a lame duck session knowing that Republicans would be in charge of the chamber starting in January 2003. A compromise quickly was reached that generally adopted the Republican position, with the added requirement that any change in union rights be put off until Congress had been notified and 10 days had passed.

The law (P.L. 107-296) in general gave the department secretary, working with the Office of Personnel Management, the authority to create an alternative personnel system or systems for the agency by regulation, although requiring that employee representatives be consulted. In some situations, mediation may be invoked. The law also required leaving existing policies in place during a transition period potentially stretching well into 2003 or beyond.

Civil Service Reforms

Both the Bush administration and Sen. George Voinovich, R-Ohio, continued to push through 2002 for several basic reforms to federal hiring, training, incentive payment and other personnel management authorities. Voinovich succeeded in attaching parts of his proposal to the law creating a Homeland Security Department. Carrying out the provisions will, in most cases, require the issuance of regulations, meaning that many of the changes will not be effective until well into 2003 if not later.

One provision reforms the competitive service hiring authority to allow alternative ranking and selection procedures, including "category rating" systems in place of creating numerical rankings and using the traditional "rule of three," in which a hiring selection must be made from the top three candidates. An appointing official may select any applicant in the highest quality category or, if fewer than three candidates have been assigned to the highest category, in a merged category consisting of the highest and second highest quality categories. Within each quality category, those with veterans preference would be listed ahead of those without that preference.

Another provision creates a permanent government-wide authority to offer employees voluntary separation incentive payments (buyouts) of up to $25,000 pretax for workforce restructuring purposes. Agencies must submit to OPM a plan outlining the intended use of the payments. They may target payments on the basis of organizational units, occupational series, geographic location, skills, knowledge or other factors related to the position.

To be eligible, employees must be in a position selected under those criteria and must be serving under a permanent appointment and have been continuously employed for at least three years. Employees must not: be a reemployed annuitant; be someone who would qualify for disability retirement; have been notified they will be involuntarily separated for conduct or performance reasons; have previously received a buyout payment or be covered by statutory reemployment rights after a transfer; or have received a student loan repayment within the previous 36 months, a recruitment or relocation bonus within the previous 24 months or a retention bonus within the previous 12 months. Employees would have to repay the full pre-tax amount if returning to government employment within five years.

The measure also creates a government-wide voluntary early retirement authority for workforce restructuring. As with buyout offers, before making early-out offers agencies must submit to OPM a plan outlining the intended use of the payments and may target payments on the basis of organizational units, occupational series, geographic location, skills, knowledge or other factors related to the position. The agency must determine that a "significant percentage" of employees otherwise would be separated or subject to an immediate reduction in pay, that the targeted positions are surplus, or that the component is undergoing a substantial restructuring.

Employees must be in a position selected under those criteria and must be serving under a permanent appointment and have been continuously employed for at least 31

days. Employees must not have been notified they will be involuntarily separated for
conduct or performance reasons.

Other provisions of the measure included:

• Creating a Chief Human Capital
Officer in most agencies responsible for setting the workforce development strategy
and aligning the agency's personnel policies
to the organization's strategic goals.

• Repealing the recertification requirements for Senior Executive Service members and raising the limit on their total
annual compensation to the rate of Level I
of the Executive Schedule, so that any
bonuses may be fully received at once
rather than spread over several years
because of pay cap considerations.

• Allowing agencies to pay for academic degree training so long as it is part of an
employee development program linked to
accomplishing the agency's strategic goals
and it "contributes significantly" to meeting
an agency training need, resolving a staffing
problem or accomplishing goals in the
agency's strategic plan. The degree must be
provided by an accredited college or university.

Pay

For executive branch employees, 2002
was another year of haggling over the size
of the pay gap with private industry and
what should be done about it, despite a
1990 law that mandated that the gap
should be virtually closed by now. The Bush
administration signaled its intentions early
in the year by recommending a 2.6 percent
January 2003 raise for federal employees
but 4.1 percent for active duty military personnel.

However, employee organizations and
their allies in Congress fought to maintain
the parity between civilian and military raises that has applied for most of the last two
decades. They succeeded in having a 4.1
percent raise for federal workers written
into both House and Senate versions of a
key appropriations bill but the Senate never
took up that bill as it hit budgetary gridlock
late in the year.

Instead, a series of stopgap funding measures that did not specify a raise amount was
enacted beginning with the October 1, 2002
start of fiscal year 2003. By underlying pay

law, that translated into a 3.1 percent
January 2003 raise, a figure that President
Bush endorsed in a late 2002 policy statement. However, civil service leaders intended to try again early in calendar year 2003 to
gain permanent enactment of the 4.1 percent amount, retroactive to the start of the
year. (Visit *www.FederalDaily.com* for an
update on the outcome of this effort.)

Another notable development occurred
when the Office of Personnel Management
issued a "white paper" on federal pay that
essentially described the current arrangement as hopelessly broken. Employee
organizations and individual employees
generally were quick to agree, but the question of what to do about the situation
remained unanswered. OPM suggested the
government rely more heavily on pay for
performance and market-based pay that
could rise—or fall—with overall demand
for skills. Employee organizations suggested
that the main problem is that over the
years, various administrations and
Congresses simply have failed to appropriate sufficient funds to pay employees at
competitive rates and that without more
money, any structural changes would do little good.

OPM said it hoped to begin a "dia-
logue" on pay-setting, but recognized that
would be a long-term process. And that dia-
logue was slow in starting since most of the
attention of the parties who otherwise
would be engaged in it spent the latter half
of the year in the Homeland Security
Department debate.

Retirement

For federal retirees, 2002 was a year
focusing mainly on what didn't happen
rather than on what did happen. Unlike in
some past years, there were no proposals to
alter the basic retirement formula or to limit
cost-of-living adjustments. However, the
January 2003 COLA, 1.4 percent, was the
smallest in four years, due to the sluggish
economy and resulting low inflation that
prevailed in most of the measuring period.

As in past years, retirees focused much
of their attention on certain provisions of
Social Security law and the tax code, and as
in the past they once again failed to con-
vince Congress to act. The tax code provision of primary interest is the one prevent-

ing federal retirees—along with other retirees—from participating in "premium conversion" arrangements in which those actively employed can pay health care premiums with pre-tax money. While a majority of House members lined up in support of a proposal to allow federal retirees to get that tax break, the bill never progressed, largely because of concern by the administration and congressional budget leaders that private sector retirees then would ask for the same break, at an unacceptable cost in lost tax revenues.

The Social Security provisions are the windfall elimination provision and the government pension offset, which primarily affect those retired under the Civil Service Retirement System. The former reduces an earned Social Security benefit for those with fewer than 30 years of "substantial" employment under that system, while the latter reduces and often eliminates Social Security spousal or survivor benefits received by anyone also drawing a benefit from a retirement system that doesn't include Social Security, such as CSRS.

Proposals in the House to soften the effect of those two provisions gathered majorities as co-sponsors, but like the premium conversion bill, never came to a vote. While financial considerations were part of the reason, the larger issue was that Congress was reluctant to touch the Social Security program in an election year. Discouraged by that failure but heartened by the high levels of support in Congress, proponents of the measures vowed to try again in 2003.

Insurance

On the insurance front, Federal Employees Health Benefits program premiums increased for the 2003 plan year at an average 11.1 percent rate, the fifth straight year that premium hikes neared or topped the double-digit range. As in past years, officials said increasing medical costs, particularly for hospitalization and prescription drugs, and the aging FEHB population were primarily to blame. They also noted that the FEHB increases were below the increases being experienced by other levels of government and by the private sector, although that was little comfort to enrollees.

The FEHB program did stabilize somewhat from previous years. Only 11 plans dropped out and only another four eliminated service areas, in contrast to the previous four years that saw a combined 168 dropouts and 37 coverage area restrictions involving some 300,000 enrollees. Officials also found it notable that four plans chose to join the program in 2003 and that several others expanded their coverage areas.

However, the persistent and significant increases in premium rates led to widespread dissatisfaction among enrollees and some members of Congress. Proposals to increase the government share of the premiums and restructure the program made no progress, however, leaving the best hopes for holding down future premiums in the hands of the carriers, who were encouraged to explore alternative premium and benefit structures.

Meanwhile, certain premiums in the Federal Employees Group Life Insurance program changed, the first revision of FEGLI premiums since 1999. The changes, effective on January 1, 2003, resulted from changing mortality and usage patterns. Rates for FEGLI Basic coverage fell slightly, as did premiums for Option B for those below age 65. However, new age bands were added to the upper levels of both Option B and Option C, resulting in significant increases in premiums for older enrollees carrying those options.

Further, the increases in Option B rates in those age categories are expected to go up again in 2004 and again in 2005.

Flexible Spending Accounts

Offsetting the increases in FEHB costs somewhat was a new program announced in late 2002 to take effect in 2003, the creation of flexible spending accounts for all executive branch employees. Such accounts previously were available only in the U.S. Postal Service, the judiciary branch and in some executive branch regulatory agencies.

The Office of Personnel Management conducted a competition lasting through late 2002 and into early 2003 for a company to administer the program, in which employees will be able to set aside through payroll withholding up to $5,000 a year for dependent care accounts and up to a separate limit—probably $3,000, but the figure remained under negotiation—for certain medical and dental expenses. The dependent care accounts are to be available for both child and elder care, while the medical and dental accounts will help pay for out of pocket costs under FEHB, as well as some medical and dental services and other expenses not covered by FEHB.

OPM prepared to make the accounts available as of July 1, 2003, with an open season starting in May for employees to make their elections for the second half of the calendar year. In calendar year 2004 and beyond, the accounts will run for full calendar years, with election periods running concurrent with the FEHB open season each preceding autumn.

As with the premium conversion arrangement for paying FEHB premiums, however, retirees were deemed ineligible to participate in FSAs.

Long-Term Care

After several years of congressional debate and more than another year of administrative work, the government in 2002 launched the Federal Long Term Care Insurance Program, the most significant new federal employee benefit since creation of the Thrift Savings Plan in the late 1980s. A partnership created by the Metropolitan Life and John Hancock insurance companies was selected as the provider, an early enrollment period was conducted in March to May and a formal open season ran for the last six months of the calendar year.

Given the newness of the benefit and the potential cost under certain circumstances, the government recognized that acceptance of the FLTCIP program would be a long-run effort. While the large majority of those eligible for the coverage passed it up during the 2002 enrollment periods, officials were stressing to eligible employees and retirees that enrollment is allowed at any time. The only difference is that after the open season, employees and their spouses are no longer eligible for "abbreviated" underwriting, which requires them to answer only limited questions about their health. Instead, they are subject to the same "full" underwriting applying to retirees and all others eligible under the program.

OPM also announced that there would

be future open seasons, although making clear that they would not occur on a regular basis. It also remained unclear whether abbreviated underwriting would again apply to active employees and their spouses in future open seasons.

Thrift Savings Plan

A set of long-awaited changes which didn't cross the finish line in 2002 involved the Thrift Savings Plan, which has been working for several years to upgrade its computer system and launch new account management features and new loan and withdrawal policies. After first announcing the changes would be effective in September, 2002, the TSP announced they would occur instead in November. Just before that date it announced that the new system still wasn't ready and that there was no target date for implementing it.

The most eagerly anticipated change is a switch from monthly valuation of accounts to daily valuation. Under the traditional system, processing for loans and withdrawals is delayed until the end of each month, as are interfund transfers. Under daily valuation, account balances will be tabulated daily and expressed in shares and share prices as well as in dollar amounts. Other important changes linked to the new system include extending the period for general purpose loans to five years, allowing partial prepayment of loans and allowing partial withdrawals and combination withdrawals after separation.

Despite those delays—the latest in a long string of them—the TSP did revise its open season schedule to make those twice-yearly election periods begin and end a month earlier than previously. That took effect with the second open season of 2002.

One other change occurring late in the year was congressional passage of a measure allowing TSP investors age 50 and older to make "catch-up" contributions like those allowed for participants in other employer-sponsored retirement savings plans. The measure, P.L. 107-304, allowed extra contributions of up to $2,000 in 2003, with the amount increasing by $1,000 each year until hitting $5,000 in 2006.

Other Issues

Telecommuting—The government continued in 2002 to encourage agencies to create more opportunities for their employees to telecommute, including offering financial incentives for agencies to use regional telecommuting centers. However, fewer than five percent of employees currently telecommute even part-time, and several studies revealed numerous roadblocks to wider acceptance of the program. Many of those related to line of control issues that discourage managers from allowing their employees to telecommute.

Special Rate Settlement—After bouncing through the federal courts for two decades, a suit for back pay for certain special rate employees reached a settlement in 2002. The settlement affects employees who were in the special rate program between 1982 and 1988 who had their raises improperly capped under a policy in effect at that time. Even with a settlement, though, mechanical issues relating to contacting affected individuals—and in some cases, their survivors—and setting up a settlement fund continued to delay final payouts into late 2003 and possibly beyond. Those payouts could range from several thousand dollars to tens of thousands of dollars in certain situations.

Contracting-Out—Early in 2002 a special panel that had been tasked with coming up with a consensus plan to improve the government's procedures for studying federal jobs for possible conversion to contract produced a report, but no consensus. Union members of the panel objected to recommendations that they said would tilt the process in favor of contractors at the cost of in-house employees. Late in the year the Bush administration proposed a series of reforms that in some cases would allow a switch to a "value" approach—in which dollar figures would not make the absolute determination. The proposed revisions also sought to speed up and streamline the decision-making process, seeking to reach a decision in 12 months. Unions opposed that proposal as well, contending that such changes would leave the program more vulnerable to waste and fraud.

Other Key Legislation

The Notification and Federal Employee Antidiscrimination and Retaliation Act (the "No Fear" Act, P.L. 107-174) required the amount of any claim, final judgment, award, or compromise settlement paid to any current or former federal employee or applicant in connection with specified anti-discrimination and whistleblower protection complaints to be reimbursed to the Treasury. It also: set requirements for the written notification of federal employees and applicants of their rights and remedies under anti-discrimination and whistleblower protection laws; required agencies to release annual reports on the number of such cases arising within them; and required each agency to post on its public website statistical data relating to equal employment opportunity complaints.

The DoD authorization bill for fiscal 2003, P.L. 107-314, made non-appropriated fund employees eligible for the Federal Long Term Care Insurance Program; extended through fiscal 2006 DoD's authority to pay involuntarily separated employees' accumulated annual leave as a lump-sum instead of biweekly and to continue temporarily paying the agency share of the Federal Employees Health Benefits Program on their behalf; opened certain security guard positions to performance by the private sector; extended a provision excluding certain expenses from the requirement that at least half of depot maintenance work be kept in-house; and required new reporting to Congress on the outcome of any DoD contracting-out cost comparison studies.

Chapter 1
Pay

Section 1—Main Federal Pay Schedules and Systems

General Schedule

The general schedule is the federal government's main pay system that sets the pay rates for employees in most "white-collar" positions. The GS pay system covers approximately half of the federal workforce. Basically, the general schedule is composed of 15 grades, or salary levels. Each grade includes ten steps through which employees advance based on satisfactory job performance and length of service. For all GS grades, the waiting periods to be advanced to each higher step (i.e., qualifying for a "within-grade increase") are as follows: 52 calendar weeks to be advanced to steps 2, 3, and 4; 104 calendar weeks to be advanced to steps 5, 6, and 7; and 156 calendar weeks to be advanced to steps 8, 9, and 10.

Position classification standards, developed by the Office of Personnel Management, are the legal basis for determining the series and grade—and consequently the pay—for the vast majority of GS positions. In most cases, a GS employee's base pay reflects the pay rate specified for the position's grade and step in the locality where the worker is employed. Disputes over the classification of a GS position that cannot be resolved within the agency can be referred to the Office of Personnel Management by either the employee or the agency. OPM is responsible for making the final decision on such an appeal, and its decision is final. There is no further right of appeal.

Supervisors of other GS employees ordinarily are classified at least one grade higher than those employees. However, this does not necessarily mean that supervisors will be paid more than each of their subordinates. The salaries of GS employees are fixed by law.

Federal Wage System

In contrast to the GS pay rates, the pay of the federal government's wage-system employees (blue-collar) is set as an hourly rate by a lead agency in accordance with the procedures established under 5 U.S.C. 5343. The law requires that hourly rates for wage system employees be adjusted from time to time consistent with the public interest in accordance with prevailing rates. The most common wage system schedule—i.e., the wage grade schedule used for most non-supervisory workers—contains 15 grades. Each of the grades includes five steps, which are set at four percent increments.

The FWS includes the full range of non-supervisory trade, craft, and laboring jobs in more than 250 occupational series. Occupations often cover more than one grade level, and many occupations typically are represented at each grade. Differences in rates of pay among wage areas reflect the fact that the prevailing cost of labor varies widely by region across the United States. It is not unusual for FWS employees who work in different wage areas to receive sometimes substantially different rates of pay even though they may have similar grade levels and job duties.

The wage system's prevailing rate determinations are made on the basis of surveys of rates paid by private employers in each local wage area for work similar to that performed by federal wage employees. Wage schedule adjustments have been capped each year since fiscal year 1979 through legislation in the budget process. In recent years, wage employees have received pay adjustments based on surveys of the prevailing rates of private sector blue collar employees in their wage area; however, because of the pay cap, these adjustments cannot exceed the average pay increase (including both base GS and average locality pay adjustments). Because wage system employees are not covered by the annual GS across-the-board pay base schedule adjustment, which is based on the BLS Employment Cost Index, the local wage survey process is critical in determining the pay for wage system workers. Wage schedules are adjusted at different times of the year according to when the local lead agency conducts the annual wage survey in each individual wage area.

U.S. Postal Service

As an independent executive branch establishment, the Postal Service operates its own pay system that has two general types of salary structures, as well as a specialized structure for rural letter carriers. The two general pay structures are: the PS (Postal Service) salary structure, which covers bargaining unit personnel, such as most clerks and carriers, mail handlers, nurses, and security personnel; and EAS (Executive and Administrative Salary) structure, which covers executives, professionals, supervisors, postmasters, technical and administrative employees, and other workers not covered by bargaining agreements. (For more information on postal service pay and policies, see the Postal Service chapter.)

Executive Schedule

The Executive Schedule governs the pay of Cabinet officers and other top federal executives. The Executive Schedule includes five levels (Level I through Level V). Several of these Executive Schedule levels are used to cap or limit pay levels of employees covered by other federal pay systems, such as the congressional and judicial salary systems. Various Executive Schedule rates also are used to establish the salary limits for general schedule employees, Senior Executive Service and employees in "Senior Level" and "Scientific or Professional" jobs, as well as administrative law judges and other federal employees in highly paid positions or occupations.

Senior Executive Service

Members of the Senior Executive Service are paid under an ES salary system that contains six pay levels: ES-1 through ES-6. The minimum SES rate (ES-1) may not be less than 120 percent of the minimum rate for GS-15, while base salaries at the highest SES level (ES-6) are limited to the pay rate established for Executive Level IV. (The pay cap for SES base pay plus locality adjustments is set at the Executive Level III rate.)

Other High-Level Systems

Administrative Law Judges—ALJs are impartial hearing officers who hear cases brought by parties whose affairs are controlled or regulated by agencies of the federal government. They operate under a merit selection system designed to protect the judge's decisional independence from undue agency influence.

Applicants must be attorneys and must have a minimum of seven years administrative law and/or trial experience involving formal administrative hearing proceedings before local, state, or federal administrative agencies, courts, or other administrative bodies. In addition, applicants must demonstrate that they have had two years of qualifying experience at a level of difficulty and responsibility characteristic of at least senior level GS-13, or one year characteristic of at least GS-14 or GS-15 federal government attorneys actively involved in administrative law and/or litigation work.

Public Law 101-509 established the ALJ pay system for former GS-15, 16, 17, and 18 ALJ positions established under Section 3105 of Title 5, United States Code. The minimum rate for ALJ positions is set at 65 percent of level IV of the Executive Schedule and the maximum rate is set at 100 percent of level IV of the Executive Schedule.

Administrative Appeals Judges—Public Law 106-554 created a new pay system for administrative appeals judges, effective in April 2001. The duties of an AAJ primarily involve reviewing decisions of administrative law judges and rendering final administrative decisions. The heads of executive agencies may fix the rates of basic pay for AAJ positions at a rate not less than the minimum rate of basic pay for level AL-3 and not more than the maximum rate of basic pay for level AL-3 of the ALJ pay system.

Senior Level/Senior Scientific and Technical Positions—These categories cover many positions classified above GS-15 that are not eligible for the Senior Executive Service due to the lack of supervisory requirements. Qualifications for the positions are determined by individual agencies and hiring generally is without competitive examination, although such examinations can be used in senior level positions. Salaries are set according to national minimum and maximum rates determined annually.

Special Salary Rates

Special salary rates may apply to federal workers employed in certain positions that the government considers difficult to fill. Special salary rates for general schedule positions have been authorized since 1954. The statutory authority for special salary rates (higher minimum rates and rate ranges) is found in 5 U.S.C. 5305. Executive Order 12748 delegates to OPM the President's authority to establish special salary rates.

Special salary rates may be authorized whenever OPM finds that the government's recruitment or retention efforts are or are likely to be adversely affected by a variety of factors, including significantly higher rates of pay offered by non-federal employers, the remoteness of the job's area or location, undesirable working conditions or duties (including exposure to toxic substances or other occupational hazards), or other circumstance that OPM considers appropriate. Once established, each special rate is reviewed at least annually and adjustments made as warranted by existing labor market conditions and agency staffing needs.

Each year, OPM and agencies employing special-rate employees conduct a review to determine the amount by which special rates will be adjusted at the time of a general increase in general schedule rates. To increase special rates by an amount equal to the general schedule raise, agencies must review the staffing situation and certify that the increased rates are needed to ensure adequate staffing. Agencies must also certify that funds are available and supply a limited amount of work force data. Agencies must submit extensive documentation of recruitment and retention problems if requesting a higher raise.

As of October 4, 2002, there were 402 special rate authorities covering 143,724 employees.

The minimum rate of a special rate range may exceed the maximum rate of the corresponding grade by as much as 30 percent. However, no special rate may exceed the rate for Executive Level V. A special rate request must be submitted to OPM by department headquarters and must be coordinated with other federal agencies with employees in the same occupational group and geographic area.

The special rate authority allows a lead agency, with the approval of OPM, to establish rates above the regular federal wage system wage schedule rates for an occupation or group of occupations experiencing or potentially experiencing recruitment or retention difficulties. Special rates are established by occupation, grade, agency, and/or geographic location. These rates will be paid by all agencies having positions for which the rates are authorized. The special rate payable may not, at any time, be less than the unrestricted rate otherwise payable for such positions under the applicable regular pay schedule.

Special rate employees get the higher of their special rate or the GS locality pay rate. If their special rate exceeds their locality rate, any locality rate adjustment will have no effect on their pay. Within grade increases are permitted for employees in these categories.

Other Pay Systems

In addition to the pay schedules or systems described above, the federal government operates numerous other pay systems. Separate pay systems, for example, are used to set salary levels for law enforcement personnel, foreign service employees, many medical personnel of the Department of Veterans Affairs, and employees of "nonappropriated fund instrumentalities," which typically are self-funding Defense Department facilities such as post exchanges or commissaries.

Also, many agencies are operating under alternative pay structures that involve pay banding and other non-standard practices (see Chapter 8) and agencies have various special pay-setting authorities available to them, some at their own discretion and some upon approval from the Office of Management and Budget and/or the Office of Personnel Management (see Section 5 of this chapter).

Section 2—General Pay Computation Procedures

Generally, most federal employees work schedules consisting of an eight-hour day, five-day, 40-hour workweek. Hourly rates of pay for general schedule employees (which are used, for example, for overtime-calculation purposes) are computed by dividing a worker's annual rate of pay by 2,087 and rounding up to the nearest cent, if one-half cent or more. To compute an employee's bi-weekly pay, the hourly rate must be multiplied by 80. If computing compensation for fractional pay periods (i.e., partially paid periods resulting from separations, retirements, use of leave without pay, etc.), the amount of pay is determined by multiplying the employee's hourly rate by the number of hours or fractions of hours.

The standard federal workday is eight hours, and the law provides overtime for work in excess of eight hours in a day, or in excess of 40 hours in the workweek. There

Maximum GS Pay Limitations

	Limit	Reference
General Schedule (excluding any locality or other geographic payment)	Level V of the Executive Schedule	5 U.S.C. 5303(f)
Special salary rates (5 U.S.C. 5305)	Minimum rate may not exceed 30% of maximum rate for grade, and maximum rate may not exceed level V of the Executive Schedule	5 U.S.C. 5305(a) and 5 CFR 530.303(a)
General Schedule, plus locality-based comparability payment	Level IV of the Executive Schedule	5 U.S.C. 5304(g)(1) and 5 CFR 531.604(b)
General Schedule, plus special pay adjustment for law enforcement officers (LEOs)	Level IV of the Executive Schedule	Section 404(c)(1) of FEPCA, 5 U.S.C. 5304(g)(1), and 5 CFR 531.302(b)
Biweekly limitation on premium pay (see note 1)	Greater of biweekly rate for Level IV or the Executive Schedule, or for GS-15, step 10	5 U.S.C. 5547(a) and 5 CFR 550.105
Aggregate limitation on pay (see note 2)	Level I of the Executive Schedule	5 U.S.C. 5307 and 5 CFR 530.203

NOTES

1. Cap does not apply in any pay period during which an employee receives premium pay for work in connection with an emergency or work deemed critical to the mission or the agency. In such cases, the aggregate of basic and premium pay for the calendar year is capped at the greater of the annual rate for GS-15 step 10 or Level IV of the Executive Schedule.

2. An employee may not receive any portion of any allowance, differential, bonus, award, or other similar payment under title 5, United States Code, in any calendar year, which when combined with the employee's basic pay would cause the employee's aggregate compensation (including premium pay) to exceed the rate for level I of the Executive Schedule at the end of the calendar year. See 5 CFR 530.202 for definitions of "basic pay" and "aggregate compensation."

also are provisions for a pay differential of 25 percent for Sunday work that falls within an employee's regularly scheduled basic workweek, and for holiday pay (100 percent of the employee's rate of basic pay) for work performed on a holiday that falls within the employee's basic workweek. Employees under the general schedule are entitled to ten percent for night work for any regularly scheduled work that falls between 6:00 p.m. and 6:00 a.m. (For details on overtime, Sunday, holiday or other premium pay, see OPM regulations found in Parts 550 and 551 of Title 5, Code of Federal Regulations.)

> Note: Special rules apply to most firefighters and to employees who receive annual premium pay for regularly scheduled standby hours.

Pay Caps

Section 1114 of Public Law 107-107 modified the biweekly and annual limitations on premium pay under 5 U.S.C. 5547, removed the separate premium pay limitation for law enforcement officers, and provided agencies with authority to waive the biweekly premium pay limitation for employees performing work critical to the mission of the agency. The revised premium pay limitations became effective on the first day of the first pay period beginning on or after April 27, 2002.

An amendment to 5 U.S.C. 5547(a) provided that an employee, including a law enforcement officer, may receive premium pay in a pay period only to the extent that the aggregate of basic pay and premium pay for the pay period does not exceed the greater of the biweekly rate for (1) GS-15, step 10 (including any applicable special salary rate or locality rate of pay), or (2) level V of the Executive Schedule. (See 5 U.S.C. 5547(a), as amended, and 5 CFR 550.105.)

An amendment to 5 U.S.C. 5547(b) provided that the biweekly premium pay cap in section 5547(a) does not apply in any pay period during which an employee, including a law enforcement officer, receives premium pay for work in connection with an emergency (including a wildfire emergency) that involves a direct threat to life or property. The amendment clarified that work in connection with an emergency includes work performed in the aftermath of the emergency. Such employees may receive premium pay only to the extent that the aggregate of basic pay and premium pay for the calendar year does not exceed the greater of the annual rate for (1) GS-15, step 10 (including any applicable special salary rate or locality rate of pay), or (2) level V of the Executive Schedule.

Another amendment to 5 U.S.C. 5547(b) provided the head of an agency with discretionary authority to waive the biweekly premium pay limitation in § 5547(a) for an employee, including a law enforcement officer, who receives premium pay to perform work critical to the mission of the agency. Such employees may receive premium pay only to the extent that the aggregate of basic pay and premium pay for the calendar year does not exceed the greater of the annual rate for (1) GS-15, step 10 (including any applicable special salary rate or locality rate of pay), or (2) level V of the Executive Schedule.

Section 3—Annual Pay Adjustments

The Federal Wage Grade System: Background

The federal wage grade system (FWS) was developed to make the pay of federal blue-collar workers comparable to prevailing private sector rates for similar positions in each local wage area. Before 1965, there was no central authority to establish wage equity for federal trade, craft, and laboring employees. Then the President ordered the Civil Service Commission (now OPM) to work with federal agencies and labor organizations to estab-

lish common job-grading standards and wage policies and practices that would ensure interagency equity in wage rates. The ultimate goal was to assure that wages would be set according to local prevailing rates, equal pay for equal work, and pay distinctions in keeping with work distinctions.

In 1972, the FWS was established in law. It created the Federal Prevailing Rate Advisory Committee (FPRAC), which is made up of agency and labor union members and has an independent chairman. FPRAC studies all matters pertaining to prevailing rate determinations and advises the director of OPM on appropriate pay policies for FWS employees.

The regular FWS pay plan for prevailing rate employees covers most trade, craft, and laboring employees in the executive branch. It does not cover Postal Service employees, or employees of private sector contracting firms.

Special pay plans cover certain employees in special circumstances. OPM authorizes special pay plans when unusual labor market conditions seriously handicap agencies in recruiting and retaining qualified employees.

WG Locality Pay Procedures

The FWS is a partnership worked out between OPM, other federal agencies, and labor organizations. OPM prescribes basic policies and procedures to ensure uniform pay setting. OPM specifies procedures for agencies to design and conduct wage surveys, to construct wage schedules, to grade levels of work, and to administer basic and premium pay for employees.

To issue common job-grading standards for major occupations, OPM occupational specialists follow specific steps to develop new standards and to update existing standards. They make full occupational studies, which include onsite visits to interview employees, supervisors, and union representatives. Specialists write standards and ask agencies and unions for comments that are carefully considered and, where appropriate, incorporated into final job-grading standards. Federal agencies are required to apply these standards.

OPM defines the geographic boundaries of individual local wage areas—there are about 130 of them, with the number varying somewhat over time—and reviews survey job descriptions to ensure that they are accurate and current. In addition, OPM works with agencies and unions to schedule annual local wage surveys in each wage area.

Each FWS wage area consists of a survey area and an area of application. A survey area includes the counties, townships, and cities where the lead agency in the wage area collects and analyzes private sector wage data to produce a wage schedule for the wage area. An area of application includes the survey area and nearby counties, townships, and cities where the wage schedule also applies.

Wage grade raises are paid at differing times of a fiscal year, varying by locality. Wage adjustments become effective in accordance with what is commonly referred to as the 45-day law. This law states that the government has 45 working days to put FWS pay adjustments into effect after each wage survey starts. Each wage schedule has a uniform effective date for all employees in a wage area, regardless of the agency. Normally, the effective date is based on the pay period cycle for the largest employer in the wage area, with the effective date set on the first day of the first pay period following the 45-day wage survey period.

For each wage area, OPM identifies a "lead" agency—in almost all cases, the Department of Defense—that employs the majority of wage grade employees in the area. The "lead" agency is responsible for conducting wage surveys, analyzing data, and issuing wage schedules under the policies and procedures prescribed by OPM. All agencies in a wage area pay their hourly wage employees according to the wage schedules developed by the lead agency. OPM does not conduct local wage surveys.

Labor organizations also play a role in the wage determination process by providing representatives at all levels of the wage determination process. The employee unions having the greatest number of wage employees under exclusive recognition designate two of the five members of a lead agency's national level wage committee. Locally, the union with the most employees under exclusive recognition in a wage area designates one of the three members of each Local Wage Survey Committee. In addition, labor organizations nominate half of the federal employees who collect wage data from private enterprise employers. A team of one labor data collector and one management data collector visits each surveyed employer.

Under the FWS, pay is based on what private industry is paying for comparable levels of work in a local wage area. Employees are paid the full prevailing rate at step 2 of each grade level. Step 5, the highest step in the FWS, is 12 percent above the prevailing rate of pay.

However, legislation may limit or delay annual wage adjustments for some FWS employees. This has been the practice in recent years, in which wage grade raises have been capped at the average general schedule amount for the fiscal year.

Wage grade pay schedules are posted online at http://www.opm.gov/oca. Click on "Salary Tables."

Monroney Amendment—Section 1113 of Public Law 107-107 reinstated a pay provision for the Department of Defense's (DoD's) blue-collar workforce commonly known as the Monroney Amendment.

The provision may cause rates of pay for FWS employees to increase when the government has large numbers of employees in specialized industries, such as aircraft maintenance, but there are insufficient private sector employees involved locally in similar work. The Monroney Amendment requires the importation of out-of-area wage data for local wage surveys in such situations.

The change did not affect prevailing rate employees of non-DoD agencies because the Monroney Amendment continued to apply to them after 1985. The National Defense Authorization Act for Fiscal Year 1986 had required the use of local survey data only for DoD schedules. Thus, in 1985-2001, DoD and non-DoD employees in some wage areas had separate wage schedules.

In FWS wage areas where the Monroney Amendment applies:

• DoD agencies implemented the change in policy on the normal effective date of the first wage schedule adjustment in each FWS wage area occurring or after December 28, 2001. Retroactive pay adjustments applied to DoD employees in wage areas with normal effective dates between December 28, 2001, and the date their agency implemented the change in policy.

• A new single schedule superseded the pre-existing two schedules on the normal effective date of the first wage schedule adjustment in each FWS wage area occurring on or after December 28, 2001. DoD agencies moved their FWS employees from their previous wage schedule to the single new wage schedule for the wage area on a grade-for-grade and step-for-step basis.

Occasionally, prevailing rate wage schedules decrease when average private sector pay rates decrease in a wage area. If the rate of pay for a DoD employee's grade and step would be lower on the single new wage schedule, and the employee was otherwise eligible for pay retention, the employee retained the rate of pay he or she held prior to the normal effective date of the new wage schedule. If an employee's retained rate in this circumstance placed the employee between two steps on the new wage schedule, the employee was placed at the higher of the two steps and pay retention ceased to apply.

GS Annual Increases: Origin and History

The federal government's base pay procedure generally calls for most employees to receive a salary or wages consisting of compensation that is specified for their position by a pay schedule for their grade, plus a locality pay adjustment. For general schedule employees, the law dictates that their annual pay adjustment consists of two parts: (1) a national, across-the-board increase; and (2) a locality-based pay adjustment.

For GS employees, the annual across-the-board increase normally is paid in January of each year (along with the locality pay adjustment). The amount of this increase is based on the annual percentage change in the Employment Cost Index, less 0.5 percent. (The ECI is a statistical measure maintained by the Bureau of Labor Statistics that measures changes in private-sector labor costs.)

Locality pay for general schedule employees was first authorized for federal workers in Federal Employees Pay Comparability Act of 1990 (Section 529 of P.L. 101-509). The locality pay increases (along with the across-the-board pay hikes) were designed to address a gap between federal and non-federal salaries that White House and congressional leaders felt was imposing a hardship on employees and leaving the government unable to compete well in the labor market. The law's goal was to bring federal pay to within virtual comparability with the private sector—within 5 percent—over nine years by using the ECI-based raises to keep federal employees generally apace with private sector wage growth while the locality component closed the officially reported pay gap.

The law put off the start of locality pay until 1994 to give time to create a locality pay system, which was a major departure from the government's traditional approach of paying the same salaries for the same work everywhere. Officials involved in setting up the new system worked for more than two years on many issues, including the designation of locality pay areas and the means of calculating local pay gaps.

Initial implementation of locality pay called for locality zones to be set up within the contiguous 48 states. These locality zones generally consisted of the government's standard metropolitan statistical areas, plus a catchall "rest of the United States" (RUS) locality. In the first year, 1994, there were 27 metropolitan zones plus RUS. For 1995, four new zones were added—Portland-Salem, Ore.-Wash., Miami-Ft. Lauderdale, Richmond-Petersburg, and Columbus, Ohio. However, in 1995 five areas that had individualized raises in 1994 were dropped because their indicated raises fell at least two-tenths of a percentage point below the figure indicated for RUS, a cutoff that the system's creators had recommended. These were Memphis, Norfolk, Oklahoma City, Salt Lake City, and San Antonio. Three new areas were added in 1997—Pittsburgh, Milwaukee and Minneapolis—and two additional areas were added in 1998—Hartford, Conn., and Orlando, Fla. In addition, the boundaries of some localities have changed somewhat over time.

However, due to funding restrictions and disagreements regarding the data used to compare federal versus private sector pay, locality pay adjustments have not reached the levels indicated by the pay law's formula. In practice, the annual federal raise has been negotiated between Congress and the White House, with part of the total raise being designated as across-the-board pay and the remainder as locality pay. The result has been that although there is variation in pay by locality, the officially reported "pay gap" has not been narrowed nearly to the extent envisioned by the law.

GS Locality Pay Procedures

The locality pay determination procedure starts with ongoing studies designed to calculate the pay gaps in each of the designated pay areas, plus the RUS locality, on which the raises are based. These surveys are done by the Bureau of Labor Statistics of more than 100 occupational levels for pay comparability between federal and non-federal employment.

Each year the Federal Salary Council, a group made up of labor union representatives and compensation experts, submits recommendations on local pay gaps to the President's Pay Agent, which consists of the Secretary of Labor, Director of the Office of Management and Budget, and the Director of the Office of Personnel Management. The Pay Agent decides the pay areas and reports on pay gaps to the President, recommending raises. The President then formally announces the raises.

Locality pay is considered basic pay for purposes of retirement, life insurance, premium pay, advances in pay and severance pay. It is not considered basic pay for other pay purposes. However, it is also used in computing lump-sum annual leave payments and workers compensation benefits.

Eligibility for locality pay is based on where an employee works, not on where the worker lives. Locality pay entitlement does not transfer with an employee who moves from one pay zone to another. Relocating employees will receive the rate of pay applying in their new workstations. Employees on details to a different pay area will continue receiving their current salaries while on such assignments. The key is the employee's official duty station of record—the employee receives the salary paid there.

Employees who receive special pay rates that exceed what they would get under the locality pay formula continue to receive the full amount of their special adjustments. They will not get extra pay due to locality increases until the locality pay in their areas exceeds any special rates they already are receiving.

Special rate employees are eligible for within-grade raises, raises related to a promotion, and similar types of increases. Depending on an agency's staffing needs, they may be granted the across-the-board annual pay raises approved for general schedule employees.

Locality pay applies only to general schedule employees in the contiguous 48 states. It does not apply overseas, nor in Alaska or Hawaii; federal employees in those locations already receive geographic pay adjustments based on cost-of-living measurements.

The pay law allows, but does not require, the President to extend locality pay to certain categories of employees not in the general schedule. These include senior level and senior executive service positions, administrative law judges, contract appeals board members, and executive branch positions where the rate of basic pay is capped at (i.e., limited to) the pay rate authorized for level IV of the Executive Schedule.

The President may not extend the locality payments to positions under the executive schedule, employees paid under the federal wage system, overseas employees, or certain other workers designated as "critical."

General schedule pay tables are posted online at http://www.opm.gov/oca. Click on "Salary Tables."

GS Locality Pay Boundaries

The boundaries for the general schedule locality pay system generally follow the lines of metropolitan statistical areas and consolidated metropolitan statistical areas. (These are standard government measures used for many purposes.) In some cases, areas that lie just outside such locality pay areas are included for fairness to the large numbers of federal employees working there.

The locality pay areas have been chosen because of their concentration of federal employees—most have at least 10,000 federal workers—not because of the size or overall population of a particular city. Thus, some large cities fall in the RUS locality, while some smaller cities that contain or are near large federal installations have locality pay rates specifically attached to them. About 60 percent of general schedule employees are within one of the metropolitan zones, with the remainder receiving the raise paid in the RUS locality.

Following are the boundaries for the locality pay areas:

Atlanta: Counties of Barrow, Bartow, Carroll, Cherokee, Clayton, Cobb, Coweta, DeKalb, Douglas, Fayette, Forsyth, Fulton, Gwinnett, Henry, Newton, Paulding, Pickens, Rockdale, Spalding, and Walton

Boston-Worcester-Lawrence: In Massachusetts, counties of Bristol, Essex, Middlesex, Suffolk

In Hampden County, Holland town

In Norfolk County, towns of Avon, Bellingham, Braintree, Brookline, Canton, Cohasset, Dedham, Dover, Foxborough, Franklin, Holbrook, Medfield, Medway, Millis, Milton, Needham, Norfolk, Norwood, Plainville, Quincy (city), Randolph, Sharon, Stoughton, Walpole, Wellesley, Weymouth, and Wrentham

In Plymouth County, towns of Abington, Bridgewater, Brockton, Carver, Duxbury, East Bridgewater, Halifax, Hanover, Hanson, Highham, Hull, Kingston, Lakeville, Marion, Marshfield, Mattapoisett, Middleborough, Norwell, Pembroke, Plymouth, Plympton, Rochester, Rockland, Scituate, Wareham, West Bridgewater, and Whitman

In Worcester County, towns of Ashburnham, Auburn, Barre, Berlin, Blackstone, Bolton, Boylston, Brookfield, Charlton, Clinton, Douglas, Dudley, East Brookfield, Fitchburg (city), Gardner (city), Grafton, Harvard, Holden, Hopedale, Lancaster, Leicester, Leominster (city), Lunenburg, Mendon, Milford, Millbury, Millville, Northborough, Northbridge, North Brookfield, Oakham, Oxford, Paxton, Princeton, Rutland, Shrewsbury, Southborough, Southbridge, Spencer, Sterling, Sturbridge, Sutton, Templeton, Upton, Uxbridge, Webster, Westborough, West Boylston, West Brookfield, Westminster, Winchendon, and Worcester (city)

In Hillsborough County New Hampshire, towns of Amherst, Bedford, Brookline, Goffstown, Greenville, Hollis, Hudson, Litchfield, Manchester (city), Mason, Merrimack, Milford, Mont Vernon, Nashua (city), New Ipswich, Pelham, Weare, and Wilton

In Merrimack County, towns of Allentown, and Hooksett

In Rockingham County, towns of Atkinson, Auburn, Brentwood, Candia, Chester, Danville, Derry, East Kingston, Epping, Exeter, Fremont, Hampstead, Hampton, Hampton Falls, Kensington, Kingston, Londonberry, New Castle, Newfields, Newington, New Market, Newton, North Hampton, Plaistow, Portsmouth (city), Raymond, Rye, Salem,

Sandown, Seabrook, Stratham, and Windham, townships of Greenland and Southhampton.

In Strafford County, towns of Barrington, Dover (city), Durham, Farmington, Lee, Madbury, Milton, Rochester, Rollingsford, and Somersworth (city)

The state of Rhode Island

In **Maine**, part of York County and towns of Berwick, Eliot, Kittery, South Berwick, and York

In **Connecticut**, part of Windham County and Thompson town

Chicago-Gary-Kenosha: In Illinois, counties of Cook, DeKalb, DuPage, Grundy, Kane, Kankakee, Kendall, Lake, McHenry, and Will

In **Indiana**, Lake and Porter Counties

In **Wisconsin**, Kenosha County

Cincinnati-Hamilton: In Ohio, counties of Brown, Butler, Clermont, Hamilton, and Warren

In **Kentucky**, counties of Boone, Campbell, Gallatin, Grant, Kenton, and Pendleton

In **Indiana**, Dearborn and Ohio Counties

Cleveland-Akron: Counties of Ashtabula, Cuyahoga, Geauga, Lake, Lorain, Medina, Portage, and Summit

Columbus: Counties of Delaware, Fairfield, Franklin, Licking, Madison and Pickaway.

Dallas-Fort Worth: Counties of Collin, Dallas, Denton, Ellis, Henderson, Hood, Hunt, Kaufman, Johnson, Parker, Rockwall, and Tarrant

Dayton-Springfield: Counties of Clark, Greene, Miami, and Montgomery

Denver-Boulder-Greeley: Counties of Adams, Arapahoe, Boulder, Denver, Douglas, Jefferson, and Weld

Detroit-Ann Arbor-Flint: Counties of Genesee, Lapeer, Lenawee, Livingston, Macomb, Monroe, Oakland, St. Clair, Washtenaw, and Wayne

Hartford: In Hartford County, towns and cities of Avon, Berlin, Bloomfield, Bristol, Burlington, Canton, East Granby, East Hartford, East Windsor, Enfield, Farmington, Glastonbury, Granby, Hartford, Manchester, Marlborough, New Britain, Newington, Plainville, Rocky Hill, Simsbury, Southington, South Windsor, Suffield, West Hartford, Wethersfield, Windsor, and Windsor Locks

In Litchfield County, towns of Barkhamsted, Harwinton, New Hartford, Plymouth, and Winchester

In Middlesex County, towns of Cromwell, Durham, East Haddam, East Hampton, Haddam, Middlefield, Middletown, and Portland

County of New London

In Tolland County, towns of Andover, Bolton, Columbia, Coventry, Ellington, Hebron, Mansfield, Somers, Strafford, Tolland, Vernon, and Willington

In Windham County, towns of Ashford, Chaplin, and Windham

Houston-Galveston-Brazoria: Counties of Brazoria, Chambers, Fort Bend, Galveston, Harris, Liberty, Montgomery, and Waller

Huntsville: Counties of Limestone and Madison

Indianapolis: Counties of Boone, Hamilton, Hancock, Hendricks, Johnson, Madison, Marion, Morgan, and Shelby

Kansas City: In Missouri, counties of Cass, Clay, Clinton, Jackson, Lafayette, Platte, and Ray

In Kansas, counties of Johnson, Leavenworth, Miami, and Wyandotte

Los Angeles-Riverside-Orange County: Counties of Los Angeles, Orange, Riverside, San Bernadino, Santa Barbara, and Ventura. Also includes the portion of Edwards Air Force Base not located within the Los Angeles-Riverside-Orange County CMSA

Miami-Ft. Lauderdale: Broward and Dade counties

Milwaukee: Cities of Milwaukee and Waukesha. Counties of Milwaukee, Ozaukee, Racine, Washington and Waukesha

Minneapolis-St. Paul: Counties of Anoka, Carver, Chisago, Dakota, Hennepin, Isanti, Ramsey, Scott, Sherburne, Washington, Pierce and Wright

In Wisconsin, St. Croix County

New York-Northern New Jersey-Long Island: In New York, counties of Bronx, Dutchess, Kings, Nassau, New York, Orange, Putnam, Queens, Richmond, Rockland, Suffolk, and Westchester

In **New Jersey**, counties of Bergen, Essex, Hudson, Hunterdon, Mercer, Middlesex, Monmouth, Morris, Ocean, Passaic, Somerset, Sussex, Union, and Warren

In **Connecticut** all of Fairfield and New Haven Counties

In Litchfield County, towns of Baylordsville, Bethlehem, Bridgewater,

Locality Raises

Pay Area	1997 Raise	1998 Raise	1999 Raise	2000 Raise	2001 Raise	2002 Raise
Atlanta	0.50	0.51	0.48	0.96	0.95	1.03
Boston	0.28	0.61	0.67	1.33	1.31	1.33
Chicago	0.48	1.02	0.73	1.43	1.39	1.45
Cincinnati	0.85	0.92	0.57	1.16	1.16	1.24
Cleveland	0.82	0.81	0.55	1.10	1.06	1.10
Columbus, Ohio	0.75	0.27	0.54	1.05	1.00	1.03
Dallas–Fort Worth	0.16	0.48	0.55	1.08	1.06	1.12
Dayton	-0.06	0.51	0.47	0.93	0.93	0.97
Denver	0.66	1.34	0.67	1.31	1.26	1.33
Detroit	0.84	1.15	0.73	1.42	1.38	1.44
Hartford	0.67	1.22	0.88	1.32	1.29	1.34
Houston	1.98	0.40	0.88	1.72	1.67	1.73
Huntsville	0.33	0.64	0.46	0.89	0.86	0.92
Indianapolis	0.44	0.14	0.44	0.89	0.86	0.92
Kansas City	0.71	0.93	0.44	0.89	0.86	0.92
Los Angeles	1.24	0.79	0.78	1.51	1.47	1.52
Miami[1]	0.77	1.07	0.62	1.23	1.21	1.27
Milwaukee[2]	1.42	0.59	0.53	1.06	1.03	1.08
Minneapolis[2]	2.36	0.76	0.58	1.14	1.12	1.18
New York	1.04	0.57	0.74	1.45	1.40	1.47
Orlando[2]	0.67	0.60	0.44	0.90	0.88	0.92
Philadelphia	0.36	0.37	0.60	1.20	1.17	1.22
Pittsburgh[1]	0.92	1.11	0.46	0.90	0.89	0.94
Portland, Ore.	0.90	1.00	0.61	1.21	1.19	1.24
Richmond, Va.	0.84	0.83	0.48	0.96	0.95	1.02
Sacramento	0.73	1.04	0.60	1.18	1.15	1.18
St. Louis	0.45	0.52	0.45	0.89	0.88	0.94
San Diego	0.30	0.83	0.65	1.29	1.25	1.29
San Francisco	1.59	1.29	0.92	1.79	1.76	1.82
Seattle	0.17	0.69	0.60	1.19	1.18	1.24
Washington, D.C.	1.03	0.15	0.58	1.14	1.11	1.17
Rest of U.S.	0.67	0.60	0.44	0.89	0.87	0.92

2003 locality increases were not available at press time, but are posted online at *www.Federal Daily.com*.

To calculate the average actual increase awarded federal employees each year, national raises (see the "General Schedule Pay Raises Since 1956" table) must be added to the pertinent locality amounts listed here.

[1] New locality in 1997. Part of RUS previously.

[2] New locality in 1998. Part of RUS previously.

Marble Dale, New Milford, New Reston, Oakville, Roxbury, Thomaston, Washington, Washington Depot, Watertown, and Woodbury

In Middlesex County, towns of Clinton and Killingworth

In **Pennsylvania**, Pike County

Orlando: Counties of Lake, Orange, Osceola, and Seminole

Philadelphia-Wilmington-Atlantic City: In Pennsylvania, Bucks, Chester, Delaware, Montgomery, and Philadelphia

In **New Jersey**, counties of Atlantic, Burlington, Camden, Cape May, Cumberland, Gloucester, and Salem

In **Delaware**, New Castle County

In **Maryland**, Cecil County

Pittsburgh: City of Pittsburgh. Counties of Allegheny, Beaver, Butler, Fayette, Washington, and Westmoreland

Portland-Salem: In Oregon, counties of Clackamas, Columbia, Multnomah, Washington, Yamhill, Marion, and Polk

In **Washington**, Clark County

Richmond-Petersburg: Counties of Charles City, Chesterfield, Dinwiddie, Goochland, Hanover, Henrico, New Kent, Powhatan and Prince George, cities of Colonial Heights, Hopewell, Petersburg, and Richmond

Sacramento-Yolo: Counties of El Dorado, Placer, Sacramento, and Yolo

St. Louis: In Missouri, Sullivan City, plus the counties of Franklin, Jefferson, Lincoln, St. Charles, St. Louis, Warren, and St. Louis city

In **Illinois**, the counties of Clinton, Jersey, Madison, Monroe, and St. Clair

San Diego: San Diego County

San Francisco-Oakland-San Jose: Counties of Alameda, Contra Costa, Marin, Monterey, Napa, San Francisco, San Mateo, Santa Clara, Santa Cruz, Solano, and Sonoma

Seattle-Tacoma-Bremerton: Counties of Island, King, Kitsap, Pierce, Snohomish, and Thurston

Washington-Baltimore: District of Columbia

In **Maryland**, the counties of Anne Arundel, Baltimore, Calvert, Carroll, Charles, Frederick, Harford, Howard, Montgomery, Queen Anne's, Prince George's, St. Mary's, and Washington and Baltimore city.

In **Virginia**, the counties of Arlington, Clarke, Culpeper, Fairfax, Fauquier, King George, Loudon, Prince William, Spotsylvania, Stafford, Warren and the cities of Alexandria, Fairfax, Falls Church, Fredericksburg, Manassas, and Manassas Park

In **West Virginia**, the counties of Berkeley and Jefferson

Rest of U.S. (RUS): The RUS locality rate is authorized for those portions of the contiguous 48 states not located within another locality pay area.

Section 4—Other Pay Increases or Actions

Within-Grade Increases

Within-grade increases are pay increases received by federal employees after they have served a specified amount of time at a certain grade level and demonstrated at least an acceptable level of performance. Within-grade increases, which also are known as "step increases," are provided for by chapter 53 of Title 5 of the U.S. Code. The Office of Personnel Management issues regulations to carry out the within-grade increase provisions.

Generally, employees who are not at the highest step of their grade are entitled to receive the within-grade raise authorized for the next step of their position as long as they: complete the required waiting period, have received at least a "fully successful" (or equivalent) rating for their most recent performance appraisal period, and did not receive an equivalent increase during the waiting period. (For a definition of "equivalent increase," see 5 CFR 531.403 and 531.407)

Waiting periods for within-grade increases for all general schedule grades are as follows:

• 52 calendar weeks to be advanced to steps 2, 3, and 4;

• 104 calendar weeks to be advanced to steps 5, 6, and 7; and

• 156 calendar weeks to be advanced to steps 8, 9, and 10.

Quality step increases are one-step increases to base pay as a form of performance recognition. See Incentive Payments and Awards, below.

Pay Upon Promotion

General Schedule—An agency that promotes an employee from one general schedule (GS) grade to another grade must set the employee's pay at a rate of the higher grade that will pay at least the equivalent of a two-step increase in the grade from which the worker was promoted.

Example: Former grade and salary, $32,135 a year; new grade and salary, $34,507 a year. The step increase is $893, so the employee must be given an increase of not less than $1,786 (two-step increments). The salary rate must equal or exceed $33,921 ($32,135 plus $1,786). When the two-step increase falls between step rates of the higher grade ($33,521 and $34,507), the higher of the two rates—$34,507—is selected.

Wage System—An agency that promotes an employee from one federal wage system grade to a higher federal wage system grade must set the employee's pay at a rate of the higher grade that will pay at least four percent more than the payline rate (normally step 2) of the grade from which promoted.

Example: (Using the wage schedule in a local wage area). Former grade and wage rate—WG-4, step 2—$6.91; new grade and wage rate—WG-5, step 2—$7.47. Four percent of the rate for WG-4, step 2, in that particular locality is 28 cents an hour ($6.91 plus $.28 = $7.19). When the one-step increase falls between step rates of the higher grade (WG-5, step 1, is $7.16 and WG-5, step 2, is $7.47), the higher of the two steps is selected—$7.47.

Grade and Pay Retention

The grade and pay retention provisions provide pay protection for employees whose grade or pay is reduced due to a management action for which they are not responsible.

Basically, these protections mean that employees can retain their current grades for two years from the date of a reduction in grade, if their placement in the lower-graded position is due to a reduction in force (if they have been at a higher grade for 52 consecutive weeks or more) or reclassification action (if their positions have been classified at the higher grade continuously for one year or more). During this two-year period, pay for these employees will not be reduced.

At the end of the two-year period, the grades of these employees will be lowered. Should their pay at that time exceed the maximum rate of their new grades, they will retain their current rate of pay except that their retained rate may not exceed 150 percent of the top rate of the grade to which they are reduced. Thereafter, if a general federal pay increase is awarded, the retained rate will be increased by 50 percent of the dollar increase in the maximum rate (e.g., step 10) of the employee's grade.

Such employees are eligible to receive the full amount of any applicable locality payment, in addition to the retained rate. If or when their pay is lower than or equal to the maximum rate of their new grades, they will be placed at the maximum rate and they will then receive the full general schedule pay increase.

An employee is not eligible for grade retention if the employee was serving under a term or temporary appointment in the position from which he or she was downgraded as a result of reduction-in-force procedures. However, the fact that the employee accepts a temporary or term appointment in conjunction with being downgraded does not affect the employee's entitlement to grade retention.

Similarly, if an employee who is already under grade retention receives a temporary or term appointment via reassignment or transfer, the employee would remain entitled to grade retention, unless one of the terminating events specified in law and regulation occur. (See 5 U.S.C. 5362(d) and 5 CFR 536.208.)

If an employee is already under grade or pay retention prior to transferring to another agency, the gaining agency generally must continue the employee's grade or pay retention entitlement, absent the occurrence of one of the terminating events set forth in law and regulation, such as a break in service of one workday or more or demotion at the employee's request. The term "demotion at the employee's request" excludes any demotion that is directly "caused or influenced by a management action." (See 5 U.S.C. 5362(d) and 5 CFR 536.208 regarding termination of grade retention and 5 U.S.C. 5363(c) and 5 CFR 536.209 regarding termination of pay retention.)

Incentive Awards and Payments

The basis for a federal agency granting an award to an individual or a group is that the contribution made benefits the government by reducing costs or improving government operations or services. Such awards may range from honorary recognition, such as a certificate or medal, to a cash award. Cash awards may be based on overall high-level performance, a special act or service, or a suggestion. Awards of over $10,000 are subject to Office of Personnel Management approval (except for IRS and the Department of Defense), while those over $25,000 are subject to Presidential approval.

Awards for suggestions, inventions, and special acts or services can be determined on the basis of benefits to the government, either tangible (measurable in dollars) or intangible (such as improved services to the public). When benefits to the government can be measured in dollars—such as reduction in production time, staff-hours, supplies, equipment, and/or space—awards sometimes are based on money saved during the first year the suggested improvement or other contribution is in effect. Performance-based cash awards, because they reward overall performance of assigned duties, typically represent a percentage of the employee's base pay and are granted as a lump-sum cash award. However, there are certain restrictions that apply when these awards are calculated as a percentage of base pay.

In designing their award programs, agencies have a responsibility to look beyond the award regulations themselves and make sure that the specific reward and incentive programs that are being proposed do not conflict with other laws or regulations. Examples of other rules that can be directly related to incentive/reward schemes are procurement, travel, Fair Labor Standards Act, and tax withholding.

Relative comparisons among individuals or groups, such as rank ordering or categorizing employees, can be used for making decisions about distributing awards. For example, agencies may limit awards to the top three producers or teams, or limit awards to those individuals or groups that exceeded certain goals. Agencies can also establish criteria for categories of awards that are given only to a selected number of recipients who best fit the criteria, although the criteria might have been met by more than one person or team.

An award program can cover both federal employees and uniformed military personnel, but only to the extent that the program covers awards for suggestions, inventions, or scientific achievements. For those categories of awards, an agency can choose to have a single program in which both civilian and military employees can participate or even a specific award for which both might be eligible. Otherwise, for all other types of awards authorized by Chapter 45 of Title 5, United States Code, military employees are excluded.

In addition to the forms of recognition described below, some agencies have developed awards to recognize individual and organizational achievement. These are used, for example, to emphasize the need for paperwork reduction, to improve safety, to increase productivity, as well as to support other management objectives. Also, a number of agencies use competitive-based awards to encourage further excellence in the performance of duties. Examples of these special awards include "Employee of the Year," "Supervisor of the Year," "Writer of the Year," etc.

Group Incentive Awards—Agencies can support continuing progress toward organizational goals by using gainsharing or goalsharing incentive programs. Gainsharing awards are designed to promote higher levels of performance through the involvement and participation of employees. As productivity improves, employees share in a portion of the financial gain. Goalsharing awards are triggered by reaching a wide variety of goals established for the group or organization as a whole.

Suggestion Programs—Some agencies have programs to reward employee ideas and innovations, although suggestion award programs are not specifically required by law or regulation. However, Congress established the suggestion award authority as the foundation of all employee incentive award authorities. Further, the program is rooted in a presumption that government-wide—not just agency-wide—benefits are to be determined and rewarded. Therefore, agencies are expected to cooperate when suggestions are referred to them from other agencies for evaluation and possible adoption, even if the receiving agency has curtailed formal procedures for its own employees.

Employees who have had the most suggestions adopted say that the way to succeed is to be sure that your suggestions promise solid improvements such as saving time, materials, or paperwork; simplifying procedures or processes; or improving services.

Other Cash Awards—Federal agencies also can make other types of cash awards to recognize exceptional performance or a significant achievement on the part of an individual employee or group of workers. Types of recognition and examples of the kind of contributions that can earn recognition include:

• Performance-based Cash Awards—Cash awards based on performance, as reflected in the employee's most recent rating of record. These awards are intended to recognize sustained levels of successful performance over the course of the rating period.

• Special Act or Service Awards—These are usually lump-sum cash awards that recognize specific accomplishments that are in the public interest and have exceeded normal job requirements. Special act or service awards are based on contributions such as work on a special project, performance exceeding job requirements on a particular assignment or task, a scientific achievement, or an act of heroism. These awards can be for individual or group contributions. On-the-spot (OTS) awards are special act or service awards which normally provide immediate recognition for employees.

• Quality Step Increases—A one-step increase to base pay, this can be granted to recognize employees in the general schedule who have received the highest available rating of record and meet agency criteria, and provide faster than normal progression through the step rates of the general schedule. Unlike other forms of monetary recognition, QSIs permanently increase an employee's rate of basic pay. No more than one QSI may be granted to an individual employee in the same 52-week period.

A quality step increase can only be granted to an employee whose most recent rating of record is Level 5, or, if covered by an appraisal program that does not use a Level 5 summary, the employee receives a rating of record at the highest summary level used by the program and demonstrates sustained performance of high quality significantly above the "fully successful" level. Employees also must meet agency-specified criteria for qualifying for a quality step increase.

A separate written justification is not required. However, OPM strongly encourages agencies to require some form of recorded justification. The agency should be able to show that the proposed recipient has performed at a truly exceptional level to justify a permanent increase in his or her rate of basic pay.

Peer nomination for quality step increases is permissible. However, some process would need to be set up to ensure that nominated employees meet the eligibility criteria. Also, under section 531.501 of title 5, Code of Federal Regulations, final authority for granting quality step increases must remain with management.

• Presidential Rank Awards—Members of the Senior Executive Service (SES) compete for Meritorious or Distinguished Rank Awards of 20 or 35 percent of base pay (senior executives are also eligible for performance bonuses of five to 20 percent of their base pay).

Section 641 of P.L. 107-67 extended eligibility for Presidential Rank Awards to senior career employees who are appointed to a position classified above GS-15 and not serving under a time-limited appointment or in a position that is excepted from the competitive service because of its confidential or policy-making character. Senior career employees are individuals who occupy Senior Level (SL) or Senior Scientific and Technical (ST) positions.

Agency heads may nominate senior career employees to be awarded the ranks of Distinguished Senior Professional for sustained extraordinary accomplishment and Meritorious Senior Professional for sustained accomplishment, in a manner similar to the nominations of career members of the SES. The eligibility criteria are consistent with criteria long-established for the SES.

Cash Surrogates—The Office of Personnel Management has concluded that cash surrogates are an appropriate option for delivering cash awards, subject to all the limitations and requirements that apply to cash awards. Examples of cash surrogates are "award vouchers" created by the agency itself that can be exchanged for currency through its imprest fund and "gift cheques" that are purchased through a vendor and that are easily and widely redeemable for cash, not merchandise. Recipients of cash surrogates must have the same freedom and control over how that award may be used as they would have over any currency or U.S. Treasury check they might otherwise receive as a cash award, including the option of saving the money or turning it over to any third party (e.g., a charity or other individual).

Cash surrogates should not be confused with merchant gift certificates.

Time-off Awards (TOAs)—A TOA is a grant of time off without charge to leave or loss of pay to an employee as an individual or member of a group. The value of a TOA is time, not money. A TOA may not be converted to cash.

Technically, there is no legal bar to offering employees a choice between cash and time-off award. However, OPM strongly recommends that agencies not offer such a choice. To do so would put the employee who opts for time-off in "constructive receipt," for tax withholding purposes, of the cash award offered. Appropriate withholding based on the cash award offered would have to be done at the time the choice is offered (i.e., when the employee reasonably would be expected to receive the cash), rather than based on the pay associated with the time off when the time off is actually taken.

Training or Equipment as an Award—An agency may provide training or purchase equipment as a form of award within a recognition program that contemplates such forms of recognition. It would be subject to all relevant training and procurement regulations, limitations, and requirements.

Honorary Awards—An honorary award is a gesture of respect given to an employee to recognize his or her performance and value to the organization. Honorary awards are generally symbolic. Many agencies include as part of their overall incentive awards programs a traditional form of high-level, formal "honor awards."

Often, such honor award programs do not use monetary recognition, but emphasize providing formal, symbolic recognition of significant contributions and publicly recognizing employees as examples for other employees to follow. They typically involve formal nominations, are granted in limited numbers, and are approved and presented by senior agency officials in formal ceremonies. The items presented, such as engraved plaques or gold medals, are principally symbolic in nature. Many honorary awards are provided to commemorate the presentation of cash or time-off awards. As mementos, such non-monetary honorary award items may be of only nominal value (e.g., simple certificates in inexpensive frames, lapel pins, paperweights). Nonetheless, all items used as honorary awards must meet specific criteria.

Informal Recognition Awards—Informal recognition awards are a type of award that may be given to reward performance that otherwise might not merit an award such as cash, time-off, or an honorary award. Agencies use these awards to provide more frequent and timely informal recognition to employees. Items presented as informal recognition awards must be of nominal value and must take an appropriate form to be used in the public sector and to be purchased with public funds.

Non-Foreign Area Allowances and Differentials

Federal white-collar and Postal Service workers in Alaska, Guam, Hawaii, the Commonwealth of the Northern Marianas, Puerto Rico, and the Virgin Islands can receive cost-of-living allowances or post differentials. The rate for these "non-foreign cost-of-living" allowances, which usually result in pay increases, is based on periodic comparative surveys of living costs. The Office of Personnel Management conducts these surveys, which basically compare living costs of workers in allowance areas with living costs of workers in Washington, D.C.

Allowances and differentials rates range from five percent (the minimum) to 25 percent (the maximum), and adjustments in allowances are made in increments of 2.5 percent.

Approximately 44,000 general schedule and U.S. Postal Service employees are eligible to receive cost-of-living allowances. Allowances are exempt from federal taxes. Neither allowances nor differentials count for federal retirement purposes.

Note: On August 17, 2000, the United States District Court of the Virgin Islands approved the settlement of *Caraballo et al v. United States*, a class-action lawsuit in which the plaintiffs contested the methodology OPM used to determine COLA rates. The decision will lead to significant changes in the way future COLAs are calculated. In addition, it provided that certain employees and former employees in non-foreign areas, except for Alaska, would be eligible for back pay. Agencies were required to notify those who were eligible by September 15, 2001. All class members were required to file a claim by February 17, 2002. For more information, go to www.opm.gov, click on Quick Index, click on Pay and Leave, then click on Non-Foreign Area Cost-of Living Adjustments.

Post differentials are allowances paid to compensate employees required to work in areas where there are extraordinarily difficult living conditions, excessive physical hardship, or notably unhealthful conditions. Differentials of 25 percent of the employee's base pay are paid in American Samoa, Guam, the Commonwealth of the Northern Mariana Islands, and Johnston, Sand, Midway and Wake Islands.

Garnishment

Debt Owed to the Government—Agencies are allowed to make deductions, within certain limits, from an employee's wages to help pay a debt owed by the worker to the federal government. Generally, under section 5514 of Title 5, United States Code, as amended by the Debt Collection Act of 1982, P.L. 97-365, federal agencies are authorized to liquidate an employee's government indebtedness by making installment deductions, or requiring the debtor's employing agency to make such deductions, in amounts not to exceed 15 percent of the employee's disposable pay.

Before any deductions may be withheld, however, the agency generally must notify the employee of its intention to collect the debt by setoff. Before making or requiring such debt-payment deductions, an agency generally must also provide notification of the employee's right to request reconsideration or a waiver of the indebtedness, and of the employee's right to an administrative hearing conducted by an individual who is not subject to the control of the head of the claiming agency. (If an agency chooses this alternative, the hearing is before an administrative law judge.)

In the event a debtor-employee retires or resigns or otherwise terminates employment before the amount of the indebtedness is completely collected, agencies are authorized to make deductions from later payments of any nature due the individual (for example, from lump-sum payments for leave or retirement contributions; see 5 CFR §550. 1101 et seq.).

The agency head may (with some exceptions) waive the repayment of an erroneous overpayment of pay or allowances (under 5 U.S.C. §5584). Employees also may question the validity of their indebtedness by filing an appeals claim.

In addition, under §124 of P.L.97-276, the government is authorized to enforce a civil judgment against a federal employee involving debts owed the U.S. government through a setoff action against the worker's pay, without having to resort to the administrative procedures applicable to a debt collection action under 5 U.S.C. §5514. The limitation on offsets of pay under a civil judgment pursuant to §124 is 25 percent of an employee's pay. Should the employee retire, resign, or terminate employment before the collection is completed, deductions may be made from later payments due the individual, such as lump-sum leave or retirement payments.

In the case of a former employee who has separated from service before the collection procedures authorized under 5 U.S.C. §5514 could be completed and put into effect, amounts may be recovered through administrative offset against any other payments due the individual from the government, pursuant to 31 U.S.C. §3711, §3716. Before an administrative offset may be carried out, the individual is generally entitled to: (1) notice of the debt and of the intent to collect it by administrative offset, (2) an opportunity to inspect the records, (3) an opportunity for review of the debt within the agency, and (4) an opportunity to reach a written agreement with the agency concerning the rate of setoff. (See Federal Claims Collection Standards in 31 CFR parts 900-904.)

The Office of Personnel Management has published regulations, at 5 CFR §831.1801 et seq., concerning setoff of an agency debt against money payable to the debtor from the Civil Service Retirement and Disability Fund. OPM's regulations require certification by the agency claiming the debt that it has complied with the applicable administrative procedures before the setoff can be carried out. Under current regulations, no more than 50 percent of a retiree's net annuity will be withheld, except in cases of fraud or misrepresentation.

OPM also has issued regulations concerning recovery of an overpayment of annuity. In such a situation, OPM generally notifies the annuitant of the amount of the overpayment, the reason(s) it occurred, the right to request reconsideration, waiver and/or compromise, and entitlement to a hearing, if any exists. There is no set limitation on the amount that may be deducted from annuity payments to recover an overpayment of annuity.

Child Support or Alimony—To enforce alimony and child support obligations, the salaries of federal and postal employees, as well as retirees' annuity payments and Social Security benefits, are subject to garnishment. For details, see Chapter 7.

General or Commercial Garnishment—Federal employee pay can be docked to satisfy private debts and state and local tax indebtedness, under a provision included in the 1993 Hatch Act reform law (P.L. 103-94). This type of general or commercial garnishment of federal pay previously had not been allowed. Up until the change, outside the postal service and a few small agencies, pay could be garnished only for child support and alimony payments.

Under the law, federal employees are entitled to similar legal protections (except for cases of tax indebtedness) afforded private-sector workers under the Consumer Credit Protection Act. That law specifies legal procedures to be followed and places limits on the percentage of an employee's salary that can be dunned.

Agencies must honor orders (writs) from any "court of competent jurisdiction," in most cases meaning state courts.

A writ must be served on the proper agency officials, who will have to notify the employee within 15 days. Agencies will have to honor writs for the collection of any legal debt of the employee and for recovery of attorney's fees, interest and court costs.

In most cases, such orders specify the total amount that must be taken from the employee's salary. Agencies will have to honor those orders up to the limits set by the consumer protection law. Generally this is up to 25 percent of net salary. In some places, however, state law sets different limits.

The percentage limits apply after mandatory deductions such as retirement contributions and taxes are taken out. Virtually all forms of pay except for suggestion awards will be counted toward the salary base.

Child support and alimony orders take priority over orders for collecting private, nonfederal debts. If more than one writ is being served, the first one will take priority.

The law applies to executive branch, postal, legislative, and judicial employees, but not to retiree annuities. Annuities can be docked only for child support, alimony and debts owed to the government.

Military Retirees: Dual Compensation Rules

Military retirees, who accept federal employment were subject, for many years, to restrictions on the amount of "dual compensation" they could receive (i.e., the combination of their military retirement pay and salary from their federal position). Generally, these retirement pay restrictions applied to all retired, regular officers who became employed in a civilian position.

However, the fiscal year 2000 National Defense Authorization Act (P.L. 106-65) repealed that provision of the Dual Compensation Act. It was estimated that the dual compensation restrictions were affecting about 6,000 retired officers. The repeal was effective October 1, 1999.

That law also removed the ceiling on combined federal income—civilian salaries plus military retired pay—which was $110,700. The removal of the ceiling also affects higher-paid enlisted retirees as well as reserve or regular officers.

Section 5—Pay Flexibilities

Agencies have considerable discretionary authority to provide additional direct compensation in certain circumstances to support their recruitment, relocation, and retention efforts. Some of these are at an agency's sole discretion while others require approval of the Office of Personnel Management and/or the Office of Management and Budget. The following summarizes some of these compensation flexibilities.

Agency-Based Discretionary Authorities

Highest Previous Rate—Upon reemployment, transfer, reassignment, promotion, demotion, or change in type of appointment, agencies may set the rate of basic pay of an employee by taking into account a rate of basic pay previously received by the individual while employed in another civilian federal position (with certain exceptions). This rate may not exceed the maximum rate of the employee's grade. (5 U.S.C. 5334(a); 5 CFR 531.202 (definition of "highest previous rate") and 531.203(c) & (d) for general schedule employees. See 5 U.S.C. 5343 and 5 CFR 532.405 for the federal wage system.)

Premium Pay, Exceptions to the Biweekly Limitation—An agency may make an exception to the GS-15, step 10, biweekly limitation on premium pay during emergencies involving a direct threat to life or property. If the agency determines that such an emergency exists, the premium pay paid to an employee performing work in connection with that emergency, when added to the employee's rate of basic pay (including any locality payment or special salary rate), must not cause his or her total pay to exceed the rate for GS-15, step 10 (including any locality payment or special salary rate), on a calendar year basis. (Note: A different limitation applies to law enforcement officers. This limitation does not apply to overtime pay earned under the Fair Labor Standards Act. This limitation does not apply to the federal wage system.) (5 U.S.C. 5547(b); 5 CFR 550.106)

Recruitment and Relocation Bonuses and Retention Allowances—See below.

Superior Qualifications and Special Qualifications Appointments—Agencies have the authority to set pay for new appointments or reappointments of individuals to general schedule positions above step 1 of the grade based on superior qualifications of the candidate or a special need of the agency. Under the federal wage system, special qualification appointments allow an employing agency to set pay at a rate above step 1 of the appropriate grade level for candidates with highly specialized skills in an occupation. Agencies must have documentation and record keeping procedures on making superior qualifications or special qualifications appointments in place to make such appointments. (5 U.S.C. 5333; 5 CFR 531.203(b) for general schedule employees. See 5 U.S.C. 5341 and 5 CFR 532.403(b) for the federal wage system.)

Travel and Transportation Expenses for Interviews and/or New Appointments—An agency, at its discretion, may pay the travel or transportation expenses of any individual candidate for a pre-employment interview or pay travel and transportation expenses for a new appointee to the first post of duty. For either payment, a decision made for one vacancy does not require a like decision for any similar future vacancies. Before authorizing any payments, the agency must consider factors such as availability of funds, desirability of conducting interviews, and feasibility of offering a recruiting incentive. (5 U.S.C. 5706b; 5 CFR part 572)

Waiver of Dual Pay Limitation—Agencies have authority to waive the limitation (40 hours per week) on aggregate basic pay, when "required services cannot be readily obtained otherwise" and "under emergency conditions relating to health, safety, protection of life or property, or national emergency." This authority enables an agency to employ a full-time federal employee in a second job or to schedule a part-time agency employee with multiple part-time appointments to work more than an aggregate of 40 hours during a week. The agency pays overtime only when an individual works more than eight hours per day or 40 hours per week for the same agency. (5 U.S.C. 5533; 5 CFR part 550, subpart E)

Referral Bonuses—Agencies can use the incentive awards authority (chapter 451 of title 5, Code of Federal Regulations) to establish a referral bonus program that provides incentives to employees who bring new talent into the agency. A referral bonus goes to the person who refers a job applicant who is selected and successfully employed, not to the new employee himself or herself.

Each agency must determine whether using referral bonuses is appropriate. OPM guidance says these bonuses might be suitable for employees whose regular job duties do not include recruitment, but who promote employment with their agency and refer potential new employees to their human resources offices. Each agency must establish the criteria it will use to determine when an employee would receive a referral bonus.

Agencies also may want to recognize the outstanding accomplishments of their employees whose job is to recruit and hire new employees. Generally, these employees would be ineligible for referral bonuses. Agencies can use their regular awards processes to develop specific incentives or recognize these employee accomplishments either through awards based on the employee's rating of record or awards given for specific accomplishments or contributions.

The law under which agencies grant referral bonuses is the general incentive awards authority in section 4503 of title 5, United States Code.

Authorities Available with OPM and/or OMB Approval

Critical Position Pay Authority—Based on a recommendation from OPM, OMB is authorized to increase the rate of basic pay for a position subject to the limit on aggregate compensation established by 5 U.S.C.

5307 and 5 CFR part 530, Subpart B. Critical pay may be authorized for a position that requires expertise of an extremely high level in a scientific, technical, professional, or administrative field or one that is critical to the agency's successful accomplishment of an important mission. Critical pay may be granted only to the extent necessary to recruit or retain an individual exceptionally well qualified for the position. (This authority does not apply to federal wage system employees.) (5 U.S.C. 5377; OMB Bul. No. 91-09)

Group Retention Allowances in Excess of 10 Percent—Upon the request of the head of an agency, OPM may approve a retention allowance in excess of 10 percent (but not to exceed 25 percent) of an employee's rate of basic pay for a group or category of employees. The agency must determine that the unusually high or unique qualifications of the employees or a special need of the agency for the employees' services makes it essential to retain the employees. The agency must also determine that a significant number of employees in the targeted category would be likely to leave the government (for any reason, including retirement) in the absence of a retention allowance. Retention allowances must be paid in accordance with the agency's previously established retention allowance plan and must be reviewed and certified annually. Retention allowances are subject to the limit on aggregate compensation established by 5 U.S.C. 5307 and 5 CFR part 530, subpart B. (5 U.S.C. 5754; 5 CFR part 575, subpart C)

Special Rates—OPM may establish higher rates of basic pay for an occupation or group of occupations nationwide or in a local area based on a finding that the government's recruitment or retention efforts are, or would likely become, significantly handicapped without those higher rates. See Special Salary Rates in Section 1.

Increased Minimum Hiring Rate (Federal Wage System)—The increased minimum hiring rate authority allows a lead agency to establish any federal wage system scheduled rate above step 1 as the minimum rate at which a new employee can be hired. When there is an increased minimum rate authorization for an occupation and grade at a particular location, all appointments must be made at the author-

ized increased minimum rate. (5 U.S.C. 5341; 5 CFR 532.249)

Special Schedules (Federal Wage System)—The special schedule authority allows OPM to establish a federal wage system schedule of rates that are broader in scope than would normally be authorized under the special rates program. Special schedules are established for specific occupations within a geographic areas when rates of pay under regular wage schedules prove insufficient for an agency to recruit or retain employees. (5 U.S.C. 5341; 5 CFR 532.254)

Unrestricted Rate Authority (Federal Wage System)—Upon the request of an agency, OPM may approve exceptions to statutory limitations on annual federal wage system pay adjustments for an occupation or group of occupations in a wage area or part of a wage area. (Requires specific authority in the pay limitation legislation; 5 CFR 532.801)

Physicians Comparability Allowance—Agencies may pay physicians comparability allowances (PCA) to recruit and retain highly qualified government physicians. In return, the physician must sign a service agreement with the agency. The head of an agency determines the size of the PCA, which may not exceed $14,000 per annum for a physician who has served as a government physician for 24 months or less or $30,000 per annum for a physician who has served as a government physician for more than 24 months. OMB approval is required. Physicians' comparability allowances are basic pay for retirement purposes if certain criteria are met. (5 U.S.C. 5948; 5 CFR part 595)

Title 38 Flexibilities for Health Care Employees—Upon the request of the head of an agency, OPM may delegate the discretionary use of certain Department of Veterans Affairs' personnel authorities under chapter 74 of title 38, United States Code, to help recruit and retain employees in health care occupations performing direct patient-care services or services incident to direct patient care. Under these delegation agreements, agencies may establish and use certain title 38 authorities such as the special salary rate, premium pay, qualifications-based grading system, and physician and dentist special pay authorities. (5 U.S.C. 5371)

Recruitment, Relocation and Retention Payments

Recruitment and relocation bonuses and retention allowances—sometimes dubbed the "three Rs"—were authorized by the Federal Employees Pay Comparability Act of 1990 (P.L. 101-509). While these payments were originally and primarily intended for general schedule positions, the Office of Personnel Management also has approved them for certain other positions, including senior-level and scientific or professional (SL/ST), Senior Executive Service (SES), and Executive Schedule positions (except agency heads) and prevailing rate (wage) employees (5 CFR Part 575). OPM approves categories upon written request from the head of the employing agency.

These payments are subject to the limit on aggregate compensation established by 5 U.S.C. 5307 and 5 CFR part 530, subpart B.

Recruitment Bonuses—Agencies may pay a recruitment bonus of up to 25 percent of basic pay to a newly appointed employee to fill a position that would otherwise be difficult to fill. Recruitment bonuses may be paid to an employee who is "newly appointed" to the federal government, including an employee reappointed with a 90-day break in service. An individual who receives a temporary appointment may be eligible as long as the appointment lasts at least six months.

Before receiving a recruitment bonus, an employee must sign a written agreement to complete a specified period of employment with the agency. The minimum allowed service period is six months. If an employee fails to complete the agreed-upon service period, he or she must repay the portion of the bonus attributable to the uncompleted period.

The bonus is paid in a lump sum. A bonus may be paid to an individual not yet employed who has received a written offer of employment and signed a written service agreement.

Before the employee enters on duty, the agency must determine in writing that, in absence of the bonus, the agency would encounter difficulty in filling the position. The agency must consider the following, as applicable: the success of recent efforts to recruit candidates for similar positions, recent turnover in similar positions, labor-

market factors, special qualifications needed in the position, and the practicality of using the superior qualifications appointment authority alone or in combination with a recruitment bonus.

An agency may target groups of positions that have been difficult to fill in the past or that are likely to be difficult to fill in the future and may make the required written determination to offer a recruitment bonus on a group basis.

The authority is in 5 U.S.C. 5753; 5 CFR part 575, subpart A.

Relocation Bonuses—Agencies may pay a relocation bonus of up to 25 percent of basic pay to an existing employee who must relocate to fill a position that would otherwise be difficult to fill. Only current employees serving in covered positions may receive a relocation bonus. Newly appointed employees are not eligible.

Before receiving a relocation bonus, an employee must sign a written agreement to complete a specified period of employment with the agency. There is no minimum service period required by OPM regulations; however, agencies may establish a minimum period under their relocation bonus plans. If an employee fails to complete the agreed-upon service period, he or she must repay the portion of the relocation bonus attributable to the uncompleted period of service. No repayment is required if the employee is involuntarily separated (for reasons other than misconduct or delinquency) or if the employee is involuntarily relocated to a different commuting area.

The bonus is paid in a lump sum. The agency may not pay the relocation bonus until the employee establishes a residence in the new commuting area.

Before the employee enters on duty in the position to which relocated, the agency must determine in writing that, in absence of the bonus, the agency would encounter difficulty in filling the position. The agency must consider the following, as applicable: the success of recent efforts to recruit candidates for similar positions, recent turnover in similar positions, labor-market factors, and special qualifications needed in the position. Under certain conditions, an agency may waive the case-by-case approval requirement for employees with a rating of at least "fully successful" (or equivalent)—for example, when these employees are part of a major organizational unit that is being relocated to a different commuting area. (Note: These groups must be approved using the same criteria that apply to individuals.)

The authority is in 5 U.S.C. 5753; 5 CFR part 575, subpart B.

Individual Retention Allowances— Agencies may make continuing (i.e., biweekly) payments of up to 25 percent of basic pay to individual employees. Before paying a retention allowance, an agency must determine that:

• the unusually high or unique qualifications of the employee or a special need for the employee's services makes it essential to retain the employee; and

• the employee would be likely to leave the federal service (for any purpose) in absence of the allowance.

The agency must document the basis for this determination in writing. An agency may not begin paying a retention allowance during the service period established by the employee's recruitment or relocation bonus service agreement. However, a relocation bonus may be paid to an employee already receiving a retention allowance.

An agency may continue payment of a retention allowance as long as the conditions giving rise to the original determination to pay the allowance still exist. However, at least once a year an agency must certify that payment of a retention allowance is still warranted. An agency may reduce or terminate an allowance if, for example, a lesser amount would be sufficient to retain the employee, the agency no longer needs the employee's services, or for budget considerations.

A retention allowance is not considered part of an employee's rate of basic pay for any purpose.

The authority is in 5 U.S.C. 5754; 5 CFR part 575, subpart C.

Group Retention Allowances—An agency may pay a retention allowance of up to 10 percent of basic pay (or up to 25 percent with OPM approval) to a group or category of employees if:

• the unusually high or unique qualifications of the employees or a special need of the agency for the employees' services makes it essential to retain the employees in the group, and

• it is reasonable to presume that there is a high risk that a significant number of employees in the targeted group would be likely to leave the federal service for any reason in absence of the allowance.

An agency must narrowly define the targeted group of employees to be paid a retention allowance using factors such as occupational series, grade level, distinctive job duties, unique qualifications, assignment to a special project, minimum agency service requirements, organization or team designation, geographic location, and performance level. An agency may not establish performance level as the sole or primary basis for authorizing a retention allowance.

An agency may pay a group-based retention allowance to any individual in the targeted group if all other conditions and requirements for payment of a retention allowance are met. For example, a retention allowance may not be paid during the service period for an existing recruitment or relocation bonus service agreement. Also, a retention allowance may not be authorized or continued if the payments would cause the employee's projected aggregate compensation in a calendar year to exceed the rate for level I of the Executive Schedule.

The authority is in 5 U.S.C. 5754, 5 CFR part 575, subpart C.

Section 6—Overtime Pay

General Overtime Pay Rights

Most general schedule and wage system employees, as well as postal employees, law enforcement personnel, and certain employees covered by other federal pay systems, are eligible for overtime pay for hours worked in excess of specified limits or premium pay for work performed outside normal schedules (e.g., Sundays, holidays, or night work).

Overtime is the general term used to describe the payments made to federal employees who work more than eight hours in a single day or in excess of 40 in one workweek. Overtime pay requirements for federal employees generally arise under either the Fair Labor Standards Act or Title 5 of the U.S. Code. In most cases, overtime is paid for work performed in excess of the daily (eight-hour) or weekly (40-hour) limits, as long as the work is officially ordered and approved by the worker's supervisor or other management official. Full-time, part-time, and intermittent employees generally are entitled to overtime pay when they work in excess of eight hours in a day, unless they are working an alternative work schedule or where the first 40 hours is their basic workweek.

Premium pay is the general term used to describe the additional pay provided to federal employees who work extra hours or whose work involves unusual situations or requirements (such as hazardous duties or night work). Examples of the most common kinds of premium pay are listed under "Types of Premium Pay."

Overtime Pay: Exempt and Nonexempt Status

Generally, the term "exempt employees" refers to those managers, professionals, and other white-collar workers who are not covered by the Fair Labor Standards Act. Under the FLSA, employees in bona fide executive, administrative, and professional positions, as well as employees in foreign areas, are considered "exempt" employees (which basically means that they are not covered by FLSA's minimum wage or overtime pay protections). However, in the federal government, many FLSA-exempt employees are compensated for their overtime work on a daily or weekly basis under Title 5 of the U.S. Code or other existing federal pay laws. This entitlement to daily overtime under Title 5 applies to most GS employees, although exceptions do exist for workers in certain categories (e.g., employees for whom the first 40 hours is the basic workweek, employees on an alternative work schedule, and employees receiving annual premium pay).

Except for certain law enforcement officers, overtime pay under Title 5 is computed at a rate of 1 1/2 times the employee's basic pay or the GS-10, step 1, rate of basic pay, whichever is lower. An exempt employee's overtime pay rate cannot exceed the GS-10, step 1 threshold. Exempt employees also are subject to an overall overtime compensation cap that bars premium payments to an individual that would cause total base pay plus premium pay to exceed the maximum biweekly pay for GS-15, step 10.

Nonexempt employees are those covered by the Fair Labor Standards Act and thus entitled to its overtime pay (and minimum wage) protections. FLSA generally provides that overtime pay be paid to all nonexempt employees for every hour worked beyond 40 in a workweek. In the federal government, all employees classified at GS-4 and below are considered nonexempt employees, along with general schedule employees in grades GS-5 through GS-10 who are not in bona fide executive, professional, or administrative positions. Similarly, wage system employees are considered nonexempt if they do not hold bona fide executive, professional, or administrative jobs. For all these nonexempt employees, overtime pay is computed at a rate of $1\frac{1}{2}$ times their "regular rate" of pay.

An employee's regular rate of pay includes basic pay, locality-based comparability payments, special pay adjustments for law enforcement officers, and certain allowances. An employee's regular rate also includes various forms of premium pay (see below), such as pay for Sunday, night, or holiday work, and hazardous/environmental differentials.

Basic Overtime Pay Computations

For overtime work in excess of eight hours a day or 40 hours a week, general schedule employees who are exempt under FLSA are paid one and a half times their rate of basic pay, up to and including the first step of GS-10. From that point on, the overtime hourly rate of basic pay is equal to $1\frac{1}{2}$ times the rate of basic pay for GS-10, step 1, with the result that most employees earning more than the GS-10/step 1 rate will receive the same hourly rate for overtime work. Also, exempt employees may not receive premium pay (e.g., Title 5 overtime, night differential, regularly scheduled standby, availability pay, Sunday, and/or holiday pay) that will cause their aggregate pay for a biweekly period to exceed the maximum rate of GS-15, step 10. A separate GS-15, step 10 annual limitation on premium pay applies to employees who are determined to be performing emergency work involving a direct threat to life or property.

These overtime limitations do not apply to overtime pay calculations resulting from extra hours worked by employees considered nonexempt under FLSA. FLSA-required overtime payments to nonexempt federal workers are not subject to the GS-10/step 1 limitation or the bi-weekly premium pay restrictions that govern the Title 5 overtime and premium payments made to federal employees.

Different hourly and bi-weekly limitations apply to certain law enforcement officers. For example, law enforcement officers whose rate of basic pay exceeds the GS-10/step 1 rate are entitled to overtime at the rate of one and one-half times either the GS-10/step 1 rate or the employee's actual hourly rate for the grade, whichever is higher.

Wage system (blue-collar) employees are paid 1 times their rate of basic pay for work in excess of eight hours a day or 40 hours a week. They also receive a 25 percent differential for Sunday work and twice their rate of basic pay for holiday work. Night shift differentials of 7 percent and ten percent are paid for regularly scheduled work on the second and third shifts, respectively. Night shift means regularly scheduled non-overtime work when a majority of the hours of such work occur between 3:00 p.m. and midnight (second shift) or between 11:00 p.m. and 8:00 a.m. (third shift).

The Fair Labor Standards Amendments of 1974, Public Law 93-259, brought many nonsupervisory federal and non-appropriated fund employees under the minimum wage and overtime pay provisions of the Fair Labor Standards Act, effective May 1, 1974.

Overtime vs. Compensatory Time Off

Compensatory time off is time off with pay under 5 U.S.C. 5543 and 5 U.S.C. 6123(a)(1) in lieu of overtime pay for irregular or occasional overtime work, or when permitted under agency flexible work schedule programs, time off with pay in lieu of overtime pay for regularly scheduled or irregular or occasional overtime work.

Compensatory time off may be approved in lieu of overtime pay for irregular or occasional overtime work for both FLSA exempt and nonexempt employees who are covered by the definition of "employee" at 5 U.S.C. 5541(2).

Compensatory time off can also be approved for a "prevailing rate employee," as defined at 5 U.S.C. 5342(a)(2).

Agencies may require that an FLSA exempt employee (as defined at 5 U.S.C. 5541(2)) receive compensatory time off in lieu of overtime pay for irregular or occasional overtime work, but only for an FLSA exempt employee whose rate of basic pay is above the rate for GS-10, step 10. Agencies may not require employees in the following categories to receive compensatory time off in lieu of overtime pay: (1) FLSA nonexempt employees; (2) prevailing rate (wage) employees (even if FLSA exempt); or (3) FLSA exempt employees whose rate of basic pay is equal to (or less than) the rate for GS-10, step 10. For these employees, compensatory time off may be granted only upon the employee's request. (See 5 U.S.C. 5543(a) and (b).)

For employees under flexible schedules, compensatory time off may be granted for regularly scheduled overtime work upon the request of the employee. It may not be required. See 5 U.S.C. 6123(a)(1).

An agency may set time limits for an FLSA exempt or nonexempt employee to take compensatory time off.

An agency may provide that an FLSA exempt employee who earns compensatory time off will lose entitlement to compensatory time off and overtime pay if it is not used within agency time limits, unless the failure was due to an exigency of the service beyond the employee's control.

If compensatory time off is not taken by an FLSA nonexempt employee within agency time limits, an agency must pay the employee for overtime work at the overtime rate in effect during the pay period in which the overtime work was completed.

One hour of compensatory time off is granted for each hour of overtime work.

FLSA Claims

Employees who believe they were incorrectly denied overtime pay may file a Fair Labor Standards Act claim with either their employing agency or with the Office of Personnel Management, but cannot pursue the same claim with both the agency and OPM at the same time. Employees who get an unfavorable decision on an administrative FLSA claim from the agency may still file a claim with OPM. However, the reverse is not true.

An FLSA pay claim is subject to a two-year statute of limitations, except in cases of a willful violation, where the statute of limitations is three years.

For more information, see the Office of Personnel Management section in Chapter 9.

Section 7—Types of Premium Pay

The term "premium pay" extends to most types of additional pay received by federal employees for working extra hours or performing work that involves unusual situations or requirements (such as hazardous duties or night work). Thus, overtime pay is considered one form of premium pay. However, in addition to overtime pay, the term "premium pay" covers a wide variety of extra payments. Listed below are examples of the most common forms of premium pay.

Sunday Premium Pay

Full-time general schedule and blue collar workers whose regular schedules require them to work on a Sunday are entitled to their rate of basic pay, plus premium pay computed at a rate of 25 percent of their basic pay rate. This Sunday premium rate generally is applicable to all non-overtime work (i.e., not in excess of eight hours per shift), although it also may apply where employees work in excess of eight hours under a fixed compressed work schedule. The Sunday work must be part of an employee's regularly scheduled basic workweek. In cases where employees work rotating shifts and the "late hour" Saturday shift extends into Sunday or an "early" Monday tour actually starts on Sunday, such workers are entitled to premium pay for the entirety of both shifts—not to exceed eight hours for each shift—even though a part of the shift work was not actually performed on Sunday.

Federal employees must actually perform work on a Sunday in order to be eligible for Sunday premium pay. Federal employees are not entitled to Sunday premium pay for periods when no work is performed, such as paid leave time, excused absences, holidays, compensatory time off, or time off granted as an incentive or performance award. Part-time and intermittent employees are not entitled to Sunday premium pay.

Holiday Pay

Employees who work on a holiday during hours that correspond to their normal tour of duty are entitled to receive holiday premium pay equal to their rate of basic pay. If employees work in excess of eight hours on the holiday or if full-time employees work during hours that do not correspond with their normal tour, they are entitled to receive their regular overtime rate of pay for hours worked in excess of eight in a day or 40 in a week.

This means that employees who work on a holiday that falls on one of their regular workdays must be paid twice their rate of basic pay for not more than eight hours of such work. Any hours worked outside an employee's regularly scheduled tour of duty on a holiday would be paid at the employee's overtime rate. An employee who is assigned to duty during holiday hours is entitled to pay for at least two hours of holiday work. An employee on a fixed compressed work schedule who is required to work on a holiday is entitled to holiday premium pay for all non-overtime hours of work

Premium pay for holiday work also will be paid in addition to night pay differential for regularly scheduled non-overtime work at night, as well as for regularly scheduled non-overtime Sunday work when an employee performs work on a holiday that occurs on a Sunday.

Night Differential Pay

Wage system employees are entitled to a night shift differential rate of 7 percent for work on a second shift, and ten percent for regularly scheduled work on the third shift. Night shift means regularly scheduled non-overtime work when a majority of the hours of such work occur between 3:00 p.m. and midnight (second shift) or between 11:00 p.m. and 8:00 a.m. (third shift). Night shift differentials are included in wage employees' basic pay rates for purposes of computing overtime pay, Sunday pay, holiday pay, severance pay, and amounts of deductions for retirement and group life insurance.

General schedule employees receive a night shift differential of ten percent of their hourly base pay when they perform regularly scheduled night work between the hours of 6:00 p.m. and 6:00 a.m. GS employees are eligible for this night differential even when excused from work on a holiday or other non-workday and for hours spent on duty while traveling. For GS employees, night differentials are paid in addition to overtime, Sunday, or holiday pay, but are not included in the rate of base pay used to compute these premium payments.

Employees regularly assigned to a night shift on a full-time basis may be paid a night differential during periods of a paid absence (both annual and sick leave). However, a GS employee is entitled to night pay differential for a period of paid leave only when the total amount of leave in a pay period, including both day and night hours, is less than eight hours.

Environmental Differential Pay

Wage system employees are entitled to environmental differentials when they are exposed to working conditions or hazards that fall within one of the categories approved by the Office of Personnel Management. The amount of the differential is equal to the percentage rate approved by OPM for the particular job category, multiplied by the rate of pay for WG-10, step 2 for the appropriated fund employees and the rate of pay for NA-10, Step 2 for the non-appropriated employees. For example, a wage system employee working on a structure at least 100 feet above the ground, deck, floor or roof of a facility or in the bottom of a tank or pit receives a differential of 25 percent, while another wage system worker performing ground work beneath a hovering helicopter is eligible for a 15 percent differential. (For a list of the exposures for which differentials may be paid, see 5 CFR 532, Subpart E, Appendix A.) Employees entitled to a differential based on actual exposure will be paid a minimum of one hour's differential pay for the exposure. For exposure beyond one hour, workers are paid in increments of one quarter hour for each 15 minutes or portion thereof in excess of 15 minutes. Employees entitled to a differential based on hours in a pay status will be paid for all hours in the pay status on the day they are exposed.

Environmental differentials are part of basic pay and are used to compute premium pay (including overtime, holiday, or Sunday pay), and the amount on which group life insurance is based. It is not part of basic pay for calculating severance pay or lump-sum annual leave payments for employees who are separating from federal service.

Hazardous-Duty Pay

GS employees are entitled to a hazardous duty pay differential if their work involves unusual physical hardships or hazards that have not already been accounted for in their job classification. "Physical hardship" means a duty that may not in itself be hazardous, but causes extreme physical discomfort or distress and is not adequately alleviated by protective or mechanical devices. Examples of such duties are tasks involving exposure to extreme temperatures for a long period of time, arduous physical exertion, or exposure to fumes, dust, or noise that causes nausea, skin, eye, ear, or nose irritation. Similarly, a "hazard" is a job situation or duty in which an employee runs the risk of suffering an accident that could result in serious injury or death.

Pay differentials for these types of assignments range from four percent of basic pay up to 25 percent, with the majority being set at 25 percent. For example, an employee working in a confined space that is subject to temperatures in excess of 110 degrees is eligible for a four percent differential, while an employee arming or disarming a propulsion system will receive a 25 percent differential. A complete schedule of these pay differentials is contained in 5 CFR 550, Subpart I, Appendix A.

Regulations at 5 CFR 550.904 allow an agency to approve payment of hazardous duty pay when the hazardous duty or physical hardship has not been taken into account in the classification of the position (i.e., the knowledge, skills, and abilities required to perform the duty are not considered in the classification of the position). If the hazardous duty has been taken into account in the classification of the position, an agency may authorize payment of hazardous duty pay only when the actual circumstances of the specific hazard or physical hardship have changed from that taken into account and described in the position description; and, when using the knowledge, skills, and abilities required for the position and described in the position description, the employee cannot control the hazard or physical hardship; thus, the risk is not reduced to a less than significant level.

Hazardous duty pay may be paid only to employees who are assigned hazardous duties or duties involving physical hardship for which a differential is authorized. It may not be paid to an employee who undertakes to perform a hazardous duty on his or her own, without proper authorization, either expressed or implied.

When an employee performs a duty for which a hazard pay differential is authorized, the agency must pay the hazard pay differential for all of the hours in which the employee is in a pay status on the day on which the duty is performed.

Hostile Fire Pay

Section 1111 of Public Law 107-107 provided the head of an executive agency with discretionary authority to pay an employee hostile fire pay. The law provides agencies with the authority to pay hostile fire pay at a rate of $150 for any month in which the employee is:

• subject to hostile fire or explosion of hostile mines;

• on duty in an area in which the employee was in imminent danger of being exposed to hostile fire or explosion of hostile mines and in which, during the period of duty in that area, other employees were subject to hostile fire or explosion of hostile mines; or

• killed, injured, or wounded by hostile fire, explosion of hostile mine, or any other hostile action.

Agencies may pay hostile fire pay to an employee hospitalized for the treatment of an injury or wound for not more than three additional months during which the employee is hospitalized. Section 5949 prohibits the payment of hostile fire pay for periods of time during which an employee receives post differentials under 5 U.S.C. 5925, because of exposure to political violence, or danger pay allowances under 5 U.S.C. 5928.

This provision is effective retroactive to September 11, 2001. The head of an executive agency may grant hostile fire pay for any hostile action that took place on or after that date.

Administratively Uncontrollable Overtime

"Administratively uncontrollable overtime" refers to work in a job that unpredictably requires substantial amounts of irregular or occasional overtime, and in which the employees generally are responsible for recognizing, without supervision, circumstances that require them to remain on duty. GS employees, other than certain criminal investigators (see "Availability Pay" below) may be granted AUO premium pay on an annual basis if their job requires substantial amounts of irregular or occasional overtime work that cannot be controlled administratively. AUO premium payments are set as a percentage of an employee's base pay, but cannot be less than 10 percent or more than 25 percent. Employees who are receiving AUO pay are not eligible for any other kinds of premium pay for irregular or occasional overtime work.

The rate of AUO pay authorized for a position is based on the average number of hours of irregular or occasional overtime work performed per week. For example, a 25 percent rate is authorized for a position that requires an average of over nine hours per week of irregular or occasional overtime work. (See 5 CFR 550.154.) Agency reviews of the percentage of AUO pay paid to employees must be conducted "at appropriate intervals," commonly every three to six months. The percentage of annual premium pay may be revised or, if appropriate, discontinued. (See 5 CFR 550.161(d).)

An employee who receives AUO pay may also receive overtime pay on an hourly basis for regularly scheduled overtime work. Regularly scheduled overtime work creates an entitlement to overtime pay on an hour-for-hour basis and generally must be officially ordered or approved by a supervisor or manager in advance of the employee's regularly scheduled administrative workweek. (See 5 U.S.C. 5542(a).)

If an employee who is engaged in law enforcement activities (including security personnel in correctional institutions) receives AUO pay and is nonexempt from (covered by) the overtime pay provisions of the Fair Labor Standards Act, he or she is entitled to additional overtime pay equal to 0.5 times the employee's hourly regular rate of pay for all hours of work in excess of

42.75 hours in a week, including meal periods within the tour of duty. Other nonexempt employees who receive AUO pay and who are not engaged in law enforcement activities are entitled to additional FLSA overtime pay equal to 0.5 times their hourly regular rate of pay for all hours of work in excess of 40 hours in a week, not including meal periods.

An employee receiving AUO pay may not receive any other premium pay (e.g., night Sunday and holiday pay) for irregular and occasional overtime hours that are compensated by AUO pay. (See 5 CFR 550.163(b).) In addition, hazardous duty pay may not be paid for irregular and occasional overtime hours of work that are compensated by AUO pay. (See 5 CFR 550.905(b).)

Temporary Assignments—Rules at 5 CFR 550.162(c)(1) provide that an agency may continue to pay AUO pay for a period of not more than 10 consecutive workdays on a temporary assignment to other duties in which conditions do not warrant AUO pay and for a total of not more than 30 workdays in a calendar year while on such a temporary assignment. An agency must discontinue an employee's AUO pay when a temporary assignment exceeds these time limits.

However, rules published in the February 13, 2002 Federal Register authorized payment of AUO pay during a temporary assignment that would not otherwise warrant the payment of AUO pay if the temporary assignment is directly related to a national emergency declared by the President. Under those rules, an agency may continue to pay AUO pay for a period of not more than 30 consecutive work days for such a temporary assignment and for a total of not more than 90 workdays in a calendar year while on such a temporary assignment. Time during which an employee continues to receive AUO pay under those provisions is not considered in computing the weekly average number of irregular overtime hours used in determining the amount of an employee's future AUO payments.

Availability Pay

Availability pay is the term used to describe the annual premium pay rate granted to certain law enforcement personnel who have criminal investigation responsibilities. Availability pay is designed to replace the use of administratively uncontrollable overtime (AUO) pay for employees in this category. Under Section 633 of Public Law 103-329, qualified criminal investigators are entitled to availability pay, which is fixed at 25 percent of basic pay (including locality pay). Higher graded law enforcement officers may be entitled to a lesser amount if their availability pay causes them to exceed the maximum earnings limitation for law enforcement officers. That limitation is 150 percent of the lesser of the minimum rate of GS-15 (including a special rate of pay or locality pay) or the rate of pay for level IV of the Executive Schedule, whichever is less. Availability pay must be paid to qualified criminal investigators who meet the legal definition of a "law enforcement officer." An annual certification must be made by both the criminal investigator and an appropriate supervisory official. The annual certification must stipulate that the investigator works, or is available to work, an annual average of two hours of "unscheduled duty" per regular workday as requested by the employing agency. Criminal investigators receiving availability pay are exempt from the minimum wage and overtime pay provisions of the Fair Labor Standards Act. The availability pay provisions became effective with the first pay period beginning on or after October 30, 1994. Section 407 of Public Law 105-277 extended coverage to special agents in the Diplomatic Security Service (DSS) of the Department of State.

Employees receiving annual availability pay remain eligible for premium pay for night, Sunday, and holiday work for regularly scheduled overtime hours not compensated by availability pay. However, they are not eligible for standby duty pay (see below). Availability pay is considered base pay only for purposes of calculating advances in pay, severance pay, workers' compensation, life insurance and retirement benefits, and Thrift Savings Plan contributions.

Standby-Duty Pay

Annual premium pay for regularly scheduled standby duty pay is paid to certain employees whose jobs require them to remain at (or within the confines of) their duty station during longer than ordinary periods of duty, a substantial part of which consists of remaining in a standby status rather than performing work.

GS employees may be eligible for annual standby duty pay if their tour of standby duty is established on a regularly recurring basis over a substantial period of time (generally at least a few months). Annual standby pay rates range from five percent up to 25 percent per year of an employee's basic pay that doesn't exceed the GS-10/step 1 cap, including any locality pay. The actual amount authorized depends on the nature of an employee's standby schedule.

Employees receiving annual standby duty pay are not eligible for overtime, night, and holiday pay, other than pay for irregular or occasional overtime work.

Firefighters Pay

Section 101(h) of Public Law 105-277 revised the methods of calculating basic pay, overtime pay, and other entitlements for federal employees whose positions are classified in the Fire Protection and Prevention Series, GS-0081, and who have regular tours of duty averaging at least 53 hours per week.

Firefighters whose regularly established workweeks average 53 hours are paid on an hourly rate. The applicable GS annual rate of pay is divided by a 2,756-hour factor to derive the "firefighter hourly rate." This factor is derived by multiplying the number of weeks in the year (52) by the FLSA weekly overtime standard (53 hours). Time-and-one-half overtime pay is provided for both FLSA-covered and FLSA-exempt firefighters for all overtime hours. For FLSA-exempt firefighters, the overtime rate is capped at 1½ times the GS-10, step 1, rate (2,087 basis), but cannot be less than the individual's firefighter rate of basic pay. Special computations are provided for firefighters whose regular tour of duty includes a basic 40-hour workweek.

Firefighters are barred from receiving payment of any other premium pay, including night pay, Sunday pay, holiday pay, and hazardous duty pay.

Rules for firefighter pay can be found in 5 CFR Parts 410, 550, 551, and 630.

Call-Back Pay

This type of premium payment is provided to wage system employees who get called back to the worksite to work extra hours after completing a tour of duty. Employees who are called back must receive a minimum of two hours of overtime pay, even if they are sent home without working that amount of time. Call-back pay rights extend to overtime work performed after hours and on an employee's scheduled day off. If the call-back occurs during regularly scheduled non-overtime work on a holiday, employees must be paid two hours of holiday premium pay instead of overtime.

Similarly, general schedule employees who are called back to the worksite to work overtime after completing their tour of duty must receive at least two hours of overtime pay or compensatory time off. This includes overtime work after hours and on days off. If the call-back occurs on a holiday, the two hour minimum also applies and the employee must be paid at least two hours of holiday premium pay. However, if a full-time employee is called back on the holiday outside the normal tour of duty, either before or after, the employee is entitled to receive a minimum of two hours of overtime pay.

Evacuation Payments

Evacuation payments are made to employees or their dependents, or both, who are ordered to be evacuated from or within the United States and certain non-foreign areas in the national interest because of natural disasters or for military or other reasons that create imminent danger to the lives of the employees, their immediate family, or their dependents. The applicable non-foreign areas are listed in the definition of "United States area" in 5 CFR 550.402. Evacuation payments are authorized for evacuations occasioned by natural disasters within the continental United States. (See 57 FR 40070, September 1, 1992.)

A separate authority applies to employees in foreign areas paid under Chapter 600 of the Department of State Standardized Regulations (Government Civilians, Foreign Areas).

When an employee has been ordered to evacuate, agency heads may make advance payments of pay, allowances, and differentials to cover a time period of up to 30 calendar days, provided the agency head or designated official determines the payment is required to defray immediate expenses incidental to the evacuation.

Evacuation payments may be made to cover a total of up to 180 calendar days (including the number of days for which payment has already been made) when employees continue to be prevented from performing their duties by an evacuation order. Employees may also receive additional allowance payments for travel expenses and subsistence expenses (i.e., per diem) to offset added expenses they incur as a result of their evacuation or the evacuation of their dependents. (See 5 CFR 550.405.)

Not later than 180 days after the effective date of the order to evacuate, or when the emergency or evacuation is terminated, whichever is earlier, an employee must be returned to his or her regular duty station or reassigned to another duty station.

Section 8—Severance Pay

General Rights and Procedures

Permanent employees who have been employed continuously for at least 12 months and who lose their jobs through no fault of their own generally are entitled to severance pay. This includes employees who are separated in a reduction in force because of abolishment of their positions, or who decline to accompany their positions in a transfer of function to another commuting area. There are some limitations on entitlement to severance pay.

For example, if a separated employee has declined a "reasonable offer" (i.e., a position in the same agency, in the same commuting area, of the same tenure and work schedule, and not more than two grades or pay levels below the employee's current position), the worker usually will not be entitled to severance pay. In addition, an employee who is entitled to an immediate annuity at the time of separation, including a reduced annuity, a disability annuity, or retired pay earned as a member of the uniformed services, is not entitled to severance pay.

For those separating employees who are eligible, the basic severance pay allowance is computed on the basis of the following formula: one week's salary for each year of the first ten years of service, with an additional two weeks' salary for each year of service beyond ten years. For employees who are over age 40, an age adjustment allowance is added to the basic allowance. This over-40 age adjustment calls for computing 2.5 percent of the basic severance allowance for each full three months of age over age 40. In both computations, full consideration is given to full quarters of a year. Military service is considered creditable service for severance pay purposes when it interrupts civilian service, and the employee returns to civilian service within the period for exercising restoration rights after military duty.

The total severance pay an employee is eligible to receive is limited to one year's pay at the rate of pay received immediately before separation. This is a lifetime limitation. Therefore, if an employee becomes eligible to receive severance pay for the second time in his federal career, the worker's severance pay entitlement ends once the sum of the two severance periods reaches 52 weeks. Severance payments are made at regular pay period intervals by the agency from which separated. Severance pay received by an employee is subject to deductions for income taxes, Medicare, and Social Security (if the employee was subject to Social Security at the time of separation).

Severance Payments and Reemployment

Severance payments end if a recipient is reemployed by the federal government (including the U.S. Postal Service) on a nontemporary basis. Upon such reemployment, the individual begins building severance credits on top of the unpaid, residual severance amount for potential future use.

In the case of temporary federal reemployment, severance payments are suspended. However, they resume when the temporary appointment expires, and continue until new federal reemployment is obtained or the severance payments are exhausted.

Exception: If the temporary appointment is full-time and begins within three days after separation from a qualifying non-temporary appointment, severance pay is terminated, not suspended. However, this type of temporary appointment is qualifying for severance pay upon the expiration of the appointment.

In the case of a former federal employee who gains non-federal employment, the worker's entitlement to federal severance pay continues until the payments are exhausted.

Resignations Pending Separation— Under 5 CFR 550.706, employees who resign because they expect to be involuntarily separated are considered to have been involuntarily separated for severance pay purposes only if they resign after receiving: a specific written notice stating that the employee will be involuntarily separated by a particular action (e.g., reduction in force) on a particular date; or a general written notice of reduction in force or transfer of function that announces that all positions in the competitive area will be abolished or

transferred to another commuting area by a particular date no more than one year after the date of the notice. If the specific or general notice is cancelled before the resignation is effected, the resignation would not be qualifying for severance pay purposes.

Inability to Perform Duties— An employee who is removed for inability to perform his or her duties may receive severance pay if the inability is caused by a medical condition that is beyond the employee's control. This determination should be made by the employing agency based on acceptable medical documentation provided by the employee.

Section 9—Standard Deductions from Pay

Compensation paid to federal employees is subject to a number of standard tax and benefit-related deductions. In addition to these mandatory deductions, various voluntary deductions may be taken, such as for federally sponsored life, health and long-term care insurance, union dues, Thrift Savings Plan investments, savings bonds and other deductions.

Civil Service Retirement

For CSRS employees, the biweekly gross salary, based on a 40-hour week, is multiplied by 7 percent to determine the civil service retirement deduction. For FERS employees, the deduction is 0.8 percent. For employees covered by the retirement systems for air traffic controllers, firefighters, and law enforcement officers, an additional 0.5 percent is deducted.

Social Security

The Social Security "FICA" (Federal Insurance Contributions Act) portion (6.2 percent) applies to the first $87,000 of the wages of FERS and CSRS-Offset employees, known as the Social Security maximum wage base. Above that threshold, CSRS-Offset employees continue to pay the deduction but the money goes into the Civil Service Retirement and Disability Fund, not the Social Security trust fund. FERS employees do not pay the FICA portion above the maximum wage base.

Medicare

A deduction of 1.45 percent of salary for

employees under all retirement systems, with no limitation on salary.

Federal Income Tax

The wage figures specified in the table on page 34 refer to wages paid after July 31, 2002. The table shows how to calculate the federal income tax withholding on an employee's biweekly gross wages. The federal government uses the percentage method of computing withholding. For more details, refer to Internal Revenue Service Circular E.

To make the computation to determine your biweekly income tax withholding under the law: (1) Multiply the number of exemptions claimed by $111.54. (The number of exemptions [withholding allowances] includes one for each personal exemption claimed, plus one special allowance for individuals or families with one employer or one spouse working, plus additional exemptions for estimated deductions-itemized deductions, alimony payments, IRA or Keogh contributions, business losses, employee business expenses, and other—see Circular E and Form W-4 for more detail). (2) Subtract this amount from your regular biweekly gross wages. (3) Then use the result to calculate your withholding tax from the tables on the following pages.

State Tax

Section 5517 of Title 5, U.S. Code, and Executive Order 10407 provide for withholding for state income tax purposes where the law of any state requires the collection of such tax and the secretary of the treasury has entered into an agreement to withhold state income taxes. Section 5516 of Title 5, U.S. Code, and Executive Order 10672 provide for withholding of income taxes for the District of Columbia when the secretary of the treasury has entered into an agreement to deduct such taxes.

Section 5520 of Title 5 of the U.S. Code provides for withholding of city or county income or employment taxes when the sec-

retary of the treasury has entered into an agreement to deduct such taxes.

Overwithholding

Where overwithholding has resulted in large refunds in past years, you may be entitled to claim additional exemptions if a similar refund is anticipated in the current year. Use Form W-4, which has a schedule to compute the exemptions.

Section 10—Flexible Spending Accounts

Flexible spending accounts, or FSAs, are employer-established benefit plans that reimburse employees for specified expenses. They are funded through salary reduction arrangements under which employees receive less take-home pay in exchange for contributions to their accounts.

Employees each year choose how much to put in their accounts, which they may use for dependent care or for medical and dental expenses other than insurance. However, there must be separate accounts for these two purposes, and amounts unused at the end of the year must be forfeited. Contributions are not subject to either income or employment taxes.

In September 2002, the Office of Personnel Management (OPM) announced that, for the first time, federal employees in the executive and legislative branches would be able to enroll in health care and childcare FSAs effective July 1, 2003. Previously, employees of the judicial branch, the U.S. Postal Service and some banking regulatory agencies had established FSAs for their employees under separate authority.

In late 2002, the government issued a solicitation to the private sector to administer the executive branch program, since the government itself has no authority to operate such a program on behalf of its own employees. Selection of a contractor in early 2003 was to be followed in May 2003 by an initial open enrollment season for participation in FSAs for the last six months of calendar year 2003.

Following the initial opportunity, open seasons are to be conducted concurrent with the annual Federal Employees Health Benefits program open season each autumn,

with employee elections effective on a calendar year basis in 2004 and thereafter.

The government is offering two types of FSAs, one covering dependent care and the other for medical and dental expenses. The maximum annual contribution to the former type is set by statute at $5,000 a year while the government's intent was to limit contributions to the latter to $3,000 a year, even though there is no statutory limit on those types of accounts. The figure was subject to negotiations with the carrier.

For dependent care expenses, money is typically drawn out from an FSA on a regular basis as costs are incurred, such as through monthly tuition charged by day care programs. Eligible costs include those incurred on behalf of a dependent listed on the participant's tax return, including dependent parents and children up to age 13.

The care must be deemed necessary for the participant to hold a job. Further, the expenses must be paid to a provider—including a day care center, at-home provider, after school program, adult day care or similar providers—that pay federal income taxes on the income they receive for providing the care. The participant must be able to show the provider's tax identification number.

For medical and dental care expense accounts, money is typically withdrawn on a sporadic basis as costs are incurred. The allowable costs include those not covered by insurance such as the Federal Employees Health Benefits program. This includes out-of-pocket charges under FEHB coverage such as co-payments and deductibles. It also includes certain medical procedures not covered—or only partly covered—by FEHB, as well as certain other health-related expenses such as transportation necessary for medical care, home or automobile renovations to accommodate a disability, certain legal fees and other costs.

In general, allowable reimbursable costs under the medical and dental accounts mirror those costs that can be deducted on an individual's federal tax return when they exceed 7.5 percent of adjusted gross income in a year. These expenses are described in IRS Publication 502, Medical and Dental Expenses. The one exception is that while premiums for long-term care insurance are deductible above that threshold, they cannot be paid from pre-tax FSA accounts.

Participation in both, either or neither type of account is strictly voluntary. Participation, or lack of it, in the government's premium conversion program—through which FEHB premiums can be paid with pre-tax money—does not affect participation in FSAs. Nor does participation or lack of it in any other voluntary government benefit program. Generally speaking, those eligible for FEHB coverage are also eligible for the FSAs. One exception is that temporary employees are eligible for health care FSAs only after completing one continuous year of service; there is no such restriction on dependent care FSAs.

Money put in FSAs is available on a "use or lose" basis. That is, any money remaining in the account at the end of a calendar year is forfeited. (Typically in private sector FSAs the money goes back to the employer; however, in the government program the money will go to the carrier.) Thus, participants need to plan carefully regarding how much money they put into the accounts.

However, the entire amount in such accounts is available from the start of a covered period, regardless of how much the employee has yet put in through payroll withholding. Thus, a participant could use up the entire amount available in the account and leave employment with no obligation to pay back the difference between what was paid in and what was drawn out in that plan year. (Typically in private sector FSAs the employer is responsible for making up the difference; however, in the government program the carrier is responsible.)

Participation in FSAs will reduce the taxable wage base for calculation of Social Security benefits. However, in most cases the reduction will be relatively minor compared with the tax savings to the individual.

Certain other features of the government's FSA program were still being decided as this issue of the Almanac went to press.

The Comptroller General has ruled that federal agencies may buy Federal Employees News Digest publications with government dollars. The decision is B-185591. For government purchase orders: Federal Employees News Digest, Inc. is a small business. Federal ID 52-0941248

INCOME TAX WITHHOLDING TABLE

SINGLE PERSON
(Including Head of Household)

If Amount of Biweekly Wage is:

Over	But Not Over	The Amount of Income Tax to be Withheld Shall be:	Of the Amount Over
$102	$329	10%	$102
$329	$1,158	$22.70 plus 15%	$329
$1,158	$2,535	$147.05 plus 27%	$1,158
$2,535	$5,585	$518.84 plus 30%	$2,535
$5,585	$12,063	$1,433.84 plus 35%	$ 5,585
$12,063		$3,701.14 plus 38.6%	$12,063

MARRIED PERSON

If Amount of Biweekly Wage is:

Over	But Not Over	The Amount of Income Tax to be Withheld Shall be:	Of the Amount Over
$248	$710	10%	$248
$710	$2,013	$46.20 plus 15%	$710
$2,013	$4,300	$241.65 plus 27%	$2,013
$4,300	$6,908	$859.14 plus 30%	$4,300
$6,908	$12,187	$1,641.54 plus 35%	$6,908
$12,187		$3,489.19 plus 38.6%	$12,187

Number of Allowances	Biweekly Deduction	Number of Allowances	Biweekly Deduction
0	$0	7	$821.17
1	$117.31	8	$938.48
2	$234.62	9	$1,055.79
3	$351.93	10	$1,173.10
4	$469.24	11 or more	Multiply number
5	$586.55		of Withholding
6	$703.86		Allowances by
			$117.31

Example: Married employee claiming four exemptions, with a biweekly gross salary of $2,500 per pay period ($65,000 annual salary).

A. $2,500 less $469.24 (4 x $117.31)	$2,030.76
B. Tax on first $2,013 (Refer to above table)	$241.65
C. Tax on remaining $17.76 ($2,030.76-2,013) x 27%	$4.80
D. Total to be withheld (Line B plus Line C)	$246.45

Your Take-Home Pay Computation Worksheet

(Deduct only those items which are applicable to you.)

Gross Bi-Weekly Pay...$ _____.___

Deduct Your Thrift Plan Contribution* ....$ _____.___

Taxable Bi-Weekly Pay ....$ _____.___

Deductions

Federal Tax...$ _____.___
(From Income Tax Withholding Table)
(Base this on "Taxable" Bi-Weekly Pay)

CSRS Employees
Retirement (7% gross bi-weekly pay)......................................$ _____.___

Medicare (1.45% gross bi-weekly pay) ....$ _____.___

FERS Employees
Retirement (0.8% gross bi-weekly pay)....................................$ _____.___

Social Security and Medicare Deduction (7.65% up to $87,000;
1.45% above $87,000) ....$ _____.___

Other Deductions

Health Insurance Premium..$ _____.___

Life Insurance Premium
($.15 per $1,000 basic coverage for non-postal employees).............$ _____.___

Optional Life Insurance Premium..$ _____.___

Union and/or Professional Dues..$ _____.___

U.S. Savings Bonds ....$ _____.___

Combined Federal Campaign Donation ....$ _____.___

Credit Unions. ....$ _____.___

Miscellaneous (Garnishments, indebtedness, etc.) ....$ _____.___

TOTAL TAX AND OTHER DEDUCTIONS ....$ _____.___

Bi-Weekly Take-Home Pay Amount......................................$ _____.___
(Before state income tax deduction)
** Note: If your state has income tax withholding,

deduct this amount here...$ _____.___

Bi-Weekly Take-Home Pay Amount.....................................$ _____.___
(After state income tax deduction)

* Thrift Plan voluntary contributions may be state taxable.

** State income tax withholding is based on gross bi-weekly pay.

Section 11—2003 Pay Tables and Schedules

Including Executive, Congressional, Judicial, Locality, Military, Historical and Others

Annual Salaries of Top U.S. Government Positions

Executive Schedule

President	$400,000 plus $50,000 official expense allowance
Vice President	$198,600
Level I Cabinet Officers	$171,900
Level II	$154,700
Level III	$142,500
Level IV	$134,000
Level V	$125,400

Congressional Salaries

Senators, Representatives, Delegates to Congress	$154,700
President pro tempore of the Senate	$171,900
Majority leader and minority leader of the Senate	$171,900
Majority leader and minority leader of the House	$171,900
Speaker of the House of Representatives	$198,600

Judicial Salaries

Chief Justice of the United States	$198,600
Associate Justices of the Supreme Court	$190,100
Circuit Judges	$164,100
District Judges	$154,700
Judges, Court of International Trade, U.S. Tax Court, U.S. Claims Court	$154,700

Senior Executive Service Salaries

Grade	Base
ES-1	$116,500
ES-2	$122,000
ES-3	$127,500
ES-4	$133,800
ES-5	$134,000
ES-6	$134,000

Please visit *www.FederalDaily.com* for updates.

> **Note:** These pay tables reflect the 3.1 percent across the board pay raise ordered by President Bush in December, 2002. For updates, please visit *www.FederalDaily.com.*

General Schedule Base Pay Table

Step	1	2	3	4	5	6	7	8	9	10
GS-1	15214	15722	16228	16731	17238	17536	18034	18538	18559	19031
2	17106	17512	18079	18559	18767	19319	19871	20423	20975	21527
3	18664	19286	19908	20530	21152	21774	22396	23018	23640	24262
4	20952	21650	22348	23046	23744	24442	25140	25838	26536	27234
5	23442	24223	25004	25785	26566	27347	28128	28909	29690	30471
6	26130	27001	27872	28743	29614	30485	31356	32227	33098	33969
7	29037	30005	30973	31941	32909	33877	34845	35813	36781	37749
8	32158	33230	34302	35374	36446	37518	38590	39662	40734	41806
9	35519	36703	37887	39071	40255	41439	42623	43807	44991	46175
10	39115	40419	41723	43027	44331	45635	46939	48243	49547	50851
11	42976	44409	45842	47275	48708	50141	51574	53007	54440	55873
12	51508	53225	54942	56659	58376	60093	61810	63527	65244	66961
13	61251	63293	65335	67377	69419	71461	73503	75545	77587	79629
14	72381	74794	77207	79620	82033	84446	86859	89272	91685	94098
15	85140	87978	90816	93654	96492	99330	102168	105006	107844	110682

Atlanta Locality Pay Table

Step	1	2	3	4	5	6	7	8	9	10
GS-1	16696	17253	17809	18361	18917	19244	19791	20344	20367	20885
2	18772	19218	19840	20367	20595	21201	21806	22412	23018	23624
3	20482	21164	21847	22530	23212	23895	24577	25260	25943	26625
4	22993	23759	24525	25291	26057	26823	27589	28355	29121	29887
5	25725	26582	27439	28296	29154	30011	30868	31725	32582	33439
6	28675	29631	30587	31543	32498	33454	34410	35366	36322	37278
7	31865	32927	33990	35052	36114	37177	38239	39301	40363	41426
8	35290	36467	37643	38819	39996	41172	42349	43525	44701	45878
9	38979	40278	41577	42877	44176	45475	46774	48074	49373	50672
10	42925	44356	45787	47218	48649	50080	51511	52942	54373	55804
11	47162	48734	50307	51880	53452	55025	56597	58170	59742	61315
12	56525	58409	60293	62178	64062	65946	67830	69715	71599	73483
13	67217	69458	71699	73940	76180	78421	80662	82903	85144	87385
14	79431	82079	84727	87375	90023	92671	95319	97967	100615	103263
15	93433	96547	99661	102776	105890	109005	112119	115234	118348	121462

Boston Locality Pay Table

Step	1	2	3	4	5	6	7	8	9	10
GS-1	17279	17855	18430	19001	19577	19916	20481	21054	21077	21614
2	19427	19888	20532	21077	21314	21941	22567	23194	23821	24448
3	21197	21903	22610	23316	24022	24729	25435	26142	26848	27554
4	23795	24588	25381	26173	26966	27759	28551	29344	30137	30930
5	26623	27510	28397	29284	30171	31058	31945	32832	33719	34606
6	29676	30665	31654	32643	33633	34622	35611	36600	37589	38579
7	32977	34077	35176	36275	37375	38474	39573	40673	41772	42872
8	36522	37739	38957	40174	41392	42609	43827	45044	46262	47479
9	40339	41684	43028	44373	45718	47062	48407	49752	51096	52441
10	44423	45904	47385	48866	50347	51828	53309	54790	56271	57751
11	48808	50435	52063	53690	55318	56945	58573	60200	61828	63455
12	58498	60448	62398	64348	66298	68248	70198	72148	74098	76048
13	69563	71882	74201	76520	78839	81158	83477	85796	88116	90435
14	82203	84944	87684	90424	93165	95905	98646	101386	104127	106867
15	96693	99917	103140	106363	109586	112809	116032	119255	122478	125702

> **Note:** These pay tables reflect the 3.1 percent across the board pay raise ordered by President Bush in December, 2002. For updates, please visit *www.FederalDaily.com*.

Chicago Locality Pay Table

Step	1	2	3	4	5	6	7	8	9	10
GS-1	17432	18014	18594	19170	19751	20093	20663	21241	21265	21806
2	19600	20065	20715	21265	21503	22136	22768	23401	24033	24666
3	21385	22098	22811	23523	24236	24949	25661	26374	27087	27799
4	24007	24807	25606	26406	27206	28006	28805	29605	30405	31205
5	26860	27755	28650	29544	30439	31334	32229	33124	34019	34914
6	29940	30938	31936	32934	33932	34930	35928	36926	37924	38922
7	33271	34380	35489	36598	37707	38816	39925	41035	42144	43253
8	36847	38075	39303	40532	41760	42988	44216	45445	46673	47901
9	40698	42054	43411	44768	46124	47481	48837	50194	51551	52907
10	44818	46312	47806	49300	50794	52289	53783	55277	56771	58265
11	49242	50884	52526	54168	55810	57452	59093	60735	62377	64019
12	59018	60985	62953	64920	66887	68855	70822	72789	74757	76724
13	70181	72521	74861	77201	79540	81880	84220	86559	88899	91239
14	82934	85699	88464	91229	93993	96758	99523	102288	105053	107817
15	97553	100805	104057	107309	110561	113812	117064	120316	123568	126819

Cincinnati Locality Pay Table

Step	1	2	3	4	5	6	7	8	9	10
GS-1	17053	17623	18190	18754	19322	19656	20214	20779	20803	21332
2	19174	19629	20265	20803	21036	21655	22273	22892	23511	24130
3	20920	21618	22315	23012	23709	24406	25104	25801	26498	27195
4	23485	24267	25050	25832	26615	27397	28179	28962	29744	30527
5	26276	27152	28027	28902	29778	30653	31529	32404	33280	34155
6	29289	30265	31242	32218	33194	34171	35147	36123	37100	38076
7	32548	33633	34718	35803	36888	37973	39058	40143	41228	42313
8	36046	37248	38449	39651	40852	42054	43256	44457	45659	46860
9	39813	41140	42468	43795	45122	46449	47776	49103	50430	51758
10	43844	45306	46767	48229	49691	51152	52614	54076	55537	56999
11	48172	49778	51384	52991	54597	56203	57809	59416	61022	62628
12	57735	59660	61584	63509	65434	67358	69283	71207	73132	75057
13	68656	70945	73234	75523	77812	80101	82390	84678	86967	89256
14	81132	83837	86541	89246	91951	94656	97360	100065	102770	105474
15	95433	98615	101796	104977	108158	111339	114520	117701	120882	124063

Cleveland Locality Pay Table

Step	1	2	3	4	5	6	7	8	9	10
GS-1	16786	17346	17904	18459	19019	19347	19897	20453	20476	20997
2	18873	19321	19947	20476	20706	21315	21924	22533	23142	23751
3	20592	21278	21964	22651	23337	24023	24710	25396	26082	26768
4	23116	23886	24657	25427	26197	26967	27737	28507	29277	30047
5	25864	26725	27587	28449	29310	30172	31034	31895	32757	33619
6	28829	29790	30751	31712	32673	33634	34595	35556	36517	37478
7	32037	33105	34173	35241	36308	37376	38444	39512	40580	41648
8	35480	36663	37845	39028	40211	41394	42576	43759	44942	46125
9	39188	40494	41801	43107	44413	45720	47026	48332	49639	50945
10	43156	44594	46033	47472	48910	50349	51788	53227	54665	56104
11	47415	48996	50577	52159	53740	55321	56902	58483	60064	61645
12	56829	58723	60618	62512	64406	66301	68195	70089	71984	73878
13	67578	69831	72084	74337	76590	78843	81096	83349	85602	87855
14	79858	82520	85182	87845	90507	93169	95832	98494	101156	103818
15	93935	97066	100197	103328	106460	109591	112722	115853	118984	122115

Note: These pay tables reflect the 3.1 percent across the board pay raise ordered by President Bush in December, 2002. For updates, please visit *www.FederalDaily.com*.

Columbus Locality Pay Table

Step	1	2	3	4	5	6	7	8	9	10
GS-1	16842	17404	17964	18521	19082	19412	19964	20522	20545	21067
2	18936	19386	20013	20545	20775	21386	21997	22608	23219	23830
3	20661	21350	22038	22727	23415	24104	24792	25481	26169	26858
4	23194	23967	24739	25512	26285	27057	27830	28603	29375	30148
5	25950	26815	27679	28544	29409	30273	31138	32002	32867	33731
6	28926	29890	30854	31819	32783	33747	34711	35675	36639	37604
7	32144	33216	34287	35359	36430	37502	38573	39645	40717	41788
8	35599	36786	37972	39159	40346	41532	42719	43906	45093	46279
9	39320	40630	41941	43252	44562	45873	47184	48494	49805	51116
10	43300	44744	46187	47631	49074	50518	51961	53405	54849	56292
11	47574	49161	50747	52333	53920	55506	57092	58679	60265	61851
12	57019	58920	60821	62722	64622	66523	68424	70324	72225	74126
13	67805	70065	72326	74586	76847	79107	81368	83628	85889	88149
14	80126	82797	85468	88139	90811	93482	96153	98824	101495	104166
15	94250	97392	100533	103675	106817	109958	113100	116242	119383	122525

Dallas-Fort Worth Locality Pay Table

Step	1	2	3	4	5	6	7	8	9	10
GS-1	16872	17436	17997	18555	19117	19447	20000	20559	20582	21105
2	18971	19421	20050	20582	20813	21425	22037	22649	23261	23873
3	20698	21388	22078	22768	23458	24147	24837	25527	26217	26907
4	23236	24010	24784	25558	26332	27106	27880	28654	29428	30203
5	25997	26863	27729	28596	29462	30328	31194	32060	32926	33792
6	28978	29944	30910	31876	32842	33808	34774	35740	36706	37672
7	32202	33276	34349	35423	36496	37570	38643	39717	40790	41864
8	35663	36852	38041	39230	40419	41607	42796	43985	45174	46363
9	39391	40704	42017	43330	44643	45956	47269	48582	49895	51208
10	43379	44825	46271	47717	49163	50609	52055	53501	54948	56394
11	47660	49250	50839	52428	54017	55606	57196	58785	60374	61963
12	57122	59027	60931	62835	64739	66643	68547	70451	72356	74260
13	67927	70192	72457	74721	76986	79250	81515	83779	86044	88309
14	80271	82947	85623	88299	90975	93651	96327	99003	101679	104355
15	94420	97568	100715	103862	107010	110157	113304	116452	119599	122746

Dayton Locality Pay Table

Step	1	2	3	4	5	6	7	8	9	10
GS-1	16678	17234	17789	18341	18896	19223	19769	20321	20344	20862
2	18752	19197	19818	20344	20572	21177	21783	22388	22993	23598
3	20459	21141	21823	22505	23187	23869	24550	25232	25914	26596
4	22968	23733	24498	25263	26028	26793	27558	28324	29089	29854
5	25697	26553	27409	28266	29122	29978	30834	31690	32546	33402
6	28644	29598	30553	31508	32463	33418	34372	35327	36282	37237
7	31830	32891	33953	35014	36075	37136	38197	39258	40319	41380
8	35252	36427	37602	38777	39952	41127	42302	43477	44653	45828
9	38936	40234	41532	42830	44128	45425	46723	48021	49319	50617
10	42878	44307	45737	47166	48596	50025	51455	52884	54313	55743
11	47110	48681	50252	51823	53394	54965	56535	58106	59677	61248
12	56463	58345	60227	62110	63992	65874	67756	69638	71520	73403
13	67143	69382	71620	73859	76097	78336	80574	82812	85051	87289
14	79344	81989	84634	87279	89925	92570	95215	97860	100505	103150
15	93330	96441	99552	102664	105775	108886	111997	115108	118219	121330

> **Note:** These pay tables reflect the 3.1 percent across the board pay raise ordered by President Bush in December, 2002. For updates, please visit *www.FederalDaily.com*.

Denver Locality Pay Table

Step	1	2	3	4	5	6	7	8	9	10
GS-1	17244	17819	18393	18963	19538	19875	20440	21011	21035	21570
2	19388	19848	20491	21035	21271	21896	22522	23147	23773	24399
3	21154	21859	22564	23269	23974	24679	25384	26089	26794	27499
4	23747	24538	25329	26120	26911	27703	28494	29285	30076	30867
5	26569	27454	28340	29225	30110	30995	31880	32765	33651	34536
6	29616	30603	31590	32577	33565	34552	35539	36526	37513	38500
7	32911	34008	35105	36202	37299	38396	39493	40590	41688	42785
8	36448	37663	38878	40093	41308	42523	43738	44953	46168	47383
9	40257	41599	42941	44283	45625	46967	48309	49651	50993	52335
10	44333	45811	47289	48767	50245	51723	53201	54679	56157	57635
11	48709	50333	51957	53581	55206	56830	58454	60078	61702	63326
12	58379	60325	62271	64217	66163	68109	70055	72002	73948	75894
13	69422	71736	74051	76365	78679	80994	83308	85623	87937	90252
14	82037	84772	87506	90241	92976	95711	98446	101181	103916	106651
15	96498	99714	102931	106147	109364	112581	115797	119014	122230	125447

Detroit Locality Pay Table

Step	1	2	3	4	5	6	7	8	9	10
GS-1	17452	18035	18615	19192	19774	20116	20687	21265	21289	21830
2	19622	20088	20738	21289	21528	22161	22794	23427	24060	24694
3	21409	22123	22836	23550	24263	24977	25690	26404	27117	27831
4	24034	24835	25635	26436	27237	28037	28838	29639	30439	31240
5	26890	27786	28682	29578	30474	31370	32266	33162	34057	34953
6	29974	30973	31972	32971	33970	34969	35968	36968	37967	38966
7	33308	34419	35529	36640	37750	38860	39971	41081	42191	43302
8	36888	38118	39348	40578	41807	43037	44267	45496	46726	47956
9	40744	42102	43460	44818	46177	47535	48893	50251	51609	52967
10	44869	46365	47860	49356	50852	52348	53844	55340	56835	58331
11	49298	50942	52585	54229	55873	57517	59161	60804	62448	64092
12	59085	61054	63024	64994	66963	68933	70902	72872	74841	76811
13	70261	72603	74946	77288	79631	81973	84315	86658	89000	91342
14	83028	85796	88564	91332	94100	96868	99636	102404	105172	107940
15	97664	100920	104175	107431	110686	113941	117197	120452	123708	126963

Hartford Locality Pay Table

Step	1	2	3	4	5	6	7	8	9	10
GS-1	17361	17940	18518	19092	19670	20010	20579	21154	21178	21716
2	19520	19983	20630	21178	21415	22045	22675	23305	23935	24564
3	21297	22007	22717	23427	24137	24846	25556	26266	26976	27685
4	23908	24705	25501	26298	27094	27891	28687	29484	30280	31077
5	26750	27641	28532	29423	30314	31206	32097	32988	33879	34770
6	29817	30811	31805	32799	33793	34786	35780	36774	37768	38762
7	33134	34239	35343	36448	37552	38657	39762	40866	41971	43075
8	36695	37919	39142	40365	41589	42812	44035	45258	46482	47705
9	40531	41882	43233	44584	45935	47286	48637	49988	51339	52690
10	44634	46122	47610	49098	50586	52074	53562	55050	56538	58026
11	49040	50675	52310	53946	55581	57216	58851	60486	62121	63757
12	58776	60735	62694	64654	66613	68572	70531	72491	74450	76409
13	69894	72224	74554	76884	79214	81544	83874	86204	88535	90865
14	82594	85347	88101	90854	93608	96361	99115	101868	104622	107375
15	97153	100392	103630	106869	110107	113345	116584	119822	123061	126299

Note: These pay tables reflect the 3.1 percent across the board pay raise ordered by President Bush in December, 2002. For updates, please visit www.FederalDaily.com.

Houston Locality Pay Table

Step	1	2	3	4	5	6	7	8	9	10
GS-1	18045	18648	19248	19845	20446	20799	21390	21988	22013	22573
2	20289	20771	21444	22013	22260	22914	23569	24224	24878	25533
3	22137	22875	23613	24351	25088	25826	26564	27302	28039	28777
4	24851	25679	26507	27335	28163	28991	29819	30646	31474	32302
5	27805	28731	29657	30584	31510	32436	33363	34289	35215	36142
6	30993	32026	33059	34092	35125	36158	37191	38224	39258	40291
7	34441	35589	36737	37885	39033	40182	41330	42478	43626	44774
8	38143	39414	40686	41957	43229	44500	45772	47043	48315	49586
9	42129	43533	44938	46342	47746	49151	50555	51959	53364	54768
10	46394	47941	49488	51034	52581	54128	55674	57221	58768	60314
11	50974	52674	54373	56073	57773	59472	61172	62872	64571	66271
12	61094	63130	65167	67203	69240	71276	73313	75349	77386	79422
13	72650	75072	77494	79916	82338	84760	87182	89604	92026	94448
14	85851	88713	91575	94437	97299	100161	103023	105886	108748	111610
15	100985	104351	107717	111083	114449	117815	121181	124548	127914	131280

Huntsville (Ala.) Locality Pay Table

Step	1	2	3	4	5	6	7	8	9	10
GS-1	16595	17150	17702	18250	18803	19128	19671	20221	20244	20759
2	18659	19102	19721	20244	20471	21073	21675	22277	22880	23482
3	20359	21037	21716	22394	23073	23751	24430	25108	25787	26465
4	22854	23616	24377	25139	25900	26661	27423	28184	28945	29707
5	25571	26422	27274	28126	28978	29830	30682	31534	32386	33238
6	28503	29453	30403	31353	32303	33253	34203	35153	36103	37053
7	31674	32729	33785	34841	35897	36953	38009	39065	40121	41177
8	35078	36247	37417	38586	39755	40925	42094	43263	44433	45602
9	38744	40036	41327	42619	43910	45202	46493	47785	49076	50368
10	42667	44089	45511	46934	48356	49779	51201	52623	54046	55468
11	46878	48441	50004	51568	53131	54694	56257	57820	59383	60946
12	56185	58058	59931	61804	63677	65549	67422	69295	71168	73041
13	66813	69040	71267	73495	75722	77950	80177	82404	84632	86859
14	78953	81585	84217	86849	89482	92114	94746	97378	100010	102642
15	92871	95966	99062	102158	105253	108349	111445	114541	117636	120732

Indianapolis Locality Pay Table

Step	1	2	3	4	5	6	7	8	9	10
GS-1	16560	17113	17664	18212	18764	19088	19630	20179	20201	20715
2	18620	19062	19679	20201	20428	21029	21630	22230	22831	23432
3	20316	20993	21670	22347	23024	23701	24378	25055	25732	26409
4	22806	23566	24326	25086	25845	26605	27365	28125	28884	29644
5	25517	26367	27217	28067	28917	29767	30617	31467	32318	33168
6	28443	29391	30339	31287	32235	33183	34131	35079	36027	36975
7	31607	32660	33714	34768	35821	36875	37929	38982	40036	41090
8	35004	36171	37338	38505	39671	40838	42005	43172	44339	45506
9	38662	39951	41240	42529	43818	45106	46395	47684	48973	50261
10	42577	43996	45415	46835	48254	49674	51093	52513	53932	55351
11	46779	48339	49899	51459	53019	54578	56138	57698	59258	60818
12	56066	57935	59804	61673	63542	65411	67280	69149	71018	72887
13	66672	68894	71117	73340	75563	77785	80008	82231	84453	86676
14	78787	81413	84040	86666	89293	91919	94546	97173	99799	102426
15	92675	95764	98853	101942	105032	108121	111210	114299	117388	120477

Note: These pay tables reflect the 3.1 percent across the board pay raise ordered by President Bush in December, 2002. For updates, please visit www.FederalDaily.com.

Kansas City Locality Pay Table

Step	1	2	3	4	5	6	7	8	9	10
GS-1	16626	17181	17734	18284	18838	19163	19708	20258	20281	20797
2	18693	19137	19757	20281	20509	21112	21715	22318	22921	23525
3	20396	21076	21755	22435	23115	23795	24474	25154	25834	26514
4	22896	23659	24422	25185	25947	26710	27473	28236	28999	29761
5	25617	26471	27324	28178	29031	29885	30738	31592	32445	33299
6	28555	29507	30459	31410	32362	33314	34266	35218	36169	37121
7	31732	32789	33847	34905	35963	37021	38079	39136	40194	41252
8	35142	36314	37485	38657	39828	41000	42171	43343	44514	45686
9	38815	40109	41403	42697	43991	45285	46578	47872	49166	50460
10	42745	44170	45595	47020	48445	49870	51295	52720	54145	55570
11	46964	48530	50096	51662	53228	54794	56360	57926	59492	61058
12	56288	58164	60041	61917	63793	65670	67546	69422	71299	73175
13	66935	69167	71398	73630	75861	78093	80324	82556	84787	87019
14	79098	81735	84372	87009	89646	92283	94920	97556	100193	102830
15	93041	96142	99244	102345	105446	108548	111649	114751	117852	120953

Los Angeles Locality Pay Table

Step	1	2	3	4	5	6	7	8	9	10
GS-1	17656	18245	18833	19416	20005	20351	20928	21513	21538	22085
2	19852	20323	20981	21538	21779	22420	23060	23701	24341	24982
3	21660	22381	23103	23825	24547	25269	25991	26712	27434	28156
4	24315	25125	25935	26745	27555	28365	29175	29985	30795	31605
5	27204	28111	29017	29923	30830	31736	32643	33549	34455	35362
6	30324	31335	32345	33356	34367	35378	36389	37399	38410	39421
7	33697	34821	35944	37068	38191	39314	40438	41561	42684	43808
8	37319	38563	39807	41052	42296	43540	44784	46028	47272	48516
9	41220	42594	43968	45342	46716	48090	49464	50838	52212	53586
10	45393	46906	48420	49933	51446	52959	54473	55986	57499	59013
11	49874	51537	53200	54863	56526	58189	59852	61515	63178	64841
12	59775	61768	63760	65753	67745	69738	71731	73723	75716	77708
13	71082	73452	75821	78191	80561	82930	85300	87670	90040	92409
14	83998	86798	89599	92399	95199	98000	100800	103600	106400	109201
15	98805	102098	105392	108685	111979	115272	118566	121859	125153	128446

Miami-Ft. Lauderdale Locality Pay Table

Step	1	2	3	4	5	6	7	8	9	10
GS-1	17108	17679	18248	18814	19384	19719	20279	20846	20870	21400
2	19236	19692	20330	20870	21103	21724	22345	22966	23586	24207
3	20988	21687	22387	23086	23785	24485	25184	25884	26583	27283
4	23561	24345	25130	25915	26700	27485	28270	29055	29840	30625
5	26361	27239	28117	28995	29873	30752	31630	32508	33386	34265
6	29383	30363	31342	32322	33301	34280	35260	36239	37219	38198
7	32652	33741	34829	35918	37006	38095	39183	40272	41360	42449
8	36162	37367	38573	39778	40984	42189	43394	44600	45805	47011
9	39941	41273	42604	43935	45267	46598	47930	49261	50592	51924
10	43985	45451	46918	48384	49850	51317	52783	54249	55716	57182
11	48327	49938	51549	53161	54772	56384	57995	59606	61218	62829
12	57921	59852	61782	63713	65644	67575	69505	71436	73367	75298
13	68877	71173	73469	75765	78062	80358	82654	84950	87247	89543
14	81392	84106	86819	89533	92246	94960	97673	100386	103100	105813
15	95740	98931	102123	105314	108505	111697	114888	118079	121271	124462

Note: These pay tables reflect the 3.1 percent across the board pay raise ordered by President Bush in December, 2002. For updates, please visit *www.FederalDaily.com*.

Milwaukee-Racine Locality Pay Table

Step	1	2	3	4	5	6	7	8	9	10
GS-1	16743	17302	17859	18412	18970	19298	19846	20401	20424	20944
2	18825	19272	19896	20424	20653	21261	21868	22476	23083	23690
3	20540	21224	21909	22593	23278	23962	24647	25331	26016	26700
4	23058	23826	24594	25362	26130	26898	27667	28435	29203	29971
5	25798	26657	27517	28376	29236	30095	30955	31814	32674	33533
6	28756	29715	30673	31632	32590	33549	34507	35466	36424	37383
7	31955	33021	34086	35151	36216	37282	38347	39412	40477	41543
8	35390	36570	37749	38929	40109	41289	42468	43648	44828	46008
9	39089	40392	41695	42998	44301	45604	46907	48210	49513	50816
10	43046	44481	45916	47351	48786	50221	51656	53091	54526	55962
11	47295	48872	50449	52026	53603	55180	56757	58334	59911	61488
12	56685	58574	60464	62353	64243	66132	68022	69911	71801	73691
13	67407	69654	71901	74148	76396	78643	80890	83137	85384	87632
14	79655	82311	84966	87622	90277	92933	95588	98244	100899	103555
15	93697	96820	99943	103066	106189	109313	112436	115559	118682	121806

Minneapolis-St. Paul Locality Pay Table

Step	1	2	3	4	5	6	7	8	9	10
GS-1	16973	17539	18104	18665	19231	19563	20119	20681	20704	21231
2	19083	19536	20169	20704	20936	21552	22168	22784	23400	24016
3	20822	21515	22209	22903	23597	24291	24985	25679	26373	27067
4	23374	24153	24931	25710	26489	27267	28046	28825	29604	30382
5	26152	27023	27894	28766	29637	30508	31380	32251	33122	33993
6	29151	30122	31094	32066	33037	34009	34981	35952	36924	37896
7	32394	33474	34553	35633	36713	37793	38873	39953	41033	42113
8	35875	37071	38267	39463	40659	41855	43051	44247	45443	46639
9	39625	40946	42267	43588	44908	46229	47550	48871	50192	51513
10	43637	45091	46546	48001	49456	50910	52365	53820	55275	56729
11	47944	49543	51141	52740	54339	55937	57536	59135	60733	62332
12	57462	59378	61293	63209	65124	67040	68955	70871	72786	74702
13	68332	70610	72888	75166	77444	79722	82000	84278	86556	88834
14	80748	83440	86132	88824	91516	94208	96900	99592	102284	104976
15	94982	98148	101314	104480	107646	110813	113979	117145	120311	123477

New York Locality Pay Table

Step	1	2	3	4	5	6	7	8	9	10
GS-1	17531	18116	18700	19279	19863	20207	20781	21361	21386	21929
2	19711	20179	20832	21386	21625	22261	22897	23533	24169	24806
3	21507	22223	22940	23657	24373	25090	25807	26524	27240	27957
4	24143	24947	25752	26556	27360	28165	28969	29773	30577	31382
5	27012	27912	28812	29712	30612	31512	32412	33312	34212	35112
6	30110	31113	32117	33121	34124	35128	36132	37135	38139	39142
7	33459	34575	35690	36806	37921	39036	40152	41267	42383	43498
8	37056	38291	39526	40761	41997	43232	44467	45703	46938	48173
9	40929	42293	43657	45022	46386	47750	49114	50479	51843	53207
10	45072	46575	48077	49580	51083	52585	54088	55590	57093	58596
11	49521	51172	52824	54475	56126	57777	59429	61080	62731	64382
12	59353	61331	63310	65288	67267	69245	71224	73202	75181	77159
13	70580	72933	75286	77639	79992	82345	84698	87051	89404	91756
14	83405	86185	88966	91746	94527	97307	100088	102868	105649	108429
15	98107	101377	104647	107918	111188	114458	117728	120998	124269	127539

Note: These pay tables reflect the 3.1 percent across the board pay raise ordered by President Bush in December, 2002. For updates, please visit www.FederalDaily.com.

Orlando Locality Pay Table

Step	1	2	3	4	5	6	7	8	9	10
GS-1	16533	17085	17635	18182	18733	19056	19598	20145	20168	20681
2	18589	19030	19646	20168	20394	20994	21594	22194	22794	23393
3	20282	20958	21634	22310	22986	23662	24338	25014	25690	26366
4	22769	23527	24286	25044	25803	26561	27320	28078	28837	29595
5	25474	26323	27172	28021	28869	29718	30567	31415	32264	33113
6	28395	29342	30289	31235	32182	33128	34075	35021	35968	36914
7	31555	32606	33658	34710	35762	36814	37866	38918	39970	41022
8	34946	36111	37276	38441	39606	40771	41936	43101	44266	45431
9	38598	39885	41172	42458	43745	45032	46318	47605	48892	50178
10	42506	43923	45340	46757	48174	49592	51009	52426	53843	55260
11	46702	48259	49817	51374	52931	54488	56045	57603	59160	60717
12	55974	57840	59705	61571	63437	65303	67169	69035	70901	72767
13	66561	68781	71000	73219	75438	77657	79876	82095	84314	86533
14	78656	81279	83901	86523	89145	91767	94390	97012	99634	102256
15	92522	95606	98690	101774	104858	107942	111026	114110	117194	120278

Philadelphia Locality Pay Table

Step	1	2	3	4	5	6	7	8	9	10
GS-1	17056	17626	18193	18757	19326	19660	20218	20783	20806	21336
2	19178	19633	20268	20806	21040	21659	22277	22896	23515	24134
3	20924	21622	22319	23016	23714	24411	25108	25805	26503	27200
4	23489	24272	25054	25837	26619	27402	28184	28967	29750	30532
5	26281	27156	28032	28908	29783	30659	31534	32410	33285	34161
6	29294	30271	31247	32224	33200	34177	35153	36130	37106	38083
7	32553	33639	34724	35809	36894	37980	39065	40150	41235	42320
8	36052	37254	38456	39658	40860	42061	43263	44465	45667	46869
9	39820	41148	42475	43802	45130	46457	47785	49112	50439	51767
10	43852	45314	46776	48238	49699	51161	52623	54085	55547	57009
11	48180	49787	51393	53000	54607	56213	57820	59426	61033	62639
12	57746	59671	61595	63520	65445	67370	69295	71220	73145	75070
13	68668	70958	73247	75536	77826	80115	82404	84693	86983	89272
14	81146	83852	86557	89262	91967	94672	97378	100083	102788	105493
15	95450	98632	101814	104995	108177	111359	114541	117722	120904	124086

Pittsburgh Locality Pay Table

Step	1	2	3	4	5	6	7	8	9	10
GS-1	16662	17219	17773	18324	18879	19205	19751	20303	20326	20843
2	18734	19179	19800	20326	20554	21158	21763	22367	22972	23576
3	20441	21122	21803	22484	23166	23847	24528	25209	25891	26572
4	22947	23711	24476	25240	26004	26769	27533	28298	29062	29827
5	25674	26529	27384	28240	29095	29950	30806	31661	32516	33372
6	28618	29571	30525	31479	32433	33387	34341	35295	36249	37203
7	31801	32861	33922	34982	36042	37102	38162	39222	40283	41343
8	35219	36393	37568	38742	39916	41090	42264	43438	44612	45786
9	38900	40197	41494	42791	44087	45384	46681	47977	49274	50571
10	42839	44267	45695	47123	48551	49979	51408	52836	54264	55692
11	47067	48637	50206	51776	53345	54914	56484	58053	59623	61192
12	56412	58292	60172	62053	63933	65814	67694	69575	71455	73336
13	67082	69318	71555	73791	76028	78264	80500	82737	84973	87210
14	79272	81914	84557	87200	89843	92485	95128	97771	100413	103056
15	93245	96354	99462	102570	105678	108786	111894	115003	118111	121219

Note: These pay tables reflect the 3.1 percent across the board pay raise ordered by President Bush in December, 2002. For updates, please visit *www.FederalDaily.com*.

Portland-Salem Locality Pay Table

Step	1	2	3	4	5	6	7	8	9	10
GS-1	16985	17552	18117	18678	19245	19577	20133	20696	20719	21246
2	19097	19550	20183	20719	20951	21568	22184	22800	23416	24033
3	20836	21531	22225	22920	23614	24308	25003	25697	26392	27086
4	23391	24170	24949	25729	26508	27287	28066	28846	29625	30404
5	26171	27043	27914	28786	29658	30530	31402	32274	33146	34018
6	29172	30144	31116	32089	33061	34033	35006	35978	36951	37923
7	32417	33498	34578	35659	36740	37820	38901	39982	41062	42143
8	35901	37098	38295	39492	40688	41885	43082	44279	45475	46672
9	39653	40975	42297	43619	44941	46262	47584	48906	50228	51550
10	43668	45124	46580	48035	49491	50947	52403	53858	55314	56770
11	47978	49578	51178	52778	54378	55977	57577	59177	60777	62377
12	57504	59420	61337	63254	65171	67088	69005	70922	72838	74755
13	68381	70660	72940	75220	77499	79779	82059	84338	86618	88898
14	80806	83500	86194	88888	91582	94276	96969	99663	102357	105051
15	95050	98219	101387	104555	107724	110892	114060	117229	120397	123565

Richmond-Petersburg Locality Pay Table

Step	1	2	3	4	5	6	7	8	9	10
GS-1	16685	17242	17797	18349	18905	19232	19778	20331	20354	20871
2	18760	19205	19827	20354	20582	21187	21793	22398	23003	23609
3	20469	21151	21833	22515	23197	23880	24562	25244	25926	26608
4	22978	23744	24509	25275	26040	26806	27571	28337	29102	29868
5	25709	26565	27422	28278	29135	29991	30848	31705	32561	33418
6	28657	29612	30567	31522	32478	33433	34388	35343	36299	37254
7	31845	32906	33968	35030	36091	37153	38215	39276	40338	41399
8	35268	36443	37619	38795	39970	41146	42322	43497	44673	45849
9	38954	40252	41551	42849	44148	45446	46745	48043	49342	50640
10	42897	44328	45758	47188	48618	50048	51478	52908	54338	55768
11	47132	48703	50275	51846	53418	54990	56561	58133	59704	61276
12	56489	58372	60255	62138	64021	65904	67787	69670	71553	73436
13	67174	69413	71653	73892	76132	78371	80611	82850	85090	87329
14	79380	82027	84673	87319	89966	92612	95258	97905	100551	103197
15	93373	96485	99598	102710	105823	108935	112048	115160	118273	121385

Sacramento-Yolo Locality Pay Table

Step	1	2	3	4	5	6	7	8	9	10
GS-1	17038	17607	18174	18737	19305	19639	20196	20761	20784	21313
2	19157	19612	20247	20784	21017	21635	22254	22872	23490	24108
3	20902	21598	22295	22992	23688	24385	25081	25778	26474	27171
4	23464	24246	25028	25809	26591	27373	28154	28936	29718	30499
5	26253	27127	28002	28877	29751	30626	31501	32375	33250	34124
6	29263	30238	31214	32189	33165	34140	35116	36091	37066	38042
7	32519	33603	34687	35771	36855	37939	39023	40107	41191	42275
8	36014	37214	38415	39615	40816	42016	43217	44417	45618	46819
9	39778	41104	42430	43756	45082	46408	47733	49059	50385	51711
10	43805	45265	46726	48186	49646	51107	52567	54027	55488	56948
11	48129	49734	51338	52943	54548	56153	57758	59363	60967	62572
12	57684	59607	61530	63452	65375	67298	69221	71144	73067	74990
13	68595	70882	73169	75456	77742	80029	82316	84603	86890	89177
14	81059	83762	86464	89166	91869	94571	97273	99976	102678	105380
15	95348	98527	101705	104883	108061	111240	114418	117596	120774	123953

Note: These pay tables reflect the 3.1 percent across the board pay raise ordered by President Bush in December, 2002. For updates, please visit www.FederalDaily.com.

St. Louis Locality Pay Table

Step	1	2	3	4	5	6	7	8	9	10
GS-1	16580	17134	17685	18233	18786	19111	19653	20203	20226	20740
2	18642	19085	19702	20226	20452	21054	21655	22257	22859	23460
3	20340	21018	21696	22374	23051	23729	24407	25085	25763	26441
4	22833	23594	24355	25116	25876	26637	27398	28158	28919	29680
5	25547	26398	27249	28100	28952	29803	30654	31505	32356	33207
6	28476	29426	30375	31324	32273	33223	34172	35121	36070	37019
7	31645	32699	33754	34809	35864	36919	37974	39029	40084	41139
8	35046	36214	37382	38551	39719	40887	42055	43224	44392	45560
9	38709	39999	41289	42580	43870	45160	46451	47741	49031	50322
10	42628	44049	45470	46891	48312	49733	51154	52575	53996	55417
11	46835	48397	49959	51520	53082	54644	56205	57767	59329	60890
12	56133	58005	59876	61747	63618	65489	67361	69232	71103	72974
13	66751	68977	71202	73427	75653	77878	80104	82329	84554	86780
14	78881	81511	84140	86770	89400	92029	94659	97289	99918	102548
15	92786	95878	98971	102064	105157	108250	111343	114436	117528	120621

San Diego Locality Pay Table

Step	1	2	3	4	5	6	7	8	9	10
GS-1	17146	17719	18289	18856	19427	19763	20324	20892	20916	21448
2	19278	19736	20375	20916	21150	21773	22395	23017	23639	24261
3	21034	21735	22436	23137	23838	24539	25240	25941	26642	27343
4	23613	24400	25186	25973	26759	27546	28333	29119	29906	30693
5	26419	27299	28180	29060	29940	30820	31700	32580	33461	34341
6	29449	30430	31412	32393	33375	34357	35338	36320	37301	38283
7	32725	33816	34907	35998	37088	38179	39270	40361	41452	42543
8	36242	37450	38658	39866	41075	42283	43491	44699	45907	47115
9	40030	41364	42699	44033	45367	46702	48036	49370	50705	52039
10	44083	45552	47022	48491	49961	51431	52900	54370	55839	57309
11	48434	50049	51664	53279	54894	56509	58124	59739	61354	62969
12	58050	59985	61920	63855	65790	67725	69660	71595	73530	75465
13	69030	71331	73633	75934	78235	80537	82838	85139	87441	89742
14	81573	84293	87012	89732	92451	95171	97890	100610	103329	106048
15	95953	99151	102350	105548	108746	111945	115143	118342	121540	124739

San Francisco-Oakland-San Jose Locality Pay Table

Step	1	2	3	4	5	6	7	8	9	10
GS-1	18111	18715	19318	19917	20520	20875	21468	22068	22093	22655
2	20363	20846	21521	22093	22340	22997	23654	24312	24969	25626
3	22218	22958	23698	24439	25179	25920	26660	27401	28141	28881
4	24941	25772	26603	27434	28265	29096	29927	30758	31588	32419
5	27905	28835	29765	30694	31624	32554	33484	34413	35343	36273
6	31105	32142	33179	34216	35253	36289	37326	38363	39400	40437
7	34566	35718	36870	38023	39175	40327	41479	42632	43784	44936
8	38281	39557	40833	42109	43385	44661	45938	47214	48490	49766
9	42282	43691	45101	46510	47920	49329	50738	52148	53557	54967
10	46562	48115	49667	51219	52772	54324	55876	57428	58981	60533
11	51159	52864	54570	56276	57982	59688	61394	63100	64805	66511
12	61315	63359	65403	67447	69491	71535	73579	75623	77666	79710
13	72913	75344	77775	80206	82636	85067	87498	89929	92360	94790
14	86162	89035	91907	94780	97652	100525	103397	106269	109142	112014
15	101351	104729	108107	111486	114864	118242	121621	124999	128377	131756

> **Note:** These pay tables reflect the 3.1 percent across the board pay raise ordered by President Bush in December, 2002. For updates, please visit www.FederalDaily.com.

Seattle Locality Pay Table

Step	1	2	3	4	5	6	7	8	9	10
GS-1	17005	17572	18138	18700	19267	19600	20157	20720	20743	21271
2	19119	19573	20207	20743	20976	21593	22210	22827	23444	24061
3	20861	21556	22251	22946	23642	24337	25032	25727	26422	27118
4	23418	24198	24978	25759	26539	27319	28099	28879	29659	30439
5	26201	27074	27947	28820	29693	30566	31439	32312	33185	34057
6	29206	30179	31153	32126	33100	34073	35047	36020	36994	37967
7	32455	33537	34619	35700	36782	37864	38946	40028	41110	42192
8	35943	37141	38339	39538	40736	41934	43132	44330	45528	46727
9	39700	41023	42346	43670	44993	46316	47640	48963	50286	51610
10	43719	45176	46634	48091	49549	51006	52464	53921	55379	56836
11	48034	49636	51238	52839	54441	56043	57644	59246	60848	62449
12	57570	59490	61409	63328	65247	67166	69085	71004	72923	74842
13	68460	70743	73025	75307	77590	79872	82154	84437	86719	89001
14	80900	83597	86294	88991	91688	94385	97082	99779	102476	105173
15	95161	98333	101505	104677	107849	111021	114193	117365	120537	123709

Washington-Baltimore Locality Pay Table

Step	1	2	3	4	5	6	7	8	9	10
GS-1	16961	17527	18091	18652	19217	19549	20104	20666	20690	21216
2	19070	19522	20154	20690	20921	21537	22152	22768	23383	23998
3	20807	21500	22193	22887	23580	24274	24967	25660	26354	27047
4	23357	24135	24914	25692	26470	27248	28026	28804	29582	30360
5	26133	27004	27874	28745	29616	30486	31357	32228	33098	33969
6	29130	30101	31072	32043	33014	33985	34956	35927	36898	37869
7	32370	33450	34529	35608	36687	37766	38845	39924	41003	42083
8	35850	37045	38240	39435	40630	41825	43020	44215	45410	46605
9	39597	40917	42236	43556	44876	46196	47516	48836	50156	51476
10	43605	45059	46513	47966	49420	50874	52328	53781	55235	56689
11	47910	49507	51105	52702	54300	55897	57495	59092	60690	62287
12	57421	59335	61249	63163	65078	66992	68906	70820	72734	74648
13	68283	70559	72835	75112	77388	79665	81941	84218	86494	88770
14	80690	83380	86070	88760	91450	94140	96830	99520	102210	104900
15	94914	98078	101242	104405	107569	110733	113897	117061	120224	123388

Rest of U.S. Locality Pay Table

Step	1	2	3	4	5	6	7	8	9	10
GS-1	16528	17080	17630	18177	18727	19051	19592	20140	20162	20675
2	18584	19025	19641	20162	20388	20988	21588	22188	22787	23387
3	20277	20952	21628	22304	22980	23655	24331	25007	25682	26358
4	22762	23521	24279	25037	25795	26554	27312	28070	28829	29587
5	25467	26316	27164	28013	28861	29710	30558	31407	32255	33104
6	28388	29334	30280	31226	32173	33119	34065	35011	35958	36904
7	31546	32597	33649	34701	35752	36804	37856	38907	39959	41011
8	34936	36101	37266	38430	39595	40760	41924	43089	44253	45418
9	38588	39874	41160	42447	43733	45019	46306	47592	48878	50165
10	42495	43911	45328	46745	48161	49578	50995	52411	53828	55245
11	46689	48246	49803	51360	52916	54473	56030	57587	59144	60700
12	55958	57824	59689	61554	63420	65285	67150	69016	70881	72746
13	66543	68762	70980	73198	75417	77635	79854	82072	84291	86509
14	78635	81256	83878	86499	89121	91742	94364	96985	99607	102228
15	92496	95579	98663	101746	104829	107912	110995	114079	117162	120245

Foreign Service Schedule

Step	Class 1	Class 2	Class 3	Class 4	Class 5	Class 6	Class 7	Class 8	Class 9
1	$85,140	$68,988	$55,901	$45,296	$36,703	$32,812	$29,332	$26,222	$23,442
2	87,694	71,058	57,578	46,655	37,804	33,796	30,212	27,009	24,145
3	90,325	73,190	59,305	48,055	38,938	34,810	31,119	27,819	24,870
4	93,034	75,386	61,085	49,496	40,106	35,854	32,052	28,654	25,615
5	95,826	77,647	62,917	50,981	41,309	36,929	33,014	29,513	26,384
6	98,701	79,977	64,805	52,511	42,548	38,038	34,003	30,399	27,175
7	101,662	82,376	66,749	54,085	43,825	39,179	35,024	31,311	27,991
8	104,711	84,847	68,751	55,708	45,139	40,354	36,075	32,251	28,831
9	107,853	87,393	70,813	57,379	46,494	41,565	37,157	33,218	29,696
10	110,685	90,015	72,938	59,101	47,889	42,811	38,272	34,864	30,587
11	110,685	92,715	75,126	60,874	49,325	44,096	39,419	35,241	31,504
12	110,685	95,496	77,380	62,700	50,805	45,419	40,602	36,298	32,449
13	110,685	98,360	79,701	64,581	52,329	46,782	41,820	37,387	33,423
14	110,685	101,311	82,092	66,519	53,899	48,185	43,075	38,509	34,425

Law Enforcement Officers
Effective January 2003
Annual Rates by Grade and Step

Step	1	2	3	4	5	6	7	8	9	10
GS-3	22396	23018	23640	24262	24884	25506	26128	26750	27372	27994
4	25140	25838	26536	27234	27932	28630	29328	30026	30724	31422
5	28909	29690	30471	31252	32033	32814	33595	34376	35157	35938
6	30485	31356	32227	33098	33969	34840	35711	36582	37453	38324
7	32909	33877	34845	35813	36781	37749	38717	39685	40653	41621
8	34302	35374	36446	37518	38590	39662	40734	41806	42878	43950
9	36703	37887	39071	40255	41439	42623	43807	44991	46175	47359
10	40419	41723	43027	44331	45635	46939	48243	49547	50851	52155

Administrative Law Judges

Grade	Base
AL-3/A	$89,200
AL-3/B	$96,000
AL-3/C	$102,900
AL-3/D	$109,800
AL-3/E	$116,600
AL-3/F	$123,400
AL-2	$130,400
AL-1	$134,000

Veterans Health Administration Pay Tables

Department of Veterans Affairs

Schedule for the Office of the Under Secretary for Health
(38 U.S.C. 7306)*

Deputy Under Secretary for Health		$144,591 **
Associate Deputy Under Secretary for Health		138,491 ***
Assistant Under Secretaries for Health		

	Minimum	Maximum
Medical Directors	$114,678	$129,972 ***
Service Directors	99,853	124,011
Director, National Center for Preventive Health	85,140	124,011

Physician and Dentist Schedule

Director Grade	$99,853	$124,011
Executive Grade	92,204	117,511
Chief Grade	85,140	110,685
Senior Grade	75,381	94,094
Intermediate Grade	61,251	79,623
Full Grade	51,508	66,957
Associate Grade	42,976	55,865

Clinical Podiatrist and Optometrist Schedule

Chief Grade	$85,140	$110,685
Senior Grade	72,381	94,094
Intermediate Grade	61,251	79,623
Full Grade	51,508	66,957
Associate Grade	42,976	55,865

Physician Assistant and Expanded-Function Dental Auxiliary Schedule ****

Director Grade	$85,140	$110,685
Assistant Director Grade.	72,381	94,094
Chief Grade	61,251	79,623
Senior Grade	51,508	66,957
Intermediate Grade	42,976	55,865
Full Grade	35,519	46,171
Associate Grade	30,565	39,733
Junior Grade	26,130	33,970

---

* This schedule does not apply to the Assistant Under Secretary for Nursing Programs or the Director of Nursing Services. Pay for these positions is set by the Under Secretary for Health under 38 U.S.C. 7451.

** Pursuant to section 7404(d)(1) of title 38, United States Code, the rate of basic pay payable to this employee is limited to the rate for level IV of the Executive Schedule.

*** Pursuant to section 7404(d)(2) of title 38, United States Code, the rate of basic pay payable to these employees is limited to the rate for level V of the Executive Schedule.

**** Pursuant to section 301(a) of Public Law 102-40, these positions are paid according to the Nurse Schedule in 38 U.S.C. 4107(b) as in effect on August 14, 1990, with subsequent adjustments.

Comparison of Pay Raises for Military,
General Schedule and Wage System Since Fiscal 1974

FY	Military	General Schedule	Wage System
74	4.8	4.8	10.2
75	5.5	5.5	8.9
76	5.0	5.0	9.0
77	4.8	4.8	8.3
78	7.1	7.1	7.9
79	5.5	5.5	5.3
80	7.0	7.0	6.4
81	11.7	9.1	9.1
82	14.3	4.8	4.8
83	4.0	4.0	4.0
84	4.0	3.5	3.5
85	4.0	3.5	3.5
86	3.0	0.0	0.0
87	3.0	3.0	3.0
88	2.0	2.0	2.0
89	4.1	4.1	4.1
90	3.6	3.6	3.6
91	4.1	4.1	4.1
92	4.2	4.2	4.2
93	3.7	3.7	3.7
94	2.2	3.09-5.62	Variable up to 3.96
95	2.6	2.28-4.28	Variable up to 3.09
96	2.4	2.05-2.82	Variable up to 2.52
97	3.0	2.24-4.66	Variable up to 3.12
98	2.8	2.44-6.52	Variable up to 2.88
99	3.6	3.54-4.02	Variable up to 3.67
2000	4.8	4.69-5.59	Variable up to 4.93
2001	3.7	3.56-4.46	Variable up to 3.83
2002	5.0-10.0	4.52-5.42	Variable up to 4.80
2003	4.1-6.5	3.1	Not available at press time

General Schedule Pay Raises Since 1956

Effective Date	Avg. (%)	Amount of Increase	Public Law
June 30, 1956		Ceiling of $16,000	84-854, July 31,1956
Jan. 1, 1958	10.00	10 percent for all employees, subject to ceiling of $17,500	84-462, June 20, 1958
July 1, 1960	7.50	7.5 percent for all employees	85-568, July 1, 1960
Oct. 11, 1962	5.50	5.5 percent for all employees Oct. 11, 1962, plus additional step for 1st 3 grades	87-793, Oct. 11, 1962
Jan. 1, 1964	3.90	3.9 percent for all employees	87-793, Oct. 11, 1962
July 1, 1964	4.20	4.2 percent for all employees	88-426, Aug. 14, 1964
Oct. 1, 1965	3.60	3.6 percent for all employees	89-301, Oct. 20, 1965
July 1, 1966	2.90	2.9 percent for all employees	89-504, July 18, 1966
Oct. 1, 1967	4.50	4.5 percent for all employees	90-206, Dec. 16, 1967
July 1, 1968	4.90	3 percent minimum, or 1/2 comparability	90-206, Dec. 16, 1967 H. Doc. 90-327
July 1, 1969	9.10	Full comparability	H. Doc. 91-131
Dec. 27, 1969	6.00	6 percent for all employees	91-231, Apr. 15, 1970
Jan. 1, 1971	6.00	6 percent for all employees	5 U.S.C. 5305.
Jan. 1, 1972	5.50	5.5 percent for all employees	92-210, Dec. 22, 1971
Jan. 1, 1973[1]	5.14	5.1 percent for all employees (annual comparability pay adjustment)	5 U.S.C. 5305.
Oct. 1, 1973	4.77	4.8 percent average increase for all employees (annual comparability pay adjustment)	5 U.S.C. 5305.
Oct. 1, 1974	5.48	5.5 percent average increase for all employees (annual comparability pay adjustment)	5 U.S.C. 5305.
Oct. 1, 1975	5.00	5 percent average increase for all employees	5 U.S.C. 5305.
Oct. 1, 1976	5.17	Increase varies from 4.24 percent to 11.83 percent (annual comparability pay adjustment)	5 U.S.C. 5305.
Oct. 1, 1977	7.05	7.05 percent average increase for all employees (annual comparability pay adjustment)	5 U.S.C. 5305.
Oct. 1, 1978	5.46	5.5 percent average increase for all employees	5 U.S.C. 5305.
Oct. 1, 1979	7.02	7.02 percent average increase for all employees	5 U.S.C. 5305.
Oct. 1, 1980	9.11	9.11 percent average increase for all employees	5 U.S.C. 5305.
Oct. 1, 1981	4.80	4.8 percent average increase for all employees	5 U.S.C. 5305.
Oct. 1, 1982	4.00	4 percent average increase for all employees	5 U.S.C. 5305.
Jan. 1, 1984	4.00	4 percent average increase for all employees	5 U.S.C. 5305.
Jan. 1, 1985	3.50	3.5 percent average increase for all employees	5 U.S.C. 5305.
Jan. 1, 1987	3.00	3 percent average increase for all employees	5 U.S.C. 5305.
Jan. 1, 1988	2.00	2 percent average increase for all employees	5 U.S.C. 5305.
Jan. 1, 1989	4.10	4.1 percent average increase for all employees	5 U.S.C. 5305.
Jan. 1, 1990	3.60	3.6 percent average increase for all employees	5 U.S.C. 5305.
Jan. 1, 1991	4.10	4.1 percent average increase for all employees	PL 101-509
Jan. 1, 1992	4.20	4.2 percent average increase for all employees	PL 101-509
Jan. 1, 1993	3.70	3.7 percent average increase for all employees	PL 101-509
Jan. 1, 1994	3.09-5.62	No national raise; locality pay system began	PL 101-509
Jan. 1, 1995	2.28-4.28	2 percent national raise plus locality pay	PL 101-509
Jan. 1, 1996	2.05-2.82	2 percent national raise plus locality pay	PL 101-509
Jan. 1, 1997	2.24-4.66	2.3 percent national raise plus locality pay	PL 101-509
Jan. 1, 1998	2.44-6.52	2.3 percent national raise plus locality pay	PL 101-509
Jan. 1, 1999	3.54-4.02	3.1 percent national raise plus locality pay	PL 105-277
Jan. 1, 2000	4.69-5.59	3.8 percent national raise plus locality pay	PL 106-58
Jan. 1, 2001	3.56-4.46	2.7 percent national raise plus locality pay	PL 106-554
Jan. 1, 2002	4.52-5.42	3.6 percent national raise plus locality pay	PL 107-67
Jan. 1, 2003	3.1	3.1 average rate for all employees	PL 101-509

[1]Effective date of Jan. 1, 1973, was subsequently changed, retroactively to Oct. 1, 1972, by Executive Order 11777 (Apr. 12, 1974), as result of court case (*National Treasury Employees Union v. Richard M. Nixon*, 492 F.2d 587). Source: Office of Personnel Management.

Note: All increases were effective the first full pay period in the indicated month except October 1962 and January 1970, which were effective October 11, 1962, and December 27, 1969, respectively.

Chapter 2
Insurance

Section 1—Federal Employees Health Benefits Program

FEHB Program: General Description

The FEHB program is open to almost all of the government's civilian employees on a voluntary basis. Exceptions are those workers who are serving their first year of federal employment under a temporary appointment, employed on an intermittent basis, or otherwise excluded by law or regulation.

The FEHB contains a number of features that make it one of the nation's leaders in the provision of health insurance. For example:

- within 60 days from the date you enter the government (or become eligible), you may enroll in a health benefits plan with group-rated premiums and benefits;
- coverage is provided without a medical examination or restrictions because of age, current health, or pre-existing conditions;
- there are no waiting periods for benefits to kick in after the effective date of enrollment;
- there is catastrophic protection against unusually large medical bills; and
- you have an annual opportunity, during annual open seasons, to enroll in a health benefits plan if you are not already enrolled, or if you are enrolled, to change to another plan or option.

The FEHB law mandates that special consideration be given to enrollees of certain FEHB plans who receive covered health services in states with a critical shortage of primary care physicians. FEHB fee-for-service insurers are required to provide benefits to plan participants in medically underserved areas who use any health care provider licensed to perform the specific medical service. The following states are medically underserved areas under the FEHB program: Alabama, Idaho, Kentucky, Louisiana, Maine, Mississippi, Missouri, Montana, New Mexico, North Dakota, South Carolina, South Dakota, Texas, Utah, West Virginia, and Wyoming.

FEHB Rules and Procedures

Under FEHB you have a wide selection of plans from which to choose. Currently, there are nearly 190 health plans in the program. One is a government-wide plan, 12 are employee organization plans (only six of which are open to all), and the rest are health maintenance organizations (HMOs). Any eligible employee may enroll in the government-wide plan. Generally, to enroll in an employee organization plan you must be a member of the organization sponsoring the plan. Some organization plans are open to all employees; others are restricted to specific agencies or occupations. HMOs are open to those who live or work within the geographic area serviced by that particular plan. Consult the plan brochure for more information.

By enrolling in an FEHB plan, employees have an opportunity to acquire protection against the cost of health care service for themselves and their families, including individuals suffering from prolonged illnesses or involved in serious accidents. Moreover, these health insurance benefits may be retained by employees after retirement, if they retire under certain conditions and meet certain requirements. (See below for "Coverage After Retirement.")

The cost of FEHB premiums is shared by the enrollees and the government, with active employees paying their share through payroll deductions and retirees through annuity deductions.

Federal and postal workers also are covered by Medicare hospital insurance (Part A) for which they pay 1.45 percent of salary each bi-weekly period. Employees become eligible for Medicare coverage when they reach age 65.

Patients' Rights

The FEHB program complies with a Patients' Bill of Rights first outlined by President Clinton in 1997 and applied to the program over the following several years. Under its provisions, consumers have the right to:

• receive accurate, easily understood information to help them make informed decisions about their health plans, professionals and facilities, including: accreditation status; compliance with state or federal licensing, certification, or fiscal solvency requirements; disenrollment rates; years in existence; corporate form; and compliance with standards (state, federal, and private accreditation) that assure confidentiality of medical records and orderly transfer to caregivers.

• information about networks and providers, including: board certification status and geographic location of all contracting primary and specialty care providers; whether they are accepting new patients; language(s) spoken and availability of interpreters; and whether their facilities are accessible to the disabled.

• a choice of health care providers that is sufficient to ensure access to appropriate high-quality health care. This includes: direct access to women's health care providers for routine and preventative health care services; direct access to a qualified specialist within the network of providers for complex or serious medical conditions that need frequent specialty care; and transitional care for those with chronic or disabling conditions or who are pregnant where the provider either drops out of the program or is terminated under the carrier's contract.

• access to emergency health care services when and where the need arises. Health plans use a "prudent layperson" standard in determining eligibility for coverage of emergency services without prior authorization.

• full participation in all decisions related to their health care. Consumers who are unable to fully participate in treatment decisions have the right to be represented by parents, guardians, family members, or other conservators.

• considerate, respectful care from all members of the health care system at all times and under all circumstances. An environment of mutual respect is essential to maintain a quality health care system. Consumers must not be discriminated against in the delivery of health care services consistent with the benefits covered in their policy or as required by law. Consumers who

are eligible for coverage under the terms and conditions of a health plan or program or as required by law must not be discriminated against in marketing and enrollment practices based on race, ethnicity, national origin, religion, sex, age, mental or physical disability, sexual orientation, genetic information, or source of payment.

• confidential communication with health care providers, and assurances of confidentiality for their personal health care information. Consumers also have the right to review and copy their own medical records and request amendments to their records.

In a health care system that protects consumers' rights, it is reasonable to expect and encourage consumers to assume reasonable responsibilities. Greater individual involvement by consumers in their own care increases the likelihood of achieving the best outcomes and helps support a quality-improvement, cost-conscious environment.

Questions, Complaints and Appeals

Questions about an individual's health insurance policy should be addressed to an employee's local personnel office. If the local personnel office needs further assistance, it should contact the designated agency insurance benefits officer at agency headquarters. OPM posts general information on the FEHB program as well as certain information on individual plans and links to Internet sites of the plans on its website at www.opm.gov/-insure/health. In addition, insurance carriers maintain toll-free numbers that can answer questions about coverage and provide plan brochures and other information. See below for "Contacting FEHB Plans."

If you don't agree with your health plan's decision regarding a claim, review and follow the directions in the disputed claims section of the brochure. This section will tell you how to ask the plan to reconsider your claim. You must explain why (in terms of the applicable brochure coverage provisions) you feel the services should be covered.

If the plan again denies the claim, read the plan's decision letter carefully. Then, check your plan's brochure again. If you still disagree with the plan's decision, the disputed claims section of the brochure will tell you how to write to the U.S. Office of Personnel

Management to ask OPM to review the claim. The address is: Office of Personnel Management, Retirement and Insurance Service, Office of Insurance Programs, P.O. Box 436, Washington, DC 20044.

OPM will review your disputed claim request and will use the information it collects from you and your plan. It will send you a final decision within 60 days. You may call the Contracts Division to check on the status of your disputed claim review by dialing the telephone number provided on the acknowledgement they send you. The Contracts Division cannot give you a decision over the phone until they have completed the review and issued a written final decision.

Decisions by the Contracts Division are the final level of OPM review. Those dissatisfied with the decisions may file a complaint in the appropriate federal district court by December 31 of the third year after the year in which you received the disputed services, drugs, or supplies.

FEHB Eligibility and Enrollment Rules

Generally, all federal and postal employees and retirees, as well as many temporary workers, are entitled to participate in the FEHB program. Enrollment in an FEHB health plan is not compulsory, and employees may decline to participate. (For a list of excepted categories of employees, see 5 CFR 890, or the FEHB Handbook at OPM's website at www.opm.gov/insure/health.)

Covered employees also include "cooperatives," those who serve "in cooperation" with nonfederal agencies and who are paid in whole or in part from non-federal funds, such as certain employees of the Agricultural Extension Service, certain Agricultural Stabilization and Conservation County Committee workers, employees transferred to public international organizations under the Federal Employees International Organization Act, and U.S. commissioners. When spouses are both government employees, each may enroll individually or one spouse may enroll for the family. However, the children of such a couple would be covered only if one spouse enrolls under the family option; enrolling individually does not cover children.

If your agency denies you coverage and offers you no supporting documentation,

look up the rule yourself in the sources mentioned above, or contact your agency's headquarters insurance officer.

At the time employees become eligible to enroll, the employing office provides: (1) an FEHB Guide (RI 70-1 for current employees, RI 70-8 for certain temporary employees, and RI 70-9 for retirees and survivors), which explains the health benefits program, compares the benefits under fee-for-service plans, and contains rates, and (2) Standard Form 2809, which is the form used by employees to enroll in a plan or elect not to enroll. Eligible employees may enroll during the annual open season or at other specified times (see below, "Table of Permissible Changes in Enrollment").

Employees in an authorized leave-without-pay or other type of non-pay status generally can continue health insurance coverage for up to one year of the non-pay period. The 365 days of non-pay status may be continuous or may be interrupted by periods in a pay status that last less than four consecutive months. Agencies must give employees the opportunity either to directly pay their share of the premiums for these periods of FEHB coverage or to incur a debt to the agency, if the agency advances their salary in the amount of the worker's share of the health premium to cover the cost of extended coverage.

FEHB open seasons for making enrollment changes are held each year from Monday of the second full workweek in November through Monday of the second full workweek in December, or as otherwise announced by the Office of Personnel Management. During an open season, employees may make enrollment decisions or changes affecting the health plan coverage of themselves and their eligible family members.

"Eligible family member" includes an employee's spouse and any unmarried dependent children under the age of 22, including legally adopted children, recognized children born out of wedlock, and foster children or stepchildren if they live with you in a regular parent-child relationship. Unmarried children may be covered regardless of their age if they are incapable of self-support because of an incapacity that began before attaining age 22. Parents or other relatives cannot be covered even though they may live with you.

In some cases, an employee's former spouse may be eligible for FEHB coverage. (For details, see 5 CFR 890, or visit OPM's website at www.opm.gov/insure.) Former spouses whose divorce occurred during the spouse's federal service should contact the agency that employed the spouse when the divorce occurred. Former spouses whose divorce occurred after the spouse's retirement should contact the Office of Personnel Management's Retirement and Insurance Service, Office of Retirement Programs, P.O. Box 17, Washington, DC 20044; (202) 606-0500.

Neither employees nor their family members will be required to pass a physical examination to enroll for health benefits. Similarly, neither employees nor their family members can be excluded from joining an FEHB plan because of age or employment in a hazardous job.

FEHB Plan Options

The FEHB program generally allows federal employees and annuitants to choose between fee-for-service plans, which work on a reimbursement model, and health maintenance organizations (HMO), which provide comprehensive health care on a pre-paid basis through contracts with physicians and hospitals in a particular geographic area. The government-wide service health benefit plan is a fee-for-service plan provided through Blue Cross and Blue Shield organizations that any employee may join. It is called a "service benefit plan" because it works on the principle of paying benefits either to the enrolled participant or directly to the doctor or hospital that provides the treatment or service. Blue Cross and Blue Shield also offers a network-only option.

Another type of FEHB fee-for-service plan is the employee organization plan. Any employee who is a member of an organization that sponsors a plan approved by the Office of Personnel Management may enroll in the plan.

In addition to the above plans, the FEHB program offers employees and annuitants the chance to enroll in a number of HMOs. Types of HMO options available to FEHB enrollees include:

• Group Practice Prepayment Plans— These plans have their own medical center or centers and their own doctors who prac-

tice as a group. Employees who live in an area where there is a group-practice pre-payment plan that participates in the FEHB program may choose to join it instead of one of the other plans.

• Individual Practice Prepayment Plans— In these plans, doctors agree to accept payments from the plan instead of requiring the patient to pay their usual charge. Like the group practice plans, these plans operate only in certain areas. Employees residing in a locality that has such an approved plan may choose to join it.

• "Mixed Model" Prepayment Plans— These are a combination of group practice and individual practice plans.

Employees seeking more detailed information about the types of benefits provided by different plans should consult the plan brochures that can be obtained from most government employment offices or from the OPM website at *http://www.opm.gov/-insure/ health/download_guides.htm.*

FEHB Premium Rates

The premium rates for FEHB plans typically change each year, following the annual contract negotiations between OPM and each insurance carrier. Any new plan rates resulting from these negotiations begin on the first day of the first pay period in January of the following year for active employees, and Jan. 1 for retirees.

FEHB premium costs are shared by the government and the participating employee or annuitant. Under the "Fair Share Formula," the maximum government contribution is set at 72 percent of the weighted average cost of all plans, not to exceed 75 percent of the cost of any specific plan. The enrollee pays for the balance of the premium cost.

The government contribution is the same for most federal employees, with the following exceptions:

• Employees appointed under the Federal Part-Time Career Act of 1978 only receive a portion of the government contribution paid to full-time employees, with the government's share pro-rated in proportion to the percentage of full-time service regularly performed.

• Temporary employees pay the full premium (both the employee and government shares).

• The U.S. Postal Service contributes an additional amount, specified in collective bargaining agreements, toward the cost of a postal service employee's enrollment.

Pre-tax Payment of FEHB Insurance Premiums

All employees in the Executive Branch of the federal government who are participating in the FEHB and whose pay is issued by an Executive Branch agency are eligible to have their premiums converted to pretax dollars. This includes deductions for retroactive coverage, payback of premiums from a prior period of LWOP and other adjustments.

This "premium conversion" arrangement results in reductions in federal income, Social Security and Medicare taxes. In many jurisdictions, state and local taxes will also be reduced. On the other hand, federal retirement, thrift savings and life insurance benefits are not affected by participation in premium conversion. For example, it does not affect base salary for the purpose of determining "high 3" salary years for retirement benefits calculation.

Participation in premium conversion is automatic. However, anyone choosing not to participate need only complete a form to opt out. That form is available from agency personnel offices. Each year during open season, employees may decide whether to participate for the following year. The participation continues uninterrupted unless the employee decides not to participate.

Eligibility for all Executive Branch employees began in October 2000. The Judiciary Branch, U.S. Postal Service, and some smaller Executive Branch agencies with independent compensation-setting authority previously implemented their own FEHB premium conversion plans.

Enrollees may change participation status in premium conversion during the annual FEHB open enrollment period, or during the calendar year upon a qualifying life event (see below).

Enrollment or participation in premium conversion ends if you terminate or are terminated from federal government employment. If you are eligible and elect to participate in Temporary Continuation of Coverage (TCC), you pay those premiums directly on an after-tax basis; premiums that are paid under TCC are not eligible for premium conversion.

While annuitants are not eligible for premium conversion, reemployed annuitants employed in positions that normally convey FEHB eligibility may participate in premium conversion. For them to do so, their FEHB enrollment must be transferred from their retirement system to the employing agency. For considerations relating to reemployed annuitants, see Chapter 4.

Premium conversion may result in somewhat lower Social Security benefits for those federal employees who pay Social Security taxes on their salaries, primarily those under the Federal Employees Retirement System. Therefore, in rare situations, it may be advantageous to pay full Social Security taxes rather than the lower ones arising from premium conversion. These rare cases do not involve employees covered by CSRS or CSRS-Offset.

An employee participating in premium conversion generally has the same flexibility as a person who chooses not to participate. Because of the tax laws, there are two exceptions. Those who waive premium conversion have the flexibility, without giving any reason, either to drop health insurance altogether or change from a self and family enrollment to self-only. Those participating in premium conversion are allowed to drop coverage, or change to self-only, only if the decision to do so comes during open season or at the time of a "qualifying life event," such as marriage or the new employment of a spouse in a job that covers the enrollee under the spouse's health insurance. Other qualifying life events include: the enrollee, spouse or dependent first become eligible for or lose entitlement to Medicare or Medicaid; a change in the enrollee's employment status or that of a spouse or dependent from either full-time to part-time, or the reverse; the start or end of an unpaid leave of absence by the enrollee, spouse or dependent; and a significant change in the cost or conditions of the spouse's health care coverage related to the spouse's employment that affects the enrollee. In certain circumstances, entering or returning from a period of unpaid leave (leave without pay, or LWOP) by the enrollee, spouse or covered dependent may constitute a qualifying life event.

Those entering a period of LWOP (more than 31 days) have the option to terminate or continue FEHB coverage. Those who elect to continue FEHB coverage must choose one of the options to pay the enrollee share of the premium. These options are pay-as-you-go (paying the enrollee share of the FEHB premium directly to the employing agency while on LWOP), and catch-up (where the agency remits the enrollee share of the FEHB premium to OPM during the period of LWOP and the enrollee repays it on return to pay status). In addition, under the IRS rules an agency may, but is not required to, offer a prepay option.

For more information on the pre-tax payment of FEHB insurance premiums, go online to *www.opm.gov/insure/health/pretaxfehb*.

Preadmission Certification Procedures

If you are enrolled in a traditional insurance plan or a health maintenance organization under the FEHB program, you need to remain up to date not only on your plan's benefits, but also on its cost containment rules and procedures. Under the FEHB, both HMOs and managed fee-for-service insurance plans have cost containment measures in place. All plans require preadmission certification of all non-emergency hospital admissions. Check your plan brochure for additional information.

If you are enrolled in a managed fee-for-service plan, the preadmission certification provision makes you responsible for ensuring that the requirement is met. You or your doctor must check with your FEHB plan before you are admitted to the hospital. If that doesn't happen, your benefits for the admission will be reduced by $500, not to exceed the cost of the admission. This means that if you do not satisfy the preadmission certification requirement before being admitted to the hospital, you will be penalized by forfeiting up to $500 in benefits your FEHB plan would otherwise pay to you.

For example, if you meet your annual deductible, then incur $1,000 in covered hospitalization charges, you will receive $800 in benefits from your FEHB plan if that plan pays 80 percent of hospitalization charges, as long as you are pre-certified to be admitted to the hospital. However, if, in that same situation, you fail to satisfy the preadmission requirement, $500 in benefits are lost as a penalty and you will receive only $300 in benefits from your FEHB plan. Avoid penalties by following your plan's cost containment provisions, specified in their FEHB brochure.

Temporary Continuation of Coverage

Temporary Continuation of Coverage (TCC) is a feature of the FEHB program that allows certain people—typically, employees who separate from employment and enrollee dependents who lose coverage—to temporarily continue their FEHB coverage after regular coverage ends. TCC enrollees must pay the full premium for the plan they select (i.e., both the employee and government shares of the premium) plus a two percent administrative charge.

Under certain conditions, federal employees and members of their families who lose their FEHB coverage due to the occurrence of a "qualifying event" are eligible for TCC. In most cases, the "qualifying event" that triggers TCC rights is an employee's separation from government service (including separations of retirees who otherwise might lose health coverage because they failed to meet length-of-enrollment requirements). However, employees are not entitled to TCC if they are involuntarily separated due to gross misconduct. Normally, the employing office is responsible for deciding whether conduct that results in an involuntary separation constitutes "gross misconduct." In such cases, the employing office must notify the worker of that fact and explain what the employee can do to appeal the decision.

Dependent children who are covered under the family enrollment of an employee, former employee, or annuitant are eligible for TCC coverage if one of the following occurs: marriage, reaching age 22 or becoming capable of self-support after age 22; or loss of status as a stepchild, foster child, or recognized natural child.

However, for a federal employee's spouse, the qualifying events triggering TCC rights are divorce and annulment of the marriage. Spouses are not eligible for TCC in their own right, even if a federal employee separates from federal service and decides not to elect TCC or if the employee dies before the spouse is entitled to survivor benefits. However, if a federal employee's marriage ends other than by death, the worker's former spouse is eligible for TCC.

A former employee's or former dependent child's election of TCC family enrollment covers the same family members of the enrollee as were covered under regular FEHB family enrollment, and the family members must continue to meet the same requirements as under a regular family enrollment. A new family member, such as a spouse or newborn child, who is added during the period of TCC enrollment also is covered as a family member.

For former spouses, family members are limited to individuals who are children of both the federal employee and the former spouse. The new husband or wife of a remarried former spouse is not covered as a family member.

Separating employees can continue TCC for up to 18 months after the date of separation. An employee's children and former spouses can continue TCC for up to 36 months after: (1) the date of the qualifying event if it occurs while the child or former spouse is covered as a family member of an employee or annuitant under a regular FEHB enrollment, or (2) the date of the employee's separation if the qualifying event occurs while the child or former spouse is covered under the TCC enrollment of a former employee.

If a child's or former spouse's qualifying event occurs while the employee is enrolled for family coverage under TCC, the child or former spouse may elect TCC in his or her own right; however, the TCC coverage may not continue beyond 36 months after the date of the worker's separation.

Except in cases of gross misconduct, separating employees who would lose FEHB coverage because of their employment termination are eligible for TCC. It is the responsibility of the worker's employing office to provide notice to the employee (within 61 days after regular FEHB enrollment terminates) of the right to enroll under TCC. Generally, separating employees must submit their TCC election notice to their employing agency within 60 days after the date of separation or within 65 days after the date of notice from the employing agency, whichever is later.

Employees should ask their agency to provide them with TCC information before or on the day they separate. TCC enrollments—and premiums—always begin on the 32nd day after an employee's regular coverage ends (which happens on the last day of the pay period in which the employee separates). The earlier the TCC enrollment form is submitted, the earlier the agency can process it, and the less likely that the worker will receive a large bill for retroactive TCC coverage.

Employees who retire and are eligible to continue their regular FEHB coverage are not eligible for TCC, since their regular FEHB coverage does not stop.

To apply for TCC, separating employees (or their child or former spouse, as applicable) must complete Standard Form 2809, Health Benefits Election Form, and submit it to their employing office within the time limit noted above. Employing offices can accept late enrollments in very limited circumstances. Enrollees are not limited to the plan or option in which they were covered when the regular FEHB coverage ended. Employees or other eligible individuals may enroll in any plan for which otherwise qualified. (Some plans require that enrollees live or work in a certain geographic area or belong to the sponsoring employee organization.)

If an employee's child wants TCC, it is the employee's responsibility to notify the employing office within 60 days after the qualifying event and supply the child's mailing address. (Since the enrollment will be in the child's name, the child must complete the election form and the child will be billed for the coverage.)

Within 14 days after it receives the information about the child, the employing office must notify the child of his or her TCC rights. The child must make his or her election within 60 days after the later of (1) 60 days after the date of the qualifying event, or (2) if you notified the employing office within 60 days after the qualifying event, 65 days after the date the child receives the notice about TCC rights from your employing office.

If the employee does not notify the employing office within the 60-day time limit, the child's opportunity to elect TCC ends 60 days after the qualifying event.

Table of Permissible Changes in Enrollment*

Events That Permit Enrollment or Change		Change Permitted			Time Limits
Code	Event	From Not Enrolled to Enrolled	From Self Only to Self and Family	From One Plan or Option to Another	When You Must File Health Benefits Election Form With Your Employing Office
1	**EMPLOYEE**				
1A	Initial opportunity to enroll.	Yes	N/A	N/A	Within 60 days after becoming eligible.
1B	Open Season.	Yes	Yes	Yes	As announced by OPM.
1C	Change in family status; for example: marriage, birth or death of family member, adoption, legal separation, or divorce.	Yes	Yes	Yes	From 31 days before through 60 days after event.
1D	Change in employment status; for example: • Reemployment after a break in service of more than three days; • Return to pay status following loss of coverage due to expiration of 365 days of LWOP status or termination of coverage during LWOP; • Return to pay sufficient to make withholdings after termination of coverage during a period of insufficient pay; • Restoration to civilian position after serving in uniformed services; • Change from temporary appointment to appointment that entitles employee receipt of Government contribution; • Change to or from part-time career employment.	Yes	Yes	Yes	Within 60 days of employment status change.
1E	Separation from Federal employment when the employee or employee's spouse is pregnant.	Yes	Yes	Yes	Enrollment or change must occur during final pay period of employment.
1F	Transfer from a post of duty within the United States to a post of duty outside the United States, or reverse.	Yes	Yes	Yes	From 31 days before leaving old post through 60 days after arriving at new post.

* See "Pre-tax Payment of FEHB Insurance Premiums" for special considerations for those participating in premium conversion.

Events That Permit Enrollment or Change		Change Permitted			Time Limits
Code	Event	From Not Enrolled to Enrolled	From Self Only to Self and Family	From One Plan or Option to Another	When You Must File Health Benefits Election Form With Your Employing Office
1G	Employee or eligible family member loses coverage under FEHB or another group insurance plan; for example: • Loss of coverage under another FEHB enrollment due to termination, cancellation, or change to self only of the covering enrollment; • Loss of coverage under another federally-sponsored health benefits program; • Loss of coverage due to termination of membership in the employee organization sponsoring the FEHB plan; • Loss of coverage under Medicaid or similar State-sponsored program; • Loss of coverage under a non-Federal health plan.	Yes	Yes	Yes	From 31 days before through 60 days after loss of coverage.
1H	Employee or eligible family member loses coverage due to the discontinuance, in whole or part, of an FEHB plan.	N/A	Yes	Yes	During open season, unless OPM sets a different time.
1I	Loss of coverage under a non-Federal group health plan because an employee moves out of the commuting area to accept another position and the employee's non-federally employed spouse terminates employment to accompany the employee.	Yes	Yes	Yes	From 31 days before the employee leaves the commuting area through 180 days after arriving in the new commuting area.
1J	Employee or covered family member in a Health Maintenance Organization (HMO) moves or becomes employed outside the geographic area from which the carrier accepts enrollments, or if already outside the area, moves or becomes employed further from this area.	N/A	Yes	Yes	Upon notifying the employing office of the move or change of place of employment.

Events That Permit Enrollment or Change		Change Permitted			Time Limits
Code	Event	From Not Enrolled to Enrolled	From Self Only to Self and Family	From One Plan or Option to Another	When You Must File Health Benefits Election Form With Your Employing Office
1K	On becoming eligible for Medicare (This change may be made only once in a lifetime.)	N/A	No	Yes	At any time beginning on the 30th day before becoming eligible for Medicare.
1L	Temporary employee completes one year of continuous service in accordance with 5 U.S.C. Section 8906a.	Yes	N/A	N/A	Within 60 days after becoming eligible.
1M	Salary of temporary employee insufficient to make withholdings for plan in which enrolled.	N/A	No	Yes	Within 60 days after receiving notice from employing office.
3	**FORMER SPOUSE UNDER THE SPOUSE EQUITY PROVISIONS**				
3A	Initial opportunity to enroll, Former spouse must be eligible to enroll under the authority of the Civil Service Retirement Spouse Equity Act of 1984 (P.L. 98-615), as amended, the Intelligence Authorization Act of 1986 (P.L. 99-569), or the Foreign Relations Authorization Act, Fiscal Years 1988 and 1989 (P.L. 100-204).	Yes	N/A	N/A	Generally, must apply within 60 days after dissolution of marriage. However, if a retiring employee elects to provide a former spouse annuity or insurable interest annuity for the former spouse, the former spouse must apply within 60 days after OPM's notice of eligibility for FEHB. May enroll any time after employing office establishes eligibility.
3B	Open season.	No	Yes*	Yes	As announced by OPM.
3C	Change in family status based on addition of family members who are also eligible family members of the employee or annuitant.	No	Yes	Yes	From 31 days before through 60 days after change in family status.
3D	Reenrollment of former spouse who cancelled FEHB enrollment to enroll in a Medicare sponsored Coordinated Care Plan (Medicare HMO), Medicaid, or similar State-sponsored program and who later was involuntarily disenrolled from the Medicare HMO, Medicaid, or similar State-sponsored program.	May Reenroll	N/A	N/A	From 31 days before through 60 days after disenrollment.

Events That Permit Enrollment or Change		Change Permitted			Time Limits
Code	Event	From Not Enrolled to Enrolled	From Self Only to Self and Family	From One Plan or Option to Another	When You Must File Health Benefits Election Form With Your Employing Office
3E	Reenrollment of former spouse who cancelled FEHB enrollment to enroll in a Medicare-sponsored Coordinated Care Plan (Medicare HMO), Medicaid, or similar State-sponsored program and who later voluntarily disenrolls from the Medicare-sponsored Coordinated Care Plan (Medicare HMO), Medicaid, or similar State-sponsored program.	May Reenroll	N/A	N/A	During open season.
3F	Former spouse or eligible child loses FEHB coverage due to termination, cancellation, or change to self only of the covering enrollment.	Yes	Yes	Yes	From 31 days before through 60 days after date of loss of coverage.
3G	Enrolled former spouse or eligible child loses coverage under another group insurance plan; for example: • Loss of coverage under another federally-sponsored health benefits program; • Loss of coverage due to termination of membership in the employee organization sponsoring the FEHB plan; • Loss of coverage under Medicaid or similar State-sponsored program (but see 3D and 3E); • Loss of coverage under a non-Federal health plan.	N/A	Yes	Yes	From 31 days before through 60 days after loss of coverage.
3H	Former spouse or eligible family member loses coverage due to the discontinuance, in whole or part, of an FEHB plan.	N/A	Yes	Yes	During open season, unless OPM sets a different time.
3I	Former spouse or covered family member in a Health Maintenance Organization (HMO) moves or becomes employed outside the geographic area from which the carrier accepts enrollments, or if already outside this area, moves or becomes employed further from this area.	N/A	Yes	Yes	Upon notifying the employing office of the move or change of place of employment.

Events That Permit Enrollment or Change		Change Permitted			Time Limits
Code	Event	From Not Enrolled to Enrolled	From Self Only to Self and Family	From One Plan or Option to Another	When You Must File Health Benefits Election Form With Your Employing Office
3J	On becoming eligible for Medicare (This change may be made only once in a lifetime.)	N/A	No	Yes	At any time beginning the 30th day before becoming eligible for Medicare.
3K	Former spouse's annuity is insufficient to make FEHB withholdings for plan in which enrolled.	No	No	Yes	Retirement System will advise former spouse of options.

4   TEMPORARY CONTINUATION OF COVERAGE (TCC) FOR ELIGIBLE FORMER EMPLOYEES, FORMER SPOUSES, AND CHILDREN.

Code	Event	From Not Enrolled to Enrolled	From Self Only to Self and Family	From One Plan or Option to Another	When You Must File Health Benefits Election Form With Your Employing Office
4A	Opportunity to enroll for continued coverage under TCC provisions: • Former employee • Former spouse • Child who ceases to qualify as a family member	 Yes Yes Yes	 Yes N/A N/A	 Yes N/A N/A	Within 60 days after the qualifying event, or receiving notice of eligibility, whichever is later.
4B	Open season: • Former employee • Former spouse • Child who ceases to qualify as a family member	 No Yes Yes	 No Yes* Yes	 No Yes Yes	As announced by OPM
4C	Change in family status (except former spouse); for example, marriage, birth or death of family member, adoption, legal separation, or divorce.	No	Yes	Yes	From 31 days before through 60 days after event.
4D	Change in family status of former spouse, based on addition of family members who are eligible family members of the employee or annuitant.	No	Yes	Yes	From 31 days before through 60 days after event.
4E	Reenrollment of a former employee, former spouse, or child whose TCC enrollment was terminated because of other FEHB coverage and who loses the other FEHB coverage before the TCC period of eligibility (18 or 36 months) expires.	May Reenroll	N/A	N/A	From 31 days before through 60 days after the event. Enrollment is retroactive to the date of the loss of the other FEHB coverage.

Events That Permit Enrollment or Change

Code	Event	From Not Enrolled to Enrolled	From Self Only to Self and Family	From One Plan or Option to Another	When You Must File Health Benefits Election Form With Your Employing Office
		Change Permitted			**Time Limits**
4F	Enrollee or eligible family member loses coverage under FEHB or another group insurance plan; for example: • Loss of coverage under another FEHB enrollment due to termination, cancellation, or change to self only of the covering enrollment (but see event 4E); • Loss of coverage under another federally-sponsored health benefits program; • Loss of coverage due to termination of membership in the employee organization sponsoring the FEHB plan; • Loss of coverage under Medicaid or similar State-sponsored program; • Loss of coverage under a non-Federal health plan.	No	Yes	Yes	From 31 days before through 60 days after loss of coverage.
4G	Enrollee or eligible family member loses coverage due to the discontinuance, in whole or part, of an FEHB plan.	N/A	Yes	Yes	During open season, unless OPM sets a different time.
4H	Enrollee or covered family member in a Health Maintenance Organization (HMO) moves or becomes employed outside the geographic area from which the carrier accepts enrollments, or if already outside this area, moves or becomes employed further from this area.	N/A	Yes	Yes	Upon notifying the employing office of the move or change of place of employment.
4I	On becoming eligible for Medicare. *(This change may be made only once a lifetime.)*	N/A	No	Yes	At any time beginning on the 30th day before becoming eligible for Medicare.

* Former spouse may change to self and family only if family members are also eligible family members of the employee or annuitant.

If someone other than the employee notifies the employing office about the child's eligibility, the employing office will notify the child of his or her TCC rights, but the child's 60-day time limit to elect TCC begins with the qualifying event, not the date of the employing office's notice of TCC rights.

Enrollees may elect either self or self and family enrollment; however, as noted above, the individuals who qualify as family members under a TCC family enrollment vary depending on whether the enrollee is a former employee, a child, or a former spouse. If individuals who are eligible for TCC cannot make an election on their own behalf due to a mental or physical disability, a court-appointed guardian may file an election for that person.

An enrollee who loses FEHB coverage other than by cancellation (including cancellation for nonpayment of premiums) has a 31-day temporary extension of coverage, at no cost, in the same enrollment category held at separation for the purpose of converting to a nongroup contract with the current health benefits plan. This is true even when the enrollee also has the right to elect temporary continuation of FEHB coverage. TCC takes effect on the day that the 31-day temporary extension of coverage ends. Coverage is retroactive to that date if the enrollment processing is completed later.

Depending on the circumstances, a timely election can be made up to 126 days after the qualifying event. A person who waits that long to enroll is billed for the entire 95-day period of retroactive coverage. In cases where the employing office accepts a late election, the period of retroactive coverage for which the enrollee is billed is even longer. If the enrollee does not pay the bill for the retroactive coverage, the TCC enrollment is canceled retroactively to the beginning date and the person is not eligible to reenroll.

FEHB and Medicare

Upon reaching age 65, most federal employees and retirees become eligible for Medicare. Generally, plans under the FEHB program help pay for the same kind of expenses as Medicare. FEHB plans also provide coverage for prescription drugs, routine physicals, emergency care outside of the United States and some preventive services that Medicare doesn't cover. Some FEHB plans also provide coverage for dental and vision care.

However, Medicare covers some orthopedic and prosthetic devices, durable medical equipment, home health care, limited chiropractic services, and medical supplies, which some FEHB plans may not cover or only partially cover.

FEHB plans are limited to paying the Medicare fee schedule amount for physician services provided to retired FEHB enrollees age 65 and over who are not enrolled in Medicare Part B. Medicare participating providers can collect no more than the Medicare fee schedule amount from these enrollees. Medicare non-participating providers can collect no more than the limiting charge amount, which is 115 percent of the fee schedule amount. This reduces both what the plan and the enrollee can be charged by doctors.

Medicare Enrollment Issues—Most Medicare-eligible persons on reaching age 65 are eligible for Part A (hospital insurance) benefits premium-free. Part A will help cover some of the costs that an FEHB plan may not cover, such as deductibles, coinsurance, and charges that exceed the plan's allowable charges. There are other advantages to enrolling in Part A, such as being eligible to enroll in a Medicare managed care plan.

Enrollees don't have to take Part B (primarily physicians' services) coverage if they don't want it, and an FEHB plan can't require them to take it. There are some advantages to enrolling in Part B:

• An enrollee must be enrolled in Parts A and B to join a Medicare + Choice plan.

• An enrollee has the advantage of coordination of benefits between Medicare and the FEHB plan, reducing out-of-pocket costs.

• An FEHB plan may waive its co-payments, coinsurance, and deductibles for Part B services.

• Some services covered under Part B might not be covered or only be partially covered by an FEHB plan.

Anyone enrolled in an FEHB HMO may go outside of the plan's network for Part B services and receive reimbursement by Medicare when Medicare is the primary payer. Those who don't enroll in Medicare as soon as they are eligible must wait for the general enrollment period (January 1 - March 31 of each year) to enroll, and Part B coverage will begin the following July 1. Their Part B premiums will go up 10 percent for each 12 months that they could have had Part B but didn't take it.

Those who didn't take Part B at age 65 because they were covered under FEHB as an active employee (or were covered under a spouse's group health insurance plan and he/she was an active employee) may sign up for Part B (generally without increased premiums) within eight months from the time the enrollee or spouse stops working or is no longer covered by the group plan. An enrollee also can sign up at any time when covered by the group plan.

Medigap Enrollment Issues—FEHB is not one of the 10 standardized Medicare supplemental insurance policies known as Medigap (and Medicare SELECT) policies. However, many FEHB plans and options will supplement Medicare by paying for costs not covered by Medicare, such as the required deductibles and coinsurance, and by providing additional benefits not provided under Medicare, such as prescription drugs, routine physicals and additional preventive care.

An FEHB enrollee generally doesn't need to purchase a Medigap policy since FEHB and Medicare will coordinate benefits to provide comprehensive coverage for a wide range of medical expenses.

Which Pays First—Medicare law and regulations determine whether Medicare or FEHB is primary (pays benefits first). Medicare automatically transfers claims information to the FEHB plan once a claim is processed, so the enrollee generally doesn't need to file with both.

An FEHB plan must pay benefits first when the enrollee is an active federal employee or reemployed annuitant and either the enrollee or covered spouse has Medicare, unless the reemployment position is excluded from FEHB coverage or the enrollee is enrolled in Medicare Part B only. An FEHB plan must also pay benefits first for the enrollee or a covered family member during the first 30 months of eligibility or entitlement to Part A benefits because of End Stage Renal Disease (ESRD), regardless

of employment status.

Medicare must pay benefits first when the enrollee is an annuitant, and either the enrollee or covered spouse has Medicare. Medicare also must pay benefits first when the enrollee is receiving workers' compensation and the Office of Workers' Compensation Programs has determined that the enrollee is unable to return to duty.

FEHB Enrollment Issues—An enrollee may change FEHB enrollment to any available plan or option at any time beginning on the 30th day before becoming eligible for Medicare. The enrollee may use this enrollment change opportunity only once. An enrollee may also change enrollment during the annual open season, or because of another event that permits enrollment changes (such as a change in family status).

Once Medicare becomes the primary payer, the enrollee may find that a lower cost FEHB plan is adequate. Also, some plans waive deductibles, coinsurance, and co-payments when Medicare is primary.

An FEHB fee-for-service plan won't necessarily cover all out-of-pocket costs not covered by Medicare. A managed fee-for-service plan's payment is typically based on reasonable and customary charges, not on billed charges. In some cases, Medicare's payment and the plan's payment combined will not cover the full cost.

Out-of-pocket costs for Part B services will depend on whether the doctor accepts Medicare "assignment." When a doctor accepts assignment, the enrollee can be billed only for the difference between the Medicare-approved amount and the combined payments made by Medicare and your FEHB plan. When a doctor doesn't accept assignment, the enrollee can be billed up to 115 percent of the Medicare-approved amount (the "limiting charge") when the FEHB plan's payment and Medicare's payment don't cover the full cost.

Although the enrollee will usually have to pay the FEHB HMO's required co-pays and deductibles, some HMOs waive such payments when Medicare is primary. However, the enrollee must still use the HMO's participating provider network to receive services and get required referrals for specialty care.

Medicare Managed Care Plan Issues—Those who enroll in a Medicare managed care plan may not need FEHB coverage because the Medicare managed care plan pays many of the same benefits. Review their benefits carefully before making a decision.

Those who provide documentation to their retirement system that they are suspending FEHB coverage to enroll in a Medicare managed care plan may reenroll in FEHB if they later lose or cancel the Medicare managed care plan coverage. Those who voluntarily cancel Medicare managed care plan coverage must wait until the next open season to reenroll in FEHB. Those who involuntarily lose coverage under the Medicare managed care plan may reenroll from 31 days before to 60 days after losing the Medicare managed care plan coverage, and their reenrollment in FEHB will be made effective the day after the Medicare managed care plan coverage ends. An involuntary loss of coverage includes when the Medicare managed care plan is discontinued or when the enrollee moves outside its service area.

The FEHB plan brochure provides specific information on how its benefits are coordinated with Medicare. In addition, OPM publication RI 75-12, "The Federal Employees Health Benefits Program and Medicare," is available in agency personnel offices. Some HMOs participating in the FEHB will coordinate to the enrollee's greater advantage for enrolling in both their FEHB HMO and their Medicare managed care plan.

FEHB, Tricare and CHAMPVA

Effective Oct. 1, 2001, coverage under the Tricare military health system was reinstated for Medicare-eligible uniformed services retirees, their survivors and eligible dependents. This 'Tricare for Life' coverage is advantageous for cost reasons to many Medicare-eligible military system beneficiaries who are covered under the FEHB.

Further, Public Law 107-14 provides beneficiaries over age 65 of the Department of Veterans Affairs (VA) with coverage secondary to Medicare under the Civilian Health and Medical Program of the Department of Veterans Affairs (CHAMPVA). CHAMPVA provides similarly attractive benefits to VA eligible beneficiaries as those benefits provided to uniformed services beneficiaries under the Tricare or Tricare for Life programs.

Annuitants and Former Spouses— Current FEHB annuitants and former spouses who are eligible for these programs may suspend (rather than cancel) their FEHB coverage and premium payments. OPM regulations published in the June 18, 2002 Federal Register allow these individuals to reenroll in the FEHB during the open season, or immediately if they are involuntarily disenrolled from the non-FEHB coverage. The intent is to allow eligible beneficiaries to avoid the expense of continuing to pay FEHB premiums while they are using other coverage, without endangering their ability to return to the FEHB in the future. Under previous FEHB regulations, an annuitant or former spouse would have to cancel his or her FEHB coverage to use other health coverage and would not be allowed to return to FEHB coverage.

The suspension provision also applies to those eligible to enroll in Tricare's Uniformed Services Family Health Plan.

Annuitants or former spouses can suspend FEHB coverage to use Tricare or CHAMPVA at any time. Annuitants can call OPM's Retirement Information Office at 1-888-767-6738 (202-606-0500 within the Washington, D.C. calling area) to obtain a suspension form. Former spouses can get the form from the employing office or retirement system maintaining their enrollment.

Eligible individuals must submit a completed suspension form and provide all necessary documentation to show eligibility for Tricare or CHAMPVA during the period beginning 31 days before and ending 31 days after the date they designate as using Tricare or CHAMPVA instead of FEHB coverage. If the documentation showing your eligibility for Tricare is received within that period, the suspension becomes effective at the end of the day before the day you designated. Otherwise, the suspension becomes effective at the end of the month in which OPM receives your documentation.

An annuitant, survivor, or former spouse may not suspend his or her own FEHB coverage while allowing family members to continue coverage under the FEHB. The coverage of all family members is suspended as well. Nor can an annuitant, survivor, or former spouse suspend his or her family members' FEHB coverage while remaining covered under the FEHB. An annuitant, survivor, or former spouse can change to self-only coverage, but this cancels all family members' coverage and takes away their future enrollment eligibility.

If you suspend FEHB coverage to use Tricare or CHAMPVA instead, you can reenroll in the FEHB for any reason during a future open season. If you are involuntarily disenrolled from Tricare or CHAMPVA, you are eligible to immediately reenroll in the FEHB. Your request to reenroll must be received within the period beginning 31 days before and ending 60 days after your Tricare or CHAMPVA coverage ends. Otherwise, you must wait until an open season.

If an annuitant dies during his or her suspended FEHB enrollment, his or her survivor will be eligible to reenroll in the FEHB as long as the annuitant was enrolled in self and family coverage when he/she suspended FEHB coverage and made arrangements to leave a survivor annuity.

Active Employees—Actively working civil service employees may not suspend their FEHB coverage to use CHAMPVA, Tricare or Tricare for Life. However, they can cancel their coverage to use CHAMPVA, Tricare or Tricare for Life. Employees who do not participate in premium conversion may cancel their enrollment at any time. For employees who participate in premium conversion, eligibility for CHAMPVA or Tricare is not a qualifying life event that would allow them to cancel their FEHB enrollment. These employees may cancel only during an annual FEHB open season.

If an employee who canceled FEHB coverage to use CHAMPVA, Tricare or Tricare for Life decides to return to FEHB coverage, the employee can do so during a future open season. If the employee loses CHAMPVA, Tricare or Tricare for Life coverage involuntarily, the employee can immediately reenroll in the FEHB.

Before an employee cancels FEHB coverage to use Tricare or Tricare for Life, the following should be considered:

• To be eligible to continue FEHB coverage after retirement, a retiring employee must be enrolled or covered under the FEHB for the five years of service immediately before retirement, or, if less than five years, for all service since the first opportunity to enroll. Employees can count their coverage under Tricare toward meeting this requirement. However, the employee must

be enrolled in an FEHB health plan on the date of retirement to continue coverage.

• If the employee dies when the cancellation is in effect, any surviving spouse will not be eligible to continue FEHB health benefits coverage.

Information about Tricare can be obtained by calling 1-888-363-5433 or by going to the Tricare website at *http://www.tricare.osd.mil*. Information about CHAMPVA can be obtained by calling 1-888-733-8387 or by going to the Department of Veterans Affairs website at *http://www.va.gov/hac*.

FEHB Coverage After Retirement

Federal employees are allowed to continue their health benefits coverage after they retire if they meet certain conditions. Generally, to continue FEHB coverage as a retiree, you must retire on an immediate annuity; and you must have been continuously enrolled under the FEHB program (or covered as a family member) for the five years of service immediately preceding your retirement or, if less than five years, for all service since your first opportunity to enroll. In rare and unusual circumstances, OPM may waive these eligibility requirements when it determines it would be against "equity and good conscience" not to allow an individual to be enrolled in FEHB as an annuitant.

OPM grants waivers to employees who have been covered under the FEHB continuously since October 1, 1996, or the beginning date of an agency's latest statutory buyout authority, whichever is later. These employees must:

• Retire during the agency's statutory buyout period; and

• Receive a buyout under the agency's statutory buyout authority; or

• Take an early optional retirement as a result of early-out authority in the agency; or

• Take a discontinued service retirement based on an involuntary separation due to RIF, directed reassignment, reclassification to a lower grade, or abolishment of position.

Employees who meet these requirements do not need to write a letter requesting a waiver. Instead, agencies must attach a memorandum to the employee's retirement application stating that the employee meets the requirements for a pre-approved waiver by OPM. That certification must include the number of the public law granting the agency's buyout authority and the beginning and ending dates of the agency's buyout period.

Employees who do not qualify for a pre-approved waiver may request a waiver on a case-by-case basis. They should explain why they believe OPM should consider them for a waiver (e.g., why they are unable to meet the five-year requirement) or why meeting it would be harmful to them. Waiver requests should be sent to the following address: Office of Personnel Management, Retirement and Insurance Service, Office of Retirement Programs, 1900 E St., N.W., Washington, DC 20415-3532.

Employees who separate and are eligible for a deferred annuity cannot begin health insurance coverage when their deferred annuity begins. Employees must retire on an immediate annuity to be eligible to continue their health insurance coverage. (For employees retiring under FERS, an immediate annuity includes one based on the minimum retirement age and ten years of service—i.e., MRA plus 10—even though the employee may postpone receipt of annuity.)

The applicable rate of a retiree's health insurance premium will be deducted from the monthly retirement annuity check. If the annuity is not enough to cover the health insurance premiums, the premiums can be paid directly to OPM.

Federal employees and retirees (excluding the Postal Service) pay the same amount for their premiums. However, when postal employees retire, they no longer receive an additional amount toward their cost of health insurance, which requires them, as retirees, to pay the same as all other federal workers and retirees.

Retirees who are enrolled for self and family can have family members continue coverage until such time as they become ineligible—for example, when a covered child reaches age 22 or marries. However, the widow(er) of a federal retiree who did not elect a survivor benefit is not eligible for FEHB insurance after the retiree's death. A deceased employee must have been enrolled for self and family at the time of death. All survivors who meet the definition

of "family member" continue their health benefits coverage under the enrollment as long as any one of them is entitled to a survivor annuity.

Under Office of Personnel Management rules (5 CFR 630.212) federal employees who are retiring because of a downsizing have the right to use their accrued annual leave to qualify for continuing their health insurance into retirement. Previously, agencies had to approve such a use of annual leave for retirement crediting purposes.

Also, Medicare-eligible federal retirees and former spouses can cancel their FEHB enrollment and enroll in a Medicare-sponsored prepaid health plan. If that plan stops participating for any reason, they can reenroll in FEHB and not lose a day of coverage. However, if they voluntarily disenroll from the Medicare plan, they may not reinstate their FEHB coverage until the annual open enrollment season. Medicare-eligible retirees interested in making this choice should contact their retirement system. Former spouses who are Medicare-eligible should get in touch with the agency that maintains their enrollment. (See also the FEHB and Medicare section above.)

Direct Payment of Premiums

For many years, annuitants and compensationers whose payments are not large enough to cover their health insurance premiums have been allowed to pay those premiums directly to the retirement system. Beginning on or after August 21, 1996, that privilege was extended to certain employees who have insufficient pay on an ongoing basis. Typically, these are employees who are in a non-pay status or whose salary after mandatory deductions is insufficient to pay the FEHB premiums.

Employing offices are required to give written notice to employees as soon as possible after the office becomes aware that they are in non-pay status or their pay is insufficient to cover premiums. The notice offers employees the choice of 1) terminating the enrollment or 2) continuing the enrollment and agreeing to pay the premiums directly or incur a debt to the agency. If the employee elects to continue the enrollment, the agency must pay OPM the premiums due on a current basis. If the written notice is not acted on and returned within 31 days

(45 days for employees residing overseas), the employing office must terminate the enrollment. Employees whose FEHB enrollment is terminated may reenroll in any FEHB plan upon returning to pay and duty status without having to wait for an Open Season or other enrollment event.

For More Information

More detailed information about the federal government's health insurance program and policies may be found in FEHB law (5 U.S.C. Chapter 89), regulations (5CFR, Part 89) or the FEHB Handbook on OPM's website at: *www.opm.gov/insure/health*.

Following is a listing of the FEHB guides published by the Office of Personnel Management to provide key information during the open enrollment periods. The OPM publications include: civil service—RI-70-1; U.S. Postal Service—RI-70-2; temporary continuation of coverage (spouse equity, etc.)—RI-70-5; individuals receiving compensation from OWCP—RI-70-6; temporary employees under 5 USC 8906a—RI-70-8; federal retirees and survivors—RI-70-9; visually impaired (large type).

Federal Employees News Digest Inc. has published a comprehensive guide to federal insurance benefits titled *Insuring Your Future: A Federal Employee's Guide to Meeting Insurance Needs*. See publication-ordering information in this *Almanac*.

Contacting FEHB Plans

Nationwide Fee-for-Service:
General
Alliance.................................. 202-939-6325
APWU 800-222-2798
Blue Cross and Blue Shield .. local phone #
GEHA 800-821-6136
Mail Handlers 800-410-7778
NALC 888-636-6252
Postmasters 703-683-5585
PBP Health Plan 800-544-7111

Nationwide Fee-for-Service:
Open to Specific Groups Only
Association Benefit Plan 800-634-0069
Foreign Service 202-833-4910
Panama Canal Area 800-548-8969
Rural Carrier Benefit Plan 800-638-8432
SAMBA 800-638-6589
Secret Service 800-424-7474

HMOs

Alabama
PrimeHealth of Alabama........ 800-236-9421
The Oath Health Plan............ 800-947-5093
Arizona
Aetna Health, Inc 800-537-9384
Health Net of Arizona, Inc 800-289-2818
PacifiCare Health Plans.......... 800-531-3341
California
Aetna Health, Inc 800-537-9384
Blue Cross HMO 800-235-8631
Blue Shield of CA Access+ .. .800-880-8086
CIGNA HealthCare of CA 800-244-6224
Health Net 800-522-0088
Kaiser Permanente 800-464-4000
PacifiCare Health Plans.......... 800-531-3341
UHP HEALTHCARE 800-544-0088
Universal Care 800-257-3087
Colorado
Kaiser Permanente 800-632-9700
PacifiCare of CO................... 800-877-9777
Connecticut
ConnectiCare 800-251-7722
District of Columbia
Aetna U.S. Healthcare, Inc 800-537-9384
CareFirst BlueChoice 866-520-6099
Kaiser Permanente 301-468-6000
MD-IPA 800-251-0956
Florida
AAv-Med Health Plan 800-882-8633
Capital Health Plan................ 850-383-3311
Foundation Health 800-441-5501
Healthplan Southeast 850-668-3000
Humana Medical Plan 888-393-6765
Total Health Choice 305-408-5823
Vista Healthplan 866-847-8235
Georgia
Aetna Health, Inc 800-537-9384
Kaiser Permanente 800-611-1811
Guam
PacifiCare Asia Pacific............ 671-647-3526
Hawaii
HMSA................................. 808-948-6499
Kaiser Permanente 808-597-5955
Idaho
Group Health Cooperative 888-901-4636
Illinois
BlueCHOICE 800-634-4395
Group Health Plan 800-755-3901
Health Alliance HMO 800-851-3379
Humana Health Plan Inc........ 888-393-6765
John Deere Health Plan 800-247-9110
Mercy/Premier Health Plans .. 800-327-0763
OSF HealthPlans................... 800-673-5222
PersonalCare's HMO 800-431-1211
UNICARE HMO 312-234-8855

Union Health Service 312-829-4224

Indiana

Advantage Health Plan, Inc.... 800-553-8933

Aetna Health, Inc 800-537-9384

Arnett HMO 765-448-7440

Health Alliance HMO 800-851-3379

Humana Health Plan 888-393-6765

M*Plan 317-571-5320

Physicians HP of N. Indiana .. 260-432-6690

UNICARE HMO 888-234-8855

Iowa

Avera Health Plans 888-322-2115

Coventry Health Care 800-257-4692

John Deere Health Plan 800-247-9110

Health Alliance 800-851-3379

Kansas

Coventry HC Kansas Cty 800-969-3343

Coventry HC Wichita/Salina .. 800-664-9251

Humana Health Plan, Inc 888-393-6765

Preferred Plus of Kansas 800-660-8114

Kentucky

Humana Health Plan 888-393-6765

United HC of Ohio, Inc 800-231-2918

Louisiana

Coventry Healthcare 800-341-6613

Vantage Health Plan 888-823-1910

Maryland

Aetna Health, Inc 800-537-9384

CareFirst BlueChoice 866-520-6099

Kaiser Permanente 301-468-6000

MD-IPA 800-251-0956

Massachusetts

Blue Chip,
 Coord Health Prtnrs.............. 401-459-5500

ConnectiCare 800-251-7722

Fallon Community
 Health Plan 800-868-5200

Michigan

Bluecare Network of MI 800-662-6667

Grand Valley Health Plan 616-949-2410

Health Alliance 800-422-4641

HealthPlus MI 800-332-9161

M-Care 800-658-8878

OmniCare............................. 800-477-6664

The Wellness Plan.................. 800-875-9355

Total Health Care 800-826-2862

Minnesota

Avera Health Plans 888-322-2115

HealthPartners 952-883-5000

Missouri

BlueCHOICE 800-634-4395

Coventry Health Care 800-969-3343

Group Health Plan 800-755-3901

Humana Health Plan, Inc 888-393-6765

Mercy/Premier Health Plans .. 800-327-0763

Montana

New West Health Plan 800-290-3657

Nevada

Health Plan of Nevada 800-777-1840

PacifiCare Health Plans.......... 800-531-3341

New Jersey

Aetna U. S. Healthcare, Inc .. 800-537-9384

AmeriHealth HMO 800-454-7651

GHI Health Plan 212-501-4444

New Mexico

Cimarron Health Plan 800-473-0391

Lovelace Health Plan 800-244-6224

Presbyterian Health Plan........ 505-923-5678

New York

Aetna Health, Inc 800-537-9384

Blue Choice 800-462-0108

C.D.P.H.P............................. 518-641-3700

GHI Health Plan 212-501-4444

GHI HMO Select 877-244-4466

HIP of Greater NY 800-447-8255

HMO Blue 800-722-7884

HMO-CNY 800-828-2887

Independent Health Assoc 800-453-1910

MVP Health Care 888-687-6277

Preferred Care 800-950-3224

Univera Healthcare............... 716-847-0881

Vytra Health Plans 800-406-0806

North Dakota

Heart of America HMO 701-776-5848

Ohio

Aetna Health, Inc 800-537-9384

AultCare HMO 330-438-6360

Blue HMO 800-228-4375

Health Plan of the Upper OH 800-624-6961

HMO Health Ohio- 800-522-2066

Kaiser Permanente 800-686-7100

Paramount Health Care 800-462-3589

SummaCare Health Plan........ 330-996-8700

SuperMed HMO.................... 800-522-2066

United Health Care of Ohio .. 800-231-2918

Oklahoma

PacifiCare Health Plans.......... 800-531-3341

Oregon

Kaiser Permanente 800-813-2000

PacifiCare Health Plans.......... 800-531-3341

Pennsylvania

 Aetna Health, Inc.................. 800-537-9384

HealthAmerica PA-Pittsburgh 800-735-4404

HealthAmerica PA-Central PA 800-788-8445

Health Net of Pennsylvania.... 877-757-9585

HealthGuard......................... 800-822-0350

Keystone Health Plan Central 800-622-2843

Keystone Health Plan East...... 800-227-3115

UPMC Health Plan 888-876-2756

Puerto Rico

Humana Health Plans	....	800314-3121
Triple-S	....	787-749-4777

Rhode Island
Blue Chip,
Coord Hlth Partners 401-459-5500

South Dakota
Avera Health Plan SD 888-322-2115
Sioux Valley Health Plan 800-752-5863

Tennessee
Aetna U. S. Healthcare, Inc .. .800-537-9384
HealthSpring 615-291-5030

Texas
Amcare Health Plans.............. 800-782-8373
FIRSTCARE 800-884-4901
HMO Blue Texas 800-833-5318
Humana Health Plan of Texas 888-393-6765
Mercy/Premier Health Plans .. 800-617-3433
PacifiCare Health Plans.......... 800-531-3341

Utah
Altius Health Plans 800-377-4161

Vermont
MVP Health Plan 888-687-6277

Virginia
Aetna Health, Inc 800-537-9384

CareFirst BlueChoice 866-520-6099
Kaiser Permanente 301-468-6000
MD-IPA 800-251-0956
Optima Health Plan 800-206-1060
Piedmont Comm. Healthcare 888-674-3368

Washington
Aetna Health, Inc 800-537-9384
Group Health Cooperative 888-901-4636
Kaiser Permanente 800-813-2000
KPS Health Plans 800-552-7114
PacifiCare Health Plans.......... 800-531-3341

West Virginia
Health Plan Upper OH Valley 800-624-6961

Wisconsin
Dean Health Plan 800-279-1301
Group Health Coop
 South Ctrl 608-251-3356
Group Health Coop
 Eau Claire 715-552-4300
HealthPartners 952-883-5000

Wyoming
WINhealth Partners 307-638-7700

Section 2—Federal Employees' Group Life Insurance Program

General Coverage Rules

The group policy coverage available to most federal employees through the FEGLI program is administered by Metropolitan Life Insurance Company under a contract with the Office of Personnel Management. Under FEGLI's basic coverage, employees are provided with two kinds of coverage: (a) group term life insurance without a medical examination (if you do not waive coverage when first eligible or if you elect it during an open enrollment period) and (b) accidental death and dismemberment insurance that provides double indemnity protection. Eligible employees are automatically covered for Basic insurance unless they specifically state in writing that they do not want it.

In addition to the Basic coverage, there are a number of optional coverages available to employees who wish to augment their own life insurance program or provide coverage for their family members. Although the premiums for optional coverages are paid for exclusively by employees, they are provided at group rates.

Basic Life Insurance

If you are an insured federal employee, the following material explains in general terms the rights and benefits available to you under the FEGLI program.

The cost of the Basic insurance is shared by the employee and the government. The employee's share is two-thirds of the cost and is withheld from the worker's salary. The employee pays 15¢ biweekly or 32.5¢ monthly per $1,000 of Basic coverage.

The government's share is one-third and is contributed from agency appropriations or other funds available to pay salaries. (However, the U.S. Postal Service contributes 100 percent of the Basic life insurance costs for its employees.)

The group policy provides two kinds of Basic insurance during employment: (a) life insurance without a medical examination (if you don't waive coverage when first eligible or if you elect it during an open enrollment period), and (b) accidental death and dismemberment insurance providing double indemnity for accidental death, and payment for accidental loss of eyesight or one or more limbs.

The Basic insurance amount equals an employee's annual pay rounded to the next higher thousand plus $2,000, with a minimum of $10,000 insurance for all those earning $8,000 or less, at all times during active employment.

The "Schedule of Basic Insurance Withholdings" shows how life insurance amounts and an employee's cost are determined at different compensation levels. Each amount of life insurance shown carries with it an equal amount of accidental death and dismemberment protection (not including the extra benefit explained below).

The amount of Basic life insurance provided under FEGLI begins to decrease once an individual retires or reaches age 65, whichever is later. The rate of decrease is two percent per month, until 25 percent of the amount you had at time of retirement is reached. However, FEGLI-covered employees are given an opportunity at the time of retirement to elect either a lower rate of reduction or no coverage reduction after attaining age 65 in exchange for their agreement to make additional premium payments. Accidental death and dismemberment coverage is not available to retirees. (See Insurance Premiums: Retirees and Compensationers, below.)

The amount of Basic life insurance available to each eligible employee under age 45 was increased commencing with the first pay period beginning on or after October 1, 1981, at no additional cost to the employee. The increase is graduated according to the employee's age.

Employees under age 36 are eligible for Basic insurance coverage in an amount equal to their annual salary rounded to the next higher thousand dollars, plus $2,000, multiplied by two. For employees in this under-36 category, a worker's FEGLI premium cost remains the same. Beginning at age 36, the multiplication factor for the amount of Basic insurance will decline by 0.1 each year, until it reaches 1.0 for employees age 45 and over.

To illustrate:

If the age of the employee is:	The appropriate factor is:
35 or under	2.0
36	1.9
37	1.8
38	1.7
39	1.6
40	1.5
41	1.4
42	1.3
43	1.2
44	1.1
45 or over	1.0

Option A— (Standard Optional Insurance)

Federal employees covered under the Basic life insurance program have the option of purchasing an additional $10,000 worth of FEGLI life insurance. The employee pays the full cost of this "standard optional insurance" coverage. The amount of the premium depends on the employee's age and is withheld from the worker's salary. For covered employees (not retirees), selection of the Option A life insurance coverage also results in an equal amount of accidental death and dismemberment protection. Retirees who reach age 65 no longer have to pay premiums, but the $10,000 optional insurance starts to decline at this point at the rate of two percent for each full calendar month until it reaches $2,500, or one-fourth of the face value. The cost is listed in the table entitled "Option A Withholdings."

Option B— (Additional Optional Insurance)

Federal employees who are insured for the Basic coverage may elect "additional optional insurance" in an amount equal to one, two, three, four, or five times their actual rate of annual basic pay (rounded to the next $1,000). The employee pays the full cost of the additional optional insurance. The premium depends on the employee's age and is withheld from salary. Accidental death and dismemberment coverage is not included in this coverage. Retirees at age 65 no longer have to pay premiums for additional optional insurance, but the amount of their coverage starts to decrease at this point at the rate of two percent each month for 50 months, at which point coverage ceases. However, a retiree may elect to keep the full amount of the additional optional insurance in force and continue to pay the full premium. Such an election may be cancelled at a later date. The cost for the additional optional insurance is listed in the table entitled "Option B Withholdings."

Option C— (Family Optional Insurance)

Federal employees insured for the Basic insurance coverage may elect family optional insurance to cover eligible family members. Eligible family members are an employee's spouse and unmarried dependent children under age 22. The coverage amount is an amount equal to up to five multiples of $5,000 for a spouse and up to five multiples of $2,500 for each eligible child. The employee pays the full cost of the family optional insurance. The premium depends on the employee's age and is withheld from the worker's salary. Accidental death and dismemberment coverage is not included in this coverage. Retirees at age 65 no longer have to pay premiums for family optional insurance, but their coverage amount starts to decrease at this point at the rate of two percent each month for 50 months, at which point coverage ceases. However, a retiree may elect to keep the full amount of the family optional insurance in force and continue to pay the full premium. Such an election may be cancelled at a later date. The cost of family optional insurance is listed in the table entitled "Option C withholdings."

Salary Changes

The amount of your Basic and Option B insurance may change if your salary rate changes. If your salary rate increases or decreases sufficiently to bring you within a different classification (as shown in the "Schedule of Basic Insurance Withholdings" table), the new amount of insurance will be effective on the date the salary rate change occurs. For premium withholding purposes, a salary rate change is deemed to occur: (1) on the stated effective date of the change or the date such change is approved, whichever is later, or (2) on the effective date of the change when a retroactive adjustment is actually the correction of an error, unless otherwise stipulated in a law providing for the change. Note: If you elect a Living Benefit (described below), salary changes will have no effect on the amount of Basic insurance.

Filing a FEGLI Claim

All notices and proofs of the death or accidental loss of a FEGLI participant should be sent to the worker's employing office, which will submit this notification to the Office of Federal Employees' Group Life Insurance (OFEGLI). The individual's employing office can supply a claim form upon request. It is the responsibility of the person to whom the benefits are payable, however, to furnish notice of loss and proof of loss within the time limits specified below.

An accident that results in loss of life, limb, or eyesight must be reported within 20 days after the incident occurs. Proof of the loss resulting from the accident must be submitted on the form provided not later than 90 days after the date of the loss. However, if it is not possible to furnish notice or proof in the time specified, the requirements will be met if such notice or proof is furnished as soon as reasonably possible.

The Office of Federal Employees' Group Life Insurance has the right to have a physician examine individuals during the period that they are claiming benefits for loss of limb or eyesight, as well as the right to require an autopsy in the event of a claim for accidental death benefits (unless the autopsy is forbidden by law).

To receive payment of the death benefits, a FEGLI participant's beneficiary or other survivor (see below) must submit a claim on the form provided and furnish written proof of the covered individual's death and of the claimant's right to payment.

All claims are settled by the Office of Federal Employees' Group Life Insurance, P.O. Box 2627, Jersey City, NJ 07303-2627, phone 1-800-633-4542, fax (201) 395-7950.

FEGLI Beneficiaries: Order of Precedence

You do not need to name a beneficiary if you are satisfied to have the death benefits of your insurance paid in the order of precedence noted below. If you are not survived by a designated beneficiary, the benefits will be paid to your widow or widower under category (1). If you have no survivor in category (1), benefits will be paid under category (2), and so on, as necessary, under the other categories.

(1) Your widow or widower.

(2) Your child or children in equal shares, with the share of any deceased child distributed among the descendants of that child.

(3) Your parents in equal shares, or the entire amount to the surviving parent.

(4) Your duly appointed executor or administrator of your estate.

(5) Your next of kin under the laws of your state of domicile at the time of your death.

If you want to name a different beneficiary or change the designation, you can do so by filing a written notice, signed and witnessed, with your employing office. Your employing office can supply appropriate forms for this purpose. However, a person who serves as a witness to this type of designation may not receive payment as a beneficiary.

In general, you do not need the consent of anyone to change your beneficiary. However, a law authorizes an exception to the standard order of precedence under the FEGLI program if a court has issued a decree of divorce, annulment, or legal separation that calls for the benefits to be paid to someone else. The court decree must be received in the employing agency before the insured's death. In the case of retirees, the same document must be received by OPM. The law also allows a court to direct the insured individual to make an irrevocable assignment of life insurance ownership to the person(s) named in the court order. However, the court documents do not themselves serve as an official assignment. The insured must still complete an Assignment of Insurance Form.

A designation of beneficiary is automatically canceled 31 days after you cease to be insured. If your insurance is continued or reinstated when you retire or while you are receiving federal workers' compensation benefits, your designation of beneficiary is placed on file in the Office of Personnel Management and remains in effect. To be valid, your designation of a beneficiary must be received by the employing office before your death.

If you name more than one beneficiary, be sure to specify the exact share you wish each person to receive. If designated beneficiaries die before you do, their rights and interests in your insurance benefits end automatically.

If any person otherwise entitled to payment as explained above fails to make a benefits claim within one year after your death, or if payment to such person within that period is prohibited by federal statute or regulation, payment may be made in the order of precedence shown above as if such person had died before you.

FEGLI Benefit Payments

FEGLI benefits generally are payable if death or accidental injury occurs while an employee or retiree is insured and proper notice and proof are presented (typically, in accordance with the claims-filing procedures outlined above). The two general types of benefit payments made under FEGLI are:

Death Benefits—The amount of your life insurance is payable in the event of your death while insured, no matter how caused.

Payment Under the Accidental Death and Dismemberment Insurance—Benefits under this type of insurance are payable if, while insured, you receive bodily injuries solely through violent, external, and accidental means (other than those noted under "Exceptions") and if as a direct result of the bodily injuries, independently of all other causes, and within 90 days afterwards you lose your life, limb, or eyesight.

The full amount of your accidental death and dismemberment insurance (equal to your Basic Insurance Amount, plus Option A coverage if you have it) is payable in the case of loss of life under such circumstances. One-half the amount of such insurance is payable to you for the loss of one limb or sight of one eye, or the full amount for two or more such losses.

For all such losses resulting from any one accident, no more than the full amount of accidental death and dismemberment insurance is payable. If a loss of a hand or foot or the sight of one eye occurs in a different accident after a previous loss of such member, the benefit payable for the subsequent loss is one-half the amount of accidental death and dismemberment insurance. The payment of benefits for any loss will not affect the amount of benefits payable for losses resulting from any subsequent accident.

Exceptions—Payment for accidental death or dismemberment will not be made if your death or loss is caused or contributed to by:

- physical or mental illness;
- the diagnosis or treatment of a physical or mental illness;
- ptomaine or bacterial infection, unless the loss is caused by an accidentally sustained external wound;
- a war (declared or undeclared), any act of war, or any aggression by armed forces, against the United States, in which nuclear weapons are being used;
- a war (declared or undeclared), any act of war, armed aggression, or insurrection, in which the employee is, at the time bodily injuries are sustained, in actual combat;
- suicide or attempted suicide;
- intentional infliction of self-injury;
- self-administration of illegal or illegally obtained drugs.
- driving a vehicle while intoxicated, as defined by the laws of the jurisdiction in which you were operating the vehicle.

Assignment of Benefits

Effective October 3, 1994, any FEGLI-covered employee, retiree, or compensationer may irrevocably assign his/her life insurance benefits to another person or persons, including an individual, a corporation or a trust. Assignment means that you transfer ownership and control of your Basic, Option A, or Option B insurance (if you have these coverages) to the assignee(s). Thereafter, life insurance premiums will continue to be withheld from your salary, annuity, or compensation payment. You will not be able to cancel your life insurance coverage or cancel the assignment. Such an assignment voids all prior designations and prohibits you from making any future designations of beneficiaries. The assignee becomes the beneficiary (unless the assignee designates someone else). Family optional insurance may not be assigned.

Assignments are generally made to comply with a court order upon divorce, for inheritance tax purposes, to obtain cash before death from a viatical settlement firm (for terminally ill individuals), or to satisfy a debt.

If you are an employee and would like to request an assignment form (RI 76-10), which contains more information, ask your personnel office for a copy. If you are a retiree, write to the Office of Personnel Management, Retirement Operations Center, Attention: RI 76-10, Boyers, PA 16017.

Note: If you assign your life insurance, you may not elect Living Benefits (see below).

Living Benefits

Effective July 25, 1995, any FEGLI-covered employee, retiree, or compensationer who has been diagnosed as terminally ill with a life expectancy of nine months or less may elect a Living Benefit. Living benefits are life insurance benefits paid to individuals while they are still living, rather than paid to a beneficiary or survivor upon the individual's death.

Only Basic insurance is available for Living Benefits. Employees may elect either a full Living Benefit—i.e., all of their Basic benefit—or a partial Living Benefit (in multiples of $1,000). Retirees and compensationers may elect only a full Living Benefit. With a full benefit, withholding of premiums for Basic insurance ceases; with a partial benefit, they are recalculated.

Living Benefits can be elected only once and an election cannot be retracted. If a full Living Benefit is elected, no Basic life insurance will remain. If a partial Living Benefit is taken (an option only available to employees), the amount of the remaining Basic insurance will be frozen. It will not change, even if there is a subsequent change in salary. However, you may assign any remaining insurance.

If you believe you qualify for and wish to elect a Living Benefit, contact the Office of Federal Employees' Group Life Insurance, P.O. Box 2627, Jersey City, NJ 07303-2627, phone 1-800-633-4542, fax (201) 395-7950. That office will send you an application form (FE-8, Claim for Living Benefits) and a calculation sheet, so you can determine the amount of Basic insurance available to you. This will take into account the age multiplication factor for employees under age 45 and the post-65 reduction for annuitants age 65 and over. The benefits received will be reduced by an amount representing interest lost to the life insurance fund because of the early payment of benefits.

If FEGLI does not approve your request for a Living Benefit, you may furnish additional medical evidence to support your claim or may reapply if future circumstance warrant.

Discontinuing FEGLI Coverage

Unless you've assigned it to someone else, you may discontinue your Basic or Optional insurance coverage at any time by providing a written waiver of insurance coverage to your employing office (or to the Office of Personnel Management in the case of a retiree). However, there are only five situations in which your insurance can be discontinued without your consent. All but one of them involve a change in employment status:

1. Separation from service other than for retirement.

2. After 12 months of non-pay status.

3. Any other employment change that results in your ceasing to be a FEGLI-eligible employee.

4. Termination of your annuity.

5. At the end of the pay period in which it is determined that your pay, after all other deductions, is insufficient to cover the required withholding for your insurance. However, you may arrange to continue your insurance coverage by making payments directly to your agency or retirement system.

Converting to an Individual Policy

If your coverage stops, you have the right to convert your FEGLI coverage under Basic and Options A and B to an individual life insurance policy without medical evidence of insurability. If you do, you will be responsible for the full amount of the premiums. There will be no government contribution. You will make your payments directly to the insurance company. Premiums will be retroactive to the end of the 31-day extension. The amount of those premiums will depend on four factors:

- the amount of insurance you apply for;
- the type of policy you apply for;
- your age; and
- the class of risk you fall into on the day following the termination of group coverage.

If you decide to convert your FEGLI coverage to an individual life insurance policy, the following conditions apply:

- The individual policy will be issued by any eligible insurance company you select that has agreed to issue such policies under the provisions of the group policy.

- The individual policy may be in any form customarily issued by the insurance company you select, with the exception of term insurance, universal life insurance, or any other type of life insurance that has an indeterminate premium. It does not include

Bi-weekly Premiums for Employees

Age Group	Option A Withholdings (per $10,000 of coverage)	Option B Withholdings (per $1,000 of coverage)	Option C Withholdings (per multiple)
Under age 35	$0.30	$0.03	$0.27
Age 35 through 39	$0.40	$0.04	$0.34
Age 40 through 44	$0.60	$0.06	$0.46
Age 45 through 49	$0.90	$0.09	$0.60
Age 50 through 54	$1.40	$0.14	$0.90
Age 55 through 59	$2.70	$0.28	$1.45
Age 60 through 64	$6.00	$0.60	$2.60
Age 65 through 69	$6.00	$0.71	$3.00
Age 70 through 74	$6.00	$0.87	$3.40
Age 75 through 79	$6.00	$1.07	$4.50
Age 80+	$6.00	$1.27	$6.00

disability or accidental death or dismemberment benefits.

• You may choose to have this individual policy written for an amount equal to or less than the total amount of life insurance you have under the group policy, including all options on the date your insurance stops.

You must make written application within 31 days after your insurance stops, or within 31 days after you receive notice of your loss of group coverage and right to convert, whichever is later. The employee is liable for the premiums retroactive to 31 days after the date of group coverage termination. The premium will be that required for the form and amount of the policy applied for at your age (at nearest birthday) and class of risk at the time. The premiums will probably be higher than those you paid under the group coverage (which reflected a government contribution for Basic insurance). At the time your insurance stops, you may obtain detailed information about your right to apply for an individual policy from: Office of Federal Employees' Group Life Insurance, P.O. Box 2627, Jersey City, NJ 07303-2627, phone 1-800-633-4542, fax (201) 395-7950.

In the event of your death (or separation if you don't convert), if you have Option C, your family members also will have a 31-day period in which they may apply for their own conversion policies. If you should die during the 31 days after the date your insurance coverage stops, a death benefit will be payable

under the group policy (subject to proof in the usual manner) in an amount equal to the amount of life insurance (excluding accidental death and dismemberment benefits) on the date your insurance stopped.

In general, if you drop your FEGLI coverage as a retiree, you may never again be covered. However, under certain circumstances, if you drop your FEGLI coverage while an employee, you may pick it up at a later date, for example, provided you are found to be medically insurable, during an open enrollment period or because a life event has changed your situation. Medical insurability must be determined by a physical examination for which you pay. Exam results are attached to an SF-2822, Request for Insurance, which your personnel office can supply. The form is filled out by you, your agency, and the doctor who does the physical exam. The doctor sends the form to OFEGLI.

Life Insurance in Retirement

If you are retiring on an immediate annuity, you may retain your Basic insurance (but not the accidental death and dismemberment coverage) if you have been covered by FEGLI's Basic life insurance for: (1) the five years of service immediately preceding the starting date of your annuity, or (2) the full period or periods of service during which the Basic life insurance was available to you (if less than five years).

You also may retain all three forms of

Monthly Premiums for Annuitants

Age Group	Option A Withholdings (per $10,000 of coverage)	Option B Withholdings (per $1,000 of coverage)	Option C Withholdings (per multiple)
Under age 35	$0.65	$0.065	$0.59
Age 35 through 39	$0.87	$0.087	$0.74
Age 40 through 44	$1.30	$0.130	$1.00
Age 45 through 49	$1.95	$0.195	$1.30
Age 50 through 54	$3.03	$0.303	$1.95
Age 55 through 59	$5.85	$0.607	$3.14
Age 60 through 64	$13.00	$1.300	$5.63
Age 65 through 70	$13.00	$1.538	$6.50
Age 70 through 74	$13.00	$1.885	$7.37
Age 75 through 79	$13.00	$2.318	$9.75
Age 80 +	$13.00	$2.752	$13.00

Optional insurance (but not accidental death or dismemberment coverage) if you are eligible to keep your Basic insurance and you have had that particular form of Optional insurance in force for not less than: (a) the five years of service immediately preceding the commencing date of your annuity, or (b) the full period of service during which that optional insurance was available to you (if less than five years).

The amount of your life insurance will be the amount you had at retirement, or until the end of the calendar month that follows your 65th birthday or retirement, whichever is later. It then may begin to reduce in value (as explained below under "Retirees and Compensationers: Coverage and Premiums.")

The above conditions also hold true if at the time your Basic life insurance would otherwise stop under conditions (1) or (2) OPM determines that you are retiring on an immediate annuity and you did not exercise your right to convert to an individual policy as described above.

Life Insurance and Workers' Compensation

If you become entitled to benefits from the Office of Worker's Compensation Programs (OWCP) for a job-related illness or injury that prevents you from working, you may continue your FEGLI coverage as an employee, including accidental death and dismemberment (AD&D) coverage for up to 12 months of non-pay status. Premiums will be withheld from your compensation.

After this 12-month period, your FEGLI coverage may be continued (but without the AD&D) if you are in receipt of benefits from OWCP and are unable to return to duty and have been insured for: (1) the coverages you wish to continue for the five years of service immediately preceding the date of your entitlement to OWCP benefits or (2) the full period of service during which the coverages were available to you (if less than five years).

You must continue Basic life insurance to continue any Optional insurance you might have. Also, the number of multiples of pay you may continue under Optional B and C insurance is limited to the highest number of multiples you had that meet the above requirements.

At the end of 12 months of non-pay status (or at separation, if earlier), you will have the opportunity to convert all or a portion of your FEGLI insurance coverage to an individual (direct-pay) policy. If eligible to continue coverage and you do not convert, premium withholdings will be made from your compensation payment. For the purposes of the FEGLI program, a compensationer is treated as an annuitant.

Retirees and Compensationers: Coverage and Premiums

Following is a summary of FEGLI's general rules governing insurance options and premium payments for federal retirees and compensationers (i.e., workers' compensation recipients).

Basic Insurance—Prior to retiring or receiving compensation, employees must make a written election as to the amount of post-65 Basic life insurance coverage they want to retain. They can obtain this election form from their employing office. With the exception of those who have elected a Partial Living Benefit, they have three choices: a 75 percent reduction, a 50 percent reduction or no reduction. Those who elected a Partial Living Benefit have only two choices: termination of the insurance and conversion to an individual policy or no reduction. The percentage reduction choices operate as follows:

• 75 Percent Reduction—This calls for coverage to be reduced by two percent a month, beginning at age 65, with an ultimate reduction to 25 percent of the basic policy value. Anyone who retires on or after January 1, 1990, must pay the same premium as active employees until age 65 (i.e., $.3358 a month per $1,000 of coverage). No further premiums will be withheld after the calendar month in which the retiree becomes 65.

• 50 Percent Reduction—This consists of a reduction of one percent a month beginning at age 65, which continues until coverage reaches 50 percent of the basic policy value. There is a higher premium charged for this lesser reduction (i.e., $.9250 per month per $1,000 of coverage until age 65 and $.60 a month per $1,000 of coverage thereafter).

• No Reduction—This choice results in a

larger premium being charged—$2.1550 per month per $1,000 of coverage until age 65 and $1.83 per month per $1,000 of coverage thereafter.

Except for those who elected a Partial Living Benefit, failure to make a written choice will result in OPM deeming the insured to have picked the 75 percent reduction.

Generally, all premiums will be withheld from annuity or compensation payments. However, annuitants and compensationers are eligible to pay the premium directly to the retirement system, if their annuity is insufficient to withhold the premiums.

If retirees who have not assigned their insurance decide to cancel their increased post-retirement coverage under the second or third items above, the amount of Basic insurance coverage and the premiums would immediately drop to the level they would have been if the retirees had originally elected the 75 percent reduction. Retirees must elect No Reduction if they previously elected a partial living benefit, and such an election may not be changed at a later date.

Optional Insurance—The face value of any Optional life insurance will be the same as the amount carried at retirement (or if a compensationer, the date your insurance would otherwise have terminated, as explained above). You must pay the full amount for any Optional insurance coverage you retain until you reach age 65. However, you may elect to keep the full amount of the Option B and C insurance in force and continue to pay the full premium. Unless the insurance has been assigned, such an election may be cancelled at a later date. Generally, the cost of optional insurance premiums will be withheld from your annuity or compensation payments.

At the end of the calendar month that follows your 65th birthday or your retirement, whichever is later, your Option A life insurance will be reduced by two percent each month until it reaches 25 percent of its face value. Option B and Option C insurance will continue to be reduced for 50 months, at which time coverage ceases

unless the retiree elects to continue premiums after age 65 or retirement.

Direct Payment of Premiums

For many years, annuitants and compensationers whose payments are not large enough to cover their insurance premiums have been allowed to pay those premiums directly to the retirement system. Beginning with the first pay period on or after October 30, 1999, employees who have insufficient pay on an ongoing basis have been given the same opportunity. Insufficient pay on an ongoing basis means that the employing agency expects that during the next six months or more, an employee's regular pay, after all other deductions, will not be enough to cover the required withholdings.

The direct pay provision does not apply to employees in a non-pay status. Those employees are entitled to continue their FEGLI coverage for free for up to 12 months (unless they are receiving workers' compensation benefits, in which case the coverage is not free). In general, at the end of 12 months in a non-pay status, FEGLI terminates.

For More Information

Although the Office of Personnel Management has overall responsibility for administering the FEGLI program, each federal agency is responsible for day-to-day operations of the program with respect to its own employees. Therefore, questions about life insurance policy should be addressed to the local personnel office or the agency insurance benefits officer at agency headquarters.

Additional information about life insurance policy is also available online at www.opm.gov/insure or in a series of program booklets: RI 76-21 for federal employees, RI 76-20 for Postal Service employees and RI 76-12 for retirees and their families.

Federal Employees News Digest Inc. has published a comprehensive guide to federal insurance benefits titled *Insuring Your Future: A Federal Employee's Guide to Meeting Insurance Needs*. See publication-ordering information in this *Almanac*.

Section 3—Federal Long-Term Care Insurance Program

The Federal Long-Term Care Insurance Program, authorized by Public Law 106-265, the Long-Term Care Security Act of 2000,

covers services that individuals may need because they are unable to care for themselves due to a chronic mental or physical condition. Included are services such as nursing home care, home health care, assisted living facilities, adult day care and personal/homemaker care. The coverage is provided by LTC Partners, LLC, a partnership of the John Hancock and Metropolitan Life insurance companies under contract with the Office of Personnel Management.

Coverage is voluntary and enrollees pay the entire cost of the premiums; there is no government contribution. The FLTCIP is "guaranteed renewable"—it cannot be canceled as long as you pay your premiums for reasons of age, change in health or any other reason, including leaving the eligible enrollment group.

Eligiblity

Individuals eligible to apply for this insurance coverage are:

• Federal employees and members of the uniformed services. This includes employees of the U.S. Postal Service and Tennessee Valley Authority, but does not include employees of the District of Columbia government. For federal and postal employees in general, if you are in a position eligible for Federal Employees Health Benefits program coverage, you are eligible for FLTCIP (whether enrolled in FEHB or not—the key is eligibility).

• Federal annuitants, surviving spouses of deceased federal or postal employees or annuitants who are receiving a federal survivor annuity, individuals receiving compensation from the Department of Labor who are separated from the federal service, members or former members of the uniformed services entitled to retired or retainer pay, and retired military reservists at the time they qualify for an annuity (also known as gray area reservists). Retired employees of the D.C. government are not included.

• Current spouses of employees and annuitants (including surviving spouses of members and retired members of the uniformed services who are receiving a survivor annuity).

• Adult children (at least 18 years old, including natural children, adopted children and stepchildren) of living employees and annuitants. Foster children are not eligible.

• Parents, parents-in-law, and stepparents of living employees (but those of annuitants are not eligible).

There is no upper age limit for who can apply for this insurance but there is a minimum age; you must be at least 18 years old at the time you submit your application.

Enrollment

Eligible individuals may enroll at any time; it is not necessary to wait for an open enrollment period. An early enrollment period was offered March 25-May 15, 2002, with an open season running July 1-December 31, 2002. Dates of subsequent open seasons are yet to be determined, although they will not be held on an annual basis. During the 2002 early enrollment and open season periods, active employees and their spouses were subject only to abbreviated underwriting.

Newly hired employees and their spouses have 60 days to enroll and use abbreviated underwriting. Afterward, they must use full underwriting.

All other enrollments are subject to full underwriting.

Underwriting

"Abbreviated" underwriting applies to newly hired employees and their spouses and also applied to all active employees and their spouses during the initial 2002 open season. (Note: It is still to be determined whether abbreviated underwriting would apply to current employees during any future open seasons or whether they will have to undergo full underwriting.)

The abbreviated underwriting application has seven health-related questions designed to determine who may be immediately eligible for benefits, or eligible for benefits within a short period of time. Spouses of active employees eligible for abbreviated underwriting also are subject only to abbreviated underwriting, although they must answer two additional questions regarding their mobility and any need for help with everyday tasks.

All other applicants are subject to "full" underwriting at all times. This means that they must answer numerous health-related and lifestyle-related questions in addition to questions asked of active employees and their spouses qualifying for abbreviated underwriting.

Benefit Choices

Enrollees can choose a maximum benefit,

the length of the policy, the type of inflation protection and the waiting period before benefits begin. They also can choose between comprehensive coverage and coverage for only facility-based care. The program offers four standardized packages known as Facilities 100, Comprehensive 100, Comprehensive 150 and Comprehensive 150+. However, enrollees may tailor their coverage as they see fit. Also, you may change coverage levels after you are first insured.

Benefit Amount—The maximum daily benefit can range from $50 to $300 a day in a multiple of $25; weekly benefit amounts also can be elected.

Length of Policy—The length of policy can be three years, five years or lifetime coverage. If you select a three-year or five-year policy, that length and the maximum weekly benefit you chose determine a "pool of money." The insurance will pay benefits until your pool of money is exhausted, a process that may take longer than the length of the policy. For example, a $700 weekly benefit and a three-year policy would produce $109,200 ($700 x 52 weeks x 3 years) for covered services. When the pool is gone, your insurance ends.

A lifetime benefit has a limitless pool of money.

Inflation Protection—Two inflation protection features are available. Under Automatic Compound Inflation Protection, your benefit would automatically increase by 5 percent every year, regardless of actual inflation. Your premiums would remain level for life, even as your weekly benefit increases.

Under the Future Purchase Option, every two years you would have the option to increase your benefits based on a medical inflation index. Your premiums would increase as your benefit increases; they further would be based on the age at that election, not the age at which you first took out the policy. If you decline more than two FPO offers, you can still apply for future inflation increases but would have to show satisfactory evidence of insurability.

You can switch from the Future Purchase Option to the Automatic Compound Inflation Protection option without proof of good health at the time of a Future Purchase Option notification if you have not declined more than two notifications in the past and

are not eligible for benefits at that time. Premiums for those who make this change will be based on age at that time and premiums already paid in, not on the standard rate tables for new enrollees.

Waiting Period—Enrollees also can choose the waiting period—also called an elimination period or deductible—which is the number of days of covered care that you (or other insurance coverage you may have) must pay for before the insurance begins to pay. The choice is either 90 days or 30 days.

Types of Coverage—Two basic types of coverage are available. A Facilities-only Plan covers care in assisted living facilities, nursing homes and inpatient hospice care. It also provides benefits for respite services in a facility. It does not cover home care.

A Comprehensive Plan covers everything a facilities-only plan covers plus care at home (formal or informal care), in adult day care centers, hospice care at home and respite services at home.

Changing Coverage Levels—You can request a decrease in your coverage at any time. You can decrease to anything that is available under the program, and your premiums (which will be based on your age at time of original enrollment) will also decrease. For example, if you have the five-year benefit period, you can decrease to a three-year benefit period. But you could not decrease to a two-year benefit period, because such a benefit period is not available under the program. You do not have to undergo new underwriting in order to decrease your coverage. However, you don't get paid-up benefits.

At any time, you also may request an increase in your coverage by contacting LTC Partners. To receive approval of a request for an increase outside of an open season, you must provide, at your expense, evidence of your good health that is satisfactory to LTC Partners. The amount of an increase is subject to what's then available under the program. If you request and LTC Partners approves an increase in your daily benefit amount (not counting an increase due to your inflation protection option), your additional premium will be based on your age and the premium rates in effect at the time the increase takes effect. Other coverage increases you request that LTC Partners approves will cause your entire premium to be based on your age and the premium rates in effect at the time the increase takes effect.

Premiums

Premiums are based on age when the enrollee buys the coverage, the benefit amount, the length of the policy, the waiting period, the type of coverage and the type of inflation protection chosen. Premiums are designed to be level for life

---

Monthly Premium Costs for $100 Maximum Daily Benefit Amount—Comprehensive Coverage

Automatic Compound Inflation Option

Age	Benefit Period		
	3 years	**5 years**	**Unlimited**
30 and under	$32.00	$38.60	$53.00
40	$43.40	$52.80	$72.80
50	$62.20	$75.80	$104.20
60	$93.20	$113.60	$154.40
70	$154.40	$187.80	$252.80
80	$369.20	$450.40	$609.20

Future Purchase Option

Age	Benefit Period		
	3 years	**5 years**	**Unlimited**
30 and under	$8.40	$9.40	$11.40
40	$12.60	$14.60	$18.60
50	$21.40	$25.00	$32.60
60	$40.60	$48.20	$62.80
70	$86.80	$103.00	$133.80
80	$258.60	$308.00	$403.40

Monthly Premium Costs for $100 Maximum Daily Benefit Amount—Facilities-Only Coverage

Automatic Compound Inflation Option

Age	Benefit Period		
	3 years	**5 years**	**Unlimited**
30 and under	$21.40	$26.40	$36.60
40	$29.40	$36.20	$50.80
50	$42.40	$53.00	$73.60
60	$64.60	$80.40	$111.00
70	$111.20	$137.80	$185.80
80	$267.60	$331.40	$445.40

Future Purchase Option

Age	Benefit Period		
	3 years	**5 years**	**Unlimited**
30 and under	$6.00	$6.60	$8.00
40	$8.60	$10.00	$12.60
50	$14.20	$17.00	$22.40
60	$27.80	$33.60	$44.80
70	$63.20	$76.80	$100.00
80	$190.80	$231.20	$302.00

Notes:

The tables above represent costs of plans taken out at ages upon receipt of application and include 90-day waiting periods before benefits begin. Enrollees may customize their choices by varying daily benefits from between $50 to $300 a day in $25 increments. Enrollees also may choose a 30-day waiting period instead.

A premium calculator is available online at www.ltcfeds.com.

---

from the time of purchase. They cannot be increased on an individual basis, only on a group basis and only with Office of Personnel Management approval.

The following figures show premium rates for policies purchased at representative ages for maximum daily benefits of $100 and with a 90-day waiting period. Remember, you are free to customize coverage by electing daily benefits of between $50 and $300 in $25 increments, may elect weekly benefits and may shorten the waiting period to 30 days. Shortening the waiting period can increase the premium by from several dollars to $100 or more a month, depending on age and benefit level chosen. Electing weekly rather than daily benefits raises the cost by several percentage points.

Alternative Insurance Plan/Service Package

Some employees and their spouses who are not approved to enroll in the insurance they originally applied for will be offered the Alternative Insurance Plan. This plan is not available to other groups who use the full underwriting application, such as annuitants. It offers nursing home only coverage with a 180 day waiting period and two-year benefit period. The Alternative Insurance Plan also has higher premiums.

If you apply for and are denied the standard insurance and are not offered the Alternative Insurance Plan, you will be offered a Service Package. This is true for everyone who applies—those using the abbreviated underwriting application and those using the full underwriting application. The Service Package is not insurance. It is a package of services, including access to a care coordinator, general information and referral services, and access to a discounted network of long term care providers and services. It costs $59 per year for an individual or a couple.

Everyone who is denied standard coverage will receive information from Long Term Care Partners to review at no obligation. The information will describe what is available in lieu of the standard insurance— either the Alternative Insurance Plan and/or the Service Package. Individuals who are offered both can decide which, if any, they wish to purchase.

On the following page is a table summarizing this information.

Types of Care Covered

Depending on whether you elect Comprehensive or Facilities-only coverage, the FLTCIP plan may cover:

• nursing home care, assisted living facility care, hospice care and respite care (temporary care if your normal caregiver needs time off), at up to 100 percent of the chosen daily benefit amount;

• home care by nurses, home health care aides, therapists or other providers and adult day care (services received in a licensed adult day care center for those unable to care for themselves during the day but able to be home at night), at up to 75 percent of the chosen daily benefit amount;

• approved care provided in the home by friends, family members and other non-licensed caregivers who don't normally live in the enrollee's home (covered for the benefit period when provided by non-family members and up to 365 days when provided by family members), at up to 75 percent of the chosen daily benefit amount;

• caregiver training, paid up to 100 percent of the chosen daily amount and up to seven times the daily amount as a lifetime benefit to train a family member or other informal caregiver to provide care;

• care coordination that can arrange for discounted services, monitor the care being given and assist with altering a plan of care as needs change; and

• alternate plans of care under certain circumstances in which care coordinators can authorize benefits for services not specifically defined as covered (such as making a home wheelchair-accessible), so long as they are deemed to meet needs and to be cost effective.

The FLTCIP does not cover:

• illnesses, treatments or medical conditions arising out of participation in a felony, riot or insurrection, from an attempted suicide while sane or insane or from self-inflicted injuries;

• care or treatment for alcoholism or drug addiction;

• care or treatment provided in a government facility unless required by law;

• care received in a hospital except in specifically designated nursing home or hospice units;

• any service or supply reimbursable under Medicare;

Your Federal Affiliation	Your Answers to Questions on Abbreviated Underwriting Application:			What You Will Be Offered
	1-	4-7	8-9	
Employee or member of the uniformed services	No	No	N/A	Standard insurance
Employee or member of the uniformed services	No	Yes	N/A	Choice of either: Alternative Insurance Plan or Service Package
Employee or member of the uniformed services	Yes	N/A	N/A	Service Package
Spouse of either an employee or member of the uniformed services	No	No	No	Standard insurance
Spouse of either an employee or member of the uniformed services	No	No	Yes	Possibly Standard insurance. If denied standard insurance, choice of either: Alternative Insurance Plan or Service Package
Spouse of either an employee or member of the uniformed services	No	Yes	N/A	Choice of either: Alternative Insurance Plan or Service Package
Spouse of either an employee or member of the uniformed services	Yes	N/A	N/A	Service Package
Everyone using the full underwriting application who is denied standard insurance	N/A			Service Package

Covered Services for Daily Benefit Amounts—If you elect a daily benefit amount, the program provides reimbursement for actual charges you incur for covered services up to the following percentages:

Covered Services Under Both the Comprehensive Option and the Facilities-Only Option	Daily Reimbursement Up To
Nursing home, assisted living facility, or hospice facility	100% of your daily benefit amount
Bed reservations	100% of your daily benefit amount—benefits limited to 30 days per calendar year
Caregiver training	100% of your daily benefit amount—benefits limited to 7 x your daily benefit amount in your lifetime
Respite services	100% of your daily benefit amount—benefits limited to 30 x your daily benefit amount per calendar year

Additional Covered Services Under the Comprehensive Option	Daily Reimbursement Up To
Formal caregiver services	75% of your daily benefit amount
Informal caregiver services	75% of your daily benefit amount—benefits for informal caregiver services provided by family members who did not normally live in your home at the time you became eligible for benefits are limited to 365 days in your lifetime
Hospice care at home	100% of your daily benefit amount
Adult day care center	75% of your daily benefit amount

Covered Services for Weekly Benefit Amounts—If you choose a weekly benefit amount, the program provides reimbursement for actual charges you incur for covered services up to the following percentages:

Covered Services Under the Comprehensive Option (Weekly Benefit Amount)	Daily Reimbursement Up To
Nursing home, assisted living facility or hospice facility	100% of your weekly benefit amount
Formal caregiver services	75% of your weekly benefit amount
Informal caregiver services	75% of your weekly benefit amount—benefits for informal caregiver services provided by family members who did not normally live in your home at the time you became eligible for benefits are limited to 365 days in your lifetime
Hospice care at home	100% of your weekly benefit amount
Adult day care center	75% of your weekly benefit amount
Bed reservations	100% of your weekly benefit amount—benefits limited to 30 days per calendar year
Caregiver training	100% of your weekly benefit amount—benefits limited to 7 x your daily benefit amount in your lifetime
Respite services	100% of your weekly benefit amount—benefits limited to 30 x your daily benefit amount per calendar year

• services or supplies for which you are not obligated to pay in the absence of insurance; or

• services provided by any person who normally lives in your home at the time you become eligible for benefits.

Benefit Eligibility Determination and Appeals

You are eligible for benefits if, after your coverage becomes effective:

• a licensed health care practitioner has certified within the last 12 months that you are unable to perform, without substantial assistance from another person, at least two activities of daily living for an expected period of at least 90 days due to a loss of functional capacity; or you require substantial supervision due to your severe cognitive impairment;

• LTC Partners agrees with that certification; and

• LTC Partners approves a written plan of care established for you by a licensed health care practitioner or its care coordinator.

Activities of daily living include eating, toileting, transferring (as from bed to chair), bathing, dressing, and bowel and bladder control. A cognitive impairment is impairment in short-term or long-term memory, orientation as to person, place and time, or deductive or abstract reasoning such that the person needs substantial supervision by another person to prevent him from harming himself or others.

You will not have to pay premiums after you have met one of those two conditions and you use the care coordination program during the waiting period you select. If you do not use the care coordination program, you will pay premiums during your waiting period, but will stop paying them after you satisfy your waiting period.

To apply for benefits, call 1-800-582-3337, TDD 1-800-843-3557. After you apply, LTC Partners may contact you, your physician or other persons familiar with your condition, access medical records and may have you examined by a licensed health care professional and/or conduct an on-site assessment.

LTC Partners will send you written notice of its decision on whether you are eligible for benefits no later than 10 business days after it receives all the information it needs. If LTC Partners determines that you are eligible for benefits, the notice will state the date as of which you are eligible for benefits and will include claim forms. At least once a year, but no more often than every 30 days, LTC Partners will reassess whether you continue to be eligible for benefits.

If LTC Partners determines that you are not eligible for benefits, the notice will provide the reason(s) for the denial and will let you know how to request a review of the denial. If that denial is upheld, you may request an appeal. The letter upholding the denial will explain the process to you.

All appeals will be reviewed by an appeals committee composed of: one or more representatives of John Hancock Life Insurance Company, one or more representatives of Metropolitan Life Insurance Company, and other person(s) if mutually agreed upon by OPM and LTC Partners.

If the appeals committee upholds the denial, and that denial is eligible for review by an independent third party, the letter upholding the denial will give you the details on requesting a review by an independent third party. For example, appeal to an independent third party is available when the appeals committee upholds a denial of your eligibility for benefits because its review indicates that you can perform five out of six activities of daily living. However, appeal to an independent third party is not available for example when the appeals committee upholds a denial of your claim for benefits because you exhausted your maximum lifetime benefit.

The decision by the independent third party is final and binding on LTC Partners.

After you have gone through this administrative review process, you may seek judicial review of a final denial of eligibility for benefits or a claim. The amount of recovery available is limited to the benefit payable; no punitive, compensatory or other damages are allowed.

Tax Treatment

This insurance coverage meets the requirements of the Health Insurance Portability and Accountability Act (HIPAA). This means you can deduct the premiums to the extent that your total qualified medical expenses exceed 7.5 percent of your annual adjusted gross income and that the benefits you receive are not considered income for tax purposes.

For More Information

Further information on the program can be obtained from LTC Partners, phone 1-800-582-3337 or TDD 1-800-843-3557 and online at *www.ltcfeds.com* and at *www.opm.gov/insure/ltc.*

In addition, Federal Employees News Digest, Inc. has published a comprehensive guide to long-term care titled *A Guide to Long-Term Care Benefits* and a comprehensive guide to federal insurance benefits titled *Insuring Your Future: A Federal Employee's Guide to Meeting Insurance Needs.* See publication-ordering information in this *Almanac.*

Chapter 3
Retirement

Section 1—Retirement Systems: General Description

Basic Federal Systems and Coverage

Most federal and postal employees are covered by a "defined benefit plan." A defined benefit plan is one that has specific criteria for determining eligibility for the benefits, as well as a formula that calculates what the benefits will be. Under such a plan, an employee's eligibility for an annuity is based on age and years of service. The formula for computing a retiree's benefits is based on years of service, average salary, and certain percentage multipliers. (See 5 CFR 831.201 for exclusions from coverage under CSRS and 5 CFR 842.104 for exclusions under FERS.)

In addition, many federal employees are covered by Social Security, which is also a defined benefit plan, although one that uses a greater number of variables to determine benefits.

At the same time, many government employees expect to supplement their retirement income by building up investment earnings in a "defined contribution plan," the government-sponsored version of which is called the Thrift Savings Plan. Benefit levels under the TSP program, like those under most 401(k) plans and other types of defined contribution programs, are based on the amount of money (i.e., contributions plus interest or investment earnings) that individual employees accumulate in their accounts.

While retirement benefit levels in defined benefit plans are not based on how much a person has contributed to the retirement fund, they are in defined contribution plans. Thus, a retiree's benefit payments under a defined benefit plan have a stable, predictable relationship to salary and service, while the payouts under defined contribution plans are far more dependent on—and sensitive to—changes in the value of the securities in which the funds are invested.

Federal civilian employees automatically participate in one of the federal retirement systems. With few exceptions, the system an employee participates in is determined by the date of hire.

FERS—Employees first hired after December 31, 1983, are automatically covered under FERS and Social Security. These employees are eligible to participate fully in the thrift savings plan, since the TSP is primarily designed to complement the coverage of FERS and Social Security.

CSRS—Generally, employees hired before 1984 are members of CSRS unless they elected coverage under FERS during one of the open seasons authorized for making such choices in 1987 and 1998.

CSRS-Offset—This option is available to employees who were originally hired before 1984 and covered by CSRS, but who left federal service and were rehired after 1983. Upon rehire, they are eligible to reenter CSRS if they have at least five years of eligible service credit under CSRS. However, if such an employee returns after having been outside federal employment for more than one year, that employee also becomes covered by Social Security. At retirement, the benefits of a CSRS-Offset employee are coordinated so that the value of the worker's Social Security benefits (i.e., those earned through federal service performed after 1983 while covered by both CSRS and Social Security) are subtracted from the individual's CSRS benefits. (The formulas for accomplishing this reduction generally work to an employee's advantage and only seldom to anyone's disadvantage.)

Returning employees eligible for reentry into CSRS, either with or without Social Security coverage, may choose coverage under FERS; such an election must be made during the first six months after rehire. Employees without five years of creditable service under CSRS are automatically enrolled in FERS with their previous service credited under that program.

Employees either automatically enrolled or who elect FERS are not subject to the offset.

TSP—Federal employees covered either by FERS or CSRS can elect to have deductions from their pay invested through the federal Thrift Savings Plan, beginning immediately after entering service. During twice-yearly open seasons, employees can specify the amounts they want invested, up to the maximums allowed. FERS participants also have additional funds invested in their behalf by their employing agencies, with amounts linked to employee deductions. Employees who terminate their TSP deductions must skip an open season before they are allowed to again authorize a deduction. (For more information, see Chapter 6.)

Retirement Systems: Basic Objectives and Design

Each of the government's major retirement benefit programs differs in terms of its basic design and in the rights granted by its provisions. Stated another way, in the FERS, CSRS, CSRS-Offset, and Social Security programs, the law specifies what a retiree's benefits will be and authorizes these payments from federal funds. The TSP also has definitions that govern participation and eligibility for benefits, but its benefit payouts are linked to the amount of money accumulated in an individual's account, which means that benefit levels are affected by investment returns to those accounts. In the main benefit programs, federal law directs that federal money be paid to individuals, under specified circumstances and in specified amounts that can be changed only by alterations in the law. In the TSP, the contributions of federal agencies and employees are credited to individual employees who, in effect, "own" their accounts, the value of which can increase (or decrease) depending on investment results over time.

CSRS—The Civil Service Retirement System currently is a comprehensive system of entitlements that provides covered federal workers with a full range of pension benefits and wage insurance protections. In addition to annuities for workers who meet age and service criteria for voluntary retirement, annuities are paid to workers whose jobs are terminated after they have reached certain specified levels of age and/or serv-

ice. Benefits also are provided to workers who become unable to perform in their positions because of a disabling condition, and to dependents of deceased workers and retirees who meet certain conditions. Benefits are adjusted annually for inflation.

Workers who leave federal employment with at least five years of creditable service and who were covered by CSRS for at least one year within the two-year period before separation retain rights to deferred benefits, beginning at age 62. However, the computation of CSRS benefit payments received at age 62 is based on the amount of service and salary base attained by the employee at the point of separation. Most workers who leave service before attaining eligibility for immediate benefits exercise their right to withdraw their contributions to the system, thereby waiving their rights to deferred benefits. Subsequently, if they take another government job or otherwise reenter federal service, they generally may recapture that service credit by repaying the amount they withdrew, plus interest.

One effect of CSRS's basic design has been to encourage the retention of workers who have not reached eligibility for immediate benefits, while encouraging employees to retire once they have achieved such eligibility. Studies have shown that in comparison to private-sector workers with similar salaries and service, CSRS participants have substantially less protection if they leave service before becoming eligible for benefits, and substantially more in terms of lifetime benefits (about one-third more, on average) if they retire shortly after becoming eligible. Disabled workers and survivors may be better or worse off under CSRS than their private-sector counterparts, depending on a number of factors.

FERS—Most federal civilian workers first hired after 1983 are automatically covered by the Federal Employees Retirement System. FERS was created as a result of Congress' decision to expand Social Security coverage to federal employment, beginning in 1984. Eventually, all federal workers will be covered by FERS, although CSRS will continue to be the government pension system for workers who retained rights to such coverage because they were employed before 1984. (According to current actuarial estimates, the CSRS system will end in the year 2070, when all beneficiaries and their survivors will have died.)

When Congress decided to include all new federal workers in Social Security, it addressed problems with the federal retirement program that could be corrected only during the design of a new system. Congressional studies had shown that disability and survivor benefits were often better for those covered by a combination of Social Security and private pensions. They had also revealed that two categories of CSRS-covered workers were at a special disadvantage when compared to their private sector counterparts: workers who left federal employment before becoming eligible for immediate benefits, and workers who retired at ages later than the average retirement age (around 61-62). Finally, virtually all CSRS benefits were shown to be more advantageous to workers at higher grades than they were to lower-wage federal employees, a direct contradiction to Congressional retirement policies for other workers.

In designing FERS, Congress continued the practice of providing salary insurance for a full range of events that a worker might encounter during a normal career. Benefits are provided for normal retirement and for circumstances that might occur earlier, such as involuntary retirement because of a reduction-in-force (RIF), disability, or benefits for survivors in cases of the death of a worker or retiree.

Except for totally and permanently disabled workers (whose benefits are generally better under FERS and Social Security than they would be if covered by CSRS), FERS benefits are added to Social Security, thereby preserving that program's objective of enhancing benefits for workers with relatively lower salaries over the course of their careers (see below). In FERS, workers who leave before eligibility for immediate benefits can begin to draw benefits at earlier ages than can workers under CSRS, thereby more closely linking their retirement benefits to the salaries they had at the point of separation.

In addition, the combination of FERS, Social Security, and the Thrift Savings Plan makes it possible for employees who work beyond the "typical" retirement age to lessen the impact on their lifetime benefits of continued employment.

CSRS-Offset—Federal and postal employees separated from service for at least one year are automatically covered by Social Security if they resume federal or postal employment after 1983. However, those workers whose prior employment spanned at least five years of creditable service under CSRS have the right to reenter that retirement system upon reemployment. To eliminate the overlap between CSRS and Social Security, Congress created a special category of coverage called CSRS-Offset. Under this approach employees contribute the same amount as they would have if they had been covered by CSRS alone. The money is divided between Social Security and CSRS. The Social Security trust fund receives the same percentage amount as is contributed for everyone else covered by that program (6.2 percent up to the Social Security taxable maximum). The civil service retirement fund receives the rest (.8 percent, except for those special category employees who pay more for coverage). When an employee's wages exceed the taxable maximum, Social Security deductions cease and CSRS deductions increase to the full CSRS rate for the remainder of the calendar year.

Note: Since the taxable wage base for Social Security purposes includes wages, such as overtime and awards, which are not counted for CSRS purposes, FICA (Federal Insurance Contributions Act) deductions may stop before CSRS deductions revert to their full rate.

Thrift Savings Plan—As part of the legislation establishing FERS, Congress created the federal Thrift Savings Plan, a tax-advantaged savings plan patterned after the "401(k)" savings plans widely available in the private-sector. Like 401(k) plans, the TSP program is designed to encourage workers to save toward their wage replacement needs. Two TSP program characteristics provide this encouragement: (1) an employee's TSP contributions from pay are deducted before income taxes are computed, and (2) the interest earned on these savings is not included as taxable income each year the account is in operation. At retirement, or under certain other circumstances (see Chapter 6), the individual pays taxes on the wages and earned interest as the account is converted to benefit payments.

Federal and postal employees covered by

CSRS or FERS are allowed to participate in TSP, although workers covered by FERS may contribute more and are eligible for another important participation inducement—agency contributions. FERS participants receive an automatic contribution to their accounts from their employing agencies of an amount equal to one percent of salary, and their agencies also will contribute additional amounts in the form of matching payments to an employee's contributions. Basically, an agency will match each dollar saved up to three percent of pay, and will contribute 50¢ for each additional dollar up to a total of five percent of pay. TSP accounts are invested in a combination of government securities and financial market instruments, and employees can control the direction (although not the actual investment) of the account.

Social Security—The Social Security system was established in 1935 in response to a growing awareness that many workers were vulnerable to economic downturns and unable to adequately prepare for income losses, especially in old age. Because primary and immediate attention was directed to those workers perceived to be most vulnerable, Social Security coverage was originally provided to workers in industrial and commercial enterprises, most of whom had no income protection when they became too old to continue employment. Federal and postal employees were excluded from Social Security. While there were several reasons for this exclusion, there is no question that the existence of the CSRS program made federal workers less in need of such coverage than other workers. This decision effectively was reversed for federal employees hired after 1983 with creation of the FERS program, which includes Social Security as a basic component.

The program, named in law as the Old Age, Survivors, and Disability Insurance program (OASDI), provides a floor of support in old age and ensures that individuals dependent on a worker's wages will not be without income if the worker dies or becomes disabled. Dependents' benefits are provided in the form of guarantees. Dependents can receive benefits based either on their own work histories or on the work histories of the primary beneficiary, up to certain specified levels. Benefits are automatically available to workers at age 62, reduced from what they would be if the worker waits until 65 to retire (climbing gradually to 67 over the first 22 years of the next century). Benefit levels are set so that, on average, workers receive approximately the same lifetime benefits regardless of whether they retire early or at the age of full benefits.

The fundamental characteristic of the Social Security program is its categorical approach to benefit entitlement. The program identifies categories of persons dependent on a specific wage, and in circumstances defined as appropriate, replaces portions of that wage with federal payments. Social Security is neither a program of enforced savings nor is it a pension. It is a distributive system of taxes and entitlements. The program collects taxes from workers (and their employers) during their work careers, and subsequently distributes the money to beneficiaries. When a person becomes a beneficiary, the taxes collected are used to fund the benefit payments made to them or their dependents or survivors.

Generally, Social Security is designed to ensure that workers with similar wages during their careers will receive similar benefits. Nevertheless some benefit rights are redistributed away from higher-paid workers toward workers with relatively lower-paid jobs; families also receive more benefits than do single workers with similar careers. Benefits are related to workers' wage increases and promotions during their careers, but benefits are also enhanced for workers whose careers yielded relatively lower wages. Couples in which only one person served as the primary earner might well receive benefits similar to a couple in which both worked. (For more information, see the Social Security section below.)

Federal Retirement Plan Financing

Federal retirement plans are primarily financed through the taxing power of the federal government. In CSRS and FERS, employee contributions provide very little of the actual program revenue necessary to meet benefit obligations. Instead, these mandatory payments are part of the criteria that must be satisfied to meet eligibility requirements. Federal and postal employee contributions to Social Security are revenues that the federal government uses to meet benefit obligations of the program; the employer share of Social Security taxes for federal and postal workers covered by the program must be raised from the general public in the same way as all other federal financial requirements. Only in TSP are all benefits directly related to contributions; payments to beneficiaries are directly related to account balances resulting from employee savings and agency matching amounts, plus interest earned through investing these combined amounts.

The Civil Service Retirement and Disability Trust Fund—Benefits in CSRS and FERS are paid from the Civil Service Retirement Disability Trust Fund, although it is important to appreciate that this federal account is not money that can be separated from the government's general financial operations. Agency money to the trust fund is mingled with various general Treasury payments, with any amounts not needed for the immediate payment of benefits retained in the Treasury as an account balance. The trust fund is a device that assures that benefit checks can be issued independent of any annual appropriations. Through a spiraling series of internal paper transactions, the Fund is automatically assured of adequate revenues to meet all benefit obligations of the fund. Thus, the impact of CSRS and FERS on federal taxpayers each year is equal to the sum of benefit payments from the program, minus the sum of employee money contributed to the program during the year.

Social Security Trust Funds—Payments for the Old Age, Survivors, and Disability Insurance benefits of Social Security are also made from a trust fund maintained as a federal financial operation. Money is collected from the payrolls of the nation's employers and employees, and amounts not needed for immediate benefit payments are held in the Treasury as an account balance.

As previously noted, the Social Security program is a public mechanism for regulating the flow of purchasing power from workers to beneficiaries, most of whom no longer work. Thus, the program's financing is fundamentally an exchange between taxpayers and beneficiaries, with the assumption that the one becomes the other as circumstances dictate.

Thrift Savings Plan—The money invest-ed by employees is deducted from pay on a pre-tax basis. Agency contributions for FERS investors are transferred from agency appropriations to the TSP. Accounts are maintained as actual account balances for individual participants at their discretion.

CSRS and FERS: General Eligibility Requirements

Under CSRS, there are two general requirements that all retiring employees must meet in order to leave their government jobs with the right to either an immediate or deferred annuity. These general eligibility requirements stipulate that employees: (1) must have at least five years of credible civilian service with the government, and (2) must have been employed under CSRS for at least one year out of the last two years preceding separation for retirement (this requirement is waived for retirements on account of disability).

Under FERS, employees only have to satisfy the first condition (i.e., five years of creditable service) to be eligible for an immediate annuity. Employees also must be covered by FERS when they retire, but no minimum final period of service is required.

To retire and draw an immediate annuity, employees also must meet one of the specified combinations of minimum age and service requirements, as well as any special requirements that may be applicable to the type of retirement they are taking.

To qualify for a deferred retirement annuity (which generally is available starting at age 62), employees must meet the general service requirements and separate from federal service for any reason (or transfer to a government position not under CSRS or FERS) before becoming eligible for an immediate annuity. Such employees also must leave all their retirement contributions in the retirement fund to be entitled to receive a deferred annuity at age 62.

Retirement Misenrollments

Public Law 106-265, the Federal Erroneous Retirement Coverage Corrections Act (FERCCA), which was enacted in 2000, addresses the problems created when federal agencies put some of their employees in the wrong retirement plan. It gives certain employees a choice of retirement plans. If you have not worked for the federal government continuously since 1983, or you have had changes in appointment types and retirement plans, you may want to ask your agency to review your retirement coverage to ensure that it is correct.

First, double-check the retirement system you are in. Look at any of your Standard Form 50s (Notifications of Personnel Actions). There's a block that shows your retirement plan. Second, determine if you might be in the wrong plan. The accompanying table shows some of the common errors, broken down by retirement plan. Those are just some of the common situations, however. If you fall under any of them—or believe there is any chance you might be misenrolled otherwise—contact your personnel office.

The Office of Personnel Management maintains a FERCCA hotline at 1-888-689-3233, available Monday through Friday from 8 a.m. to 6 p.m. Eastern time for those with specific questions about the law as well as a website with information and the option to register for placement on a list of those who believe they are misenrolled, *http://www.opm.gov/benefits/correction/*. FERCCA rules are found at 5 CFR parts 831, 839, 841, and 846.

Available Relief—The FERCCA law provides several options for those who are found to be misenrolled. Depending upon what the retirement coverage error was and how long an employee was in the wrong retirement plan, FERCCA may provide an employee one or all of the following:
- a choice between retirement plans;
- a new opportunity for make-up contributions to the employee's Thrift Savings Plan account;
- lost earnings on make-up contributions already made as well as those made in the future;
- payment for certain expenses and losses related to correction of a retirement coverage error; and
- an opportunity to receive credit for civilian or military deposit service by taking an actuarial reduction in the employee's retirement benefit, instead of paying a deposit.

Those whose errors are discovered after they retired generally have the same choices under FERCCA that active employees have. If an employee, former employee, or retiree would have had a choice under FERCCA but died before making an election, then the survivor can make that election instead. A recent decision by OPM has authorized payment of

If your retirement plan is:	you may be in the wrong plan if you:
CSRS	Worked for the government before 1984, but your first appointment under CSRS was after 1983; or Left federal employment for more than a year at any time after 1983.
CSRS or CSRS-Offset	Have a temporary appointment limited to a year or less, a term appointment, or an emergency indefinite appointment; or Have no federal civilian employment before 1984; or Do not have a career or career conditional appointment and you work on an intermittent basis. (See the work schedule block on your SF-50.)
CSRS-Offset	Did not work for the government for a total of five years before 1987. (Don't count your military service.) Exception: If you worked under CSRS, left the government, and your agency placed you in CSRS-Offset on your return, your CSRS-Offset coverage is probably correct if you had five years of government service when you left.)
FERS	Have a temporary appointment limited to a year or less; or Do not have a career or career conditional appointment and you work on an intermittent basis; or Have worked for the government under a retirement plan continuously since December 31, 1983, unless you elected to transfer to FERS during the 1987 or 1998 FERS open seasons.

If your agency put you in:	And you belonged in:	Then you may choose between:
CSRS or CSRS-Offset	FERS Social Security only	CSRS-Offset and FERS coverage CSRS-Offset and Social Security-only coverage
FERS	CSRS CSRS-Offset Social Security only	FERS and CSRS coverage* FERS and CSRS-Offset coverage* FERS and Social Security-only coverage*

*If you already had this choice, you do not have an opportunity to change your election under FERCCA.

The following chart summarizes the types of errors that do not trigger an election right:

You are in:	And you belong in:	Your coverage must be corrected to:
CSRS-Offset	CSRS	CSRS
CSRS	CSRS-Offset	CSRS-Offset
Social Security-Only	CSRS	CSRS
Social Security-Only	CSRS-Offset	CSRS-Offset
Social Security-Only	FERS	FERS

interest under FERCCA for retirees. Those who elect a retirement plan that increases their annuity will be paid interest on the difference between the two rates. The interest will be retroactive to April 1, 2002, and will be paid up through the current date. The interest will be payable at variable rates.

Also, FERCCA does not affect you:
• if you worked under the wrong plan for less than three years after December 31, 1986;
• if you belonged in FERS and your agency corrected your records when it discovered the error and you later separated and took a refund of all FERS retirement deductions;
• if you belonged in FERS and your agency corrected your records when it discovered the error and you chose to withdraw your TSP contributions; or
• if you received a payment ordered by a court or provided as settlement of a claim for losses resulting from a retirement coverage error, you may not make an election under FERCCA unless you repay the amount you received or OPM waives repayment.

Certain employees whose agency placed them in FERS in error could choose to remain in FERS when the agency discovered its error. If they declined FERS, the agency placed them in the correct retire-ment plan (CSRS, CSRS-Offset, or Social Security only). If you already had this opportunity, FERCCA does not give you an opportunity to change your decision.

Social Security—If you should have had Social Security coverage during your federal employment, then you must have Social Security coverage in addition to your federal retirement coverage. If your agency incorrectly put you in CSRS when it should have put you in CSRS-Offset, it must correct your retirement coverage to CSRS-Offset. The Social Security law requires you to have Social Security coverage. Likewise, if your agency incorrectly put you in CSRS-Offset when it should have put you in CSRS, it must correct your retirement coverage to CSRS because you are not eligible for Social Security coverage during your federal employment. You cannot choose to keep your Social Security coverage. However, Social Security will give you credit for all but the last three years before your record was corrected.

Thrift Savings Plan—If you are erroneously covered by FERS and you choose to move out of FERS, FERCCA allows you to keep the employee contributions you made to your TSP account in your TSP account even if the contributions exceeded the maximum CSRS investment. However, all agency contributions that were made to your account and the attributable earnings must be removed from your account if you do not remain under FERS.

If you choose FERS coverage under FER-CCA, you may make up employee contributions that you could have made had you been correctly covered by FERS. In addition, you will receive the agency automatic (1 percent) contributions and agency matching contributions that you should have received had you been correctly covered by FERS. Finally, you will receive lost earnings on both your employee and agency make-up contributions. (Prior to FERCCA, lost earnings were payable only on agency make-up contributions.) The lost earnings on both employee and agency contributions will be determined the same way lost earnings are determined on agency make-up contributions under TSP regulations.

Erroneous FERS Coverage of Less Than Three Years—OPM Benefits Administration Letter 02-103 of May 7, 2002, provided instructions for correcting errors involving erroneous FERS coverage that lasted for less than three years of service. It included instructions for correcting errors where an employee is in FERS by mistake and can choose to stay in FERS. These are sometimes called "deemed FERS" elections (see 5 CFR §846.204(b)(2)).

A deemed FERS error is one where the employee is automatically put in FERS and should have been put in CSRS, CSRS-Offset, or Social Security-only with a six-month opportunity to elect FERS coverage. Agencies had been correcting deemed FERS coverage errors since 1993. However, FERCCA changed some of the procedures for correcting retirement coverage when the employee is erroneously put in FERS.

FERCCA changed the service credit rules for employees who owe deposits or redeposits for military or civilian service that they performed before the coverage error. The employee can still pay the deposit or redeposit under normal rules. However, if the employee does not pay the military or civilian deposit or redeposit, the military or civilian service is used in the computation of the employee's retirement benefit and the benefit will be reduced by an amount that is actuarially determined.

FERCCA also changed some of the rules regarding TSP contributions. Any contributions an employee made to his or her TSP account while erroneously covered under FERS may remain in the employee's TSP account. Earnings associated with the employee's contributions may also remain in the employee's TSP account. Agency contributions made while the employee was erroneously covered under FERS, and associated earnings, still must be removed from the employee's TSP account if the employee declines FERS coverage. Although FERCCA allows payment of lost earnings on employee make up TSP contributions in some situations, it does not permit payment of lost earnings when the employee was erroneously placed in FERS.

If the error lasted for less than three years of service, agencies must correct the error. The employee has no choice regarding his or her retirement coverage.

If the employee already chose whether he or she wanted to be deemed to have elected FERS, or if the employee was given a notice but failed to respond, then the employee does not get an opportunity to make another election.

If an employee was put in FERS during a period that the employee would have had an opportunity to elect FERS, an agency must now go back and give the employee a chance to elect FERS. If the employee decides that he or she wants FERS coverage, the effective date of the FERS coverage is retroactive to the date that the employee was erroneously put in FERS.

If You Are or Might Be Misenrolled—If you are not sure you are or were in the right retirement plan:

If you are in:	And you belong in:	You are considered to have elected:
CSRS or CSRS-Offset	FERS	CSRS-Offset
FERS	CSRS, CSRS-Offset or Social Security-Only	FERS
CSRS or CSRS-Offset	Social Security-Only	CSRS-Offset

• If you are an employee, your employer has your personnel records and will review them to determine whether an error has been made. Therefore, you should notify your employer's human resources office if you believe an error has been made in your case. Notify your current employer even if you believe the error occurred while you were employed at another agency.

• If you are not currently employed by the government, you should notify OPM at: Office of Personnel Management, Retirement Operations Center, Post Office Box 45, Boyers, Pennsylvania 16017. You can also contact OPM by electronic mail at *FERC-CA@OPM.GOV*. Notify OPM regardless of whether you are a retiree, survivor, or separated employee.

You may get additional information about the FERCCA and may enroll in the FERCCA database online at *www.opm.gov/benefits/correction*.

Assistance Available—Agencies are under orders to provide counseling and other types of assistance to employees in discovering any misenrollments and in deciding what to do should a misenrollment be discovered. In 2001, OPM contracted with Klynveld Peat Marwick Goerdeler (KPMG) to provide counseling to individuals eligible for relief under FERCCA.

Once an individual is determined to have been misenrolled, counselors provide a written election summary including the election options available to that person, the details of the financial benefits under each option and a printout of employment and payroll history. The individual will be asked to review the material, provide any other pertinent information to the counselor and ask questions about the options, through telephone calls, written correspondence and face-to-face counseling.

After the individual makes an election, the counselor prepares an implementation package including instructions to the pertinent agency offices.

Deadlines—Employees who have a choice of retirement plans under FERCCA have a deadline of six months from the date the employee receives formal notice explaining his or her FERCCA options. If your qualifying retirement coverage error was previously corrected, the time limit for making an election expired on December 31, 2002. If your qualifying retirement coverage error was not previously corrected and you fail to make an election within the time limit, your retirement coverage is summarized in the accompanying chart.

If your qualifying retirement coverage error was previously corrected and you fail to make an election within the time limit, you are considered to have elected to remain in your current retirement plan.

Your election is irrevocable once your employer or OPM processes it. If you do not make a timely election, the resulting coverage is also irrevocable.

Your election is effective on the date that the retirement coverage error first occurred. This means that your election will be retroactive, or will change your retirement coverage for a period of service in the past.

Appeal Rights—You can appeal these decisions to the Merit Systems Protection Board: your employer's determination that your error is not subject to FERCCA rules; your employer's determination that you are not eligible to elect retirement coverage under the rules; and OPM's denial of your request for a waiver of the time limit for making an election. You may not seek review of a decision under any employee grievance procedures, including those established by chapter 71 of title 5, United States Code, and 5 CFR part 771.

After exhausting your administrative remedies, you may bring a claim against the government under section 1346(b) or Chapter 171 of Title 28, United States Code. You may also bring a claim against the government under any other provision of law if your claim is for amounts not otherwise provided for under FERCCA rules.

Death Before Retirement

Under CSRS, no lump-sum death benefit is payable immediately to a currently employed worker's survivors who qualify for an annuity. A lump-sum death benefit may be payable later if annuity amounts paid out do not equal a retiree's contributions, plus interest.

Under FERS, a "basic" death benefit is payable to an actively employed worker's surviving spouse. The amount is equal to an indexed lump-sum figure ($24,330.97 in 2003), plus 50 percent of the employee's final or high-3 average salary (larger of the two). This basic death benefit may be paid in a lump sum or in 36 monthly installments. Survivors may also be eligible for monthly annuity payments.

Under CSRS and FERS, if you leave no survivors who qualify for an annuity, your retirement contribution, plus interest, is paid as a lump sum that includes the following:

• **CSRS:** Retirement deductions withheld from your pay, redeposits of refunds previously paid, deposits for civilian service where no deductions were taken, deposits for post-1956 military service and interest on deductions through December 31, 1956 (if any). Note: In the case of an employee or former retiree who dies with less than five years of creditable service, interest is paid to the date of separation (or transfer to a position not covered by CSRS) on any amount over one year of service.

• **FERS:** Retirement deductions (including CSRS Interim and CSRS-Offset) withheld from pay, deposits for civilian service performed before January 1, 1989, deposits for post-1956 military service, redeposits of CSRS refunds previously made, the balance left after the return of excess deductions (civilian and military), and the variable interest on deductions and deposits if the service covered totals at least one year. Note: For transferees with a CSRS component, interest on the CSRS component of the lump sum accrues under CSRS rules.

Retirement: Main Types and Eligibility Conditions

Employees who meet the general eligibility criteria may qualify for several different types of retirement benefits. Generally, the availability of any of these alternative forms of retirement depends on a variety of factors. For the majority of employees, the most significant criteria involve a worker's attainment of certain minimum age and length of service requirements. However, the availability of some other types of retirement may depend on factors like an individual's health or physical ability to work (e.g., a disability retirement) or a worker's employment situation (e.g., a discontinued service retirement during a reduction-in-force).

The types of retirement generally available to federal employees include:

Voluntary Retirement—When federal employees meet the age and service requirements for a voluntary retirement, they may retire at any time with an immediate, full annuity. (This kind of voluntary retirement also is known as a "nondisability" or "standard" retirement.) For CSRS-covered employees who meet the general eligibility requirements (see above), voluntary retirement is an option once the following minimum age and creditable service requirements are satisfied: age 62, five years service; age 60, 20 years service; and age 55, 30 years service.

FERS-covered employees who meet the general minimum requirement (i.e., five

FERS Benefits Payable to Surviving Spouses of Employees Who Die in Service

More than 18 months but less than 10 years	1. Lump Sum payment of $24,328.94 (Effective 12-1-2002) indexed to the CPI*
	 Plus
	 2. Lump Sum of higher of:
	   a. ½ of annual basic pay at time of death,
	   -or-
	   b. ½ of high-3 average salary
	     Plus
	 3. Any Social Security benefits that may be payable
	   Plus
	 4. Any thrift plan death benefits

10 or more years of service	1, 2, 3 and 4 above *plus* 5. A survivor annuity equal to 50% of the employee's basic annuity under FERS.

* #1 and #2 may be taken in a lump sum or over a period of time.

years creditable service) are eligible for a standard or voluntary retirement once they meet certain minimum age and service requirements. The minimum retirement ages for unreduced FERS benefits are: age 62 with five years' service, age 60 with 20 years' service, and age 55 (for individuals born before 1948) with 30 years' service. FERS-covered employees born in or after 1948 also may qualify for unreduced benefits if they have at least 30 years' service and meet the special Minimum Retirement Age (MRA) requirements established for unreduced annuities. These MRA standards generally establish the earliest age at which employees may qualify for unreduced annuities (with 30 years' service) or reduced annuities if they have between ten and 29 years of creditable service.

Under FERS, a worker may separate after completing ten years of service and reaching the minimum retirement age, and delay application for benefits in order to diminish applicable reductions for attaining benefits before age 62.

Deferred Retirement—This is another form of retirement that normally is taken on an optional basis. Under CSRS, former employees who leave their money in the retirement fund are eligible for an annuity that starts at age 62 if they have completed at least five years of creditable civilian service and were covered by CSRS for at least one year within the two-year period immediately before separating.

Under FERS, workers are eligible for deferred benefits if they leave service after having completed five years of service covered by retirement deductions. Deferred benefits are payable at age 62, or at the minimum retirement age with at least ten years of service. Separated workers electing the deferred benefit at the MRA with at least ten years of service will have a computation as if they were retiring at that point, including the applicable reductions of five percent for each year of age under age 62.

Deferred annuitants under CSRS and FERS are not eligible to participate in the FEHB program or to acquire FEGLI coverage. However, once their annuity begins, they will get annual cost-of-living adjustments (COLAs). In addition, they will be eligible to provide a survivor annuity for their spouses.

Disability Retirement—Federal and postal workers covered by CSRS or FERS who become unable to continue in their federal or postal positions because of the onset of a disabling condition generally are eligible for a disability retirement. Under CSRS and FERS, federal and postal employees no longer able to perform in their positions (or other vacant positions at the same grade or pay level) are assumed to be disabled for federal or postal service, even though they might be able to hold some other job. This "occupational" definition of disability is different than that used by Social Security.

Employees generally must meet all of the following conditions to be eligible for disability retirement.

• If CSRS-covered, they must have completed at least five years of civilian service to be eligible for disability benefits (the comparable figure for FERS-covered employees is 18 months).

• They must, while employed subject to either retirement system, have become totally disabled for useful and efficient service in the position occupied or any other vacant position of the same grade or pay level for which they otherwise are qualified.

• Their application for disability retirement must be filed with the Office of Personnel Management in accordance with specified time limits.

Early Retirement—Generally, there are two kinds of early retirement under which federal employees may be able to leave their jobs with an immediate (but possibly reduced) annuity, even though they have not met the normal age and service requirements. Both CSRS and FERS contain special provisions that allow employees who do not meet the normal age and service requirements to retire early. The basic purpose of these early retirement options or procedures is to assist an agency in carrying out a personnel reduction or downsizing operation with minimal workforce disruptions. These early retirement options typically are extended to employees who are facing an involuntary separation, transfer to another commuting area, or an immediate reduction in their rate of basic pay. By allowing employees who meet certain criteria to retire early, an agency can create vacancies that, in turn, can be filled by employees who would otherwise be separated or downgraded.

The two basic kinds of early retirement that may be made available to certain employees are:

• *Early Voluntary Retirement*—An agency may make this type of "early out" option available during a downsizing operation, such as a reduction-in-force or reorganization, to employees who meet certain minimal age and service requirements; i.e., employees must be at least age 50 with 20 (or more) years of creditable service or they can qualify at any age if they have at least 25 years of creditable service. Generally, CSRS retirees who are under age 55 will have their annuities reduced by one-sixth of one percent for each full month they are under age 55 (i.e., two percent per year). Once they reach age 55, such retirees will not have their annuities increased to compensate for the reduction.

• *Discontinued Service Retirement*—A "discontinued service retirement" is an involuntary retirement that provides an immediate annuity to employees who are separated (i.e., retired) against their will. Just as with an early voluntary retirement, employees are not eligible for a discontinued service annu-

ity if they are separated for cause on charges of misconduct or delinquency. The final responsibility for determining whether a separation is in fact involuntary for purposes of receiving a discontinued service annuity rests with OPM. Other than their involuntary nature, DSRs are similar in many respects to an early voluntary retirement. They have the same minimal age and service requirements (i.e., age 50 with 20 years, any age with 25 years), but are subject to several additional requirements or procedures.

While both types of early retirement are often triggered by the same personnel pressures (RIF, reorganization, transfer of function, etc.), they differ in several important respects. For more details, see Early Retirement, below.

Annuity Bar for Security Offenders

Public Law 83-769, as amended by Public Law 87-299, prohibits payment of federal retirement benefits to persons (or their survivors) who have committed certain specified offenses or acts involving national security. While they are barred from receiving annuities by law, their retirement contributions, with interest, will be refunded.

Section 2—Employee Contributions

Required Contributions from Employees

Over an employee's career, the contributions for retirement that are deducted from a worker's pay represent a substantial sum of money. Yet, in spite of their importance to employee retirement, the contributions to CSRS, FERS, and Social Security do not constitute savings. Contributions made to the various federal retirement programs are a part of the eligibility criteria that must be met to qualify for benefits.

These contributions are an "admission ticket" to the programs; except in certain special circumstances the amounts an employee contributes have no direct bearing on the amount of benefits the worker will receive. In some circumstances, employees must pay to capture service for use in the computation of benefits, but in these cases the amounts required bear no relation to the value in the benefit compu-

tation of the captured service. Only in the TSP, which essentially is a savings program, is there a direct relationship between contributions and benefits.

CSRS, FERS and Social Security all require different amounts of payment from participating employees. However, it is important to note that the increases in retirement contributions mandated by the Budget Reconciliation Act of 1997, which caused contributions to increase by .25 percent of salary in 1999 and another .15 percent of salary in 2000 were rolled back by P.L. 106-346, effective on the first day of the first pay period beginning on or after January 1, 2001. That law returned the withholding rates for CSRS and FERS employees, other than members of Congress, to those in effect before 1999.

CSRS—Most employees covered by CSRS pay 7.0 percent of their basic pay to participate in the program. (Employees in certain special categories, such as law enforcement officers and firefighters, contribute 7.5 percent.) Included in the amount of basic pay subject to the 7.0 percent (or 7.5 percent) deduction are salaries for regularly scheduled work. Excluded are differentials for special services such as night duty, and payments for bonuses, allowances, overtime, and lump-sum payments for unused leave. A worker's CSRS contributions are credited to the program under the employee's name, and records are kept of the amounts paid and the salaries earned at the time they were paid.

FERS—Employees covered by FERS pay at a rate of total basic pay that, combined with the OASDI portion of Social Security taxes, equals 7.0 percent. The contribution rate for FERS payments is 0.8 percent of basic pay. (The rate for special category employees, such as law enforcement officers and firefighters, is 1.3 percent.) Thus, employees with federal or postal pay below the Social Security wage base ($87,000 in 2003) pay the same in terms of their combined payments to the two programs as CSRS participants pay to the single CSRS retirement program. Above the Social Security wage base, FERS employees do not pay the 6.2 percent OASDI component but continue paying the FERS component of 0.8 percent (1.3 percent for special rate category employees).

CSRS-Offset—Employees covered by CSRS-Offset pay into the civil service retirement fund an amount that, when combined with the OASDI portion of the Social Security taxes, equals 7.0 percent of their basic pay. Employees pay 0.8 percent of their salary to CSRS on pay below the Social Security wage base ($87,000 in 2003), and 7.0 percent on any basic pay that exceeds the wage base. (For special category employees, such as law enforcement officers and firefighters, these contribution rates are 1.3 percent and 7.5 percent.) Thus, unlike FERS participants, when CSRS-Offset participants earn wages above the Social Security wage base, those wages continue to be subject to mandatory deductions of 7.0 percent (or 7.5 percent), all of which is credited under CSRS.

Social Security—Federal and postal employees first hired after 1983 are automatically covered by Social Security. The taxes to that program are levied against that portion of all wages that do not exceed an amount called the "contribution and benefit base" (wage base). The annual wage base is adjusted each year to reflect increases in average wages throughout the national economy. All wages up to that amount ($87,000 in 2003) are subject to the Social Security OASDI tax of 6.20 percent. Wages from all covered employment during the year are included in the wage base. Federal and postal workers who have wages earned outside the government will have those counted toward the maximum, (although their nonfederal employer will continue to deduct Social Security taxes). Employees are entitled to a refund of the excess amount of Social Security taxes collected on their combined federal wages and outside earnings (i.e., taxes on the excess over the wage base limit) when they file their annual income tax returns.

Medicare—All federal and postal employees regardless of retirement system coverage pay 1.45 percent of all salary toward Medicare. This deduction is not a retirement contribution since the money goes toward Medicare health insurance coverage, not retirement benefit coverage. However, the Medicare deduction commonly is considered a standard part of an individual's mandatory deductions from salary. In many cases the Medicare tax (also called the Hospital Insurance deduction) is lumped together with the OASDI contribution for those covered by Social Security and the two collectively are termed the Social Security deduction, even though only the OASDI portion goes toward the Social Security trust fund.

Refunds of Contributions at Separation

Employees who leave federal or postal service before becoming eligible for immediate retirement benefits under CSRS or FERS have the option of either leaving their retirement contributions in the retirement fund or withdrawing them in total. To be eligible for a refund of contributions, an employee must have been separated from the service for at least 31 days. Separated employees may apply for a refund up to 31 days before their 62nd birthday, provided they don't return to federal service in a position that provides retirement coverage.

Note: if a court order awards benefits to a former spouse, a separated employee may not be eligible for a refund.

Under both CSRS and FERS, refunds of contributions for employees who served less than one year do not receive any interest. Under CSRS, contributions withdrawn by former employees with more than one year but less than five years of service at separation are refunded with interest, computed at three percent. Withdrawn amounts for separating employees with more than five years of service do not include interest. Under FERS, all refunds for service of more than one year do include interest, which is based on variable interest rates determined by the Treasury Department.

A separated employee who exercises the right to withdraw contributions waives the right to collect further benefits from either CSRS or FERS. In fact, a separated FERS employee who takes a refund can never recapture that service. It is permanently lost for retirement computation purposes. On the other hand, a former CSRS employee may recapture that service after returning to a covered position in the federal government. In general, it may be recaptured by repaying the withdrawn amount, plus interest.

In any event, the withdrawal of contributions should be done with caution. The rights to future benefits through a deferred retirement are often more valuable than the dollar amount of the contributions. In fact, the older the worker is at separation, the more likely the annuity benefits lost will exceed the value of the contributions, even after taking into account the amount of interest that could be earned by investing those contributions.

For more information about re-deposits of refunded contributions, see Section 3.

Note: Employees are never entitled to a refund of Social Security taxes, except for the inadvertent collection of taxes above the maximum taxable amounts (wage base) in any year (which might occur if a worker holds two jobs in the same taxable year).

CSRS Voluntary Retirement Contributions

Voluntary contributions are optional payments employees may make to the Civil Service Retirement and Disability Fund in addition to the regular retirement deductions taken from their salary. These voluntary contributions to the Fund earn market-rate interest. The interest earned is tax-deferred.

On retirement, the contributions, plus interest, may be used to purchase an additional annuity. This VC annuity is added to the regular annuity an employee would normally receive. Alternatively, all contributions may be withdrawn, with interest, at any time. However, once a refund is taken, an employee generally may not participate in the VC program again.

Who May Make Voluntary Contributions— The VC program is open only to CSRS-covered individuals, including CSRS-Offset. Active employees covered under CSRS or retired employees whose applications for retirement are being adjudicated may make voluntary contributions, provided the "Application to Make Voluntary Contributions," SF 2804, has been approved by OPM. (Note: Even if employees opened a voluntary contributions account before separating from service, they cannot make any additional contributions following separation except during the period that they are eligible to actually receive a retirement annuity and have filed an application for that annuity with OPM.)

No moneys will be accepted until the SF 2804 is approved. OPM will not approve an application from anyone who, although otherwise eligible, has: (1) not deposited amounts covering all civilian service performed by the applicant (including any refund of contributions) or (2) previously received a refund of voluntary contributions, unless the applicant was separated for more than three calendar days and was again employed in a position subject to the CSRS after the refund was paid. Note that employees covered by or retiring under the Federal Employees' Retirement System (FERS) are not eligible to make voluntary contributions.

Voluntary Contribution Rules and Procedures— As long as employees are eligible, they may make voluntary contributions at regular intervals or whenever they wish. However, these cannot be deducted from an employee's salary. Each payment must be in multiples of $25 (i.e., $50, $75, $100, etc.) Employees should not attempt to make payments before their application has been accepted by OPM. If they do, their payment will be returned. Once an application is accepted, the employee will be assigned an account number and OPM will provide instructions for making payments.

An employee's VC program contributions cannot be more than ten percent of the total of basic civilian salary received as of the date any contribution is made. Employees cannot make contributions based on anticipated future earnings. OPM will compute an employee's limitation when the worker retires or closes out the account. While OPM generally will accept an employee's VC contributions, when the worker retires or closes out an account, any amount found to be in excess of the worker's limit will be refunded, without interest.

Employees may apply for and be paid a refund of all (not just a part) of their voluntary contributions, plus earned interest, at any time before they retire and receive an additional annuity. Note that they will not receive interest on the amount of their deposits that exceed the ten percent limitation. If they are paid such a refund, they cannot again make voluntary contributions unless they are separated for more than three calendar days and are then reemployed in a position subject to CSRS.

Interest on Voluntary Contribution Accounts—Voluntary contributions currently earn interest based on the average yield earned by new investments purchased by the Civil Service Retirement and Disability Fund during the preceding fiscal year (see Interest Rates table in next section). Interest on voluntary contributions begins to accrue on the date they are deposited by OPM and is compounded on December 31 of each year. OPM provides an annual account statement to each employee who has made voluntary contributions.

Additional Annuity for Oneself—Voluntary contributions, with interest, may be used to purchase an additional annuity. The amount of this VC annuity depends on the age at which you retire. If you retire at age 55 or younger and do not elect an additional survivor annuity, each $100 will buy you $7 a year of a VC annuity. This amount increases by 20¢ for each full year you are over 55 at the time you retire. Thus, if you retire at age 60, each $100 will buy $8 a year of VC annuity; at age 62, $8.40 a year; and so forth. The VC annuity is payable as long as you stay retired, but is not increased by cost of living adjustments (COLAs).

Additional Survivor Annuity—If you decide to use your voluntary contributions to buy an additional annuity for yourself, you have the option of electing a survivor annuity for your spouse or any other person. If you do, your VC annuity will be reduced and, at your death, your survivor will be paid half of your reduced VC annuity for the rest of his or her life. The reduction in your VC annuity depends on the difference in ages between you and the person named to receive the survivor benefit.

The reduction is ten percent of your VC annuity, plus an additional five percent for each full five years the person is younger than you. Maximum reduction is 40 percent.

Example: Suppose you are 57 years old at retirement and have voluntary contributions of $25,000, including interest. Your VC annuity would be $154 per month ($25,000 divided by $100 = 250 multiplied by $7.40 = $1,850 per year, divided by 12 months = $154, rounded down). If you provided a survivor annuity for someone who is age 50, your VC annuity would be reduced by 15 percent, to $131 per month ($1,850 - $277.50 (15 percent) = $1,572 per year, divided by 12 months = $131, rounded down). Your survivor would receive $65 per month after you died ($1,572.50 x .5 = $786.25 per year, divided by 12 months = $65, rounded down).

Refunds of VC Contributions—As an alternative to buying an additional annuity, employees may withdraw their total VC program contributions, plus interest, at any time and for any reason. Partial refunds are not permitted. Once an account is closed out, it can never be opened again, unless the person has been separated from the government for more than three days and is reemployed in a CSRS-covered position.

Generally, those who take a refund of their voluntary contributions account may roll the interest portion into an IRA or qualified employer retirement plan to defer income taxes. The rollover options depend on the amount of interest payable on the employee's account.

For More Information—A FEND publication, *Increase Your CSRS Retirement Income: A Guide To The Voluntary Contribution Program*, is the only comprehensive guide to this important, yet much overlooked benefit available to federal and postal employees under CSRS. It provides a step-by-step description of the program's features and tells how you can use the program to your best advantage. It also includes copies of the vital forms that can be hard to come by in personnel offices. See publication-ordering information in this *Almanac*.

Section 3—CSRS and FERS: Service Credit Rules

Creditable Service: General Rules

All periods of service as an employee of the federal government are creditable under CSRS or FERS. To be considered a federal employee, an individual must be (1) engaged in performing federal functions under authority of an Act of Congress or Executive Order, and (2) hired by a federal officer in his or her official capacity as such, and (3) working under the supervision and direction of a federal officer. Non-deduction service performed after December 31, 1988, cannot be credited under FERS rules for any purpose.

Service performed as an employee of the District of Columbia government is creditable under CSRS and FERS, for individuals hired by the D.C. government before October 1, 1987.

Service also is creditable for employees who hold federal appointments, are engaged in activities jointly administered by the United States and a state or other outside agency, and are under the supervision and control of federal officials. However, if such persons are not federally appointed or are supervised and controlled by officials of the state, land grant college, or other cooperating organization, the service is not considered federal for retirement purposes.

Employees in a leave-without-pay status can generally credit up to six months in any calendar year toward retirement.

Congress also has authorized federal retirement credit for employment in agricultural stabilization and conservation county committees.

Persons engaged in relief project employment sponsored by the various agencies (CWA, WPA, etc.) in the 1930s were non-federal employees for retirement purposes. Credit is allowed for service on these agencies' administrative force and on the administrative force of nationwide projects sponsored by such agencies.

More detailed information about service credits and related policies can be found in the *CSRS and Fers Handbook for Personnel and Payroll Offices*. Questions about service credit should first be addressed to the local personnel office or the designated agency retirement counselor at agency headquarters.

To request a formal determination of service credibility, you should complete an Application to Make Deposit or Redeposit (SF 2803) for CSRS (or Application to Make Service Credit Payment (SF 3108) for FERS) and submit it to: Office of Personnel Management, Retirement Operations Center, Boyers, PA 16017.

Unused Sick Leave: CSRS Credit

Employees covered under CSRS are allowed a credit for unused sick leave for annuity-computation purposes. With one exception, this credit for unused sick leave is not available to FERS-covered employees (see below).

Generally, under CSRS rules, the service of an employee who (1) retires on immediate annuity or (2) dies leaving a widow or widower entitled to a survivor annuity is increased by the days of unused sick leave that the worker accrued under a formal leave system. The days of unused sick leave added are used only in counting the number of years and months of service for annuity-computation purposes. The unused sick leave cannot be added in computing the employee's average salary or for meeting the minimum length of service for retirement eligibility.

In general, an employee is charged eight hours of sick leave for a day's absence, 40 hours for five days (one week), and 160 hours for 20 days (one month). In an effort to provide retirees with 12 equal monthly payments during a given year, OPM treats all months as having 30 days. Thus, 360 days equals one year. To find the retirement-credit value of each sick leave day, OPM divides 360 into the congressionally mandated number of work hours in a year, which is 2087.

The net result is that 5.797+ hours of sick leave equals one day. For convenience, OPM uses a conversion chart based on six-hour days, inserting five-hour days at appropriate intervals so that the totals add up. For example, an employee with 1,003 hours of unused sick leave is credited with an additional five months and 23 days for purposes of computing the worker's annuity. A slight variation in crediting of unused sick leave applies to an employee who has an uncommon tour of duty. (See the table which shows how OPM converts unused sick leave into increased service time.)

Employees making these computations should remember that the extra days (i.e., beyond a full month) of sick leave credit may only be counted for another month of credit if, when added to the extra days credit earned through regular service, the total amounts to 30 days or more. If this is not the case, the extra days on either end are dropped.

Chart for Converting Unused Sick Leave Into Increased Service Time Credit for Higher Annuities

(CSRS Employees Only)*

No. of Days	1 Day & Up	1 Mo. & Up	2 Mo. & Up	3 Mo. & Up	4 Mo. & Up	5 Mo. & Up	6 Mo. & Up	7 Mo. & Up	8 Mo. & Up	9 Mo. & Up	10 Mo. & Up	11 Mo. & Up
0	—	174	348	522	696	870	1044	1217	1391	1565	1739	1913
1	6	180	354	528	701	875	1049	1223	1397	1571	1745	1919
2	12	186	359	533	707	881	1055	1229	1403	1577	1751	1925
3	17	191	365	539	713	887	1061	1235	1409	1583	1757	1930
4	23	197	371	545	719	893	1067	1241	1415	1588	1762	1936
5	29	203	377	551	725	899	1072	1246	1420	1594	1768	1942
6	35	209	383	557	730	904	1078	1252	1426	1600	1774	1948
7	41	214	388	562	736	910	1084	1258	1432	1606	1780	1954
8	46	220	394	568	742	916	1090	1264	1438	1612	1786	1959
9	52	226	400	574	748	922	1096	1270	1444	1617	1791	1965
10	58	232	406	580	754	928	1101	1275	1449	1623	1797	1971
11	64	238	412	586	759	933	1107	1281	1455	1629	1803	1977
12	70	243	417	591	765	939	1113	1287	1461	1635	1809	1983
13	75	249	423	597	771	945	1119	1293	1467	1641	1815	1988
14	81	255	429	603	777	951	1125	1299	1472	1646	1820	1994
15	87	261	435	609	783	957	1130	1304	1478	1652	1826	2000
16	93	267	441	615	788	962	1136	1310	1484	1658	1832	2006
17	99	272	446	620	794	968	1142	1316	1490	1664	1838	2012
18	104	278	452	626	800	974	1148	1322	1496	1670	1844	2017
19	110	284	458	632	806	980	1154	1328	1501	1675	1849	2023
20	116	290	464	638	812	986	1159	1333	1507	1681	1855	2029
21	122	296	470	643	817	991	1165	1339	1513	1687	1861	2035
22	128	301	475	649	823	997	1171	1345	1519	1693	1867	2041
23	133	307	481	655	829	1003	1177	1351	1525	1699	1873	2046
24	139	313	487	661	835	1009	1183	1357	1530	1704	1878	2052
25	145	319	493	667	841	1015	1188	1362	1536	1710	1884	2058
26	151	325	499	672	846	1020	1194	1368	1542	1716	1890	2064
27	157	330	504	678	852	1026	1200	1374	1548	1722	1896	2070
28	162	336	510	684	858	1032	1206	1380	1554	1728	1901	2075
29	168	342	516	690	864	1038	1212	1386	1559	1733	1907	2081

How to Use This Chart: To find the increased service time credit for unused sick leave, use the following formula: find the number of hours of unused sick leave. In the horizontal column you will find the number of months and in the vertical column the remaining number of days. For example, 441 hours equals 2 months and 16 days. Another example: 1455 hours equals 8 months and 11 days.

* FERS employees may not convert unused sick leave for extra retirement credit.

As an example, the situation described above demonstrated that 1,003 hours of unused sick leave translated into five months and 23 days of service credit. If the employee in that case had seven or more extra days credited during their career service, the total would add up to the 30 days needed to obtain one month additional credit for retirement purposes. On the other hand, if the worker had earned less than seven extra days during the regular service, the 23 days would be discarded. This situation also could work the other way. An employee's regular service could translate, for example, into 20 extra days. If this employee's sick leave accumulation turned out to give him ten or more extra days, he also would get an extra month's credit for retirement purposes. There is no upper limit to the amount of sick leave time that can be credited toward CSRS retirement.

Under FERS, unused sick leave is not creditable for annuity computation purposes. However, individuals who transferred to FERS with a CSRS annuity component may receive credit for the amount of unused sick leave they had at the date of transfer or the date of retirement, whichever is less. For example, a CSRS employee with 15 years' CSRS service transferred to FERS with a sick leave balance of 1,000 hours and retired with 1,500 hours of sick leave would receive a service credit for 1,000 hours for purposes of computing the CSRS annuity component. On the other hand, if that same employee retired with 700 hours, only that number of hours would be credited.

Redeposit Service

Employees who took a refund of their retirement contributions before October 1, 1990, and return to federal service must repay that money, plus interest, before the period of time covered by the refund can be credited in the computation of their annuity benefits. They may still count the time involved for determining their eligibility to retire and for determining their "high-3" average salary. However, no credit will be allowed in the computation of their annuity unless they have repaid the entire amount owed by the time they retire.

Employees who took a refund after October 1, 1990, and return to service have an important alternative to repayment. Such workers can either repay the outstanding amount plus any interest before retiring or elect to have their annuity actuarially reduced. The reduction is based on an employee's age at the time of retirement and calculated so that over a probable (actuarial) lifetime, the total difference in the annuity would equal the outstanding amount. To make this calculation "present value factors" are used. For example, a retiring employee age 55 would have a present value factor of 211.4, which would be divided into the amount owed to determine the monthly annuity reduction. If he owed $16,000, the monthly reduction would be $79.69. (See the Present Value Factors table.)

Nondeduction Service: Credits and Deposits

Employees who performed creditable service before October 1, 1982, for which no CSRS deductions were made are entitled to receive credit for this service in the computation of CSRS annuity benefits without being subject to a requirement that they make a deposit to cover that period of service. However, if they do not make a deposit for the period of non-deduction service, the annuity otherwise payable will be reduced by an amount equal to ten percent of the amount unpaid, plus accrued interest.

Employees generally are required to make a deposit, with interest, for entire periods of non-deduction (previously referred to as optional) service performed on or after October 1, 1982, before such service can be used in the CSRS annuity computation. If a deposit is not made, the service will still be creditable for purposes of establishing entitlement to an annuity. Such employees will not be able to elect to have their annuities reduced by ten percent of the amount owed for non-deduction service performed on or after October 1, 1982. Moreover, if a deposit is not made for such service, no credit will be allowed for that period of service for purposes of computing the individual's annuity.

Under FERS rules, periods of non-deduction service performed after December 31, 1988, cannot be credited for any purposes.

Payments to Capture Nondeduction Civilian Service

To receive full credit under CSRS for service for which no retirement deductions were made, a deposit must be made of the outstanding amount, plus applicable interest. If no deposit is made for non-deduction service performed before October 1, 1982, the service will count toward eligibility for retirement and will be used to compute the annual annuity. However, this annuity will be reduced by ten percent of the total deposit owed, including interest. If the service was performed after September 30, 1982, that service counts toward eligibility for retirement, but will not be used in determining total creditable service for annuity-computation purposes.

Under FERS, non-deduction service performed before January 1, 1989, will not count for eligibility or computation purposes, unless the employee makes the required deposit, including interest.

The outstanding deposit amount is equal to the deduction that would have been made to the applicable retirement system at the time the service was performed. Generally, this amount is computed at a seven percent rate for CSRS deductions and 1.3 percent for FERS deductions.

OPM has added a calculator to its website that can be used to estimate the amount you must pay to get retirement service credit for such non-deduction service. For information, go to *www.opm.gov/benefits*.

> Note: In general, the circumstances that led to service being performed without deductions from pay being required were eliminated at the time FERS was enacted..

Creditable Military Service

As a general rule, military service in the armed forces of the United States is creditable for retirement purposes under CSRS and FERS if it was active service, was terminated under honorable conditions, and was performed before separation from a civilian position under the retirement system. This covers service in the Army, Navy, Air Force, Marine Corps, and Coast Guard, including the service academies. It also covers service after June 30, 1960, in the Regular Corps or Reserve Corps of the Public Health Service; after June 30, 1961, as a commissioned officer of the National Oceanic and Atmospheric Administration; and, after August 1, 1990, in any full-time National Guard duty that interrupts creditable civilian

service and is followed by reemployment.

An exception to the general rule cited above is that no credit for any military service is given to an employee who receives military retired pay unless that pay has been awarded: (a) on account of a service-connected disability incurred in combat with an enemy of the United States, or (b) on account of a service-connected disability caused by an instrumentality of war and incurred in the line of duty during a period of war, or (c) under the provisions of Chapter 67, Title 10, U.S.C. (pertaining to retirement from a reserve component of the Armed Forces), or in the case of CSRS participant if it was performed after December 1956 and Social Security benefits are payable. Generally, employees who are receiving military retired pay must elect to waive the retired pay in order for their military service to be added to their civilian service for purposes of computing their federal annuity. If employees do not waive their military retired pay, their retirement rights will be based on their civilian service only and the period of military service will not be included in computing their annuity. However, under certain circumstances, employees may receive both military retired pay and the civil service annuity at the same time.

Receipt of Social Security benefits has no effect on granting civil service retirement credit for military service performed before January 1, 1957. (For information on contributions that must be made to purchase credit for military service performed on or after January 1, 1957, see below, "Payments to Capture Military Service Credit.")

For information on earnings during military service, write to the appropriate address:

Army
DFAS-Indianapolis Center
Attn: DFAS-IN/F JESR
8899 East 56th St.
Indianapolis, IN 46249-0875
Phone: (317) 510-2800
Fax: (317) 510-5575

Navy
DFAS-Cleveland Center
Attn: DFAS-CL/FMCS
1240 E. 9th St.
Cleveland, OH 44199-2055
Phone: (216) 522-5974
Fax: (216) 522-6924

Air Force

DFAS-Denver Center
Attn: DFAS-DE/FJY
6760 E. Irvington Place
Denver, CO 80279-3000
Phone: (303) 676-7408
Fax: (303) 676-6218

Marines
DFAS-Kansas City Center
Attn: DFAS-KC/FBL
1500 E. 95th St.
Kansas City, MO 64197-0001
Phone: (816) 926-7652
Fax: (816) 926-7648

National Oceanic and Atmospheric Administration (NOAA)
NOAA Commissioned Personnel Center
1315 East-West Hwy., Rm. 12100
Silver Spring, MD 20910-2382

Coast Guard Pay and Personnel Center
444 S.E. Quincy St.
Topeka, KS 66683-3591
Phone: (785) 357-3570
Fax: (785) 295-2544

Public Health Service
Division of Commissioned Personnel
Compensation Branch
Parklawn Bldg., Rm. 4-50
5600 Fisher Lane
Rockville, MD 20857
Phone: (301) 594-2693
Fax: (301) 594-2711

Air National Guard
Air National Guard Readiness Center
ANGRC/FMF
3500 Fetchet Ave.
Andrews AFB, MD 20762-5157
Phone: (301) 836-8861

Air Force Reserve
HQ AFRES/ACFM
Robins AFB, GA 31098-6001
Phone: (912) 327-1436

Payments to Capture Military Service Credit

The military began deducting Social Security from military pay on January 1, 1957. Congress enacted a law in 1982 giving employees the opportunity to make a deposit into their civilian retirement system for active military time served after that date (no deposit is required for service before that date). Individuals who make the deposit are entitled to credit for the military service under both the Social Security sys-

tem and the applicable civilian retirement system.

Military service for this purpose is honorable active service in the following uniformed services: Army, Navy, Air Force, Marine Corps, and Coast Guard and after June 30, 1960, in the Commissioned Corps of the Public Health Service, and after June 30, 1961, service in the Commissioned Corps of the National Oceanic and Atmospheric Administration and its predecessor agency.

You also may receive credit for Army National Guard or Air National Guard service that is followed by federal civilian reemployment that occurs after August 1, 1990, when all of the following conditions are met:

• the service must interrupt civilian service creditable under CSRS or FERS and be followed by reemployment in accordance with the appropriate chapter of the laws concerning veterans benefits;

• it must be full-time, not inactive duty; and

• it must be under a specified law and you must be entitled to pay from the U.S. (or have waived pay from the U.S.) for the service.

No interest will be computed if a deposit for military service is made within two years after the date you first became employed. If the deposit is not completed in the two-year period, interest will be posted to your account one year after the two-year period; thus the total effective interest-free period is three years minus one day. Any interest charged is assessed at the rates listed in the Interest Rates table.

Any required deposit for post-1956 military service must be made before retirement in order for it to be creditable for eligibility or computation for retirement purposes. If you die as an employee, your surviving spouse will have the option to make a deposit for your military service for purposes of calculation of survivor benefits.

If you are retired military, you may combine your active duty military service and civilian service for one annuity. This requires a deposit into the civilian retirement system for the active military service and you must waive your military retired pay effective with the beginning of the civilian annuity. There are two exceptions to the requirement to waive military retired pay: You do not have to waive your military retired pay if it was awarded for a disability incurred in combat or caused by an instrumentality of war, or awarded for reserve service under Chapter 67, Title 10.

In sum, a period of military service may be credited for title to and computation of federal retirement and death benefits, subject to the following conditions:

• the military service was performed before the date of separation upon which title to an annuity is based;

• it was active duty;

• it was not included in the computation of military retired pay, or if it was included in retired pay, the retired pay was awarded based on disability incurred in combat with an enemy of the United States or caused by an instrumentality of war and incurred in the line of duty during a period of war; or granted under the provisions of Chapter 67, Title 10, of the U.S. Code;

• it was honorable service; and

• a deposit is made for post-1956 military service (see below for special considerations for those first employed under CSRS before October 1, 1982).

FERS—If you are covered under FERS, you will receive retirement credit for mili-

Interest Rates

Payments to CSRS and FERS to capture or recapture service—including military, nondeduction, or service for which contributions were withdrawn—entail additional amounts for interest. This interest varies depending upon the circumstances associated with the outstanding contributions. Note: Prior FERS service cannot be recaptured by those currently under FERS.

In most cases, interest on contributions to capture or recapture service is charged at the following rates:

Prior to 12/31/47	4.0%
1/1/48 to 12/31/84	3.0%
1985	13.0%
1986	11.125%
1987	9.0%
1988	8.375%
1989	9.125%
1990	8.75%
1991	8.625%
1992	8.125%
1993	7.125%
1994	6.25%
1995	7.0%
1996	6.875%
1997	6.875%
1998	6.75%
1999	5.75%
2000	5.875%
2001	6.375%
2002	5.5%
2003	5.0%

Exceptions to the above rates are: (1) Nondeduction service earned before October 1, 1982, and redeposits of refunds made before October 1, 1982: Interest is charged at three percent in all years; and (2) Military service—Interest is only charged beginning two years after the beginning of civilian employment.

tary service only if a deposit for military service is made. For periods of active duty service prior to January 1, 1999, the deposit equals 3 percent of basic military pay (not allowances) you received for the post-1956 military service, for periods of service performed during 1999, the deposit equals 3.25 percent, for periods of service performed during 2000, the deposit equals 3.40 percent, and after December 31, 2000, the deposit is 3 percent of base pay.

FERS with a CSRS Component—If you transferred to FERS and have a CSRS component, you continue to be under the CSRS military deposit rules (see below) for service performed before the transfer. The earliest interest begins to accrue is October 1, 1986, or your third anniversary of entry into a CSRS position (if no CSRS component, interest begins to accrue two years from the date of transfer to FERS; posted on the third year).

If you are not eligible for Social Security at age 62, no deposit is required for the military service performed after January 1, 1957. If you were first hired on or after October 1, 1982, a deposit is required regardless if eligible for Social Security. Note: OPM will only check with Social Security for eligibility the year that you turn age 62 or at retirement, if later.

CSRS—If you were first employed under CSRS on or after October 1, 1982, you will receive retirement credit for post-1956 military service only if a deposit for the military service is made. For periods of active duty service prior to January 1, 1999, the deposit equals 7 percent of basic military pay (not allowances) you received for the post-1956 military service, for periods of service performed during 1999, the deposit equals 7.25 percent, for periods of service performed during 2000, the deposit equals 7.40 per-

cent, and after December 31, 2000, the deposit is 7 percent of base pay.

If you were first employed under CSRS before October 1, 1982, you have two options:

• making the deposit for the post-1956 military service; or

• receiving service credit but having your annuity recomputed at age 62 to eliminate post-1956 military service. Any survivor annuity payable to your spouse after your death would also be recomputed to eliminate all credit for post-1956 military service when he/she attains age 60 and becomes eligible for Social Security benefits. (This reduction, known as "Catch-62," only occurs if you are eligible for Social Security. If you do not currently have enough quarters to be eligible for Social Security benefits and will not have enough quarters by age 62, there is no advantage to making a deposit for the post-1956 military service.)

Making the Deposit—Complete Form RI-20-97, Estimated Earnings During Military Service, and mail it to the appropriate military finance center identified above, with a copy of your DD Form(s) 214, Report of Transfer or Discharge. The completed form or letter showing the estimated earnings will be returned to you. Take that letter, a copy of your DD Form(s) 214 and form SF 2803 (CSRS) or SF 3108 (FERS), to your local payroll office to request an estimate of deposit required. Your payroll office will compute the amount you owe, including interest, and arrange with you to make the payment in a lump sum or on a schedule of regular payments. Any required deposits for military service must be made to your employing agency before you separate for retirement.

Section 4—Computation of CSRS and FERS Benefits

General Procedure

Under both CSRS and FERS, the two essential variables that must be determined when calculating the amount of an employee's basic federal retirement annuity are: the worker's "high-3" average pay (see below) and the years of creditable federal service accumulated by the employee (see above). Armed with these two essential fig-

ures, individuals can apply the different formulas specified under CSRS and FERS for computing an annual or monthly annuity benefit.

Keep in mind that other variables can affect annuity computations, including election of a survivor annuity (see below), failures to make required service deposits or redeposits (see above), or inclusion of an additional annuity related to voluntary contributions (see above).

High-3 Salary Base

The amount of an employee's annuity depends primarily upon the worker's "high-3" average pay (which includes locality pay) and length of service. "High-3" average pay is the highest average annual pay produced by the employee's basic pay rates during any three consecutive years of service. In most cases, the last three years of service will be the highest average pay. However, employees may use any three consecutive years of service, if a larger "high-3" pay base can be obtained.

In computing this high-3 figure, keep in mind that within-grade pay increases are part of basic pay, but additional pay, such as overtime and allowances, is not.

CSRS and FERS: Basic Annuity Computations

CSRS Formula—"Standard" retirement benefits under CSRS generally are available to workers at age 55 with 30 years service, at age 60 with 20 years, or at age 62 with five years.

There are three parts to the CSRS basic annuity formula. If employees have more than ten years of service, all the parts apply. If they have less than ten years of service, only parts A and B apply. The same "high-3" average pay is used in all three parts.

A. Take: 1½ percent of the "high-3" average pay and multiply the result by service up to five years.

B. Add: 1¾ percent of the "high-3" average pay multiplied by all years of service over five and up to ten.

C. Add: 2 percent of the "high-3" average pay multiplied by all service over ten years.

Example: Individual employee who has 30 years' service, and "high-3" average pay of $40,000.

A. 1.5 percent x $40,000 x 5 = $3,000
B. 1.75 percent x $40,000 x 5 = $3,500
C. 2 percent x $40,000 x 20 = 16,000
    Basic Annuity = $22,500

This formula produces the basic CSRS annuity, which generally cannot exceed 80 percent of an individual's "high-3" average pay. Contributions that employees have made to the retirement fund above that amount are refunded at the time of retirement. However, for CSRS retirees, there is no upper limit to the amount of unused sick leave that they can add to their years of service. As a result, a CSRS-covered retiree who has lengthy service and a lot of sick

Earned CSRS Retirement Percentages Based on Years of Service

Years of Service	Percent of High 3–Year Average Earnings	Years of Service	Percent of High 3–Year Average Earnings	Years of Service	Percent of High 3–Year Average Earnings	Years of Service	Percent of High 3–Year Average Earnings
5	7.50%	15	26.25%	25	46.25%	35	66.25%
6	9.25%	16	28.25%	26	48.25%	36	68.25%
7	11.00%	17	30.25%	27	50.25%	37	70.25%
8	12.75%	18	32.25%	28	52.25%	38	72.25%
9	14.50%	19	34.25%	29	54.25%	39	74.25%
10	16.25%	20	36.25%	30	56.25%	40	76.25%
11	18.25%	21	38.25%	31	58.25%	41	78.25%
12	20.25%	22	40.25%	32	60.25%	42	80.00%
13	22.25%	23	42.25%	33	62.25%	43	80.00%
14	24.25%	24	44.25%	34	64.25%		

*Annuity in excess of 80%, which is produced by credit for unused sick leave, is payable in the case of CSRS employment. See *CSRS and FERS Handbook for Personnel and Payroll Offices*, Chapter 50 for further details.

leave may actually receive an annuity greater than 80 percent.

FERS Formula—Like CSRS, the FERS computation formulas for an immediate, unreduced retirement benefit are based on an employee's age, "high-3" average salary, and years of creditable service at retirement. Generally, FERS-covered employees are eligible for immediate, unreduced retirement benefits once they: reach age 62 and have five years of creditable service, reach age 60 and have 20 years' creditable service, or attain the "minimum retirement age" (see below) and accumulate the specified years of service. There is an enhanced benefit formula for those who work to age 62 and later. Here are the formulas:

• If under age 62: 1% x "high-3" average salary x length of service

• If at least 62 years old (and at least 20 years' service): 1.1% x "high-3" average salary x years of service

Examples:

(1) Individual who is age 57 and has 30 years of creditable service and a $40,000 "high-3" salary:

1.0% x $40,000 x 30 = annuity of $12,000

(2) Individual age 62, 20 years of creditable service, and $35,000 high-3 salary

1.1% x $35,000 x 20 = annuity of $7,700

FERS "MRA+10" Reduced Benefit— FERS-covered workers also may retire with an immediate annuity when they reach their MRA (see below) and have accumulated at least ten years of creditable service. However, this special "MRA+10" retirement option (which only applies to FERS-covered employees) also provides for a five percent annuity reduction for each year the worker is under age 62 at retirement.

Example: Individual is age 58, has ten years of creditable service, and a $38,000 high-3 average salary

1.0% x $38,000 x 10 = $3,800 - 20% (four years under age 62) = annuity of $3,040

A worker may separate after completing 10 years of service and reaching the MRA and delay application for benefits in order to diminish applicable reductions for receiving benefits before age 62. The former worker retains the right to re-enroll in a health benefits plan under FEHB. This right is also extended to any eligible survivors if the former worker dies before making application for benefits.

Minimum Retirement Age

Generally, the minimum retirement age (MRA) for employees who have accumulated 30 years of creditable service was age 55 until the year 2003, when it began to climb by two months per year (paralleling the scheduled gradual rise in the age for receiving unreduced benefits under Social Security). Thus, the MRA will reach age 56 in 2009, where it will remain through the year 2020; beginning in 2021 it will resume rising by two months per year, until it reaches 57.

You can determine your Minimum Retirement Age by referring to the following chart:

If you were born	your MRA is
before 1948	55
in 1948	55 and 2 months
in 1949	55 and 4 months
in 1950	55 and 6 months
in 1951	55 and 8 months
in 1952	55 and 10 months
1953–1964	56
in 1965	56 and 2 months
in 1966	56 and 4 months
in 1967	56 and 6 months
in 1968	56 and 8 months
in 1969	56 and 10 months
1970 or after	57

Computing Annuities with FERS and CSRS Components

Employees who will have both CSRS and FERS components to their annuities (for example, those who transferred from CSRS to FERS during one of the open seasons in which that was allowed) will have part of their annuities computed using the CSRS general formula. Generally, these employees can calculate their "FERS Combined Basic Annuity" by computing their CSRS basic annuity component and adding this figure to their basic annual FERS component.

Example: Individual who is age 60 with a $30,000 high-3 salary, and has 25 years applied to CSRS component and five years applied to FERS component.

(1) Compute Basic Annual CSRS Component:

1.5 percent x $30,000 x 5 = $2,250
1.75 percent x $30,000 x 5 = $2,625

2.0 percent x $30,000 x 15 = $9,000 CSRS Component $13,875

(2) Compute Basic Annual FERS Component:
1.0 percent x $30,000 x 5 = $1,500

(3) Add the two to determine FERS Combined Basic Annuity:
$13,875 + $1,500 = Annuity of $15,375

Computing CSRS-Offset Benefits

When a CSRS-Offset employee becomes eligible for retirement benefits, the annuity is calculated in exactly the same way that it would be for any CSRS participant. However, if and when the employee becomes eligible to receive Social Security benefits, the CSRS annuity is reduced ("offset") to take that portion of the Social Security benefit attributable to CSRS-Offset service into account. Here's the way it works. The Social Security Administration takes the federal earnings for the period when the individual was covered by both Social Security and CSRS and computes two Social Security benefit amounts—the first with those earnings included, and the second with those earnings excluded. These two amounts are sent to OPM, which determines the CSRS-Offset amount.

The offset reduction will be the lesser of:

(1) The difference between the Social Security monthly benefit amount with and without CSRS-Offset service (service after December 31, 1983, covered under the interim CSRS provisions or CSRS-Offset provisions); or

(2) The product of the Social Security monthly benefit amount, with federal earnings, multiplied by a fraction where the numerator is the employee's total CSRS-Offset service rounded to the nearest whole number of years and the denominator is 40.

Social Security benefit X $\dfrac{\text{Total Yrs of Offset Svc}}{40}$

Example: The following example shows how the offset would be computed for an employee with three years and eight months of Offset service:

First computation: (a) Social Security monthly benefit with federal months of Offset service=$600; (b) Social Security monthly benefit without federal Offset serv-

ice=$550; (c) the difference is $50.

Second computation: (a) Social Security amount with federal earnings = $600 x four years (nearest whole year to three years eight months) = $2,400 divided by 40 = $60.

Since the offset is determined by taking the *lesser* amount of the two computations, the reduction in this case would be based on the first computation method—or $50.

If the individual has Social Security coverage in the private sector, the amount of reduction in the CSRS benefit will generally be less than the Social Security benefit to which the individual will be entitled. If ineligible for Social Security benefits at age 62, CSRS employees continue to receive their full CSRS benefits.

Computing Deferred Retirement Benefits

General CSRS Rules—Under CSRS, former employees who leave their money in the retirement fund are eligible for an annuity at age 62 if they have completed at least five years of creditable service and were covered by CSRS for at least one year within in the two-year period immediately before separating.

The computation of benefits will be based on their "high-3" salary at the time of separation. It will not be adjusted for inflation. As a result, the value of the annuity will have eroded. The amount of this deferred benefit erosion depends on the time an employee has to wait for the deferred annuity to start. If there is a long delay before it begins, the older rates of pay may provide only a small benefit in current dollars.

Deferred annuitants under CSRS and FERS are not eligible to participate in the FEHB program or to acquire FEGLI coverage. However, once their annuity begins, they will get annual cost-of-living adjustments (COLAs). In addition, they will be eligible to provide a survivor annuity for their spouses.

General FERS Rules—Workers covered under FERS are eligible for deferred benefits if they leave service after having completed five years of service covered by retirement deductions. Deferred benefits are payable at age 62, or at age 55 with at least ten years of service. Separated workers electing the deferred benefit at 55 with at least ten years of service will have a computation as if they were retiring at that point, including the applicable reductions of five percent for each year of age under age 62. Nevertheless, because the computation will be performed earlier, there is less erosion of the relationship between the "high-3" base and the point in time at which the computation is performed. Thus, it is generally to the advantage of the retiree to exercise the option to take the deferred retirement at the earliest possible date rather than waiting until age 62, when full benefits are payable.

> Note: A worker separating from federal service with at least 10 years of service before reaching the MRA or separated with at least 5, but less than 10 years of service, will not be eligible to continue any health benefits or life insurance coverage he or she had while employed.

Special Retirement Supplement—FERS contains an additional benefit computation for workers retiring at the MRA with at least 30 years of service. This Special Retirement Supplement, which is determined using a complex formula that estimates the Social Security benefits earned through federal or postal employment under FERS, is intended to replicate the Social Security benefit payable at age 62. The following classes of employees are entitled to the supplement:

• Voluntary retirement at the minimum retirement age (55-57) with at least 30 years of service.

• Voluntary retirement at age 60 with at least 20 years of service.

• Discontinued service retirement when the retiree attains the minimum retirement age (55-57).

• Members of Congress at age 50 with at least 20 years of service or 25 years of service at any age when they attain the minimum retirement age (55-57).

• Military Reserve technicians who are age 50 with at least 25 years of service who lose their military status.

• Law enforcement officers, air traffic controllers, and firefighters.

The Special Retirement Supplement is paid as an annuity until you reach age 62. If you transferred to FERS from CSRS, you must have at least one full calendar year of FERS-covered service to qualify for the supplement.

This supplement was created by Congress to bring FERS participants nearer

to the treatment of workers covered by CSRS. Unlike FERS, CSRS participants do not directly qualify for Social Security benefits through federal or postal employment (except for CSRS-Offset participants). Because CSRS benefits do not include Social Security, an "implied" Social Security benefit exists so that CSRS retirement benefits roughly approximate the benefits of workers in the private-sector who are covered by Social Security and a private-sector pension. Yet, under CSRS, that implied Social Security amount is payable before the earliest age for drawing the Social Security retirement benefit; i.e., age 62.

The CSRS definition of eligibility, in combination with the CSRS formula, allows participants to retire before age 62 and receive benefits above what they would receive were they to be covered by a "typical" private-sector arrangement, in which the Social Security portion of the benefit would not become payable until age 62.

When Congress created FERS, it established the annuity supplement for workers who retire after full careers in federal and postal employment, but before age 62.

If you have earnings from wages or self-employment that exceed the Social Security annual exempt amount under the Earnings Test (see Social Security section), your Special Retirement Supplement will be reduced or stopped.

The supplement payable to law enforcement officers, firefighters, air traffic controllers, and military reserve technicians who lose military status is not tested for earnings until they attain the minimum retirement age (55-57).

Commencing Date of Annuities

Under CSRS, employees or members of Congress who retire with three or fewer days of service in the month in which they retire will have their annuities commence the following day; otherwise their annuities will become effective on the first day of the following month. This "first-of-the-month after" provision does not apply to survivor annuities, disability annuities, or those discontinued service annuities based on involuntary separation under either system. These annuities will commence on the day after separation, death, or last day of pay, as appropriate. For employees with a gap between the date of separation and the beginning date of annuity, and who are eligible to continue health and life insurance into retirement, premiums will not be required between the end of the pay period in which the employee separates and the commencing date of annuity.

Under FERS, all annuities based on voluntary retirements begin on the first day of the following month.

Applying for Retirement and Survivor Benefits

Retirement benefits are not paid automatically. Employees or survivors must apply for them. Employees (or survivors of employees who die in service) should contact their agency personnel offices.

Separated employees or survivors of retirees living in the Washington, D.C., area must call OPM at (202) 606-0500, TDD (202) 606-0551. Those living elsewhere should use OPM's toll-free number: 1-888-767-6738 (TDD 1-800-878-5707). Or they may write to the following address:

U.S. Office of Personnel Management
Retirement Operations Center
P.O. Box 45
Boyers, PA 16017-0045

CSRS-covered employees may appeal OPM's retirement decisions directly to the Merit Systems Protection Board, rather than first requesting reconsideration by OPM, under rules published in the April 28, 1997, *Federal Register*. This appeals procedure is designed to streamline the processing of disputed cases and to make the rules governing CSRS employees the same as those applying to FERS workers.

Survivors of Current Employees— Notify the employee's office of his or her death. That office will call the agency's servicing personnel office.

The agency will contact OPM via fax or through its website (www.opm.gov), using a CSRS Death-in-Service Quick Pay form or a FERS Basic Death-in-Service form. That will allow OPM to begin making expedited interim payments to the survivors. The agency will also provide the surviving spouse with the necessary forms to complete the process. These include the application for death benefits and life insurance. The agency will be responsible for assisting the survivor to complete the paperwork. Once the forms are submitted, OPM will be the survivor's point of contact.

Survivors of Retired Employees—To speed up the time required for survivors of federal retirees to receive their benefits, OPM's Survivor Express allows the payment of a survivor annuity as soon as the survivor reports the retiree's death. The survivor then has 30 days in which to submit the

---

Commonly Used Retirement Forms

The following forms should be available to employees in their agency personnel offices:

	CSRS	FERS
Application for Death Benefits	SF 2800	SF 3104
Application for Immediate Retirement	SF 2801	SF 3107
Application for Refund of Retirement Deductions	SF 2802	SF 3106
Application to Make Deposit or Redeposit	SF 2803	SF 3108
Application to Make Voluntary Contributions	SF 2804	n/a
Designation of Beneficiary	SF 2808	SF 3102
Documentation in Support of Disability Retirement	SF 3112	SF 3112

Many of these forms may be downloaded from OPM's website at www.opm.gov/forms.

Separated employees who wish to retire on a deferred annuity must write to OPM at the following address to get the appropriate application form, OPM Form 1496A for CSRS and OPM Form RI 92-19 for FERS:

U.S. Office of Personnel Management
Retirement Operations Center
P.O. Box 45
Boyers, PA 16017-0045

---

required documentation; the forms will be supplied by OPM. This approach also speeds up the time needed to process life insurance claims and change health insurance enrollments.

Getting Answers to Retirement Questions

Information about retirement policy is provided in the *CSRS and FERS Handbook for Personnel and Payroll Offices*. Current employees must contact their agency personnel offices or retirement counselors for retirement information and for forms relating to retirement. OPM does not have current records and cannot assist employees.

OPM handles inquiries from or about civil service annuitants. You may contact OPM by e-mail, phone, in writing, or through OPM's website at *www.opm.gov*. See How to Contact OPM for more information.

All inquiries should include the name of the former federal or postal employee, the individual's claim number, date of birth, and Social Security number. This data will allow OPM to provide the most prompt response.

While it is possible to get answers to urgent inquiries by telephone, OPM strongly recommends that only questions that are reasonably uncomplicated and that do not require the review of records be telephoned in. A report of the death of a civil service annuitant is an example of an uncomplicated administrative matter that is easily handled via the telephone. Simple inquiries will be answered by the Retirement Information

Office on: 1-888-767-6738. This office is open on standard business days from 7:30 a.m. to 7:45 p.m. Eastern Time. Annuitants with hearing impairments who have TDD equipment should call 1-800-878-7507. Reports of a death may be made by calling 1-888-767-6738 at any time, day or night. Local callers must dial (202) 606-0500. TDD callers must dial (202) 606-0551.

Individuals who want to report a specific incident of waste, fraud, or abuse of civil service annuity benefits can call the "Hot Line" on: (202) 606-2423 or 606-0232.

When an inquiry is complex, requires the review of records, or seeks to alter records, OPM strongly recommends inquiring by letter. This is not only less expensive, but also will help get answers quicker. Most written inquiries should be addressed to: U.S. Office of Personnel Management, Retirement Operations Center, Boyers, PA 16017. This is where retirement records are maintained. OPM's staff at Boyers can answer a wide range of retirement-related questions. If it is necessary for an inquiry to be referred to the staff in Washington, D.C., the necessary records will be forwarded from Boyers with the inquiry.

If the individual can identify the exact nature of his or her inquiry the individual can use the information under Addresses for Specialized Retirement Functions to determine if the appropriate office has a special address. Otherwise, always refer a written inquiry to the Retirement Operations Center.

Section 6—Early Retirement

Definition of Terms

Both CSRS and FERS contain special provisions that allow employees who do not meet the normal age and service requirements to retire early. The purpose of this early retirement option is to assist an agency in carrying out personnel or workload changes with minimal disruption to the work force. This section covers the two general types of early retirement: (1) voluntary and (2) involuntary (commonly referred to as discontinued service retirement, or DSR). While both types of retirement are often triggered by the same personnel pressures (e.g., a RIF, reorganization, transfer of func-

tion, etc.), they differ in several important respects.

Whether the early retirement is voluntary or involuntary, the following definitions apply:

Reduction in Force—A reduction-in-force (RIF) action means the release of a competing employee from his or her competitive level by furlough for more than 30 days, separation, demotion, or reassignment requiring displacement, which is required because of a lack of work, shortage of funds, insufficient personnel ceiling, reorganization, an individual's exercise of reemployment or restoration rights, or reclassification due to erosion of duties when it occurs within 180 days of a formally announced RIF in a competitive area.

Furlough—Under RIF procedures, a furlough means the placement of an employee in a temporary nonduty/nonpay status for more than 30 consecutive calendar days or more than 22 workdays if done on a non-continuous basis, but not for more than one year when the action is based on one of the RIF reasons and is not in accordance with pre-established conditions of employment.

Reorganization—Reorganization means the planned elimination, addition, or redistribution of functions or duties in an organization.

Transfer of Function—Transfer of function means: (1) transfer of the performance of a continuing function from one competitive area and its addition to one or more other competitive areas, except where the function involved is virtually identical to functions already being performed in the other competitive area(s) affected, or (2) the movement of the competitive area in which the function is performed to another commuting area.

Function—Function means all or a clearly identifiable segment of an agency's mission, including all integral parts of that mission, regardless of how it is performed.

Local Commuting Area—A local commuting area is one that usually constitutes a single area for employment purposes. It includes any population center (or two or more neighboring ones) and the surrounding localities in which people live and reasonably can be expected to travel back and forth daily in their usual employment.

Early Voluntary Retirement

An agency or segment of an agency that is undergoing a major RIF, a major reorganization, or a major transfer of function may ask OPM to permit early voluntary retirement for its employees. Such a request must be in writing. OPM then determines whether the authority should be granted. If it agrees, OPM designates the specific geographic area(s) or occupation(s) covered by the RIF retirement option and stipulates limited period of time during which the option will remain in effect. The agency may, at its discretion, end the time period earlier.

General Eligibility Requirements—When OPM determines that an agency is undergoing a major RIF, a major reorganization, or a major transfer of function, an eligible employee may apply to retire on an immediate annuity if he or she satisfies the general age and service requirements and meets certain other conditions. This means an employee must:
- be at least 50 years old with at least 20 years of creditable service; or
- be any age with at least 25 years service;

Note: Accrued annual leave (and unused sick leave for CSRS employees only) may not be added to meet either of the service requirements listed above.

- meet the minimum civilian service requirement, which is at least five years of creditable civilian service;

Note: If a CSRS employee has the minimum five years of creditable service, creditable military service may be used to meet the balance of service necessary for an early voluntary retirement. FERS employees with post-1956 military service cannot use it to meet the service requirement unless they make a deposit for it before retirement.

- separate from a position subject to either CSRS or FERS coverage. However, this cannot be a time-limited appointment;
- if covered by CSRS, meet the "one-out-of-two" requirement; i.e. be covered by CSRS for at least one year within the two-year period immediately preceding the separation on which the annuity is based. This one year does not have to be continuous;

Note: There is no "one-out-of-two" requirement for FERS employees.

- have served in a position covered by OPM authorization for at least 31 calendar days before the agency's initial request to OPM and must have remained continuously on the rolls without a break in service of more than four days since that time; and
- separate by the end of the last day of the early-out period authorized by OPM or the last day permitted by the agency, if it ends the period earlier.
- The employee must not be in receipt of a decision of involuntary separation for misconduct or unsatisfactory performance.

Withdrawal of Application to Retire—Since optional retirement is a form of voluntary separation, submitting a retirement application is equivalent to submitting a resignation. As a result, a retiring employee has the same rights as any other employee involved in a voluntary action. This means that you can establish the date on which your retirement will take place (as long as it is within the period set) or withdraw it if you change your mind before the separation is effective.

Discontinued Service Retirement

A discontinued service retirement (DSR) is an involuntary retirement that provides an immediate annuity to employees who are separated against their will. Employees who are separated for cause on charges of misconduct or delinquency are not eligible for a discontinued service annuity.

DSRs can lessen the impact of an involuntary separation of a long-service employee. The final responsibility for determining whether a separation is in fact involuntary for discontinued service annuity purposes rests with OPM. Whether a separation is voluntary depends on all the facts on a particular case. It is the true substance of the action that governs, not the methods followed or the terminology used. Note: If it is later discovered that

a separation does not meet the standard for a DSR, that separation may be canceled, or an annuity denied or terminated.

Examples of Involuntary Separation: Separations that are involuntary for DSR purposes include, but are not limited to, separations for:
- reduction-in-force (RIF);
- abolishment of position;
- lack of funds;
- expiration of an incumbent's term of office;
- unacceptable performance (unless due to the employee's misconduct);
- transfer of function outside the commuting area;
- reassignment outside the commuting area when there is no mobility agreement;
- failure to continue to meet qualification requirements of the position (provided the separation is non-disciplinary and the action is initiated by the agency);
- separation during probation because of failure to qualify due to performance (not misconduct);
- separation of a National Guard technician because of loss of military membership or the rank required to hold the National Guard position; and

---

How to Contact OPM

OPM provides retirement information on the Internet. You will find retirement brochures, forms and other information at www.opm.gov/retire. This website has up-to-date information about a wide range of retirement topics. You can also use OPM's "Service Online" function at this website to:
- Change you mailing address;
- Start or change Direct Deposit of your payments to your account in a financial organization;
- Set up allotments of your payments to more than one checking or savings account;
- Buy, change, or stop U.S. Savings Bonds;
- Request a duplicate tax-filing statement (1099R);
- Change your Personal Identification Number (PIN) for accessing OPM's automated systems; and
- Establish, change, or stop an allotment to an organization.

You can contact the retirement system by e-mail at retire@opm.gov. There you can obtain assistance with any action you wish to take, inform OPM of the death of an annuitant, or make general comments. If OPM needs further information or documents to accomplish your business, they will let you know by e-mail. This is especially helpful to you if you live outside the United States.

Address for General Inquiries
U.S. Office of Personnel Management
Retirement Operations Center
P.O. Box 45, Boyers, PA 16017-0045

Addresses for Specialized Retirement Functions

Circumstance	*Special Address*
1. For questions about mailing or payment address for those already on the annuity roll. Changes can be made in writing or by calling (202) 606-0500,Washington, D.C. metro area or toll-free 1-888-767-6738, TDD 1-800-878-5707. The annuitant must make the call or sign the written request.	U.S. Office of Personnel Management Change of Address Section P.O. Box 440 Boyers, PA 16017-0440
2. To report non-receipt of annuity, lump sum, or refund payment, call (202) 606-0500, Washington, D.C. metro area or toll-free 1-888-767-6738, TDD 1-800-878-5707.	U.S. Office of Personnel Management P.O. Box 7815 Washington, DC 20044-7815
3. To have monthly annuity payments sent to a bank by direct deposit, call 1-888-767-6738 or have your bank complete a form SF1199A and send it to OPM.	U.S. Office of Personnel Management P.O. Box 440 Boyers, PA 16017-0440
4. General inquiries about federal and state income tax.	U.S. Office of Personnel Management P.O. Box 45 Boyers, PA 16017-0045
5. To change amount of income tax withheld, call Annuitant Express at 1-800-409-6528. Use a touch-tone telephone and be prepared to give your PIN number. If you don't have a touch-tone phone, call (202) 606-0500, Washington, D.C. metro area or toll-free 1-888-767-6738, TDD 1-800-878-5707, or write. No special form is required.	U.S. Office of Personnel Management Retirement Operations Center P.O. Box 45 Boyers, PA 16017-0045
6. (a) For questions involving health insurance for annuitants not related to open season.	U.S. Office of Personnel Management Health Benefits Branch Washington, DC 20415-3532
(b) For open season questions.	P.O. Box 809 Washington, DC 20044-0809.
7. For questions involving garnishment or apportionment of annuities, bankruptcies, alimony, or child support.	U.S. Office of Personnel Management Court Order Benefits Branch Washington, DC 20415-3560
8. To report the death of an annuitant or survivor annuitant, call (202) 606-0500, Washington, D.C. metro area or toll-free 1-888-767-6738, TDD 1-800-878-5707 or write.	U.S. Office of Personnel Management Retirement Operations Center P.O. Box 45 Boyers, PA 16017-0045
9. For questions related to student benefits.	U.S. Office of Personnel Management Washington, DC 20415-2309
10. For questions related to: (a) marital survey, (b) income survey for disability annuitants, or (c) waiver of annuity, or representative payee survey.	U.S. Office of Personnel Management Retirement Surveys Branch Washington, DC 20415-2309
11. For questions concerning reconsideration of the collection of overpayments.	U.S. Office of Personnel Management Retirement Operations Center P.O. Box 45 Boyers, PA 16017-0045
12. To send payments for deposits, and overpayments (debts).	U.S. Office of Personnel Management P.O. Box 7125 Washington, DC 20044
13. To report changes in Social Security benefits for FERS disability and survivor benefits.	U.S. Office of Personnel Management P.O. Box 200 Boyers, PA 16017-0200

14. To report changes in the status of Workers' Compensation benefits.

U.S. Office of Personnel Management
Operations Center
Boyers, PA 16017

15. For questions concerning the collection of overpayments from former annuitants and other individuals who are not receiving monthly benefits.

U.S. Office of Personnel Management
Receivables Management Branch
Rm. 3H30
Washington, DC 20415

16. For questions related to suspected waste, fraud, or abuse in CSRS or FERS, or call one of the Hotlines–(202) 606-2423 or 606-0232.

U.S. Office of Personnel Management
Retirement Inspections Branch
Washington, DC 20415-3564

• removal from the Senior Executive Service (SES) for less than fully successful performance.

Among the situations that do not constitute a basis for a DSR are reclassification to a lower grade as a result of prior misclassification or the application of a new standard (including the correction of title, series and/or grade) and resignation because of ill health. In the latter case, it is qualifying if the employee is removed by adverse action or equivalent procedures (or retires after a decision to remove has been issued), because of illness resulting in one or more of the following:

• continued absence;
• inability to perform his or her duties; or
• endangering his or her health or that of other employees.

Requirement for Specific Written Notice: To qualify for discontinued service retirement, an employee must receive a specific written notice of a proposed involuntary separation. The notice must be directed to the individual employee and must:

• inform the employee that he or she faces involuntary separation from his or her position from the federal service;
• specify the reason for the proposed action (i.e., impending organizational change, etc.); and
• state the date proposed action is to be effective.

General Eligibility Requirements—The eligibility requirements to retire for CSRS and FERS employees facing involuntary separation are essentially the same as those for early voluntary retirement. In brief, the employee must:

• meet the age and service requirements;
• meet the minimum civilian service requirements, which is at least five years of creditable civilian service;
• separate from a position subject to

either CSRS or FERS coverage;
• if covered by CSRS, meet the "one-out-of-two" requirement. There is no "one-out-of-two" requirement for FERS employees; and
• not decline a reasonable offer of another job.

Reasonable Offer: A job that meets all of the conditions below is a "reasonable offer."

• The agency offer of the position must be in writing.
• The employee must meet established qualification requirements for the position.
• The offered position must be in the employee's agency, including an agency to which the employee with his/her function is transferred in a transfer of function between agencies.
• The offered position must be within the employee's commuting area, unless the employee is under a geographic mobility agreement.
• The offered position must be the same tenure, i.e., same service (competitive, excepted, SES, etc.), same type (career, permanent, indefinite, etc.), and same work schedule (full-time, part-time, etc.).
• The offered position must not be lower that the equivalent of two grade/pay levels below the employee's current grade or pay level. The grade or pay level for an employee who is not under grade retention is the grade or pay level of the position currently occupied. The grade or pay level of an employee who is under grade retention is the retained grade or pay level.

Retirement Options—When an employee qualifies for more than one type of retirement, the employee is entitled to apply for the option he or she prefers. That choice may depend on the employee's interest in subsequent federal employment. For example, if the employee is already eligible to retire and voluntarily exercises that option, pay on reemployment will be reduced by the amount of the annuity. On the other hand, if the retirement is for discontinued service after an involuntary separation, the annuity is terminated and the employee acquires a new retirement right, unless the reemployment is excluded from retirement coverage.

Eligibility for Severance Pay—While a separation that meets discontinued service criteria also meets the severance pay criteria, severance pay is not payable in situations in which the employee is eligible for discontinued service retirement.

Other Early Retirement Rules and Considerations

Use of Accrued Annual Leave—Federal employees who are about to lose their jobs due to downsizing can, at their discretion, use their accrued annual leave to qualify for retirement eligibility, under rules issued by the Office of Personnel Management in the March 10, 1997, Federal Register and made final on May 13, 1998. Previously, agencies had the right to approve such use of accrued annual leave for retirement-eligibility purposes.

Credit for Unused Sick Leave—CSRS employees will receive credit for unused sick leave in their annuity computation, but only after they have met the basic requirements for early retirement. FERS employees receive no credit for unused sick leave.

Former CSRS employees who transferred to FERS will receive credit for the amount of sick leave at the time of their transfer or at the time of retirement, whichever is less. The sick leave credit is applied to the CSRS portion of their annuity.

Annuity Computations—In general, annuities for early voluntary and discontinued service retirees are calculated in the same way as those for employees who have completed a full career (see above). However, there are some exceptions.

Factors for Determining Reduction in Basic Annuity Under CSRS

Age at Separation and at Least 1 Day Over	0 Mo.	1 Mo.	2 Mo.	3 Mo.	4 Mo.	5 Mo.	6 Mo.	7 Mo.	8 Mo.	9 Mo.	10 Mo.	11 Mo.
40	.7017	.7033	.7050	.7067	.7083	.7100	.7117	.7133	.7150	.7167	.7183	.7200
41	.7217	.7233	.7250	.7267	.7283	.7300	.7317	.7333	.7350	.7367	.7383	.7400
42	.7417	.7433	.7450	.7467	.7483	.7500	.7517	.7533	.7550	.7567	.7583	.7600
43	.7617	.7633	.7650	.7667	.7683	.7700	.7717	.7733	.7750	.7767	.7783	.7800
44	.7817	.7833	.7850	.7867	.7883	.7900	.7917	.7933	.7950	.7967	.7983	.8000
45	.8017	.8033	.8050	.8067	.8083	.8100	.8117	.8133	.8150	.8167	.8183	.8200
46	.8217	.8233	.8250	.8267	.8283	.8300	.8317	.8333	.8350	.8367	.8383	.8400
47	.8417	.8433	.8450	.8467	.8483	.8500	.8517	.8533	.8550	.8567	.8583	.8600
48	.8617	.8633	.8650	.8667	.8683	.8700	.8717	.8733	.8750	.8767	.8783	.8800
49	.8817	.8833	.8850	.8867	.8883	.8900	.8917	.8933	.8950	.8967	.8983	.9000
50	.9017	.9033	.9050	.9067	.9083	.9100	.9117	.9133	.9150	.9167	.9183	.9200
51	.9217	.9233	.9250	.9267	.9283	.9300	.9317	.9333	.9350	.9367	.9383	.9400
52	.9417	.9433	.9450	.9467	.9483	.9500	.9517	.9533	.9550	.9567	.9583	.9600
53	.9617	.9633	.9650	.9667	.9683	.9700	.9717	.9733	.9750	.9767	.9783	.9800
54	.9817	.9833	.9850	.9867	.9883	.9900	.9917	.9933	.9950	.9967	.9983	1.0000

To find out the impact of retiring early, first determine your basic annuity using the standard formula then multiply it by the factor that reflects your age at retirement. The product will be your reduced annuity. For example: If you calculated that you would receive an annuity of $40,000 but would be retiring at age 50 and ten months, your reduced annuity would be $36,372 ($40,000 x .9183). Note: Official OPM table is actually set forth in six decimal places.

Civil Service Retirement Table for CSRS Employees
Monthly Annuities Computed Under Basic Formulae

(Second line of each salary level reflects annuity with 55 percent survivor benefit deduction.)

Basic annuity is subject to reduction if (a) deductions are not in the fund for any service since August 1, 1920, (b) retirement—except for disability—is before age 55, (c) a survivor-type annuity is elected at retirement.

Highest 3 Year Average Salary	YEARS OF CREDITABLE SERVICE																	Amounts For Each Add'l Yr. Unlisted
	5	10	15	16	17	18	19	20	21	22	23	24	25	30	35	40	42	
20,000	125	271	438	471	504	538	571	604	638	671	704	738	771	938	1,104	1,271	1,338	33
	122	264	416	446	476	506	536	566	596	626	656	686	716	866	1,016	1,166	1,266	
23,000	144	311	503	541	580	618	656	695	733	771	810	848	886	1,078	1,270	1,461	1,538	38
	140	304	475	510	544	579	613	648	682	717	751	786	820	993	1,165	1,338	1,407	
26,000	163	352	569	612	655	699	742	785	829	872	915	959	1,002	1,219	1,435	1,652	1,739	43
	158	339	534	573	612	651	690	729	768	807	846	885	924	1,119	1,314	1,509	1,587	
30,000	188	406	656	706	756	806	856	906	956	1,006	1,056	1,106	1,156	1,406	1,656	1,906	2,006	50
	183	388	613	658	703	748	793	838	883	928	973	1,018	1,063	1,288	1,513	1,738	1,828	
33,000	206	447	722	777	832	887	942	997	1,052	1,107	1,162	1,217	1,272	1,547	1,822	2,097	2,207	55
	201	425	672	722	771	821	870	920	969	1,019	1,068	1,118	1,167	1,415	1,662	1,910	2,009	
36,000	225	488	788	848	908	968	1,028	1,088	1,148	1,208	1,268	1,328	1,388	1,688	1,988	2,288	2,408	60
	219	461	731	785	839	893	947	1,001	1,055	1,109	1,163	1,217	1,271	1,541	1,811	2,081	2,189	
40,000	250	542	875	942	1,008	1,075	1,142	1,208	1,275	1,342	1,408	1,475	1,542	1,875	2,208	2,542	2,675	66
	244	510	810	870	930	990	1,050	1,110	1,170	1,230	1,290	1,350	1,410	1,710	2,010	2,310	2,430	
43,000	269	582	941	1,012	1,084	1,156	1,227	1,299	1,371	1,442	1,514	1,586	1,657	2,016	2,374	2,732	2,876	72
	262	547	869	934	998	1,063	1,127	1,192	1,256	1,321	1,385	1,450	1,514	1,837	2,159	2,482	2,611	
46,000	288	623	1,006	1,083	1,160	1,236	1,313	1,390	1,466	1,543	1,620	1,696	1,773	2,156	2,540	2,923	3,076	76
	280	583	928	997	1,066	1,135	1,204	1,273	1,342	1,411	1,480	1,549	1,618	1,963	2,308	2,653	2,791	
50,000	313	677	1,094	1,177	1,260	1,344	1,427	1,510	1,594	1,677	1,760	1,844	1,927	2,344	2,760	3,177	3,344	83
	304	632	1,007	1,082	1,157	1,232	1,307	1,382	1,457	1,532	1,607	1,682	1,757	2,132	2,507	2,882	3,032	
53,000	331	718	1,159	1,248	1,336	1,424	1,513	1,601	1,689	1,778	1,866	1,954	2,043	2,484	2,926	3,368	3,544	88
	323	668	1,066	1,145	1,225	1,304	1,384	1,463	1,543	1,622	1,702	1,781	1,861	2,258	2,656	3,053	3,212	
56,000	350	758	1,225	1,318	1,412	1,505	1,598	1,692	1,785	1,878	1,972	2,065	2,158	2,625	3,092	3,558	3,745	93
	341	705	1,125	1,209	1,293	1,377	1,461	1,545	1,629	1,713	1,797	1,881	1,965	2,385	2,805	3,225	3,393	

Avg. Salary																	
60,000	375	813	1,313	1,513	1,613	1,713	1,813	1,913	2,013	2,113	2,213	2,313	2,813	3,313	3,813	4,013	100
	366	754	1,204	1,384	1,474	1,564	1,654	1,744	1,834	1,924	2,014	2,104	2,554	3,004	3,454	3,634	
63,000	394	853	1,378	1,588	1,693	1,798	1,903	2,008	2,113	2,218	2,323	2,428	2,953	3,478	4,003	4,213	105
	384	790	1,263	1,452	1,546	1,641	1,735	1,830	1,924	2,019	2,113	2,208	2,680	3,153	3,625	3,814	
66,000	413	894	1,444	1,664	1,774	1,884	1,994	2,104	2,214	2,324	2,434	2,544	3,094	3,644	4,194	4,414	110
	394	827	1,322	1,554	1,619	1,718	1,817	1,916	2,015	2,114	2,213	2,312	2,807	3,302	3,797	3,995	
70,000	438	948	1,531	1,765	1,881	1,998	2,115	2,231	2,348	2,465	2,581	2,698	3,281	3,865	4,448	4,681	116
	416	876	1,401	1,611	1,716	1,821	1,926	2,031	2,136	2,241	2,346	2,451	2,976	3,501	4,026	4,236	
73,000	456	989	1,597	1,840	1,962	2,085	2,205	2,327	2,449	2,570	2,692	2,814	3,422	4,030	4,639	4,882	122
	433	912	1,460	1,679	1,788	1,898	2,007	2,117	2,226	2,336	2,445	2,555	3,102	3,650	4,197	4,416	
76,000	475	1,029	1,663	1,916	2,043	2,169	2,296	2,423	2,549	2,676	2,803	2,929	3,563	4,196	4,829	5,083	126
	450	949	1,519	1,747	1,861	1,975	2,089	2,203	2,317	2,431	2,545	2,659	3,229	3,799	4,369	4,597	
80,000	500	1,083	1,750	2,017	2,150	2,283	2,417	2,550	2,683	2,817	2,950	3,083	3,750	4,417	5,083	5,350	133
	473	998	1,598	1,838	1,958	2,078	2,198	2,318	2,438	2,558	2,678	2,798	3,398	3,998	4,598	4,838	
83,000	519	1,124	1,816	2,092	2,231	2,369	2,507	2,646	2,784	2,922	3,061	3,199	3,891	4,582	5,274	5,551	138
	489	1,034	1,657	1,906	2,030	2,155	2,279	2,404	2,528	2,653	2,777	2,902	3,524	4,147	4,769	5,018	
86,000	538	1,165	1,881	2,168	2,311	2,455	2,598	2,741	2,885	3,028	3,171	3,315	4,031	4,748	5,465	5,751	143
	506	1,071	1,716	1,974	2,103	2,232	2,361	2,490	2,619	2,748	2,877	3,006	3,651	4,296	4,941	5,199	
90,000	563	1,219	1,969	2,269	2,419	2,569	2,719	2,869	3,019	3,169	3,319	3,469	4,219	4,969	5,719	6,019	150
	529	1,119	1,794	2,064	2,199	2,334	2,469	2,604	2,739	2,874	3,009	3,144	3,819	4,494	5,169	5,439	
93,000	581	1,259	2,034	2,344	2,499	2,654	2,809	2,964	3,119	3,274	3,429	3,584	4,359	5,134	5,909	6,219	155
	546	1,156	1,853	2,132	2,272	2,411	2,551	2,690	2,830	2,969	3,109	3,248	3,946	4,643	5,341	5,620	
96,000	600	1,300	2,100	2,420	2,580	2,740	2,900	3,060	3,220	3,380	3,540	3,700	4,500	5,300	6,100	6,420	160
	563	1,193	1,913	2,201	2,345	2,489	2,633	2,777	2,921	3,065	3,209	3,353	4,073	4,793	5,513	5,801	
100,000	625	1,354	2,188	2,521	2,688	2,854	3,021	3,188	3,354	3,521	3,688	3,854	4,688	5,521	6,354	6,688	167
	585	1,241	1,991	2,291	2,441	2,591	2,741	2,891	3,041	3,191	3,341	3,491	4,241	4,991	5,741	6,041	
110,000	688	1,490	2,406	2,773	2,956	3,140	3,323	3,506	3,690	3,873	4,056	4,240	5,156	6,073	6,990	7,356	183
	641	1,363	2,188	2,518	2,683	2,848	3,013	3,178	3,343	3,508	3,673	3,838	4,663	5,488	6,313	6,643	

The above figures are rounded to the nearest dollar.

Example illustrating computations: Assume an Average Salary of $40,000 at 24 years of service:

For 1st 5 years use:	1 1/2% x $40,000 x 5	=	$3,000.00
For 2nd 5 years use:	1 3/4% x $40,000 x 5	=	$3,500.00
For balance of 14 years use:	2% x $40,000 x 14	=	$11,200.00
Total annual annuity		=	$17,700.00

Divide by 12 (months) = $1,475 a month. If a survivor annuity is elected, the monthly annuity would be reduced to $1,350.

Federal Employees' Retirement System (FERS) Table

Monthly Basic Annuity Amounts Based on "High-3" Salary And Years of Service For Employees

(Second line of each salary level reflects annuity with 50 percent survivor benefit deduction.)

Basic annuity is subject to reduction if (a) deductions are not in the fund for any service since August 1, 1920, (b) retirement—except for disability—is before age 55, (c) a survivor-type annuity is elected at retirement.

Highest 3-Year Average Salary	YEARS OF CREDITABLE SERVICE																	Amounts For Each Add'l Yr. Unlisted
	5	10	15	16	17	18	19	20	21	22	23	24	25	30	35	40	42	
20,000	83	167	250	267	283	300	317	333	350	367	383	400	417	500	583	667	700	16
	75	150	225	240	255	270	285	300	315	330	345	360	375	450	525	600	630	
23,000	96	192	288	307	326	345	364	383	403	422	441	460	479	575	671	767	805	19
	86	173	259	276	293	311	328	345	362	380	397	414	431	518	604	690	725	
26,000	108	217	325	347	368	390	412	433	455	477	498	521	542	650	758	867	910	21
	98	195	293	312	332	351	371	390	410	429	449	468	488	585	683	780	819	
30,000	125	250	375	400	425	450	475	500	525	550	575	600	625	750	875	1,000	1,050	25
	113	225	338	360	383	405	428	450	473	495	518	540	563	675	788	900	945	
33,000	138	275	413	440	468	495	523	550	578	605	633	660	688	825	963	1,100	1,155	27
	124	248	371	396	421	446	470	495	520	545	569	594	619	743	866	990	1,040	
36,000	150	300	450	480	510	540	570	600	630	660	690	720	750	900	1,050	1,200	1,260	30
	135	270	405	432	459	486	513	540	567	594	621	648	675	810	945	1,080	1,134	
40,000	167	333	500	533	567	600	633	667	700	733	767	800	833	1,000	1,167	1,333	1,400	33
	150	300	450	480	510	540	570	600	630	660	690	720	750	900	1,050	1,200	1,260	
43,000	179	358	538	573	609	645	681	717	753	788	824	860	896	1,075	1,254	1,433	1,505	36
	161	323	484	516	548	581	613	645	671	710	742	774	806	968	1,129	1,290	1,355	
46,000	192	383	575	613	652	690	728	767	805	843	882	920	958	1,150	1,342	1,533	1,610	38
	173	345	518	552	587	621	656	690	725	759	794	828	863	1,035	1,208	1,380	1,449	
50,000	208	417	625	667	708	750	792	833	875	917	958	1,000	1,042	1,250	1,458	1,667	1,750	41
	188	375	563	600	638	675	713	750	788	825	863	900	938	1,125	1,313	1,500	1,575	
53,000	221	442	663	707	751	795	839	883	928	972	1,016	1,060	1,104	1,325	1,546	1,767	1,855	44
	199	398	596	636	676	716	755	795	835	875	914	954	994	1,193	1,391	1,590	1,670	
56,000	233	467	700	747	793	840	887	933	980	1,027	1,073	1,120	1,167	1,400	1,633	1,867	1,960	46
	210	420	630	672	714	756	798	840	882	924	966	1,008	1,050	1,260	1,470	1,680	1,764	

Avg. Annual Salary	250	500	750	800	850	900	950	1,000	1,050	1,100	1,150	1,200	1,250	1,500	1,750	2,000	2,100	
60,000	250	500	750	800	850	900	950	1,000	1,050	1,100	1,150	1,200	1,250	1,500	1,750	2,000	2,100	50
	225	450	675	720	765	810	855	900	945	990	1,035	1,080	1,125	1,350	1,575	1,800	1,890	
63,000	263	525	788	840	893	945	998	1,050	1,103	1,155	1,208	1,260	1,313	1,575	1,838	2,100	2,205	52
	236	473	709	756	803	851	898	945	992	1,040	1,087	1,134	1,188	1,418	1,654	1,890	1,985	
66,000	275	550	825	880	935	990	1,045	1,100	1,155	1,210	1,265	1,320	1,375	1,650	1,925	2,200	2,310	55
	248	495	743	792	842	891	941	990	1,040	1,089	1,139	1,188	1,238	1,485	1,733	1,980	2,079	
70,000	292	583	875	933	992	1,050	1,108	1,167	1,225	1,283	1,342	1,400	1,458	1,750	2,042	2,333	2,450	58
	263	525	788	840	893	945	998	1,050	1,103	1,155	1,208	1,260	1,313	1,575	1,838	2,100	2,205	
73,000	304	608	913	973	1,034	1,095	1,156	1,217	1,278	1,338	1,399	1,460	1,521	1,825	2,129	2,433	2,555	61
	274	548	821	876	931	986	1,040	1,095	1,150	1,205	1,259	1,314	1,369	1,643	1,916	2,190	2,300	
76,000	317	633	950	1,013	1,077	1,140	1,203	1,267	1,330	1,393	1,457	1,520	1,583	1,900	2,217	2,533	2,660	63
	285	570	855	912	969	1,026	1,083	1,140	1,197	1,254	1,311	1,368	1,425	1,710	1,995	2,280	2,394	
80,000	333	667	1,000	1,067	1,133	1,200	1,267	1,333	1,400	1,467	1,533	1,600	1,667	2,000	2,333	2,667	2,800	66
	300	600	900	960	1,020	1,080	1,140	1,200	1,260	1,320	1,380	1,440	1,500	1,800	2,100	2,400	2,520	
83,000	346	692	1,038	1,107	1,176	1,245	1,314	1,383	1,453	1,522	1,591	1,660	1,729	2,075	2,421	2,767	2,905	69
	311	623	934	996	1,058	1,121	1,183	1,245	1,307	1,370	1,432	1,494	1,556	1,868	2,179	2,490	2,615	
86,000	358	717	1,075	1,147	1,218	1,290	1,362	1,433	1,505	1,577	1,648	1,720	1,792	2,150	2,508	2,867	3,010	71
	323	645	968	1,032	1,097	1,161	1,226	1,290	1,355	1,419	1,484	1,548	1,613	1,935	2,258	2,580	2,709	
90,000	375	750	1,125	1,200	1,275	1,350	1,425	1,500	1,575	1,650	1,725	1,800	1,875	2,250	2,625	3,000	3,150	75
	338	675	1,013	1,080	1,148	1,215	1,283	1,350	1,418	1,485	1,553	1,620	1,688	2,025	2,363	2,700	2,835	
93,000	388	775	1,163	1,240	1,318	1,395	1,473	1,550	1,628	1,705	1,783	1,860	1,938	2,325	2,713	3,100	3,255	77
	349	698	1,046	1,116	1,186	1,256	1,325	1,395	1,465	1,535	1,604	1,674	1,744	2,093	2,441	2,790	2,930	
96,000	400	800	1,200	1,280	1,360	1,440	1,520	1,600	1,680	1,760	1,840	1,920	2,000	2,400	2,800	3,200	3,360	80
	360	720	1,080	1,152	1,224	1,296	1,368	1,440	1,512	1,584	1,656	1,728	1,800	2,160	2,530	2,880	3,024	
100,000	417	833	1,250	1,333	1,417	1,500	1,583	1,667	1,750	1,833	1,917	2,000	2,083	2,500	2,917	3,333	3,501	83
	375	750	1,125	1,200	1,275	1,350	1,425	1,500	1,575	1,650	1,725	1,800	1,875	2,250	2,625	3,000	3,150	
110,000	458	917	1,375	1,467	1,558	1,650	1,742	1,833	1,925	2,017	2,108	2,200	2,292	2,750	3,208	3,667	3,850	92
	413	825	1,238	1,320	1,403	1,485	1,568	1,650	1,733	1,815	1,898	1,980	2,063	2,475	2,888	3,300	3,465	

Example illustrating an average annual salary at 24 years of service: 1% of $33,000 = $330, times 24 (years of service) = $7,920 annual annuity or $660 monthly. If the employee opted at retirement to elect a survivor annuity, his monthly annuity would be reduced by 10% to $594. (Employees who continue to serve at age 62 or older with 20 years of service will have their annuity computed at 1.1 percent. For example, the same employee in the example above who retires at age 62 or older would have an annual annuity of $8,712 or $726 monthly. If a survivor annuity is elected, the monthly annuity would be $653.40).

• CSRS: If the retiring employee is under age 55, the annuity rate is reduced by one-sixth of one percent for each full month (two percent a year), the worker is under age 55. The reduction is permanent and will not be eliminated when the individual becomes age 55.

• FERS: There is no annuity reduction for FERS employees under age 55 who take an early voluntary retirement. However, if the FERS employee has a CSRS component, that portion of the annuity will be reduced in the same way it is for full CSRS employees. Once again, that reduction will be permanent.

> Note: In general, a FERS-covered employee taking an early voluntary retirement or DSR will receive a retiree annuity supplement when he or she reaches the minimum retirement age (MRA).

Commencement of Annuities—An early retiree's annuity payments begin in accordance with the following rules:

Early Voluntary Retirement—Under CSRS, the annuity of an individual who was in a pay status for three days or fewer in the month of retirement begins the day after separation or the day after pay ceases and the age and service requirements are met. For individuals who were in a pay status four or more days in the month of retirement, annuities begin on the first day of the month following retirement. Under FERS, regardless of the date of separation, annuities begin on the first day of the month following separation.

Discontinued Service Retirement—Under CSRS and FERS, the annuity of an individual who is involuntarily separated begins on the earlier of the day after separation or the day after pay ceases and the worker meets the age and service requirements for an annuity.

Cost-of-Living Adjustments (COLAs)—All CSRS and FERS annuities are increased annually by COLAs. However, the laws governing their application to the two systems are different. See below for information on how and when COLAs are granted.

Eligibility to Continue Insurance—An employee's decision about whether to take an early voluntary retirement depends on many factors. Among these is a determination of whether the worker's insurance coverage will continue. (See Chapter 2 for rules on continuing these benefits into retirement.)

Survivor Annuities—The rules governing the provision of a survivor annuity to a surviving spouse of an early voluntary or discontinued service retiree are the same as those for an employee who retires after completing a full career.

Lump Sum Annual Leave Payment—All employees leaving the government will receive a lump sum payment for their unused annual leave. The amount is based on the hourly rate of pay being received on the date of separation from the government. For tax purposes, the lump sum payment is treated like salary. Deductions from the total will include federal income tax at the 28 percent rate, applicable state and local taxes, the Medicare hospital insurance tax. If the retiree is covered by FERS or CSRS-Offset, Social Security tax will also be withheld.

Taxability of Retirement Income—All retirement annuities are treated as ordinary income in the year they are received. However, a small portion of an annuity is non-taxable. Additional information is contained in IRS Publication 721, Comprehensive Tax Guide to U.S. Civil Service Retirement Benefits. To obtain a copy of the IRS publication, call 1-800-TAX-FORM (1-800-829-3676).

Disposition of Thrift Savings Plan (TSP) Account Balance—All those who leave government service have full entitlement to all their TSP contributions and related earnings. They will be provided a full range of withdrawal options at separation.

Potential Consequences of Early Retirement—Those who retire early may be more attractive to a prospective employer. For one thing, since they have an income from retirement, they can be more flexible in negotiating a salary. In addition, if they continue to carry their health and life insurance, the employer won't have to pick up that cost.

Employees who are eligible for optional retirement because they have completed a full career, still may choose to go out on a DSR, if that option is available. While the amount of annuity will be the same, there is an advantage in taking a DSR if they return to the federal service. Their annuity will simply stop and they will begin earning a regular salary. When they retire again, their annuity will be computed on their total years of service and what is often a larger "high-3" years of average salary.

Employees who go out on an early voluntary retirement and return to work for the federal government will have their salary reduced by the amount of their annuity. Their full annuity will resume once they leave government. In addition, they may be eligible for either an annuity supplement or a recomputed annuity, depending on the amount of time they worked. (See Chapter 4.)

While the annuity of those taking early retirement will stop if they return to work for the federal government, it will continue in full if they go to work for the private sector, or for a state or local government.

On the other hand, the annuities of employees who are involuntarily separated and return to work for the federal government will be terminated. When the annuity stops, the individual has the same status as any other federal employee in an equivalent position and with a similar service history. In general, when such employees again leave government service, their annuities will be reinstated, unless they are entitled to an immediate or deferred annuity based on the new separation.

Note: An employee who works more than one year, but does not meet the age and service requirements for an immediate annuity, may only get a deferred annuity.

Advantages and Disadvantages of Early Retirement

Although employees who meet the age and service requirements may not need to take an early retirement, it could be to their advantage to do so. For instance, they will receive an annuity payment every month for the rest of their lives. Their annuities will be increased by a cost-of-living-adjustment (COLA) once a year. In addition, if they have been enrolled in the FEHB program for five years before retirement (or from their first opportunity to enroll), they will receive the

same health insurance coverage at the same cost as when they were employed. The same is true for life insurance under FEGLI.

There also are potential downsides to taking an early retirement. Obviously, employees who don't complete a full career won't receive a full retirement benefit. As a result, their annuity may be insufficient to meet their needs, especially if they have no expectation of further employment.

Further, CSRS employees under age 55 will have their annuity permanently reduced for every month they are under that age. That's one-sixth of one percent per month or 2 percent per year. There is no reduction under FERS. However, those who transferred to FERS and will receive a combined CSRS and FERS annuity, will have that reduction imposed on the CSRS retirement portion.

Regardless of whether an individual retires voluntarily or under a DSR, his or her spouse will be entitled to a survivor annuity. A full survivor annuity for CSRS survivors is 55 percent of the basic, unreduced annuity. For FERS it is 50 percent.

While an individual may choose to provide a reduced annuity for the spouse, it may only be done if the spouse consents to the reduction in writing. Further, the spouse's signature must be notarized. (See Retirement Annuities and Survivor Benefits.)

A former spouse also may be eligible for a survivor annuity if the marriage was dissolved on or after May 7, 1985, and a qualifying court order is on file with OPM awarding the benefit.

Applying for Early Retirement

Employees who are eligible for an optional, early voluntary or discontinued service annuity should fill out an *Application for Immediate Retirement* (Standard Form 2801 under CSRS, SF 3107 under FERS) and file it with the appropriate office of their agency.

Section 6—Disability Retirement

General Description

This section discusses the benefit rights of federal and postal workers covered by CSRS or FERS who become unable to continue in their federal or postal positions because of the onset of a disabling condition.

Under both CSRS and FERS, benefits are payable to federal and postal employees no longer able to perform in their positions. Because federal and postal workers are hired from a register of qualified applicants, and because they must serve a probationary period before attaining career status, a worker exhibiting an inability to perform in his/her position (or for other vacant positions at the same grade or pay level) is assumed to be disabled for federal or postal service, even though that worker might be able to hold some other job. This "occupational" definition of disability is different than that used by Social Security.

Under Social Security's rules, a worker is not eligible for benefits as a result of the loss of a job due to the inability to perform due to a disabling condition. Instead, to qualify for disability benefits under Social Security, a worker generally must be no longer able to work in any job because of a disability. This additional distinction of "total and permanent" disability means that federal or postal workers covered under FERS have the additional protections provided by Social Security to individuals dependent upon the wages of a worker who becomes totally and permanently disabled.

Eligibility Rules for Disability Retirement

Federal employees must meet the following conditions to be eligible for disability retirement:

• CSRS employees must have completed at least five years of creditable federal civilian service, while FERS employees must have completed at least 18 months of federal civilian service that is creditable under FERS.

• You must, while employed in a position subject to the CSRS or FERS, have become so disabled that you are prevented from performing useful and efficient service in your current position. (Useful and efficient service means fully successful performance of the critical or essential elements of the position—or the ability to perform at that level—and satisfactory conduct and attendance.)

• The disability must be expected to last at least one year.

• Your agency must certify that it is unable to accommodate your disabling medical condition in your present position and that it has considered you for any vacant position in the same agency, at the same grade or pay level, and within the same commuting area, for which you are qualified for reassignment. (An employee of the Postal Service is considered not qualified for reassignment if the reassignment is to a position in a different craft or is inconsistent with the terms of a collective bargaining agreement covering the employee.)

• You, or your guardian or other interested person, must apply for disability retirement before your separation from service or within one year afterward. The application must be received by OPM within one year of the date of your separation. This time limit can be waived only in instances involving incompetence.

• If you are a National Guard Technician being separated from your position because of a disability that disqualifies you from membership in the National Guard or from holding the military grade required for your employment, special provisions may apply. Contact your employing agency for the necessary information.

• If covered by FERS, you must apply for Social Security disability benefits. OPM must receive a receipt or notice of approval or disapproval of disability benefits from the Social Security Administration before any disability annuity benefits can be paid. If the application for Social Security disability benefits is withdrawn for any reason, OPM will dismiss the FERS disability retirement application upon notification by the SSA.

The general requirement that an employee must have within the two-year period preceding separation from service, completed at least one year of civilian service subject to retirement deductions to be eligible for an annuity is not applicable in the case of an employee retiring due to disability. (See 5 USC 8333(b).)

In general, the employee must make application for disability retirement; however, there are instances where the employing agency has an obligation to file an application on behalf of the employee. The agency must file a disability application when all of the following conditions exist:

• The agency has medical documentation that shows that a disease or an injury prevents the employee from performing successfully in his or her current position, or in any other vacant position in the agency, at the same grade or pay level and tenure in the commuting area for which the employee is qualified for reassignment.

• The agency has issued a decision to remove the employee because of deficient performance, conduct, or attendance.

• The employee is institutionalized or,

based on a review of medical and other documentation, the agency concludes that the employee is unable to file the application.

• The employee has no personal representative or guardian.

• No immediate family member is willing to file the disability retirement application on behalf of the employee.

Time Limits and Appeal Rights

If the application is made by the agency, it must be filed with the Office of Personnel Management before the employee is separated from the service. If it is made by the employee, guardian, or some other interested person, it must be made before the worker's separation from service or within one year thereafter. This time limit may be waived in certain cases involving incompetence.

For CSRS employees, Standard Form 2801, Application for Immediate Retirement, is used in making application for disability retirement; for FERS employees, form SF3107 is used. In addition, both CSRS and FERS employees must document the disability on a Standard Form 3112.

Based on its examination of the submitted documents, the Office of Personnel Management decides whether a disability retirement is warranted. Generally, applicants have the burden of proving that they meet all of the requirements for disability retirement and are responsible for insuring that all documents are submitted within time limits. However, in the case of employees who have been removed for physical inability to perform, there is a presumption that the worker meets the requirements for disability retirement.

If OPM denies the application, the employee can ask for reconsideration by submitting a written and signed request. The request must be received by OPM within 30 days of the issuance of the initial decision. The applicant may submit additional medical or other information at the reconsideration stage. OPM then reevaluates the decision taking any additional information into account.

A final denial of an application by OPM can be appealed to the Merit Systems Protection Board within 35 days of the reconsideration decision. The MSPB hearing officer reviews the case and issues a written decision

based on the preponderance of the evidence. The applicant can then appeal to the three-member Board and from there to the U.S. Court of Appeals for the Federal Circuit.

Disability Determination Process

The agency should render every assistance to the employee in completing the application by helping the employee to select the type of annuity best suited to his or her circumstances, explaining the effect of making deposit or redeposit, obtaining the necessary statement from the employee's supervisor or manager, explaining the requirement of a physician's statement, and getting a statement from the employee to accompany the application showing any unverified prior service with other agencies. Employees insured under the Federal Employees Group Life Insurance law who retire on account of disability may retain basic life insurance coverage as an annuitant only if they have been insured for the five years of service immediately preceding retirement or the full period(s) of service during which the basic life insurance was available (if less than five years). Also, employees who retire on account of disability may continue their health benefits enrollment into retirement if they have been enrolled (or covered as a family member) under the Federal Employees Health Benefits program for the five years of service immediately preceding retirement (or their entire period of service since their first opportunity to enroll).

In certain cases, retiring employees may be eligible for waivers of the general FEHB five-year participation requirement. (See Chapter 2 for rules covering these benefits.)

In general, employees eligible for benefits under the Federal Employees' Compensation Act (i.e., workers' compensation system) and the civil service retirement law may choose whichever benefits work to their advantage.

As noted above, before you can be considered eligible for disability retirement benefits, you must have five years of creditable civilian service under CSRS (or 18 months under FERS). Then, your employing agency must determine that you are not qualified for reassignment to any other vacant position within your agency and your commuting area at the same grade or pay level of the position you currently occupy. In addition, you or someone acting for you must file an application for disability retirement with OPM either before you leave federal service or within one year after you leave. This time limit can be waived only when an employee is mentally incompetent upon leaving the federal service or becomes mentally incompetent within one year after leaving. In such a situation, the application will be accepted by OPM if filed within one year from the date the employee is restored to competency or a guardian is appointed, whichever is earlier.

You are "disabled" when the information submitted indicates that there is a deficiency, caused by disease, injury, or illness, of sufficient degree to preclude useful and efficient service. "Useful and efficient service" means (1) either acceptable performance of the critical or essential elements of the position or the ability to perform at that level; and (2) satisfactory conduct and attendance. Service that is not "useful and efficient" is a level of performance or attendance which, if it were to continue, would warrant denial of a within-grade increase, demotion, separation, or other remedial action.

If you refuse reassignment to a position at the same grade or pay level in the same commuting area, your refusal terminates the agency's obligation to identify any other vacant position and may disqualify you from further consideration for disability retirement.

A claim for disability retirement must include documentation that clearly and specifically establishes:

• a deficiency in service with respect to performance, conduct, or attendance, or in the absence of any actual service deficiency, a showing that the medical condition is incompatible with either useful service or retention in the position;

• a medical condition defined as a disease or an injury caused the service deficiency;

• the duration of the medical condition, both past and expected, and a showing that the condition, in all probability, will continue for at least a year;

• inability to render useful and efficient service arose while serving in covered employment;

• inability of employing agency to make reasonable accommodation to the medical condition; and

• the absence of another position, within the employing agency and commuting area, at the same grade or pay level and tenure, to which the employee is qualified for reassignment.

Your agency will provide assistance in obtaining the required forms to obtain statements from your supervisors and attending physicians and proof that your condition prevents you from performing useful and efficient service. If you are found to be disabled as outlined above, you will be allowed to retire on disability. Up to the age of 60, you will be subject to periodic medical reevaluations to determine whether the disabling condition continues to exist, and an annual review of your earnings to make an official determination of whether you are "restored to earning capacity."

An individual's status as an employee is not affected by the act of his or her agency in applying for the employee's disability retirement. Pending decision on the application, the employment status is determined under the normal rules relating to employees.

Unless the employee has already been separated, the OPM will notify the agency of the action of allowance or disallowance of the claim. If disability retirement has been allowed, the agency should take the proper steps to effect the separation.

Periodic Medical Examinations

Unless the OPM determines that the disability is permanent in character, a disability annuitant must undergo periodic medical reevaluation until reaching age 60. If an annuitant fails to submit to a required medical examination, payment of his or her annuity is suspended until continuance of the disability is established satisfactorily. A finding of permanent disability normally eliminates the necessity for such examinations (unless special circumstances warrant such a requirement)..

CSRS Disability Computations

A CSRS-covered disability retiree is entitled to an "earned" annuity computed under the general formula. However, the law guarantees a minimum annuity to employees who retire because of disability. If the "earned" annuity is less than the guaranteed minimum, the minimum generally becomes the basic annuity.

The guaranteed minimum is not a fixed amount but varies from one employee to another, depending on age, service, and average salary. It is the lesser of the following:

• 40 percent of the employee's "high-3" average salary; or

• the amount obtained under the general formula after increasing the actual creditable service by the time remaining from the commencing date of annuity to the date of the employee's 60th birthday.

Most employees under age 60 who retire on disability are entitled to guaranteed minimum annuities. The guaranteed minimum annuity formula gives no advantage to an employee who has reached the age of 60, since the general annuity computation formula will be applied if a larger annuity would result. However, employees who are in receipt of military retired or retainer pay or compensation from the Department of Veterans Affairs in lieu of retired or retainer pay are not eligible for the guaranteed minimum disability annuity. (This limitation on benefits does not apply to military retired pay awarded on account of a service-connected disability incurred in combat with an enemy of the United States or caused by an instrumentality of war and incurred in line of duty during a period of war as defined by section 301 of Title 38; or to retired pay awarded under Chapter 67 of Title 10 (reserve retirement)).

The following examples, which relate to the accompanying "Minimum Guaranteed Disability Retirement Table," illustrate the basic points of computing disability retirement annuities.

1. John E. Jones, five years service, age 45, average salary $18,000.
   Actual service—5 years
   Years to age 60—15 years
   Total—20 years
   Guaranteed disability retirement annuity—$6,525 per year.

2. Pete X. Smith, 20 years service, age 50, average salary $24,000.
   Actual service—20 years
   Years to age 60—10 Years
   Total—30 years
   Guaranteed disability retirement annuity—$9,600 per year.

3. Jane V. Doe, 25 years service, age 50, Average salary $32,000.
   Actual service—25 years

Years to age 60—10 years
Total—35 years
Guaranteed disability retirement annuity—$12,800 per year.
Actual Earned Annuity, 25 years service—$14,800 (the amount to be paid).

Enhanced Benefits—Because of a court decision, Pitsker and Rogers v. Office of Personnel Management, 234 F.3d 1378 (Fed. Cir. 2000), OPM in 2002 began allowing enhanced disability annuities for CSRS disability annuitants and their survivors where the disability annuitant performed at least 20 years of law enforcement officer or firefighter service.

FERS Disability Computations

Disability benefits under FERS are computed differently depending on the retiree's age and amount of service at retirement. In addition, FERS disability retirement benefits are recomputed after the first twelve months and again at age 62, if the annuitant is under age 62 at the time of disability retirement.

If at disability retirement you are already 62 years old, or you meet the age and service requirements for immediate voluntary retirement, you will receive your "earned" annuity based on the general FERS annuity computation—i.e., 1 percent of your "high-3" average salary multiplied by your years and months of service. If you are at least 62 years old at retirement and have completed at least 20 years of service, your annuity will be computed as 1.1 percent of your high-3 average salary multiplied by your years and months of service.

If at disability retirement you are under age 62 and not eligible for voluntary retirement, you will receive the following benefit:

(1) For the first 12 months—60 percent of your high-3 average salary, minus 100 percent of any Social Security disability benefits.

(2) After the first 12 months—40 percent of your high-3 average salary, minus 60 percent of any Social Security disability benefits. (Note: You are entitled to your earned annuity—1 percent of your high-3 average salary multiplied by your years and months of service—if it is larger than your disability annuity computed under either of the previously mentioned formulas.)

(3) When you reach age 62—The FERS disability benefit is again recomputed. An

Minimum Guaranteed Disability Retirement Annuity Table

Lesser of: 40% of high-3-year average pay or computed amount based on years of service plus years to age 60; actual earned annuity if greater.

High 3-Year Average Salary		If service to date *plus* number of years to age 60 equals- TOTAL YEARS OF SERVICE					
Full Amount	40%	10	15	20	25	30	35
15,000	6,000	2,438	3,938	5,438			
16,000	6,400	2,600	4,200	5,800			
17,000	6,800	2,763	4,463	6,163			
18,000	7,200	2,925	4,725	6,525			
19,000	7,600	3,088	4,988	6,888			
20,000	8,000	3,250	5,250	7,250			
21,000	8,400	3,413	5,513	7,613			
22,000	8,880	3,575	5,775	7,975	22 YEARS AND		
23,000	9,200	3,738	6,038	8,338			
24,000	9,600	3,900	6,300	8,700	OVER		
25,000	10,000	4,063	6,563	9,063			
26,000	10,400	4,225	6,825	9,425			
27,000	10,800	4,388	7,088	9,788	SAME AS		
28,000	11,200	4,550	7,350	10,150			
29,000	11,600	4,713	7,613	10,513	40% OF		
30,000	12,000	4,875	7,875	10,575			
31,000	12,400	5,038	8,138	11,238	HIGH 3-YEAR		
32,000	12,800	5,200	8,400	11,600			
33,000	13,200	5,363	8,663	11,963			
34,000	13,600	5,525	8,925	12,325	AVERAGE		
35,000	14,000	5,688	9,188	12,688			
36,000	14,400	5,850	9,450	13,050	SALARY		
37,000	14,500	6,013	9,713	13,413			
38,000	15,200	6,175	9,975	13,775	OR ACTUAL		
39,000	15,600	6,338	10,238	14,138			
40,000	16,000	6,500	10,500	14,500	EARNED		
41,000	16,400	6,663	10,763	14,863			
42,000	16,800	6,825	11,025	15,225			
43,000	17,200	6,988	11,288	15,588	ANNUITY		
44,000	17,600	7,150	11,550	15,950			
45,000	18,000	7,313	11,813	16,313	I F		
46,000	18,400	7,475	12,075	16,675			
47,000	18,800	7,638	12,338	17,038	GREATER		
48,000	19,200	7,800	12,600	17,400			
50,000	20,000	8,125	13,125	18,125			
55,000	22,000	8,938	14,438	19,938			
60,000	24,000	9,750	15,750	21,750			
65,000	26,000	10,563	17,063	23,563			
66,000	26,400	10,725	17,325	23,925			
68,000	27,200	11,050	17,850	24,650			
70,000	28,000	11,375	18,375	25,375			

Note the following conclusions from the above table:

A. Up to 22 years service (actual plus years to age 60) the computed annuity generally is the minimum guaranteed annuity and would apply.

B. After approximately 22 years of service (actual plus years to age 60) your minimum guaranteed annuity is based on 40% of the 3-year high average pay.C. However, if actual earned service exceeds 22 years, then such actual service computed in the regular manner, without further adjustments, would be the applicable formula to your advantage.

artificial retirement benefit is calculated for the retiree, assuming the retiree worked to age 62. Thus, actual service is added to the time spent on the disability rolls to age 62. The total time is then multiplied by 1 percent. The total percentage amount is multiplied by the high 3 average salary existing at the onset of disability increased by all FERS cost of living adjustments payable from that time to age 62.

From the second year forward, the FERS disability benefit is indexed by the FERS cost of living formula, which generally reflects the change in the Consumer Price Index minus one percentage point.

Due to the intertwining of FERS and Social Security, applicants for disability benefits under the FERS program also are required to apply for Social Security disability benefits. The government cannot pay any FERS benefits, even interim payments pending final adjudication of the claim, until the Office of Personnel Management receives proof of a Social Security disability application.

Social Security Disability

Social Security applies a stricter definition of disability than does federal retirement: you must be so severely disabled that you cannot perform any substantial gainful work, and the disability is expected to last at least one year or to result in death. Benefits do not begin until after a five-month waiting period. Social Security disability benefits continue until the beneficiary dies or converts to Social Security retirement at age 65, or until SSA determines that the beneficiary is no longer eligible due to earned income (the earning thresholds vary by type of disability but overall are very low) or improvement in the medical condition. SSA conducts "continuing disability reviews" at least once every three years on beneficiaries whose medical improvement is possible or expected; where medical improvement is not expected, they are conducted every seven years.

The Social Security Administration sometimes awards disability benefits after the individual has begun receiving FERS disability annuity payments. In these cases, the annuitant should notify OPM of the monthly Social Security benefit and the effective date of the payments. Overpayments sometimes occur when

OPM does not know an annuitant has been awarded a retroactive Social Security benefit after being placed in a payment status under FERS. The annuitant would have to pay back any overpayment to OPM. Thus, applicants should forward to OPM an application receipt or notice of allowance or disallowance from SSA as soon as it is received.

The individual should apply for Social Security disability benefits close to his or her last day of pay, which is the last day of work for Social Security purposes. Individuals on annual, sick or donated leave are considered still in a pay status. Those who apply to SSA too early while still in a work status likely will be denied a benefit because of their substantial gainful work. In that situation, the individual would have to reapply once ending work and submit evidence of the new SSA application to OPM.

Individuals should apply for Social Security disability benefits, not Supplemental Security Income (SSI).

Applicants also should take care to report information regarding benefits received from the Office of Workers Compensation Programs due to a job-related illness or injury. OPM needs this information because law prohibits the receipt of both a FERS annuity and compensation for total or partial disability under the Federal Employees Compensation Act.

Survivor Benefits

CSRS Rules—A survivor annuity is calculated in the same way as it is for any other retiree—typically, 55 percent of the amount of the annuity before reduction for a survivor benefit election, although lower amounts can be elected. If you are single and have no dependent children or former spouse eligible for benefits, there would be no monthly survivor annuity benefit payable. In this case, a lump sum of your retirement contributions would be paid to your survivors under the order of precedence.

Survivor benefits of CSRS-Offset employees may be subject to an offset equal to the value of the offset service in the Social Security survivor benefit. The offset only applies if the survivor is eligible for Social Security benefits based on your employment.

FERS Rules—If you were married and

worked for the federal government for at least 18 months, your surviving spouse may receive a lump sum payment. The lump sum payment (which is called the basic employee death benefit) is an amount equal to one half of your annual pay rate at death or one half of your high-3 average pay, plus an annually-indexed lump-sum amount.

If you had 10 years of federal service, your surviving spouse may also qualify for a monthly survivor benefit. The amount of a survivor annuity depends on the age of the disability retiree who died. If death occurred after age 62, the annuity is computed the same as it would be for the survivor of any other retiree; i.e., 50 or 25 percent (whichever the couple elected) of the amount of the annuity before reduction for a survivor benefit election. If the retiree died before age 62, a special computation is used in which the retiree's earned annuity is increased by the amount of time between retirement and age 62 and the average salary is increased by annual inflation adjustments the annuitant received. The survivor then receives either 50 or 25 percent of that amount as an annuity.

If you die after completing 18 months of civil service, your dependent children may also receive a survivor annuity benefit if they are not receiving Social Security benefits.

Social Security Rules—Social Security may pay survivor benefits to your surviving spouse and dependent children. For your spouse to qualify for benefits, he or she must be age 60, or between the ages of 50 and 59 and disabled, or any age and caring for a child under age 16 or a disabled child. Children may qualify for benefits if they are under age 18 (or under age 19, if in high school) or disabled. Dependent parents and former spouses may also qualify for survivor benefits. The amount of the benefit depends on your Social Security earnings and the number of survivors eligible for benefits. The Social Security spousal benefit may be reduced if the survivor is eligible for benefits based on his or her own employment and that employment was not covered by Social Security (such as employment under CSRS).

A lump sum of $255 is payable to your surviving spouse provided the two of you were living together at the time of your death or he/she is entitled to survivor benefits. If there is no surviving spouse, the lump sum is paid to children who are eligible for benefits. Otherwise, the lump sum is not payable.

Recovery or Restoration of Earning Capacity

After a disability retirement is approved, the Office of Personnel Management may periodically review eligibility for continued payments. Any disability annuitant under age 60 may have his or her eligibility reviewed at any time OPM considers it necessary.

OPM contacts the annuitant and requests a current report from his or her physician concerning the status of the medical condition on which the retirement was based. OPM also asks for information regarding current employment status. Those who do not respond to such notices can have their annuities suspended. Therefore, it is important that OPM be kept current on any changes in mailing addresses. You may do this by phone or e-mail, or by sending notification of address changes to OPM, Change of Address Section, P.O. Box 440, Boyers, PA 16017-0440. Include the retirement claim number (CSA number).

The annuitant is responsible for paying any expenses involved in answering OPM's request for medical evidence.

Annuitants who are over age 60 can be found recovered from a disability, but only if they specifically request a review of their own eligibility. The annuitant must furnish OPM with medical evidence showing recovery from the disability.

An annuity will be discontinued at the end of one year from the date of a medical examination or report showing recovery, or upon reemployment in the federal government, whichever comes first.

If you are under age 60, your disability annuity will be discontinued if OPM determines that you are able to earn a certain level of income. Each year, OPM sends a questionnaire to disability annuitants under age 60 to determine their earnings for the previous year. OPM verifies reported earnings with the IRS. All disability annuitants under age 60 are required to complete the survey form, which normally is mailed early in the year. Failure to respond can result in suspension of the annuity.

Under both CSRS and FERS, earning capacity is considered restored if, in any one calendar year, the annuitant's income from wages and self-employment is at least 80 percent of the current rate of base pay for the position from which he or she retired. That rate is calculated as of December 31 of the year for which the income is being compared. Base pay for this purpose includes the amount of pay subject to retirement deductions, including locality pay and certain types of premium pay. It does not include bonuses, allowances, overtime pay and various differentials.

If, before reaching age 60, a disability annuitant recovers, or is restored to earning capacity, his or her annuity payments will be continued temporarily to afford an opportunity to seek reemployment. In cases of restoration of earning capacity, disability annuity payments are ended six months from the end of the calendar year in which income exceeded the 80 percent earnings limitation, or upon reemployment with the federal government, whichever comes first. In cases of recovery, benefits end one year from the date of a medical exam showing recovery. OPM notifies annuitants in advance of the decision to stop payments, including information on eligibility for any other benefits. Generally, terminations and suspensions of benefits are effective July 1 of each year.

If an annuitant who is found to be recovered or restored to earning capacity is not reemployed in the government in a position under either retirement system, he or she shall be considered, except for service credit purposes, as involuntarily separated from the service as of the date the annuity was discontinued. Such annuitants will be entitled to discontinued-service retirement or deferred retirement if either is applicable in the individual's case.

A disability annuity can be reinstated at the same rate in effect when it was terminated under the following conditions:

• If the annuity stopped because of an individual's restored earning capacity, it can be reinstated effective at the beginning of the year following any calendar year in which earning capacity fell below the 80 percent figure, provided that the medical condition on which the disability was approved still exists, the annuitant was not reemployed in the federal service, was not medically recovered, and is not age 62 or older. Those age 62 or older may be entitled to a deferred annuity.

• If the annuity stopped because of an individual's recovery from disability, it may be reinstated as of the date of a current medical exam showing the disability has recurred and that the condition is worse than at the date of recovery, provided the annuitant was not reemployed in the federal service, was not restored to earning capacity, and is not age 62 or older. Those age 62 or older would be entitled to a deferred annuity.

Federal Reemployment Rules

Disability retirees whose medical condition has improved may apply for reemployment with the federal government for any position for which they are qualified. The law does not require the former employing agency or any other agency to offer a position. However, those found to be recovered or restored to earning capacity may be eligible for a job referral under the Interagency Career Transition Assistance Plan, which gives eligible individuals priority for vacancies over other candidates from outside the agency. The selection priority lasts one year from the date of an OPM letter determining medical recovery or restoration to earning capacity.

Disability annuities can continue after reemployment only under certain conditions:

• Those under age 60 who are reemployed in either a position of different tenure or at a lower salary rate from the position from which they retired can have their annuities continued, but their salaries will be reduced by the amount of the annuity, and the 80 percent earnings limitation remains in effect. The earnings figure used in such calculations is the gross salary for the position, not the reduced amount being received. (Those under age 60 who are reemployed in a position similar in tenure and pay from the position from which they retired will be deemed to be recovered from their disability and their annuity payments will stop.)

• Those reemployed at age 60 or above will have their annuity payments continue, but their salary will be reduced by the amount of the annuity. There is no limitation on the amount of earnings someone aged 60 and above can receive.

Disability annuitants must tell the agency in which they are seeking reemployment that they are disability annuitants. Those who become reemployed must notify the OPM Retirement Operations Center, Boyers, PA, 16017.

Taxation of Disability Benefits

Under current law, there is no federal tax benefit unless the taxpayer is totally disabled for all gainful employment. Since OPM's decision on your application must be based only on whether you are disabled for your current position, or a vacant position of equal grade or pay, a finding of disability by OPM may not meet the Internal Revenue Service's criteria for a tax-exempt benefit. If your application is based partly on the belief that civil service disability retirement will result in a tax advantage, you should check with your local Internal Revenue office for current tax information.

Section 7—Alternative Form of Annuity: Lump-Sum Benefit

General Description

From its inception in 1986, the "Alternative Form of Annuities" provision allowed workers entering retirement to receive a payment equal to the value of the contributions they made to the retirement program over their careers. (During the first two years of the provision, the lump sums were paid in one payment. During the last years, the lump sums were paid in two installments, except in the case of individuals with life-threatening conditions, who continued to receive it as one payment.)

Public Law 103-66 eliminated the lump-sum option as of October 1, 1994, for everyone except those who have life-threatening conditions resulting in a life expectancy of less than two years and who are not taking disability retirement. The following medical conditions provide prima facie evidence of life-threatening afflictions or critical medical conditions for the purposes of qualifying for a lump-sum payment:

Metastatic and/or inoperable neoplasms, aortic stenosis (severe), class IV cardiac disease with congestive heart failure, respiratory failure, corpulmonale with respiratory failure, emphysema with respiratory failure, severe cardiomyopathy-class IV, aplastic anemia, uncontrolled hypertension with hypertensive encephalopathy, cardiac aneurysm not amenable to surgical treatment, agranulocytosis, severe hepatic failure, severe Hypoxic brain damage, severe portal hypertension with esophageal varices, AIDS (active, not AIDS-Related Complex or only seropositivity), life-threatening infections (encephalitis, meningitis, rabies, etc.), scleroderma with severe esophageal involvement, amyotrophic lateral sclerosis (rapidly progressive), hemiplegia with life-threatening complications and quadriplegia with life-threatening complications.

If a medical condition other than those listed above is claimed, OPM will review the physician's certification to determine whether the cited condition is life-threatening.

In exchange for the lump-sum payment, the law requires that the recipient's monthly annuity be reduced so that the present value of the benefits received under this alternative is the same as the present value of the annuity they would have otherwise received.

The reduction is pegged to an individual's age at retirement and is based on life-expectancy tables and assumptions about the future of the economy known as "present value factors." This is true even though the only people now eligible for the Alternative Form of Annuity are those whose life expectancy is short. The sum used to compute subsequent retirement benefits under the Alternative Form of Annuity is equal to the employee's total contributions to FERS or CSRS, without interest.

Following is an example of how such a lump-sum payment is computed for an eligible CSRS employee retiring at age 55 with 30 years of service and a total contribution of $34,160. In this case, the lump-sum payment will reduce the amount of the monthly annuity received during retirement. The employee's initial or basic annuity computed from the CSRS formula would be $23,513 per year, which amounts to $1,959 per month. The actuarial adjustment made to the monthly annuity to take into consideration the lump-sum payment is dependent on the retiree's age. For example:

Age: 55
Actuarial adjustment
(present value factor): 221.4
Monthly annuity (initial): $1,959

Present Value Factors

Present value factors apply to retirees who elect to provide survivor annuity benefits to a spouse based on post-retirement marriage and to retiring employees who elect the alternative form of annuity, owe certain redeposits based on refunds of contributions for service before October 1, 1990, or elect to credit certain service with non-appropriated fund instrumentalities.

Age	Value Factor		Age	Value Factor	
	CSRS	FERS		CSRS	FERS
40	280.4	176.8	66	157.7	148.0
41	276.4	176.3	67	153.0	143.8
42	272.7	175.9	68	148.1	139.5
43	268.8	175.4	69	143.2	135.2
44	264.1	174.6	70	138.3	130.8
45	259.0	173.5	71	133.4	126.5
46	254.0	172.5	72	128.6	122.1
47	249.3	171.8	73	123.5	117.5
48	244.8	171.0	74	118.4	112.9
49	239.3	169.8	75	113.1	108.1
50	233.8	168.6	76	107.9	103.4
51	229.5	168.2	77	102.6	98.4
52	225.4	168.0	78	97.9	94.1
53	221.0	167.8	79	93.4	90.0
54	216.2	167.3	80	88.5	85.4
55	221.4	167.0	81	83.4	80.6
56	206.6	166.7	82	78.4	75.9
57	201.9	166.6	83	73.8	71.6
58	197.2	166.7	84	69.4	67.4
59	192.5	166.8	85	64.6	62.9
60	187.9	167.3	86	60.3	58.7
61	183.1	167.7	87	57.1	55.7
62	177.9	165.8	88	54.6	53.3
63	172.9	161.3	89	51.9	50.8
64	167.8	156.9	90	48.7	47.7
65	162.5	152.3			

Reduction ($34,160 divided by 221.4) = $154.30

Yields adjusted monthly annuity: $1,804.70

The reduction also takes into consideration the election of survivor benefits:

Monthly annuity (initial computation, reduced for survivor annuity): $1,785.97

Reduction ($34,160 divided by 221.4) = $154.30

Yields adjusted monthly annuity with survivor benefits: $1,631.67

IRA Rollovers

Lump-sum distributions received after January 1, 1993, may be "rolled over" into IRA accounts. Recipients should arrange a direct account-to-account transfer to avoid the 20 percent federal tax withholding that otherwise would apply.

Section 8—Specific Annuity Rules Applying to Special Groups

CSRS Special Group Rules

Law Enforcement and Firefighter Personnel—If you are an employee whose duties are primarily in the following categories:

• The investigation, apprehension, or detention of persons suspected or convicted of offenses against the criminal laws of the United States, or

• The control and extinguishment of fires or the maintenance of fire fighting apparatus and equipment, you may voluntarily retire if you are age 50 or over, and have completed at least 20 years of such service. Retirement is mandatory at age 57 with at least 20 years of such service. Agency heads are authorized, in the public interest, to except employees from mandatory retirement until age 60. Employee and agency contributions to the Civil Service Retirement and Disability Fund are 7.5 percent.

The basic annuity of an employee who retires under the special provision for law enforcement and/or firefighter personnel is figured by taking 2 1/2 percent of the "high-3" average pay and multiplying the result by 20 years of law enforcement and/or firefighter service, plus 2 percent of the high-3 average pay multiplied by all service over 20 years (including credit for sick leave). Also, they take no cut in annuity for retiring under age 55. Public Law 92-297 extended this provision to air traffic controllers and P.L. 100-92 to flight service station specialists.

Air Traffic Controllers—Effective May 16, 1972, an air traffic controller must be separated from the service on the last day of the month in which he or she becomes age 56. However, the law does not apply to a person appointed as an air traffic controller by the Department of Transportation before May 16, 1972, or by the Department of Defense before September 12, 1980. Air traffic controllers are entitled to optional retirement at age 50 with 20 years as ATC or any age with 25 years as ATC. An ATC retiring under this provision is guaranteed an annuity of no less than 50 percent of his or her high-3 average pay.

Retirement of Legislative Officials and Employees—Members of Congress and employees of the Congress, being elective or appointive officials and employees in the legislative branch of the federal government, are included within the civil service retirement system if they so choose and under certain circumstances. In most respects the system's provisions for members of Congress and congressional employees parallel those for federal employees generally, but there are these major differences.

Except for personnel of the Architect of the Capitol and of the Botanical Garden, they are not automatically covered under the system as are other federal personnel. They become subject to the obligations and benefits of the system only if and when they file written elections to do so. The payroll reduction rate for members of Congress is 8.5 percent of salary (CSRS) and 1.8 (FERS). The deduction rate for congressional employees will be one-half percent lower.

Their civil service annuities are computed under a special modification of the standard annuity formula, in each instance, as follows:

• Member of Congress: A member retiring with at least five years of service as a member, as congressional employee, or both, and with his or her last five years' civilian service covered by deductions or deposit, is afforded a basic annuity computed as 2 1/2 percent of high-3 average salary and multiplied by years of member service, military service (for which not receiving retired pay) performed while on leave of absence as member during war or national emergency, other military service (for which not receiving retired pay) up to five years, and congressional employee service. The basic annuity may not exceed 80 percent of the final salary.

• Congressional employee: A congressional employee, with at least five years of service in that capacity, or as a member of Congress, or both, and with his or her last five years' civilian service covered by deductions or deposit, retiring from the congressional employee position or from any position wherein he or she is subject to the Retirement System, is afforded basic annuity consisting of: 2.5 percent of high-3 average salary and multiply by years of all congressional employee service plus creditable military service not exceeding five years; and any prior service as member of Congress. The basic annuity may not exceed 80 percent of high-3 average salary, except if the additional percentage is produced by unused sick leave.

Congressional staff and members of Congress are able to designate survivor benefits under the same rules and reductions as are available to other employees covered by the program. However, members of Congress who die between leaving office and becoming eligible for retirement benefits leave their survivors with entitlement rights as if they were eligible for retirement on the day of their deaths, provided that they have not withdrawn their contributions to the program.

CSRS/FERS Benefits at a Glance

Provision	Civil Service Retirement System (CSRS)	Federal Employees Retirement System (FERS)
Basic Annuity: Retirement		
Basic plan design	Defined benefit	Defined benefit not "integrated," i.e., it is fully added to Social Security
Required employee retirement contributions	7.0% retirement contribution plus 1.45% Medicare on all pay	Social Security tax (6.2% FICA on pay up to $87,000, plus 1.45% Medicare on all pay) plus 0.8% retirement contribution
Vesting (retirement)	5 yrs. for retirement	Same as CSRS
Salary base	Avg. of high-3 yrs. salary	Same as CSRS
Retirement benefit (accrual rate)	1.5% x first 5 yrs. of service; 1.75% x second 5 yrs. of service; 2.0% x yrs. of service beyond 10	High-3 years average salary formula times 1%, times years of service, or 1.1% at age 62 with 20 years of service
Unreduced retirement benefits	Age 55 with 30 yrs. of service; age 60 with 20 yrs. of service; age 62 with 5 yrs. of service	Age 62 and 5 yrs. of service; age 60 and 20 yrs. of service; or "minimum retirement age" (MRA) plus 30 years. MRA = 1987-2002, age 55; 2002-2008, increases 2 mos. per yr., 2009-2020, age 56; 2021-2026 increases 2 mos. per yr.; 2027 and after, age 57.
Reduced retirement benefits	N/A	MRA and 10 yrs. of service. Reduced by 5% for yrs. under age 62
Optional (RIFs or re-organizations) or involuntary early retirement; age and reductions	Age 50 with 20 yrs. of service; any age with 25 yrs. of service. Benefit reduced 2.0% for each yr. under age 55	Unreduced benefits at age 50 with 20 yrs. of service; any age with 25 yrs. of service
Deferred retirement	At least 5 yrs. of service; accrued benefit payable at age 62	Unreduced benefit at age 62, if employee had 5 yrs. of civilian service at termination and did not get refund of contributions, or upon attaining the MRA and had 30 yrs. of service at separation, or is age 60 with 20 yrs. of service at separation. Reduced benefit available upon reaching the MRA to vested employee with 10 yrs. of service
Pre-62 supplement for early retirement	N/A	Payable at retirement (but no earlier than MRA) until age 62; approximately equal to projected Social Security benefit payable

Provision	Civil Service Retirement System (CSRS)	Federal Employees Retirement System (FERS)
		at age 62, attributable to federal service Supplement is subject to earnings test, similar to the test used by Social Security at age 62, reducing supplement if retiree has earned income in excess of an annually adjusted exempt amount ($11,520 in 2003,wage-indexed)
Refunds	Option to withdraw sums contributed at separation with benefits forfeited, unless subsequently made redeposit when reemployed in a covered position. May elect actuarial reduction for refunded service that ended before October 1, 1990.	Option to withdraw contributions, plus interest, at separation with benefits irrevocably forfeited
Cost-of-living adjustments (COLAs)	Payable to all annuitants. Annually, full rate of inflation measured by CPI:	Payable only to regular retirees over age 62, or disabled (after first yr.) and survivors at any age.

Increase in CPI	Annual COLA percentage
Up to 2%	Same as CPI increase
2% to 3%	2%
3%+	CPI increase minus one percentage point

Disability Benefits

Provision	Civil Service Retirement System (CSRS)	Federal Employees Retirement System (FERS)
Vesting (disability)	5 yrs. of service	18 mos. of service
Definition of disability	Unable to do own job or vacant position at same grade or pay level in same agency and commuting area	Same as CSRS
Disability benefit amounts	Annuity earned at onset, or if greater, the lower of (1) 40% of salary base, or (2) the annuity that would be paid projecting service to age 60 at the same salary base. Benefits increased annually by full CPI	For the first yr. of eligibility, 60% of high-3 pay minus 100% of any Social Security payable. After the first yr., 40% of high-3 pay minus 60% of any Social Security payable. No COLAs provided first yr.; thereafter, COLAs provided on the same basis as for retirees aged 62 and over

Provision	Civil Service Retirement System (CSRS)	Federal Employees Retirement System (FERS)
Retirement benefits after disability	Disability pension continues for life unless 1) restored to earning capacity before age 60 or 2) no recovery before normal retirement age	At age 62 the annuity will be re-computed. For the retirement re-computation, the per. of disability would be credited toward yrs. of service, and average pay would be increased to reflect COLAs applicable during that period
Preretirement death benefit—spouse	At death of worker with at least 18 mos. of service, surviving spouse receives 55% of the accrued bene-fit, or, if larger, the lesser of (1) 55% of 40% of salary base, or (2) 55% of the accrued annuity with service projected to age 60 at same high-3	At death of worker with at least 18 mos. but less than 10 yrs. of service, the benefit is a one-time payment of $24,328.94 plus one-half of the deceased worker's final annual pay. If the deceased worker had 10 or more yrs. of service, an annuity is also payable equal to 50% of the accrued annuity
Preretirement death benefit—children	Unrelated to annuity. Annually adjusted amount varies by number of chil-dren and whether or not orphaned by one or both parents. Children must be (1) unmarried, (2) under age 18 or 22 if in school, or (3) any age and incapable of self-support if disability started before age 18.	The amount in excess, if any, of payments to children under CSRS (to all children in family) over the children's Social Security benefits.
Postretirement death benefit—spouse	Annuity to married retiree automatically reduced by 2.5% of first $300 monthly plus 10% of remainder unless jointly waived, but raised to unreduced level after death or divorce of spouse (unless otherwise stipulated in a divorce decree).	Annuity to retiree reduced by 10% (or 5% if lower benefit is jointly elected) to provide a survivor annuity, unless jointly waived but raised to unreduced level after death or divorce of the spouse, unless otherwise stipulated in a divorce decree
	Benefit equal to 55% of the annuity received by the retiree at the time of death, excluding the reduction for survivor election and including any reduction for in-voluntary early retirement. No Social Security for federal employment	If the survivor is under age 60 and Social Security survivor benefits are not payable, benefits are lesser of (1) current CSRS or (2) 50% (25% if elected) of accrued annuity plus a Social Security "equivalent." When Soc. Sec. survivor benefits are payable, FERS pays 50% (25% if elected) of the deceased retiree's annuity.
Postretirement death benefits—children	Same as preretirement death	Same as preretirement death

Provision	Civil Service Retirement System (CSRS)	Federal Employees Retirement System (FERS)
Thrift Savings Plan (TSP)		
Eligibility	Every 6 mos. employees have an open season to begin or change contrib. Newly hired employees may join at the 2nd open season (6-12 mos. after hire.)	Same as CSRS
Contributions:		
by employees	Employees may contribute up to 8% of pay, with no employer match	Employees may contribute up to 13% of pay
by agencies	N/A	Agency automatically contributes amount equal to 1% of pay into each employee's account Agency also matches employee contributions: 1st 3% of pay = $1 per $1; next 2% of pay = $0.50 per $1
Vesting	Full and immediate vesting	Full and immediate vesting of all except the 1% automatic agency contribution. This automatic contribution becomes vested at 3 yrs. of service for career civil servants, 2 yrs. of service for non-career senior executive service and political (schedule C) appointees, Members and congressional staff
Investments: Employee may elect to invest own account in:		Same as CSRS

G Fund: special government securities

F Fund: Bond index fund consisting of US. Treasury, corporate, and federally sponsored agency notes and bonds and mortgage-backed securities

C Fund: a stock index fund (invested in diversified common stock portfolio designed to replicate Standard & Poor's 500 stock index).

I Fund: international stock index fund invested in the shares of Barclays EAFE Index Fund, which holds common stocks of all the companies represented in the Europe, Australasia, and Far East stock index, and whose contributions are invested in the EAFE Index Fund regardless of gains or losses in the international markets. It also includes temporary investments in G Fund securities.

S Fund: medium and small company stock fund that tracks the returns of the Wilshire 4500 stock index, which includes those U.S. stocks that are not found in the S&P 500 index. It invests in shares of the Barclays Extended Market Index Fund, which holds common stocks of companies in the Wilshire 4500 index.

A "member of Congress" for retirement system purposes includes a Senator, Representative in Congress, Delegate from a Territory, the Resident Commissioner from Puerto Rico, and the Vice President (see 5 USC 2106).

A "congressional employee" for retirement system purposes includes employees of the Senate and House of Representatives, employees of the various committees of Congress, elective officers of the Senate or House who are not members of Congress, legislative counsels and their employees, Architect of the Capitol and United States Botanical Garden personnel, employees of the Congressional Record Index Office and the Capitol Guide Service, Official Reporters of Debates in the Senate and their employees, members of the Capitol Police force, and any employee of the Vice President or of any member of Congress whose salary is disbursed by the Secretary of the Senate or the Clerk of the House.

FERS Special Group Rules

In general, the rules defining membership in a special group are the same for FERS and CSRS. However, because of the coordination of FERS and Social Security, the benefits received by special groups are different under FERS.

Firefighters, Law Enforcement Officers and Air Traffic Controllers—Employees in these categories are eligible for:

• Unreduced benefits at age 50 and 20 years of service, or any age and 25 years of service.

• Annuity is 1.7 percent of high-3 pay multiplied by years of service up to 20, 1.0 percent times years over 20. Supplement paid to age 62, equals estimated Social Security benefit earned in federal service, earnings-tested above minimum retirement age. Annual COLA percentage applies at all ages. Employees contribute additional 0.5 percent of pay.

Special Note for CSRS-to-FERS Transfers—Law enforcement, firefighter and air traffic controller personnel who have switched from CSRS coverage to the FERS retirement plan and retire under these special annuity provisions are entitled to "restart" the FERS annuity calculation clock. This means that these CSRS transferees can use the higher FERS computation rate of 1.7 percent when multiplying all their years of FERS-covered service in these positions (up to the specified maximum of 20). Generally, an employee's years of CSRS-covered service as a law enforcement officer, firefighter or air traffic controller do not count toward the 20-year limit on using FERS higher 1.7 percent computation rate when calculating the FERS component of the worker's federal retirement annuity.

Example: An employee works six years in

Who Can Get Benefits

When a worker is fully insured, monthly retirement insurance benefits can be paid to: the worker age 62; children under age 18 (or up to age 19 if a full-time secondary school student); disabled children 18 or over who were disabled before 22; and a spouse of any age caring for the worker's child under age 16; a spouse 62 or older (including divorced spouses).

When a worker is fully insured, monthly survivor insurance benefits can be paid to: children (as described above), and a surviving spouse or surviving divorced spouse of any age caring for the worker's children under age 16; a surviving spouse or surviving divorced spouse 60 or older; dependent parents 62 or older.

When a worker is currently insured, but not fully insured, monthly survivor insurance benefits can be paid to children and surviving spouse or surviving divorced spouse (as described above) of any age caring for worker's children under age 16 or disabled before age 22.

When a worker is insured for disability, monthly benefits can be paid to the worker, children (as described above), and a spouse of any age caring for these children under age 16; a spouse 62 or older.

a CSRS-covered law enforcement position before transferring over to the FERS system in 1987. The worker's service credit clock for purposes of using FERS higher computation rate is reset or re-triggered at the point of the retirement plan transfer. Thus, the employee can accumulate up to 20 years of FERS service computed at the 1.7 percent rate. In addition, the CSRS component of the worker's combined annuity will reflect six years of CSRS service computed at the 2.5 percent rate.

Keep in mind, however, that only the years and months of actual law enforcement service can be counted as creditable service for purposes of these special provisions. For example, time spent in military service or amounts of unused sick leave (for CSRS service-computation purposes) cannot be computed at the higher calculation rates.

Military Reserve Technicians—Employees in this category are eligible for special benefits if they are separated due to termination of military service after age 50 and 25 years of service. In general, they get an unreduced annuity with supplement to 62, earnings-tested above MRA.

Members of Congress and Congressional Employees—These classes contribute an additional 0.5 percent of pay. For members of Congress only, unreduced annuity at age 50 and 20 years of service, or any age and 25 years of service. Annuity is 1.7 percent of high-3 x years of service up to 20, 1.0 percent x years over 20. Earnings-tested supplement paid from minimum retirement age (MRA) to age 62.

Section 9—Social Security Benefits

General Description

Social Security is one of the three legs of the Federal Employees Retirement System (FERS), a civil service annuity and the Thrift Savings Plan being the other two. Many employees under the Civil Service Retirement System (CSRS) also are eligible for Social Security benefits, due either to their employment outside the government in Social Security-covered jobs, or through spousal or survivor rights. However, there are offsets, called the Government Pension Offset (GPO) and the Windfall Elimination Provision (WEP), that often reduce or even eliminate Social Security benefits for CSRS employees.

A person must work and pay taxes into Social Security to get something out of it, except for those who benefit as a dependent or survivor of someone else. Working and paying the taxes build up credits toward coverage; most people need 40 credits (10 years of work) to qualify. Younger people need fewer credits to be eligible for disability benefits or for their family members to be eligible for survivor benefits if they should die before achieving the normally required credits.

Most workers earn many more credits than are needed to be eligible for Social Security. These credits do not increase the eventual Social Security benefit. However, the income earned will increase the benefit. The amount of a Social Security benefit is based on factors including date of birth, type of benefit being applied for, and, most important, the individual's earnings.

A person with sufficient credits and born prior to 1938 is eligible for full Social Security retirement benefits at age 65. For individuals born in 1938 or later, the age for full retirement increases according to the person's year of birth. For example, the full retirement age for a person born in 1942 is 65 years and 10 months. The retirement age for persons born in 1960 and later is 67 years.

However, reduced benefits remain available to those with sufficient coverage credits as early as age 62. For individuals who take early retirement, benefits are permanently reduced based on the number of months they will receive checks before reaching full retirement age. If the person's full Social Security retirement age is 65, the reduction for starting Social Security at age 62 was about 20 percent; at age 63, 13⅓ percent; and at age 64, it was about 6⅔ percent. (As of January 1, 2003, all such individuals are already at least 65 years of age.)

Social Security not only pays a benefit to the retiring worker but also potentially to the worker's spouse and any eligible children. The spouse and child's benefits are payable while the retired worker is still living and do not affect the level of the worker's benefit. However, the spouse will not receive this benefit if he or she is eligible for his or her own Social Security benefit that exceeds the level of the spouse benefit. The

Social Security Retirement Benefits table displays the individuals entitled to benefits and their levels. Primary Insurance Amount (PIA) is a Social Security term used to describe the actual Social Security benefit.

Social Security benefits are inflation proof and increase automatically as the cost-of-living rises. Cost-of-living adjustments are made each January.

Coverage of Federal Employees

All federal employees hired after December 31, 1983, are covered by Social Security and will pay Social Security taxes. This also includes employees with previous federal service (other than rehired annuitants) if their break in service was a year or longer. Certain previously hired federal employees will be covered under Social Security after December 1983, including:

• legislative branch employees who were not covered by the CSRS on Dec. 31, 1983;

• all members of Congress, the President, and the Vice-president;

• sitting federal judges; and

• most high-level political appointees, including non-career members of the senior executive service.

Also covered are pre-1984 employees who chose to join the FERS system. In addition, other pre-1984 federal employees may qualify for benefits under both the CSRS and Social Security, because of pro-

tection acquired in other ways. A pre-1984 federal employee may earn Social Security credits in several ways, including:

• while working under Social Security as a temporary federal employee;

• through work under Social Security before entering the CSRS;

• by working evenings or weekends under Social Security while employed full time under civil service;

• by operating a small business in addition to his or her full-time permanent job under civil service;

• through employment or self-employment under Social Security after retirement or resignation from a civil service job; and

• through military service that has been covered since 1957.

Also, many career federal employees have protection for themselves and their children based on their spouses' work under Social Security, in addition to the protection earned by their own work under the CSRS. However, under certain circumstances, spouse's Social Security benefits are offset because of the government pension they receive (see below).

Federal employees (such as those in temporary positions) who are not covered under a federal retirement system are generally covered under Social Security. Further, basic pay for military service after 1956 is also covered under Social Security. Therefore, the military pay for federal employees who are military reservists on active duty for training is cov-

Social Security Contribution Rates

Contribution Rate Schedule for Employees and Employers, Each				Contribution Rate for Self-Employed*			
Percent of Covered Earnings				Percent of Covered Earnings			
Years	Retirement, Survivors & Disability Insurance Rate (Percent)	Hospital Insurance Rate (Percent)	Total	Years	Retirement, Survivors & Disability Insurance Rate (Percent)	Hospital Insurance Rate (Percent)	Total
1985	5.7	1.35	7.05	1985	11.40	2.70	14.10
1986–1987	5.7	1.45	7.15	1986–1987	11.40	2.90	14.30
1988–1989	6.06	1.45	7.51	1988–1989	12.12	2.90	15.02
1990 and after	6.2	1.45	7.65	1990 and after	12.40	2.90	15.30

*Self-employed also got credits, starting at 2.7 percent for 1984, and declining slowly through 1989. Credits disappeared in 1990, replaced by a new method of deducting SECA taxes for income-tax purposes.

ered under Social Security. Beginning January 1, 1988, wages paid for inactive duty service are covered wages for Social Security purposes. In addition to coverage for basic pay for military service after 1956, servicemen may also have wages under Social Security of $160 per month for military service between September 16, 1940, and December 31, 1956, "deemed" wages of $300 per calendar quarter for service from 1957 through 1977, and deemed wages of $100 for each full $300 of annually reported wages up to the $1,200 maximum per year for service from 1978 on. A law effective January 1, 2002, eliminated deemed military wage credits for members of the uniformed services for all years after calendar year 2001. Deemed wage credits will continue to be given for appropriate earnings for periods prior to calendar year 2002.

Earning Social Security Credits

In general, if a person was paid $50 or more for full or part-time work during a calendar quarter of a year before 1978, he received one quarter of coverage for his work up to a max of four per year. In 1978, a quarter of coverage was credited (up to a maximum of four) for each $250 in annual earnings. After 1978, the amount required for a quarter of coverage (now called "credits") began to rise to reflect increases in average wages. In 2003, a person earns one credit for each $890 in earnings, up to the yearly maximum of four credits.

Work in commerce and industry has earned Social Security credit since 1937. Effective in 1951 other types of work—including some self-employment—came under the law. Because the Social Security law has been expanded over the years to bring almost all work under the program, some federal employees have some Social Security credit for past work. This credit should not be overlooked; it counts toward Social Security benefits.

Fully Insured—Forty credits, which can be earned in as little as 10 years of full or part-time work, is all that anyone needs to be insured for retirement and survivors insurance benefits. That amount of credits ensures that at least some amount of Social Security benefits will be paid to the worker and the employee's family members or survivors. For workers who reached age 62 before 1991, fewer than 40 credits were required to be fully insured. The general rule is that a person is fully insured if that person has at least one credit (whenever acquired) for every full calendar year elapsing after 1950 (or elapsing after the year in which the person attained age 21, if attainment is after 1950) up to but not including, the year in which the person becomes disabled, attains age 62, or dies, whichever occurs earliest. A rule of thumb for finding the number of credits you will need to be fully insured is to simply count the number of elapsed years in this period.

Currently Insured—A person is termed currently insured if he or she has Social Security credit for work in at least six calendar quarters during the 13-quarter period ending with the calendar quarter in which he or she dies, becomes entitled to retirement benefits, or becomes disabled before death. Certain benefits—including those to

Social Security Retirement Benefits

Categories Insurance	% Primary Insurance Amount (PIA)
Worker	
• Age 65–67	100
• Age 62	80–70
Spouse and/or Divorced Spouse	
• Age 65–67	50
• Age 62	37.5–25
• Any age with eligible child	50
• Eligible child*	50

* Eligible child is defined as: 1. unmarried; 2. under age 18; 3. under 19 if in high school; 4. any age if disabled before 22.

young survivors—can be paid on just this amount of Social Security credit. To be considered fully insured for Social Security benefits all workers born after 1929 need 40 credits, regardless of when earned. (Workers born before 1929 need fewer credits depending on their date of birth.)

Insured for Disability—A person who has enough work credit may qualify for monthly disability insurance benefits for himself/herself and his/her family if he/she has 20 Social Security credits in the 10 years just before he or she became disabled and is fully insured. (Workers under age 31 may qualify with fewer credits.) Blind disabled workers need be only fully insured.

Degree of Disability on Which Benefits Can Be Paid—To get disability insurance benefits, the worker must have, in addition to the necessary work credit, a physical or mental impairment so severe that it makes him or her unable to do any "substantial" work. Generally, a job that pays $700 or more per month is "substantial." This impairment must be a kind that will show up in medical examinations and tests, and it must be expected to continue or has lasted for at least 12 months or result in death. The disabling conditions must have lasted for at least five full months before

benefits can be paid. Application for benefits can be made earlier, however.

Self-employment is covered by Social Security. Credit toward insured status is earned for any year in which net earnings are at least equal to the amount for a credit of coverage. However, federal employees operating a small business during non-work hours should be reporting their earnings from the activity if the net earnings are $400 or more. They must pay Social Security taxes on these earnings, and will get Social Security credit for their part-time work.

Paying Taxes and Reporting Earnings

The employer is responsible for withholding the employee's share of the Social Security tax, adding an equal amount, remitting the tax to the IRS, and reporting the employee's earnings. Earnings are reported annually. When a report reaches the Social Security Administration's record keeping headquarters, each person's earnings are credited to his or her individual earnings record, which is identified by the name and number appearing on the Social Security card.

Self-employed persons are responsible for reporting their own earnings—and earn-

Social Security Credit Needed to Be Fully Insured

A worker who reached age 62 in:	Will need this number of quarters of coverage:	Which is equivalent to this period of work under Social Security:
1975	24	6 years
1976	25	6¼ years
1977	26	6½ years
1978	27	6¾ years
1979	28	7 years
1980	29	7¼ years
1981	30	7½ years
1982	31	7¾ years
1983	32	8 years
1984	33	8¼ years
1985	34	8½ years
1986	35	8¾ years
1987	36	9 years
1988	37	9¼ years
1989	38	9½ years
1990	39	9¾ years
1991 and after	40	10 years

ings of their employees—for Social Security purposes. Self-employment earnings must be reported as a part of filing an annual income tax return and taxes are paid through this return.

Federal employees who net as much as $400 a year from part-time self-employment must pay Social Security taxes on their earnings from self-employment—and will in turn get the Social Security credit due them.

The Social Security Contribution Rates table shows the amount of Social Security taxes of recent years. These taxes apply on earnings up to $87,000 in 2003.

Each year, Social Security sends a personal Social Security Statement to everyone age 25 or older, who is not already receiving benefits on his or her earnings record and for whom the agency can obtain a current address. The statement is mailed about three months before the person's birthday.

The statement is intended to help workers plan their financial future by providing an updated record of their earnings that are posted to Social Security records and estimates of benefits the worker and family may be eligible to receive now and in the future. If the person has any work that's not covered by Social Security (such as federal or state employment) the statement will not show those earnings. Therefore, the benefit estimates will not reflect the WEP or the GPO (see below).

You can get a statement by calling Social Security at 1-800-772-1213 or by requesting one through SSA's Internet site, *www.ssa.gov.*

Monthly Benefit Payments

When a worker has enough Social Security credits, the following benefits may be paid:

• monthly retirement insurance benefits for him or her, and benefits for dependent family members;

• monthly disability insurance benefits (up to retirement age) for him or her, and benefits for dependent family members; and

• monthly survivor insurance benefits for the family when he or she dies, plus a lump-sum death payment in some cases.

A person eligible for benefits based on his or her own earnings and also for bene-

fits as a family member or survivor (generally as a wife or widow) will receive the full amount of his or her own benefit, plus an amount equal to any excess of the other benefit over his or her own—in effect, the larger of the two.

The amounts of all Social Security benefit payments are based on a worker's average earnings under Social Security during a certain number of years specified in the law. Since a career federal employee will usually work only a relatively short period under Social Security, or will have only part-time earnings under Social Security, his average earnings will be relatively low and so will his benefits.

Monthly benefits payable to the worker and his or her family members or survivors are subject to a maximum family benefit amount that varies directly with the worker's benefit level.

Computation of Social Security Benefits

Social Security benefits are based upon a worker's career earnings. The more a worker earns up to the wage base and the longer a worker earns such amounts the higher the Social Security benefit. The maximum number of years used to compute career earnings is 35. For those born before 1929, the number of years used to compute career earnings is determined by adding the number 6 to the last two digits of the worker's year of birth. For example, Social Security would use 31 years of earnings for an individual born in 1925, 25 + 6 = 31.

By the time an individual is eligible for Social Security benefits, the dollar amounts of the individual's actual earnings, particularly in the early years, will appear quite small. So the Social Security system requires that the yearly earnings be indexed upwards to reflect current dollars. The number of required yearly indexed earnings are totaled, dropping out the lowest earnings years to arrive at the required number of years to compute the Social Security benefit. The total earnings are then divided by the number of months in those years, resulting in the Average Indexed Monthly Earnings (AIME).

Once the AIME is determined an annual Social Security formula is applied, resulting in the Primary Insurance Amount—the full Social Security benefit. For example, the Social Security formula applied to a worker's AIME who was 62 in 2003:

- 90 percent of the first $606 of the AIME, plus
- 32 percent of the AIME in excess of $606 through $3,653, plus
- 15 percent of the AIME over $3,653

Note the different percentage amounts in each of the three levels. These show how individuals at lower income levels receive higher percentages of their salaries than those at higher levels. The dollar amounts in the above formula change every year, but the percentages remain the same.

Other computations, such as reductions for retiring before the full retirement age, are rounded to the next lowest $0.10. After all computations are performed, the benefit is rounded to the next lowest dollar (unless already at an even multiple of the dollar).

Full Retirement Age—The usual retirement age for people retiring now is age 65. Social Security calls this "full retirement age," and the benefit amount that is payable is considered the full retirement benefit. Because of longer life expectancies, the full retirement age will be increased in gradual steps until it reaches age 67. This change started in 2003, and it affects people born in 1938 and later.

Age To Receive Full Social Security Benefits

Year of Birth	Full Retirement Age
1937 or earlier	65
1938	65 and 2 months
1939	65 and 4 months
1940	65 and 6 months
1941	65 and 8 months
1942	65 and 10 months
1943-1954	66
1955	66 and 2 months
1956	66 and 4 months
1957	66 and 6 months
1958	66 and 8 months
1959	66 and 10 months
1960 and later	67

Approximate Monthly Retirement Benefits If the Worker Retires At Full Retirement Age With Steady Lifetime Earnings

Worker's Age in 2001	Worker's Family	Low Earnings[1]	Average Earnings[2]	High Earnings[3]	Maximum Earnings[4]
45	Retired worker only	$690	$1,137	$1,509	$1,873
	Worker-spouse[5]	$1,035	$1,705	$2,263	$2,809
	Replacement rate[6]	60%	45%	37%	28%
55	Retired worker only	$690	$1,137	$1,509	$1,817
	Worker-spouse[5]	$1,035	$1,705	$2,263	$2,725
	Replacement rate[6]	60%	45%	37%	27%
65	Retired worker only	$635	$1,049	$1,363	$1,536
	Worker-spouse[5]	$952	$1,573	$2,044	$2,304
	Replacement rate[6]	56%	41%	34%	24%

[1]Low earnings are determined to be $13,711.43 for 1999 and later.

[2]Average earnings are determined to be $30,469.84 for 1999 and later.

[3]High earnings are determined to be $48,751.7 for 1999 and later.

[4]Maximum earnings are greater than or equal to the OASDI wage base, the maximum earnings subject to the Social Security tax, and are determined to be $84,900 for 2002.

[5]Your spouse is assumed to be the same age as you, receives a benefit equal to one-half of yours and spouse may qualify for a higher benefit based on personal earnings.

[6]Replacement rate is the percentage of income represented by benefits.

Note: The accuracy of these estimates depends on the worker's actual earnings, which may vary significantly from those assumed. *Source: Social Security Administration*

Early Retirement—You can start your Social Security benefits as early as age 62, but the benefit amount you receive will be less than your full retirement benefit. If you take early retirement, your benefits will be permanently reduced based on the number of months you will receive checks before you reach full retirement age. For example, if your full retirement age is 67, the reduction for starting your benefits at 62 will be about 30 percent; at age 63, about 25 percent; at age 64, about 20 percent; at age 65, about 13⅓ percent; and at age 66, about 6⅔ percent.

As a general rule, early retirement will give you about the same total Social Security benefits over your lifetime, but in smaller amounts to take into account the longer period you will receive them.

Delayed Retirement—Each additional year you work adds another year of earnings to your Social Security record. Higher lifetime earnings also may result in higher benefits when you retire.

In addition, your benefit will be increased by a certain percentage if you delay retirement. These increases will be added in automatically from the time you reach your full retirement age until you start taking your benefits, or you reach age 70. The percentage varies depending on your year of birth, ranging from a 3 percent increase per year retirement is delayed for those born before 1924 to 8 percent per year for those born in 1943 and later.

Social Security Disability Benefits

In addition to retirement benefits, Social Security pays benefits to disabled workers. To be eligible for disability benefits, the worker must have worked long enough and recently enough under Social Security to qualify for disability benefits.

The number of credits of coverage necessary to be eligible for disability benefits must be equal to the number of years from the time the worker turned age 22, or after 1951 if later, to date of disability. Thus, a worker born in 1941 who became disabled in 1987 must have 25 credits of coverage to be eligible for disability benefits.

Current requirements provide that a worker must have been covered under the

Approximate Monthly Disability Benefits If the Worker Became Disabled In 2001 And Had Steady Lifetime Earnings

Worker's Age in 2001	Worker's Family	Low Earnings[1]	Average Earnings[2]	High Earnings[3]	Maximum Earnings[4]
25	Disabled worker only	$690	$1,137	$1,509	$1,821
	Worker-spouse-child[5]	$970	$1,706	$2,264	$2,731
35	Disabled worker only	$690	$1,137	$1,509	$1,831
	Worker-spouse-child[5]	$970	$1,706	$2,264	$2,747
45	Disabled worker only	$690	$1,137	$1,509	$1,815
	Worker-spouse-child[5]	$970	$1,706	$2,264	$2,723
55	Disabled worker only	$690	$1,137	$1,507	$1,738
	Worker-spouse-child[5]	$970	$1,706	$2,260	$2,607
64	Disabled worker only	$661	$1,091	$1,420	$1,599
	Worker-spouse-child[5]	$933	$1,637	$2,131	$2,399

[1]Low earnings are determined to be $13,711.43 for 1999 and later.

[2]Average earnings are determined to be $30,469.84 for 1999 and later.

[3]High earnings are determined to be $48,751.7 for 1999 and later.

[4]Maximum earnings are greater than or equal to the OASDI wage base, the maximum earnings subject to the Social Security tax, and are determined to be $84,900 for 2002. Maximum family disability benefit.

Note: The accuracy of the illustrated amounts depends on the worker's actual earnings, which may vary from those assumed. *Source: Social Security Administration*

Social Security system for a certain period of time just prior to the onset of disability. For example, an individual older than age 31 must be covered by Social Security for 20 of his or her last 40 credits of employment. Those under age 31 need fewer credits.

Once a Social Security-covered worker becomes disabled, he or she must apply to the Social Security Administration (SSA) for benefits. SSA determines whether the worker meets the definition of disability. Disability is defined as being so severely physically or mentally impaired that he or she cannot perform any substantial gainful activity and the disability is expected to last at least 12 months or result in death.

The following table shows the levels of disability benefits and who is eligible for them:

Categories	% of PIA*
• Disabled Worker	100
• Spouse and/or Divorced Spouse	50
• Retirement age	

with no child in care	37.5-50
• Any age with eligible child in care	50
• Eligible child	50

(* Primary Insurance Amount)

Social Security Survivor Benefits

The Social Security system also pays benefits to survivors of workers. For a worker's survivors to be eligible for survivor benefits, the worker must be either fully insured or currently connected to the covered work force. In this case, however, the current connection requirement is that the worker be covered by Social Security for six quarters of the last 13.

The following table displays the eligible survivors of a fully insured worker and the amounts to which they are entitled:

Categories	% of PIA*
• Widow(er) or Divorced Spouse— Full Retirement Age	100

Approximate Monthly Benefits Payable to Survivors if the Worker Died in 2001 With Steady Lifetime Earnings

Worker's Age in 2001	Worker's Family	Low Earnings[1]	Average Earnings[2]	High Earnings[3]	Maximum Earnings[4]
35	Spouse-one child[5]	$1,036	$1,706	$2,264	$2,760
	Spouse-two children[6]	$1,036	$2,076	$2,640	$3,219
	One child	$518	$853	$1,132	$1,380
	Spouse aged 60[7]	$493	$813	$1,079	$1,315
45	Spouse-one child[5]	$1,036	$1,706	$2,264	$2,728
	Spouse-two children[6]	$1,036	$2,076	$2,640	$3,128
	One child	$518	$853	$1,132	$1,364
	Spouse aged 60[7]	$493	$813	$1,079	$1,300
55	Spouse-one child[5]	$1,036	$1,706	$2,260	$2,606
	Spouse-two children[6]	$1,036	$2,076	$2,636	$3,040
	One child	$518	$853	$1,130	$1,303
	Spouse aged 60[7]	$493	$813	$1,077	$1,242

[1]Low earnings are determined to be $13,711.43 for 1999 and later.

[2]Average earnings are determined to be $30,469.84 for 1999 and later.

[3]High earnings are determined to be $48,751.7 for 1999 and later.

[4]Maximum earnings are greater than or equal to the OASDI wage base, the maximum earnings subject to the Social Security tax, and are determined to be $84,900 for 2002.

[5]Amounts shown also represent benefits payable to two children if no parent survives or if no payment is paid because the surviving parent has substantial earnings.

[6]Maximum family benefit amount.

[7]Spouse is assumed to be age 60 in the year of the worker's death.

Note: The accuracy of the illustrated amounts depends upon the worker's actual earnings, which may vary significantly from those assumed. *Source: Social Security Administration*

- Widow(er) or Divorced
  Surviving Spouse—Age 60
  Full Retirement Age 71.5-100
- Disabled Widow(er) or
  Divorced Surviving   ..
  Spouse—Age 50-59 .... 71.5
- Widow(er) or Divorced
  Surviving Spouse Under Age
  60 Caring for Eligible Child 75
- Eligible child 75
- Dependent Parents 82.5

(* Primary Insurance Amount)

Eligible survivors of a worker who was only currently connected to the work force and not fully insured is limited to a spouse with eligible children and the children. Note in either case, spouses with no dependent children receive no survivor benefit. Where the worker was fully insured, the spouse would receive a survivor benefit when the spouse turned age 60 or age 50 if disabled.

> Note: A surviving spouse or divorced sur-
> viving spouse receives an unreduced ben-
> efit at full retirement age. At age 60 the
> benefit is reduced to 71.5%. All ages in
> between are reduced proportionately.
> Full retirement age for surviving spouses
> and divorced surviving spouses is:

Year of Birth	Full Retirement Age
1939 or earlier	65
1940	65 and 2 months
1941	65 and 4 months
1942	65 and 6 months
1943	65 and 8 months
1944	65 and 10 months
1945-1952	66
1953	66 and 2 months
1954	66 and 4 months
1955	66 and 6 months
1956	66 and 8 months
1957	66 and 10 months
1958 and later	67

Eligible survivors of a worker who was only currently connected to the work force and not fully insured is limited to a spouse with eligible children and the children. Note in either case, spouses with no dependent children receive no survivor benefit. Where the worker was fully insured, the spouse would receive a survivor benefit when the spouse turned age 60 or age 50 if disabled.

Dependent Benefits

Family Protection—Monthly Social Security checks also are paid to certain fam-

ily members of a worker who has retired, become disabled or who has died.

Retirement or Disability—Monthly payment can be made to a retired or disabled worker's:

- unmarried children under 18 (or up to age 19 if a full-time secondary school student);
- children 18 or over who were severely disabled before 22 and who continue to be disabled;
- wife or husband 62 or over, including a divorced wife or husband 62 or over if married for 10 years prior to divorce;
- spouse under 62 who is caring for worker's child under 16 (or disabled) who's eligible for a benefit based on the retired or disabled worker's earnings.

Survivors—Monthly payments can be made to a deceased worker's:

- unmarried children under 18 (or up to age 19 if a full-time secondary school student);
- son or daughter 18 or over who was severely disabled before 22 and remains disabled;
- widow or widower 60 or older, including a divorced widow or widower 60 or older if married for 10 years prior to divorce;
- widow(er), or surviving divorced mother or father if caring for worker's child under 16 (or disabled) who is getting a benefit based on the earnings of the deceased worker;
- widow(er) 50 or older, including a divorced widow or widower married for 10 years prior to divorce, who becomes disabled not later than seven years after worker's death, or within seven years after he or she stops getting checks as a widow or widower caring for worker's children; and
- dependent parents 62 or older.

A divorced spouse age 62 or older may be eligible for benefits even if the worker is not currently receiving benefits. The worker must be at least age 62, the spouse must be divorced from the worker for at least two years, and the marriage must have lasted for 10 years.

The Earnings Test

If you're receiving Social Security retirement or survivors benefits and still working, you can earn a certain amount of money while receiving benefits. However, depending on your age, your benefits will be reduced if you earn over certain limits. This is the so-called Earnings Test.

Your earnings in (and after) the month

you reach your full retirement age will not affect your Social Security benefits. However, your benefits will be reduced if your earnings exceed certain limits for the months before you reach your full retirement age—65 for persons born before 1938 and gradually increasing to 67 for persons born in 1960 or later.

If you're under full retirement age, $1 in benefits will be deducted for each $2 in earnings you have above the annual limit ($11,520 in 2003).

In the year you reach your full retirement age, your benefits will be reduced $1 for every $3 you earn over a different annual limit ($30,720 in 2003) until the month you reach full retirement age. Starting with the month you reach full retirement age, you can receive your full benefits with no limit on your earnings. These limits increase each year as average wages increase.

Only your wages count toward Social Security's earnings limits. If you're self-employed, SSA counts only your net earnings from self-employment. Non-work income such as other government benefits, investment earnings, interest, pensions, annuities and capital gains don't count. If you're self-employed, income counts when you receive it—not when you earn it—except if it is paid in a year after you become entitled to Social Security and was earned before you became entitled to Social Security. For example, if you started getting Social Security in June 2002 and you received some money in February 2003 for work you did before June 2002, it will not count against your 2003 earnings limit. However, if the money you received in February 2003 was for work you did after June 2002, it would count against your 2003 earnings limit.

If you're not self-employed, income counts when it is earned, not when it is paid. If you have income that you earned in one year but the payment was deferred to the following year, it does not count as earnings for the year you receive it. Some examples of deferred income include accumulated sick or vacation pay and bonuses.

A special rule applies to earnings for one year, usually the first year of retirement, for those who retire in a year after having already earned more than the yearly earnings limit. Under this rule, you can receive a full Social Security check for any whole month you are retired and earn under the limit, regardless of your yearly earnings.

At any time during the year, if you see that your earnings will be different from what you had estimated, you should call SSA to revise your estimate. This will help SSA keep the amount of your Social Security benefits correct.

If other family members get benefits on your Social Security record, the total family benefits may be affected by your earnings. This means SSA may withhold not only your benefits, but those payable to your family as well. But, if you get benefits as a family member, your earnings affect only your own benefits.

More information is available in the leaflet, *How Work Affects Your Benefits (Publication No. 05-10069)*, available from Social Security.

Windfall Reduction Benefit Computation

If you will receive a pension from a job where you didn't pay Social Security taxes, and you also have enough Social Security credits to be eligible for retirement or disability benefits, a modified formula may be used to figure your benefit amount. This modified formula will give you a lower Social Security benefit, but it will not affect your other pension. This reduction is also known as the "Windfall Elimination Provision."

Who Is Affected—The modified formula affects workers who reach 62 or become disabled after 1985 and first become eligible after 1985 for a monthly pension based in whole or in part on work not covered by Social Security. You are considered eligible to receive a pension if you meet the requirements of the pension, even if you continue to work. Therefore, if you become eligible to receive the pension prior to 1986, the Windfall Elimination Provision will not affect you.

The modified formula will be used in figuring your Social Security benefit beginning with the first month you get both a Social Security benefit and the pension based on employment not covered by Social Security.

Why a Different Formula Is Used—Since the beginning of the Social Security program, lower-paid workers have received larger benefits in relation to their earnings than higher-paid workers. However, because of the way benefits were computed, people who worked only part of their lives in jobs covered by Social Security had their benefits computed as if they were long-term, low-wage workers. These workers received the advantage of higher Social Security benefits, in addition to their pensions from work not covered by Social Security. In 1983, the Social Security law was changed to eliminate this advantage.

How It Works—Social Security benefits are based on the worker's average monthly earnings adjusted, or "indexed," for changes in national average earnings. When Social Security figures your benefits, it separates your average indexed monthly earnings into three amounts and multiplies the figures using three factors.

For example, for a worker who turns 62 in 2003, the first $606 of average indexed monthly earnings is multiplied by 90 percent; from $606 to $3,653 is multiplied by 32 percent; and over $3,653 by 15 percent.

In the modified formula, the 90 percent factor is reduced. The reduction was phased in for workers who reached age 62 or became disabled between 1986 and 1989. For those who reach 62 or become disabled in 1990 or later, the 90 percent factor is reduced to 40 percent.

However, if you have 30 or more years of "substantial" Social Security earnings, Social Security uses the regular formula to figure your benefit. If you have 21–29 years of "substantial" Social Security earnings, they use the modified formula, but it will affect you less than if you have fewer years of covered earnings. For people with 21–29 years of substantial Social Security earnings, the first factor in the formula is reduced as follows:

Years of Social

Security Earnings	First Factor
30 or more	90 percent
29	85 percent
28	80 percent
27	75 percent
26	70 percent
25	65 percent
24	60 percent
23	55 percent
22	50 percent
21	45 percent
20 or less	40 percent

For the modified formula, you are considered to have a year of substantial earnings if your earnings equal or exceed the figures shown for each year in the chart below.

Year	Earnings
1937–50	$ 900
1951–54	900
1955–58	1,050
1959–65	1,200
1966–67	1,650
1968–71	1,950
1972	2,250
1973	2,700
1974	3,300
1975	3,525
1976	3,825
1977	4,125
1978	4,425
1979	4,725
1980	5,100
1981	5,550
1982	6,075
1983	6,675
1984	7,050
1985	7,425
1986	7,875
1987	8,175
1988	8,400
1989	8,925
1990	9,525
1991	9,900
1992	10,350
1993	10,725
1994	11,250
1995	11,325
1996	11,625
1997	12,150
1998	12,675
1999	13,425
2000	14,175
2001	14,925
2002	15,675
2003	16,125

Note: Total credited earnings from 1937–50 are divided by $900 to get the number of years of coverage (maximum of 14 years)

Some Exceptions—The modified formula does not apply to survivors' benefits. It also does not apply to you if:

• you are a federal worker hired after December 31, 1983;

• you were employed on January 1, 1984, by a nonprofit organization that was required to be covered under Social Security on that date;

• you met the eligibility requirements for an immediate federal retirement before

January 1, 1986;
- your only pension is based solely on railroad employment;
- your only work where you did not pay Social Security taxes was before 1957; or
- you have 30 or more years of "substantial" earnings under Social Security.

Guarantee—A guarantee is provided to protect workers with relatively low pensions. It provides that the reduction in the Social Security benefit under the modified formula cannot be more than one-half of that part of the pension attributable to earnings after 1956 not covered by Social Security.

If you have questions or need more information about the modified benefit formula for workers with pensions from non-covered work, contact Social Security at 1-800-772-1213.

Government Pension Offset (GPO) for Spousal Benefit

If you worked for a federal, state or local government where you did not pay Social Security taxes (such as CSRS retirement), some or all of a Social Security spouse's or widow(er)'s benefit for which you may be qualified may be offset under the GPO, sometimes called the "Public Pension Offset."

The offset will reduce the amount of your Social Security spouse's or widow(er)'s benefits by two-thirds of the amount of your non-Social Security annuity. In other words, if you get a monthly civil service pension of $600, two-thirds of that, or $400, must be used to offset your Social Security spouse's or widow(er)'s benefits. If you're eligible for a $500 widow(er)'s benefit, you'll receive $100 per month from Social Security ($500 – $400= $100).

If you take your annuity in a lump sum, the offset is figured as if you chose to receive regular monthly benefits.

The following individuals are exempt from the GPO:
- Any state, local or military service employee whose government pension is based on a job where he or she was paying Social Security taxes on the last day of employment. (Some government entities were not initially covered by Social Security, but chose to participate in Social Security at a later date.)
- Anyone whose government pension is not based on his or her own earnings.
- Anyone who received or who was eligible to receive a government pension before December 1982 and who meets all the requirements for Social Security spouse's benefits in effect in January 1977.
- Anyone who received or was eligible to receive a federal, state or local government pension before July 1, 1983, and was receiving one-half support from her or his spouse.
- Federal employees, including Civil Service-Offset employees, who have mandatory Social Security coverage. (Civil Service-Offset employees are federal employees rehired after December 31, 1983, following a break in service of more than 365 days and who had five years of prior CSRS employment.)
- Federal employees who chose to switch from CSRS to the Federal Employees Retirement System (FERS) on or before December 31, 1987, as well as those employees who were allowed to make a belated switch to FERS through June 30, 1988. Employees who switched outside of these periods, including those who switched during the open season from July 1, 1998, through December 31, 1998, need five years under FERS to be exempt from the government pension offset.

Delayed Retirement Credits

There is a delayed retirement credit, which currently is 6 percent for each year a worker who reaches retirement age and does not receive benefits because the individual is still working (up to age 70). This credit will be gradually increased to eight percent for workers who reach retirement age in 2008 or later. Note that the percentage changes depending on the year of birth.

One-Time Death Benefit Payment

A one-time payment of $255 can be made to the widow or widower who was living in the same household as the worker in the month of death or who was eligible to receive monthly benefits at the time of the worker's death (excluding a divorced spouse). In the absence of a widow or widower, the payment can be made to any child of the deceased worker who is eligible for benefits for the month of death as a surviving child. The payment can be made if the worker is either currently or fully insured.

Applying for Social Security Benefits

Call 1-800-772-1213 to apply for benefits or to make an appointment to visit any Social Security office to apply in person. You also can apply online for retirement, disability, or spouse's benefits at *www.ssa.gov/apply-forbenefits*. Depending on your circumstances, you will need some or all of: your Social Security number; your birth certificate; your W-2 forms or self-employment tax return for the previous year; your military discharge papers if you had military service; your spouse's birth certificate and Social Security number if he or she is applying for benefits; children's birth certificates and Social Security numbers, if applying for children's benefits; proof of U.S. citizenship or lawful alien status if you (or a spouse or child is applying for benefits) were not born in the U.S.; and the name of your bank and your account number so your benefits can be directly deposited into your account. You will need to submit original documents or copies certified by the issuing office.

Disability Benefits—You may apply for disability benefits by phone, mail or by visiting a Social Security office or online at www.ssa.gov/applyforbenefits. While you may receive back benefits from the date you became disabled, they are limited to one year before the date you filed for benefits. It generally takes longer to process claims for disability benefits than other types of Social Security claims—from 60 to 90 days.

Required information may include: the Social Security number and proof of age for each person applying for payments including your spouse and children, if they are applying for benefits; names, addresses, and phone numbers of doctors, hospitals, clinics and institutions that treated you and dates of treatment; names of all medications you are taking; medical records from your doctors, therapists, hospitals, clinics and caseworkers; laboratory and test results; a summary of where you worked and the kind of work you did; your W-2 forms or self-employment tax return for the previous year; and dates of prior marriages if your spouse is applying.

Appeals—If you disagree with a decision made on your claim, you can appeal it. The steps you can take are explained in the fact sheet, The Appeals Process (Publication No. 05-10041), available from Social Security. You have the right to be represented by an attorney or other qualified person of your choice. More information is in the fact sheet, *Your Right to Representation* (Publication No. 05-10075), available from Social Security.

When Benefit Payments Start

Retirement Insurance Benefits—Retirement insurance benefits are available to covered workers as early as age 62. If benefits are paid before full retirement age, the monthly amount is permanently reduced up to 30 percent at 62 to make up for the longer time benefits will be received. Benefits may be refigured at full retirement age to take into account months for which no payment was made (for example, due to work).

When children and a spouse caring for these children are eligible for benefits, their payments can usually start the first month in which the worker is entitled to benefits. Benefits to each child continue until he or she reaches 18, or up to age 19 if still a full-time elementary or secondary school student unless he/she marries at an earlier age. Benefits to a child disabled before 22 continue as long as the child is disabled. Benefits to the spouse continue until the youngest child reaches 16 or marries younger. The amount of his or her benefit is not reduced because of age under retirement age.

When a spouse does not have in his or her care children of his or her spouse who are entitled to benefits, his or her payments do not start until age 62 or the month his or her spouse starts getting retirement benefits, when this is later. If the spouse takes the benefit before he or she reaches retirement age, his or her monthly amount will be permanently reduced up to 35 percent at 62 to make up for the longer time his or her benefits will be paid. Benefits to a spouse under age 62 begin no earlier than the first month throughout which he or she has an entitled child under 16 or disabled in care. Benefits for a worker or spouse at age 62 can begin no earlier than the first month throughout which he or she is age 62.

Survivor Benefits—Monthly benefits to dependent parents, children and a widow or widower caring for the children can start with the month of the worker's death.

When no dependent children are entitled to benefits, a surviving spouse gets benefits as early as age 60, but in a reduced amount. If he or she is disabled, reduced benefits can be paid as early as age 50. Full widow's or widower's benefits are payable if the surviving spouse waits until full retirement age. Dependents at age 62 are eligible for survivor benefits. Benefits to parents are not reduced in amount.

Disability Insurance Benefits—If a worker meets the disability requirements of the law (amount of work and extent of disability), he or she can get disability insurance benefits for the period of disability after a five-month waiting period, and, if the disability continues up to retirement age, when they are converted to old-age insurance benefits.

When a worker gets disability insurance benefits, payment to his or her children and spouse caring for the children can usually start with the first month in which the worker is entitled to benefits.

When the disability benefits cease, the benefits to family members also stop.

When no children are eligible for payments, a wife or husband is not eligible for payments until age 62, when he or she can get reduced benefits based on age.

Contacting Social Security

There are more than 1,300 Social Security district offices located throughout the country. Addresses of these offices are listed in telephone directories under "Social Security Administration." The address of the nearest office can also be obtained from your postmaster, by calling Social Security's toll-free number 1-800-772-1213, or by accessing www.ssa.gov. The lines are busiest early in the week and early in the month. When you call, have your Social Security number handy.

Individuals can also contact the toll-free

telephone number with general questions about Social Security benefits, lost Social Security checks, misplaced Social Security cards and so on. You can speak to a service representative between the hours of 7 a.m. and 7 p.m. on business days. If you have a "touch-tone" phone, recorded information and services are available after 7 p.m. weekdays and all day on weekends and holidays. People who are deaf or hard of hearing may call a toll-free "TTY" number, 1-800-325-0778, between 7 a.m. and 7 p.m. on business days.

Social Security offers a selection of free pamphlets that may be obtained by Internet, telephone, letter or a visit to a local office.

You also can obtain Social Security information and some services on the Internet, www.ssa.gov. The site allows you to:

• Plan your financial future by linking to the "Benefits Planner" for valuable information about retirement benefits and options you'll want to consider; you also can calculate your benefit.

• Subscribe to e-News and get the most up-to-date news about Social Security programs and benefits, as well as annual cost-of-living information.

• Apply for retirement, disability or spouse's benefits online and save a trip to your local Social Security office.

• Check out the Social Security Statement page if you have questions about it.

• Download and print Social Security publications.

• Locate your local Social Security office.

• Correct or change your name on your Social Security card or get a replacement card by requesting an Application for Social Security Card (Form SS-5).

Chapter 4
Post-Retirement

Section 1—Survivor Benefits

General Types of Survivor Annuities

Under CSRS and FERS, as part of the overall wage insurance protection provided federal and postal workers, survivors of employees who die, after the workers have met certain minimum service requirements, are eligible to receive benefits. Survivors also have special rights under the Thrift Savings Plan (see Chapter 6). In addition, Social Security also provides wage insurance to the families of deceased workers covered by that program (see the Social Security section in Chapter 3).

Under both CSRS and FERS, retiring federal employees can make provisions that will ensure the continuation of benefits to survivors in the event of the death of the retiree. Generally, this is accomplished by making reductions in the amount of a retiree's annuity to offset part of the cost of the additional protection afforded survivors. The value of the survivor protection is generally greater than the cost of the reduction to the annuity. In other words, an annuitant selecting a survivor option pays part of the cost of the option by taking a reduction, and the remainder of the cost is borne by the system.

On average, in both CSRS and FERS, the annuitant bears about one-half the cost, and the system the other half. Therefore, annuitants should view the claims advanced by various suppliers of private insurance-based survivor coverage with care, given the difficulty in offering a benefit that could exceed the value of the federal subsidy to the CSRS and FERS survivor benefit.

The basic types of survivor annuity options available to federal retirees include:

Annuity With Survivor Benefit to Widow, Widower, or Former Spouse—If you are married when you retire, the OPM will compute full survivor benefits for your spouse unless you and your spouse elect less than the full survivor amount (or no survivor annuity) at the time of your retirement. A court order awarding a survivor annuity to a former spouse (from whom you were divorced after May 7, 1985) reduces the maximum amount that can be paid to a current spouse. If there is no court order in effect, you may still elect to provide a survivor annuity for a former spouse; however, if you are married, you may do so only with the consent of your current spouse.

Under CSRS, you may use your entire annuity or any portion of it as a base for your annuity. Upon your death after retirement, your survivor will receive an annuity of 55 percent of your full annuity or whatever portion of it you and your spouse jointly specified in writing as the base for the survivor annuity.

Under FERS, there are only two survivor annuity options, 50 percent or 25 percent of your full annuity. You may not elect the lower percentage unless your spouse agrees to it in writing. In all cases, the amount of the survivor annuity is keyed to a percentage of the annuity base, before the reduction noted below is taken. The survivor annuity on which the computation is based will reflect all cost-of-living adjustments up to the time of death. This benefit to your widow or widower will continue until she or he dies or remarries. However, remarriage of a widow or widower who is at least age 55 does not terminate the survivor annuity. Also, if the annuity of such a widow or widower is terminated because of remarriage before age 55, the survivor annuity may be restored if the remarriage is dissolved by death, annulment, or divorce. The former spouse can also remarry after age 55 without loss of benefits, but if the former spouse remarries before age 55, the benefit cannot be reinstated if the remarriage ends.

If you accept the Annuity With Survivor Benefit to Widow, Widower, or Former Spouse, your annuity will be reduced by:
• 2.5 percent of the first $3,600 used as a base for survivor annuity; plus

• 10 percent of any amount over $3,600 used as a base for the survivor annuity.

Under CSRS, you may use all of your annuity or any portion of it as a base for your annuity. Upon your death after retirement, your survivor will receive an annuity of 55 percent of your full annuity or whatever portion of it you and your spouse jointly specified in writing as the base for the survivor annuity. The amount of the survivor annuity is keyed to a percentage of the annuity base, before the reduction noted above is taken. Your spouse's benefit will continue until death, or until remarriage before age 55.

Survivor Annuity for a Former Spouse—Under certain circumstances, a survivor annuity may be paid to a former spouse of a retiree. For example, a court order may award a survivor annuity to a former spouse. If you are married, the maximum amount that can be paid to your current spouse will be reduced. If there is no court order in effect, you may still elect to provide a survivor annuity to a former spouse; however, if you are married, you may do this only with the consent of your current spouse.

Annuity Without Survivor Benefit—This type of annuity option is available to all retiring employees. It provides annuity benefits to you only. If upon retirement you elect this type of annuity, no survivor benefits may be paid to your widow or widower. If a retiring married employee elects an annuity without survivor benefits or a reduced annuity with survivor benefits based on less than all of the employee's annuity, the employee must provide OPM with either: (1) the spouse's signed and notarized consent to the loss of or reduction in survivor benefits, or (2) a request for waiver of spousal consent by the OPM. The spousal consent requirement can be waived, if the spouse's whereabouts are unknown or a court finds that consent is not appropriate.

Note: If you choose an annuity without survivor benefits, your spouse and any other family members covered under your Federal Employees Health Benefits plan will lose that coverage upon your death unless they are otherwise eligible for coverage. In addition, they will lose the ability to initially enroll in the Federal Long Term Care Insurance Program, unless otherwise eligible for coverage.

Annuity With Benefit to Named Person Having an Insurable Interest—If you are in good health when you retire, you may elect an Annuity With Benefit to Named Person Having an Insurable Interest (a relative or former spouse, for example). Upon your death after retirement, and for the rest of his or her life, the person named as having an insurable interest will receive an annuity equal to 55 percent under both CSRS and FERS of your reduced annuity.

If you elect an Annuity With Benefit to Named Person Having an Insurable Interest, your annuity will be reduced by a percentage amount that depends on the difference between your age and the age of the person you name, as shown on the accompanying table. However, if the person named as having an insurable interest dies before you, your annuity will be restored to its unreduced rate upon written request to the retirement system.

The insurable interest option is not available to persons who retired on a federal

Insurable Interest Annuity Reduction

Age of Person Named in Relation to That of Retiring Employee	Reduction in Annuity of Retiring Employee
Older, same age, or less than 5 years younger	10%
5 but less than 10 years younger	15%
10 but less than 15 years younger	20%
15 but less than 20 years younger	25%
20 but less than 25 years younger	30%
25 but less than 30 years younger	35%
30 or more years younger	40%

civil service disability.

This election may be changed to a reduced annuity with a survivor benefit to widow or widower if you marry after retirement. Your written request for such a change must be received in the OPM no later than one year (or two years if married after February 26, 1986, or retired after May 6, 1985) after you marry. Once a change in election is accepted by the OPM, it cannot be changed.

Death Benefits when No One is Eligible for Survivor Annuity

If you leave no survivors who can qualify for a survivor annuity, a lump-sum death benefit consisting of the annuity accrued to date of death is generally payable immediately. Also, if the total annuity paid to you is less than your contributions to the retirement fund, the difference represents a balance payable as an immediate lump-sum death benefit.

If you leave survivors who qualify for a survivor annuity, no lump-sum death benefit (other than unpaid annuity accrued to date of death) is payable immediately. A lump-sum death benefit may be payable later if, when the survivors' annuities end, the total annuity paid to you and the survivors is less than your contributions to the retirement fund. Also, a widow(er) under FERS who had elected to receive a death benefit in installments may take the present value of the remaining payments in a single payment. (5 CFR Part 843.309) The amount payable is the difference between the total annuity paid and your contributions.

Order of Beneficiaries—A lump-sum death benefit is payable to the person or persons indicated below:

First: to the beneficiary designated by you;

Second: if you do not designate a beneficiary, to your widow or widower;

Third: if you leave no widow or widower, to your child or children in equal shares, with the share of any deceased child distributed among the descendants of that child;

Fourth: if none of the above, to your parents (or parent);

Fifth: if none of the above, to the executor or administrator of your estate;

Sixth: if none of the above, to your next of kin who may be entitled under the laws of the state in which you are domiciled at the time of your death.

You do not need to designate a beneficiary to receive the lump-sum death benefit unless you wish to name a person or persons not mentioned in the order of precedence shown above (or unless you wish to name a person who is mentioned but in a different order or for a different share). A designation of beneficiary is for lump-sum death benefit purposes only and does not affect the right of any person who can qualify for a survivor annuity. A designation of beneficiary must be in writing (Standard Form 2808 under CSRS; SF3102 under FERS), and must be received by the Office of Personnel Management before your death.

If you designate a beneficiary, remember to keep your designation current. Changes in your family or employment status without a corresponding change in your beneficiary designation may result in a settlement other than you intended.

For more information on what you'll need to ensure that your survivors receive all the benefits that you've earned for them, obtain a copy of FEND's *Understanding Survivor Benefits.* Both CSRS and FERS versions are available. To get your copy, use the ordering information included in this Almanac, or call 1-800-989-3363.

Section 2—Changes in Survivor Elections

Changing the Survivor Election for Your Spouse after Retirement

If you are married at retirement, you may change your decision not to provide a survivor annuity, or you may increase the survivor annuity amount. You may change your election if, not later than 30 days after

the date of your first regular monthly payment, you file a new election in writing. You should write to: Office of Personnel Management, Retirement Operations Center, Boyers, PA 16017-0001.

Your first regular monthly payment is the first annuity check payable on a recurring basis (other than an estimated payment or an adjustment check) after OPM has computed the regular rate of annuity payable and has paid the first regular annuity amount.

If you change your election to anything less than the maximum survivor benefit, you must get your spouse's consent to the election, or request that OPM waive the spousal consent requirement.

When the 30-day period following the date of your first regular monthly payment has passed, you can only change your election in writing no later than 18 months after the beginning date of your annuity. In addition, you must pay (1) a deposit representing the difference between the reduction for the new survivor election and the original survivor election, plus (2) a percentage of your annual annuity. Under FERS, this percentage is 24.5 percent of your annual annuity (at retirement) if you are changing from no survivor benefit to a full (50 percent) survivor benefit, and 12.25 percent if you are changing from none to a partial (25 percent) benefit or from a partial benefit to a full benefit. Under CSRS, this percentage is 24.5 percent of the amount of the increase from the original base to the new survivor base. Interest on the deposit must also be paid, chargeable at the same rate used for other retirement system deposits and redeposits (see the Interest Rates table in Chapter 3).

Electing Survivor Benefits for a Spouse Acquired After Retirement

If you get married after retirement, you can elect a reduced annuity to provide a survivor annuity for your spouse, if you contact the OPM to request the benefit within two years of the date of the marriage. (Note: If you retired before May 7, 1985, and married before February 27, 1986, the time limit is one year.) To be eligible for a survivor benefit in this circumstance, the spouse must have been married to you for at least nine months (one year if married before November 8, 1984, and retired before May 7, 1985) before your death, or, if married less than nine months, be the parent of a child born to the marriage, or your death must have been accidental. You may elect either a full survivor annuity or a partial survivor annuity. If you remarry the same person you were married to at retirement and that person consented to either no survivor annuity or a partial survivor annuity, you cannot elect a sur-

vivor annuity greater than the amount provided in your original election.

There will be two reductions in your annuity if you elect to provide the survivor benefit. One will be the reduction to provide the survivor benefit. The amount of the reduction depends on whether you have elected to provide a full survivor annuity or a partial survivor annuity. The reduction to provide the survivor benefit will be eliminated if your marriage ends.

The other reduction in your annuity is a permanent actuarial reduction to pay the survivor benefit deposit. The deposit equals the difference between the new annuity rate and the annuity paid to you for each month since retirement, plus 6 percent interest. The reduction is determined by dividing the amount of the deposit by an actuarial factor for your age on the date your annuity is reduced to provide the survivor benefit. The actuarial reduction will not be eliminated from your annuity if your marriage ends.

Electing Survivor Benefits for a Former Spouse if Your Marriage Terminates After Retirement

If your marriage terminates after retirement, you can elect a reduced annuity to provide a survivor annuity for your former spouse, if you contact OPM to request the benefit within two years of the date of the termination of the marriage. You may elect either a full survivor annuity or a partial survivor annuity. However, if you were married to that individual at retirement and he or she consented to either no survivor annuity or a partial survivor annuity, you cannot elect a survivor annuity greater than the amount provided in your original election. In addition, a former spouse who remarries before reaching age 55 is not eligible for a former spouse survivor annuity.

The same reductions are applied as those for a spouse acquired after retirement.

Changing an Insurable Interest Annuity Election for a Current Spouse to a Regular Survivor Annuity Election

If a former spouse's court-ordered survivor annuity will prevent your current spouse from receiving a survivor annuity that is sufficient to meet his or her anticipated needs, you may have elected an insurable interest annuity for your current spouse at retirement. If the former spouse later loses entitlement to the court-ordered survivor annuity, you can request that the reduction in your annuity to provide the insurable interest annuity be converted to the regular survivor annuity reduction. Your current spouse would then be entitled to the regular survivor annuity.

Termination of the Reduction in Your Annuity to Provide a Survivor Benefit

Current Spouse—The reduction in your annuity to provide a survivor annuity for your current spouse stops if your marriage ends because of death, divorce, or annulment.

Former Spouse—The reduction in your annuity to provide a survivor annuity for a former spouse stops if the former spouse dies, if the former spouse remarries before reaching age 55, or under the terms of the court order that required you to provide the survivor annuity for the former spouse when you retired. (Modifications to the court order issued after you retire do not affect the former spouse survivor annuity.)

Insurable Interest—The reduction in your annuity to provide an insurable interest annuity stops if the person you name to receive the insurable interest annuity dies or if the person you name is your current spouse and you change your election because a former spouse has lost entitlement to a survivor annuity. The reduction also ends if, after you retire, you marry the insurable interest beneficiary and elect to provide a spousal survivor annuity for that person. If you marry someone other than the insurable interest beneficiary after you retire and elect to provide a survivor annuity for your spouse, you may elect to cancel the insurable interest reduction at that time.

Section 3—Cost of Living Adjustments (COLAs)

General Rules and Procedures

The annual adjustments to annuities to reflect changes in the cost-of-living represent one of the most important provisions in federal retirement programs. Studies show that private-sector pensions replace about one-third or less of the lost purchasing power of the benefits paid from those plans. In contrast, CSRS and Social Security return annuities to their full value each year (unless specifically modified by changes in law), and FERS provides almost full inflation protection.

Under P.L.103-66, COLAs for 1994, 1995 and 1996 were delayed three months. Thus, the adjustment was shown in April checks in each of those years.

Initial cost-of-living adjustments for newly retired employees are prorated depending on the month in which their annuity begins. For example, to get the full January 2003 COLA, a retiree or survivor annuity must have begun no later than December 31, 2001. Those whose annuities began after that date got one-twelfth of the increase for each month they received benefits before the effective date of the COLA, which was December 1, 2002.

If the COLA will cause an annuity to exceed the pay rate for GS-15, Step 10, at the highest locality pay possible, the adjustment will be capped at that figure. However, if an individual's final salary (or "high-3" average salary, if higher) increased by all cumulative average general schedule salary increases from the commencing date of his or her annuity to the COLA date is greater than the highest rate for GS-15, step 10, this latter amount will be the annuity cap.

Cumulative GS increases are used in all cases, even though the individual may have been employed under a different pay system. While this cap applies to any increases added to an already-existing annuity, in no instance will an annuity that presently exceeds the cap be reduced.

CSRS COLAs

The cost-of-living increases for civil service retirees and survivor annuitants normally are effective each December, payable in January checks. The percentage increases of these COLAs will be determined by the average CPI/W (Consumer Price Index for Urban Wage Earners and Clerical Workers) for the third quarter of each year over the third quarter average CPI/W index of the previous year.

Retiree COLAs of Recent Years

Federal Employees Retirement System

Year	Rate	Year	Rate	Year	Rate
2003	1.4	1998	2.0	1992	2.0
2002	2.0	1997	2.0	1991	2.7
2001	2.5	1996	2.0*	1990	4.4
2000	2.0	1995	2.0*	1989	3.7
1999	1.3	1994	2.0*	1988	3.0

Civil Service Retirement System

Year	Rate	Year	Rate	Year	Rate
2003	1.4	1998	2.1	1992	3.0
2002	2.6	1997	2.9	1991	3.7
2001	3.5	1996	2.6*	1990	5.4
2000	2.4	1995	2.8*	1989	4.7
1999	1.3	1994	2.6*	1988	4.0

* Delayed three months until April of each year, under P.L. 103-66.

FERS COLAs

The following FERS benefits are increased annually by cost of living adjustments:

• retirement benefits payable to retirees age 62 and older;

• retirement benefits payable to law enforcement officers, firefighters, air traffic controllers, military reserve technicians who lost their military status due to medical reasons and who were age 50 with at least 25 years of service, and special CIA employees;

• survivor benefits; and

• disability retirement benefits.

The amount of the increase depends upon the annual change in the Consumer Price Index for Urban Wage Earners and Clerical Workers (CPI/W). If it increases by 3 percent or more in any year, the benefits in the above table are increased by the CPI/W minus 1 percentage point. If the CPI/W increases by 2 percent to 3 percent, the adjustment will be two percent. If the CPI/W increase is 2 percent or less, the adjustment will equal the CPI/W.

Section 4—Reemployment of Annuitants

General Rules

Federal retirees may be reemployed in any position for which they are qualified unless they have accepted a buyout incentive payment to retire. In that case, the law bars reemployment for five years, including under a personal services contract type arrangement, unless the full (pre-tax) amount of the buyout is repaid. Note: Former employees of the Department of Defense are only barred from accepting a personal services contract for one year.

In general, annuity payments and salaries of returning annuitants may not be combined and the salaries of those reemployed annuitants who retired voluntarily will be offset by the amount of the annuity. Those who retired early under a discontinued service retirement will have their annuity suspended for the period of reemployment.

Reemployed annuitants who have recovered from disability or who were involuntarily separated are subject to mandatory deductions under CSRS or FERS. CSRS reemployed annuitants whose annuities are subtracted from their pay may elect to have deductions made; retirement deductions are mandatory for FERS reemployed annuitants.

The Office of Personnel Management maintains an online Federal Reemployment Readiness Form at *http://apps.opm.gov/patriots/index.htm* for those interested in returning to government service. OPM forwards completed forms to the appropriate federal agencies, which contact interested individuals directly when they are able to match skills with their mission needs.

Reemployment to Meet Exceptional Needs

The Federal Employees Pay Comparability Act of 1990 permits OPM to authorize retired military and federal civilian personnel to be employed without offset of pay or annuity when such employment is needed to meet exceptional needs in recruiting or retaining qualified candidates for particular positions or under unusual circumstances. There are two conditions under which OPM may authorize exceptions to the reduction in pay or annuity normally required for either military or civilian retirees: (1) for temporary employment that is necessary due to an emergency involving a direct threat to life or property or other unusual circumstances (which may be delegated to agencies), and (2) on a case-by-case basis for employees in positions for which there is exceptional difficulty in recruiting or retaining a qualified employee.

Reemployment as an Expert or under a Personal Services Contract

Some federal annuitants are rehired under "personal services" contracts, whose terms vary greatly among agencies, occupations and locations. In some cases such contracts can make the individuals eligible for certain benefits. In addition, some annuitants are rehired under a special non-competitive appointment authority for experts and consultants. See the Hiring and Placement section in Chapter 8.

Effect on CSRS Annuity

If Annuity Stops—Reemployment with the government will cause your annuity to stop if:
• you are a disability annuitant whom OPM has found recovered or restored to earning capacity prior to reemployment;
• you are a disability annuitant who was not disabled for your National Guard Technician position but were awarded disability annuity because you were medically disqualified for continued membership in the National Guard;
• your annuity is based on an involuntary separation (other than a separation that was required by law based on your age and length of service or a separation for cause

on charges of misconduct or delinquency) and your new appointment is permanent in nature (for example—career, career-conditional, or excepted); or
• you receive a Presidential appointment subject to retirement deductions.

If your annuity stops as the result of your reemployment with the government, your status will be that of a regular employee.

If your new appointment gives retirement coverage:
• the coverage will be CSRS if you had CSRS coverage when you retired, and you are reemployed within one year of your retirement.
• the coverage will be CSRS-Offset (CSRS and Social Security coverage) if you had CSRS-Offset coverage when you retired, you are reemployed more than a year after your retirement, or you are appointed to a senior position that is subject to mandatory Social Security coverage.

You will be eligible to transfer to FERS if you are reemployed after a break in service of more than three days and your new appointment is neither temporary nor intermittent.

When your reemployment ends, a new determination about your rights to retirement benefits will be made. Your prior retirement benefit generally has no impact on your new retirement benefit.

If you meet all the requirements for an immediate retirement, your benefit will be computed as though you are retiring for the first time. (Note: The unused sick leave balance used in the initial retirement computation will be added to the unused sick leave balance when your reemployment ends.)

Generally, you will have to wait until age 62 to receive a deferred annuity if you do not qualify for an immediate retirement benefit when your reemployment ends.

In rare situations, an annuity based on an involuntary retirement may be reinstated when your reemployment ends. The annuity will be reinstated if:
• you were reemployed after more than one year of your initial retirement, and
• your reemployment lasted less than one year.

A disability annuity may be reinstated when your reemployment ends if:
• you have not reached age 62,
• you were reemployed more than one year after you separated for disability retirement,

• your reemployment lasted less than one year, and your disability has recurred, or your earnings capacity falls below the 80 percent limitation.

If Annuity Continues—If your annuity does not stop under the rules above, then you will continue to receive it while you are working. Your pay will be reduced by the amount of annuity paid for the period you work. If you do not work full time, the reduction in pay will be adjusted proportionately. However, some pay is not subject to this reduction for annuity. Pay is not reduced for annuity for a period during which you have elected to receive injury compensation benefits in lieu of annuity or when you receive a lump-sum payment of annual leave on separation.

Effect on FERS Annuity

If Annuity Stops—Reemployment with the government will cause your annuity to stop if:

• you are a disability annuitant whom OPM has found recovered or restored to earning capability prior to reemployment; or

• you are a disability annuitant who was not disabled for your National Guard Technician position but were awarded disability annuity because you were medically disqualified for continued membership in the National Guard.

When your annuity stops, you have the same status as any other federal employee employed in an equivalent position with a similar service history. Your retirement coverage will be FERS.

When you again leave federal service, you will be entitled to either an immediate or deferred FERS annuity based on this new separation. Generally, the annuity will be computed on the basis of your service and salary history at the time of the future separation from federal service.

If Annuity Continues—If your annuity does not stop under the provisions above, you will continue to receive it while you are working. Your pay will be reduced by the amount of annuity paid for the period you worked. If you do not work full-time, the reduction in pay will be adjusted proportionately.

However, some pay is not subject to this reduction for annuity. Pay is not reduced

for annuity for a period during which you have elected to receive injury compensation benefits in lieu of annuity, or when you receive a lump-sum payment of annual leave on separation. Unless your reemployment is on an intermittent basis, retirement deductions will be withheld from your pay. The retirement deductions are a percentage of your basic pay, before it is reduced for annuity.

Supplemental and Recomputed Annuities

Reemployment may increase your retirement and death benefits. As a reemployed annuitant, you can earn either a supplemental annuity or a re-determined annuity. A supplemental annuity is an annuity that is added on to your present annuity. A re-determined annuity is a recomputed annuity that takes the place of your present annuity.

If you work as a reemployed annuitant on a full time, continuous basis for at least one year, you may be entitled to a supplemental annuity. If you work part time, you must work a proportionately longer period to earn a supplemental annuity. If your reemployment continues for at least five years, or the part-time equivalent, you may elect a re-determined annuity.

Intermittent service cannot be counted in establishing eligibility for a supplemental or re-determined annuity and cannot be used in the computation of a supplemental annuity.

If you die while reemployed, after becoming eligible for either a supplemental or re-determined annuity, your surviving spouse may have his or her survivor benefit either increased or recomputed.

Note: CSRS reemployed annuitant service cannot be credited in a supplemental or re-determined annuity unless a deposit is paid after separation, or retirement deductions are withheld. If you are reemployed in a full-time or part-time position, you may elect to have retirement deductions withheld from your pay. The amount of retirement deductions or deposit is a percentage of your basic pay before it is reduced for annuity. Retirement deductions are mandatory for FERS reemployed annuitants.

Disability Retirees

If Under Age 60—If you are reemployed on a permanent basis in a position equivalent in grade and pay to the position from which you retired, or if you are reemployed subject to medical and physical qualification standards equivalent to those of the position from which you retired, OPM may find that you have recovered from your disability.

If you are reemployed in a position that is not equivalent to the one you held at retirement, your annuity will continue and your salary will be offset by the amount of your annuity for the period of reemployment. You will be subject to the 80 percent earnings limit. You reach the 80 percent earnings limit if, in any calendar year, your income from wages and self-employment is at least 80 percent of the current rate of basic pay for the position from which you retired.

The pay of the position in which you are reemployed, prior to the offset of annuity, will be included as earnings in determining whether you are restored to earning capacity and your annuity must stop.

Receipt of, or continued entitlement to receive, full or partial injury compensation during reemployment, when those benefits are based on the same injury or medical condition that is the basis for OPM's award of disability retirement, is considered conclusive evidence (unless there is contravening medical evidence) that you have not recovered from your disability.

If Age 60 or Over—If you are a disability retiree age 60 or older at the time of reemployment, your annuity payments will continue and your salary will be reduced by the amount of your annuity. There is no limit on the amount of earnings you may receive. You will not be found recovered on the basis of your employment unless you specifically request to be found recovered.

Exceptions

Not all of the above rules apply to all reemployed annuitants. You should ask your employing agency for information about special retirement rules that may apply to you if you are reemployed:

• under special provisions for positions for which there is exceptional difficulty in recruiting or retaining a qualified employee or there is a direct threat to life or property, or other unusual circumstances warranting emergency employment;

• on an interim basis, as a consequence of an administrative or judicial body reviewing the grounds for your separation;

• as a Presidential appointee to a position that is permanent in nature;

• as a former Member of Congress who separated from Congressional service with more than five years of service as a Member of Congress;

• as a Justice or Judge of the United States, as defined by Section 451 of Title 28 of the United States Code; or

• under another retirement system for federal employees.

Health Insurance

If your annuity stops upon reemployment, your Federal Employees Health Benefits program coverage as an annuitant stops, too. If your appointment is one that gives you eligibility for FEHB coverage, you can enroll in FEHB when you are reemployed.

If your annuity continues after you are reemployed, your FEHB coverage as an annuitant continues and withholding of premiums continues to be made from your annuity payment.

Under Section 125 of the Internal Revenue Code, pre-tax benefits available in the FEHB—so-called "premium conversion," in which premiums are paid with pre-tax money—are only available to current employees. Thus, annuitants and compensationers whose FEHB premiums are deducted from annuities and benefits are not eligible to participate in premium conversion. However, special rules apply to reemployed annuitants. They become eligible for premium conversion as active employees upon their reemployment and become eligible for the tax savings.

Reemployed annuitants enrolled in the FEHB automatically participate in premium conversion, provided they are employed in a position that conveys FEHB eligibility and by an agency covered by premium conversion.

Agencies must deduct FEHB premiums on a pre-tax basis, unless the rehired annuitants waive participation in premium conversion. Reemployed annuitants have an initial opportunity to waive their participation in premium conversion. The waiver will be effective on the first day of the first pay period after the date the employing office receives it.

All participants in premium conversion must have their FEHB premiums deducted from their pay as employees, not from their retirement annuities. To allow eligible reemployed annuitants an opportunity to participate in premium conversion, their FEHB enrollment must be transferred from their retirement system to their employing agency.

Newly hired reemployed annuitants who are not enrolled in FEHB may participate in premium conversion if they are rehired in a position that conveys eligibility for FEHB coverage. They may enroll in FEHB under the same terms as any newly hired employee and will automatically participate in premium conversion unless they file a waiver.

Life Insurance

If your annuity stops upon reemployment, your Federal Employees Group Life Insurance as an annuitant stops without a right to convert to an individual policy. You acquire life insurance coverage as an employee under the same conditions as any other employee who is rehired in the federal service.

If your annuity continues after you are reemployed, you retain the life insurance you have as a retiree. However, if the type of appointment you have makes you eligible for FEGLI coverage as an employee, Basic life insurance, Standard Optional insurance, and the Family Optional insurance are suspended. They will be resumed at the same rate when the reemployment ends, except for any applicable reductions that normally begin at age 65.

During your reemployment, you will have Basic, Standard Optional, and Family Optional as an employee (including Accidental Death and Dismemberment coverage, where applicable) and withholding of premiums will be made from your pay. The cost of Additional Optional insurance, if you have it, will continue to be withheld from your annuity payment unless you request that it also be suspended so that you can have Additional Optional insurance as an employee. If you choose to have Additional Optional insurance as an employee, you will be subject to the same conditions as other employees who are rehired.

If you die during the period of reemployment, your survivor will receive either the amount of Basic Life insurance you had as an employee or the amount of the suspended Basic Life you had as an annuitant, whichever is larger. If you have Standard Optional insurance, the amount you have as an employee is the amount payable if you die as a reemployed annuitant. If you have Additional Optional insurance as an employee rather than as an annuitant, the amount you have as an employee is the amount payable if you die as a reemployed annuitant. If you had Additional Optional as an annuitant, that is the amount payable.

> Note: If you retire and are reemployed under a temporary appointment without a break in service or a break in service of three days or less, you are eligible for FEGLI coverage as an employee. If the break in service before the temporary appointment begins is more than three days, you are not generally eligible for FEGLI coverage as an employee.

Caution: Any waiver or declination of insurance you file as a reemployed annuitant will affect your suspended life insurance as an annuitant as well as the coverage you have as an employee.

When you leave the reemployment, you can keep insurance you acquired because of the reemployment if:
- you qualify for a supplemental annuity or you acquire a new annuity right; and
- you have had the insurance (or number of multiples, in the case of Additional Optional insurance) as an employee (including the time as a reemployed annuitant) for at least the five years of service immediately preceding your separation from the reemployment (or for all periods of service during which you were eligible for the insurance, if less than five years).

If you keep insurance you acquired during the reemployment, the suspended insurance of the same type terminates.

Thrift Savings Plan

If you are rehired to a position covered by FERS or CSRS or an equivalent retirement plan, the following rules apply:

If your break in service is less than 31 full calendar days, you are not eligible to withdraw your account. If you are a FERS participant, your new agency should start making its automatic (one percent) contribution immediately. Whether you are FERS or CSRS, your own contributions to your account should continue automatically when you are rehired. (Check your earnings and leave statement.) If the agency's or your own contributions do not resume, contact the agency's personnel office.

If your break in service is 31 or more full calendar days, you are eligible, but not required, to withdraw the portion of your account that is attributable to your previous employment. If you wish to withdraw that portion of your account, the TSP office must receive your Withdrawal Request while you are still separated from government service.

If you had requested a withdrawal to begin at a future date and you are rehired before that date, the TSP will not process your withdrawal. Also, if you are receiving a series of monthly payments from the TSP and are subsequently rehired, the monthly payments will stop. However, annuity payments will continue despite your rehire.

If you are rehired but are not covered by FERS or CSRS or an equivalent retirement plan, the rules outlined above that apply to participants with a break in service of 31 or more full calendar days apply to you.

Buyouts

An individual who received a voluntary separation incentive, or buyout, payment and who comes back to work for the government of the United States within five years must repay the entire pre-tax payment. This includes employment with any part of the federal government, including the Postal Service. Repayment for reemployment with the federal government may be waived by the Office of Personnel Management only in rare instances where the individual involved possesses unique abilities and is the only qualified person available. There is no authority to approve a waiver of repayment for buyout takers who wish to enter into personal services contracts with the federal government.

If you retired with a buyout payment and are considering returning to work with any part of the government, ask the agency where you want to work about the effect of reemployment payment you received.

Typically reemployed annuitants are not eligible to receive buyouts from those positions. For details, see the Buyouts section in Chapter 8.

Employment in the Private Sector

Your employment outside the federal service will not affect your basic annuity payments unless you're receiving a disability annuity and are under age 60, as explained above. If you are receiving a FERS Special Retirement Supplement, it will be reduced based on how much you earn over the annual Social Security Earnings Test limit; also note that the Earnings Test applies to any Social Security component received after age 62 (see Chapter 3).

If you are employed with a company that contracts with or receives grants from the federal government, special restrictions may apply. Contact the ethics office of your former agency, or contact the Office of Government Ethics, Suite 500, 1201 New York Avenue, N.W., Washington, DC 20005-3917, phone (202) 208-8000, online at www.usoge.gov. Also see the OGE Section in Chapter 9.

Chapter 5
Leave and Other Benefits

Section 1—Paid Time Off

Annual and Sick Leave: General Rules

The federal government has made provisions for authorized absence from work, usually through earned leave, for most of its employees. These provisions, spelled out in chapter 63 of Title 5, U.S. Code, enable employees to take off for vacations or personal business, or when they are ill.

The leave law applies to most civilian employees of the government. Among those employees who are exempt from the leave law are congressional employees and those workers who do not have established tours of duty.

Except for emergencies, an employee's use of annual leave generally must be authorized in advance, usually by the employee's immediate supervisor.

Authorization for sick leave, because of its nature, is not usually obtained in advance, except for cases where employees know they will be unable to work because of medical, dental, or optical examinations or treatment, an operation, a period of convalescence, a lengthy illness, or something similar.

Employees absent from work because of illness may be required to submit administratively acceptable evidence that they were ill and unable to work for periods in excess of three workdays or for a lesser period when determined necessary. The agency may require a medical certificate.

Charges for annual and sick leave are normally in increments of one hour. However, an agency may on its own initiative, or on the basis of union negotiations, establish a policy for charging leave in lesser amounts.

Advanced Leave—At the discretion of the agency, a maximum of 30 days of sick leave may be advanced to an employee with a serious disability or ailment or for purposes related to the adoption of a child. A maximum of five days of sick leave may be advanced for family care or bereavement purposes.

Supervisors may grant advance annual leave consistent with agency policy. The amount of annual leave that may be advanced is limited to the amount of annual leave an employee would accrue in the remainder of the leave year. Employees do not have an entitlement to advanced annual leave. In most cases, when an employee who is indebted for advanced annual or sick leave separates from federal service, he or she is required to refund the amount of advanced leave for which he or she is indebted.

RIF Situations—In reduction-in-force and other restructuring situations, an employee may use annual leave to establish initial eligibility for retirement or to continue health insurance coverage into retirement so that the employee may remain on the agency's rolls after the effective date employee would otherwise have been separated. Employees may not use advanced annual leave for these purposes, but only accrued or restored annual leave that has been credited to their account before the effective date of a RIF or relocation and annual leave earned while in a paid leave status after the effective date of the RIF or relocation. In a RIF situation, whatever retention standing an employee had when these rights are exercised remains in force until the RIF is completed. Once employees exercise these rights and they are retained under this authority, they may not use any other type of leave.

Annual and Sick Leave: Accrual and Use

Annual leave is earned on the basis of years of federal service, including creditable military service. Full-time employees with 15 years or more service earn 26 days of annual leave a year; those with three but less than 15 years earn 20 days; and those with less than three years earn 13 days. Normally, part-time employees with 15 years or more service earn one hour of annual leave for each ten hours in a pay status, those with three but less than 15 years earn one hour for each 13 hours in pay status, and those with less than three years earn one hour for each 20 hours in pay status.

Full-time employees earn 13 days sick leave a year; part-time workers earn one hour of sick leave for each 20 hours in a pay status.

Employees are permitted to accumulate annual leave, but within certain limitations. The law permits most employees to accumulate 30 days of annual leave, although overseas employees are allowed to accumulate 45 days. Under this system, employees have to "use or lose" their excess leave by the end of the leave year with certain exceptions. Employees with an authorized accumulation in excess of 30 days who return to a position with a 30-day maximum accumulation limit are allowed to retain their excess annual leave until used. Special rules apply to SES members.

In determining annual leave accrual rate for military retirees, credit for military service is limited to service during a war, or in a campaign or expedition for which a campaign badge is authorized, unless the retiree was retired on the basis of combat disability, or was employed on November 30, 1964, in a federal civilian position to which the annual and sick leave laws apply, and has not had a break in service of more than 30 days thereafter (5 USC 6303(a)).

Generally, when employees transfer between positions, accrued amounts of annual and sick leave are transferred to the new employing agency. When employees transfer to agencies with a different leave system, the leave normally is transferred, sometimes on an adjusted basis.

New employees may use their annual leave as they earn it during their first 90 days if their appointments are for 90 days or longer.

There is no limit on the amount of sick leave that can be accumulated. Employees who leave federal service are not entitled to lump-sum payments for unused sick leave. However, if workers are reemployed in the federal service after December 2, 1994, the amount of previously accumulated, unused sick leave is re-credited to their accounts (unless it was previously forfeited due to reemployment before Dec. 2, 1994). (Prior to 1994, the allowable period of separation was three years.)

Retirees under the Civil Service Retirement System are entitled to a credit for the amount of unused sick leave they've accumulated at the time of retirement for purposes of calculating their service credits used in computing retirement annuities. With one exception, this sick leave credit, which has been effective since October 20, 1969, does not apply to annuity calculations of employees covered by the Federal Employees Retirement System. The exception is that those who transferred to FERS with a CSRS annuity component may receive credit for the amount of unused sick leave they had at the date of transfer or the date of retirement, whichever is less.

Restoration of Forfeited Annual Leave

Agencies may restore annual leave that was forfeited because it was in excess of the maximum leave ceilings if the leave was forfeited because of an administrative error, exigency of the public business, or sickness of the employee, under Section 6304 (d) of Title 5, U.S.C. An agency must restore the annual leave in a separate leave account.

The employing agency determines what constitutes an administrative error, that an exigency is of major importance and that excess annual leave cannot be used, or that the annual leave was forfeited because of a period of absence due to an employee's sickness or injury that occurred late in the leave year or was of such duration that the excess annual leave could not be rescheduled for use before the end of the leave year. (Note: Leave years do not run concurrent with calendar years. Typically a leave year ends a number of days into the succeeding calendar year.)

An agency typically may consider for restoration annual leave that was forfeited due to an exigency of the public business or sickness of the employee only if the annual leave was scheduled in writing before the start of the third biweekly pay period prior to the end of the leave year.

An employee must schedule and use restored annual leave not later than the end of the leave year ending two years after:
• the date of restoration of the annual leave forfeited because of administrative error;
• the date fixed by the head of the agency

or designee as the date of termination of the exigency of the public business; or

• the date the employee is determined to be recovered from illness or injury and able to return to duty.

Restored annual leave that is not used within the established time limits is forfeited with no further right to restoration. Administrative error may not serve as the basis to extend the time limit within which to use restored annual leave. This is so even if the agency fails to establish a separate leave account, fix the date for the expiration of the time limit, or properly advise the employee regarding the rules for using restored annual leave, absent agency regulations requiring otherwise.

On March 4, 2002, the Office of Personnel Management issued in the Federal Register regulations to provide that employees who forfeited excess annual leave because of their work to support the nation during the national emergency declared after the September 11, 2001, terrorist attacks on the World Trade Center and the Pentagon were deemed to have scheduled their excess annual leave in advance. Such employees were entitled to restoration of their annual leave under the rules.

A similar grant of authority made in 1999 that permitted use or lose annual leave to be restored to employees who were determined to be necessary to the Y2K conversion effort expired at the end of leave year 2002.

Lump-Sum Payments at Separation or Retirement

Employees receive a lump-sum payment for accrued annual leave when they separate from federal service or may elect to receive a lump-sum payment when they enter on active duty with the armed forces. Under the rules stipulated in 5 U.S.C. 5551, the amount of this lump-sum payment must equal the pay employees would have received if they had remained employed until their annual leave ran out.

Generally, upon separation from federal employment, employees are entitled to payment for annual leave credited to their accounts, including the carry-over balance, the unused leave accrued during the year, and any unused restored leave. In the event of an employee's death, survivors are enti-tled to payment for all annual leave credited to the employee at time of death. (Postal Service regulations provide for lump-sum payments for unused accumulated annual leave, but place certain restrictions upon payment for leave accrued during the year of separation.)

The types of pay included in a lump-sum payment are those that an employee would have received on a biweekly basis had he or she remained in federal service on annual leave, excluding allowances that are paid for the sole purpose of encouraging an employee to remain in government service. These are: basic pay; locality pay or other similar geographic adjustment; within-grade increase (if waiting period met on date of separation); across-the-board annual adjustments; administratively uncontrollable overtime pay, availability pay, and standby duty pay; night differential (for wage system employees only); regularly scheduled overtime pay under the Fair Labor Standards Act for employees on uncommon tours of duty; supervisory differentials; non-foreign area cost-of-living allowances and post differentials; and foreign area post allowances. If a statutory pay adjustment becomes effective during the employee's lump-sum leave period, the lump sum is adjusted to reflect the increased rate beginning on the effective date of the pay adjustment.

In calculating a lump-sum payment, an agency projects forward an employee's annual leave for all the workdays the employee would have worked if he or she had remained in federal service. By law, holidays are counted as workdays in projecting the lump-sum leave period. If an employee is reemployed in the federal service prior to the expiration of the period of annual leave (i.e., the lump-sum leave period), he or she must refund the portion of the lump-sum payment that represents the period between the date of reemployment and the expiration of the lump-sum period. An agency re-credits to the employee's leave account the amount of annual leave equal to the days or hours of work remaining between the date of reemployment and the expiration of the lump-sum leave period.

SES Members: Annual Leave Rules

Members of the Senior Executive

Service are subject to special annual leave rules and procedures, most of which became effective October 13, 1994, with enactment of Section 201 of the Government Management Reform Act of 1994 (GMRA), Public Law 103-356.

Ninety-day (720 hour) Limit on Leave Accumulation—GMRA established a new 90-day (720-hour) limit on the amount of annual leave both current and future Senior Executive Service (SES) members may carry over from one leave year to the next. Since the inception of the Senior Executive Service, SES members had been exempt from the normal annual leave accumulation ceilings of 30 days (240 hours) and 45 days (360 hours) applicable to most federal workers and to overseas employees contained in 5 U.S.C. 6304. The law did include a grandfather clause allowing current SES members with accumulated annual leave balances in excess of 90 days to retain their excess annual leave as their "personal leave ceiling" (see below).

SES Personal Leave Ceiling—If the amount of accrued leave and accumulated annual leave in an SES member's leave account as of October 13, 1994, was in excess of 90 days, that amount became his or her personal leave ceiling. Amounts of annual leave that are advanced or restored to SES members are not included in their personal leave ceiling. Restored annual leave is placed in a separate leave account and must be used within a two-year period.

The personal leave ceiling is subject to reduction under the rules in 5 U.S.C. 6304(c). An SES member's personal leave ceiling must be reduced by the number of hours used in excess of the number of hours earned during the previous year. Once the personal leave ceiling falls below 90 days (720 hours), it is eliminated and the SES member becomes subject to the 90-day (720-hour) limit.

"Use or Lose" Leave—If an SES member begins a new leave year with 720 or more hours of annual leave and earns more annual leave than used in that leave year, the excess leave hours will be forfeited at the beginning of the succeeding leave year. All SES members are subject to the "use or lose" rules for the forfeiture of excess annual leave under 5 CFR 630.302 for any leave earned and not used in a leave year that is in excess

of the new 720-hour ceiling. Thus, SES members who have 1,000 hours as a personal leave ceiling at the start of a leave year and earn 100 hours more than they use in that year will lose those 100 hours, and their personal leave ceiling will remain at 1,000 hours at the beginning of the next leave year.

SES members are eligible for the temporary restoration (normally for two years) of annual leave forfeited because of exigencies of the public business or sickness, as described above.

Lump-sum Payments at Separation or Retirement—At the time of an SES member's separation or retirement, all unused accrued annual leave is payable as a lump-sum at the rate of pay in effect. If an SES pay adjustment becomes effective during the employee's lump-sum leave period, the lump-sum payment is adjusted to reflect the increased rate beginning on the effective date of the pay adjustment.

Holidays

Government workers are entitled to the following ten regular holidays each year (also see Leave Chart in back of book):

- New Year's Day, January 1
- Martin Luther King, Jr.'s Birthday, 3rd Monday in January
- Presidents Day, 3rd Monday in February
- Memorial Day, last Monday in May
- Independence Day, July 4
- Labor Day, 1st Monday in September
- Columbus Day, 2nd Monday in October
- Veterans Day, November 11
- Thanksgiving Day, 4th Thursday in November
- Christmas Day, December 25

When Inauguration Day falls within the regularly scheduled tour of duty of an employee in the Metropolitan Washington, D.C., area, it is observed as a holiday. There is no provision for an "in lieu of" day when an employee is not scheduled to work on Inauguration Day.

When a holiday falls on a non-workday outside a full-time employee's 40-hour basic workweek or the employee's basic work requirement for the week, the day to be treated as the employee's holiday is the workday immediately preceding the non-workday. There are four exceptions:

(1) When the non-workday is Sunday (or "in lieu" of Sunday), the next workday is

the "in lieu of" holiday;

(2) There is no provision in law for an "in lieu" of holiday if Inauguration Day falls on a non-workday; and

(3) Under Public Law 104-201, an agency head may issue rules under which a different "in lieu of" holiday may be designated than would otherwise be required for full-time employees under compressed work schedules. These rules would be issued when the head of the agency determines that a different "in lieu of" holiday is necessary to prevent an adverse agency impact, as defined in 5 U.S.C. 6131(b) (This authority became effective on September 23, 1996.); and

(4) Whenever Monday is designated as a holiday, the first regularly scheduled workday in the week is the holiday for a federal employee working overseas whose basic workweek includes Monday but is not the typical Monday through Friday work schedule found in the United States. This has the effect of providing three-day weekends (Friday, Saturday, and Sunday) for employees working overseas whose basic workweek is Sunday through Thursday. This authority became effective on October 17, 1998.

Time Off as an Incentive

Federal employees are eligible for paid time off as an incentive. Agencies may grant employees time off from duty, without loss of pay or charge to leave, to recognize excellent employee performance.

Agencies may grant time-off awards alone or in combination with monetary or non-monetary awards to recognize the same kinds of employee contributions. Time-off awards are not intended to replace other awards.

Agencies may choose to exclude certain categories of employees from eligibility for time-off incentives (for example, SES members or intermittent employees). However, unless agencies make such an exclusion, all federal employees who meet the definition of employee under 5 U.S.C. 2105 are eligible for time-off awards. Similarly, agencies may choose to restrict the kinds of contributions that time-off awards will be used to recognize.

If a scale of benefits is used, agencies are to avoid creating an equivalency between time-off awards and cash awards. Under no circumstances may a time-off award be converted to a cash payment.

Section 2—Paid Leave: Other Authorized Uses

Military Leave

Permanent or temporary indefinite full-time government employees in the National Guard or the reserve accrue 15 days of military leave each fiscal year for use when called for active duty or active duty training. As a result of the DoD Authorization Act of 1990, employees may also use accrued military leave for inactive-duty training. They get their regular civilian pay plus military pay on days of military leave. Part-time career employees accrue military leave at a proportionate rate to the number of hours in their regularly scheduled workweek. Unused military leave accumulates for use in succeeding years but no more than 15 days may be carried over into a new fiscal year. Permanent or temporary indefinite federal employees, when called to duty as Guard members or reservists for purposes related to public safety, are also entitled to leave not to exceed an additional 22 workdays in any calendar year, with military pay for any portion of the 22 days so

used being offset against civilian pay for the same period. Employees may choose to use annual leave instead of military leave for any of the 22 work days, and no offset against civilian pay will be made.

Further, Reserve and National Guard Technicians are entitled to 44 workdays of military leave for duties overseas under certain conditions.

The 15 days of military leave are credited to a full-time employee on the basis of an eight-hour workday. A full-time employee working a 40-hour workweek will accrue 120 hours (15 days x 8 hours) of military leave in a fiscal year, or the equivalent of three 40-hour workweeks. Military leave for active duty or inactive duty training is pro-rated for part-time employees and for employees on uncommon tours of duty based proportionally on the number of hours in the employee's regularly scheduled biweekly pay period.

The minimum charge to leave is one

hour. An employee may be charged military leave only for hours that the employee would otherwise have worked and received pay.

Employees who request military leave for inactive duty training (which generally is 2, 4, or 6 hours in length) are charged only the amount of military leave necessary to cover the period of training and necessary travel. Members of the Reserves and the National Guard are no longer charged military leave for weekends and holidays that occur within the period of military service.

An employee's civilian pay typically remains the same for periods of military leave including any premium pay minus Sunday premium pay an employee would have received if not on military leave.

Military Leave for Funeral Honors Duty—Section 563 of Public Law 107-107 permitted employees to use the 15 days of military leave provided under that section for "funeral honors duty" as described in Section 12503 of Title 10 and Section 115 of Title 32, United States Code. This entitlement became effective on December 28, 2001. Each agency is responsible for administering the use of military leave for funeral honors duty for its employees.

Court Leave

Federal employees called to court as witnesses on behalf of the U.S. government, the District of Columbia, or a state or local government, or to serve on a jury, are authorized to receive pay during such absence from work status without charge to leave.

Court leave includes periods of absence in which employees are summoned to appear as witnesses on behalf of a private party in a judicial proceeding to which the United States, the District of Columbia, or a state or local government is a party. Any fees payable for such service must be collected and turned in to the employing agency. Any payments designated as expenses by the court or other appropriate authority may be retained.

Leave for Bone Marrow or Organ Donation

Federal employees are entitled to take up to seven days of paid leave in a calendar year (in addition to sick or annual leave) to serve as a bone marrow donor and up to 30 days of paid leave in a calendar year to serve as an organ donor.

Absence for Funerals of Federal Law Enforcement Officers or Firefighters

Federal law enforcement officers or firefighters are entitled to be excused from duty to attend the funeral of a fellow law enforcement officer or firefighter, under Section 642 of Public Law 103-329, which amended section 6327 of Title 5, U.S.C. Under these rules, a law officer's or firefighter's attendance at such a service is to be considered official duty, and the agency may pay the employee's travel, transportation, and subsistence expenses as provided under 30 U.S.C. 1345.

Sick Leave to Care for Family Members

Employees can use their sick time for family members—defined as a spouse, spouse's parents, children and their spouses, parents, brothers and sisters and their spouses, and others whose close association creates the equivalent of a family relationship—who have conditions for which an employee would qualify for sick leave himself or herself, if afflicted personally. This includes care for a family member who is incapacitated as a result of physical or mental illness, injury, pregnancy, childbirth or medical, dental or optical examination or treatment.

Employees may use up to five days of sick leave per year for that purpose. Those who wish to use more than five days for that purpose, however, must have a reserve of sick leave of at least 80 hours, or ten days' worth. In no case may an employee use more than 13 days of sick leave to care for family members in a year.

Under the same limitations, employees may use any or all of the 13 days of sick leave to make arrangements for or attend the funeral of persons meeting the definition of a family member.

Part-time employees and employees under uncommon tours of duty are eligible to use the leave on a basis proportional to that of full-time employees.

Beginning June 20, 2000, an employee may use a total of up to 12 administrative workweeks of sick leave each year to care for a family member with a serious health condition. If an employee previously has used any portion of the 13 days of sick leave for gener-

Other Helpful Resources from *Federal Employees News Digest*

FINANCIAL AND RETIREMENT PLANNING

Your Financial Guide

Your Financial Guide is a plain-English, step-by-step financial planning manual designed for the special needs of federal and postal employees. In simple, clear language, this book will help you put your financial affairs in order. It takes the mystery and complexity out of financial planning, plus it shows you how to care for your family after your death. Includes a number of financial and estate planning tools, numerous worksheets and personal record organizers. $17.95

CSRS/FERS Benefits Calculator 2003 – Personal PLUS Version

Find out if you'll have a gap in retirement income! The CSRS and FERS Benefits Calculator enables federal and postal employees to perform a quick and thorough analysis of all the factors and timing that affect retirement benefits and investigate all the variables to determine the best strategy for retirement. Now also includes long-term care calculator. PC software on CD-ROM. Free updates throughout 2003 included. $29.95. Professional Version available for multiple client files (ideal for managers, personnel offices, insurance agents and financial planners). $119.95

FEND's Financial Planning Kit

43.90

Includes: one copy of *Your Financial Guide* and one copy of the *2003 CSRS/FERS Benefits Calculator Personal Plus*. (see descriptions of these products above) $39.95 (savings of $7.95 off individual pricing).

Federal Employees Resource CD

This information-packed CD-ROM includes helpful resources such as a Federal Benefits Calculator, Retirement Income Gap Calculator, Government Form Library, Helpful Web Link Directory, plus much more! Requires PC with CD-ROM drive. $9.95

Your Retirement: How to Plan for It, How to Enjoy It
Get your own personal retirement counselor! *Your Retirement* is a
comprehensive retirement planning guide. It will assist you in
calculating your pension, retirement timetables, health and life
insurance needs, Social Security options, survivor benefits, and more.
It gives crucial guidance on issues many people don't consider until
it's too late to make a difference. Both CSRS and FERS versions
are available. $12.95

INSURANCE AND LIFE CHANGES

A Guide to Long-Term Care Benefits: Preparing for the New Federal LTC Benefits Package
This guide provides an easy-to-read overview of the most important
LTC insurance options and considerations facing federal employees.
It also clears up much of the confusion regarding long-term care with
updated information on the nuts and bolts of the new Federal Long
Term Care Insurance Program (FLTCIP). $9.95

Insuring Your Future
Many federal employees are insured through the federal
government's health, life and disability insurance programs and feel
pretty comfortable with that insurance. But is it enough? This book
clarifies the strengths and weaknesses of the government's major
insurance programs and explains when federal employees may want
to supplement that insurance. It also explains the federal long-term
care insurance program and professional liability insurance and how
these protections may be important to federal employees. $9.95

Divorce and Your Federal Benefits
This guide provides an overview of the rules governing the impact
of divorce on retirement and other benefits offered by the federal
government. Armed with this information, federal workers and their
spouses who are facing a divorce should be able to conduct the
necessary discussions and negotiations of financial matters in a
business-like manner. $19.95

CAREER AND WORKPLACE ESSENTIALS

Civil Service Handbook for Ex-Military Personnel: Expand Your Benefits, Enhance Your Career

This new publication is designed to help current and retired federal employees who have military service, either from past active duty or from current Reserve or Guard duty – as well as active duty and retired military personnel who may be considering taking a government job. The guide pulls together the previously scattered information about military and federal employee benefits into one place. $12.95

10 Steps to a Federal Job

10 Steps to a Federal Job will help you understand how to apply for jobs in government. Anyone who is a U.S. Citizen can apply for a job in government. There are thousand of jobs in information technology, administration and customer service, as well as scientific and technical fields. The CD-ROM accompanying the publication contains sample resumes, KSAs and The Resume Place's popular Federal Resume, KSA and Cover Letter builders. Simply fill in the fields and "build" your resume content for a federal job. $38.95

Electronic Federal Resume Guidebook

Get hired and get promoted as a civilian with the Army, Air Force, Navy and Marines and other DoD agencies with the best possible resume for Resumix and new automated recruitment and hiring systems. Tips on crafting effective electronic resumes for automated recruitment systems often used in government. Includes CD Rom with e-resumes plus job search tools. $44.95

Federal Resume Guidebook

This big book of federal resumes (24 samples) and KSA writing has everything you need to apply for a federal job, including understanding a job announcement, step-by-step instructions for writing a standout federal resume, and great chapters on KSAs, SES, ECQs, and cover letters. Also contains a valuable chapter on editing and converting the lengthy SF-171 descriptions into short, concise, accomplishment-based copy. Written for both federal employees seeking advancement as well as first-time federal job seekers. $36.95

Federal Job Dispute Procedures

Federal Job Dispute Procedures is an updated and extensively revised guide to the federal employee complaint and appeal processes. It provides both general and specific information on a wide range of the most common complaint and dispute situations, including: discrimination, unfair personnel actions, sexual harassment, pay errors or problems, whistle blowing, discipline for misconduct, performance-based actions, injury compensation, veteran's rights, money-related disputes, and reductions in force. $14.95

Federal Worker's Compensation Guide

The *Federal Worker's Compensation Guide* gives you the advanced knowledge you need to know before an injury on the job happens. The *Guide* provides up-to-date-information on the FECA program, including an easy-to-read summary of the benefits available, a plain-English examination of the procedures for filing claims, and includes the conditions employees must meet to be entitled to FECA benefits. $14.95

Federal Employees News Digest

Stay informed of changes affecting your career, your workplace and your future! Get an early warning on what's happening now.and what's coming next! With a subscription to the *News Digest* – serving federal employees for more than 50 years – you have a direct line to the facts, and time to prepare. The *News Digest* covers all aspects of your federal job including pay, retirement, contracting out, career advancement, benefits, job rights, workplace policies, court decisions, and much more. $97.00

NEW!

FEDERAL EMPLOYEES RESOURCE CD
Just 9.95!*
(plus shipping and handling)

Order this information-packed CD-ROM** and get these helpful
resources:

• Federal Benefits Calculator
This "light" version of our CSRS/FERS Benefits Calculator allows
you to determine retirement eligibility, calculate retirement annuity
and other basic calculations, plus get useful reports projecting your
benefits into retirement.

• Retirement Income Gap Calculator
Allows you to project all income and outgoing monies during your
retirement years to determine if you will have a shortfall (or gap) in
income vs. expenses.

• Government Form Library
Virtually every form you'll ever need in 2003 for retirement, TSP
and much more.

• Helpful Web Link Directory
An up-to-date list of additional information resources available on
the Web.

• Plus much more!

---

* Price for CD is just $6.00 with the purchase of the *2003 Federal Employees Almanac*

** System Requirements:
PC with CD-ROM drive
Windows: 95, 98, ME, NT, 2000, XP
Minimum Screen Resolution: 600 x 800 pixels
Windows Compatible Mouse / Pointing Device

Federal Employees
News Digest INC.

Have you had a taste of FederalSoup?

If not, you're missing out!

Sponsored by Federal Employees News Digest, FederalSoup.com (**www.FederalSoup.com**) provides a free forum for federal workers to share, debate and discuss work-related issues with one another. Visit this federal community and join thousands of other federal employees in active discussions in the following forums:

- **Inside the News**
- **Financial and Retirement Planning**
- **Career Planning and Development**
- **Postal Employees**
- **You be the Judge**
- **Q&A**

FederalSoup.com
A place to share, debate and discuss.

al family care or bereavement purposes in a leave year, that amount must be subtracted from the 12-week entitlement. If an employee has already used 12 weeks of sick leave to care for a family member with a serious health condition, he or she cannot use an additional 13 days in the same leave year for general family care purposes. An employee is entitled to a total of up to 12 weeks of sick leave each year for all family care purposes. However, in order to use more than 40 hours of sick leave for any family care purpose, an employee must maintain a balance of at least 80 hours of sick leave at all times.

Sick Leave for Adoption

Section 629 (b) of Public Law 103-329 amended 5 U.S.C. 6307 to permit employees to use sick leave for purposes related to the adoption of a child. This provision became effective on September 30, 1994.

Home Leave

Home leave is a special category of leave that employees who serve abroad earn in addition to their annual leave. Generally, employees are entitled to home leave only when they have completed a basic service period of 24 months of continuous service abroad. The granting of home leave is at the discretion of each agency.

An agency may grant home leave in combination with other leaves of absence according to existing agency policy. An employee may only use home leave in the United States, the Commonwealth of Puerto Rico, or a territory or possession of the United States.

Home leave may only be taken during a period of service abroad, or within a reasonable period after the employee's return from service abroad when the worker is expected to return to service abroad immediately or on completion of an assignment in the United States. Also, employees are entitled to have their home leave account transferred or recredited to their accounts when they move between agencies or are reemployed without a break in service of more than 90 days.

Employees working abroad can accrue from five to 15 days of home leave per 12 months of service abroad, depending on the overseas post of duty. (For more detailed information on home leave, see 5 U.S.C. 6305; 5 CFR Part 630, subpart F; and your agency's policy.)

Section 3—Leave Sharing

General Leave Sharing Rights

Leave sharing for federal employees began in 1988 under P.L. 100-566, which authorized a five-year test of voluntary leave transfer and voluntary leave bank programs. The "Federal Employees Leave Sharing Amendments Act of 1993," effective February 5, 1994 (P.L. 103-103), made permanent the programs. The act requires all agencies to operate a leave transfer program, allows all agencies to establish leave banks at any time, permits employees to participate in both programs if available, eliminates the requirement to count any advanced leave an employee may have when determining whether the employee qualifies to be a leave recipient, and permits leave recipients who exhaust transferred leave to use leave accrued while in a shared leave status.

Participation in either program is strictly voluntary. Agencies may not coerce employees to participate or refrain.

In any leave year, an employee may donate not more than one-half of the amount of annual leave he or she would accrue during the leave year. For employees with "use or lose" annual leave, the employee may donate the lesser of one-half of the annual leave he or she would accrue in a leave year or the number of hours remaining in the leave year for which the employee is scheduled to work and receive pay.

While using donated leave, a leave recipient may accrue no more than 40 hours of annual leave and 40 hours of sick leave in "set-aside accounts." The leave in the set-aside accounts will be transferred to the employee's regular leave accounts when the medical emergency ends or if the employee exhausts all donated leave.

Leave Transfer Program

The leave transfer program is designed to help employees who are experiencing a medical or family emergency and who have exhausted all of their available leave. They can receive donations of annual leave from fellow employees to help ease financial hardships that would be caused by being forced to take extended leave without pay or resigning from their jobs. Donated annual leave may not be used to care for a newborn unless the child is ill.

An employee wishing to receive leave under this program must make written application to the agency describing the reasons why the leave is needed and may be required to submit certification from physicians or other appropriate experts to provide justification. The expected absence without available paid leave must be at least 24 hours, or, in the case of part time employees, at least 30 percent of the average number of hours in the employee's normal bi-weekly tour of duty.

To make a donation, an employee submits a request to the agency that a specified number of hours of his or her accrued annual leave be transferred to a specified recipient. Annual leave may not be transferred to the donor's immediate supervisor.

An employee who receives and uses donated leave continues to be paid at his or her pay rate as if in work status. When the medical emergency ends, unused transferred leave is restored to the donors on a prorated basis.

Transferred leave under the leave-sharing program is not a tax deduction for the donor, but its dollar value is taxable to the recipient when it is used.

Leave Bank Program

Under the leave bank program, employees may make a special contribution of annual leave to the agency's leave bank in order to become leave bank members. Should such a member then experience a medical or family emergency, he or she can apply to the leave bank for withdrawal of annual leave from the bank. Donated annual leave may not be used to care for a newborn unless the child is ill. Banked leave also can be distributed to fellow employees in much the same way as under the leave transfer program.

In agencies that have leave banks the

employee joins by making a written application to the agency's "bank board," which runs the program. The minimum leave contribution each year normally is four hours for those with less than three years of service, six hours for those with between three and 15 years and eight hours for those with 15 or more years. A leave donor may contribute generally no more than half of the amount of annual leave he or she would be entitled to accrue during the year.

To withdraw leave, a leave bank member must make written application to the bank board describing why the leave is needed, and may be required to provide certification from physicians or other appropriate experts. Rules for the expected minimum absence are the same as those described above for the leave transfer program. However, unused excess leave donated through a leave bank is restored to the bank and is not returned to the original donor.

When the medical emergency ends, any annual leave withdrawn from the bank and not used is returned to the bank.

Emergency Leave Transfer Program

In the event of a major disaster or emergency that results in severe adverse effects for a substantial number of employees, the President may direct OPM to establish an emergency leave transfer program. Under such a program, employees in any executive branch agency may donate a designated amount of leave for use by employees of their own or another agency. Agencies also may make similar donations from their existing leave banks under a leave transfer program established by OPM. Employees approved as leave recipients will be able to use donated leave without having to exhaust their own accrued annual and sick leave. This type of emergency leave transfer program is in addition to the voluntary leave transfer and leave bank programs described above. The emergency leave transfer program was authorized by Section 9004 of P.L. 105-18, which added Section 6391 to Title 5, U.S.C.

Section 4—Unpaid Leave

Leave Without Pay

Leave without pay (LWOP) is a temporary non-paid status and absence from duty that,

in most cases, is granted at the employee's request. It may be granted whether or not the employee has annual or sick leave to his credit. In most instances, granting LWOP is a matter of supervisory discretion and may be limited by agency internal policy. Employees, however, have an entitlement to LWOP in the following situations:

• The Family and Medical Leave Act of 1993 (FMLA, Public Law 103-3, February 5, 1993), provides covered employees with an entitlement to a total of up to 12 weeks of unpaid leave (LWOP) during any 12-month period for certain family and medical needs. (See 5 CFR part 630, subpart L.)

• The Uniformed Services Employment and Reemployment Rights Act of 1994 (P.L. 103-353) provides employees with an entitlement to LWOP when employment is interrupted by a period of service in the uniformed service. (See 5 CFR 353.106.)

• Executive Order 5396, July 17, 1930, provides that disabled veterans are entitled to LWOP for necessary medical treatment.

Other uses for which LWOP may be approved are an employee's desire to enroll in academic courses or training that would be of benefit to the agency or protection of employee status and benefit eligibility pending action on claims for disability retirement or injury compensation. Employees may not be in a pay status while receiving workers' compensation payments from the Department of Labor.

Generally, the effects of LWOP are different for an employee who is granted LWOP to serve as a full-time officer or employee of certain employee organizations or one who is temporarily assigned to either a state or local government or to an institution of higher learning, than for an employee who is granted LWOP for personal reasons. Employees should be aware that LWOP affects their entitlement to or eligibility for certain federal benefits.

Service Computation Date—Except for absence due to military service or because of compensable injury, when an employee has been on leave without pay for six months or less during any calendar year, he is given service credit for that period and the service computation date is not affected. No credit for government service will be given for any portion of LWOP in excess of six months during the same calendar year.

Impact on Annual and Sick Leave— Under 5 CFR 630.208, full-time employees who accumulate 80 hours of LWOP must have their credits for annual and sick leave reduced by an amount equal to the amount of leave that they would earn during the pay period in which accumulated LWOP equals 80 hours.

If employees continue in an extended LWOP status, they will not earn any more sick or annual leave until such time as they return to a pay status. If the accumulated LWOP for full-time employees equals less than 80 hours at the end of the last pay period of the leave year, the LWOP is dropped and the employees are entitled to earn annual and sick leave until they once again accumulate 80 hours of LWOP in the new leave year.

Life Insurance—Basic and optional life insurance continue without cost to the employee while he or she is in non-pay status for up to 12 months, at which time the insurance is terminated. The 12 month LWOP status may be continuous or broken by periods of less than four consecutive months in pay status.

If the employee has four or more consecutive months during which he or she received some pay in each pay period after a period of non-pay status, the employee is entitled to begin the 12 month continuation of insurance again. For exceptions to this, refer to the FEGLI Program Handbook, available at www.opm.gov/insure/life/handbook.

Health Insurance—Generally, an employee's health insurance enrollment may be continued for up to 365 days of LWOP status. However, employees on LWOP remain responsible for payment of the employee share of the cost of enrollment for every pay period during which the enrollment continues.

If an employee in non-pay status returns to pay status for less than four consecutive months, then returns to non-pay status, the employee does not begin a new period of 365 days during which he or she is entitled to continue the health benefits enrollment. Instead, the second non-pay period is treated as a continuation of the first. If an employee is in a pay status during any part of a pay period, the entire pay period is not counted toward the 365-day limit. On the other hand, if the employee returns to pay status for at least four consecutive months during which he or she is paid for at least part of each pay period, the employee will be entitled to begin a new period of up to 365 days continuation of enrollment while in non-pay status.

For exceptions to this, see the *FEHB Program Handbook*, available at *www.opm. gov/insure/handbook/fehb01.htm.*

Excused Absences

With few exceptions, agencies determine administratively the situations in which they will excuse employees from duty without charge to leave. Each department or agency has discretion to excuse employees from their duties without loss of pay or charge to leave. OPM advises that the granting of excused absence should be limited to those situations in which the employee's absence is not specifically prohibited by law and, as determined by the agency, satisfies one or more of the following criteria: (1) the absence is directly related to the department or agency's mission; (2) the absence is officially sponsored or sanctioned by the head of the department or agency; (3) the absence will clearly enhance the professional development or skills of the employee in his or her current position; or (4) the absence is brief and is determined to be in the interest of the agency. Agencies should review their internal guidance on excused absences and applicable collective bargaining agreements.

Some of the more common situations in which agencies usually approve excused absence are for donating blood, for closing because of extreme weather conditions, for attending meetings for the benefit of the federal service, and for voting.

Government departments and agencies are urged to allow employees sufficient time off to register and vote in federal, state, county, or municipal elections, to the extent that it does not interfere seriously with operations. As a general rule, where the polls are not open at least three hours either before or after an employee's regular hours of work, an amount of excused leave (no charge to annual leave) may be granted which will permit the employee to report to work three hours after the polls open or leave work three hours before the polls close, whichever requires the lesser amount of time off. If an employee's voting place is beyond normal commuting distance and vote by absentee ballot is not permitted, the employee may be granted sufficient time off (not to exceed one day) in order to be able to make the trip to the voting place to cast a ballot. Time off in excess of one day must be charged to annual leave or leave without pay.

Volunteer Activities—In limited circumstances, employees may be granted excused absences to participate in volunteer activities. See Volunteer Activities in Chapter 8.

Family and Medical Leave Act

The 1993 Family and Medical Leave Act (Public Law 103-3) provides federal employees with unpaid leave for family and medical purposes. The law provides for 12 administrative workweeks of unpaid leave during any 12-month period for the following conditions:

• birth of a son or daughter and care of newborn (within one year after birth),

• placement of a son or daughter with the employee for adoption or foster care (within one year after placement),

• care for a spouse, son, daughter, or parent with a serious health condition; or,

• serious health condition that makes the employee unable to perform the duties of his or her position.

To be eligible, employees must have completed at least one year of civilian service with the government. Temporary and intermittent employees are excluded from the coverage. The law prohibits any interference with the employee's right to take this special leave through coercion, intimidation, or threat.

The unpaid family and medical leave is in addition to the employee's paid annual and sick leave or any compensatory time off available to the employee. The employee may offset some of the unpaid leave under this law by substituting annual or sick leave, as appropriate.

Employees wishing to request family or medical leave need to provide up to 30 days advance notice if this is practicable. As a rule, an employee may not invoke his or her entitlement to FMLA leave retroactively. However, if an employee and his or her personal representative are incapable of invoking the employee's entitlement to FMLA during the entire period of absence from work, the employee may retroactively invoke entitlement to FMLA within two days after returning to work.

When leave is being requested for a serious health condition, or to care for a seriously ill child, spouse or parent, the leave may be taken intermittently or on a reduced work schedule without the agency's approval.

An employee is expected to make a reasonable effort to schedule treatment, subject to the approval of the health provider, so as not to disrupt unduly the operations of the agency. In the case of a serious illness the agency may transfer the employee to another position that better meets the needs of the agency and the employee.

Also, where the request for leave is based on a medical problem, an agency may require medical certification with the date of the onset, prognosis, and statement of need for care. An employee must provide medical documentation within 15 calendar days. If this is not possible, despite the employee's diligent, good faith efforts, medical certification must be provided within a reasonable period of time, but no later than 30 calendar days after the date the agency requests such certification.

If the agency doubts the validity of the original certification of eligibility, it may require a second opinion. Cost of the second opinion would be paid by the agency. If the second opinion varies from the first opinion, the agency may require a third opinion. The third opinion is final and binding.

Several conditions are attached to return to employment upon completion of unpaid leave. An employee using the unpaid leave is entitled to be returned to the same or equivalent position with equivalent benefits, pay, status and other terms and conditions of employment. Under the law, this leave cannot result in the loss of any employment benefit accrued before leave began.

Further, the law does not entitle any returning employee to the accrual of any employment benefits other than those to which the employee would have been entitled if the leave had not been taken.

The law requires the government to continue health insurance benefits for employees taking this leave at the same level and under the same conditions as would be in effect if the employees had continued on the job. Employees who don't return to work from leave must pay the government back for health premiums it paid while they were on this leave.

Agencies retain the right to have a uniformly applied policy that requires employees who use FMLA medical leave for their own serious health condition to obtain certification from a health care provider confirming their ability to return to work. During the period of leave, an agency also can require periodic status reports on the employee's ability or intention to return to work. (For more information about FMLA rights, see OPM's website at *www.opm.gov/oca/leave.htm*, or OPM's regulations at 5 C.F.R. Part 630, Subpart L, as well as your own agency's FMLA policies.)

Time Off for Family Obligations

Where possible, federal employees should be allowed to take up to 24 hours of unpaid leave annually to meet routine, but important, family obligations, according to an April 11, 1997, Presidential memorandum to the heads of executive departments and agencies. Examples of the family obligations that employees might use such leave grants for include: participation in children's school activities, accompanying children or elderly relatives to routine medical or dental appointments, and helping elderly relatives make living arrangements related to housing, meals, banking services, and similar activities. The President also asked agencies to cooperate, where possible, with employees' requests to schedule paid leave or time off (such as annual or sick leave, compensatory time off, or credit hours under flexible work schedules) to allow them to participate in these family activities.

However, this is not an entitlement. According to OPM's follow-up guidance, federal supervisors already had discretion to grant workers time off for such purposes, but the President's memo was designed to "make supervisors more sensitive to employees' needs." Such requests by employees, OPM stressed, "should continue to be evaluated in terms of whether the employee's services are required or can be spared during the time period covered by the leave request." However, as a general rule, such requests should be granted, OPM said, "unless circumstances exist that would severely limit an agency's ability to accomplish its mission."

An agency may require employees to provide "administratively acceptable" evidence supporting their family-obligation leave requests, such as certification of medical appointments or similar evidence of a scheduled school activity or need to make arrangements for an elderly relative. Agencies may keep records of such leave, but are not required to do so.

> Note: There is no order of precedence dictating how or when employees may use or request time off under the federal government's various family-friendly leave policies. For example, a supervisor may not require an employee to use leave without pay to cover time off for routine child-care or elder care purposes.

The heads of departments and agencies are to support its employees' commitment to community service and ensure that all employees are aware of the various flexibilities available to them to participate in volunteer activities. Federal departments and agencies may review their work scheduling practices and leave scheduling policies to make maximum use of existing flexibilities, when possible, to allow federal employees to plan and take time off to participate in volunteer activities and perform community service.

Work Schedule Adjustments for Religious Observances

To the extent that modifications in work schedules do not interfere with accomplishing an agency's mission, federal agencies must approve employee requests to adjust work schedules for the purpose of taking time off without charge to leave or entitlement to overtime pay when employees' personal religious beliefs require that they abstain from work during periods of a workday or workweek.

Any employee who elects to work alternative hours for this purpose is entitled to an equal amount of time off (hour for hour) from his or her scheduled tour of duty. An employee may work such alternative hours (compensatory time) before or after the grant of compensatory time off.

A grant of compensatory time off must be repaid by the appropriate amount of work within a reasonable period.

Section 5—Federal Employees' Compensation Act (Workers' Compensation Benefits)

General Rules and Procedures

The Federal Employees' Compensation Act is the law governing the payment of workers' compensation benefits to civilian employees of the United States who suffer a disability due to personal injury (including occupational disease) sustained while in the performance of duty. Damage to or destruction of medical braces, artificial limbs, and other prosthetic devices incidental to a job-related personal injury is also compensable. The act also provides for the payment of benefits to dependents if a job-related injury or disease causes the employee's death.

FECA is administered by the Office of Workers' Compensation Programs (OWCP) in the Labor Department, through district offices located throughout the United States. Its website is http://www.dol.gov/esa /regs/compliance/owcp/fecacont.htm. FECA forms are found at http://www.dol.gov/esa/ regs/compliance/owcp/forms.htm.

All injuries, including disease proximately caused by employment, sustained while in the performance of duty by civilian employees of the United States (with the exception of non-appropriated fund employees), are covered. Coverage is provided by special legislation to Peace Corps and VISTA volunteers, federal petit or grand jurors, volunteer members of the Civil Air Patrol, Reserve Officer Training Corps cadets, Job Corps, Neighborhood Youth Corps and Youth Conservation Corps enrollees, and non-federal law enforcement officers under certain circumstances (e.g., situations involving crimes against the United States). Temporary employees are covered on the same basis as permanent employees.

The employee must provide medical and factual evidence to establish the essential elements of a claim. These elements generally include proof that the claim was filed within FECA's statutory time requirements, the injured or deceased person was an employee within the scope defined by FECA, the employee sustained an injury or disease, the employee was in the performance of duty when the injury occurred, and the employee's compensable condition resulted from the injury.

Benefits cannot be paid if a worker's injury or death is caused by the injured employee's intoxication or willful misconduct or by an intent to bring about the injury or death of oneself or another.

All injuries should be reported, since a seemingly minor injury may develop into a more serious condition. For protection, the employee should file a report of the injury with the immediate supervisor when it occurs. Benefits will not be paid unless an injury is reported.

A traumatic injury is defined as a wound or other condition of the body caused by external force, including stress or strain. The injury must be caused by a specific event or incident or series of events or incidents within a single day or work shift.

An occupational disease is defined as a condition produced in the work environment over a period longer than one workday or shift. It may result from systemic infection, repeated stress or strain, exposure to toxins, poisons, fumes, or other continuing conditions of the work environment.

Diseases and illnesses aggravated, accelerated, or precipitated by the employment are covered. The employee must submit medical and factual evidence that establishes that the employment aggravated, accelerated, or precipitated the condition.

A recurrence of an employment-related disability is covered if an injured employee is again disabled as a result of the original injury or occupational disease.

FECA Coverage Rules

Federal employees generally are eligible for FECA coverage regardless of the length of time they've been on the job or the type of position held. Compensation payments can be made after wage loss begins and medical evidence shows that the employee is unable to perform the duties of his or her regular job.

An employee who sustains a disabling traumatic injury is entitled to continuation of regular pay (COP) for a period not to exceed 45 calendar days. This is considered

salary for all intents and purposes, including tax deductions, and not compensation. In order to be eligible for COP, written notice of injury must be filed within 30 days of the injury.

Schedule awards are FECA payments that are provided for specified periods of time for the permanent loss, or loss of use, of certain parts and functions of the body. Partial loss or loss of use of these parts and functions is compensated on a proportional basis. Before payment of a schedule award can be considered, the condition of the affected part of the body must reach maximum improvement. This determination involves a medical judgment that the condition has permanently stabilized.

FECA Compensation Payments

Total disability benefits may be paid to injured workers to compensate them for lost wages after the end of a continuation-of-pay period or from the beginning of pay loss. An employee who receives disability payments will be notified by letter of the amount of compensation to be paid, including the pay rate used as a basis and the resulting compensation rate. Compensation payments for total disability may continue as long as the medical evidence substantiates total disability.

No compensation is payable for the first three days of wage loss unless the disability exceeds 14 days after the expiration of COP, where COP is payable, or the injury results in permanent impairment. Injured employees may use sick or annual leave credited to their account if so desired, in which event FECA compensation does not begin until the expiration of leave. Use of personal leave should only be necessary in extreme circumstances.

Monetary compensation is based on the monthly pay of the injured employee at the time of the injury, at the time the disability begins, or at the time a compensable disability recurs (if such recurrence begins more than six months after the injured employee resumes regular full-time employment with the United States), whichever is greater.

FECA compensation generally is calculated at two-thirds of the employee's monthly pay rate if he or she has no

Labor Department District Offices
Workers' Compensation Programs

U.S. Dept. of Labor, OWCP District Office Address	Jurisdiction
District No. 1 — Boston JFK Federal Building Rm. E-260 Boston, MA 02203 617-624-6600 617-624-6605 Fax	Connecticut, Maine, Massachusetts, New Hampshire, Rhode Island, and Vermont
District No. 2 — New York 201 Varick St. Rm. 740 New York, NY 10014 646-264-3000 646-264-3006 Fax	New Jersey, New York, Puerto Rico, and the Virgin Islands
District No. 3 — Philadelphia Curtis Center Ste. 715 East 170 S. Independence, Mall West Philadelphia, PA 19106-3308 215-861-5481*, 5482 215-861-5453 Fax	Pennsylvania, Delaware, and West Virginia
District No. 6 — Jacksonville 214 N. Hogan St., Ste. 1006 Jacksonville, FL 32202 904-357-4777 904-357-4778 Interactive Voice Response System	Alabama, Florida, Georgia, Kentucky, Mississippi, North Carolina, South Carolina, and Tennessee
District No. 9 — Cleveland Rm. 851 1240 E. 9th St. Cleveland, OH 44199 216-357-5100 216-357-5378 Fax	Indiana, Michigan, and Ohio
District No. 10 — Chicago 8th Floor, 230 S. Dearborn St. Chicago, IL 60604 312-507-7157* 312-596-7145 Fax	Illinois, Minnesota, and Wisconsin
District No. 11 — Kansas City City Center Square 1100 Main St. Ste. 750 Kansas City, MO 64105 816-502-0301 816-502-0314 Fax	Iowa, Kansas, Missouri, and Nebraska
District No. 12 — Denver 1999 Broadway., Ste. 600 Denver, CO 80202 720-264-3000* 720-264-3064 Fax	Colorado, Montana, North Dakota, South Dakota, Utah, and Wyoming

District No. 13 — San Francisco 71 Stevenson St. San Francisco, CA 94105 *or write to:* P.O. Box 3769 San Francisco, CA 94119-3769 415-848-6700 415-848-6830 Fax	Arizona, California, Hawaii and Nevada
District No. 14 — Seattle 1111 Third Ave., Ste. 650 Seattle, WA 98101-3212 206-398-8100 206-398-8151 Fax	Alaska, Idaho, Oregon, and Washington
District No. 16 — Dallas 525 S. Griffin St., Rm. 100 Dallas, TX 75202 972-850-2300 972-850-2310 Interactive Voice System 972-850-2301 Fax	Arkansas, Louisiana, New Mexico, Oklahoma and Texas
District No. 25 — Washington, DC 800 N. Capitol Street, N.W., Rm. 800 Washington, DC 20211 202-513-6800* 202-513-6806 Fax	D.C., Maryland and Virginia; all areas outside the U.S., its possessions, territories and trust territories; and all special claims

* The Interactive Voice Response System can be accessed from this number

dependents, or three-fourths of the pay rate if married or with one or more dependents.

For FECA benefit purposes, a dependent is: a wife or husband residing with the employee or receiving regular support payments from him or her; an unmarried child who lives with the employee or who receives regular support payments from him or her who is under age 18, or if over age 18 is incapable of self-support due to physical or mental disability; a student between 18 and 23 years of age who has not completed four years of post-high school education and who is regularly pursuing a full-time course of study; and a parent who is wholly dependent on the employee.

Locality, night differential, hazard, premium, holiday, and Sunday pay are included in determining the pay rate on which compensation is based, although overtime pay is not. The maximum payment per month cannot exceed three-fourths of the highest rate of basic pay provided for grade GS-15.

Minimum monthly compensation for total disability cannot be less than three-fourths of the lowest basic monthly pay level for GS-2, or the employee's monthly pay, whichever is less, except for increases resulting from cost-of-living adjustments.

If, as the result of an on-the-job injury, an employee returns to work at a lower rate of pay, compensation for loss of earning capacity is paid at the rate of two-thirds (without dependents) or three-fourths (with dependents) of the loss of earning capacity. The wage earning capacity of a partially disabled employee is determined by actual earnings, or if the employee has no actual earnings, an amount determined by OWCP taking into consideration the nature of the injury and other factors that affect the capacity to earn wages.

Compensation for disability cannot be paid concurrently with an annuity (including a lump-sum payment) under the Civil Service Retirement System, or the Federal Employees' Retirement System, or any other law providing retirement benefits in lieu of those provided under the CSRS or FERS. An employee entitled to both types of benefits (i.e., retirement and FECA) must make an election; however, a new election may be made whenever it is to the employee's advantage to do so. (For more detail, see the section below entitled "Disability Retirement vs. FECA Benefits.")

Health Insurance Coverage—Under provisions of the Federal Employees' Health

Benefits Act, employees, former employees, and survivors of deceased employees who meet certain requirements may continue their health benefits coverage while in receipt of disability or death compensation. The employee's or survivor's share of the cost of the FEHB insurance is withheld from the compensation.

Cost-of-Living Adjustments—For individuals who have been in receipt of compensation benefits for more than one year, those benefits are increased effective March 1 of each year by any percentage change in the Consumer Price Index published for December of the preceding year.

Schedule Awards

FECA may pay a scheduled award for a permanent impairment to certain members or functions of the body (such as loss of use of an eye or arm, or loss of function or removal of a kidney due to injury). The amounts payable are specified by the Federal Employees Compensation Act.

Schedule awards can be paid during a period where the employee is receiving federal salary or retirement benefits, is working for private industry, or is self-employed. Employees may not receive wage loss compensation and schedule awards benefits concurrently for the same injury.

If an employee sustains a period of temporary total disability during the course of the award, it may be interrupted to pay the period of disability; the schedule award will resume afterwards. If an employee dies during the course of a schedule award from causes unrelated to the compensable injury, his or her dependents are entitled to two-thirds of the balance of the award.

Schedule award amounts vary from 15 weeks to 312 weeks of compensation for total loss or loss of use of designated body parts. There is an additional award for serious disfigurement of the head, face or neck.

Medical Care Benefits

FECA covers all medical care that an employee needs to recover from the effects of a work-related injury, including hospitalization, nursing service, prosthetic appliances, and services of an attendant when required in severe injuries. The employee has the right to initially select a physician to provide medical services, appliances, and supplies. The term "physician" includes surgeons, podiatrists, dentists, clinical psychologists, optometrists, chiropractors (to the extent that such services are reimbursable under the Act), and osteopathic practitioners within the scope of their practice as defined by state law. Payments for chiropractic services are limited to treatment consisting of manual manipulation of the spine to correct a subluxation that has been verified by an X-ray. A physician whose license to practice medicine has been suspended or revoked by a state licensing or regulatory authority is not a physician within the meaning of this section during the period of such suspension or revocation.

Medical care coverage also extends to the necessary cost of transportation and expenses incident to securing medical services, appliances and supplies. Medical care for a compensable injury may be continued after a beneficiary accepts a retirement annuity. Bills for injury-related medical expenses should be submitted promptly. No bill will be paid for expenses incurred if the bill is submitted more than one year beyond the end of the calendar year in which the expense was incurred, or more than one year beyond the end of the calendar year in which the claim was first accepted as compensable, whichever is later.

Vocational Rehabilitation—A permanently disabled employee may be provided with vocational rehabilitation services and an additional allowance may be paid for necessary maintenance in an amount not to exceed $200 per month while the employee is undergoing an approved course of training. Also, an employee will be paid compensation at the rate for total disability while pursuing an OWCP-approved training course.

Survivor and Death Benefits

When an employee dies as a result of a job-related injury, the individual's surviving spouse and dependents may qualify for monthly compensation benefits. The surviving spouse must be living with or dependent for support on the injured worker at the time of death (or living apart for reasonable cause or because of the employee's desertion).

If no children are eligible, a deceased worker's surviving spouse would receive 50 percent of the employee's salary. If there are children, a surviving spouse would receive 45 percent of the worker's salary, plus an additional 15 percent for each child up to a total of 75 percent of salary. If there is no widow or widower, FECA compensation for the first child is 40 percent of the employee's salary and each additional child is entitled to 15 percent of the employee's salary, up to a maximum of 75 percent, payable on a share and share alike basis.

In rare instances, parents, minor brothers and sisters, and grandparents and grandchildren who were totally dependent on the deceased employee at the time of death, may be entitled to a small portion of survivor benefits. Payments are not made after a beneficiary marries or completes four years of study beyond high school.

When survivors are eligible from OPM, they may be eligible for both death compensation benefits and a survivor annuity from OPM. They must elect which of the two benefits they wish to receive.

Survivor benefits will be reduced if the employee was covered under FERS and the survivors are eligible for Social Security benefits based on the employee's federal employment.

FECA provides for payment of reasonable burial expenses, up to a maximum of $800. Apart from any funeral or burial expenses, a separate sum of $200 is paid to the personal representative of a deceased employee for reimbursement of the costs incurred in terminating the deceased worker's status as an employee of the United States.

Recovery and Job Restoration

OWCP requires most individuals receiving FECA disability benefits to undergo medical examinations once a year. The evaluation usually is done by the employee's own physician. OWCP may, however, require the employee to be examined by another physician. FECA compensation will be terminated if medical evidence is submitted that indicates that the employee no longer has residual limitations from the accepted condition and can return to the former job without limitations; or the individual's employer makes a suitable job offer which is unreasonably refused by the employee. OWCP will determine both the suitability of the job offer and the reasonableness of a worker's refusal.

Receipt of a schedule award—i.e., an OWCP payment for a permanent impairment of a specified body member, function, or organ—does not necessarily mean the individual has recovered for purposes of job restoration rights. It only means that part of the employee's body is considered to have reached maximum medical improvement.

FECA benefit payments can be suspended if the employee does not cooperate with a specific directive from OWCP (such as a request to report for medical examination) or fails to respond within 30 days to a request for information on employment/earnings, dependents, or the receipt of dual benefits. Similarly, FECA compensation can be suspended if a beneficiary in a death case fails to respond to a request for information on continuing entitlement, such as verification of student status. Where an individual's response to such requests is subsequently received, OWCP may reinstate benefits retroactive to the date of suspension, if appropriate.

Job Restoration Rights—If employees recover from their disability within one year from the date they became entitled to FECA payments, they have the right to return to their former jobs or an equivalent position. Even if their period of disability extends beyond one year, employees have priority placement rights to their former or equivalent positions.

The restoration rights of employees who sustain compensable injuries fall into four separate categories depending on the length and extent of recovery. Other factors affecting restoration rights are the timeliness of the application for restoration, the employee's performance and conduct prior to the injury, and the availability of positions.

Full recovery is determined by a decision to terminate FECA benefits on the basis that the employee is medically able to resume regular employment. For purposes of restoration rights, a position with the same seniority, status, and pay means a position that is equivalent to the former one in terms of pay, grade, type of appointment, tenure, work schedule, and, where applicable, seniority. An employee's standing in the organization, such as first or second supervisory level, is not a factor.

The four categories are:
• *Fully recovered within one year.* Employees who fully recover within one year

from the date compensation began have mandatory restoration rights to their former job or an equivalent position. This basic entitlement is to a position in the former commuting area. If a suitable vacancy does not exist, the restoration right is agency-wide. Employees must apply for restoration immediately and must be restored immediately and unconditionally by their former agency.

• *Fully recovered after one year.* If full recovery takes longer than one year from the date compensation begins, injured employees are entitled to priority consideration for their former position or an equivalent one, provided they apply for restoration within 30 days of the date compensation ends. Priority consideration means the agency enters the individual on its reemployment priority list. If the agency cannot place such individuals in their former commuting area, they are entitled to priority consideration for an equivalent position elsewhere in the agency.

• *Physically disqualified.* FECA compensationers who are medically unable to return to their former occupation, but who are able to do other work, are considered to be physically disqualified. Such individuals are entitled, within one year of the date compensation begins, to be placed in a position that most closely approximates the seniority, status, and pay to which they otherwise would be entitled, depending on the circumstances of the case. These restoration rights are agency-wide. After one year, such individuals are entitled to the same restoration rights as individuals who fall into the "partially recovered" category described below. Physically disqualified employees typically have a permanent medical condition, such as the loss of an arm, that disqualifies them for their old or an equivalent position and makes it unlikely that they will ever be able to return to the former position.

• *Partially recovered.* In contrast to a physically disqualified worker, a partially recovered employee is expected to fully recover eventually. These individuals, who have not yet fully recovered but are able to work in some capacity, are entitled to be considered for employment in the former commuting area. The agency must make every effort to place the employee, but there is no absolute right to restoration. If the individual is restored at a lower grade or pay level, OWCP will make up the differ-

ence in pay, or the agency may elect to pay the employee at the former rate. If such employees later fully recover, they are entitled to the restoration rights of a fully recovered employee, based on the timing of the recovery. Partially recovered employees have an obligation to seek employment within their capabilities. If a partially recovered employee refuses to accept a suitable job offer, OWCP may terminate compensation. OWCP determines whether an agency job offer is suitable according to the individual's medical restrictions, education, and vocational background.

Claims-Filing Time Limits

Written report of a work-related injury must be given within 30 days to the employee's immediate superior and a claim for disability or death compensation must be filed within three years. The time limitations do not apply to: (1) minors until they reach the age of 21 or have had a legal representative appointed and (2) incompetent individuals while they are incompetent and have no duly appointed legal representative. In cases of latent disability, the time limitations do not begin to run until the employee has a compensable disability and is aware, or reasonably should be aware, that the disability is causally related to employment. A claim for disability or death compensation filed after the three-year period may not be allowed, unless the immediate superior had actual knowledge of the injury or death within 30 days, or written notice of the injury or death was properly given within 30 days.

Administration and Appeals

The Act is administered by the Office of Workers' Compensation Programs (OWCP) of the U.S. Department of Labor. Further information regarding the law may be obtained online at *http://www.dol.gov/esa/regs/compliance/owcp/fecacont.htm* or by writing to the:

Office of Workers'
Compensation Programs
U.S. Department of Labor
Washington, DC 20210

The adjudication and payment of claims is decentralized into the district offices of the OWCP. Inquiries concerning specific cases should be directed to the appropriate district office.

An employee or survivor who disagrees with a final determination of OWCP may, within 30 days after the date of the decision, request an oral hearing from the Branch of Hearings and Review. The hearing will be informal and will be held at a convenient location. You may be represented at the hearing by any person authorized by you in writing. As soon as possible after the hearing, a copy of the OWCP representative's decision will be mailed to you. You will have the right to appeal this decision. The request for hearing should be addressed to the Office of Workers' Compensation Programs, Branch of Hearings and Review, P.O. Box 37117, Washington, DC 20013-7117. Section 8124(b)(1) of the Act provides entitlement to a hearing only before reconsideration.

In lieu of an oral hearing, you may request a review of the written record by an OWCP representative at which you may submit additional written evidence in support of your claim. The request should be sent to the address above. You may not have both an oral hearing and a review of the written record on the same issue.

If you have other evidence you believe to be pertinent, you may ask the OWCP to reconsider the decision. No special form is required, but the request must be in writing and state clearly the grounds upon which reconsideration is requested. Also, the request must be accompanied by evidence not previously submitted, such as medical reports, affidavits, or statements. In order to ensure that you receive a new and independent evaluation of the evidence, your case will be reconsidered by persons other than those who made the original determina-

tion. Request for reconsideration, along with new evidence, should be addressed to the office servicing your case. Reconsideration may be requested within one year of the most recent decision on the merits of the claim, whether or not a hearing has been held. Where reconsideration is initially requested, you are not entitled to a hearing.

If you believe that all available evidence has been submitted, you have the right to appeal to the Employees' Compensation Appeals Board for review of the decision. Review by the Appeals Board is limited to the evidence of record. No new evidence may be submitted to the Board. Request for review by the Appeals Board should be made within 90 days from the date of the decision and should be addressed to the Employees' Compensation Appeals Board, U.S. Department of Labor, 200 Constitution Ave., N.W., Rm. N-2609, Washington, DC 20210. If you should request a hearing or reconsideration by the Office of Workers' Compensation Programs as indicated above, the 90-day period within which you may request review by the Appeals Board will run from the date of any later decision by the OWCP. For good cause shown, the Appeals Board may waive the failure to file within 90 days if application is made within one year from the date.

Decisions of the ECAB are final and may not be appealed to federal or state courts.

Federal Employees News Digest Inc. publishes a comprehensive guide to understanding rights and rules under the injury compensation program called the *Federal Workers' Compensation Guide* and a monthly newsletter called the *Federal Workers' Compensation Update*. See publication-ordering information in this Almanac.

Section 6—Disability Retirement vs. FECA Benefits

General Relationship

For many federal employees, workers' compensation benefits and disability retirement are closely related issues, but it is important to realize that these two benefit programs are very different. Each has its own set of eligibility and procedural rules, and the two are administered by different agencies—the Labor Department's Office of Workers' Compensation Programs in the case of Federal Employees Compensation Act bene-

fits, and the Office of Personnel Management in the case of disability retirement. An employee's right to receive benefit payments under one program does not ensure entitlement to benefits under the other. However, as long as their injury or illness is work-related, many disabled federal workers find that they may be eligible for benefits under both.

Because employees often must decide whether to draw benefits from one or the other, it can be important for a worker to understand both programs and how they relate to each other. However, the two administering agencies operate independently and have made few efforts to integrate the two programs. Little official information is available that allows a direct comparison of both programs and the guidance employees need to understand them as they relate to one another.

The information below provides general comparisons of the two programs. Be sure to check pertinent sections of this Almanac (particularly the discussions of CSRS vs. FERS differences in Chapter 3), as well as the official guidance and publications issued by OPM and OWCP, for further details if needed.

Benefit Differences and Choices

Two fundamental points are essential to a clear understanding of the differences between injury compensation benefits under FECA and disability retirement coverage under either CSRS or FERS:

• Disability retirement benefits are payable whether or not the employee's disabling disease or injury was job-related, while workers' compensation benefits are paid only if the cause of the disabling condition was job-related.

• Employees generally may not receive annuity payments from OPM and FECA payments from OWCP for the same period of time, but must elect one type of benefit (the limited exceptions to this rule are explained below).

Faced with the dual compensation choice between a disability annuity and FECA payments, many disabled employees choose the FECA benefit, primarily because it usually amounts to a higher payment. That's because FECA's disability payment formula typically is more generous, and workers' compensation benefits are tax-free. However, there are exceptions, as well as other considerations, which might cause an individual to choose a disability retirement benefit instead.

Note that a disabled employee's election between workers' compensation benefits and an annuity is not irrevocable. Individuals may switch between the two systems if it is to their advantage to do so. OPM considers an election of benefits in death cases to be irrevocable, however.

Individuals should be aware that their election of one type of benefit could result in some disadvantages. For example, an individual who files a disability retirement application with OPM and who is entitled to an annuity, but elects to receive FECA benefits in lieu of an annuity, is still considered an annuitant. Unless the person's entitlement to an annuity ends (for example, because of recovery from the disabling condition), upon reemployment with the federal government, the worker becomes subject to the rules governing reemployed annuitants. Being subject to these rules may be disadvantageous if the individual is reemployed at a lower grade or on a part-time basis or does not work long enough to gain eligibility for a supplemental annuity.

There is a final consideration for employees who are facing a FECA/disability retirement choice, but who also are eligible for standard optional retirement. They sometimes choose disability retirement instead of standard retirement on a belief that disability retirement is more favorable. However, the benefits under the two generally are the same. Moreover, the choice of disability retirement has certain disadvantages: the requirement to prove eligibility through medical and other evidence and the vulnerability of recipients under age 60 to loss of benefits due to restoration of earning capacity or medical recovery. Also, those who owe a redeposit for a period of service ending before October 1, 1990, may have an actuarial reduction in a standard annuity in lieu of making the redeposit, while those retiring on disability must make the redeposit in order to receive credit for the service.

On the other hand, certain job restoration rights that do not apply to standard optional retirement do apply to disability retirement, which could be a consideration for those who think they might want to return to federal employment after retirement.

Impact of Separation

Upon leaving federal employment, separated employees who have applied for workers' compensation benefits also must apply for disability retirement to preserve their annuity rights under CSRS or FERS. Employees who are found eligible for both FECA benefits and disability retirement must then choose between them. Applying for disability retirement benefits is the only way in which the future annuity rights of separated employees (and their survivors) will be fully protected. Except in cases of mental incompetence, the disability retirement application of a separated employee must be received by OPM within one year of the date of separation from federal service. All medical evidence submitted to OWCP in connection with a FECA claim and any OWCP evaluation of the claim should be included with a disability retirement claim.

Former employees who are receiving FECA payments and who do not file a timely retirement application will not be eligible for disability retirement benefits if and when their workers' compensation benefits stop. In such cases, former employees also will not be eligible to temporarily continue health benefits coverage. In addition, their survivors' rights to death benefits would not be established.

The one-year limit does not apply to applications for non-disability retirement benefits. Thus, separated employees who are eligible for a normal retirement annuity based on age and years of service need not apply for a disability annuity to protect their retirement benefit rights. (However, such employees may want to consider filing a disability annuity application to preserve their survivors' rights to annuity benefits and continued health insurance coverage, in the event they die before filing for retirement and workers' compensation benefits are not payable to their survivor on a continuing basis.)

Benefit Payment Procedures

If an injured or disabled employee applies and is found eligible for disability retirement benefits, OPM will begin annuity payments as long as OWCP has not awarded workers' compensation benefits by the time the retirement claim has been adjudicated. If OWCP subsequently decides the worker is entitled to workers' compensation benefits, an annuitant who elects to receive the FECA payments must reimburse OPM for any annuity payments received in the interim. Typically, OWCP will withhold the amount of annuity payments received from the worker's WC benefits to reimburse OPM.

If annuitants choose to receive workers' compensation benefits, OPM will suspend payment of their retirement benefits during the period that FECA benefits are paid. However, if the compensation benefits end for any reason, including the worker's personal choice, OPM will reinstate the annuity if the individual is still entitled to a disability retirement; i.e., has not recovered from the disability or has not been restored to earning capacity.

Retirement benefits are payable under certain circumstances where compensation benefits are not payable. For instance, retirement benefits may be payable to a former spouse if a court order provides for such an award, but FECA benefits are not payable to a former spouse as a result of a court order. In addition, if a deceased employee's widow or widower remarries before age 55 and that marriage ends, the survivor's retirement benefit may be reinstated (provided the survivor has not received a refund of the employee's retirement contributions). However, a FECA benefit will not be reinstated in those circumstances.

Simultaneous FECA and Retirement Payments

In very limited circumstances, federal employees may receive a concurrent payment of annuity and FECA benefits for the same period of time. Circumstances in which such dual payments can occur include:

• The employee is receiving a scheduled award under FECA. A scheduled award is usually paid when there is a disability resulting from the loss, or loss of use, of a function or member of the body (such as a hearing loss or the loss of an arm). However, if the award is based on total or partial disability (i.e., a non-scheduled award), the employee may not receive an annuity during the same period that he is receiving FECA benefits. (If an employee is receiving civil service annuity payments and a schedule award is changed to a non-schedule FECA benefit, he must immediately notify OPM. Any overpayment of FECA benefits or annuity he receives is subject to collection by the OPM or OWCP.)

• The employee is receiving FECA benefits due to the death of another person and is eligible for annuity on the basis of his own federal service.

• FECA payments are suspended because he is receiving a financial settlement from the party directly responsible for the injury (e.g., a third-party settlement). In this instance, his annuity may be paid during the period that his OWCP benefits are suspended.

• An employee may receive FECA compensation concurrently with military retirement or retainer pay, subject to the reduction of such pay in accordance with 5 U.S.C. 5532(b).

Refunds of Retirement Contributions

Separated employees who are not entitled to an annuity, including individuals who have elected to receive workers' compensation benefits in lieu of a disability annuity, may receive a refund of their federal retirement contributions. However, in applying for such a refund, keep the following points in mind:

• Separated CSRS employees who receive a refund forfeit all annuity rights stemming from the period of service covered by the refund (including survivor benefits), unless they later are reemployed in a position subject to CSRS and make the required redeposit.

• Payment of a refund under FERS permanently eliminates retirement rights based on the period of FERS service the refund covers. Unlike CSRS, FERS does not allow reemployed workers to make a deposit of refunded retirement money to regain credit for the refunded service.

Taking a retirement contribution refund following a FECA award can be risky. While employees may believe that a job-related injury is permanent and that FECA benefits will continue for their lifetime, the payment of FECA benefits may be interrupted or ended because of a change in the employee's medical condition, the availability of suitable work, or rehabilitation. Thus, a retirement contribution refund could imperil a worker's ability to qualify for an annuity in the future that includes the period of work covered by the refund. In addition, if your FECA benefit is terminated, your Federal Employees' Group Life Insurance coverage, if any, also would end without the right to convert to an individual policy.

Impact on Retirement Service Credits

An employee who is in a leave-without-

pay (LWOP) status while in receipt of FECA benefits will receive full credit for the LWOP period for purposes of retirement annuity computations of annuity (as well as high-3 average salary purposes). An employee's use of LWOP while in receipt of FECA benefits is not subject to the normal LWOP limitation of six months in each calendar year for annuity crediting purposes. Thus, when a separated employee (not annuitant) returns to federal service, that portion of the separation when the employee received FECA benefits is deemed to be a period of LWOP during which the employee is receiving FECA benefits, and is fully creditable for future annuity computation and high-3 average salary purposes.

However, no period of separation, even one in which the employee received FECA benefits, may be used as a credit for purposes of meeting the requirement that a CSRS employee complete one year of covered service in the two-year period immediately preceding a non-disability retirement.

Survivor Benefit Considerations

A surviving spouse and dependent children will qualify for compensation death benefits from OWCP if an employee dies because of a job-related injury or illness. Although they also may be eligible for survivor annuity benefits from the CSRS or FERS system, the two benefits are not payable for the same period of time. A survivor must elect which of the two benefits he or she wishes to receive. Most survivors will choose compensation benefits instead of a survivor annuity because compensation normally pays a higher amount.

If electing compensation benefits, they may also elect to receive a lump-sum payment of the employees contributions to the retirement fund. The lump sum is paid under a statutory order of precedence: first, to the designated beneficiary; if none designated, to the surviving spouse; if none, to the child or children and descendants of deceased children, by representation; if none, to any surviving parents; if none, to the duly appointed executor or administrator of the estate; if none, to the next of kin. (If a survivor elects a survivor annuity under disability retirement, the annuity is calculated in the same way as it is for any other retiree.)

In addition, survivors of FERS-covered employees who elect to receive FECA compensation are not eligible for the basic employee death benefit.

Impact on TSP Participation

The federal government's retirement Thrift Savings Plan only accepts participant contributions from basic pay, which means that TSP participants must be in an active "employed" status. If the agency changes a FECA recipient's status to separated, he or she becomes eligible to elect a TSP withdrawal. On the other hand, if the FECA recipient's status is never changed from inactive, the individual is eligible for in-service withdrawals.

Disability retirees may not contribute to the TSP. They are eligible for post-service TSP withdrawal options

Section 7—Unemployment Compensation

Basic unemployment insurance rights and income-security protections for some five million federal civilian employees and ex-service members are provided for in Title 5, Chapter 85, of the U.S. Code (formerly Title XV of the Social Security Act). The program of unemployment compensation for federal civilian employees has been effective since January 1, 1955; the program of unemployment compensation for ex-service members since October 27, 1958. While administrative responsibility for both programs rests with the Secretary of Labor, the actual payment of unemployment compensation is made by state employment security agencies from funds provided by the federal government.

Unless they work in one of the rare types of civilian employment exempt by federal law, government workers are entitled to UC payments if they are civilian or military employees of the United States or civilian employees of any instrumentality wholly or partially owned by the U.S.

Employees do not pay a tax or payroll contribution for unemployment insurance coverage. Instead, the U.S. government pays the costs of UC coverage. Unemployment benefits are paid to claimants by a state employment security agency under the provision of that state's employment security law. Each federal agency (and branch of the military service) is billed for and deposits quarterly into a special Treasury account an amount equal to benefits paid by state agencies to former employees of the federal agency or branch of military service. State agencies draw funds from the account as needed to pay benefits to eligible claimants.

UC Benefit Eligibility Criteria

Under all state laws, you must have had a sufficient qualifying employment or earnings during the time specified by the state law as the "base period" (in the majority of states, a 12-month period beginning less than 18 months before you file a claim); you must be unemployed; you must register for work, file a claim and continue to report to the local office as directed; you must be able to work and be available for immediate referral to full-time suitable work. All state laws provide for disqualification if you voluntarily quit a job without good cause; if you are discharged for misconduct connected with your work; or if you refuse a suitable job without good cause.

If a determination is made that you are ineligible for or disqualified from benefits, you have the right of appeal provided in the applicable state law. If you believe that the information reported by a federal agency is incorrect, you can ask for a review by that agency. The federal agency also has a right to appeal a decision made in your favor.

If you've received a lump-sum payment for terminal annual leave and/or severance payments, your UC benefit eligibility for the period covered by such payments is determined by the law of the state to which your federal service and wages are assigned. Some state laws deny or reduce unemployment benefits to individuals for the duration of the period they receive such income; others disregard the terminal leave and/or severance pay periods in determining eligibility for benefits.

Ex-military service members separated after July 1, 1981, must meet the following federal criteria. "Federal service" means active service (not including active duty in a reserve status unless for a continuous period of 90 days or more) in the armed forces or the commissioned corps of the National Oceanic and Atmospheric Administration, if with respect to that service

(A) the individual was discharged or released under honorable conditions (and, if an officer, did not resign for the good of the service); and

(B) (1) the individual was discharged or released after completing his first full term of active service, which the individual initially agreed to serve, or (2) the individual was discharged or released before completing such term of active service—

(a) for the convenience of the government under an early release program,

(b) because of medical disqualification, pregnancy, parenthood, or service-incurred injury or disability,

(c) because of hardship, or

(d) because of personality disorder or inaptitude, but only if the service was continuous for 365 days or more.

UC Benefit Payments

Your weekly benefit amount and the number of weeks payable depend on the law of the state that has jurisdiction over your claim. State laws provide varying amounts, depending on an individual's earnings, and varying maximum periods in a benefit year. In some states weekly amounts are increased by allowances for dependents. (See state U.I. laws table.) After regular benefits are exhausted, additional weeks of extended benefits may be available in accordance with state law if unemployment is at a specified high level.

The federal law (26 USC 3304) requires states, at a minimum, to reduce the weekly benefit amount of any individual by the amount, allocated weekly, of any "governmental or other pension, retirement or retired pay, annuity, or any other similar periodic payment based on the previous work of such individual." This requirement applies only to payments made under a plan maintained or contributed to by a base-period or chargeable employer. In addition, states may disregard pension payments if the base-period employment did not affect eligibility for or increase the amount of the pension. Also, states are permitted to reduce benefits on less than a dollar-for-dollar basis to take into account the contributions made by the worker to the plan from which payments are made. State law for pension offsets may exceed the min-

imum requirements of the federal law.

UC Claims-Filing Procedures

Your benefit rights based on federal civilian employment will generally be determined by the law of the state in which you had your last official station, including the District of Columbia, the Commonwealth of Puerto Rico, and the Virgin Islands. However, the law of the state of your residence will govern your benefit rights if:

• your last official station in civilian employment was outside the United States, and you are a citizen of the United States at the time such employment is performed; or

• you worked in employment covered under the law of the state in which you reside and establish a claim after termination of your federal civilian employment.

(Your benefit rights based on federal military service and wages will be determined under the law of the state in which you file your first claim establishing a benefit year after your last period of federal military service. "State" laws include those of the District of Columbia, the Commonwealth of Puerto Rico, and the Virgin Islands.)

As soon as you are separated from federal civilian (or military) employment, visit the nearest local public employment and claims office of the state employment security agency to register for work and claim unemployment benefits. These offices offer job placement, testing, counseling services; they have information on job opportunities locally and in other sections of the country, and will make every effort to find suitable work for you in government or private industry. If there is no office in your locality, ask the postmaster for the address of the nearest office.

Employees (including military personnel) who are terminated abroad may not file a UC claim until they return to the "states" which, for the purpose, includes the 50 states, the District of Columbia, the Commonwealth of Puerto Rico, and the Virgin Islands.

If the claim is based on federal civilian employment, your Standard Form 50 notice of personnel action or other documents showing that you were separated from federal employment should be brought to the local UC office, although states are required to take claims even without any records.

Records should include SF-50, 52, W-2 Forms, Earnings and Leave Statements. You also will need any Standard Form 8 issued to you since the beginning of the "base period" (see explanation below) of the state which will determine your benefit rights because the form gives the address of the payroll/personnel office that has your records. (If military personnel, bring DD Form 214, Copy No. 4, and/or other separation documents.)

If you do not already have a Social Security account number, you should get one as soon as possible. However, you may start your claim without a number. Benefits will be withheld pending receipt of the number.

If you willfully make a fraudulent claim, you are subject to a fine or imprisonment, or both. If you have made a mistake in giving information when you filed your claim, notify the local office as soon as you discover the mistake, in order to avoid penalties.

Section 8—Medicare

General Rules

Medicare is a health insurance program for people ages 65 or older, people with end-stage renal disease (permanent kidney failure requiring dialysis or a transplant) and some people with disabilities under age 65. It is administered by the Centers for Medicare and Medicaid Services (formerly known as the Health Care Financing Administration), a subagency of the Health and Human Services department. Local Social Security Administration offices take applications for Medicare and provide general information about the program. Information is available online at www.medicare.gov.

Medicare has two types of coverage— hospital insurance (Part A) and medical insurance (Part B). Hospital insurance helps pay for inpatient hospital care and certain follow-up care after you leave the hospital. Medical insurance helps pay for your doctor's services, outpatient hospital care, and some other medical services and supplies that Part A does not cover.

Federal and postal workers pay 1.45 percent of their salaries for coverage under Medicare's hospital insurance. If you are age 65 or older, you are eligible for hospital insurance if you have government service (alone or in combination with private-sector service) that equals the amount of work needed for Social Security benefits at age 62 (even though you are not also eligible for Social Security benefits). In no case will any individual need more than ten years of government service (alone or in combination with private-sector service) to be eligible for Medicare's hospital insurance at age 65. You must file an application at your local Social Security office.

Medicare eligibility starts at age 65 for you and your spouse. Therefore, if you have a younger spouse, it may be advisable to continue under one of the low-option Federal Employees Health Benefits program plans until the spouse reaches age 65. If you are still working at age 65, that insurance coverage will continue as primary insurer, with Medicare as the secondary insurer until you retire. If your spouse reaches age 65 while you are still working, the federal health insurance coverage will also continue as primary insurer for your spouse. For information about the relationship between Medicare and the Federal Employees Health Benefits program, and how that relationship might affect your decisions under Medicare and/or FEHB, see the Health Insurance section in Chapter 2.

Employees under age 65 who retire on disability may be eligible for hospital insurance. You must file an application for such disability coverage with your local Social Security Administration office. The disability must conform to the disability standards set by Social Security, which generally require that an individual be unable to engage in any substantial gainful activity. However, if you have permanent kidney failure, even if you are still able to work, you may be able to obtain Medicare coverage.

You can get Part A at age 65 without having to pay premiums if: you are already receiving retirement benefits from Social Security or the Railroad Retirement Board; you are eligible to receive Social Security or Railroad benefits but have not yet filed for them; or you or your spouse had Medicare-covered government employment.

If you are under 65, you can get Part A without having to pay premiums if: you have received Social Security or Railroad

Retirement Board disability benefits for 24 months; or you are a kidney dialysis or kidney transplant patient.

While you do not have to pay a monthly premium for Part A if you meet one of those conditions, you must pay for Part B if you want it (in 2003, $58.70). It is deducted from your Social Security or civil service retirement check.

Medicare Eligibility and Enrollment

You don't need any work credits to get Medicare medical insurance. Almost anyone who is 65 or older or who is eligible for hospital insurance can enroll for medical insurance.

If you are receiving Social Security benefits, you will be automatically enrolled for medical insurance unless you say you don't want it at the same time you become entitled to hospital insurance.

There is a seven-month initial enrollment period for medical insurance. This period begins three months before you turn 65 and ends three months after that month. For example, if you are eligible for medical insurance in July, your initial enrollment period starts April 1 and ends October 31.

If you don't take medical insurance during your initial enrollment period and then later decide you want it, you can sign up during a general enrollment period. A general enrollment period is held January 1 through March 31 of each year. But if you enroll during a general enrollment period, your protection won't start until the following July and your monthly premium will be ten percent higher than the basic premium for each full 12-month period you could have had medical insurance but were not enrolled.

A special enrollment period is provided if you are covered under a group health plan when you are first eligible to get Medicare. The plan coverage must be based on your current or active employment or the current or active employment of your spouse. (If you are disabled, the plan coverage may be based on the current or active employment of any family member.) It cannot be a plan for retired people. Under the special enrollment period rules, you may enroll in medical insurance during any month that you are covered under the group health plan or you may enroll during the eight-month period that begins the first full month that you are no longer covered under the group health plan based on current employment.

If you enroll while covered under the group health plan or during the first full month you no longer have group health plan coverage based on current or active employment, medical insurance begins the month you file your application, or at your option, the first day of any of the following three months. If you enroll during the balance of the special enrollment period, medical insurance begins the month after the month of enrollment. In addition, all months during which you are covered under the group health plan based on current or active employment will not be counted as months during which you could have had medical insurance in determining if your premium should be increased.

Hospital Insurance Benefits

Medicare hospital insurance can help pay for medically necessary inpatient hospital care and inpatient care in a skilled nursing facility, home health care, and hospice care.

For inpatient hospital or skilled nursing facility care, a benefit period starts when you enter a hospital. It ends when you have been out of a hospital or other facility that provides skilled nursing or rehabilitation services for 60 days in a row. After that you begin a new benefit period the next time you enter a hospital. There is no limit to the number of benefit periods you can have for inpatient hospital or skilled nursing facility care. However, special limited benefit periods apply to hospice care.

If you need inpatient care, hospital insurance helps pay for up to 90 days in any participating hospital in each benefit period. For the first 60 days, hospital insurance pays for all covered services except for the first $840. You pay this $840 deductible only once in each benefit period. For the 61st through 90th day, hospital insurance pays for all covered services except for $210 a day.

If you ever need more than 90 days of hospital care in any benefit period, you can use some or all of your 60 "reserve days." Reserve days are not renewable. Once you

Medicare Cost Sharing and Premium Amounts for Supplementary Medical Insurance (Part B) Since Program's Inception

Annual Deductible		Coinsurance	Monthly Premiums For Enrollee (Aged and Disabled)[1]
Beginning Each July Until 1984			
1966	$50	20%	$3.00
1970	50[2]	20[2]	5.30
1975	50	20[4]	5.30
1980	50	20	9.60
1981	50[5, 6]	20[6]	11.00
1982	75	20[7]	12.20
1984	75	20	14.60[3]
1985	75	20	15.50
1987	75	20	17.90
1988	75	20	24.80
1989	75	20	31.90
1990	75	20	28.60
1991	100	20	29.60
1992	100	20	31.80
1993	100	20	36.60
1994	100	20	41.10
1995	100	20	46.10
1996	100	20	42.50
1997	100	20	43.80
1998	100	20	43.80
1999	100	20	45.50
2000	100	20	50.00
2001	100	20	50.00
2002	100	20	54.00
2003	100	20	58.70

[1] Beginning July 1973 for the disabled.

[2] Professional inpatient services of pathologists and radiologists not subject to deductible or coinsurance, beginning in April 1968.

[3] Beginning in January for current and succeeding years.

[4] Home health services not subject to coinsurance, beginning July 1972.

[5] Home health services are not subject to deductible.

[6] Same as footnote[2], but only when physician accepts assignment.

[7] Effective October 1, 1982, professional inpatient services of pathologists and radiologists are subject to coinsurance and deductible.

use a reserve day, you never get it back. For each reserve day you use, hospital insurance pays for all covered services except for $420 a day.

Covered services include semiprivate room, all meals, regular nursing services, operating and recovery room costs, hospital costs for anesthesia services, intensive care and coronary care, drugs, lab tests, X-rays, medical supplies and appliances, rehabilitation services, and preparatory services related to kidney transplant surgery.

Under special conditions, hospital insurance can help pay for care in a psychiatric hospital, a U.S. nonparticipating hospital, or a qualified Canadian or Mexican hospital.

If you need inpatient skilled nursing or rehabilitation services after a hospital stay, hospital insurance helps pay for up to 100 days in a participating skilled nursing facility in each benefit period. You must have been in the hospital for at least three days and meet certain other conditions.

Hospital insurance pays for all covered services for the first 20 days and all but $105 a day for up to 80 more days. Covered services include semiprivate room, all meals, regular nursing services, rehabili-

Medicare (Part A): Hospital Insurance-Covered Services Per Benefit Period

Services	Benefit	Medicare Pays**	You Pay**
HOSPITAL STAYS Semiprivate room and board, general nursing, and miscellaneous hospital services and supplies.	First 60 days	All but $840	$840
	61st to 90th day	All but $210 a day	$210 a day
	91st to 150th day*	All but $420 a day	$420 a day
	Beyond 150 days	Nothing	All costs
POSTHOSPITAL SKILLED NURSING FACILITY CARE You must have been in a hospital for at least three days, enter a Medicare-approved facility generally within 30 days after hospital discharge, and meet other program requirements. (2)	First 20 days	100% of approved amount	Nothing
	Additional 80 days	All but $105 a day	Up to $105 a day
	Beyond 100 days	Nothing	All costs
HOME HEALTH CARE Medically necessary skilled care, home health aide services, medical supplies, etc.	Part-time or intermittent nursing care and other services for as long as you meet criteria for benefits.	100% of approved amount; 80% of pproved amount for durable medical equipment.	Nothing for services; 20% of approved amount for durable medical equipment.
HOSPICE CARE Full scope of pain relief and support services available to the terminally ill.	As long as doctor certifies need.	All but limited costs for outpatient drugs and for inpatient respite care.	$5 for outpatient prescription drugs and 5% of the Medicare-approved amount for inpatient respite care.
BLOOD	Unlimited if medically necessary.	All but first three pints per calendar year.	For first 3 pints.***

* 60 reserve days may be used only once.

** These figures are for 2003 and are subject to change each year.

*** To the extent the blood deductible is met under one part of Medicare during the calendar year, it does not have to be met under the other part.

Note: A benefit period begins on the first day you receive service as an inpatient in a hospital and ends after you have been out of the hospital or skilled nursing facility for 60 days in a row or ÉÉ remain in a skilled nursing facility but do not receive skilled care there for 60 days in a row.

Neither Medicare or Medigap insurance will pay for most nursing home care.

Medicare (Part B): Medical Insurance-Covered Services Per Calendar Year

Services	Benefit	Medicare Pays**	You Pay**
MEDICAL EXPENSE Doctor's services, outpatient medical and surgical services and supplies, physical and speech therapy, diagnostic tests, durable medical equipment, etc.	Medicare pays for medical services in or out of the hospital.	80% of approved amount (after $100 deductible); 50% of approved charges for most outpatient mental health services.	$100 deductible,* plus 20% of approved amount and charges above approved amount.** 50% of aproved charges for outpatient mental health care.
CLINICAL LABORATORY SERVICES Blood tests, urinalysis, and more	Unlimited if medically necessary.	Generally 100% of approved amount.	Nothing for services.
HOME HEALTH CARE Medically necessary skilled care, home health aide services, medical supplies, etc.	Part-time or intermittent nursing care and other services for as long as you meet criteria for benefits.	100% of approved amount; 80% of approved amount for durable medical equipment.	Nothing for services; 20% of approved amount for durable medical equipment.
OUTPATIENT HOSPITAL SERVICES Reasonable and necessary services for the diagnosis or treatment of an illness or injury.	Unlimited if medically necessary.	Medicare payment based on hospital costs.	A coinsurance or fixed copayment amount that may vary according to the service.
BLOOD	Unlimited if medically necessary.	80% of approved amount (after $100 deductible and starting with 4th pint).	First three pints plus 20% of approved amount for additional pints (after $100 deductible).***

* Once you have had $100 of expense for covered services, the Part B deductible does not apply to any other covered services you receive for the rest of the year.
** The amount by which a physician's charge can exceed the Medicare-approved amount is limited by law.
*** To the extent the blood deductible is met under one part of Medicare during the calendar year, it does not have to be met under the other part.

197

tation services, drugs, medical supplies, and appliances.

Under certain conditions, hospital insurance can pay for hospice care for people with a terminal illness. Covered services include physician services, nursing care, outpatient drugs for pain relief and symptom management, short-term inpatient care, therapies and homemaker-home health aide services. There is a co-payment of up to $5 for outpatient prescription drugs. You also pay 5 percent of the Medicare-approved payment amount for inpatient respite care.

Hospital insurance can pay the approved cost of home health visits from a participating home health agency. You must be confined to your home and meet certain other conditions. The number of home health visits covered by Medicare varies with each illness or injury.

Covered services include part-time skilled nursing care, physical therapy, and speech therapy. If you need one or more of those services, hospital insurance also covers part-time services of home health aides, occupational therapy, medical social services, and medical supplies and equipment.

Medical Insurance Benefits

Medicare's medical insurance helps pay for your doctor's services and supplies that are not covered by the hospital insurance provided under the program. Each year, as soon as you meet the annual medical insurance deductible, medical insurance generally will pay 80 percent of the approved charges for other covered services you receive during the rest of the year. The annual deductible is $100.

Medical insurance covers doctors' services no matter where you receive them in the United States—in a doctor's office, the hospital, your home, or elsewhere. Covered doctor's services include surgical services, diagnostic tests and X-rays that are part of your treatment, medical supplies furnished in a doctor's office, services of the office nurse, and drugs which are administered as part of your treatment and cannot be self-administered.

Note: Medicare payment for laboratory services by your doctor will be made only when the doctor takes "assignment," i.e., agrees to accept Medicare payment as payment in full.

Medicare does not cover delivery of hospitalization or medical services outside the United States, except under special circumstances in Mexican and Canadian hospitals.

Medical insurance covers outpatient hospital services you receive for diagnosis and treatment of an illness or injury, such as care in an emergency room or outpatient clinic of a hospital.

Medical insurance can cover an unlimited number of home health visits if all required conditions are met.

Under certain conditions or limitations, medical insurance also covers: ambulance transportation; artificial limbs and eyes; chiropractors' treatment for subluxation of the spine; diagnostic testing prior to a hospital stay; durable medical equipment such as wheelchairs or oxygen equipment for use in your home; home dialysis equipment, supplies, and periodic support services; home and office services of independent physical therapists; independent laboratory tests (when performed under "assignment" as described above); optometrists' services for fitting of corrective lenses after cataract surgery; oral surgery (but not routine dental care); outpatient maintenance dialysis; outpatient physical therapy and speech pathology services; outpatient psychiatric services; pneumococcal, influenza and hepatitis B vaccinations; podiatrists' services; therapeutic shoes for certain individuals with diabetes; surgical dressings, splints, casts, colostomy supplies, and braces; training for home dialysis; x-rays and radiation treatments.

Medicare Health Plan Choices

Medicare health plan choices include the Original Medicare Plan and Medicare + Choice. Medicare + Choice plans include managed care plans (health maintenance organizations) and private fee-for-service plans. No matter how you get your Medicare benefits, you are still in the Medicare program. In every Medicare health plan you pay the monthly Medicare Part B premium and you get all the Medicare Part A and Part B covered services.

Original Medicare Plan—The Original Medicare Plan is also known as "fee-for-service." This plan, offered by the federal government, is available nationwide. You are usually charged a fee for each health care service or supply you get.

If you are in the Original Medicare Plan, you may go to any doctor, specialist, or hospital that accepts Medicare. Generally, a fee is charged each time you get a service.

You pay a deductible amount for your health care each year before Medicare pays its part. Then Medicare pays its share and you pay your share (coinsurance). After you get a health care service, you get an explanation of Medicare benefits or a Medicare summary notice that lists the amount you may be billed.

What you pay out-of-pocket depends on whether your doctor or supplier agrees to "accept assignment" (i.e., bill only up to certain maximums for Medicare reimbursement), how often you need health care, what type of health care you need, whether you get health care while traveling outside of the United States (since in most cases you would pay for this care), and whether you get services or supplies not covered by Medicare.

To help cover the costs the Original Medicare Plan does not cover, you can keep employer health coverage (such as Federal Employees Health Benefits program coverage), or buy a "Medigap" policy (Medicare Supplement Insurance). A Medigap policy fills gaps in Original Medicare Plan coverage. In all states except Massachusetts, Minnesota and Wisconsin, a Medigap policy must be one of ten standardized policies. Two of the standardized policies may have a high deductible option. In addition, any standardized policy may be sold as a "Medicare SELECT" policy. Medicare SELECT policies usually cost less because you must use certain hospitals and doctors except in emergencies.

Medicare + Choice—Medicare managed care plans and private fee-for-service plans—collectively called Medicare + Choice—often offer benefits in addition to those provided under the Original Medicare Plan. Enrollees also get all regular Medicare-covered services and all Medicare rights and protections. However, these plans are not available in all areas.

If you have Medicare, you can join either of these types of plans if: you have both Part A and Part B; you live in the service area of the plan; and you do not have End-Stage Renal Disease (permanent kidney failure requiring dialysis or a kidney transplant).

What you pay out-of-pocket depends on whether the plan charges a monthly premium in addition to the Part B premium, how much the plan decides you must pay for each visit, the type of health care you need and how often you get it, and how much the plan charges for extra benefits.

A Medicare managed care plan, sometimes called an HMO, is a health plan offered by private insurance companies. Medicare pays a set amount of money every month to the private insurance company. In most managed care plans, you can only go to certain doctors and hospitals that agree to treat members of the plan. Generally, you can only see a specialist when you get a referral from your primary care doctor.

Some managed care plans offer a point-of-service option allowing enrollees to go to other doctors and hospitals outside the plan. Most of the time this option costs more, and gives more choices.

A private fee-for-service plan is a Medicare health plan offered by a private insurance company. Medicare pays a set amount of money every month to the private insurance company. The private insurance company provides health care coverage to people with Medicare who join this plan. The insurance company, rather than the Medicare program, decides how much it pays, and how much the enrollee pays, for services. Enrollees can go to any doctor or hospital that accepts the plan's payment.

In a private fee-for-service plan, you may pay more if the plan lets doctors, hospitals, and other providers bill you more than the plan pays for services. If this is allowed, there may be a limit to what they can charge, and you must pay the difference.

Chapter 6
Thrift Savings Plan

Section 1—General TSP Rules and Procedures

Open Seasons

Twice a year during the TSP open seasons, each April 15-June 30 and October 15-December 31, employees may begin participation, terminate participation or alter their contribution amounts (until the second open season of 2002, the open seasons ran each May 15-July 31 and November 15-January 31).

Newly hired employees have a 60-day window to begin participating. If they miss that opportunity, they must wait until the next open season. Agency automatic and matching contributions for newly hired Federal Employees Retirement System participants become effective in the second "election period" following their employment. An "election period" is the last calendar month of an open season, the earliest any transactions chosen during that open season can become effective. Thus, depending on how the date of hiring coincides with an open season, the wait for automatic and matching contributions could be as long as nearly a year.

Employees may stop contributing to the TSP at any time. However, if they do, they must skip one open season before they can resume contributions.

Valuation of Accounts

At the end of each month, the TSP conducts a valuation of accounts. Accountings include any new investments made by actively employed investors, any loan or withdrawal activity, interfund transfers, and the changes in the value of the funds themselves due to investment earnings or losses. When the TSP switches to a new computer system—possibly to occur in 2003—accounts will be tabulated every business day and balances will be shown as shares and share prices as well as in dollar amounts.

Allocating Ongoing Investments

Investors may allocate ongoing investments at any time by using the ThriftLine automated phone system (504-255-8777), the TSP website, www.tsp.gov, or by submitting Form-50 to the TSP Service Office.

Interfund Transfers

Investors may transfer money from one TSP investment fund to another at their discretion. This applies both to actively employed investors and those retired or separated.

Investors may make interfund transfers through the TSP's website, www.tsp.gov, by using the automated ThriftLine system (504-255-8777) or by filing Form TSP-30, Interfund Transfer Request, and submitting it to the TSP Service Office. Generally, transfer requests must be received by the TSP by the 15th of each month in order to be effective at the end of that month; otherwise the transaction will occur at the end of the following month.

When the TSP switches to a new computer system—possibly to occur in 2003—if you request an interfund transfer on the Web site or the ThriftLine, your request will normally be processed and posted to your account within two business days and if you use Form TSP-30, your request will normally be processed and posted to your account within two business days of the day it is received by the TSP.

Investors who have not previously invested outside the Government Securities (G) Fund must sign a statement acknowledging risk before moving money into any of the other funds.

Transfers into the TSP

Transfers are allowed into the TSP from private-sector 401(k) and similar stock incentive and profit sharing plans. As a practical matter, this provision primarily affects Federal Employees Retirement System participants since most participants under the Civil Service Retirement System by definition joined the government before use of such programs became a widespread practice in the private-sector. The policy further allows transfers from individual retirement accounts established to hold such money from 401(k) plans and similar accounts after leaving private-sector employment, but does not allow transfers into the TSP from funds in other types of IRAs.

A TSP participant who would like to transfer money into the TSP should check with a representative of his or her former plan or IRA to ensure that the distribution is considered an eligible rollover distribution. The TSP cannot accept after-tax money.

For purposes of these transactions, there is a distinction between a transfer and a rollover. A transfer occurs when the participant instructs the qualified retirement plan or conduit IRA to send all or part of his or her eligible distribution directly to the TSP instead of issuing it to the participant. A rollover occurs when the qualified retirement plan or IRA makes a distribution to the participant (after withholding the mandatory 20 percent federal income tax) and the participant deposits all or any part of the gross amount of the distribution into the TSP within 60 days after receiving it.

The TSP can accept a transfer from:
• A qualified retirement plan. This is either a qualified trust described in section 401(a) of the Internal Revenue Code which is tax exempt under IRC 501(a) or an IRC 403(a) annuity plan. A qualified retirement plan generally includes defined contribution plans such as money purchase plans, profit sharing plans, employee stock ownership plans, stock bonus plans and other plans that have provisions for cash or deferred arrangements under section 401(k) of the IRC and may include a distribution from a qualified benefit plan.
• A conduit IRA. This is an individual retirement account described in IRC 408(a) or an individual retirement annuity described in IRC 408(b) that contains only funds transferred or rolled over from a qualified retirement plan and earnings on those amounts. Thus, it cannot contain funds contributed to it directly by the participant. Consequently, an IRA will not qualify as a conduit IRA if the participant has mixed regular contributions or funds from other sources with the rollover distribution from the retirement plan.

The TSP can accept a rollover from the participant. A rollover can only be accepted within 60 calendar days of the date the participant received the eligible rollover distribution from a qualified plan or conduit IRA. The rollover must be in guaranteed funds made payable to the TSP.

Money rolled over or transferred into the TSP is allocated according to the participant's most current contribution allocation. It becomes part of the TSP employee contributions and will be subject to the same plan rules as all other employee contributions into the account. The money does not count against the annual dollar cap imposed on regular employee contributions.

Contributions, Matches and Limits

Employees may contribute to the TSP on a pay period basis either in percentage-of-salary amounts or whole dollar amounts. Through most of 2003, CSRS employees may contribute up to 8 percent of basic pay biweekly and FERS employees may contribute up to 13 percent of basic pay, subject to a dollar cap discussed below.

The percentage limits are rising by 1 percentage point during each autumn open season under a phase-out schedule enacted in 2000 (P.L. 106-361). Note that there is a lag time between an election to increase withholdings and the effective date of that change; the earliest an election made in an open season can be effective is the last month of that open season. Thus, an election made in an open season starting October 15 becomes effective no sooner than the first full pay period starting in December.

The TSP traditionally limited contributions to 5 percent for CSRS employees and 10 percent for FERS employees, subject to the annual tax code dollar contribution limit. However, P.L. 106-361 enacted a phase-out of percentage limits. Beginning with the open season that started May 15, 2001, FERS-covered workers were able to invest up to 11 percent of pay each period, while CSRS-covered workers were allowed to contribute up to 6 percent. In the November 15, 2001-January 31, 2003 open season, those limits were increased to 12 and 7 percent, respectively. The open season dates changed after the first open season of 2002 to begin each April 15 and October 15. Thus, investments of up to 8 percent for CSRS investors and up to 13 percent for FERS investors were allowed effective in the autumn 2002 open season, effective as early as the first full pay period of December 2002.

The TSP contribution limits will rise by a further 1 percent each autumn open season until hitting 10 percent for CSRS and 15 percent for FERS in the autumn 2004 open season and will be eliminated effective with the autumn 2005 open season. The agency matching contribution system is unaffected by the phase-out of the percentage limits, and the total employee contributions remain subject to the annual IRS limit.

Lump-sum contributions—other than transfers and rollovers as described above—are not permitted.

While retirees and separated participants may leave their accounts open and continue to transfer money among the investment funds, they may not make further investments.

The government partially matches contributions by FERS employees. Contributions are matched dollar for dollar for the first three percent of pay contributed per pay period, and then 50 cents on the dollar for the next two percent of pay contributed per pay period. The employing agency also makes an automatic one percent contribution for FERS-covered employees, whether or not they have decided to contribute their own money to a TSP account.

Employee contributions are subject to the annual "elective deferral limit" (for 2003, $12,000). This annual limit traditionally has affected only highly paid FERS employees, although as the percentage limits are phased out, it will become a factor for highly paid CSRS employees and for less highly paid FERS employees as well. Once the dollar cap is reached for a year, employee investments are shut off—as are the agency matching (although not automatic) contributions for FERS employees. Thus, FERS employees may need to adjust their total contribution so that they receive the advantage of full agency matching contributions throughout the year, rather than allowing their contributions—and the associated matching contributions—to stop before the end of the year because the employee contribution limit has been exceeded. That consideration does not apply to CSRS employees, since they receive no government contributions in any case.

Amounts transferred into the TSP from 401(k) and similar plans and from conduit individual retirement accounts holding proceeds of such plans do not count against the dollar limit; nor do government contributions for FERS investors.

The dollar contribution limit is scheduled to rise to $13,000 in 2004, $14,000 in 2005 and $15,000 in 2006.

Contributions to a TSP account generally can come only from payroll deductions; therefore money in an IRA generally cannot be rolled over to a TSP account. The exception is transfers into the TSP from 401(k) and similar plans as well as from conduit IRAs holding proceeds of such plans.

Employees participating in the TSP remain eligible to contribute to an IRA. However, government retirement plans like CSRS and FERS are considered to be retirement plans for the purpose of IRA eligibility, so rules governing IRA contribution limits and tax deductions may apply. Check with a tax advisor.

Catch-Up Contributions—Under legislation enacted late in 2002 (P.L. 107-304), TSP investors age 50 and older may make "catch-up" contributions of up to $2,000 in 2003, with the amount increasing by $1,000 each year until hitting $5,000 in 2006 and adjusted for inflation thereafter. These contributions are on top of the percentage of salary or dollar limits that otherwise would apply to an individual.

Catch-up contributions must be made through payroll withholding and were to be allowed beginning with the TSP open season starting April 15, 2003, if not earlier.

Enactment of the provision put TSP participants on equal footing with employees of private sector companies offering similar tax-preferred retirement savings programs. Under a 2001 tax reform law, those plans were authorized to allow such contributions effective in 2002, but separate legislation was needed to make that authority applicable to the TSP.

They are termed catch-up contributions because the intent is to allow investors who did not have such plans available to them throughout their working careers to supplement their retirement savings.

Vesting Requirements

TSP's vesting requirements apply only to FERS participants. If you are a FERS participant, you must work for the federal government for a certain number of years to be entitled to (or "vested" in) the agency's automatic, one percent contributions in your account and the earnings on those contributions.

Most FERS employees become vested in the automatic contributions after three years of federal civilian service. FERS employees in congressional and certain non-career positions become vested in the automatic contributions after completing two years of federal civilian service. If you leave government service before meeting the vesting requirement for your automatic contributions, those contributions and their earnings will be removed from your account and forfeited to the TSP.

If you are a FERS participant, you are always vested in your own contributions (and their earnings) as well as the matching contributions your agency makes (and the earnings on them). If you die before leaving government service, your entire TSP account will be vested automatically.

CSRS participants receive no agency contributions, so they are always vested in all the money in their accounts.

Automatic Cashout of Small Accounts

If your vested account balance is $3,500 or less after your agency reports you have left the government, you are subject to the TSP automatic cashout procedures unless you make an election. When the TSP switches to a new computer system—possibly to occur in 2003—that threshold will drop to $200. Other withdrawal options are not available for these accounts.

Spousal Rights

The spouses of TSP participants are granted certain rights under the Federal Employees' Retirement System Act of 1986. (Generally, the term "spouse" includes a separated spouse.) If you are married and your vested account balance is more than $3,500, these spousal rights requirements must be satisfied before you can withdraw your account. (See below for a review of TSP's withdrawal rules and procedures.)

If you are a married FERS participant, your spouse is entitled by law to a survivor annuity. This annuity is a joint life annuity, with 50 percent survivor benefits, level pay-

ments, and no cash refund feature. If you want to purchase a different type of annuity or choose to withdraw your account in a single payment or a series of monthly payments, your spouse must sign a notarized statement waiving his or her right to the required annuity. (If your current spouse has previously waived the right to this survivor annuity, you do not have to obtain his or her signature again if you change your election.)

If you are a married CSRS participant, the TSP must notify your spouse of your withdrawal and any change in election.

Under certain circumstances exceptions may be made to the spouse's right to a survivor annuity (FERS) or notice (CSRS). If the whereabouts of your spouse are unknown, or if there are exceptional circumstances that make it inappropriate for you to obtain your spouse's signature, you may apply for an exception to the spouse waiver and notice requirements by submitting Form TSP-16, Exception to Spousal Requirements, and the required documentation. The criteria for supporting a claim on the basis of exceptional circumstances are strict. The fact that there is a separation agreement, a prenuptial agreement, a protective order, or a divorce petition does not in itself support a claim of exceptional circumstances.

For more information on establishing an exception to the spousal rights requirements, see Form TSP-16 or get a copy of "Background Information on Exceptions to Spousal Requirements," available through personnel offices, the TSP website at www.tsp.gov, or Thrift Savings Plan Service Office, P.O. Box 61500, New Orleans, LA 70161-1500.

Court Orders

The TSP must honor a valid court order that awards all or part of your TSP account to a former or separated spouse. The TSP must also honor a valid order that enforces obligations to pay child support or alimony. Your withdrawal will not be processed while the TSP is reviewing an order. If the TSP determines that an order is valid and applies to your TSP account, it will comply with the order before your withdrawal is processed.

For more information about court orders, see Chapter 7. You should also get the booklet *Information About Court Orders* and the notice *"Tax Treatment of Thrift*

Savings Plan Payments Made Under Qualifying Orders," available through personnel offices, the TSP website at *www.tsp.gov*, or Thrift Savings Plan Service Office, P.O. Box 61500 New Orleans, LA 70161-1500.

Tax Status of Investments

An employee's own contributions to the TSP reduce the worker's taxable current income. In effect, an employee's contributions reduce the individual's gross salary for federal income tax purposes. For example, if employees who have a $30,000 salary contribute 5 percent of their pay ($1,500) to the TSP, their gross salary is reduced to $28,500 for federal income tax purposes. Most state and local governments apply the same rule. Current exceptions are the states of Pennsylvania and New Jersey. To be sure about state and local taxes, employees should check with state and local government taxing authorities.

Social Security taxes, however, are applied to an employee's total salary. Thus, in the example above, the Social Security tax would be applied to the $30,000 base salary. All agency contributions and earnings in participant accounts are sheltered from taxes until withdrawn.

Upon withdrawal, the amount paid to an employee is subject to different tax rules depending upon how the account is withdrawn.

You must treat amounts paid to you from your TSP account as taxable income for federal income tax purposes in the year in which such payments are made. TSP annuity purchases and direct transfers by the TSP to other eligible plans are not payments made directly to you and are not subject to these rules.

The tax law contains complex rules for the payment of federal income tax and tax withholding on payments from plans such as the TSP.

Military Reserve TSP Accounts

Under P.L. 106–65, members of the Ready Reserve or National Guard of the Army, Navy, Air Force, Marine Corps, Coast Guard, Public Health Service, and the National Oceanic and Atmospheric Administration in any military pay status (as well as regular active duty members of those services) can contribute to the TSP. Such accounts must be established by submitting to the applicable service a separate election form called the TSP-U-1 during a TSP open season. Military TSP accounts have generally the same tax treatment and the same investment, loan and withdrawal options as civilian accounts.

Federal and postal employees who are Reservists can have both a civilian TSP account and a uniformed services TSP account. When civilian federal employees enter military active duty, they cannot make any contributions to their civilian TSP accounts while on LWOP or separated from the civilian position. As active duty service members, though, they can contribute to a military TSP account, without the benefit of matching contributions from their branch of service.

Those with two accounts have their accounts treated separately for most purposes. For example, to move money between funds, they must submit two interfund transfer requests, one for each account. However, the accounts are combined for the tax code dollar limit ($12,000 in 2003) on annual contributions and in determining the amount the participant is eligible to borrow from the TSP.

Members of the uniformed services have access to the TSP loan program. However, Reservists who drill only monthly should think seriously before taking a loan from their military accounts because they may be unable to repay the loan in the time frame required by law. Employees are prohibited from repaying a uniformed services TSP loan from civilian pay, or vice versa.

Only pay for active military service can be contributed to a military TSP account. In 2003, the percentage limit is 8 percent of the basic pay earned in military status each month. Reservists also may be able to contribute all or any whole percentage of any special or incentive pay (including reenlistment or other bonuses) received, up to the tax code dollar limit. To contribute from military special pay, incentive pay, or bonuses, the participant must be contributing from military basic pay.

Contributions from tax-exempt pay such as combat zone pay are not subject to the dollar limit but they do count against the percentage maximum. Any earnings attributable to those contributions will be taxable upon withdrawal.

Once an employee separates from either the uniformed services or federal civilian service, the employee will be able to combine the TSP accounts by contacting the TSP Service Office.

Catch-Up Contributions for Reservists

Employees who perform uniformed service and then later are restored to their civilian positions may make up any contributions to a civilian Thrift Savings Plan account they missed because of the military service. The amount of contributions is determined by using the TSP election form (Form TSP-1) in effect immediately before entry into military service, unless the employee submits a new Form TSP-1 to terminate the contributions or make an election for any open season that occurred during military service. The amount of money they can retroactively contribute to their civilian accounts will be offset by any contributions they made to their uniformed services TSP account while on active duty.

Both makeup and current contributions must be invested in the funds requested on the current Form TSP-1. All makeup contributions must be deducted from future pay.

Those in the Federal Employees Retirement System will receive retroactive agency matching contributions as they make up their employee contributions. FERS participants receive agency automatic (1 percent of salary) contributions regardless of whether they make up employee contributions. Retroactive earnings are credited on retroactive agency contributions but not on makeup employee contributions.

Account Information

There are several ways to access information regarding a TSP account. The TSP ThriftLine, (504) 255-8777, is an automated telephone service that is available 24 hours a day, seven days a week from touchtone phones (callers may opt out of the automated system to speak to a customer service representative during normal business hours). The TSP website (www.tsp.gov) also offers account holders information of a general and specific nature. For certain services callers or visitors must have their personal identification number (PIN) and Social Security number.

On both the ThriftLine and website you may: make an interfund transfer, change or request personal identification number, check on status of loan or withdrawal request, determine current account balance and amount available for loan, allocate future contributions, check the status of an outstanding loan, and obtain a loan prepayment amount.

When the TSP switches to a new computer system—possibly to occur in 2003—the website additionally will allow visitors to begin and in some cases complete a loan or withdrawal request, and to re-amortize a loan. Whether you will be able to complete a loan or withdrawal through these automated services will depend on whether your request requires your spouse's signature or additional documentation.

At the beginning of each open season, employees receive the Thrift Savings Plan Update, which contains information concerning the plan and the activities permitted in the open season. Under the new computer system the TSP also will issue quarterly account statements for the periods ending March 31, June 30, September 30, and December 31 containing a detailed summary of the activity in the account, including any loan activity.

For current employees, the primary contact for TSP information is the agency personnel office. The TSP Service Office is the primary contact for participants who have left federal service.

Thrift Savings Plan Service Office
National Finance Center
P.O. Box 61500
New Orleans, LA 70161-1500
Phone: (504) 255-6000
TDD: (504) 255-5113

The TSP Service Office can answer questions about your account and send you TSP withdrawal materials to supplement the withdrawal package provided by your agency upon your separation from federal service. Submit your withdrawal forms directly to the TSP office.

In addition, Federal Employees News Digest Inc. has published a comprehensive guide to understanding investment options, strategies and withdrawal rules called *Your*

Guide to the New Thrift Savings Plan. See publication-ordering information in this Almanac.

Federal Retirement Thrift Investment Board

The TSP is managed by an independent federal agency—the Federal Retirement Thrift Investment Board. The Board consists of five members who serve in a part-time capacity. They are nominated by the President and confirmed by the Senate.

The agency is administered by a full-time executive director, appointed by the Board. Board operations are funded first by departing employees' forfeiture of the agency's automatic one percent account contributions. These funds are turned over to the Board because FERS-covered employees who work less than three years are not vested in the one percent contribution or its earnings. (In the case of FERS-covered congressional workers and certain non-career employees vesting takes only two years.)

If these forfeitures by terminating employees are not sufficient to pay the Board's expenses, then the Board pays its remaining administrative expenses from earnings on all participant and agency contributions.

James B. Petrick is Executive Director of the Federal Retirement Thrift Investment Board. The Board's address is 1250 H St., N.W., Washington, DC 20005.

Section 2—TSP Investment Options and Fund Performance

General Investment Options

There are five investment funds for TSP accounts:

G Fund—investments in short-term, non-marketable U.S. Treasury securities.

C Fund—large-capitalization U.S. stocks.

F Fund—a bond index fund consisting of a mix of government and corporate bonds.

S Fund—small and mid-capitalization U.S. stocks.

I Fund—mostly large-capitalization foreign stocks.

All employees may elect to invest any portion of their current account balances or future contributions in any or all of the funds. All participants also may make interfund transfers. An interfund transfer is the movement of all or some of the money in a participant's account among the funds.

The G Fund is managed by the Thrift Investment Board's staff. The Board has contracted with Barclays Global Investors to manage the S, I, C and F Funds.

How Returns Are Calculated

G Fund—By definition, the G Fund never can have a losing month. All investments in the fund earn interest at a rate equal to the average of market yields on Treasury marketable securities with four or more years to maturity.

G Fund returns are reduced by administrative expenses, which are about 0.06 percent, or $.60 for every $1,000 invested.

C, S, I and F Funds—The C, S, I and F Funds can post gains or losses. The capital gain or loss consists of these elements:

• the change in the price of the stocks in the equity index funds (C, S and I Funds) or the notes in the U.S. Debt Index Fund (F Fund);

• dividend (C, S and I Funds) or interest (F Fund) income credited to the funds;

• interest on short term investments while contributions are awaiting investment;

• income from lending securities (C, S and I Funds) or notes and bonds (F Fund) on a short-term basis;

• administrative expenses, including management fees paid to Barclays, which are about 0.06 percent, or $.60 for every $1,000 invested in the C and F Funds and about 0.05 percent, or $.50 for every $1,000 invested, in the S and I Funds; and

• trading costs.

In addition, the I Fund fluctuates relative to the U.S. dollar's value against the currencies of the countries in whose stock markets that fund has investments.

Government Securities Investment (G) Fund

The G Fund consists exclusively of investments in short-term, non-marketable U.S. Treasury securities specially issued to the TSP by the Treasury. The Treasury holds the assets of the G Fund in trust. Maturities range from one day on business days to four days over holiday weekends.

The G Fund rate is set monthly by the Treasury; all G Fund investments earn interest at that rate for the month. Since the G Fund is invested in short-term securities regardless of the rate, the value of securities does not fluctuate.

The G Fund rate is calculated by the Treasury using the closing market bid prices of approximately 100 Treasury securities on the last day of the previous month. These prices are used to calculate the yield on each security. The yield of each security has a weight in the G Fund rate calculation based on the market value of each security. The larger the dollar amount for a security, the larger the weight in the calculation.

The net result is that the G Fund is a weighted average of yields on Treasury notes and bonds with a weighted average maturity of about 14 years. The G Fund rate formula is the same as that used for the calculation of the interest rate for the investments of the Social Security and civil service retirement trust funds.

The table below shows the actual fund rates of return since 1988, the first full year of operation of the fund, after deducting administrative expenses. These are the rates used in the allocation of earnings to participants' accounts. There is no assurance that future rates of return for the fund will resemble any of these rates.

Annual G Fund Return Rates, 1988-2002

1988	8.81%
1989	8.81%
1990	8.90%
1991	8.15%
1992	7.23%
1993	6.14%
1994	7.22%
1995	7.03%
1996	6.76%
1997	6.77%
1998	5.74%
1999	5.99%
2000	6.42%
2001	5.39%
2002	5.00%

Annual compounded rate of return, 1993-2002: 6.24%

Common Stock Index Investment (C) Fund

The C Fund is invested in the Barclays Equity Index Fund and tracks the S&P 500 index, which provides a representative measure of stock market performance of 500 companies traded in U.S. stock markets, primarily on the New York Stock Exchange. These stocks represent more than 100 separate industries grouped into four major sectors: industrials, utilities, financials and transportation. The stocks in the S&P 500 make up about three-fourths of the market value of the U.S. stock markets.

The companies in the index are selected by S&P primarily based on their representation in their industry groupings, not because they are expected to have superior stock price performance relative to the stock market in general or to any other companies in particular. Instead, the measure is designed to be a representative gauge of U.S. stock market performance. The makeup of the index varies from time to time.

The weighting of stocks in the S&P 500 index is based on each stock's total market value—its market stock price per share times the number of shares outstanding—relative to the market value of the other stocks in the index. The result is that the companies with high market value have a disproportionate effect on the direction of the index.

The table below shows the actual fund rates of return since 1988, the first full year of operation of the fund, after deducting administrative expenses. These are the rates used in the allocation of earnings to participants' accounts. There is no assurance that future rates of return for the fund will resemble any of these rates.

Annual C Fund Return Rates, 1988-2002

1988	11.84%
1989	31.03%
1990	-3.15%
1991	30.77%
1992	7.70%
1993	10.13%
1994	1.33%
1995	37.41%
1996	22.85%
1997	33.17%
1998	28.44%
1999	20.95%

2000	−9.14
2001	−11.94%
2002	-22.05%

Annual compounded rate of return, 1993-2002: 9.29%

Fixed Income Investment (F) Fund

The F Fund is invested in the Barclays U.S. Debt Index Fund, which tracks the LBA index, a measure of the performance of the major bond markets in the U.S. The LBA index consists of high quality fixed income securities with maturities of more than one year, including government, mortgage-backed and corporate bonds.

The government sector represents half of the total, primarily Treasury issues, but also including some agency-issued obligations. The Treasury sector contains all public obligations with maturities of at least one year and an outstanding par value of at least $100 million. The agency sector is made up of all publicly issued obligations of federally sponsored agencies such as the Federal Home Loan Bank System with maturities greater than one year and an outstanding par value of at least $100 million.

Mortgage-backed securities constitute about another 30 percent of the LBA index. These securities include fixed rate pass-through securities backed by agencies such as Ginnie Mae, Fannie Mae and Freddie Mac.

The corporate sector represents the remainder of the LBA index and contains all publicly issued fixed rate investment grade securities of U.S. companies with maturities of at least one year and an outstanding par value of at least $100 million. These are securities rated at least BBB by Standard & Poor's or Baa by Moody's Investors Service. This sector also includes Yankee bonds, U.S. dollar-denominated securities issued or guaranteed by foreign or international entities within the U.S.

The table below shows the actual fund rates of return since 1988, the first full year of operation of the fund, after deducting administrative expenses. These are the rates used in the allocation of earnings to participants' accounts. There is no assurance that future rates of return for the fund will resemble any of these rates.

Annual F Fund Return Rates, 1988-2002

1988	3.63%
1989	13.89%
1990	8.00%
1991	15.75%
1992	7.20%
1993	9.52%
1994	-2.96%
1995	18.31%
1996	3.66%
1997	9.60%
1998	8.70%
1999	-0.85%
2000	11.67
2001	8.61%
2002	10.27%

Annual compounded rate of return, 1993-2002: 7.49%

Small Capitalization Stock Index Investment (S) Fund

The S Fund is invested in the Barclays Extended Market Index Fund, which tracks the Wilshire 4500. The Wilshire 4500 represents about a quarter of the market value of the U.S. stock market, consisting of medium and small companies whose stocks are not in the S&P 500, which the C Fund tracks. The Wilshire 4500 actually reflects more than 6,000 securities.

After excluding illiquid stocks (those not traded frequently) and stocks selling at less than $1.00 per share, Barclays buys stocks of all the companies in the index with market values greater than $1 billion, in the same proportion as the publicly available market value of that stock relative to the publicly available market value of the rest of the index. For stocks with market values below $1 billion, Barclays uses a sampling technique.

The largest market sectors within the Wilshire 4500 are financials, industrials, information technology, consumer discretionary and health care. Energy, telecommunications services and utilities make up most of the rest.

Since the S Fund was launched only in May 2001, it does not have a track record like those of the three original TSP funds, the C, G and F Funds. Below are the returns since 1993 in the Barclays Extended Market Index Fund, in which the S Fund is invested. That fund generally tracks the underlying Wilshire 4500 within about a percentage point variation per year; one notable exception occurred in 2000, when the Wilshire 4500 was down 15.67 percent while the Barclays fund was down 8.76 percent.

Annual S Fund Return Rates, 1993-2002

1993	13.54%
1994	-3.22%
1995	33.66%
1996	18.52%
1997	26.61%
1998	7.51%
1999	32.70%
2000	–8.76%
2001	9.04%
2002	-18.14%

Annual compounded rate of return, 1993-2002: 9.86%

International Stock Index Investment (I) Fund

The I Fund is invested in the Barclays EAFE Index Fund, which consists of the stocks of companies in 20 countries representing nearly half the value of the world stock markets (the U.S. stock market represents nearly all of the rest). The primary source of earnings is the net changes in the prices of stocks, although at times foreign currency exchange rates relative to the U.S. dollar can be a more significant component of the results than stock price gains or losses. Dividend income is another source of earnings.

The Barclays EAFE Index Fund holds common stocks of all the companies represented in the Morgan Stanley Capital International EAFE (Europe, Australasia and Far East) stock index, and uses a passive investment strategy of replicating the performance of the index. For each country in the index, MSCI selects the common stocks of companies that together represent 60 percent of the value of that company's stock market, comprising about two dozen industry groups within 10 economic sectors.

Each country's weighting in the EAFE index is based on the total market value of its stock market relative to the market value of the stock markets of the other countries in the index. In turn, the weightings of the stocks in the EAFE index are based on each stock's total market value relative to the market value of the other stocks of that country which are included in the index. Like the S&P 500, the EAFE index is considered a big company

index, containing large international companies.

Since the I Fund was launched only in May 2001, it does not have a track record like those of the three original TSP funds, the C, G and F Funds. Below are the returns since 1992 in the Barclays EAFE Index Fund, in which the I Fund is invested. That fund generally tracks the underlying EAFE within about a percentage point variation per year.

Annual I Fund Return Rates, 1992-2002

1992	-9.92%
1993	31.59%
1994	7.67%
1995	10.90%
1996	6.27%
1997	1.46%
1998	20.46%
1999	26.81%
2000	–14.11%
2001	-21.94%
2002	-15.98%

Annual compounded rate of return, 1993-2002: 3.84%

Investment Performance Information

The Thrift Investment Board provides several sources of information about the investment performance of the TSP funds. Each open season, the Board produces an Open Season Update. This brochure is distributed by employing agencies to every federal employee. It includes multi-year investment performance information.

The semi-annual TSP Highlights provides the most recent ten-year performance summary as well as monthly detail on the TSP funds and the related securities and indexes.

The TSP issues participant statements quarterly, for the periods ending each March 31, June 30, September 30 and December 31.

Every month, the Board publishes a Monthly Returns fact sheet, which is available from agency personnel and payroll offices and through the TSP's website at *www.tsp.gov*.

In addition, Federal Employees News Digest Inc. has published a comprehensive guide to understanding investment options, strategies and withdrawal rules called *Your Guide to the New Thrift Savings Plan*. See publication-ordering information in this Almanac.

Section 3—TSP Loans and In-Service Withdrawals

General Eligibility Criteria

To be eligible to borrow money from their TSP accounts, participants must be currently employed in a pay status and meet the following criteria:

• Their TSP account must have at least $1,000 in employee contributions and associated earnings.

• Their outstanding loan balance must be within the limits specified in federal tax law.

• The amount left in their paycheck after the loan repayment and other deductions must equal at least ten percent of their basic pay.

• They must document expenses for the allowed purposes (described below) or demonstrate financial hardship.

FERS employees must get spousal consent, while the spouses of CSRS-covered employees must be notified of the loan application by the Thrift Board.

Loan Rules and Requirements

General purpose loans are available for a repayment period of one to four years. Documentation supporting the amount of the loan request is not required. When the TSP switches to a new computer system—possibly to occur in 2003—the maximum repayment period will be five years.

Loans for the purchase of a primary residence are still available for a repayment period of one to 15 years. Documentation is required for residential loans. Do not specify a loan type unless you are applying for a residential loan.

You can request a loan by filing Form TSP-20, Loan Application. Under the new computer system, investors also will be able to initiate and in some cases complete a loan application on the ThriftLine, (504) 255-8777, or through the TSP website, ***www.tsp.gov***.

Maximum Loan Amount—The maximum amount a TSP participant can borrow is limited by the Federal Employees' Retirement System Act of 1986 and the Internal Revenue Code.

Federal employees can never borrow more than the amount of their own contributions and their earnings.

If there is not a TSP loan outstanding during the past year and contributions and earnings are $10,000 or less, then the account holder can borrow up to the full amount of his or her contributions.

If there is not a TSP loan outstanding during the past 12 months, or if contributions in the account and their earnings are greater than $10,000, several calculations must be done to determine the top loan amount. Worksheets are available from the TSP.

No more than $50,000 may be borrowed.

Payment includes interest; the rate is the G Fund rate at the time the loan application is received. Payment typically is made through payroll deductions, but prepayment in full is permitted. Under the new computer system prepayment in part also will be permitted.

At separation from service, a borrower must repay loan in full, or the unpaid balance and any unpaid interest will be declared a taxable distribution (may be subject to ten percent early withdrawal penalty).

In-Service Withdrawals

You can withdraw funds from your TSP account for two reasons while still employed by the federal government: (1) financial hardship (documentation is required), and (2) a one-time single payment (of all or part of your account) for employees over age 59½. The in-service withdrawal for employees under age 59½ will be subject to early withdrawal penalties.

In-service withdrawals also are subject to state income taxes. Excise taxes also may apply in certain situations.

Age-based withdrawals are subject to mandatory 20 percent federal income tax withholding unless the payment is transferred into an individual retirement account or other qualified retirement savings plan. Financial hardship in-service withdrawals are not subject to mandatory 20 percent federal income tax withholding but those funds are not transferable to an IRA or similar tax-favored retirement savings plan.

Note: When the TSP switches to a new computer system—possibly to occur in 2003—a partial post-separation withdrawal option will be allowed; however it will not be available to those who took an age-based in-service withdrawal.

While withdrawals offer an additional means to access a TSP account while still employed (in addition to the availability of loans), withdrawals and loans serve different purposes and have unique rules. One primary difference is that while money drawn out as a loan must be repaid into the TSP account, money taken out as an in-service withdrawal may not be repaid. Thus, an in-service withdrawal permanently depletes the account while a loan does not.

The minimum amount under either type of in-service withdrawal is $1,000. Spouses have certain rights in withdrawals, even if the couple is separated at the time. For FERS employees, the law requires spousal consent. Spouses of CSRS employees will be notified by the TSP before an in-service withdrawal is made. Further, if there is a court order against your account, such as one to enforce alimony or child support payments, the TSP will place a hold on the account and an in-service withdrawal can't be made until the court order process has been satisfied.

The two types of withdrawals differ in several ways.

Age-Based Withdrawals

Age-based withdrawals are available at age 59½. The investor need not document any need or reason for making the withdrawal and may withdraw all or a portion of the vested account balances.

Only one age-based withdrawal is allowed and, as noted above, those who take one will be ineligible for partial withdrawals after separation. They do remain eligible for a later TSP loan or financial hardship withdrawal, however, and there is no restriction on continued investment in the TSP after-

ward as long as they remain in service. An age-based withdrawal may be transferred to an IRA or similar retirement savings plan.

The form to use is Form TSP-75/75-T, Age-Based In-Service Withdrawal Request.

Financial-Hardship Withdrawals

Financial hardship withdrawals have no age limit but require the participant to demonstrate a hardship. Investors can withdraw their own contributions and the earnings on those contributions (but not agency automatic or matching contributions or their associated earnings) up to the amount of the documented hardship. The application form requires information on monthly income and expenses plus documentation for any extraordinary expenses.

There is no limit on the number of financial hardship withdrawals an individual can make, although they can be no closer together than six months. TSP participants may not make contributions to the TSP for six months afterward, starting about 45 days after the TSP has made the disbursement, depending on your payroll cycle. For FERS employees, this means losing agency matching contributions, although agency automatic contributions (1 percent of salary) will continue.

As noted above, financial hardship withdrawals are not subject to mandatory 20 percent federal income tax withholding and are not eligible for transfer to an IRA or similar plan. A financial hardship withdrawal taken under age 59½ is subject to a 10 percent early withdrawal penalty tax on the total amount received directly from the TSP, including any amount withheld for taxes.

The form to use is Form TSP-76/75-T, Financial Hardship In-Service Withdrawal.

Section 4—Post-Service Withdrawals from TSP Accounts

General Withdrawal Rights and Procedures

All TSP participants who separate from federal service have the same TSP withdrawal options, regardless of their eligibility for retirement benefits.

When you separate from federal service, you become eligible to withdraw your TSP account. You can choose to receive a TSP life annuity, a single payment, or a series of

monthly payments. You can ask to have your payments begin as soon as possible or you can specify a future date. You can ask to have the TSP transfer all or a part of a single payment or, in some cases, a series of monthly payments, to an IRA or other eligible retirement plan. You also may leave your account in the TSP when you separate, and make a withdrawal decision later on.

For special rules applying to those rehired after retirement, see the Reemployment of Annuitants section in Chapter 4. For special rules applying to those rehired after separation before eligibility for retirement see the Separation Before Retirement Eligibility section in Chapter 8.

Withdrawal Options

There are three basic ways to withdraw your TSP account: (1) have the TSP purchase a life annuity for you, (2) receive your account in a single payment, and (3) receive your account in a series of monthly payments.

You can have the TSP transfer all or part of a single payment (and in some cases a series of monthly payments; see Transferring Your TSP Account, below) to an IRA or other eligible retirement plan.

When the TSP switches to a new computer system—possibly to occur in 2003—participants will be able to combine the options. Payment(s) will begin as soon as the full withdrawal is made. In addition, participants will be able to make partial withdrawals designated for one of these options while leaving the remainder in their accounts. The exception will be those who made in-service age-based withdrawals; they could not make a partial withdrawal after separation.

Single Payment—You can withdraw your account balance in a single payment, with part or all of it transferred to an individual retirement account or other eligible plan.

A Series of Monthly Payments—You can withdraw your account in a series of substantially equal monthly payments. You can choose:

• A specific dollar amount per month or a selected number of months. In both of these options, you will receive payments in the amount that you request until your entire account balance has been paid to you. The amount of the monthly payments that you request must be $25 or more.

• Monthly payments computed by the TSP based on an IRS life expectancy table. Your initial payment amount is based on your account balance at the time of the first payment and your age. The TSP will recalculate the amount of your monthly payments every year based on your account balance at the end of the preceding year and your age.

When the TSP switches to a new computer system—possibly to occur in 2003—the option for payments based on a selected number of months will be eliminated, investors will be able to change the amount of a designated dollar amount withdrawal often as annually and they will have a one-time lifetime opportunity to change a life expectancy-based withdrawal to a payout based on a dollar amount.

You can transfer your account balance among the TSP investment funds while you are receiving monthly payments. If you have investments outside the G Fund, remember that investment losses could cause your account balance to decrease, which could reduce either the amount of your monthly payments or their duration, depending on which option you chose.

You also can change to a final single payment, change the proportion that is transferred to an IRA or other eligible retirement plan, or change the IRA or plan to which your payments are sent.

If you are receiving a series of monthly payments from your account when you become 70½, you will be subject to IRS minimum distribution requirements.

Life Annuity—A TSP annuity is a monthly benefit paid to you for life. If your account balance is at least $3,500, you can have the TSP use your account balance to purchase an annuity for you from the TSP's annuity provider. If your account balance is less than $3,500, you can request an annuity with a specific future date; however, your account must be at least $3,500 before the annuity can be purchased.

When a TSP investor decides to purchase an annuity, the money used to buy it is taken out of the TSP and turned over to the annuity provider, currently the Metropolitan Life Insurance Company. The annuity provider, not the TSP, is responsible for paying the annuity and providing any needed services regarding the annuity. These services include information about income tax withholding, reporting of payments to the IRS and instructions about how to keep account records up to date. After an annuity is purchased, the recipient cannot change the election or terminate the annuity.

The TSP offers three basic types of annuities:

• **single life**—an annuity paid only during

the recipient's lifetime
- **joint life with spouse**—an annuity paid to the recipient while both the recipient and spouse are alive. When either dies, an annuity will be paid to the survivor for his or her life.
- **joint life with someone other than spouse**—an annuity paid to the recipient while the recipient and a person chosen by the recipient, other than the spouse, are alive. This person must have an "insurable interest" in the recipient. When either dies, an annuity will be paid to the survivor for his or her life.

Joint life annuities may provide either a 100 percent or 50 percent survivor benefit. This means that monthly payments will continue in the same amount (100 percent) or be reduced by half (50 percent) to you or to your joint annuitant when either one of you dies.

Several annuity features can be combined with the basic annuity types. These are:
- **increasing payments**—the amount of the monthly payment may increase up to 3 percent each year, depending on the change in the consumer price index.
- **cash refund**—if the recipient (and the joint annuitant, if applicable) dies before receiving payments equal to the amount of the account balance used to purchase the annuity, the designated beneficiary will receive a cash refund of the difference between the sum of the payments made and the amount used to purchase the annuity.
- **10-year certain**—if the recipient dies within 10 years of the start of the annuity, the beneficiary receives the payments for the remaining portion of the 10-year period.

Spousal Rights to Annuities

FERS Participants—The spouse of a married FERS participant has the right to a joint and survivor annuity, even if the spouses are separated. If the participant elects any withdrawal option (including annuity options) other than the joint life annuity with spouse with a 50 percent survivor benefit, level payments and no cash refund, the spouse must waive this annuity option.

If the participant is not able to locate the spouse, or if exceptional circumstances make it inappropriate for the spouse to sign a waiver, the TSP may grant an exception to the required waiver. The participant must complete TSP Form 16, Exception to Spousal Requirements and provide supporting documentation as described on that form.

CSRS Participants—The TSP must send a notice to the spouse of a married CSRS participant before an annuity is purchased, even if the spouses are separated, stating which annuity option the participant has chosen. If the participant is not able to locate the spouse, the TSP may grant an exception to the required waiver. The participant must complete TSP Form 16, Exception to Spousal Requirements and provide supporting documentation as described on that form.

Court Orders—Under either FERS or CSRS, if the TSP has received a valid court order that awards a portion of the TSP account to a former spouse or separated spouse or a valid court order that requires payment for enforcement of child support or alimony obligations, the TSP will comply with that order before the annuity is purchased. The TSP will notify the participant of any court orders received that affect the account.

Approximate Monthly Annuity Payments
Per $1,000 of Plan Balance

| | Single Life Annuities | | Joint Life Annuities | |
| | Life | 10 Years Certain | 100% Spouse | 50% Spouse |
Age	Only	& Life	Same Age	Same age
50	$6.90	$6.84	$6.40	$6.90
55	$7.27	$7.16	$6.62	$7.27
60	$7.77	$7.59	$6.93	$7.77
65	$8.51	$8.17	$7.38	$8.51
70	$9.57	$8.90	$8.05	$9.57
75	$11.11	$9.75	$9.04	$11.11

Monthly Annuity Amounts

The factors that affect the amount of the monthly payments are:

• the annuity options chosen;
• the age of the participant when the annuity is purchased;
• the age of the spouse or other joint annuitant, if an annuity with survivorship rights is elected;
• the balance of the TSP account used to purchase the annuity; and
• market interest rate levels when the annuity is purchased.

In general, the single life-only annuity option will pay the largest monthly benefit; a joint and 100 percent survivor annuity with annual increases and a cash refund will pay the smallest monthly benefit.

An annuity will be purchased from a private insurance carrier 30 days before payment is to start. The Thrift Board has estimated the annuity rates in the table entitled "Approximate Monthly Annuity Payments Per $1000 of Plan Balance," which uses an assumed interest rate of six percent. The Board also has an annuity calculator available on its website, www.tsp.gov. The calculator can estimate single and joint life annuities spanning annuitant ages 50 to 75 and joint annuitant ages of up to ten years older and younger than the annuitant. It also takes into account variations in market interest rates.

Withdrawal Requests

What Your Agency Must Do—When you leave the government, your agency is required to give you a TSP Withdrawal Package that contains a tax notice and the forms you will need.

Your agency must also notify the TSP that you have left the government by submitting to the TSP a Separation Code and the date of your separation. The TSP cannot start your withdrawal process until your agency reports this information.

What the TSP Service Office Will Do—When information about your separation is received, the TSP office will send you current account and withdrawal information and the tax notice (unless the TSP has already received a withdrawal election from you). If you do not receive this information within 60 days after leaving the government, contact your former agency to make sure it has submitted a Separation Code and the date of

your separation to the TSP.

If you have an outstanding TSP loan at the time your agency reports your separation, the TSP Service Office will notify you. An outstanding loan will delay your withdrawal, because you cannot withdraw your account until you have repaid your loan in full or a taxable distribution to you has been declared.

What You Should Do—Read the TSP's Withdrawal Booklet and the tax notice provided by your agency. When you are ready to make an election—but not before you separate from service—complete Form TSP-70, Withdrawal Request.

Send Form TSP-70 (and Form TSP-70-T, if appropriate) to the TSP Service Office. Make sure your forms are complete and correct before you mail them. The TSP Service Office won't accept changes over the telephone.

Transferring Your TSP Account

Your TSP account is a portable retirement benefit. This means that, when you leave federal service, you can have the TSP transfer your account to an IRA or other eligible retirement plan (for example, a 401(k) plan of a new employer). Check with your new employer to see if its plan can accept your transfer. You will continue to defer taxes on the amounts transferred. In this way, your savings will continue to accrue tax-deferred earnings until you withdraw your money.

If you choose to receive your account in a single payment, you can have the TSP transfer all or part of your account balance to an IRA or other eligible retirement plan. The amount not transferred will be paid directly to you.

If you choose to have the TSP pay out your account in a series of monthly payments, in some cases you can have the TSP transfer all or part of each monthly payment to an IRA or other plan. The TSP can transfer monthly payments that are expected to last less than ten years and are not based on the IRS life expectancy table.

Thus, if you choose a dollar amount, the TSP will use a factor to determine whether your payments are expected to last less than ten years, taking into account the effect of future earnings (at an assumed annual rate of eight percent). The factor is equal to your account balance divided by the dollar amount you requested. If the factor is 85 or more, your payments cannot be transferred, and the TSP Service Office will so notify you. You can use your current account balance to estimate whether your payments will be eligible for transfer, but remember that your account balance will be different when the TSP applies the factor at the time of the first payment.

To request a transfer, complete Form TSP-70, Withdrawal Request, indicating that you want a transfer. Also, you and the financial institution or administrator of the plan that is to receive your money must both complete Form TSP-70-T, Transfer Information. You cannot use the forms of the financial institution or plan because the TSP won't accept them. If you indicate on Form TSP-70 that you want the TSP to transfer your payment(s), but you do not submit a properly completed Form TSP-70-T, you will be notified and your election will be canceled. You will then have to submit another Form TSP-70.

You can submit Form TSP-70-T even if you did not indicate that you wanted a transfer when you submitted Form TSP-70. However, your Form TSP-70-T must be received in time to be processed before the scheduled payment date, or your withdrawal will be paid directly to you.

Some financial institutions and plans have minimum transfer amounts. You should verify that the financial institution or plan will accept the transfer of your payment(s) before you request a transfer.

You can also receive directly any payments that are eligible to be transferred and roll them over to an IRA or other eligible retirement plan within 60 days. However, there may be tax consequences.

Taxation of Withdrawals

Amounts paid from a TSP account are taxable income for federal and other tax purposes in the year or years in which payment is made. Depending on the withdrawal method chosen, different withholding rules apply. For example, there is a mandatory 20 percent federal income tax withholding on certain payments unless the account holder asks the TSP to transfer the payments to an individual retirement account or other eligible retirement plan.

For withholding purposes, payments are classified as three types:
• eligible rollover distributions,

• periodic payments; and
• non-periodic payments.

Federal income tax withholding rules are different for each (the TSP does not withhold amounts for state or local income taxes).

Eligible Rollover Distributions—The following types of payments are considered eligible rollover distributions:
• single payment of the entire account;
• in-service age-based withdrawal payments;
• automatic cashout payment;
• monthly payments when the account is expected to be paid out in less than 10 years (except those computed by the TSP according to the IRS life expectancy table);
• a final single payment made after a series of monthly payments;
• amounts paid directly to you after the complete withdrawal of your account (e.g., the payment of a late contribution to your account);
• death benefits paid to the spouse of a deceased participant; and
• court-ordered payments made to a spouse or former spouse.

Any amount paid directly to the recipient is subject to 20 percent federal income tax withholding, which cannot be waived. The recipient may elect to have an amount in addition to the 20 percent withheld through IRS form W-4P, Withholding Certificate for Pension or Annuity Payments, and submitting it to the TSP Service Office, National Finance Center, Thrift Savings Plan Service Office, P.O. Box 61500, New Orleans, LA 70161-1500.

The recipient can avoid withholding on all or any portion by having the TSP transfer that amount to an IRA or other eligible retirement plan. However, the recipient cannot avoid withholding on any amount that was received directly, even if it is then rolled over to an IRA or other eligible plan.

For information on rollovers, see Transferring Your TSP Account.

Periodic Payments—The following types of payments are considered periodic payments:
• monthly payments when the account is expected to be paid out in 10 years or more; and
• monthly payments computed according to the IRS life expectancy table.

Withholding for periodic payments is based on the assumption that the recipient is married and claiming three withholding allowances. The recipient may elect to have a different amount, or none, withheld through IRS form W-4P, Withholding Certificate for Pension or Annuity Payments, and submitting it to the TSP Service Office, National Finance Center, Thrift Savings Plan Service Office, P.O. Box 61500, New Orleans, LA 70161-1500.

Notes on Annuities: Special considerations apply to annuities, which also are considered periodic payments (they are treated as ordinary income because the money in a TSP account was contributed on a tax-deferred basis, and all earnings on the account were tax deferred). The recipient will receive information about making a withholding election from the annuity provider at the time the annuity is purchased. Annuity payments are not subject to the IRS early withdrawal penalty, even if the recipient is under age 55 when payments begin.

Notes on Monthly Payments: Monthly payments can be treated as either eligible rollover distributions or periodic payments. In sum, monthly payments expected to be made for less than 10 years are treated as eligible rollover distributions while those expected to be made for 10 years or more or calculated based on the life expectancy are treated as periodic payments. Payments based on life expectancy will be treated as periodic no matter how long they last. For payments based on a number of months, withholding is based on the number of months chosen. Treatment of payments based on a dollar amount is determined by a formula that determines, based on an assumed annual 8 percent earnings rate, whether the payments are expected to last more or less than 10 years. A payment resulting from changing from monthly payments to a single final payment is treated as an eligible rollover distribution.

Non-Periodic Payments—The following types of payments are considered non-periodic payments:

• required minimum distributions paid either separately or together with an eligible rollover distribution, a transfer or a TSP annuity purchase;

• minimum distribution payments made to a recipient who is also receiving a series of monthly payments;

• death benefits paid to someone other than the spouse of the participant; and

• court-ordered payments made to someone other than the spouse or former spouse, including court-ordered child support payments.

The TSP will withhold 10 percent for federal income tax from these payments. The recipient may elect to have an additional amount, or none, withheld through IRS form W-4P, Withholding Certificate for Pension or Annuity Payments, and submitting it to the TSP Service Office, National Finance Center, Thrift Savings Plan Service Office, P.O. Box 61500, New Orleans, LA 70161-1500.

Early Withdrawal Penalty—In addition

TSP Forms and Materials for Separated Participants

To withdraw your account:
• Form TSP-70, Withdrawal Request (including Form TSP-70-T, Transfer Information)
• Form TSP-16, Exception to Spousal Requirements
• Withdrawing Your TSP Account
• Thrift Savings Plan Annuities

To keep your account information up to date:
• Form TSP-3, Designation of Beneficiary
• Form TSP-9, Change of Address for Separated Participants

For beneficiaries to receive your account:
• Form TSP-17, Application for Account Balance of Deceased Participant
• Important Tax Information About Thrift Savings Plan Death Benefit Payments

Other information:
• Using the Thriftline and TSP Web Site
• Important Information Regarding Transfers of the TSP to Eligible Retirement Plans
• Information About Court Orders

to ordinary income tax, in certain situations an early withdrawal tax of 10 percent applies on amounts received directly from the TSP, unless such payments are transferred or rolled over.

For those who separate or retire before the year in which they reach age 55, the penalty tax will apply on all amounts received before becoming age 59½. There are two exceptions. The penalty tax is not imposed on annuity payments, payments made because of death or payments to disability retirees. Also, payments based on life expectancy are not subject to the penalty tax even for those separating or retiring before the year in which they reach age 55 (however, those who change from such payments to a final single payment before age 59½ or within five years of the date of the first payment, whichever is later, must pay the penalty tax on all payments received before age 59½.

For Further Information—See the TSP publication, "Important Tax Information about Payments from your TSP Account," available in personnel offices, through the TSP's website, *www.tsp.gov*, or the National Finance Center, Thrift Savings Plan Service Office, P.O. Box 61500 New Orleans, LA 70161-1500.

Reporting Changes in Personal Information

Until your TSP account is completely withdrawn, you must keep the TSP informed of any changes in your mailing address and other personal information maintained by the TSP. Otherwise, you may not receive your participant statements and other important mailings. You should also inform the TSP of any address change through January following the year your account is closed so that you will receive tax reporting information.

Before you separate from service, your agency personnel office is responsible for updating your TSP account records. After separation, you must report changes to the TSP Service Office as follows:

To change your address, submit Form TSP-9, Change of Address for Separated Participants. You can also change your address for your TSP account by writing to the TSP Service Office. Your dated and signed letter must contain your Social Security number and your date of birth, which will be used to identify your account. If you submit withdrawal forms, your new address on the forms will automatically update your TSP account records.

To change your name, submit Form TSP-15, Change in Name.

Section 5—Leaving Your Money in the TSP

General Rules and Procedures

After you leave federal service, you can leave your entire account balance in the TSP until April 1 of the calendar year after you reach age 70½, subject to the restrictions described below. You do not need to submit any forms until you are ready to make a withdrawal election, unless your account balance is $3,500 or less or you are approaching the required date of election explained below.

When you are ready to choose an option and date for your withdrawal, you can contact the TSP office for current tax information and withdrawal forms, if you need them. Submit Form TSP-70, Withdrawal Request.

If you make an election for a partial withdrawal with a specific future payment date, the TSP will notify you four months before that date to confirm your election and will provide you with current withdrawal and tax information. Your account will continue to accrue earnings and you can continue to change the way your money is allocated among the TSP investment funds by making interfund transfers.

Restrictions on Leaving Your Money in the TSP

TSP participants who want to leave their investments and earnings in a TSP account should keep the following rules in mind:

Contributions and Loans—You cannot make any additional contributions to your account after you leave federal service, and you can no longer borrow from your account.

Required Election and Payment Date—You must elect a withdrawal option before March 1 of the calendar year after you turn age 70½. Additionally, when you make your election, you cannot choose a future date for your withdrawal that is later than April of the year following the year in which you turn 70 ½. If you depart from government service after this date, any election you make must be for an immediate payment.

Required Minimum Distributions— The IRS requires that you begin to receive payments from your account by April 1 of the year following the year that you become 70½. Your minimum distribution will be calculated based on your account balance and your age, using IRS Table V: "Ordinary Life Annuities One Life-Expected Return Multiples," which can be found at 26 CFR subsection 1.72-9. The TSP will notify you before this situation applies to you and send you the notice "Information About Your Thrift Savings Plan Required Minimum Distribution" at that time. You also may ask your personnel office or the TSP office for a copy of this information.

Minimum distribution amounts cannot be transferred to an IRA or other eligible retirement plan. If you are receiving monthly payments from your account, your payments may be adjusted at the beginning of the year to ensure that the required minimum amount is distributed. If you are having all or part of your monthly payments transferred, the TSP will make direct payments to you at the beginning of each year and suspend the transfer of payments until sufficient direct payments have been made to you to fulfill the minimum distribution requirements.

Section 6—Death Benefits

Beneficiary Designations

You may designate beneficiaries to receive your TSP account in the event of your death. If you do not designate beneficiaries for your account, it will be distributed according to the standard order of precedence. (However, if you die after the TSP office receives a completed annuity request for you, benefits will be provided in accordance with your annuity selection.)

To name a beneficiary or beneficiaries for your account, mail Form TSP-3, Designation of Beneficiary, to the TSP Service Office; your form must be received by the TSP Service Office before your death. (A will is not valid for the disposition of your TSP account; if no designation of beneficiary form has been submitted, a standard order of precedence will apply as described below.)

Distributions and Order of Precedence

The share of any designated beneficiary who dies before you die will be distributed proportionally among the surviving designated TSP beneficiaries. Your Designation of Beneficiary will be void if none of the designated beneficiaries is alive at the time of your death. In that case, the standard order of precedence will be followed. The beneficiary procedure specified by the order of precedence is as follows: your widow or widower; if none, to your child or children equally, and descendants of deceased children by representation; if none, to your parents equally or the surviving parent; if none, to the appointed executor or administrator of your estate; if none, to your next of kin who is entitled to your estate under the laws of the state in which you resided at the time of your death.

If there are any changes in your family status (marriage, divorce, birth, death, etc.), you may want to make changes in your beneficiary designation. To change or cancel a previous designation, mail a new Form TSP-3 to the TSP Service Office.

For your beneficiaries to receive your account, Form TSP-17, Application for Account Balance of Deceased Participant, must be submitted to the TSP Service Office together with a certified copy of your death certificate.

Chapter 7
Divorce, Legal Separation, and Annulment

Section 1—Benefits Impact of Divorce

Basic Effects of Divorce or Separation

Broadly speaking, a court order related to a federal or postal employee's divorce, annulment, or legal separation can:

• Divide a Civil Service Retirement System (CSRS) or Federal Employees Retirement System (FERS) annuity;

• Block or divide a refund of CSRS or FERS employee retirement contributions;

• Provide a survivor annuity payable upon the death of an employee or retiree;

• Permit a former spouse to continue health insurance coverage under the Federal Employees Health Benefits program;

• Require employees or retirees to assign their Federal Employees' Group Life Insurance coverage to a former spouse or children; or

• Require payment to the former spouse from a Thrift Savings Plan account.

In addition, a court order may require that a federal employee's pay or retirement benefits be garnished for alimony or child support.

Special rules and procedures apply to divorce and similar proceedings involving federal and postal benefits. At the outset, it is essential to recognize that CSRS and FERS are exempt from the Employee Retirement Income Security Act (ERISA), which generally governs marriage-related court orders affecting private-sector workers. Thus, court orders that are commonly used to divide private-sector benefits, called "Qualified Domestic Relations Orders" (or QDROs), may not be valid in proceedings involving federal or postal employees or retirees. If a court issues its order in the form of QDRO, the order may be acceptable for OPM processing if the court specifically states that it has considered the terminology and requirements of the federal employee benefit laws and regulations and that the terms and provisions of the order "are governed by the standard conventions" of those federal employment laws and rules.

Similarly, benefit allocations commonly used under ERISA may not be allowable or acceptable for OPM processing purposes. For example, under ERISA, a former spouse's share of a retirement benefit can begin when the employee reaches the minimum retirement age, even if the employee is still working. However, this arrangement is not available under the CSRS or FERS systems, both of which refuse to allow court orders to affect a retirement benefit until the benefit is actually payable to the former employee. Similarly, the TSP governing board has special rules for distributions from TSP accounts under which standard court orders may not achieve the desired effect.

Likewise, it is very important that any court orders or agreements intended to award a survivor annuity reflect the intent of the parties and conform to law and regulations. While court orders can be changed before the employee retires or dies, in general they cannot be modified to affect survivor benefits once the employee dies or has retired.

During the early stages of any legal proceedings, individuals involved in a divorce or marital separation also need to know how to obtain relevant information. For example, to get necessary information about an active employee's work history, pay, or other required information, the employing agency, not OPM, normally is the proper source of information about the worker's service with that agency. However, if the worker's federal employment history includes previous service with a different agency, information about the individual's retirement fund contributions for the earlier service is held at OPM.

For retirees and separated employees, OPM is the appropriate source for information similar to that available from individual agencies about active employees. OPM also has annuity rate information about retirees. OPM will release such information only in response to a subpoena signed by a judge or a release signed by the retiree or former employee. The subpoena or release should be sent to: Associate Director, Retirement and Insurance Service, Office of Personnel Management, P.O. Box 16, Washington, DC 20044-0016.

Requested information that an employing agency can provide in response to a subpoena signed by a judge, or a release signed by the employee, includes a statement of retirement system coverage, amount of money withheld by the agency to the employee's credit in the retirement fund, and an annuity estimate using service to date. The requirements for obtaining information vary among agencies.

Agencies can prepare estimates of benefits that the employee has already earned. However, such estimates are not considered binding on the government. Also, an employing agency will not provide estimates that would require speculation about events such as promotions. Nor will it determine the "present value" of employee entitlements since they involve various economic and mortality assumptions.

Likewise, the government will not become involved in determining the proper division of benefits between spouses. To guide attorneys in preparing court orders, the Office of Personnel Management has published a Handbook for Attorneys on Court Ordered Retirement, Health Benefits, and Life Insurance, which may be purchased from the Superintendent of Documents by calling (202) 512-1800.

Effect on Designations of Beneficiary

A divorce does not affect a designation of beneficiary that was filed at some earlier time. An employee or retiree who has designated a now former spouse to receive life insurance or retirement lump sum benefits must file new designations for any benefits that become payable to go to someone else. Designations of beneficiary may be changed at any time.

The life insurance designation of beneficiary for both retirement systems is SF 2823. To designate a beneficiary for any lump-sum benefit that may remain after a retiree's death, the CSRS form is SF 2808, the FERS form is SF 3102. Retirees may obtain these forms from the Office of Personnel Management by calling (202) 606-0550 or online at *www.opm.gov/forms*.

Section 2—Impact on Retirement Benefits

General Considerations

In the event of a divorce, separation, or annulment, the most common ways that the courts divide a federal worker's retirement benefits are awards to the former spouse of payments from a retiree's monthly annuity, a portion of an employee's refund of retirement contribution, and rights to a survivor annuity. Awards of "insurable interest" annuities are also sometimes are made.

OPM has detailed requirements for those types of court orders it considers acceptable for processing. OPM will not honor court awards that don't comply with those rules or with underlying federal law (which generally takes precedence over state law). For example, state courts lack the authority to prevent OPM from paying a retired employee an annuity that is required by law—or to delay the payment of such annuities. On the other hand, OPM will honor court orders that direct it to pay the annuity to the court, an officer of the court acting as a fiduciary, or a state or local government agency pending the outcome of a divorce or legal separation proceeding.

The address for delivery of court orders affecting retirement benefits is Office of Personnel Management, Retirement and Insurance Service, P.O. Box 17, Washington, DC 20044-0017.

OPM must comply with the terms of a properly filed court order for processing, even if the retiree and the former spouse agree that they want OPM to pay an amount different from the amount specified in the court order. Thus, OPM will not honor a request from a former spouse, a retiree, or both jointly that an amount either greater or less than the amount provided in the court order be withheld from an employee annuity or a refund of employee contributions to the retirement fund. Any change requires that an amended court order be filed with OPM.

Payment of Portion of Retiree's Annuity

A court order can apportion or divide a CSRS or FERS retirement benefit as a result of a divorce, legal separation, or annulment of marriage. The court order must expressly direct OPM to pay a portion of the retiree's monthly CSRS or FERS benefits to the former spouse. The spouse's share must be stated as a fixed amount, a percentage or fraction of the annuity, or in terms of some other formula whose value is readily apparent from the face of the order and information in the government's files. The spousal share cannot exceed the amount payable to the retiree after deductions for taxes and insurance.

A former spouse's right to payments from a retiree's annuity ends with the retiree's death. For the former spouse to continue receiving payments after the retiree's death, the retiree must elect, or the court order must provide for, a survivor annuity.

The federal government generally makes payments from an annuity only when all conditions necessary for payment of the annuity are met, including a worker's separation from a covered position with immediate eligibility for an annuity and the employee's submission of an annuity application. Money that is held by an employing agency or OPM and that may be payable at some future date is not available for payment under court orders directed at annuities.

A former spouse, personally or through a representative, must apply to OPM in writing to be eligible to begin receiving a court-awarded portion of an employee annuity. No special form is required, but the application must include a certified copy of the court order, the individual's certification that the order is currently in force, information sufficient for OPM to identify the employee or retiree, and current mailing addresses of the former spouse and the annuitant. When the court order requires termination of the payments if the former spouse remarries, OPM also needs a statement certifying that a remarriage has not occurred, that the former spouse will notify OPM within 15 days of any remarriage, and that the former spouse will be personally liable for any overpayment resulting from a remarriage.

To be acceptable to OPM, a court-ordered award of spousal benefits must expressly divide the employee annuity, provide for payment of the apportioned share to the former spouse, and provide OPM with sufficient information to compute the amount of the former spouse's monthly benefit. The amount must be expressed as a fixed amount, a percentage or fraction of the annuity, or in some other readily understandable formula. OPM prefers that such orders specify that it make the payments directly to the former spouse, although a court order directing the employee or separated employee to arrange for OPM to pay the former spouse also is considered acceptable.

If the order awards a former spouse a lump-sum amount from the annuity and does not state a monthly rate at which the lump sum should be calculated, OPM will pay the former spouse equal monthly installments of 50 percent of the gross annuity until the lump-sum amount is paid in full.

The former spouse's share will be increased by the same cost-of-living adjustment formula that governs COLA increases for the retiree's annuity.

Payments to the former spouse will be discontinued if the retiree's annuity payments are suspended or ended. If the individual's annuity payments are later restored, payments to the former spouse also will resume under the terms of a court order that is in effect at that time. However, a retiree may not deprive a former spouse of payment by causing suspension of payment of the annuity.

A former spouse's portion of an annuity typically ends on:

• a date on which the court order requires termination;

• the issuance of a court order invalidating the original order or amending it to stop payment; or

• the death of the retiree or (in most cases) the former spouse.

OPM will honor a court order that directs it to continue paying a former spouse's share after such individual's death in the form of payments made to the court, an officer of the court, the former spouse's estate, or one or more of the retiree's children. However, it will not honor an order directing it to continue annuity payments to the former spouse after the death of the retiree, absent express language granting the former spouse survivor annuity rights.

Refunds of Retirement Contributions

A court order may provide for payment of all or part of a refund of an employee's retirement plan contributions to the worker's former spouse. A court order also may block payment of a refund to the employee, but only if the order also grants a survivor annuity or a portion of a retiree annuity to a legally separated or former spouse.

Refunds of employee contributions are payable only if all of the conditions necessary for payment of the contributions to the separated employee have been met. Generally, these include the individual worker's separation from a covered position, application for payment of the refund, and immediate entitlement to a refund.

A former spouse, personally or through a representative, must apply in writing to be eligible for a court-awarded portion of a refund of an employee's retirement contribution. No special form is required, but the application letter must be accompanied by a certified copy of the court order, a certification that the court order is currently in force, information sufficient to identify the employee or separated employee, and current addresses of both the separated employee and former spouse.

Generally, OPM must receive the documentation no later than the last day of the second month before payment of the refund. If the documentation is incomplete, OPM will notify the former spouse and require full documentation within 15 days.

A court order dividing a refund of employee contributions must expressly award a former spouse a portion of any refund, identify the retirement system affected, and provide OPM with sufficient information to compute the former spouse's share. The specified portion can be expressed as a fixed amount, a percentage or fraction of the refund, or in another readily understandable formula. OPM will not accept an order that requires it to examine or interpret a state statute or a

court decision on a different case to compute the former spouse's share. OPM prefers that orders specify that it make the payments directly to the former spouse, although an order directing the employee or separated employee to arrange for OPM to pay the former spouse is acceptable.

A court order barring payment of a refund will be honored only if it expressly directs OPM not to pay a refund of employee contributions it awards, or a prior court order has awarded the former spouse a survivor annuity or a portion of the employee's annuity; and payment of the refund to the employee would prevent a required payment to the former spouse under an order for a survivor annuity or a portion of the employee's annuity.

Survivor Annuity to Former Spouse

A monthly survivor annuity may be payable to a former spouse after the death of the employee or annuitant if provided by court order. An employee or retiree is required to provide such an annuity if such payments are stipulated in a divorce agreement or annulment ending a marriage after May 6, 1985. The provision of a former spouse survivor annuity results in a reduction to the retiree's monthly benefit amount.

A retiring employee may voluntarily elect to provide a survivor annuity to a former spouse. However, if the employee has remarried, this voluntary election may only be made if the worker's current spouse consents to it.

Court orders must expressly award a former spouse a survivor annuity or expressly direct an employee or retiree to elect to provide a former spouse with a survivor annuity. As with the other types of spousal benefits, the court's award must provide sufficient information so that OPM can determine the amount of the former spouse's monthly benefit, using only the express language of the court order. Orders that would require OPM to examine or interpret a state statute or a court decision on a different case to compute the former spouse's share are unacceptable.

In cases where an actively employed individual dies, a court-ordered survivor benefit is payable to a former spouse if the deceased employee has completed at least

18 months of creditable civilian service, and dies while enrolled under CSRS or FERS coverage. Under CSRS, a survivor annuity is payable to the former spouse. Under FERS, a lump sum death benefit is payable, and a survivor annuity also is payable if the employee had at least ten years of creditable service.

If a separated former employee dies before gaining eligibility for a CSRS retirement, no survivor annuity can be paid to a former spouse, regardless of the terms of any court order. In certain limited circumstances, a FERS survivor annuity may be payable to a former spouse if a separated former employee dies before retirement.

OPM will not honor court awards awarding lump-sum payments (other than the FERS basic employee death benefit) to a former spouse upon the death of an employee or retiree. Nor will it honor awards allowing the retiree or former spouse to pay for the reduction in a retiree's annuity by any means other than withholding from the annuity.

The maximum possible combined totals of all current and former spouse survivor annuities are 55 percent of the self-only annuity amount payable under CSRS or 50 percent of the amount paid under FERS. Thus, a court order awarding a survivor annuity to a former spouse invariably reduces the amount that can be paid to a current spouse of the employee or retiree at the time of death. This means that if the maximum percentage of an annuity has been awarded to a former spouse (or former spouses, if the worker had more than one), the employee's current spouse will not receive any survivor benefit (unless the former spouse loses entitlement to benefits due to death, remarriage before age 55, or under the terms of a court order). If less than the maximum percentage (i.e., 55 or 50 percent) has been awarded, a current spouse will be entitled to a survivor benefit that amounts to the difference between the maximum survivor annuity permitted and the amount allocated to a former spouse. The current spouse's entitlement would increase if the former spouse loses entitlement.

Survivor annuities to former spouses are increased according to the same cost-of-living adjustment formulas applied to the CSRS or FERS annuity.

A former spouse's survivor annuity continues for life unless entitlement is lost due to the individual's remarriage before age 55 or under terms of the court order. An annuity to a former spouse that ends due to an individual's remarriage cannot be restored, even if that marriage ends in annulment or divorce.

Insurable Interest Annuity

An insurable interest election can be made at retirement to provide a current or former spouse with additional survivor benefits if the retiree is in good health and no court order prohibits it. Choosing this option causes an additional reduction in the retiree's annuity that is based on the difference in ages between the retiree and the named beneficiary. When an insurable interest survivor annuity stops because the beneficiary dies, it has no effect on any other survivor annuity. An insurable interest annuity to a former spouse continues for life regardless of remarriage.

Garnishment of Benefits

Garnishment is a legal process under state law for enforcing existing legal obligations. Benefits under the Civil Service Retirement System or the Federal Employees Retirement System can be garnisheed only for alimony, child support, or in cases of child abuse. The garnishment must conform to all state law requirements for garnishment actions involving private employers, and is subject to the limitations in Title 5, Code of Federal Regulations, Section 581. For further information, see Section 6 below.

Restrictions

The maximum possible combined total of all current and former spouse survivor annuities equals 55 percent of the rate of a self-only annuity under the Civil Service Retirement System. The maximum possible annuity is 50 percent under the Federal Employees Retirement System. A court order awarding a survivor annuity to a former spouse reduces the maximum that can be paid to the spouse married to the annuitant at the time of death. An insurable interest election can be made at retirement to provide a current spouse with additional survivor benefits if the retiree is in good health.

It is very important that provisions intended to award a survivor annuity both reflect the intent of the parties and conform to law and regulations. While orders can be changed before the employee retires or dies, in general they cannot be modified to affect survivor benefits after the employee retires or dies.

State court orders cannot affect several types of benefits payable under CSRS and FERS. OPM must pay any accrued annuity that is not paid before a retiree's death and any unexpended balance of an employee's retirement contributions that are paid as a death benefit in accordance with the order of precedence established by federal law. Similarly, eligibility for children's survivor benefits is governed entirely by federal law and cannot be affected by State court orders.

Orders Affecting Military Retired Pay

Individuals who receive military retired pay often are barred from receiving credit for their military service for CSRS or FERS retirement purposes unless they elect to waive the military retirement benefit and have their military service added to civilian service in computing their CSRS or FERS annuity. If employees with military retired pay rights are subject to a court order awarding a former spouse a portion of their military retirement, they cannot receive military service credit for CSRS or FERS benefit purposes without consenting to continue paying former spouses the amount they would receive from the military pay center, if the military retired pay arrangement had continued.

OPM's General Process

OPM authorizes retirement benefit pay-ments to former or separated spouses according to provisions of court orders it considers acceptable for processing under applicable law and regulations. If OPM views the order as not acceptable, the parties must return to state court to seek modifications.

To claim court-ordered benefits from OPM, former spouses (or their legal representatives) are responsible for:

- filing a certified copy of the court order and all other required supporting information with OPM;
- keeping OPM advised of current mailing addresses of both the former spouse who is claiming benefits and the federal employee/retiree whose benefits are being affected;
- notifying OPM of any changes in circumstances that could affect the individual's entitlement to benefits; and
- submitting all disputes with the employee/retiree to the appropriate state court for resolution.

Once OPM determines that a court order is acceptable, the agency will do the following:

- inform the former spouse that the court order is acceptable, when spousal benefits will begin to accrue (if known), how much the monthly benefit will be and how it was computed, and that if the individual disagrees, a clarifying court order must be obtained; and
- inform the employee, retiree, or other interested party that the former spouse has applied for benefits, that the court order is acceptable for processing, when payment will commence (if appropriate), and in what amount and computed under which formula. Individuals who want to contest the validity or amount must submit a court order that either invalidates or amends the one submitted by the former spouse.

Section 3—Impact on Health Insurance Coverage

General Eligibility Rules

A former spouse who is awarded a portion of a CSRS or FERS annuity or a survivor annuity by a qualifying court order, even though the benefit is not yet payable, may be eligible to enroll for health benefits coverage under the Federal Employees Health Benefits program. However, the former spouse is not eligible to retain coverage under the employee's or retiree's own family enrollment.

A former spouse's continued entitlement to FEHB coverage is based on the court order requirements for a former spouse annuity. Children's eligibility for FEHB coverage is controlled by federal law and cannot be affected by a state court order.

A court order granting the former

spouse a portion of the retiree's annuity provides the former spouse with a monthly payment after the employee retires and continued FEHB coverage until the employee dies. A court order that grants a survivor annuity provides the former spouse with continued FEHB coverage until the former spouse dies, but the annuity does not begin until the employee/retiree dies. A court order providing a portion of the retirement annuity and a survivor annuity ensures an annuity payment from the date of retirement or death and continued FEHB coverage until the former spouse dies.

Individuals who qualify as a former spouse must enroll in FEHB coverage in their own right and must pay both the employee's and the government's share of the premium. Those who are receiving survivor annuity benefits will have the premium cost withheld from the annuity, otherwise the former spouse must pay the cost of such health coverage directly to the OPM.

For a former spouse of an active or retired employee to continue FEHB coverage after a divorce, four basic requirements must be met. The former spouse must:

• have been covered as a family member under the employee/retiree's FEHB enrollment for at least one day during the 18 months before the end of the marriage;

• be entitled to receive a portion of the retirement annuity after the employee retires or a survivor annuity at the time the employee/retiree dies;

• within 60 days after the end of the marriage, apply to the employment office of the agency where the employee worked and provide written notice that he or she wants to continue FEHB coverage under the spouse equity provisions of the FEHB law. If the marriage ended after retirement, that notice must be sent to OPM's retirement system; and

• not remarry before age 55.

General Coverage Procedures

Coverage begins on the first day of the pay period after the agency's employment office or the retirement system receives all properly completed qualifying documents—i.e., a Standard Form 2809 or a signed statement with enough information to execute enrollment—and satisfactory proof of eligibility. Former spouses whose divorce occurred during the spouse's federal service should contact the employing agency, while former spouses whose divorce occurred after the spouse's retirement should contact the Office of Personnel Management, Retirement and Insurance Service, Office of Retirement Programs, P.O. Box 17, Washington, DC 20044, phone (202) 606-0500.

To avoid a potential break in coverage, former spouses might want to apply for temporary continuation of FEHB coverage pending a decision on their eligibility for ongoing coverage as a former spouse. Under the temporary continuation of coverage rules, individuals must pay the full cost of the FEHB premiums, plus a two percent administrative fee.

Former spouses who do not meet the criteria for ongoing FEHB coverage may continue temporary coverage for three years from the date the marriage ended. To be eligible for temporary continuation, they need only have been covered by FEHB at some time during the 18 months before the marriage dissolved. The application must be filed within 60 days after the divorce or annulment. They are eligible to convert to a non-group health benefits contract when their temporary continuation of coverage ends.

A former spouse who meets the requirements for ongoing FEHB coverage may elect self-only or family insurance. A family enrollment covers only the former spouse and unmarried, dependent, natural, or adopted children of both of the former marriage partners, as long as the children are not otherwise covered under FEHB. To be considered a dependent, a child must be under age 22 or incapable of self-support because of a mental or physical disability existing before age 22. Coverage as a family member may be denied if evidence calls the child's paternity or maternity into doubt or shows that the employee or annuitant did not recognize the child as his or her own (despite a willingness to support the child).

A former spouse's entitlement to FEHB coverage, if based on entitlement to survivor benefits, normally continues for life. However, a former spouse's FEHB enrollment may end, subject to a 31-day coverage extension for conversion to an individual contract, when any of the following occur:

• a court order ceases to provide entitlement to a survivor annuity or to a portion of a retirement annuity;

• the former spouse remarries before age 55;

• the employee or annuitant on whose service the benefits are based dies and no survivor annuity is payable to the former spouse;

• a separated employee on whose service the benefits are based dies before the requirements for a deferred annuity have been met;

• an employee on whose service benefits are based leaves federal service before establishing title to an immediate or deferred annuity; or

• a refund of retirement contributions is paid to the separated employee on whose service the benefits are based.

If any of those events occur before the three-year eligibility for temporary continuation of coverage expires, the former spouse can change to temporary continuation enrollment for the remainder of that period.

The coverage of a former spouse's family member ends, subject to a 31-day extension of coverage for conversion to an individual contract, when the individual ceases to be an eligible family member (as defined above) or when the former spouse ceases to be enrolled, unless the family member is entitled as a survivor annuitant to continued enrollment or is entitled to continued coverage under the enrollment of another person.

A former spouse may cancel enrollment at any time. However, former spouses who cancel their enrollment may not later reenroll. A former spouse whose enrollment is terminated because of nonpayment of premiums generally may not reenroll.

Section 4—Impact on Life Insurance Coverage

General Rules and Procedures

The Office of Federal Employees Group Life Insurance must pay benefits in accordance with the terms of a valid court decree of divorce, annulment, or legal separation, or the terms of a court order or court-approved property settlement agreement relating to such a court decree, regardless of whether the insured individual actually completes a designation complying with the court order.

To be valid, the court order must be a certified copy. The appropriate office must receive the certified copy on or after July 22, 1998, and before the insured's death and it must expressly provide for someone to receive your FEGLI benefits.

If a valid court order is in effect, the insured individual cannot change his/her designation, unless the person(s) named in the court order agrees in writing or unless the court order is later modified.

If you are an employee, you must file the court order with your human resources office. If you receive benefits from the Department of Labor, Office of Workers Compensation Programs and you have been receiving these benefits for less than 12 months and you are still on the agency's rolls as an employee, you also must file the form with your agency's human resources office. If you are a retired employee, or you are on compensation and are separated from your agency or have been receiving compensation for 12 months or more, you must file the form with the Office of Personnel Management, Retirement Operations Center, P.O. Box 45, Validation Section, Boyers, PA 16017-0045.

The date of the court order itself is not relevant. But the date the agency or retirement system (as applicable) received the court order is relevant. If someone submitted a court order before July 22, 1998, it is not valid and OFEGLI cannot honor it. If you turned in an order before that date you do not have to get a new court order. You can submit the old one again. As long as it is a certified copy and you submit it to the appropriate office before the insured dies, it should be acceptable.

You can submit a court order if you are an employee, an annuitant, a former spouse, the former spouse's attorney or anyone else.

The insured can cancel coverage even if there is a court order on file. However, he or she cannot submit a new designation to void the court order. If there is a valid court order on file, you may not change or submit a designation of beneficiary unless the person(s) named in the decree, order, or agreement agrees in writing or unless the decree, order or agreement is modified.

A court order cannot serve as an assignment of life insurance. A court order can direct that the insured individual assign (give up ownership of) his/her life insurance coverage under FEGLI. But unless and until the insured individual files a valid assignment form (RI 76-10), the insurance is not assigned. This is different than a designation. If valid, a court order can serve as a designation of beneficiary for life insurance purposes even if the insured individual doesn't complete a designation form.

Court-Ordered Assignment

As part of a divorce or separation proceeding, a court may order federal employees or retirees to designate a former spouse as the beneficiary of FEGLI benefits coverage. However, under FEGLI, insured individuals may change their designation of beneficiary at any time. Moreover, FEGLI law preempts state law, as well as court orders based on state law, that conflict with FEGLI policy. Thus, to avoid a situation in which a divorced FEGLI policyholder could circumvent a court award by changing the designated beneficiary or even canceling the coverage at a later date, many courts will issue an order requiring an assignment of FEGLI coverage to a former spouse. This assignment option has been available under FEGLI since 1994.

Such court orders may require that FEGLI benefits be assigned either to a former spouse or children. An assignment of benefits transfers ownership of FEGLI coverage to the assignee. The individual who makes the assignment no longer has control over the insurance coverage and can no longer designate beneficiaries. Assignments are irrevocable, and apply to three types of FEGLI coverage: Basic, Option A (standard option) and Option B (additional optional) insurance. Assignment may not be used for Option C (family optional) insurance coverage.

An assignment automatically cancels a prior designation of beneficiary.

The policyholder, not the employing agency or OPM, is responsible for executing the assignment. This is accomplished by filling out Form RI 76-10, which is available at most agency personnel offices. Retirees may obtain a copy by contacting Office of Personnel Management, Retirement Operations Center,

Attention: RI 76-10, Boyers, PA 16017. The form also is available online at *www.opm.gov/forms*. OPM does not have authority to enforce a court order directing the assignment of FEGLI coverage. It is the responsibility of the court-designated assignee to ensure that the policyholder has complied with a FEGLI assignment order.

If a FEGLI assignment order is issued, policyholders who own more than one type of coverage must assign all of the insurance (except for family optional), not just part. An assigning policyholder may not name contingent assignees in the event the primary assignee dies first. If the assignment of the insurance is to two or more persons, the individual must specify percentage shares, rather than dollar amounts or types of insurance, to go to each assignee.

Policyholders who assign benefits continue to be insured under the FEGLI program. Premiums will continue to be withheld from their salary, annuity, or compensation payments. However, they may not cancel their life insurance coverage or revoke the assignment.

A determination as to whether the FEGLI proceeds should be included in the insured's gross estate is made by the Internal Revenue Service at the time of the insured's death. Individuals should refer to tax laws and IRS regulations in attempting to determine the tax consequences of a FEGLI assignment and may wish to obtain a ruling from the IRS.

The insured person retains the right to elect new insurance coverage, though all new insurance coverage (except for family optional insurance) would be subject to an existing assignment. The assignor also retains the right to decide, at the time of retirement or upon the receipt of workers' compensation benefits, to maintain more than the minimum percentage of his or her basic life insurance. However, the right to choose a Living Benefit is lost.

The assignment voids all prior beneficiary designations and prohibits the insured person from making any future designations of beneficiaries. Once FEGLI insurance is assigned, the assignee becomes the beneficiary unless he or she designates someone else. The assignee may not elect a Living Benefit.

In addition to designating beneficiaries, an assignee may convert the insurance to an individual policy if the insured person's eligibility for group insurance ends (e.g., the insured leaves government employment). Assignees also may cancel the insurance or reduce the amount of coverage. When insurance is assigned to more than one person, all must convert their shares to an individual policy when eligibility for group insurance ceases. Similarly, all must consent to a coverage cancellation or reduction.

Each assignee (and beneficiary of an assignee) is responsible for keeping the insured's employing office informed of his or her current address. The employing office will notify assignees of their conversion rights in the event group insurance coverage ends.

The value of assigned insurance increases or decreases in accordance with any automatic increases or decreases in the value of the coverage.

An assignment is effective on the date the insured's employing office receives a completed, signed, and witnessed assignment. For retirees, this information should be sent to the Office of Personnel Management, Retirement Operations Center, Boyers, PA 16017.

An assignment of benefits should not be confused with a designation of beneficiary. If there has been no assignment of benefits, a divorce does not affect a previously filed designation of beneficiary. An employee or retiree who has designated a former spouse to receive life insurance benefits must file new designations for any benefits that become payable to go to someone else. Beneficiary designations do not convey any policy-ownership rights under FEGLI and may be changed at any time unless there was an assignment of benefits.

The insurance designation form is Standard Form 2823. For Civil Service Retirement System retirement employees, the form is SF 2808. For the Federal Employees Retirement System, this form is SF 3102. Employees may obtain these forms from their personnel offices. Retirees may obtain them from the U.S. Office of Personnel Management by calling (202) 606-0500. The forms also are available online at *www.opm.gov/forms*.

Section 5—Impact on Thrift Savings Plan Accounts

Divorce, Separation, or Annulment Decrees

A court decree can award a portion of a Thrift Savings Plan account to someone other than the participant. The TSP will honor such orders if they are issued in connection with a divorce, annulment, or legal separation. It also honors preliminary court orders made prior to a decree that freeze a participant's TSP account, as well as subsequent court orders amending a decree.

The TSP governing board will honor any divorce, annulment, or separation order that meets its regulations. TSP compliance with such orders generally depends on three conditions being met:

• The court order must expressly relate to a participant's TSP account; general terms such as "all retirement benefits" or "government benefits" are not adequate. Similarly, the language of the order must refer to the individual participant's account or account balance, rather than to a benefit.

• The order must provide a means for calculating the affected person's entitlement, either by awarding a specific dollar amount

to be paid from the account or dividing the account by a percentage or fraction. It also should include a date or event from which the amount is to be calculated.

• The order must be to a person other than the participant, such as the participant's current or former spouse, an attorney, dependent children, or other dependents of the participant. The payment cannot be made to any person from whom the participant eventually can gain access to the money, must specify the award to be made to each person, and may not be made to creditors.

An order that requires payment at a future date may be acceptable, if it is currently possible to calculate the amount of the entitlement and the award provides for interest or earnings to be paid on the amount due until the future payment date.

When the TSP Service Office receives a court order, the account of the participant will be frozen. This means that the participant will not be allowed to receive a loan from the account or withdraw from it, except to meet IRS minimum distribution requirements. However, other account activity, such as investments and interfund transfers, may continue.

If the order is not complete, the board will inform the parties and will unfreeze the account within 30 days if no complete copy is received in that time. The board will issue a decision to the party submitting the order, including a determination of whether the order is qualifying, a statement on the effect that compliance would have on the account, a description of the way any entitlement was calculated, and the circumstances under which any required payment will be made.

The amount of an entitlement can change after the original award is calculated due to investment losses, loan payments, and other factors. The amount of payment cannot exceed the vested account balance at the time of payment. Interest or earnings won't be paid on the amount of the entitlement unless the court order specifically provides for it. The amount of an entitlement won't be segregated or invested separately pending payment. The participant retains the exclusive right to invest the funds in the account.

The board will make only one disbursement. It will not make a series of payments even if the court order requires it. The payee may not choose among standard TSP withdrawal options, but may have the money transferred to an individual retirement account or other eligible retirement plan. If the money is paid to a spouse or former spouse and is not directly rolled over into an IRA, it will be subject to a mandatory 20 percent federal income tax withholding. If the payment is made to someone other than the spouse or former spouse, it is subject to ten percent federal income tax withholding (unless another amount is specified by filing a Form W-4P) and cannot be rolled over to an IRA. The distributions are not subject to early withdrawal penalties.

Court orders relating to a TSP account should be sent to: Thrift Savings Plan Service Office, National Finance Center, P.O. Box 61500, New Orleans, LA 70161-1500.

Child Support or Alimony Decrees

The TSP also will enforce orders for outstanding child support or alimony. The TSP will comply with a court order or legal process for the enforcement of a participant's legal obligations to provide child support or make alimony payments under the following conditions:

• The legal process must be a writ, order, summons, or similar process in the nature of a garnishment that is issued by a court, an authorized official acting under court authority, or an authorized state agency.

• The legal process must expressly relate to the TSP in that it must indicate a clear intent to deal with the TSP as distinct from other retirement benefits.

• The legal process must demonstrate that its purpose is to enforce the participant's legal obligation to provide child support or make alimony payments.

• The legal process must require the board to pay a stated dollar amount from a participant's TSP account or must require the board to freeze the account in anticipation of an order to pay from the account.

The TSP board will not honor a legal process that requires payment of non-vested money or that requires a series of payments.

When it receives a document that purports to be a qualifying legal process, the board will freeze the participant's account. No withdrawals or loans will be allowed until the account is unfrozen. Other account activity, including contributions and interfund transfers, may continue. If the board determines that the document is incomplete, it will request a complete copy from the party that submitted the document. If a complete copy is not received within 30 days, the account will be unfrozen.

On receipt of a complete document, the TSP board will advise the submitting party and the participant of its determination, including whether the document is a qualifying legal process, the effect that compliance will have on the account, the amount to be paid, and tax and withholding information.

Payment will be made only to the persons or entities specified in the process. If the payment is to be made to a participant's spouse or former spouse, the money may be transferred into an individual retirement account.

A payment cannot exceed the participant's vested account balance, excluding any outstanding loan amount. The entire amount must be disbursed at one time.

Such orders or legal processes should be submitted to the TSP Record Keeper, Thrift Savings Plan Service Office, National Finance Center, P.O. Box 61500, New

Orleans, LA 70161-1500. Receipt by an employing agency or other government office does not qualify.

Tax Liability

The tax liability for payments made under qualifying orders depends upon whether the person being paid is either a current or former spouse or someone else. If payment is made to a current or former spouse, it will be taxable income to that individual. However, if payment is made to someone else (such as to a child for child support or to an attorney for payment of attorney's fees) it will be taxable income to the TSP participant from whose account the payment is made.

If you are a current or former spouse, you may want to consider whether you should transfer all or part of your payment to a traditional individual retirement account or to an eligible employer plan. If you are also currently a TSP participant, you may be able to transfer the payment to your TSP account. You should also consider whether you can use the 10-year averaging tax option.

Further information on the tax implications is found in the TSP publication "Tax Treatment of Thrift Savings Plan Payments Made Under Qualified Orders," available at personnel offices, the Thrift Savings Plan Service Office, National Finance Center, P.O. Box 61500, New Orleans, LA 70161-1500, or online at *www.tsp.gov*.

Section 6—Garnishment for Child Support or Alimony

General Rules and Procedures

To enforce alimony and child support obligations, the salaries of federal and postal employees, as well as retirees' annuity payments and Social Security benefits, are subject to garnishment, under Section 659 of Title 42, U.S. Code (Public Law 93-647 as amended by Public Law 95-30 and Public Law 104-193). Similarly, their pay or annuity is subject to withholding under state law and under any other legal process brought by a state agency administering a program to enforce an individual's legal obligations to provide child support and alimony. (Separate rules apply to child support and alimony orders affecting the Thrift Savings Plan; see preceding section.)

While it should be noted that the federal provisions do not preempt state or local law regarding the bringing of civil actions to enforce support and maintenance obligations, Congress has set maximum limitations on the percentage of wage or benefit payments that may be subject to garnishment.

Legal orders that the government will honor include any writ, order, summons, notice to withhold income, or similar garnishment process. This includes attachments, a writ of execution, court-ordered wage assignments, or orders by a child support agency. Enforceable orders include those issued by a court (or court official) of competent jurisdiction or a state agency authorized to issue income-withholding notices under state or local law.

OPM is authorized to comply with the terms of a court decree, order, or property settlement in connection with the divorce or legal separation of an individual who is eligible for benefits under the Civil Service Retirement System, under Section 8345(j) of Title 5, U.S. Code (Public Law 95-366). Civil service retirement benefits must be specifically divided by divorce decree or court order to qualify for payment under this law. A similar provision for individuals eligible for benefits under the Federal Employees Retirement System (FERS) is contained in section 8467 of Title 5 (Public Law 99-335).

Former spouses of federal employees or annuitants may be entitled to receive all or a portion of the spousal survivor annuity or lump-sum refund that may become payable based upon the employee's or annuitant's service, under Sections 8339(j), 8341(h), and 8342(j) of Title 5. With only limited exceptions, these rights apply only to former spouses who were still married on or after May 7, 1985, to an employee or annuitant who retired, died, or took a lump-sum refund on or after that date. The statutes permit such a division of the survivor annuity to be made, subject to restrictions, by agreement between the employee and the former spouse at the time of retirement or within two years thereafter, or a division of the annuity or lump-sum benefit pursuant to a court order or court-approved property settlement incident to a decree of divorce or annulment. A court order or court-approved settlement pursuant to a decree of legal separation may divide the lump-sum benefit, but not the annuity.

Similar provisions establishing entitlement rights for certain former spouses to all or a portion of spousal survivor annuity benefits or lump-sum refunds payable under the Federal Employees Retirement System (FERS) are contained in sections 8417, 8445 and 8424(b) of Title 5. These provisions of the FERS system, enacted by Public Law 99-335, were effective January 1, 1987.

The types of active employee payments that are subject to garnishment include virtually all forms of pay, ranging from basic pay to various forms of premium pay, special allowances and awards, overtime, differentials, special pay adjustments, incentives, and severance pay. Also subject to garnishment are retirement benefits, dependents' or survivors' benefits, refunds of retirement contributions, employee and government contributions to the Thrift Savings Plan, and injury compensation payments.

However, certain types of payments are not subject to garnishment. These include compensation for death under any federal program, benefit payments under "black lung" programs, and Department of Veterans Affairs-paid pensions and service-connected disability or death benefits. Also exempt are reimbursements for expenses incurred by an individual in connection with employment such as travel, transportation, relocation and storage expenses, per diem, along with such allowances and payments as post differentials and allowances, allowances for uniforms, living in foreign areas, education for dependents, maintenance, home service transfer, quarters, and remote worksites.

In determining the amount of disposable income that can be garnisheed, certain mandatory payments are excluded. These include payments for debts owed to the United States, mandatory retirement deductions, Medicare deductions, health insurance premiums, and deductions for basic (but not optional) life insurance under the Federal Employees Group Life Insurance program.

Maximum Garnishment Amounts

Public Law 95-30 established the following general limitations on amounts that can be garnished to enforce a support obligation. Unless state or local law provides a lower maximum garnishment limitation, the maximum amounts subject to garnishment are:

• Fifty percent of the obligor's aggregate disposable earnings for any workweek, where the obligor asserts by affidavit or other acceptable evidence that he or she is supporting a spouse, a dependent child (or both), other than the former spouse and/or child for whose support the order is issued. The amount may increase to 55 percent if the garnishment is to enforce a support order for a period that is 12 weeks prior to that workweek. An obligor is considered to be supporting a spouse, dependent child, or both, when providing more than half of their support.

• Sixty percent of the obligor's aggregate disposable earnings for any workweek, where the obligor fails to assert by affidavit or otherwise establish that he or she is supporting a spouse, dependent child, or both, other than a former spouse, child, or both, for whose support the order is issued. The amount may increase to 65 percent if the garnishment is to enforce a support order for a period that is 12 weeks prior to that workweek.

Where obligors submit evidence that they are supporting a second spouse, child, or both, copies of this evidence will be sent by the governmental entity to the garnishor or the garnishor's representative, as well as to the court or other authority together with notification that the obligor's support claim will be honored. Garnishors who disagree with an obligor's support claim should refer the matter to the court or other authority for resolution.

Procedures

The garnishment order or similar legal process should state on its face that it is to enforce an obligation to provide child support or to make alimony payments. The legal notice must include the garnishee's name, date of birth, Social Security or retirement claim number, employment status, and the employing component and official duty station. If the information submitted is deemed insufficient, the legal order will be returned to the issuer with an explanation of the deficiency.

For active employees, a legal notice of garnishment or similar support order must be served on the appropriate agency office designated to receive such orders or, if none has been designated, on the agency head (offices designated to accept garnishment orders are listed in 5 CFR 581.501). If the notice is not directed to any particular official within the entity or if it is addressed to the wrong individual, the recipient must forward the legal process to the designated agent. However, valid service is not accomplished until the notice is received in the office of the designated agent. The government is not liable for any costs or damages resulting from an agency's failure to timely serve process or to correct faulty service of process.

In the case of retired civil service employees, the garnishment order should be sent by certified or registered mail, return receipt requested, to the Office of Personnel Management's Court Order Benefit Section, P.O. Box 17, Washington, DC 20044.

When a valid order is received, the government will notify the obligor that legal process has been served. The notice will describe the maximum garnishment limitations, request evidence needed to determine the applicable limitation, and inform the obligor of the amount that will be withheld if he or she fails to submit such evidence.

The government will comply with valid legal orders unless they would require withholding of funds not eligible for garnishment. Where notice is received that the obligor has appealed either the legal process or the justification for the underlying alimony or child support order, payment of money subject to the legal process will be suspended unless the law of the jurisdiction prohibits it. The money will continue to be withheld and will be retained by the government until an order is received to resume payments or otherwise disburse the suspended amounts. Payments will not be suspended if the law of the jurisdiction where the appeal was filed requires compliance while an appeal is pending.

The government will not vary its normal pay or disbursement cycles to comply with a garnishment order.

The government will comply with an order that requires withholding for the payment of attorney fees, interest or other costs, as long as it expressly provides for those payments and the award is within the authority of the court, official, or agency issuing the order.

Section 7—References

The provisions of law that govern CSRS benefits are in sections 8341, 8342, 8345, and 8346, of Title 5 of the United States Code. The law governing FERS benefits is in Sections 8401, 8424, 8445, 8467, and 8470 of Title 5. The regulations covering both CSRS and FERS benefits are in part 838 of Title 5, Code of Federal Regulations.

The law on continuing Federal Employees Health Benefits program coverage for former spouses is in Sections 8901 and 8905 of Title 5 of the United States Code. Regulations are in Subpart H of part 890 of Title 5 of the Code of Federal Regulations.

Assignments of Federal Employees Group Life Insurance (FEGLI) coverage are authorized by Section 8706 of Title 5, United States Code. Regulations are found in Subpart I of Part 870 of Title 5 of the Code of Federal Regulations.

OPM's regulations on garnishment are in Parts 581 and 582 of Title 5, Code of Federal Regulations.

The Federal Retirement Thrift Investment Board's regulations governing court orders are in Part 1653 of Title 5, Code of Federal Regulations. A pamphlet, Information About Court Orders, is available at personnel offices, from the Thrift Savings Plan, 1250 H St., N.W., Washington DC 20005, and through the TSP's website at *www.tsp.gov*.

Federal Employees News Digest Inc. has published a comprehensive guide called *Divorce and Your Federal Benefits*. See publication-ordering information in this *Almanac*.

The Comptroller General has ruled that federal agencies may buy Federal Employees News Digest publications with government dollars. The decision is B-185591. For government purchase orders: Federal Employees News Digest, Inc. is a small business. Federal ID 52-0941248.

Federal Employees News Digest Inc. has published a comprehensive guide called *Divorce and Your Federal Benefits*. To order, visit *www.FederalDaily.com* or call (800) 989-3363.

Chapter 8
Employment Procedures and Policies

Section 1—Hiring and Placement

Applying for a Federal Job

Applicants for federal jobs—including currently employed federal workers seeking other positions—should submit an "Optional Application for Federal Employment–OF 612," a resume, or use any other written format of their choice, including computer-generated forms to apply for federal jobs.

An online resume service at www.USAJOBS.opm.gov allows applicants to create, save, print and submit resumes on line. Whatever format they choose, applicants must be sure to include all the information requested on both the vacancy announcement and in a flyer called "Applying for a Federal Job." Such information includes identification, job-related qualifications, personal data needed to satisfy general legal requirements, and applicant preferences such as work location and schedule. The "Optional Application for Federal Employment," OF 1510, also contains information about how to apply for federal jobs. The OF 1510 can be obtained from local OPM employment information offices, by calling (478) 757-3000, or via the Internet at *www.opm.gov/forms*.

An agency may require the use of special forms when filling unique jobs with specialized requirements through automated systems, and when recruiting exclusively from its own employees. Federal employment information is also available through the phone system at (478) 957-3000.

(For a listing of resources and databases providing information on federal employment opportunities, see the Federal Employment Information Resources section in this chapter.)

Candidate Assessment and Probation

The government uses two basic types of hiring procedures. The traditional method, called register hiring, which built up standing inventories of candidates, has been in decline in recent years as the nature of the government as an employer has changed from one that employed large numbers of people doing essentially the same work to one seeking specific skills for unique positions. The government increasingly uses "case examining," which entails advertising and filling jobs one at a time.

Under register hiring, an examining office establishes in advance a list of qualified candidates in rank order (including additional points added for veterans preference). Some registers accept candidates at all times, while others are open to new candidates only at specified intervals. Individuals usually apply "blind" for any jobs that open up on the register and are referred from the top of the registers when managers request lists of eligible candidates (called certificates of eligibles, or simply certificates). Hiring from a register is most commonly used when there is a need to fill many similar jobs at many locations, either on a continuing or one-time basis.

Under case examining, positions are advertised and applications are accepted where there is a specific job opening or multiple similar openings. Applicants are being considered for a specific position at a specific place. Candidates are still numerically scored and referred in rank order.

In addition to those two methods, many agencies have alternative hiring authorities under demonstration projects and other alternative personnel practices (see Alternative Personnel Practices section below).

Because of a 1995 amendment to 5 U.S.C. 1104, the Office of Personnel Management delegated authority to agencies to examine for all their positions (except for administrative law judges). Some 700 agency organizations have examining authority; these "delegated examining units" decide what assessment tools to use and how to use them, subject to OPM regulations.

OPM also maintains employment service centers, which assess and refer candidates for agencies on a fee for service basis.

There are three basic approaches to preappointment applicant assessment:

233

• written and performance tests;

• a review of each applicant's training and experience (done manually or via an automated system); and

• interviews and reference checks.

Federal managers and human resources staffs in the delegated examining units typically use some combination of these three methods.

Many hiring decisions must comply with the "rule of three" and veterans preference. The rule of three requires managers to select from among the top three available candidates on the list the examining office gives to them. Persons eligible for veterans preference ("preference eligibles") have additional points added to their earned passing scores, and then are listed ahead of persons without preference points whose earned scores are equal to the augmented scores of the preference eligibles. Under certain circumstances preference eligibles are placed ahead of all other eligible candidates (see the Veterans Employment Benefits section of this chapter).

Traditionally, candidate assessment has been focused on the extent to which individuals possessed the knowledge, skills, abilities, and other factors ("KSAOs" but more often called "KSAs") required to do the job. In KSAs:

• knowledge is a body of information applied directly to the performance of a function;

• skill is an observable competence to perform a learned psychomotor act;

• ability is a competence to perform an observable behavior or a behavior that results in an observable product; and

• other includes less easily measured traits such as promptness and honesty.

However, in recent years attention increasingly has been focused on measuring "competencies." OPM defines competency as an "observable, measurable pattern of skills, knowledge, abilities, behaviors, and other characteristics that an individual needs to perform work roles or occupational functions successfully."

Matching Federal Job Applicants to Vacancies

Step	Performed by	Assessment tools used
1. Determine whether each applicant is eligible for the job	OPM employment service center or agency delegated examining unit	OPM qualification standards
2. Score candidates and determine their referral order	OPM employment service center or agency delegated examining unit	Vary by assessing office, job, and skill level (grade) being filled
3. Select from among the referred candidates.	Manager with authority to make selections	Typically, interviews and reference checks
4. Retain or separate during probation	Supervisor or higher manager	Job performance

As shown in the accompanying table, candidate assessment—including continuing assessment in the probationary period after the actual hiring—is typically a four-step process.

Step 1—done by a delegated examining unit or an OPM service center—involves measuring applicants against the appropriate qualifications standard established or approved by OPM to determine whether they meet the basic qualifications for the job. Certain other reviews also usually occur at step 1 but sometimes are conducted later in the process. These include reviews of medical or physical examinations and reviews of background or personal history information that may bear on an individual's eligibility, suitability, or fitness for federal employment. Applicants still under consideration after step 1 have been found basically qualified for the vacant job and are now candidates.

Under step 2, candidates are further assessed to determine their relative qualifications to perform the work of the job. Using assessment tools considered appropriate for the job to be filled, the examiner scores the candidates to determine the order in which they will be referred for selection. It is not unusual for subject matter experts from the hiring organization to take part in or even actually conduct this step, particularly in hiring for jobs in higher grades. Score order ("ranking") is critical to candidates' opportunities to be hired because of its importance to the operation of the rule of three and veterans preference, as described above.

Actual selection—step 3—places considerable discretion in the hands of individual federal managers. The most common way managers gain additional information about job candidates is through interviews, which may be either structured or unstructured, review of candidates' employment applications and supplemental materials and interviews with current and former supervisors.

The post-appointment probationary period—step 4—also is largely the responsibility of supervisors or managers. Every new federal employee is subject to a probationary period. The probationary period is one year long, except for rare instances involving organizations that have received authority to establish probationary periods of different (usually longer) periods of time. This post-appointment assessment approach is based on observation of actual performance on the job.

During this period, the employee's performance will be monitored, with emphasis on helping the individual succeed. Appropriate training may be provided as needed and efforts will be made to help the individual correct any deficiencies.

An employee who does not meet acceptable standards may be removed during the probation without formal procedures that apply to non-probationers. For example, probationers lack the full rights to appeal adverse actions against them to the Merit Systems Protection Board or under negotiated grievance procedures. At the end of the period they gain full due process rights.

Employees who have completed a satisfactory probationary period normally do not have to complete another.

If the agency determines that the employee on a probationary period after promotion into a managerial or supervisory position is unsuited to the demands of the position, the law and OPM regulations require that the worker be placed in a non-supervisory position of no lower grade and pay than the one the employee left to accept the supervisory position. Adverse action procedures do not apply in such a case and there is no right of appeal to the Merit Systems Protection Board.

This probationary period is not to be used to assess technical ability or program knowledge not directly related to supervisory or managerial performance. Individual agencies may set the length of the probationary period, subject to the proviso that it be of reasonable fixed duration, appropriate to the position, and uniformly applied. (Most agencies have adopted a one-year probationary period for all supervisory and managerial positions.) Employees who complete a supervisory/managerial probationary period may not be required to serve another such probationary period regardless of the number of agencies, occupations, or positions in which they serve.

Types of Appointments

Individuals are hired—formally, "appointed"—into government jobs through a number of different authorities. The type of appointment in turn can affect employee rights in some areas, particularly rights to appeal adverse actions (see the Merit Systems Protection Board section in Chapter 9). The category of appointment is designated on the employee's form SF-50, kept in the personnel file.

Competitive Service—In general, the competitive service covers all civil service positions except those:

• specifically excepted from the competitive service;

• to which appointments are made by nomination for confirmation by the Senate; and

• in the Senior Executive Service

In addition, some career positions in government outside the Executive Branch may be designated as competitive service by statute.

The typical method to enter competitive service positions is by appointment through the competitive examining process. Jobs announced under this process are open to the public.

Competitive service status confers certain advantages in job competitions and protections. Current career and career-conditional employees (see below) may be appointed by transfer. Former career and career-conditional employees may be appointed by reinstatement, but time limits may apply. Transfer and reinstatement eligibles may be required to compete under the merit promotion program. Competitive service employees in general gain the right to appeal to the Merit Systems Protection Board after completing a one-year probation.

Career-conditional Appointments—A career-conditional appointment leads, after three years of substantially continuous service, to a career appointment. For the first year, the employee serves a probationary period.

Excepted Service—Certain positions are excepted from the competitive service by law, by executive order, or by the Office of Personnel Management, typically on grounds that it is not appropriate to conduct examinations for such positions. Appointments to such positions do not confer competitive status. Positions excepted by the Office of Personnel Management are placed in one of three schedules—A, B, or C—after a study of all pertinent facts (such as duties, pay, and location of the position) has been made.

• **Schedule A** is for positions for which it is not practical to hold any examinations, such as chaplains, certain positions in isolated localities, and attorney positions.

• **Schedule B** is for positions for which competitive examinations are impractical. Examples are positions filled by students in cooperative education programs.

• **Schedule C** is for positions that are of a policy-determining nature or that involve a close personal relationship between the incumbent and an agency's head or key officials. No examinations are given for Schedule C positions.

In addition to those distinctions, some positions are designated as excepted on grounds that the individual in the position could not establish ability to perform the job through testing but can establish competency through actual on-the-job performance. This authority most commonly is used for those with certain disabilities.

Some agencies are entirely excepted service. These agencies have their own hiring systems that establish the evaluation criteria they use in filling their internal vacancies. In many cases these procedures parallel those commonly used for competitive service hiring.

If you are interested in employment with an excepted service agency, you should contact that agency directly. The Office of Personnel Management does not provide application forms or information on jobs in excepted service agencies or organizations.

Major excepted service agencies include Federal Reserve System, Board of Governors, Central Intelligence Agency, Defense Intelligence Agency, Department of State foreign service positions, Federal Bureau of Investigation, General Accounting Office, Agency for International Development, National Security Agency, U.S. Nuclear Regulatory Commission, Postal Rates Commission, U.S. Postal Service, Tennessee Valley Authority, United States Mission to the United Nations, Department of Veterans Affairs, Health Services and Research Administration.

In addition, legislative and judicial branch employment falls under the excepted service, as does employment with international organizations such as the International Monetary Fund, UN agencies and the World Bank.

Excepted service employees who are not veterans may not appeal adverse personnel actions against them to the Merit Systems Protection Board unless they have completed two years of current continuous service under other than a temporary appointment limited to two years or less. Service in temporary appointments may not be combined with permanent excepted service to meet this requirement.

Interchange Agreements—OPM and an excepted service agency having an established merit system may enter into an agreement, known as an interchange agreement, prescribing conditions under which employees may be moved from one system to the other. Such agreements exist with respect to many of the agencies listed above.

To be eligible for career or career-conditional appointment under an interchange agreement, a person must:

• be currently serving under an appointment without time limit in the other merit system or have been involuntarily separated from such appointment without personal cause within the preceding year;

• be currently serving in or have been involuntarily separated from a position covered by an interchange agreement (some agreements do not cover all positions of the other merit system); and

• have served continuously for at least one year in the other merit system prior to appointment under the interchange agreement, except that an employee of the Defense Nuclear Facilities Safety Board must have served continuously for at least two years with the Board under an appointment without time limit.

A person must be appointed to the competitive service without a break in service of one workday, except that a person may be appointed within one year after being involuntarily separated from the other merit system. The qualification standards (including internal placement provisions, subject to 5 CFR 335) and requirements, appointing documents, and determinations for these appointees are the same as for transfer of employees within the competitive service.

Eligible persons may be considered for appointment to positions in the same manner that other individuals are considered for noncompetitive appointment. The appointments are not subject to the merit promotion provisions of 5 CFR Part 335 unless required by agency policy.

Persons appointed to competitive positions under the interchange agreements will receive career or career-conditional appointments, depending on whether they meet the three-year service requirement for career tenure or are exempt from it under 5 CFR 315.201(c). Service that begins with a person's current permanent appointment in the other merit system counts toward the three-year service requirement for career tenure. Interchange agreements do not authorize temporary or term appointments.

Interchange agreements provide for two-way movement. This means that career and career-conditional employees are eligible for employment in the other merit system with which OPM has agreements under similar conditions. A career or career-conditional employee who is not eligible for appointment under an interchange agreement may be eligible for appointment consideration under other appointment procedures of the other merit system.

Term Appointments—In general, term appointments may be made for nonpermanent work that will last for more than one but not more than four years. However, OPM may extend term appointments beyond the four-year limit when clearly justified.

Appointments of Foreign Service Employees—Agencies may noncompetitively appoint current and former foreign service employees who:

• have served in the foreign service under an unlimited, career-type appointment;

• immediately before separation from that appointment, have completed at least one year of continuous service without a break of a work day under one or more nontemporary foreign service appointments, which may include the service that made the employee eligible for career-type appointment;

• meet the qualification standard and other requirements governing appointment to the competitive service, except they are not required to compete in a competitive examination, or under internal merit staffing procedures unless an agency's policies require them to do so; and

• are appointed to the competitive service within three years of separation from a foreign service career-type appointment, but the time limit does not apply to a person entitled to veterans' preference or one who has completed three years of substantially continuous service under one or more nontemporary foreign service appointments immediately before separation from unlimited, career-type appointment.

Appointments Leading to Noncompetitive Conversion—Several governmentwide appointing authorities permit agencies to noncompetitively convert employees to career or career-conditional appointments from excepted or temporary appointments. These include:

• Veterans Readjustment Appointments under 38 U.S.C. 4214; 5 CFR Part 307; 5 CFR 315.705

• Disabled Veterans under 5 U.S.C. 3112; 5 CFR 316.402(b)(5); 5 CFR 315.707

• Severely Physically Handicapped and Mentally Retarded Persons under Executive Order 12125; 5 CFR 3.1(b); 5 CFR 213.3102(t); 5 CFR 213.3102(u); 5 CFR 315.709

• Student Career Experience Program (formerly the "Co-op Program") under Executive Order 12015; 5 CFR 213.3202(a), (b), and (d)

• Presidential Management Intern program under Executive Order 12364; 5 CFR 213.3102(ii); 5 CFR Part 362; 5 CFR 315.708

In addition, some agencies have their own conversion authorities based on specific provisions of law.

Appointment as an Expert or Consultant—Rules governing expert and consultant appointments are found at 5 CFR 304. In general, they allow an agency to grant an excepted service appointment to a qualified expert or consultant to a position that requires only intermittent and/or temporary employment. The appointments are excepted from competitive examination, position classification and pay rules and may be for a limited time period or without time limit.

Agencies may not use the authority to make appointments to a position requiring Presidential appointment, to the Senior Executive Service, to perform managerial or supervisory work (with some exceptions), to make final decisions on substantive policies or otherwise function in the agency chain of command, to do work performed by the agency's regular employees, to fill in during staff shortages, or solely in anticipation of giving that individual a career appointment.

Rates of pay are determined by the head of the agency, subject to a cap of the GS-15, step 10 rate in that locality. Individuals appointed under this authority are entitled to sick and annual leave, holidays and are subject to offsets of pay if they are reemployed federal annuitants. These appointments are distinct from personal services contract-type arrangements (see below).

Special Hiring and Placement Programs

Career Intern Program—The Federal Career Intern Program, created under Executive Order 13162, is intended primarily for positions at grade levels GS-5, 7, and 9.

It applies to placement both from outside and inside federal agencies and is designed as a recruitment and career development tool.

In general, individuals are appointed to a two-year internship that involves a formal training and development program. Internships can extend beyond two years with Office of Personnel Management approval. Upon successful completion of the internships, the interns may be eligible for permanent placement within an agency. Career interns are not required to serve a probationary period following their conversion to the competitive service; the two years the employees spend on the excepted appointment serve as the employee's probationary period. If the employee fails to complete the program for reasons unrelated to misconduct or suitability, the agency is obligated to place the employee back in a position of equivalent status, tenure, and pay at the position the employee left.

Appointments are not subject to Interagency Career Transition Assistance Program requirements. Agencies have discretion over how they apply veterans' preference when making career intern appointments.

An agency may use the program for any occupation as long as it has determined that the occupation lends itself to a formal training and development component. Initial appointments can be made at any grade level for which the agency has a formal training program in place. There is no limitation on promotion potential.

Individuals interested in career intern opportunities must contact specific agencies directly.

Hiring of the Disabled—The Rehabilitation Act of 1973 (P.L. 93-112, as amended) requires federal agencies to develop plans for the hiring, placement, and advancement of persons with disabilities.

To facilitate employment, federal agencies may use either competitive or special appointing authorities. Realistic standards, based on the tasks of a position, require that applicants possess only the qualifications necessary for safe and efficient performance of the essential duties of a particular position. Reasonable accommodation also must be considered in determining an applicant's ability to perform the essential duties of a job.

Special appointing authorities include:

(1) a 700-hour "trial" appointment, which gives individuals an opportunity to demonstrate their ability to perform a job, (2) Schedule A, section 213.3102(u), an excepted authority for severely physically disabled persons who have completed a 700-hour trial period or who have been certified to a position by a state or Department of Veterans Affairs vocational rehabilitation counselor and (3) a Schedule A, section 213.3102(t) excepted appointment for persons with cognitive disabilities and have been certified to a position by a state vocational rehabilitation counselor. Persons successfully completing two years in a continuing position under (2) and (3) above may be noncompetitively converted to a competitive appointment on the recommendation of their supervisors.

Agencies generally may not use any employment test or other selection criterion that tends to screen out qualified individuals with handicaps or any class of individuals with handicaps. They also generally may not conduct a preemployment medical examination and may not ask an applicant whether the applicant has a handicap or inquire into its extent or nature.

An agency may, however, make preemployment inquiries into an applicant's ability to meet the essential functions of the job, or the medical qualification requirements if applicable. Agencies may condition a job offer on the results of a medical exam if all entering employees are subject to such exams. An agency may invite applicants for employment to indicate whether and to what extent they are handicapped for purposes of generating records for its affirmative action program.

An agency may not discriminate against applicants or employees who are qualified individuals with handicaps due to the inaccessibility of its facility.

Persons with certain emotional disabilities may be considered for appointment under Schedule B, section 213.3202 (k). This authority does not provide for noncompetitive conversion to a competitive appointment.

Certain veterans also may be considered under special hiring programs for disabled veterans with disability ratings of 30 percent or more or Vietnam Era Veteran Readjustment Act opportunities.

The Rehabilitation Act of 1973, as amended, requires agencies to provide reasonable accommodations to qualified employees or applicants with disabilities, unless doing so would cause an undue hardship to the agency. (An undue hardship means that a specific accommodation would require significant difficulty or expense.) A reasonable accommodation is any change to a job, the work environment, or the way things are usually done that allows an individual with a disability to apply for a job, perform the essential job functions, or enjoy equal access to benefits available to other individuals in the workplace.

Federal agencies are required by Executive Order 13164 to develop written procedures for providing reasonable accommodation. Different agencies place responsibility for reasonable accommodation in different offices. Contact the agency's personnel office, reasonable accommodation coordinator, civil rights office, or EEO office to request a copy of the agency's written procedures.

Hispanic Employment Initiative—On September 18, 1997, the Office of Personnel Management issued a memorandum to agencies that raised concerns about Hispanic underrepresentation in the federal workforce outlining a plan to improve the representation. The plan encourages agencies to:

• support and implement the White House Initiative on Educational Excellence for Hispanic Americans;

• provide employment information to students, faculty, and the Hispanic community;

• use the Presidential Management Intern (PMI) Program for recruiting, converting, and advancing Hispanic college graduates;

• participate in the Hispanic Association of Colleges and Universities National Internship Program;

• use the flexibilities of the Student Educational Employment Program to bring Hispanic students into agency's shortage category occupations, as well as other occupations;

• develop mentoring programs to motivate young people to pursue higher education and federal careers;

• promote participation of Hispanic employees in career development programs;

• assess agency needs for full-time, part-time, or collateral Hispanic Employment Program (HEP) managers and ensure that HEP managers are integral members of the agency's management team; and

• incorporate these activities into agency's Federal Equal Opportunity Recruitment Program accomplishment report to OPM.

Presidential Management Interns— The Presidential Management Intern program is designed to attract outstanding masters and doctoral-level students to the federal service. Students who complete a graduate degree (masters or doctoral-level degree) from an accredited college or university are eligible to be nominated by their schools if they meet the following criteria:

• demonstrate exceptional academic achievement;

• demonstrate a capacity for leadership;

• demonstrate the potential for future professional growth; and

• demonstrate a commitment to a career in the analysis and management of public policies and programs.

Interns are placed in jobs at the GS-9 or GS-11 levels. During the two-year internship, agencies arrange for on-the-job training and other developmental opportunities such as seminars, briefings and conferences. Federal agencies also provide interns with at least one rotational assignment. Interns earn annual leave and sick leave, are paid for federal holidays, are covered under the Federal Employees Retirement System and may elect life insurance, health insurance and Thrift Savings Plan options. The internships commonly lead to permanent, full-time appointments through noncompetitive conversion.

For further information, contact the PMI Program Office, Philadelphia Service Center, William J. Green, Jr. Federal Building, 600 Arch St., Room 3400, Philadelphia, PA 19106-1596, phone (215) 861-3027, fax (215) 861-3030, online *http://www.pmi.opm.gov/*.

White House Fellows—The White House Fellows Program offers fellowships at the GS-14 level in cabinet-level agencies, the Executive Office of the President or the Vice President's office for those demonstrating academic and/or professional excellence. The fellowships are for one year and primarily go to those relatively early in their working careers. For more information, go to *http://www.whitehousefellows.gov/*.

Outstanding Scholar and Bilingual/ Bicultural Programs—The Outstanding Scholar and Bilingual/Bicultural programs were established by a consent decree approved by the United States District Court for the District of Columbia on November 19, 1981. The decree resolved a class-action suit that was filed in 1979 and is now known as *Angel G. Luevano, et al., v. Janice R. Lachance, Director, Office of Personnel Management, et al.* The plaintiffs alleged that the Professional and Administrative Career Exam (PACE), which the government had been using to hire into about 120 occupations at the GS-5 and GS-7 levels, had adverse impact on the employment of African Americans and Hispanics for reasons that were not job-related.

Although the Outstanding Scholar and Bilingual/ Bicultural programs are aimed at addressing underrepresentation of African Americans and Hispanics, the programs have never been restricted to those designated minority groups.

To achieve its intent, the *Luevano* consent decree depends on agencies to focus their recruiting on sources that would increase the pool of African American and Hispanic candidates for employment. Actual hiring decisions must not be made on the basis of race or national origin except in situations that meet all of the requirements established by the Supreme Court in its 1995 ruling in *Adarand Constructors v. Pena*.

The Outstanding Scholar and Bilingual/Bicultural programs may be used to hire into only certain positions at grades GS-5 and GS-7. Only those positions which were subject to the PACE exam are covered by the consent decree. The Outstanding Scholar and Bilingual/Bicultural programs are used as supplements to competitive examining. They typically are not used unless an agency has an established pattern of competitive selection into the covered jobs or is currently making competitive selections into those jobs. There is neither a requirement nor an authority to use either program to hire only persons from the designated minority groups.

The Outstanding Scholar program may be used to appoint those college graduates from accredited schools who obtained a grade point average of 3.5 or higher on a 4.0 scale for all undergraduate courses completed toward a baccalaureate degree. It can also be used to appoint those who stand in the upper 10 percent of a baccalaureate graduating class, or of a major university subdivision such as a College of Arts and Sciences. These appointments may be made without going through an examination procedure for jobs at grades GS-5 and GS-7 in covered occupations.

To be selected through this program, a candidate must meet both the eligibility requirements for the Outstanding Scholar program and the qualification standards for the position.

Rating and ranking are not required, so neither the "rule of three" nor veterans' preference are applied. There are requirements, however, that the positions be announced, that displaced employees be given preference, and that the program only be used as a supplement to competitive examining.

In the Bilingual/Bicultural program, an agency may appoint applicants who obtain a passing score in an examination, without further regard to rank, provided that:

• the job is one in which interaction with the public or job performance would be enhanced by having bilingual and/or bicultural skills and is at grade GS-5 or GS-7 in a covered occupation; and

• the agency has determined through use of a reasonable questionnaire or interview that the applicant to whom appointment is to be offered has the required level of oral Spanish language proficiency and/or the requisite knowledge of Hispanic culture. Agencies must maintain documentation that these requirements have been met.

Unlike the Outstanding Scholar program, the Bilingual/Bicultural program requires that applicants receive a passing score through the alternative examining procedure. The examining procedure is OPM's rating schedule used in case examining. A candidate who meets the minimum qualifications for the position will be rated as having passed the examination.

Temporary Positions

An agency may make a temporary limited appointment when it needs to fill a temporary position that is not expected to last

more than one year or a permanent position that will be temporarily vacant. These appointments may be extended for one additional year up to a maximum of two years. Temporary employees can work on a full-time, part-time, seasonal, or intermittent basis.

Federal employers are prohibited from using temporary employees to avoid the costs of employee benefits or ceilings on permanent employment levels. Federal employers also cannot use temporary employment as a tryout or trial period prior to permanent employment. In addition, federal employers cannot circumvent the competitive examining process by appointing an individual on a temporary basis when that individual is not among the list of qualified applicants certified for permanent appointment. Finally, under OPM regulations, federal employers generally cannot use a temporary appointment to refill positions that were previously filled with such an appointment for an aggregate of 24 months over the preceding three years.

Agencies can use the appointing authority to: (1) fill a short-term position that is not expected to last longer than one year; (2) meet an employment need that is scheduled to be terminated within 24 months for such reasons as abolition, reorganization, contracting of the function, anticipated reduction in funding, or completion of a specific project or peak workload; or (3) fill positions temporarily when the positions are expected to be needed for the eventual placement of permanent employees who would otherwise be displaced from other parts of the organization.

Seasonal positions involve annually recurring periods of work lasting less than six months or 1,040 hours, and intermittent positions are positions in which work recurs at sporadic or irregular intervals so that an employee's tour of duty cannot be scheduled in advance of the administrative work week. Seasonal and intermittent positions are exempt from the general time limits of temporary appointments.

Office of Personnel Management rules issued in 1994 generally created a two-year limit for individual temporary appointments in both the competitive and excepted service. To extend a temporary limited appointment in the same position beyond the maximum of two years, agency officials must request and obtain approval from OPM.

Temporary limited employees can serve for continuous years under different temporary appointments or in the same appointment without an extension from OPM. If it involves a break in service of three days or less, an agency can reappoint or convert a temporary limited employee from one temporary appointment to another temporary appointment many times over a period of years and not conflict with OPM's regulations. In addition, after three days have elapsed after a temporary appointment ends, an agency can rehire the employee using a new temporary limited appointment as long as it does not involve the same basic duties, the same major subdivision of the agency, and the same local commuting area as the original appointment.

Pay and Benefits—Temporary limited employees receive some rights and benefits but are not entitled to many of the rights and benefits available to permanent federal employees. Temporary limited employees, like permanent employees, receive full salary based on the grade and step of the position they occupy, annual pay adjustments, and overtime and premium pay. They also generally earn annual and sick leave if they work a full-time or part-time schedule. Part-time employees earn annual and sick leave on a prorated basis. Seasonal employees can work full time or part time.

Because intermittent employees have no fixed work schedule, they do not earn annual and sick leave. Temporary limited employees are not eligible for military leave or family and medical leave.

Retirement and life insurance benefits are not provided to temporary limited employees. These employees cannot participate in the Thrift Savings Plan. To be eligible for health insurance benefits, they must complete one year of current continuous employment, excluding any break in service of five days or less. Once eligible, they must pay the entire cost of the insurance premium. The government does not contribute toward the cost of health insurance for temporary limited employees as it does for permanent federal employees.

Temporary limited employees in the general schedule do not receive within-grade pay increases. However, some blue-collar temporary limited employees are eligible for within-grade pay increases. Temporary limited employees cannot be converted to permanent positions, and the time served in a temporary limited position is not creditable service for federal retirement.

Temporary limited employees with appointments for 90 days or less do not earn annual leave; however, those who work beyond the 90 days become eligible for leave from the beginning of the appointment.

Temporary limited employees contribute to Social Security and Medicare.

Part-Time Positions

Permanent part-time employees are those workers who have career or career-conditional appointments (or permanent appointments in the excepted service), work less than full-time schedules each week under a prearranged schedule, and are eligible for fringe benefits. By law (5 U.S.C. 3402), nearly every federal agency is required to have a program for part-time employment.

Part-time work schedules are fixed and arranged by management to meet the agency's needs. Agencies can vary a part-time employee's schedule as necessary to meet workload requirements.

As a result of the Federal Employees Part-Time Career Employment Act of 1978 (P.L. 95-437), a person who becomes employed as a permanent part-time employee on or after April 8, 1979, must have a work schedule of from 16 to 32 hours per week or from 32 to 64 hours per pay period if the employee is permitted to work under a flexible or compressed work schedule. (In special circumstances, agencies can employ workers for less than 16 hours per week.) Agencies can increase the hours worked above 32 for a limited time to meet workload or training needs but the employee's schedule must remain at 32 hours per week or less.

An employee who was working a permanent part-time schedule before April 8, 1979, may work any schedule of less than 40 hours per week as long as the employee remains in that or any other permanent part-time position without a break in part-time service. A detail or temporary promotion to a full-time position does not count as a break in part-time service.

In most agencies, temporary variations

in the arrangement of a part-timer's workdays or hours are handled by an agreement between the part-time employee and the supervisor. In such cases, there is usually no requirement that a new personnel action form (SF 50) be issued. The number of hours worked each day would merely be reflected on the employee's time and attendance card.

If a position with the desired number of hours is available, employees can switch between part-time and full-time schedules (and the reverse) in two ways: (1) non-competitively, by requesting a change in their work schedule, or (2) filing under merit promotion procedures, if required by the agency's promotion plan. A request for a schedule change must be submitted to management for approval.

Other employment issues involving part-time workers include:

Pay—A part-time worker's gross pay is computed by multiplying the employee's hourly rate by the number of hours worked during the pay period. Pay adjustments and withholding amounts are generally prorated according to the amount of gross pay. Part-time employees generally are entitled to receive overtime pay (for work totaling more than eight hours a day or 40 hours a week). Compensatory time may also be granted in such situations. If a holiday falls on a day part-timers are scheduled to work, they are paid for the number of hours they normally would be scheduled to work.

Leave—Part-time employees earn annual leave according to the number of hours they work per pay period. A regularly scheduled part-time employee with less than three years' service earns one hour of annual leave for each 20 hours in a pay status. Employees who have between three and 15 years of service earn one hour of annual leave for each 13 hours in pay status. With 15 or more years' service, they earn one hour for each ten in pay status. Sick leave accrues at the rate of one hour for each 20 hours in a pay status. Hours in a pay status include non-overtime hours up to 80 hours in a biweekly pay period. Any excess balance in these multiples is carried over to the next pay period.

Service Credits—Permanent part-time employees receive a full year of service credit for each calendar year worked for the

purpose of retirement eligibility, date of career tenure, completion of probationary period, within-grade pay increases, change in leave category, and time-in-grade restrictions on advancement. Part-time work is prorated, however, to determine experience for qualification requirements.

Benefit Coverage—Permanent part-time employees are eligible for:

• **Retirement**—Annuities are based on an employee's length of service and the highest average annual pay received for any three consecutive years. By law, retirement benefits are prorated for part-time service performed on or after April 7, 1986.

• **Life Insurance**—Permanent part-timers are eligible for the federal employee's group life insurance program. The actual amount of insurance for which an employee is eligible is based on annual salary, but in any case not less than $10,000..A part-timer's annual salary is the amount of hours scheduled to work times pay rate.

• **Health Benefits**—Federal Employees Health Benefits program coverage is the same as that provided for full-time employees but the employee cost for the premiums is greater for people who became permanent part-time employees on or after April 8, 1979. For these employees the government contribution is prorated according to the number of hours the part-timer is scheduled to work. For example, a part-timer scheduled for 20 hours a week will pay the employee's share of the premiums plus one half the government's share. Part-timers on board before April 8, 1979, can continue to receive the same federal contributions as full-time employees for as long as they remain part time without a break in service.

Appeal Rights—Part-time employees have the same rights as full-time employees when disciplinary action is taken against them. The reduction in scheduled hours is not subject to adverse action procedures.

Classification and Job Grading Standards

Position classification standards and guides developed by OPM are the legal basis for determining the series and grade and, consequently, the basic pay for General Schedule positions. Actual basic pay rates for the various grades are set each year on the basis of comparisons with private-sector pay rates for the same levels of work.

Position classification standards are developed for broad occupational groupings. For example, one standard contains grading criteria for all professional physical science occupations, including chemistry, geology, physics, metallurgy, oceanography, etc. These position classification standards are called "job family standards." Some of them cut across occupational fields and provide guides for the classification of categories of work, such as that performed by supervisors or research scientists.

Position classification standards now exist in three basic formats:

• The Factor Evaluation System (FES). Under the FES, grades are assigned to positions based on a comparison of a position's duties and responsibilities to nine evaluation factors. These are knowledge required, supervisory controls, guidelines, complexity, scope and effect, personal contacts, purpose of contacts, physical demands, and work environment. Position grades are determined by the sum of point values assigned to the nine factors as they occur in a specific job.

• The Point-Factor Format. Like the FES, under this format, grades are assigned to positions based on a comparison of a position's duties and responsibilities to a given set of classification factors. Each factor has prescribed progressive levels with corresponding points. Position grades are determined by the sum of point values assigned to the factors. This format is primarily used for guides, such as the General Schedule Supervisory Guide and the Research Grade Evaluation Guide.

• The Narrative Guide. Under this format, the 15 grade-level concepts taken from Title 5, U. S. Code, are described in terms of the nature of the position's assignment, level of responsibility, and certain subfactors, e.g., originality required, supervision received, scope of assignments, etc. Most position classification standards in the narrative format also contain illustrations of actual work situations at various grade levels. Positions are classified by matching a job's duties and responsibilities with the most appropriate grade-level criteria in the standard. Position classification standards that are now in the narrative format will be replaced with job family standards in the FES format as OPM

updates and streamlines the federal position classification system.

Job grading standards, also developed by OPM, are the basis for grading trade and labor positions under the Federal Wage System. Salary levels for the various grades are determined for each local wage area by a survey of private-sector rates in that area. Job grading standards are developed for separate occupations, such as aircraft mechanic, machinist, and electrician, and for jobs that cross occupational lines, such as trades helper and supervisor.

Both the position classification and job grading standards are available in CD-ROM format from the Superintendent of Documents, Government Printing Office, Washington, DC 20402. They are also available at OPM's website, *www.opm.gov*, in most federal personnel offices and many depository libraries.

For information on how to appeal a job classification, see the Office of Personnel Management section in Chapter 9.

Holding More Than One Job

Additional Federal Job—In some limited situations, a federal civilian employee can hold more than one federal job. [Refer to section 5533 of Title 5, United States Code (U.S.C.), and subpart E of part 550 of Title 5, Code of Federal Regulations (CFR).] The law allows an individual to have more than one federal appointment, but limits the pay an employee can receive from multiple federal civilian jobs except when:

• the work schedules of all jobs total no more than 40 hours of work a week, Sunday to Saturday (excluding overtime); or

• an authorized exception exists.

This means an employee on leave without pay (LWOP) from one position may be paid for another. Paid leave, however, counts toward the 40-hour-per-week limitation. Authorized exceptions to the limitation on paying an employee for more than 40 hours a week include:

• exceptions in law; for example with the agency's approval a civilian employee can work for the U.S. Postal Service. (39 U.S.C. section 1001(d))

• emergency services relating to health, safety, protection of life or property, or national emergency;

• expert and consultant jobs when working different hours as an intermittent employee; and

• fees paid on other than a time basis (e.g., lump-sum pay for a report, research product, or service not based on the hours or days worked).

Also, in unusual circumstances, federal agencies can make exceptions to obtain required personal services when they cannot be readily obtained otherwise. (5 CFR section 550.504(a))

Additional Non-Federal Job—Under 2635 of Title 5, CFR, federal employees may not engage in outside employment or activities that conflict with official duties and responsibilities. Many federal agencies have written policies that allow outside employment, especially when it is not related to the federal work and will not result in, or create the appearance of a conflict of interest. Agency policies may require employees to receive prior approval for outside employment even when co-workers have similar outside jobs. Ask your supervisor, agency ethics official, and agency personnel office for further information.

Employment of Relatives

By law, no public official of the government (including a member of Congress) may appoint, employ, promote, or advance, or advocate the appointment, employment, promotion, or advancement of a relative in the agency in which the official is serving or over which he or she exercises jurisdiction or control. A relative appointed, employed, promoted, or advanced in violation of these restrictions may not be paid.

"Relative" for the purpose of these restrictions means a public official's father, mother, son, daughter, brother, sister, uncle, aunt, first cousin, nephew, niece, husband, wife, father-in-law, mother-in-law, son-in-law, daughter-in-law, brother-in-law, sister-in-law, stepfather, stepmother, stepson, stepdaughter, stepbrother, stepsister, half brother, or half sister. In addition to this legal restriction, most agencies have adopted code-of-conduct regulations aimed at controlling the appearance of impropriety and other prohibited actions. These regulations vary; some are narrowly focused while others are quite broad and may govern the employment of relatives.

Reinstatement Rights

Individuals who were involuntarily separated from the federal government for various reasons not relating to performance or conduct have certain rights to reenter the competitive service work force without competing with the public in a civil service examination. You may apply for any open civil service examination, but reinstatement eligibility also enables you to apply for federal jobs open only to "status" candidates—that is, current federal employees.

If you have held a career or career-conditional appointment at some time in the past, there is no time limit on reinstatement eligibility for those who:

• have veterans' preference; or

• acquired career tenure by completing three years of substantially continuous creditable service.

If you do not have veterans' preference or did not acquire career tenure, you may be reinstated within three years after the date of your separation. Reinstatement eligibility may be extended by certain activities that occur during the three-year period after separation from your last career or career-conditional appointment. Examples of these activities are:

• federal employment under temporary, term, or similar appointments;

• federal employment in excepted, non-appropriated fund, or Senior Executive Service positions;

• federal employment in the legislative and judicial branches;

• active military duty terminated under honorable conditions;

• service with the District of Columbia government prior to January 1, 1980 (and other service for certain employees converted to the District's independent merit system);

• certain government employment or full-time training that provided valuable training and experience for the job to be filled; and

• periods of overseas residence of a dependent who followed a Federal military or civilian employee to an overseas post of duty.

Persons who are reinstated must meet the qualification standards and requirements applicable to the appointment in question. They also must meet the time-in-grade restrictions on promotion if they are reinstated in a position paid under the general schedule and served in a nontemporary GS position any time within the previous 52 weeks before reinstatement. Additionally, if the reinstatement is to a higher-grade job or to a position with more promotion potential, they must rank among the best qualified under merit promotion procedures.

As in the case of transfers, former employees who want to be reinstated must depend mainly on their own efforts to locate vacancies for which they are qualified, and the burden is on them to interest the appointing officer in effecting a reinstatement.

Reinstatement eligibility does not guarantee you a job offer. Hiring agencies have the discretion to determine the sources of applicants they will consider.

Individuals usually apply to agencies in response to vacancies announced under the merit promotion program. Some agencies accept applications only when they have an appropriate open merit promotion announcement, while others accept applications at any time. If you are seeking a higher grade or a position with more promotion potential than you previously held, generally you must apply under a merit promotion announcement and rank among the best-qualified applicants to be selected. Status applicants include individuals who are eligible for reinstatement.

To establish your reinstatement eligibility, you must provide a copy of your most recent SF 50, Notification of Personnel Action, showing tenure group 1 or 2, along with your application. You may obtain a copy of your personnel records from your former agency if you recently separated.

The Federal Records Center is the depository for official personnel folders of persons no longer in the federal service. Federal agencies, generally, transfer employment records to the Federal Records Center 30 days after the employee has been separated from service. Requests for this information should be directed to: Federal Records Center, National Archives and Records Administration, 111 Winnebago Street, St. Louis, Missouri 63118, phone (314) 538-5761.

Such inquiries should include your full name under which formerly employed, Social Security number, date of birth, and to the extent known, former federal employing agencies, addresses and dates of such employment. The Privacy Act of 1974 (5 USC 552a) and the Office of Personnel Management require a signed and dated written request for information from federal records. No requests for information from personnel or any other type of records will be accepted by telephone or e-mail.

You must meet the qualification requirements for the position. You also must meet the suitability standards for federal employment. If you were removed for cause from your previous federal employment, it will not necessarily bar you from further federal service. The facts in each case as developed by inquiry or investigation, will determine the person's fitness for re-entry into the competitive service.

There are no maximum age limits for appointment to most positions in the competitive service. Some jobs, such as law enforcement officers and firefighters, do have limits.

Certain positions in the competitive service such as guard, messenger, elevator operator, and custodian have been restricted by law to veterans entitled to preference. Generally, a non-veteran may not be reinstated to such positions if qualified veterans are available.

A former employee who did not complete a required probationary period during previous service under the appointment upon which his/her eligibility for reinstatement is based is required, in most cases, to serve a complete one-year probationary period after reinstatement.

Special rules apply for those seeking reinstatement after being called to active military duty returning after recovery from a work-related illness or injury or who were separated in a reduction-in-force.

Transfer Rights

Career and career-conditional employees are eligible to transfer from one federal agency to another as long as certain conditions are met. Generally, the employees must be in the competitive service or excepted service operating under merit systems approved by the Office of Personnel Management for an interchange agreement.

Federal employees who want to transfer to another agency must locate vacancies for which they are qualified.

Employees with career or career-conditional tenure need not be on a civil service register (list of eligibles for a certain kind of position) to be considered for a transfer. Such employees may be transferred to other jobs in the competitive service without again taking a competitive examination. They must meet qualification standards and requirements applied in making noncompetitive actions and depending upon the job, may have to rank among the best qualified under merit promotion procedures. They must also meet the time-in-grade requirements when a higher grade job under the general schedule is involved.

The general rule is that no employee may transfer or be promoted or reassigned within three months after the employee's latest career or career-conditional appointment from a list of eligibles except to a position at the same or a lower grade, in the same line of work, and in the same geographical area.

Transfer of Function (When Jobs Move)

A transfer of function takes place when a continuing function moves to another organization, or when the entire organization moves to another geographical location. A "function" is always a clearly identifiable activity of the agency's mission, consisting of substantial authorities, powers, and duties.

Not every organizational relocation of work is a transfer of function. A transfer of function takes place only when, after the transfer, the gaining organization undertakes a new class of activity. (For example, when an agency realigns geographic boundaries so that an installation performing a particular function begins to handle that function for a broader geographic area, no transfer of function occurs. Instead, the gaining organization simply assumes responsibility for another part of the same function or class of activity, but with different geographic boundaries.) Also, no transfer of function takes place when activities, assignments, or functions shift within an organization; this is a "reorganization."

If the transfer of function will require the losing organization to have a reduction in force, the competing employees in the function must be given the opportunity to transfer with the function instead of being separated or downgraded by RIF in the losing organization. This is the only situation in which employees have the right to transfer with their function—when the alternative in the losing organization is separation or downgrading. An employee properly identified with a function to be transferred who refuses to transfer may be separated by adverse action procedures.

If the transfer of function results in the identification of more employees than the gaining organization needs to perform the function and the employee cannot be retained in the losing organization, the gaining organization may be required to have a reduction in force. In a reduction in force in this situation, the employees coming in with the function have a right not only to compete among themselves for retention in the function, but also to compete with employees already in the organization. In other words, the provision of the transfer of function regulations for the transfer of competing employees before any necessary reduction in force means the gaining organization must treat the incoming employees as its own in the reductions in force. Employees separated under these circumstances go on the reemployment priority list of the gaining organization rather than the losing organization.

Agencies use two methods to identify employees with a transferring function: Method One must be used to identify each position to which it is applicable. Method Two is used to identify positions and employees only when Method One is not applicable.

Method One specifies that employees are identified with a transferring function if they perform the function during at least half of their work time, or if the function they perform includes their grade-controlling duties.

Method Two applies to employees who perform the function during less than half of their work time and are not otherwise covered by Method One. Under Method Two, the losing organization must determine the number of positions needed to perform the transferring function. To determine which employees are identified for transfer, the losing organization must establish a reduction in force-style retention register that includes the name of each employee who performed the function. Competing employees listed on the retention register are identified for transfer in the inverse order of their retention standing. If for any retention register this procedure would result in separation or demotion by reduction in force at the losing organization of any employee with higher retention standing, the losing organization must identify employees on that retention register for transfer in the order of their retention standing.

The losing organization may permit other employees to volunteer for transfer with the function in place of employees identified under Methods One or Two. However, these other employees may be transferred only if no employee identified under Methods One or Two is separated or demoted solely because a volunteer transferred in place of him or her to the gaining organization.

In a transfer involving a geographic relocation, there is no advantage to employees in saying they will move with the activity when they know they will not. However, unless they are sure that they will not move, they should accept the offer of transfer. This assures them a job in the new location, but it does not keep them from looking for a job in the home area. An employee may later change an initial acceptance offer without penalty if the employee declines before the transfer of function effective date. Employees who decline to transfer with their function can be separated for that reason and may appeal to the Merit Systems Protection Board. Although they are not placed on the agency reemployment priority list, they may be entitled to placement through the Career Transition Assistance Plan (CTAP) and the Interagency Career Transition Plan (ICTAP) if they are career or career-conditional employees.

Employees whose permanent duty station changes and who start working in a different pay area will be eligible for locality pay as long as their permanent duty stations are in the 48 contiguous states. Their pay may go up or down (depending on the rates in effect at the new duty station) since locality pay is based on the non-federal salaries in each pay area.

An employee has no right to appeal a transfer of function per se to the Merit Systems Protection Board. However, he or she may raise a transfer of function issue as part of an appeal of a subsequent RIF action that the employee believes resulted from the transfer of function.

Overseas Employment

Many federal jobs overseas are filled by U.S. citizens, the rest by citizens of the host nations. Most jobs overseas are with the Defense and State departments.

Generally, overseas employees get special post differentials or cost-of-living allowances but do not receive general schedule locality pay. In foreign areas, quarters allowances are also provided if government housing is not available. In most areas overseas government quarters are not provided and no quarters allowance is paid. In general, overseas employees are entitled to paid vacations, sick leave with pay, retirement coverage and free travel for themselves and their dependents.

More information may be obtained from the OPM fact sheet EI-10 "Federal Employment Overseas" available via the Federal Job Opportunities Bulletin Board. Information also can be found on OPM's website at *www.opm.gov*.

There are also possible job openings in international organizations that are not part of the U.S. government but in which the United States holds membership. They include the International Monetary Fund, Recruitment and Training Division, 700 19th St., N.W., Washington, DC 20431; Organization of American States, Office of Personnel, Room 1025, 1735 I St., N.W., Washington, DC 20006; Pan American Health Organization, 525 23rd St., N.W., Washington, DC 20037; United Nations Secretariat, Office of Personnel and Recruitment Services, New York, NY 10017; and World Bank and IFC, Recruitment Division, 1818 H St., N.W., Washington, DC 20433.

Judicial/Legislative Branch Employment

Positions in the judicial branch and the legislative branch share many of the same benefits as executive branch workers. Employees of those two branches generally are covered under the federal retirement systems, Federal Employees Group Life Insurance Program, Federal Employees

Health Benefits Program, leave and holiday rules, workers' compensation, unemployment compensation, the Thrift Savings Plan and many other executive branch policies.

Still, there are significant differences in the treatment of judicial and legislative branch employees versus those employed in the executive branch. For example, where most executive branch employees have the right to appeal removals and other disciplinary and administrative actions against them, legislative and judicial workers generally do not. There are few legal limitations on the removal or discipline of court and congressional employees.

Judicial Branch—Judicial branch employees are employed as "excepted service" workers as defined in 5 U.S.C. § 2105(a), that is, they serve at the pleasure of the courts, and therefore can be, as a general rule, fired "at will." By statute, employees of a district court clerk's office are appointed and removed by the clerk with approval of the court (28 U.S.C. § 751(b)). Law clerks and secretaries to district judges are appointed by the individual judge (28 U.S.C. § 752).

Approximately three-quarters of court employees are covered under the Court Personnel System (CPS). Those not covered include chambers staff, court reporters, court unit executives, chief deputies, and district pro se law clerks. CPS provides the court with guidelines for three major areas of human resource administration: job classification, compensation, and qualification standards.

Under CPS, the most significant departure from the executive branch is in the area of compensation, which features a 12-level, 61-step table. The first 24 steps cover what is called the developmental range, while the remainder apply to the full performance range. The full performance range allows once-per-year salary progression for employees who are at or above step 25 based on longevity and acceptable level of performance. At the same time, there is provision for court units to create a "pay for performance" policy to replace the longevity factor. In addition, provision has been made for special occupational pay rates, longevity bonuses, and adjustments based on locality and changes in the Employment Cost Index (ECI).

In general, the courts are not subject to civil rights laws, including Title VII of the Civil Rights Act and the Age Discrimination in Employment Act. Nor are the courts covered by rules issued by the Equal Employment Opportunity Commission. The Judicial Conference of the United States, however, has adopted some rules modeled after these laws, although appeal rights are not provided to court workers.

The courts may promote or demote employees under their own internal procedures, which may be found in the Guide to Judiciary Polices and Procedures (Volume I-C, Chapter X, Subchapter 1531.1).

The Judicial Conference of the United States, created in 1922, governs court employment matters. The Chief Justice of the United States is the presiding officer of the Conference.

Legislative Branch—Legislative branch positions generally fall into one of two categories: positions filled by elected representatives on their personal staffs and in the congressional committee structure, and positions in legislative support agencies and other offices supporting the general structure of Congress. Positions in the former category generally are "at will" positions with few job protections except what the member or committee provides through internal office practices. Positions in the latter category typically carry somewhat greater protections.

Employment decisions regarding personal staffs of members of Congress, including hiring, promotion and removal, are at the discretion of the elected member, typically acting through a chief of staff or administrative assistant. Individual members also set their own office's policies on pay and leave, often tracking executive branch policies, if only loosely. There is some informal coordination of benefit policies among those offices through internal Capitol Hill associations.

Positions on congressional committee staffs are similarly controlled by the committee chairman, typically acting through the committee staff director, and by members of the committee. The allocation of positions generally tracks the membership split on the committee between the parties, which in turn reflects the split in the chamber as a whole.

Positions in legislative support agencies such as the Architect of the Capitol, Library of Congress and General Accounting Office also are excepted service positions, although they tend to track executive branch policies more closely and most of those positions are career in nature. Hiring typically is done through personnel offices much like the ones in the executive branch. Links to those agencies are at *http://thomas.loc. gov/.*

Personal Services Contracts

Some federal agencies use "personal services contracts" to fill special needs, particularly those requiring special expertise and/or that are likely to be of relatively short duration. In many cases, federal annuitants are reemployed under such arrangements, which often involve consulting type work.

Personal services contracts are subject to restrictions under the Federal Acquisition Regulation (37.104) which states that the government in general is required to obtain its employees by direct hire under the competitive appointment or other procedures required by civil service laws. Specific legislative authority is required for the acquisition of services by contract.

A personal services contract may create varying types of relationships between the government and the individual, acting either as a sole agent or as an employee of a contractor. The terms of the contract, and in some cases the manner of its administration, determine the level of compensation and the length of the expected relationship. In general, those hired under personal services contracts are not eligible for federal benefits unless explicitly authorized by statute and by the contract's terms.

Insurance—In general, those paid on a contract or fee basis are excluded from health, life and long term care insurance coverage. However, you are eligible for Federal Employees Health Benefits coverage when you are a United States citizen, appointed by a contract between you and the federal employing authority which requires your personal service, and paid on the basis of units of time, or a personal services contractor employed by the Department of the Treasury.

Retirement Crediting—In general, to gain service credit for Civil Service Retire-

ment System purposes an individual must be an "employee" as defined by 5 U.S.C. § 2105(a). See 5 U.S.C. §§ 8331(1)(A), 8332(a). The definition of "employee" for purposes of Federal Employees Retirement System benefits is found in 5 U.S.C. § 8401(11), which defines the term by reference to the definition of "employee" for CSRS benefits under chapter 83 found in 5 U.S.C. § 8331(1). Section 8331(1) in turn defines the term by reference to 5 U.S.C. § 2105(a).

An "employee" is defined as an individual who has been appointed by an authorized federal employee or officer into the civil service, engages in the performance of a federal function under authority of law or an executive act, and, while engaged in the performance of the duties of his position, is subject to the supervision of federal officials. All three of these elements must be met for an individual to be a federal employee. The individual must establish his entitlement to retirement credit by preponderant evidence. See *Horner v. Acosta*, 803 F.2d 687, 691 (Fed. Cir. 1986).

Typically, the "appointment" requirement alone excludes personal services contractors because they are not appointed to federal positions but rather their services are engaged under a procurement arrangement. Under the *Horner v. Acosta* decision, an appointment must be "definitive and unequivocal."

Section 110 of Public Law 100-238 provides for the creditability of service performed under personal service contracts in computing benefits under CSRS in instances where the employing agency certified to the Office of Personnel Management that it intended through the personal service contract that the employee was to be considered as having been appointed to a position in which the employee would be subject to CSRS.

Review by the Merit Systems Protection Board of a claim for service credit pursuant to a personal services contract is limited to determining that, in making its decision, OPM properly relied upon the certification or noncertification of the employing agency head whether service credit should be awarded. See *Werley v. Office of Personnel Management*, 39 M.S.P.R. 686 (1989).

Buyouts—Individuals who took buyout

separation incentive payments must repay the entire pre-tax amount if returning to work for the government within five years, including as a personal services contractor. Unlike the rules governing reemployment as an appointed federal employee, there is no provision for waiver of this requirement for those returning as personal services contractors.

Performance Payments—Personal services contracts can be written to allow for performance-contingent payments.

Section 2—Work Scheduling

Alternative Work Schedules

Federal agencies are allowed by law (Chapter 61 of Title 5, United States Code) to establish alternative work schedules (AWS) that fall into one of two categories: flexible work schedules or compressed work schedules. About a quarter of executive branch employees work under AWS schedules.

A flexible work schedule breaks the workday into components of flexible time bands and core time. During the flexible time bands, the employee selects arrival and departure times for the workday. The core time is the period of time in the schedule during which the employee must be present at work or account for those hours with leave, credit hours, or compensatory time off. The establishment of these flexible work schedules is at the discretion of the agency and, if a union represents the affected employees, are negotiable with the union.

In some flexible schedule programs, employees may earn and use "credit hours" under rules established by the agency or negotiated with the union. Subsequently, employees may use earned credit hours to shorten the length of another workday or workweek. An agency may permit a maximum of 24 credit hours to be carried over from one pay period into the next. Some types of flexible work schedules (e.g., a "maxiflex, 5/4-9") allow employees to structure their work schedules to enable them to take one or more days off during the pay period while still fulfilling their basic work requirement.

Under a compressed work schedule, full-time employees fulfill the 80-hour biweekly work requirement in less than ten days by increasing the number of hours in a workday. The two most common compressed work schedules are the 4-10 and the 5/4-9 schedules. Employees on a 4-10 schedule work four, ten-hour days each work week. Employees on the 5-4/9 schedule work nine hours each day for eight days and work eight hours for one day. In addition to their weekends, the employees get one additional day off each pay period.

Compressed work schedules are fixed work schedules implemented one of two ways. A compressed work schedule may be established by the agency in a non-union unit if a majority of the affected employees vote to be included. In a unionized unit, a compressed work schedule program is arrived at through negotiations with the union.

An agency may not combine features of flexible work schedules and compressed work schedules into a "hybrid" work schedule program.

Flexible Work Schedules—The basic work requirement of a flexible work schedule is the number of hours, excluding overtime hours, an employee must work or otherwise account for by leave, credit hours, holiday hours, excused absence, compensatory time off, or time off as an award. A full-time employee must work 80 hours/biweekly pay period, or a multiple of this requirement, as determined by the agency head. Agencies also may establish daily or weekly basic work requirements. A part-time employee works fewer hours than a full-time employee within a specified period of time, as determined by the agency head consistent with 5 U.S.C. 3401 through 3408 and 5 CFR part 340.

In general, the tour of duty comprises all hours and days for which flexible and core hours have been designated. The tour of duty defines the limits within which an employee must complete his or her basic work requirement. Overtime hours are not included in the definition of a tour of duty for employees under AWS.

The types of FWS vary significantly. Agencies have the authority to establish flexible and core hours to meet their needs. Temporary changes in the tour of duty may be made under the terms of a negotiated agreement, if applicable, or agency policy.

For employees under FWS programs,

overtime hours are all hours of work in excess of eight hours in a day or 40 hours in a week which are officially ordered in advance by management. The requirement that overtime hours be officially ordered in advance also applies to nonexempt employees under the Fair Labor Standards Act (FLSA). Employees on flexible work schedules may not earn overtime pay as a result of including "suffered or permitted" hours (under the FLSA) as hours of work. See 5 CFR 551.401(a)(2).

Management may order an employee who is covered by an FWS program to work hours that are in excess of the number of hours the employee planned to work on a specific day. If the hours ordered to be worked are not in excess of eight hours in a day or 40 hours in a week at the time they are performed, the agency, at its discretion, may permit or require the employee to: take time off from work on a subsequent workday for a period of time equal to the number of extra hours of work ordered; complete his or her basic work requirement as scheduled and count the extra hours of work ordered as credit hours; or complete his or her basic work requirement as scheduled if the agency policy permits.

An agency may grant compensatory time off in lieu of overtime pay at the request of the employee (including prevailing rate employees and nonexempt employees) under a flexible work schedule. (See 5 U.S.C. 6123(a).) Compensatory time off, in lieu of overtime pay, may not be required for any prevailing rate employee; any employee who is nonexempt from the FLSA; or any FLSA-exempt employee whose rate of basic pay is equal to or less than the rate for GS-10, step 10.

If an employee's tour of duty includes eight or more hours available for work during daytime hours (i.e., between 6 a.m. and 6 p.m.), he or she is not entitled to night pay even though he or she voluntarily elects to work during hours for which night pay is normally required (i.e., between 6 p.m. and 6 a.m.). Night differential will not be paid solely because a prevailing rate employee elects to work credit hours, or elects a time of arrival or departure at a time of day when night differential is otherwise authorized, except that prevailing rate employees are entitled to night differential for regular-

ly scheduled nonovertime work when a majority of the hours of a FWS schedule for a daily tour of duty occur during the night. (See 5 U.S.C. 5343(f) and 6123(c)(2).)

Under an FWS program, a full-time employee who is relieved or prevented from working on a day designated as a holiday (or an "in lieu of" holiday) by federal statute or executive order is entitled to his or her rate of basic pay on that day for eight hours. (See 5 U.S.C. 6124.) If a holiday falls on a day during a part-time FWS employee's tour of duty and the employee is relieved or prevented from working on that day, the employee is entitled to his or her rate of basic pay for the typical, average, or scheduled number of hours of work for that day toward his or her basic work requirement (not to exceed eight hours).

A full-time employee under an FWS program who performs non-overtime work on a holiday (or a day designated as the "in lieu of" holiday) is entitled to his or her rate of basic pay plus premium pay equal to his or her rate of basic pay for that holiday work. Holiday premium pay is limited to a maximum of eight hours. An employee under an FWS program who works during non-overtime and non-holiday hours that are part of the employee's basic work requirement on a holiday is paid his or her rate of basic pay for those hours of work.

A full-time employee who performs regularly scheduled nonovertime work, a part of which is performed on Sunday, is entitled to Sunday premium pay for the entire daily tour of duty, not to exceed eight hours. It is possible for an employee to have two daily tours of duty that begin or end on the same Sunday.

Paid time off during an employee's basic work requirement must be charged to the appropriate leave category, credit hours, compensatory time off, or to excused absence if warranted. There is no requirement that employees use flexible hours for medical or dental appointments or other personal matters if the employee wishes to charge this time to leave. To the extent permitted by the agency, an employee may choose to charge time off during flexible hours to an appropriate leave category or use credit hours when time off is scheduled during flexible hours in order to preserve leave.

The head of an agency may grant excused absence with pay to employees covered by an FWS program under the same circumstances as excused absence would be granted to employees covered by other work schedules. For employees on a flexible work schedule, the amount of excused absence to be granted should be based on the employee's established basic work requirement in effect for the period covered by the excused absence.

When an employee covered by an FWS program is assigned to a temporary duty station using another schedule—either traditional or AWS—the agency may allow the employee to continue to use the schedule used at his or her permanent work site (if suitable) or require the employee to change the schedule to conform to operations at the temporary work site.

When a Fair Labor Standards Act (FLSA)-exempt or nonexempt employee under an FWS program is in a travel status during the hours of his or her regularly scheduled administrative workweek, including regularly scheduled overtime hours, that time is considered to be hours of work and must be used for the purpose of overtime pay calculations, as applicable. Note, however, that overtime hours are initially scheduled for work, not travel.

Compressed Work Schedules—The tour of duty for employees under a CWS program is defined by a fixed schedule established by the agency. Although agencies may change or stagger the arrival and departure times of employees, there are no provisions for employee flexibility in reporting or quitting times under a CWS program.

There is no legal authority for credit hours under a CWS program. The law provides for credit hours only for flexible work schedules. See 5 U.S.C. 6121(4).

For a full-time employee under a CWS program who is exempt from the FLSA, overtime hours are all officially ordered and approved hours of work in excess of the compressed work schedule. For a full-time employee who is covered by the FLSA (non-exempt), overtime hours also include any hours worked outside the compressed work schedule that are "suffered or permitted." For a part-time employee, overtime hours are hours in excess of the compressed work schedule for a day (but must be more

than eight hours) or for a week (but must be more than 40 hours).

Employee requests for compensatory time off in lieu of overtime pay may be approved only for irregular or occasional overtime work. Compensatory time off may not be approved for an SES member. Mandatory compensatory time off is limited to FLSA-exempt employees (who are not prevailing rate employees) whose rate of basic pay is greater than the rate for GS-10, step 10, and only in lieu of overtime pay for irregular or occasional overtime work. See 5 U.S.C. 5543(a)(2).

An employee is entitled to night pay for regularly scheduled night work performed between the hours of 6 p.m. and 6 a.m. The regular rules under 5 U.S.C. 5343(f) apply in determining the majority of hours for entitlement to night pay for prevailing rate employees.

A full-time employee on a CWS who is relieved or prevented from working on a day designated as a holiday (or an "in lieu of" holiday) by federal statute or executive order is entitled to his or her rate of basic pay for the number of hours of the compressed work schedule on that day. (See 5 CFR 610.406(a).) If a holiday falls on a day during a part-time employee's scheduled tour of duty and the employee is relieved or prevented from working on that day, the employee is entitled to his or her rate of basic pay for the number of hours he or she normally would have been scheduled to work that day. (See 5 CFR 610.406(b).)

A full-time employee under a CWS program who performs nonovertime work on a holiday (or a day designated as the "in lieu of" holiday) is entitled to basic pay plus premium pay equal to his or her rate of basic pay for the work that is not in excess of the employee's compressed work schedule for that day. (See 5 CFR 610.407.) Since CWS schedules are fixed schedules, employees must not be required to move their regularly scheduled days off solely to avoid payment of holiday premium pay or to reduce the number of holiday hours included in the basic work requirement. See 5 U.S.C. 6101(a)(3)(E).

A part-time employee under a CWS program is entitled to holiday premium pay only for work performed during his or her compressed work schedule on a holiday. A part-time employee scheduled to work on a day designated as an "in lieu of" holiday for full-time employees is not entitled to holiday premium pay for work performed on that day, since part-time employees are not entitled to "in lieu of" holidays. (See 5 CFR 610.406(b).)

A full-time employee who performs nonovertime work during a tour of duty, a part of which is performed on Sunday, is entitled to Sunday premium pay for his or her entire tour of duty on that day. A part-time employee is not entitled to premium pay for Sunday work.

Paid time off during an employee's basic work requirement must be charged to sick or annual leave unless the employee used other paid leave or accumulated compensatory time

off, or unless excused absence is approved.

The head of an agency may grant excused absence with pay to employees covered by a CWS program under the same circumstances as excused absence would be granted to employees covered by other work schedules.

When an employee covered by a CWS program is assigned to a temporary duty station using another work schedule—either traditional or AWS—the agency may allow the employee to continue to use the schedule used at his or her permanent work site (if suitable) or require the employee to change the schedule to conform to operations at the temporary work site.

Comparison of Flexible and Compressed Work Schedules

Flexible Work Schedules	Compressed Work Schedules
Basic Work Requirement The basic work requirement for a full-time employee is 80 hours in a biweekly pay period. Agencies also may establish daily or weekly work requirements. The agency head determines the number of hours a part-time employee must work in a specific period. Agencies may permit employees to complete their basic work requirement in less than 10 workdays.	A full-time employee must work 80 hours in biweekly pay period and must be scheduled to work on fewer than 10 workdays. A part-time employee has a fixed schedule of fewer than 80 hours in a biweekly pay period and must be scheduled to work on fewer than 10 workdays.
Tour of Duty The tour of duty defines the limits within which an employee must complete his or her basic work requirement.	The tour of duty is defined by the fixed compressed work schedule established by the agency.
Credit Hours Hours may be worked in excess of the basic work requirement at the option of the employee to vary the length of the workday or workweek. Not all FWS programs provide for credit hours.	The law provides credit hours only for flexible work schedules. There is no legal authority for credit hours under a CWS program. See 5 U.S.C. 6121(4).
Overtime Work Overtime work consists of hours of work that are officially ordered in advance and in excess of 8 hours in a day or 40 hours in a week, but does not include hours that are worked voluntarily, including credit hours, or hours that an employee is "suffered or permitted" to work which are not officially ordered in advance. (See 5 CFR 551.401(a)(2).)	For a full-time employee, overtime work consists of all hours of work in excess of the established compressed work schedule. For a part-time employee, overtime work must be hours in excess of the compressed work schedule for the day (more than at least 8 hours) or for the week (more than at least 40 hours).

Flexible Work Schedules	Compressed Work Schedule
Compensatory Time Off An agency may, at the request of an employee, approve compensatory time off in lieu of overtime pay for non-SES employees. (See 5 U.S.C. 6123(a)(1).) Mandatory compensatory time off is limited to FLSA-exempt employees (who are not prevailing rate employees) whose rate of basic pay is greater than the rate for GS-10, step 10. (See 5 CFR 550.114(c).)	Compensatory time off may be approved in lieu of overtime pay only for irregular or occasional overtime work by an "employee" as defined in 5 U.S.C. 5541(2) or by a prevailing rate employee as defined in 5 U.S.C. 5342(a)(2), but may not be approved for an SES member. Mandatory compensatory time off is limited to FLSA-exempt employees (who are not prevailing rate employees) whose rate of basic pay is greater than the rate for GS-10, step 10.
Night Pay For GS and other employees covered by 5 U.S.C. 5545(a), agencies must pay night pay for those hours that must be worked between 6 p.m. and 6 a.m. to complete an 8-hour daily tour of duty. Agencies must also pay night pay for all designated core hours worked between 6 p.m. and 6 a.m. and for any regularly scheduled overtime work between those hours.	The regular rules governing entitlement to night pay, at 5 CFR 550.121 and 122, apply. (See 5 CFR 532.505 for prevailing rate employees.)
Pay for Holiday Work Holiday premium pay for nonovertime work is limited to a maximum of 8 hours in a day for full-time or part-time employees. A part-time employee scheduled to work on a day designated as an "in lieu of" holiday for full-time employees is not entitled to holiday premium pay for work performed on that day.	Holiday premium pay for nonovertime work is limited to the number of hours normally scheduled for that day. A part-time employee scheduled to work on a day designated as an "in lieu of" holiday for full-time employees is not entitled to holiday premium pay for work performed on that day.
Pay for Sunday Work A full-time employee who performs regularly scheduled nonovertime work during a period of duty, part of which is performed on Sunday, is entitled to Sunday premium pay (125 percent of the rate of basic pay) for the entire period of work up to 8 hours. (See 5 CFR 550.171.) A part-time employee is not entitled to Sunday premium pay for Sunday work. (See 5 U.S.C. 5546 (a), 46 Comp. Gen. 337 (1966), and 5 CFR.610.111(d).)	A full-time employee who performs regularly scheduled non-overtime work during a period of duty, part of which is performed on Sunday, is entitled to Sunday premium pay (125 percent of the rate of basic pay) for the entire scheduled period of duty that day. (See 5 U.S.C. 6128(c) and 5 CFR 610.111(d).) A part-time employee is not entitled to premium pay for Sunday work.

Holidays	
A full-time employee prevented from working on a holiday (or an "in lieu of" holiday) is entitled to pay for 8 hours for that day. A part-time employee prevented from working on a holiday is entitled to pay for the number of hours he or she would have worked but for the holiday, not to exceed 8 hours. When a holiday falls on a nonworkday of a part-time employee, there is no entitlement to pay for an "in lieu of" holiday. (See 5 U.S.C. 6124.)	A full-time employee prevented from working on a holiday (or an "in lieu of" holiday) is entitled to pay for the number of hours of the compressed work schedule for the employee on that day. A part-time employee prevented from working on a holiday is entitled to pay for the number of hours of the compressed work schedule on that day. When a holiday falls on a nonworkday of a part-time employee, there is no entitlement to pay or an "in lieu of" holiday. (See 5 CFR 610.406 and Comptroller General opinion B-217080, June 3, 1985.)
Excused Absence	
The amount of excused absence to be granted an employee covered by an FWS program should be based on his or her typical schedule.	All compressed work schedules are fixed schedules. The regular agency practices applicable to administration of excused absence apply.
Temporary Duty	
The agency may allow an employee covered by an FWS program to continue the existing schedule, modify that schedule, or require him or her to follow the schedule used at the temporary work site.	Same as Flexible Work Schedules
Travel	
Time spent in a travel status is considered to be hours of work only as provided in 5 CFR 550.112(g) or 5 U.S.C. 5544 (prevailing rate employees) for FLSA exempt employees, and as provided in 5 CFR 550.112(g) or 5 U.S.C. 5544 and 551.422 for nonexempt employees. Agencies may find it advisable to establish procedures to revert employees to standard fixed schedules when traveling.	Same as Flexible Work Schedules
Application in Unorganized Units	
Agencies may unilaterally install FWS programs in unorganized units. There is no requirement for a vote of affected employees.	In an unorganized unit, a majority of affected employees must vote to be included in a CWS program. (See 5 U.S.C. 6127(b).)
Determining Hardships	
Since FWS programs generally provide employees the flexibility to continue to work traditional schedules, the agency is not required to consider exclusion of an employee from the FWS program for personal hardship.	An employee for whom a CWS program would impose a personal hardship may request to be excluded from the program. The request must be submitted to the agency in writing. The agency must determine whether a personal hardship exists. If so, the employee must be excepted from the CWS program or reassigned to the first position that meets the criteria in 5 U.S.C. 6127(b)(2)(B).

When a Fair Labor Standards Act (FLSA)-exempt or nonexempt employee under a CWS program is in a travel status during the hours of his or her regularly scheduled administrative workweek, including regularly scheduled overtime hours, that time is considered to be hours of work and must be used for the purpose of overtime pay calculations, as applicable. Note, however, that overtime hours are initially scheduled for work, not travel.

Job Sharing for Part-Time Workers

Job sharing is a form of part-time employment in which the schedules of two part-time employees are arranged to cover the duties of a single full-time position—for example, each job sharer may work a portion of the day or week. In some cases, job-sharing provides part-time schedules that otherwise would not be available.

There is no definitive list of jobs "suitable" for job-sharing, and no law or regulation limits part-time or job-sharing to specific jobs or grade levels. Any job may be filled by a part-time employee or by a team of job-sharers when the arrangement meets the needs of the agency and the employee(s).

How Job-Sharing Develops—A proposal can come from a full-time employee who wants to reduce work hours, from a team of job-sharers, or from a supervisor who wants to consider filling a vacancy with job sharers. When an employee's request for part-time cannot be accommodated because of the need for full-time coverage, job-sharing may well be an option. The personnel office should be able to help the supervisor look at the pros and cons of various arrangements.

The first place to look is in the office (or a related office) where the employee works to see if another employee is interested. The contact point in the agency's personnel office may also be keeping a list of employees who want to reduce their work hours. Employees often conduct their own search by contacting organizations and placing ads.

An agency may post a vacancy announcement to let employees know of the job-sharing opportunity, but competition under agency merit promotion procedures is generally not required when an employee moves to a position with a different work schedule as long as the positions are at the same or lower grade level and have no more promotion potential.

Other Considerations—When two job-sharers at the same grade level are jointly responsible for all the duties and responsibilities of the full-time position, there is no need to restructure the position. Each team member should have a copy of the original position description to which a statement has been attached to show that the incumbent is a job-sharer jointly responsible for carrying out all the duties and responsibilities of the position.

When the job-sharers will be individually responsible only for portions of the job, or when the job-sharers are at different grade levels, separate position descriptions are required to reflect the actual duties and responsibilities of each employee. Each job-sharer must have a position description that accurately reflects his or her duties and responsibilities.

The decision on whether job-sharers should be jointly responsible for the entire position or only for separate functions depends on the job and the abilities of the job-sharing team. To determine the arrangement for a particular job, the supervisor should examine the position description and decide which tasks will be shared; i.e., handled by whichever team member is on duty, and which will be assigned to a specific individual, based on skills and experience.

Specific work schedules depend on the nature of the job and the needs of the office and the job-sharing team. Almost any reasonable arrangement is possible if it meets the needs of the supervisor and the job-sharers. Work schedules for job-sharers can be from 16 to 32 hours per week and can be varied in the same way as other part-time employees.

Each member of a job-sharing team must have his or her own performance standards. These will be identical if the job-sharers are jointly responsible for the entire position. Each job-sharer must be evaluated separately although the evaluation will often be based on work to which both have contributed. To make the supervisor's job easier, it would be wise to build in a mechanism for determining the relative contributions of each job-sharer.

In a reduction in force, part-time and job-sharing employees have assignment rights only to part-time positions. (Similarly, full-time employees have assignment rights only to full-time positions.)

Flexiplace (Telecommuting)

Telecommuting means working at home or another approved location away from the regular office. A telecommuting center is a multi-agency facility that provides a geographically convenient office setting as an alternative to the employee's regular office.

Individual agency practices vary greatly, but telecommuters usually work away from their principal office one or more days a week, with the schedule being set by the supervisor according to office needs and any union agreement. Most telecommuting employees spend at least part of their workweek at the regular office to improve communication, minimize isolation, and use facilities not readily available offsite.

Telecommuting is a management option rather than an employee entitlement. Work suitable for telecommuting depends on a job's content, rather than title. Telecommuting is especially appropriate for work that requires thinking and writing, telephone intensive, or computer-oriented tasks. A Presidential memo of July 26, 2000, directed agencies operating customer service call/contact centers, processing claims and financial transactions and conducting similar activities to identify positions that can be relocated to home-based or other off-site facilities and that can be filled by qualified individuals, including those with significant disabilities.

Work may not be suitable for telecommuting in situations where it would be too costly for the agency to implement or where the employee needs to have extensive face-to-face contact or frequent access to materials that cannot be removed from the regular office. At the same time, an agency may place its equipment and/or pay for the installation of telephone lines in an employee's home.

Each agency sets up its own approval process, but generally the immediate supervisor must agree to a specific employee's request. A telecommuting employee should be an organized, highly disciplined self-starter who requires minimal supervision and has a performance appraisal of at least fully successful. Employees are not to be caring for children when they are working at home. Teleworkers may follow alternative work schedules.

Agencies are encouraged to develop their telework programs in coordination with their unions and other stakeholders. Telework affects conditions of employment and agencies must consult and negotiate with unions, as appropriate, regarding telework programs.

Subject to any applicable union agreement, management decides whether the employee can work off-site, depending on the nature of the position and the characteristics of the employee. Management has the right to end an employee's use of the telework option if, for example, the employee's performance declines or if the arrangement no longer meets the organization's needs. A supervisor may require an employee to work at the main worksite on a day scheduled for an alternative worksite if the needs of the office so require.

Generally speaking, organizations are not required to provide equipment at home-based worksites. Each agency establishes its own policies on the provision and installation of equipment. Generally, the government is responsible for the service and maintenance of government-owned equipment. Teleworkers using their own equipment are responsible for its service and maintenance.

An employee may be reimbursed for business related long distance phone calls over the employee's personal phone approved by the supervisor. Agencies also may provide employees with government telephone credit cards.

Government employees suffering from work related injuries and/or damages at the alternative worksite are covered under the Military Personnel and Civilian Employees Claims Act, the Federal Tort Claims Act, or the Federal Employees Compensation Act (workers' compensation).

OPM recommends that the regular office remain the official duty station for such purposes as special salary rates, locality pay adjustments, and travel. The existing rules on hours of duty, pay, leave, and overtime generally apply. Telecommuting employees are covered by the Federal Employees Compensation Act (i.e., workers' compensation benefits). A telecommuting employee usually signs an agreement with the supervisor that stipulates the conditions and duration of the arrangement.

The General Services Administration has established a network of interagency telecenters in communities surrounding Washington, D.C. Legal authority for the telecenters is provided in Public Law 103-123, which provided funding for the acquisition, lease, construction, and equipping of flexiplace telecommuting centers in the Washington D.C. area. In addition, employees may have access to centers in other areas not operated by the federal government.

Public Law 106-346 required that each executive agency must establish a policy under which eligible employees of the agency may participate in telecommuting "to the maximum extent possible without diminished employee performance." The requirements are being phased in across the federal work force over four years, beginning in 2001.

Under that instruction, each agency must take a fresh look at the barriers that inhibit the use of this option, and actively work to remove them and increase actual participation. While the law recognizes that not all positions are appropriate for telecommuting, each agency must identify those positions that are conducive to telecommuting in a manner that focuses on broad, objective criteria.

Agencies must also identify and overcome any obstacles to telecommuting, such as reluctant managers who may lack trust in their employees or who may perceive a loss of control over their employees. Once an agency has established eligibility criteria, employees who meet them and who wish to participate must be allowed that opportunity if they are satisfactory performers and if other management conditions are met.

OPM and GSA maintain a joint Internet site at www.telework.gov that has links to OPM and GSA telework information, policy guidance, agency telework policies, guidelines for designing and implementing telework programs, answers to frequently asked questions, and telework conference announcements and registration information.

Family-Friendly Schedules and Work Arrangements

A July 11, 1994, Presidential memo directed agencies to establish a program to encourage and support the use of flexible family-friendly workplace arrangements. The memorandum challenged agencies to expand opportunities for workers to participate in flexible work arrangements, including job sharing, career part-time employment, alternative work schedules, and telecommuting both from home and satellite work locations.

A June 21, 1996, follow-up memorandum directed agencies to review their family-friendly programs and, to the extent feasible, expand them to provide their employees with the following:

• assistance in securing safe, affordable, quality child care;

• elder care information and referral services;

• flexible hours that will enable them to schedule their work and meet the needs of their families, including encouragement to parents to attend school functions and events essential to their children;

• opportunities to telecommute, when possible, and consistent with their responsibilities;

• policies and procedures that promote active inclusion of fathers as well as mothers;

• an effective mechanism by which employees can suggest new practices that strengthen families and provide for a more productive work environment; and

• leadership and participation in these policies and programs at the highest level of the agency.

The full text of these memoranda is available for downloading from the Internet at *http://www.opm.gov/wrkfam* or by contacting OPM at (202) 606-5520.

Preventive Health Services and Screenings

A January 4, 2001, Presidential memo directed agencies to review their policies and make maximum use of existing work schedule and leave flexibilities to allow federal employees to take full advantage of health screening programs and other effective preventive health measures. Such flexibilities include promoting alternative work schedules (flexible and compressed work schedules), granting leave under sick and annual leave programs, and granting excused absence to employees to participate in agency-sponsored preventive health activities.

In addition, in the case of an employee with fewer than 80 hours (two weeks) of accrued sick leave, the memo directed agencies to establish a policy that provides up to four hours of excused absence each year for participation in preventive health screenings.

Volunteer Activities

A Presidential memo of April 22, 1998, directed federal agencies to make maximum use of existing flexibilities to allow federal employees to plan and take time off to perform community service as the public business permits. Each department and agency must inform its employees of the various flexibilities available to them to participate in volunteer activities.

Guidance from the Office of Personnel Management states that agencies are encouraged to make appropriate use of this flexibility in responding to requests for changes in work schedules or time off to allow employees to engage in volunteer activities, while giving due consideration to the effect of the employee's absence or change in duty schedule on work operations and productivity.

Agencies have the flexibility to approve a variety of work arrangements for employees seeking to engage in volunteer activities during normal work hours, including alternative work schedules and use of credit hours (hours within a flexible work schedule that an employee elects to work in excess of his or her basic work requirement) so as to vary the length of a workweek or workday. Employees may use credit hours to fulfill their basic work requirement, thereby gaining time off from work to pursue volunteer activities and for other purposes. If a department or agency authorizes credit hours under its flexible work schedules program, a maximum of 24 credit hours may be carried over from one pay period to another.

Employees seeking to participate in volunteer activities during basic working hours may be granted annual leave, leave without pay, compensatory time off, or, in limited circumstances, excused absence. When employees request annual leave to perform volunteer service, agencies must be as accommodating as possible in reviewing and approving such requests consistent with regulations in 5 CFR part 630, subpart C, Annual Leave, and applicable collective bargaining agreements.

At the discretion of the agency, leave without pay (LWOP) may be granted to employees who wish to engage in volunteer activities during normal working hours. As with annual leave, OPM encourages departments and agencies, whenever possible, to act favorably upon requests by employees for LWOP to perform volunteer services. However, LWOP is deemed appropriate for extended periods only if the employee is expected to return to his or her job at the end of the LWOP.

Agencies may approve requests from employees for compensatory time off in exchange for performing an equal amount of time in irregular or occasional overtime work. For employees under flexible work schedules, departments and agencies may approve employee requests for compensatory time off for both regularly scheduled and irregular or occasional overtime work.

Each department or agency has discretion to excuse employees from their duties without loss of pay or charge to leave (excused absence or administrative leave). It is the responsibility of each department or agency head to balance support for employees' volunteer activities with the need to ensure that employees' work requirements are fulfilled and that agency operations are conducted efficiently and effectively. Agencies should review their internal guidance on excused absence and applicable collective bargaining agreements.

Part-time employment or job-sharing may also be approved for employees who request such arrangements in connection with performing volunteer service.

While managers, supervisors, and other agency officials may encourage employees to become more involved in volunteer activities, 5 U.S.C. 6132 provides that employees may not be coerced for the purpose of interfering with their legal rights under flexible and compressed work schedules.

Conflict of interest laws and related regulations governing outside employment for compensation also apply to federal employees who engage in volunteer activities. Hatch Act restrictions apply to employees who are on duty, as well as to those on paid or unpaid leave.

Departments and agencies are encouraged to recognize their employees who volunteer their skills to help others, although usually not in the form of cash or paid time off.

Lunch Breaks

Lunch is an approved period of time in a nonpay and nonwork status that interrupts a basic workday or a period of overtime work for the purpose of permitting employees to eat or engage in permitted personal activities. Agencies are allowed to establish their own policies, including whether lunch breaks will be required or permitted during overtime hours and whether they will be required or permitted for part-time employees.

Agency policies must follow certain rules. For example, a meal period may not exceed one hour. In addition, an agency may not combine a regular lunch break with a rest period just before or right after lunch, because a rest period is considered part of the regular paid workday. Also, when employees aren't excused for a lunch break or are called back to work during the break, they must be paid for the work done during that time. Employees who are on-call may have to stay on the premises to eat lunch, even though they won't be paid for that time.

Weather Dismissal Policy

During weather emergencies, agencies determine closing and related policies and announce the policies to employees and the local media. The decision to have federal employees report to work as scheduled, or to implement any one of several work schedule options, generally is made several hours before normal starting time, although changes can be made during the working day as events warrant.

The categories are:

• Federal agencies are open—Employees are expected to report to work on time. (Means federal agencies will open on time and employees are expected to report for work as scheduled.)

• Federal agencies are operating under an unscheduled leave policy—Employees may take leave without prior approval. (Means federal agencies will open on time, but employees not designated as emergency employees may take annual leave or leave without pay (LWOP) without the prior approval of their supervisors. Employees should inform their supervisors of their intentions. Employees designated as emergency employees are expected to report for work on time.)

• Federal agencies are operating under an adjusted home departure—Employees are requested to leave home a specified number of hours later than their normal departure time. (Means federal agencies will open on time, but non-emergency employees should adjust their normal home departure time consistent with the announcement. Employees designated as emergency employees are expected to report to work on time.)

• Federal agencies are operating under an adjusted home departure/unscheduled leave policy—Employees are requested to leave home a specified number of hours later than their normal departure time, and may take leave without prior approval. (Means federal agencies will open on time, but non-emergency employees who arrive late will be excused without loss of pay or charge to leave. Employees not designated as emergency employees may take annual leave or LWOP without the prior approval of their supervisors. Employees should inform their supervisors if they plan to take annual leave or LWOP. Employees designated as emergency employees are expected to report for work on time.)

• Federal agencies are closed—(Means employees not designated as emergency employees are excused from duty without loss of pay or charge to leave. Employees designated as emergency employees are expected to report for work on time.)

To determine the amount of excused absence to grant employees who experience commuting delays, agencies should consider such factors as distance, availability, and mode of transportation, and the success of other employees in similar situations.

Workdays on which a federal activity is closed are nonworkdays for leave purposes. Because leave cannot be charged for non-workdays (5 U.S.C. 6302(a)), employees who are on leave approved before the closure also must be granted excused absence. This does not apply to employees on LWOP, on military leave, on suspension, or in a nonpay status on the workday before and after the closure. These employees are not entitled to excused absence and should remain in their current status.

An employee on an alternative work schedule (AWS) whose AWS day off is the same workday on which a federal activity is closed is not entitled to another AWS day off "in lieu of" the workday on which the federal activity was closed (Comptroller General opinion B-217080, June 3, 1985). Furthermore, there is no basis for an agency to grant an excused absence to such an employee on the AWS day off.

Individual employees affected by unusual levels of temperature to the extent that they are incapacitated for duty, or to the extent that continuance of duty adversely affects their health, may be granted annual or sick leave.

Agencies are advised to consider such matters as the physical requirements of the positions involved as well as the temperature of the work areas before excused absences may be granted.

Excused absences should be limited to extreme situations.

Emergency Dismissals or Closings (Wash., D.C. Area Only)—In those rare situations that require a late work arrival or early dismissal due to severe inclement weather or other types of emergency situations, OPM may authorize an "adjusted home departure" or "adjusted work dismissal." Under this approach, the time period an employee will be excused from work will be guided by the employee's normal departure times from home or work.

An adjusted home departure policy permits employees to leave their homes later than their normal time. For example, if OPM announces that employees should delay their normal departure time by two hours, those who normally leave for work at 7:00 a.m. would delay departure until 9:00 a.m. Non-emergency employees who arrive late will be excused without loss of pay or charge to leave.

An adjusted work dismissal policy permits employees to leave work early relative to their normal departure times. For example, a three-hour early dismissal authorized by OPM as a result of an approaching snowstorm would allow an employee who normally leaves at 5:00 p.m. to leave at 2:00 p.m.

Section 3—Evaluation and Advancement

Performance Appraisal Systems

Federal employees are subject to periodic appraisals of their job performance, under Performance Management Regulations issued by the Office of Personnel Management. These performance appraisal procedures can have an impact on a wide variety of personnel and employment decisions affecting federal workers. Under the performance management rules, agencies must establish performance appraisal systems that:

• provide for periodic appraisals of job performance;

• encourage employee participation in establishing performance standards; and

• use appraisal results as a basis for personnel actions affecting employees.

The performance appraisal systems set up and used by agencies must be designed to:

• establish performance standards that will permit accurate evaluations of job performance on the basis of objective criteria related to the job;

• communicate to each employee the performance standards and critical elements of the employee's position with respect to initial appraisal periods, and thereafter at the beginning of each following appraisal period;

• evaluate each employee on such standards during the appraisal period;

• recognize and reward employees whose performance so warrants;

• assist employees in improving unacceptable performance; and

• reassign, demote, or remove employees who continue to have less than acceptable performance, but only after such workers are given an opportunity to demonstrate acceptable performance. (An "acceptable level of performance" means "a level above unacceptable.")

The appraisal systems must be based on objective, job-related criteria and performance standards must be developed for each element of the job on which an employee is to be evaluated.

Performance standards are the expressed measure of the level of achievement established by management for duties and responsibilities of a position or group of positions. Performance standards may include, but are not limited to, elements such as quantity, quality, timeliness, and manner of performance. Agencies are encouraged to have employees participate in establishing their standards.

Managers and supervisors will rate subordinates on the elements of the job. Employees who perform at an unacceptable level in one or more of the critical elements will be given the opportunity to improve, with supervisory help. If adequate improvement does not occur, the agency may take action to remove or reduce the grade of the employee.

If an employee's most recent rating of record (formal summary rating) is below Fully Successful (level 3), the agency is required to deny the employee's within-grade increase.

Employees have the right to be consulted regarding the setting of performance standards and critical elements and unions have the right to negotiate procedures under which bargaining unit employees are consulted. However, the final determination of what job performance standards and critical elements will be set for a job is not a negotiable issue between unions and an agency, and management has the right to set the performance standards and critical elements as it sees fit. Of course, should removal or demotion result from application of employees' job performance standards, they would have regular appeal rights to the Merit Systems Protection Board or through their unions via a negotiated grievance procedure, if applicable.

Each department and agency sets up its own performance appraisal system based on OPM's general regulations.

When an employee fails to meet an acceptable level of performance on a critical element, the first steps an agency must take are corrective in nature. These could include counseling, remedial training, and more direct supervision. When employees fail to improve their performance with respect to one or more critical elements, and after having been given a reasonable time to demonstrate acceptable performance, an agency may take action to remove or reduce the grade of such workers.

Employees so affected are entitled to 30 days advance written notice that identifies the specific instances of unacceptable performance and the critical elements involved in each instance. The employee is also entitled to be represented by an attorney or other representative; a reasonable time to answer orally and in writing; and a written decision within 30 days after the expiration of the notice period. Agencies may extend the initial notice period as circumstances warrant.

At the point where the agency decides to take adverse action, employees have the right to appeal to the MSPB based on the nature of their appointment and the type of position occupied. Employees represented by unions that have negotiated grievance procedures in their contracts with management, may elect to file a grievance under the negotiated grievance procedure rather than appeal to MSPB, but not both.

OPM and the General Accounting Office (on a selected basis) must review performance evaluation systems to assess their compliance with the requirements outlined above.

Additional information is available online at OPM's Performance Management Clearinghouse at *http://apps.opm.gov/perform/clearing*.

Training and Professional Development

Training and professional development can be an essential element of a federal employee's career advancement. Agencies keep records of approved training in their training files, procurement records, and electronic personnel records. Agencies use their records for planning and evaluation purposes. You also should keep your own record of any significant programs, whether sponsored by your agency or taken on your own.

Agencies may:

• pay training and education expenses from appropriated funds or other available funds for training needed to support program functions;

• reimburse employees for all or part of the costs of training or education;

• share training and education costs with employees;

• pay travel expenses for employees assigned to training;

• adjust an employee's normal work schedule for educational purposes not related to official duties;

• use funds appropriated for travel expenses to pay for employees' expenses to attend meetings, if the meetings concern functions or activities for which the appropriation is made, or will contribute to improved conduct, supervision, or management of the functions or activities;

• allow employees to accept payment, or reimbursement, of travel, subsistence and other expenses incident to attending meetings from a nonprofit organization; and

• pay an employee's membership fee in a professional organization if the membership in the association is an incidental by-product of meeting attendance that the agency pays, or purchase an organizational membership in the association or society.

The Government Employees Training Act (Public Law 85-507, codified in Title 5, United States Code, Chapter 41), makes available to most federal agencies the authority to train employees, thereby recognizing that investments in workforce development are essential to achieving an agency's mission and performance goals by improving employee and organizational performance.

The law was reinforced in 1967 by Executive Order 11348, which states that it is the policy of the United States "to develop its employees through the establishment and operation of progressive and efficient training programs, thereby improving public service, increasing efficiency and economy, building and retaining a workforce of skilled and efficient employees, and installing and using the best modern practices and techniques in the conduct of the government's business."

Under the training law, department and agency heads are required to regularly assess the workforce's needs for skills essential to meet mission and performance requirements. The review is an ongoing assessment process that is an integral part of human resource planning. Its purpose is to help ensure that the expenditure of public funds to develop an organization's human resources is directly linked to: (a) fulfilling the organizational mission, (b) improving productivity, and (c) providing quality products and service to the public.

The Federal Workforce Restructuring Act of 1994 amended the Government Employees Training Act to expand the definition of training from that of directly related to the performance of "official duties" to any training that is "mission-related."

Public Law 106-58 prohibits use of appropriated funds for training that is offensive to federal employees and unnecessary in the execution of their official duties. This includes training associated with religious or quasi-religious and "new age" belief systems, training that induces high levels of stress unrelated to the employees' work environments, and training meant to change employees' personal values or lifestyle outside the workplace.

Workforce development needs may be met through an agency's own facilities, other government facilities such as interagency or shared training, or non-government facilities, whichever is found to be most effective. Agencies are required to open their training programs to employees of other agencies when the sharing of training would result in better training, improved service, and savings to the government. This includes agency sharing of technology-based learning programs.

Travel, per diem, and transportation are training expenses governed by 5 U.S.C. 4109(a)(2)(A) and (B). The provisions in law that pertain to paying all or some of the costs of tuition and other training expenses apply to paying travel expenses. This means that the agency decides which travel expenses it will pay for employees assigned to training.

Meeting Learning Needs—Employee's performance-based learning needs may be met by planned work experience, details, and developmental assignments, on-the-job-learning and supervised practice, training and education provided through agency facilities, other government facilities, and nongovernment facilities, coaching and mentoring and self-study.

Emphasis is placed on using the most economical means available to satisfy agency needs for performance improvement. Interagency training is used instead of internal training when this would result in better training, improved service, or savings to the government. Emerging technologies are used to deliver just-in-time learning and performance support.

Each agency is required by law to have a process in place for determining its performance improvement needs and for administering its human resource development program. A typical process might include the following:
• identifying the required or desired performance of the agency, organizational unit, occupational group, or individual employee;
• determining the difference between the required or desired performance and the actual or current performance;
• exploring the causes or reasons for the performance gap and determining if the required or desired level of performance should be attained through training or other methods, such as modifying systems and work procedures;
• evaluating information derived from the assessment of learning needs and using the findings to make decisions about human resource development investments;
• involving management and employees at all levels in the planning and implementing human resource development activities; and
• integrating performance-based individual and organizational learning with other human resource management functions and operating systems activities, as appropriate.

Human Resource Development Programs—Human resource development programs may be authorized to:
• orient employees to the federal service, their agencies and organizational assignments, and conditions of employment;
• guide new employees to effective performance during their probationary period;
• provide knowledge and skills to improve job performance;
• prepare employees with demonstrated potential for increased responsibility in meeting future staffing requirements;

• provide continuing professional and technical training to avoid knowledge/skill obsolescence (e.g., keeping the skills of scientists, doctors, engineers, lawyers, registered nurses, computer programmers, procurement specialists, plumbers, electricians, and clerical employees current);
• implement reorganizations, changing missions, and administration initiatives;
• develop the managerial workforce focusing on competencies identified as essential to effective performance at supervisory, managerial, and executive levels (e.g., communication, interpersonal skills, human resource management, technology management, financial management, planning and evaluation, and vision);
• provide education leading to an academic degree if necessary to assist in the recruitment or retention of employees in occupations in which there are existing or anticipated shortage of qualified personnel, especially in those areas requiring critical skills; and
• provide for the career transition, training, and/or retraining of employees displaced by downsizing and restructuring.

Training Related to Official Duties— Agencies are authorized to pay, or reimburse you for, all or a part of the necessary expenses of training related to official duties. This includes tuition, books, supplies, and travel. It also means that you can share with your agency costs of training that benefits both the agency and you. For example, the agency could pay half the cost of a college course, while you pay the other half. However, the agency may not pay for training that is unrelated to your official government duties.

Your agency also may approve a meeting or conference as a developmental activity if the content is pertinent to your official functions and activities and it is evident that you will derive developmental benefits by attending.

There are a wide variety of basic education, skills development, and career enhancement programs tailored to agency needs and resources. Some of these are adult basic education programs; the Veterans Readjustment Appointments Program; apprenticeship programs; administrative, technical, and professional career ladder programs; and career transition programs.

Agencies may provide training in basic job-related skills. They can also sponsor training courses in local schools under the adult basic education program. These courses may be given at government expense either during or after working hours.

Although training must be related to your official duties, your agency can prepare you for anticipated future assignments or to accomplish special agency initiatives. You can receive training leading to promotion if you were competitively selected for training under your agency's merit promotion program.

Your agency may pay for training that prepares you for an examination, if the training is relevant to improving your performance. Under Public Law 107-107, an agency may at its discretion pay for expenses for employees to obtain professional credentials, including expenses for professional accreditation, state-imposed and professional licenses, professional certification, and examinations to obtain such credentials.

Your supervisor may adjust your customary workweek to allow you to take courses not sponsored by the agency if additional costs to your agency will not be incurred, completion of the course will better equip you for work in the agency, and there will not be appreciable interruption of work.

Normally you are in full pay status while participating in agency or interagency training programs. However, training law prohibits paying overtime to Title 5 employees who are in training or while they are traveling to training. If salary payments continue during the training period, the annual and sick leave regulations apply. Normal workdays falling within academic recess periods should be charged to leave unless you devote such periods to study or research or unless you are returned to a work status.

If you feel you have been unjustly denied permission to attend training, you may use your agency's procedures if the matter cannot be resolved at the supervisory level and your agency has not set up a separate system for this purpose.

When you are assigned to training, your agency may require that you sign an agreement to continue employment in your agency for a period of time. If you do not complete the agreement, you may have to repay the agency for your training expenses.

Your supervisor should be able to provide you with the necessary guidance on training matters or be able to refer you to appropriate sources.

The Federal Executive Institute (FEI) and the Management Development Centers work to develop career leaders for the federal government. The facilities offer residential learning environments and are staffed with program directors, seminar leaders, and facilitators.

The goals of the management development centers are to create, share, and apply knowledge and skills to address the challenges faced by public sector organizations and develop the values and competencies that are the foundation of public service, transcending individual professions and missions. Trainees, primarily supervisors, managers, and executives, study at the centers for between several days to four weeks. The centers also offer customized programs either on-site or at agency locations, as well as consulting services for identifying and addressing organizational challenges.

Eastern Management Development Center
101 Lowe Drive
Shepherdstown, WV 25443-9601
Phone: 304-870-8000
Fax: 304-870-8001
Email: emdc@opm.gov

Western Management Development Center
Cherry Creek Place
3151 South Vaughn Way, Suite 300
Aurora, CO 80014-3513
Phone: 303-671-1010
Fax: 303-671-1018
Email: wmdc@opm.gov

The FEI serves as the government's development center for senior executives. FEI brings SES members and GS-15s together for courses that help executives develop broad corporate viewpoints, understand their constitutional roles, and enhance skills.

Trainees work individually, in teams, and as a group with FEI faculty. The FEI faculty comprises a wide range of professionals from academia and private consulting and training organizations, along with executives in residence—senior government leaders on special assignment at the Institute.

FEI's Leadership for a Democratic Society courses help participants build a healthier working culture by exchanging ideas on improving program performance and addressing areas of interagency cooperation and conflict with colleagues from other departments.

FEI's Center for Executive Leadership provides courses directed toward executive competencies development, with a special emphasis on team building and organizational growth, and generates ongoing opportunities for lifelong learning.

Federal Executive Institute
1301 Emmet Street
Charlottesville, VA 22903-4899
Voice: 434-980-6200
TDD: 434-980-6299
Fax: 434-979-1030
Email: fei@opm.gov

Course catalogs and other information are available online at *http://www.opm.gov*.

Government Online Learning Center— The GOLC is a government-wide e-training site designed to provide one-stop access to e-training. The site contains free courses ranging in topics from communication to project management, along with additional products and services, some free and some for a fee. The GOLC website is at *http://www.golearn. gov/*.

Meetings Related to Agency Functions or to Improve Conduct of Agency Activities—Training law provides an exception to the prohibition in 5 U.S.C. 5946(1) on using appropriated funds to pay employee expenses for attending professional meetings. Under 5 U.S.C. 4110 an agency may use funds appropriated for travel expenses to pay for employees' expenses to attend meetings if the meetings concern functions or activities for which the appropriation is made, or will contribute to improved conduct, supervision, or management of the functions or activities.

Memberships in Professional Organizations—Statute (5 U.S.C. 5946(1)) prohibits using appropriated funds to pay for individual employee memberships in professional associations and societies. However, association membership is often included in registration fees for a conference or meeting. If the agency pays the registration fees, the employee's membership in the association is an incidental by-product of meeting attendance. In addition, agencies may purchase an organizational membership in the association or society for a specific agency position

and the incumbent in that position may use that membership.

Reimbursement of Meeting Expenses— A provision of training law (5 U.S.C. 4111) allows agencies to establish procedures under which employees may accept payment, or reimbursement, of travel, subsistence and other expenses incident to attending meetings from a non-profit organization. Accepting meeting expenses must not compromise the integrity of the employee or represent a payment for services rendered to the non-profit organization prior to the meeting. Prior approval from a designated high level agency official is required, often following a consultation with, or review by, the designated agency ethics official.

Academic Degrees—In most circumstances, an agency may not pay for an employee's academic degree. However, to develop an employee's knowledge and skill, an agency may pay for academic courses related to an employee's official duties. If in accomplishing this training, an employee earns an academic degree, the degree is an incidental by-product of the training.

In addition, 5 CFR Part 410 permits agencies to authorize and pay for training leading to an academic degree when necessary to assist in the recruitment or retention of employees in shortage occupations, especially those with critical skills. This is an exception to a continuing statutory prohibition of training civilians for the sole purpose of obtaining a degree. The detailed documentation requirements that must be satisfied before approving training which will lead to a degree under this exception are contained in 5 CFR Part 410.

There is a distinction between the academic degree program exception under the law and the use of tuition assistance for one or more college courses directly related to the individual or organizational performance. The intent of tuition assistance is not to fund employee degrees but to have each request evaluated on a case-by-case basis. In some cases, college training may be the only source, or the most cost-effective source when compared to alternatives.

Training Unrelated to Official Duties— Agencies may adjust an employee's normal work schedule for educational purposes. This authority allows the employee to take courses not related to his or her official duties. A special tour of duty is permissible if the following conditions are all met:

- It will not appreciably interfere with work accomplishment.
- The agency incurs no additional personal services costs.
- Course completion will equip employee to more effectively work in the agency.
- The employee receives no premium pay while on the special tour of duty, even if premium pay would be otherwise payable.

Promotions

A promotion is a change to a higher grade and should not be confused with periodic "within-grade increases" or "quality step increases," which provide salary increases within the scheduled rates of the grade. Opportunities for advancement often occur when new positions are established because of reorganization, added program responsibilities or when an employee vacates a position. Competition among employees is generally required.

For promotion from one general schedule position to another in the competitive service, the employee must also meet time-in-grade requirements. Generally, for advancement to positions at GS-12 or above, the candidate must have completed a minimum of 52 weeks in a position no more than one grade lower than the position to be filled. For advancement to positions at GS-6 through GS-11, candidates must have completed a minimum of 52 weeks in a position no more than two grades lower when the position is classified at two-grade intervals; no more than one grade lower when the position is classified at one-grade intervals; or no more than one or two grades lower when the position is classified at one-grade intervals but has a mixed interval promotion pattern.

Advancement to positions up to GS-5 have no time restrictions if the position to be filled is no more than two grades above the lowest grade the employee had held within the preceding 52 weeks.

Each agency is required to have a Merit Promotion Plan conforming to OPM requirements and details how promotions are made in the agency. To be eligible for promotion, employees generally must meet the position's qualification requirements and, if applicable, time-in-grade requirements, the time-after-competitive-appointment restriction, and requirements for fully successful performance. Awards can be part of promotion consideration.

Promotions are made either competitively (in which case the candidate competes with others for the job), or noncompetitively. Examples of noncompetitve promotions are situations where employees are promoted because (a) they are in a career ladder that provides for successive promotion up to an established full performance level, or (b) their position is reclassified at a higher grade due to the addition of higher-level duties and responsibilities.

Merit Promotion—The purpose of the federal merit promotion policy is to ensure the selection of the best qualified candidates through a system of open competition based on relative ability, in accordance with the requirements of the Merit System Principles in Title 5, United States Code. Responsibility for the day-to-day operation of the merit promotion program rests primarily with individual agencies, but is subject to requirements prescribed by the Office of Personnel Management. These requirements apply only to the competitive civil service and basically describe when competition is required and how it is to be carried out.

The rules that government agencies must use in deciding whom to promote or hire for a vacant position are provided in Section 335.103 of Part 335 of Title 5, Code of Federal Regulations. These regulations require that each agency adopt and administer a program designed to ensure a systematic means of selecting for promotions according to merit. As part of the program, agencies must develop merit promotion plans that cover all positions to which promotions are made. Each agency is also responsible for ensuring that its merit promotion plans operate compatibly with each other. The plans must be in writing with copies available to all job candidates.

In addition to specifying the positions that are covered, agency merit promotion plans must establish areas of consideration that are sufficiently broad to ensure the availability of high-quality candidates, taking into account the nature and level of the positions to be filled. Additionally, under the Veterans

Employment Act of 1998, preference eligibles or veterans who have been separated under honorable conditions from the armed forces after three or more years of continuous active service may compete for vacancies under merit promotion procedures when an agency accepts applications from individuals outside of its own workforce.

Agency merit promotion plans also specify the methods that will be used to evaluate applicants for promotion as well as to select employees for training that leads to promotion. Moreover, these plans outline management's right to use selection procedures to select or not select from among any particular group of best-qualified candidates. This right includes the right to select from other appropriate sources, such as reemployment priority lists, reinstatements, transfers, handicapped applicants or applicants from outside the government who are certified as eligible by agency delegated examining units or OPM.

By regulation, in deciding which source or sources to use, agencies are responsible for determining which source is the most likely to provide candidates who will best help the agency meet its mission objectives and affirmative action goals. Areas of consideration are sometimes affected by negotiated agreements between agencies and employee unions. These agreements may place limits on the area of consideration that can be used to fill vacancies under certain conditions.

Most often, vacancies are filled in one of three ways. If a current employee is chosen to fill a vacancy and the selection involves an increase in the selectee's grade level, then the process is governed by the competitive merit promotion regulations. If the person selected is already at the grade level of the job being filled or was once at that grade level, that person can be noncompetitively selected for the job. If the selectee is not a federal employee, competitive procedures that are in most ways analogous to those used in the merit promotion process govern the selection process. In actual practice, a number of basic steps typically occur whenever an agency has a vacancy to fill.

Career Ladder Promotion—This type of promotion occurs when competitive hiring procedures are used to select someone to fill what is often a lower level trainee position with the purpose of developing the selectee to fill a higher level full-performance position. It is also a merit promotion in the sense that the individual must meet certain performance criteria to gain the promotion.

Position Reclassifications and Grade Change—Occasionally, federal employees may be given work assignments that change the level of difficulty, responsibility, or qualification requirements of their positions. When this change in duties is recognized as a continuing assignment, the affected employee's position description normally is rewritten and the position is analyzed and evaluated. If this process determines that the employee's new assigned duties are sufficiently different, the worker's position may be reclassified.

When a position is changed and placed in a higher grade in this way, the incumbent may be eligible for a noncompetitive promotion in accordance with the agency's merit promotion plan.

Executive Core Qualifications

The Executive Core Qualifications are required for entry to the Senior Executive Service and are used by many departments and agencies in selection, performance management, and leadership development for management and executive positions. Thus, developing skills in these areas can be crucial for individuals who aspire to the SES ranks. They are:

• Leading Change—The ability to develop and implement an organizational vision that integrates key national and program goals, priorities, values, and other factors. This includes the ability: to balance change and continuity; to continually strive to improve customer service and program performance within the basic government framework; to create a work environment that encourages creative thinking; and to maintain focus, intensity and persistence, even under adversity.

• Leading People—The ability to design and implement strategies that maximize employee potential and foster high ethical standards in meeting the organization's vision, mission, and goals.

• Results Driven—Accountability and continuous improvement. It includes the ability to make timely and effective decisions and produce results through strategic planning and the implementation and evaluation of programs and policies.

• Business Acumen—The ability to acquire and administer human, financial, material, and information resources in a manner that instills public trust and accomplishes the organization's mission, and the ability to use new technology to enhance decision making.

• Building Coalitions/Communications—

The ability to explain, advocate, and express facts and ideas in a convincing manner and to negotiate with individuals and groups internally and externally. It also involves the ability to develop an expansive professional network with other organizations and to identify the internal and external politics that impact the work of the organization.

Section 4—General Employment Policies

Security Clearances

Requirements that federal employees hold security clearances authorizing their access to classified information can affect individuals either before or after they are employed by the federal government. In some jobs in certain agencies, possession of a security clearance is a mandatory condition of employment. In other situations, a currently employed worker may need access to classified information only on a temporary or short-term basis.

Executive Order 12968 of August 2, 1995, "Access to Classified Information," created a government-wide policy on security clearances designed to replace differing rules in use by various agencies. The order set new standards and guidelines for determining who may have clearances and conducting background investigations. It also established a government-wide policy on employee appeals of denials or revocations of clearances and contained a policy statement on nondiscrimination in granting of clearances.

Key features of the order are:

Access to Classified Information— Persons shall not be granted access to classified information unless they have been determined to be eligible for access by agency heads or designated officials based upon a favorable adjudication of an appropriate investigation of their background, have a demonstrated need-to-know, and have signed an approved nondisclosure agreement.

All employees are subject to investigation by an appropriate government authority prior to being granted access to classified information and at any time during the period of access to ascertain whether they continue to meet the requirements for access.

All employees granted access to classified information shall be required as a condition of such access to provide to the employing agency written consent permitting access by an authorized investigative agency, for such time as access to classified information is maintained and for a period of three years thereafter, to relevant financial records, consumer reports and records maintained by commercial entities within the United States pertaining to any travel by the employee outside the United States. Information may be requested where there are reasonable grounds to believe, based on credible data, that the employee or former employee is, or may be, disclosing classified information in an unauthorized manner to a foreign power or agent of a foreign power; information the employing agency deems credible indicates the employee has incurred excessive indebtedness or has acquired a level of affluence that cannot be explained by other information; or circumstances indicate the employee had the capability and opportunity to disclose classified information that is known to have been lost or compromised.

Financial Disclosure—Agencies shall designate each employee, by position or category where possible, who has a regular need for access to classified information that, in the discretion of the agency head, would reveal: the identity of covert agents; technical or specialized national intelligence collection and processing systems; the details of any code, cipher, or cryptographic system or equipment; particularly sensitive special access programs; or especially sensitive nuclear weapons design information.

Those employees may not be granted access unless the employee: files with the head of the agency a financial disclosure report, including information with respect to the spouse and dependent children of the employee, as part of all background investigations or reinvestigations; is subject to annual financial disclosure requirements, if selected by the agency head; and files relevant information concerning foreign travel, as determined by the Security Policy Board.

Eligibility Determinations—Except in agencies where eligibility for access is a mandatory condition of employment, eligibility for access to classified information shall only be requested or granted based on a demonstrated, foreseeable need for access. Eligibility for access to classified information may be granted where there is a temporary need for access, such as one-time participation in a classified project of a given duration provided the appropriate investigative standards have been satisfied. Access to classified information shall be terminated when an employee no longer has a need for access.

No employee shall be deemed to be eligible for access to classified information merely by reason of federal service or contracting, licensee, certificate holder, or grantee status, or as a matter of right or privilege, or as a result of any particular title, rank, position, or affiliation.

The United States government does not discriminate on the basis of race, color, religion, sex, national origin, disability, or sexual orientation in granting access to classified information. In determining eligibility for access, agencies may investigate and consider any matter that relates to the determination of whether access is clearly consistent with the interests of national security. No inference concerning the investigative and adjudicative standards may be raised solely on the basis of the sexual orientation of the employee.

No negative inference concerning the investigative and adjudicative standards in this section may be raised solely on the basis of mental health counseling. Such counseling can be a positive factor in eligibility determinations. However, mental health counseling, where relevant to adjudication of access to classified information, may justify further inquiry to determine whether other access eligibility standards are satisfied.

Appeals Procedure for Denials or Revocations of Clearances—Applicants and employees who are determined to not meet the standards for access to classified information shall be provided with:

• as comprehensive and detailed a written explanation of the basis for that conclusion as the national security interests of the United States and other applicable law permit;

• any documents, records, and reports upon which a denial or revocation is based, within 30 days upon request and to the extent the documents would be provided if requested under the Freedom of Information Act (5 U.S.C. 552) or the Privacy Act (3 U.S.C. 552a);

• information of their right to be represented by counsel or other representative at their own expense; to request any documents, records, and reports as described above upon which a denial or revocation is based; and to request the entire investigative file, as permitted by the national security and other applicable law, which, if requested, shall be promptly provided to the employee prior to the time set for a written reply;

• a reasonable opportunity to reply in writing to, and to request a review of, the determination;

• written notice of and reasons for the results of the review, the identity of the deciding authority, and written notice of the right to appeal;

• an opportunity to appeal in writing to a high level panel, appointed by the agency head, comprised of at least three members, two of whom shall be selected from outside the security field. Decisions of the panel shall be in writing, and final except for a personal involvement by the agency head; and

• an opportunity to appear personally and to present relevant documents, materials, and information at some point in the process before an adjudicative or other authority, other than the investigating entity, as determined by the agency head. A written summary or recording of such appearance shall be made part of the applicant's or employee's security record, unless such appearance occurs in the presence of the appeals panel described above.

Determinations of Need for Access—A determination that an employee does not have, or no longer has, a need for access is discretionary and shall be conclusive.

Reinvestigation Requirements—Employees eligible for access to classified information shall be the subject of periodic reinvestigations and may also be re-investigated if, at any time, there is reason to believe that they may no longer meet the standards for access.

Employee Education and Assistance—The head of each agency shall establish a program for employees with access to classified information to educate them about individual responsibilities and to inform them about guidance and assistance available concerning issues that may affect their eligibility for access to classified information, including sources of assistance for employees who have questions or concerns about financial matters, mental health, or substance abuse.

Employee Responsibilities—Employees granted eligibility for access to classified information shall: protect classified information in their custody from unauthorized disclosure; report all contacts with persons, including foreign nationals, who seek in any way to obtain unauthorized access; report all violations of security regulations to the appropriate security officials; and comply with all other security requirements.

Employees are encouraged and expected to report any information that raises doubts about another employee's continued eligibility for access to classified information.

Sanctions—Employees shall be subject to appropriate sanctions if they knowingly and willfully grant eligibility for, or allow access to, classified information. Sanctions may include reprimand, suspension without pay, removal, and other actions in accordance with applicable law and agency regulations.

HIV/AIDS in the Workplace

In May 1995, the Office of Personnel Management issued policy guidelines to assist federal agencies in establishing effective programs and policies in dealing with Acquired Immune Deficiency Syndrome (AIDS) and Human Immunodeficiency Virus (HIV). In part, these guidelines were based on guidelines previously issued by the Public Health Service's Centers for Disease Control.

The guidelines state that employees with HIV/AIDS must be allowed to continue working as long as they are able to maintain acceptable performance and do not pose a safety or health threat to themselves or others in the workplace. If the HIV infection results in medical conditions that impair an employee's ability to perform safely and effectively, the agency should treat the employee the same way it would any other employee suffering from a serious illness.

Employees may not refuse to work with fellow employees or clients who are HIV-infected or diagnosed with AIDS and they may not engage in behavior that creates an uncomfortable or hostile environment for them. Co-workers who engage in this type of conduct may be subject to disciplinary action under the provisions of the Rehabilitation Act of 1973, as amended in 1992 to conform with the Americans with Disabilities Act of 1990. Supervisors are responsible for making sure that the agency's HIV/AIDS workplace policies are understood and complied with.

Nevertheless, the concerns of these employees should be taken seriously and should be addressed with appropriate information and counseling. In addition, employees, such as health care personnel, who may come into direct contact with the body fluids of persons having HIV/AIDS are to be provided with appropriate information and equipment to minimize the risks of such contacts.

Employees who object to attending HIV/AIDS training based on a personal religious belief or practice may request to be exempted. Title VII of the 1964 Civil Rights Act and Equal Employment Opportunity Commission regulations (29 CFR 1605.2) state that employers have an obligation to accommodate the religious practices of an employee unless the employer can demonstrate that accommodation would result in undue hardship on the conduct of its business.

Employees with HIV/AIDS may request sick leave, annual leave, or leave without pay to pursue medical care or to recuperate from the ill effects of their medical condition. The agency should make its determination on whether to grant leave the same way it would for other employees with medical conditions. In addition, employees with HIV/AIDS are entitled to a total of 12 administrative weeks of unpaid leave under the Family and Medical Leave Act of 1993. Under the Federal Employees Leave Sharing Amendments Act of 1993, they may also participate in leave bank programs run by their agency after their own leave has been exhausted.

Employees with HIV/AIDS can continue their coverage under the Federal Employees Health Benefits (FEHB) Program and/or the Federal Employees' Group Life Insurance (FEGLI) Program in the same manner as other employees. Although the law requires that employees in leave-without-pay status for 12 continuous months will have their FEHB and FEGLI coverage terminated, the employee does have the privilege of converting to private policies without having to undergo a medical examination.

Under the FEGLI Living Benefits Act of 1994, federal employees who are diagnosed as terminally ill with a life expectancy of nine months or less may elect to receive all or a portion of their FEGLI basic life insurance as a "living benefit." For more information, see the Life Insurance section.

Employees with HIV/AIDS may be eligible for disability retirement if their medical condition warrants and if they have the requisite years of federal service to qualify. OPM makes every effort to expedite applications where the employee's illness is in an advanced stage and is life threatening.

HIV/AIDS-related policies or programs that would affect the working conditions of bargaining unit employees are proper subjects for collective bargaining.

For further information regarding OPM's HIV/AIDS policy guidelines, contact the Office of Work/Life Programs, Health Services Team, Office of Personnel Management, 1900 E St., N.W., Rm. 7412, Washington, DC 20415, phone (202) 606-1269, FAX (202) 606-0967.

Administrative Grievances

In non-union settings, administrative grievance processes are generally available for matters not ordinarily appealable elsewhere, such as suspensions of under 14 days. Agencies have a great deal of latitude in the design of such programs, but in general they provide a route to present a complaint and receive fair consideration, which may involve hearings, fact-finding and other information gathering techniques.

Union-represented employees also may use administrative grievance processes if there is no negotiated grievance procedure or where such a procedure excludes the matter at issue.

Decisions on administrative grievances are final.

For information on negotiated grievances, see the Labor-Management Relations section in this chapter.

Drug Testing

The Drug-Free Federal Workplace Program was mandated in 1986 by Executive Order 12564. It required all agencies to develop a program including testing, education, and rehabilitative services through an Employee Assistance Program (EAP). The Mandatory Guidelines for Federal Workplace Drug Testing Programs were published in 1988 and revised in 1994. Every agency now has a plan in place that spells out the extent of the agency's efforts to make the workplace drug free.

There are six drug testing situations:
• random testing, including unannounced testing of employees in positions designated because of safety or security-sensitive issues;
• applicant testing, normally for positions requiring random testing;
• reasonable suspicion testing, when performance or conduct problems and unusual behavior suggest that drugs may be involved;
• post-accident testing, after a serious accident;
• follow-up testing, for those who have already tested positive or otherwise identified themselves as drug users; and,
• voluntary testing for those willing to be included in the random testing pool.

Employees who come forward and admit illegal drug use prior to being tested or otherwise are found to be using illegal drugs are not immediately disciplined. However, this "safe harbor," which is designed to provide such workers with an opportunity to undergo rehabilitation, also provides for mandatory follow-up testing.

Agencies must comply with the disciplinary instructions of E.O. 12564, which require the following actions in cases of confirmed positive drug tests:

• removal from sensitive positions;
• mandatory EAP referrals for assessment and rehabilitation;
• mandatory initiation of discipline on a first finding of illegal drug use; and
• mandatory initiation of removal from the federal service upon a second finding of illegal drug use.

All agencies follow essentially the same type of procedures and follow a model plan that was developed by the Department of Health and Human Services, the Office of Personnel Management, and the Department of Justice. Differences from one agency to another are found primarily in the types of positions tested. More extensive guidance on this program is available from OPM's Employee Health Services Branch at (202) 606-1269.

Child Care

Many federal agencies provide on-site child development centers; there are approximately 100 worksite child care centers in federal buildings controlled by the General Services Administration and many hundreds more child care programs operated by the Defense Department, which generally are open to enrollment of children of civilian employees along with those of uniformed military personnel.

The Office of Personnel Management publishes the Handbook of Child and Elder Care Resources, which provides employees, managers, and employee assistance counselors with information about organizations and agencies across the country that can help employees locate quality child (and elder care) services.

Public Law 106-58, Section 643, created authority for federal agencies to provide subsidies to their lower-income employees for certain child care expenses. The law and implementing regulations published in the Federal Register on March 14, 2000, allow agencies flexibility in determining eligibility and procedures under the program.

Executive agencies may use any appropriated funds, including revolving funds, ordinarily used for salaries for this purpose. Agencies determine the amount of funds they are willing to allocate for this purpose. Federal employees interested in participating in this program should contact the individual or organization named on their agency's announcements to get more information about any tuition assistance program operating there. If their child is not yet enrolled in child care, employees should identify a licensed and/or regulated child care provider of either center-based or family child care, and assure there is a space for their child before applying for tuition assistance.

The subsidy is not limited to enrollment in government centers but is open to all licensed and/or regulated child care. If employees already have their child(ren) enrolled in licensed and/or regulated child care (center-based or family child care), and they wish to receive tuition assistance, they should fill out the tuition assistance application forms and submit them to the person or organization named on the agency's form.

Employees may be required to apply for the tuition assistance subsidy on an annual basis. Employees must be prepared to provide copies of their recent pay stubs and latest IRS tax submissions. If a family receives local and/or state child care subsidies, they must indicate the source and the amount on their application.

Agencies can choose to administer the program themselves or they can enter into an agreement or contract with an organization that provides scholarship services. Regardless of who administers the program, the decision about which model to use for determining eligibility and the amount of the subsidy is the responsibility of the agency.

Each agency has the discretion to determine who qualifies. Agencies may choose a particular definition for one location and a different definition at another location. In general, agencies consider the total family income and that the amount of subsidy would be reduced by any current state and/or local subsidy the parents/guardians currently receive. Agencies also determine the amount of tuition assistance for each eligible employee. They may use a sliding scale, prescribe a sum based on a percentage of total family income or a percentage of child care costs, or use another model.

Child care subsidies are generally taxable as income to the employee who benefits from them. However, if an agency implements the child care subsidy program as a dependent care assistance program as described in section 129 of the Internal Revenue Code, amounts of up to either $2,500 or $5,000 may be excluded from gross income.

Elder Care

Unlike child care, federal agencies do not host on-site elder care facilities, nor do they offer subsidies for employees to pay the costs of such care. Many agencies do, however, have programs at the workplace to ease the stress that caregiving employees experience. In most cases these efforts are directed by the agency's work/life coordinator.

The scope and number of programs vary by agency. They typically include resource and referral programs, on-site seminars and other information sessions, employee assistance programs, and support groups. Some agencies provide briefings to supervisors and managers on the need to support those with elder care responsibilities, including guidance on allowable flexibilities.

OPM encourages agencies to use personnel flexibilities available to federal employees to ease the burden of elder care such as part-time employment, flexible work schedules, compressed work schedules, leave programs, and telework.

Further information on referral services is available online at http://www.opm.gov/wrkfam.

Payment of Expenses to Obtain Professional Credentials

Section 1112 of Public Law 107-107 amended Chapter 57 of Title 5, United States Code, by adding a new § 5757 that provides agencies with discretionary authority to use appropriated funds or funds otherwise available to the agency to pay for expenses for employees to obtain professional credentials, including expenses for professional accreditation, State-imposed and professional licenses, and professional certification, and examinations to obtain such credentials. Agencies may not use this authority on behalf of any employee occupying or seeking to qualify for appointment in any position that is excepted from the competitive service because of the confidential, policy-determining, policy-making, or policy-advocating character of the position.

Student Loan Repayments

Student loan repayment authority in 5 U.S.C. 5379 (5 CFR part 537) permits agencies to repay the student loans of federal employees to attract or keep highly qualified individuals. These payments (before taxes) can be up to $6,000 a year and $40,000 lifetime. To receive student loan repayment benefits, an employee must sign a service agreement to remain in the service of the agency for a period not less than three years.

This authority is used at the discretion of the agency. Those interested in participating in the program must contact the agency in which they work or wish to work for further details. Agencies choosing to use this flexibility must establish a plan describing how this incentive will be implemented within that agency. Agencies can use the incentive in conjunction with other recruitment and retention incentives.

Public Law 106-398 made several changes to the law, including removing the limitation of the incentive to professional, technical, or administrative personnel, removing the limitation of the incentive to employees covered under general schedule pay rates, and broadening the types of loans that qualify.

The repayment authority is limited to federally-insured student loans made by educational institutions or banks and other private lenders authorized by the Higher Education Act of 1965 and the Public Health Service Act. The Higher Education Act covers guaranteed student loan programs such as Stafford Loans, Supplemental Loans, Plus Loans, Federal Consolidation Loans, Defense Loans, National Direct Student Loans and Perkins Loans. Loans covered under the Public Health Service Act include Nursing Student Loan Program loans, Health Profession Student Loan Program loans, and Health Education Assistance Loan Program loans.

The level of academic degree for which a student loan was obtained is not a consideration in determining eligibility for the incentive, nor is whether a degree, diploma, or certificate was earned. The repayment authority does not exclude employees who have defaulted on their student loans from receiving this benefit. However, agencies may exclude them.

Part time employees and excepted service employees (except Schedule C), assuming they are otherwise eligible, can receive student loan repayment benefits. However, temporary employees and term employees with less than three years remaining on their appointments are not eligible.

Agencies are not required to make payments in one lump sum. They may if they choose, but doing so may result in a large tax liability for the recipient of the student loan repayment benefit.

Tax withholdings must be deducted or applied at the time any loan repayment is made. Tax withholdings may not be amortized or assessed later than when the loan repayment is made.

The three-year service requirement begins when the first payment is made by the agency to the holder of the loan. The three-year service agreement is established in statute and may not be pro-rated. Any employee who does not meet the service requirement is required to reimburse the government. However, agencies may waive recovery if they determine it to be against equity and good conscience or contrary to the public interest.

Public Transit Subsidies

As a general rule, the federal government cannot subsidize an employee's cost of commuting to or from work. Section 629(a), Title IV-General Provisions of Public Law 101-509, constitutes a specific legal exception to this general rule. It provides that federal agencies may participate in any program established by a state or local government that encourages employees to use public transportation. Such programs may involve the sale of discounted transit passes or other incentives that reduce the cost to the employee of using public transportation. The provisions of Section 629 were made permanent in 1993 (P.L. 103-172), which also encouraged agencies to provide nonmonetary incentives for alternatives to commuting, such as telecommuting.

The law establishing the transit subsidy program is permissive in nature by allowing but not mandating federal agencies' participation in state or local government programs (including, for example, those sponsored by transit districts, authorities, etc., created by a state or local government)

designed to encourage the use of public transportation. This may be as general as participating in state or local government sponsored events promoting the use of public transportation or as specific as providing reduced cost incentives to the employee.

Federal agencies that choose to offer reduced cost incentives to their employees may use appropriated funds, if otherwise available, to subsidize up to $100 of federal employees' public transportation costs per month. There is no specific appropriation to cover this expense, however. The cost must be absorbed from other appropriated funds.

Employer operated and employee operated vanpools as well as private or public transit operated vanpools may qualify.

Under tax law, such subsidies are tax-free to the employee so long as the value is $100 a month or less (with changes to the Consumer Price Index, the monthly limit may increase in increments of $5). Any amount, up to the monthly tax-free limits, by which an employee elects to reduce compensation to fund either transit or vanpool benefits, is not subject to the Federal Insurance Contributions Act (FICA; that is, Social Security), the Federal Unemployment Tax Act (FUTA), and federal income tax withholding. These amounts may also be exempt from city or state income taxes. For pre-tax program participants, since FICA would not be collected on the amount of compensation that is exchanged for the benefit, employees under the Federal Employees Retirement System may experience a minimal reduction in their Social Security benefits at retirement. The tax implications are the same whether the employee receives a direct cash payment or a transit pass worth a certain amount.

Federal agencies that elect to participate in the program are required to set up safeguards that preclude any improprieties in the use of federal funds and to limit program participation to eligible federal employees. Agencies are required to consult, as appropriate, with their respective labor organizations.

Under Executive Order 13150 of April 21, 2000, all federal employees in the national capital region are eligible to receive a benefit equal to their commuting costs, not to exceed $100 a month, in the form of passes or vouchers purchased by the agency with appropriated funds. As part of a three-year pilot program under the order, all employees nationwide of the Departments of Transportation and Energy and the Environmental Protection Agency may also receive these same benefits, purchased with agency appropriated funds.

Employees located outside the national capital region are permitted to reduce their pre-tax income by an amount equal to their transit or vanpool expenses up to a maximum of $65 per month. The agency accumulates these withholdings and purchases the vouchers, passes, or fare media on behalf of the employees, and then distributes this fare media directly to the participating employees.

Further information on transit subsidies is available online at www.fta.dot.gov/.

Parking Costs—Federal agencies may elect to reimburse employees for their qualified parking expenses at or near transit stations, park-and-ride lots, or vanpool staging areas, using employee pre-tax salary funds, up to a maximum cost of $175 per month. Appropriated funds may not be used for these purposes unless exceptional circumstances exist.

Parking costs are treated separately from transit costs, even if they are incurred in conjunction with an employee's use of public transit or vanpools. Agencies also may provide such parking at the agency's office for vanpools and carpools. Agencies that make cash reimbursements for parking must establish a bona fide reimbursement arrangement to establish that their employees have, in fact, incurred such expenses. Agency provision of single occupancy vehicle parking is not consistent with the intent of the executive order, but may be permitted under other authority.

Combined Federal Campaign

Authorized by 5 CFR 950, the Combined Federal Campaign (CFC) is the government's only annual fund-raising drive. Once a year, employees are given the opportunity to contribute to eligible charities of their choice. They may select from among hundreds of eligible national, international, and local charitable organizations. Eligibility for participating national and international groups is determined by

the Office of Personnel Management and the Office of CFC Operations. Local organization eligibility is determined by committees of federal employees in each CFC throughout the country.

Employees who wish to donate receive a pledge card on which they state the amount they wish to give and the charitable organization(s) participating in the campaign to which they wish their contributions to go. Most employees choose to participate through payroll deductions. If they do, CFC contributions are deducted each pay period and sent to the charity or charities of choice by the local campaign office.

Dates for the CFC drive are decided locally, but most take place between September 1 and December 15. Annual campaigns usually run for about six weeks. Pledges are deducted from the donor's paycheck starting in the first pay period of the following year. Participation by federal employees in the CFC is strictly voluntary. Federal regulations stipulate than managers cannot solicit form those they supervise. Neither may 100 percent participation goals be set nor may donations be required in a certain amount. Also contributor lists cannot be sold or leased, and lists of non-contributors cannot be compiled and used for any purpose.

Information about CFC policies is available at www.opm.gov/cfc. Questions may be addressed to the Office of Deputy Director, OPM, 1900 E St., N.W., Washington, DC 20415.

Telephone Use

Rules governing use of federal telephones are found in 41 CFR Part 101-35. The general policy is that all telephone calls placed over government-provided and commercial long distance systems that will be paid for or reimbursed by the government must be used to conduct official business only. Official business calls may include emergency calls and other calls the agency determines are necessary in the interest of the government.

To the maximum extent practicable, federal employees must place calls on government-provided long distance telephone systems and services instead of using commercial toll services. The following practices are prohibited and a willful violation may result in criminal, civil, or administrative action, including suspension or dismissal:

• Use of any government system or service, or any other telephone service, where the government pays the cost of the long distance call, for other than official business, except emergency calls and calls the agency determines are necessary in the interest of the government.

• Making an unauthorized long distance telephone call with the intent to later reimburse the government.

• Unauthorized use of telephone call detail data.

Telephone calls may be authorized when they: do not adversely affect the performance of official duties by the employee or the employee's organization; are of reasonable duration and frequency; and could not reasonably have been made at another time; or are provided for in a collective bargaining agreement.

Personal long distance calls that must be made during working hours may be made over the commercial long distance network if consistent with the criteria above and they are: charged to the employee's home phone number or other non-government number (third-number call); made to an 800 toll-free number; charged to the called party if a non-government number call); or charged to a personal telephone credit card.

If it is cost-effective to do so, agencies collect for any unauthorized calls: the value of the call, computed on the basis of commercial long distance rates rounded to the nearest dollar; and an additional amount rounded to the nearest dollar to cover administrative costs of determining that the call was unauthorized and processing the collection. Reimbursing the government for unauthorized calls does not exempt an employee from potential administrative, civil, or criminal action.

Individual agencies have their own policies on using telephone facilities and services. Many of these policies allow for a certain amount of local phone calling for routine personal purposes and for some government-paid long-distance calls for personal purposes, for example by employees on travel. The directives also include individual agency procedures for collection and reimbursement for unauthorized calls.

Freedom of Information Act

Under the Freedom of Information Act (5 U.S.C. Subsection 552) individuals may request from agencies documents that otherwise might not be disclosed or published by the U.S. government.

While some documents and information are protected from disclosure for national security, business confidentiality, personal privacy, or other reasons, millions of other reports, correspondence, and regulations may be released.

Agencies have an obligation, under this 1966 statute, to make a reasonable effort to search for and turn over copies of records they have decided are releasable. If an individual's request is denied, the agency must state the reason, and there are formal administrative appeal rights for such denials.

The law specifies only two requirements for requesting information: (1) requests must "reasonably describe" the document sought, and (2) they must be made in accordance with an agency's published FOIA procedures.

Agencies have up to 20 working days to answer an FOIA request and must "promptly" provide information deemed releasable. They may charge reasonable search fees, copying fees, and, in the case of commercial-use requests, fees for the review of records.

Requesters can apply for a waiver of fees under a "public interest" standard. Agencies have up to 20 working days to decide an appeal of a denial and to inform the individual that he or she may bring a court action to challenge it.

The Justice Department publishes two books, the *Freedom of Information Case List*, which contains an alphabetical listing of FOIA judicial decisions, and the *Freedom of Information Act Guide & Privacy Overview*, which contains the "Justice Department Guide to the FOIA," as well as an overview discussion of the provisions of the Privacy Act. Federal employees who do FOIA work for their agencies may obtain single copies free by calling (202) 514-5105. Other individuals may obtain copies by writing to the Superintendent of Documents, U.S. Government Printing Office, Washington, DC 20402, or by calling (202) 512-1800. Ask for the Freedom of Information Case List.

Privacy Act

The Privacy Act of 1974 gives federal employees several rights with regard to records that are part of what the Act calls a "system of records." A system of records under the Privacy Act means "a group of any records under the control of any agency from which information is retrieved by the name of the individual or by some. . . identifying particular assigned to the individual."

The Act allows federal employees to inspect and receive copies of their files, subject to various exemptions that an agency may claim if it has published regulations pursuant to the exemptions.

Employees can request correction or amendment of any Privacy Act-covered information about them that the employee feels is in error. If the agency does not correct the record, the employee can appeal the agency's denial to a person whose name and address should be provided in the denial letter. If the employees lose such an appeal, they have the right to file a brief statement giving reasons for disputing the record, which will accompany the record if it is sent somewhere else by the agency.

Agencies are also required to publish public notices of all systems of records maintained.

The law requires agencies to obtain an employee's written permission prior to disclosing to other persons or agencies information about the individual, unless such disclosures are specifically authorized under the Act. Information can be disclosed without an individual's consent, for example, under circumstances in which: disclosure would be required under the Freedom of Information Act; disclosure is to an employee or officer of the agency that maintains the record who has a need for the information to perform official duties; disclosure is pursuant to a "routine use" as published in the agency's public notice of the system of records containing the information; disclosure is to another agency for a specific civil or criminal law enforcement activity in response to the written request of the agency head; disclosure is pursuant to a showing of compelling circumstances affecting the health or safety of an individual; or disclosure is made pursuant to a court order.

The Privacy Act generally bars the release of personal information such as names and home addresses to unions. However, the information can be provided without the employee's consent if there are no other adequate alternative means of communicating with bargaining unit members.

Agencies are required by the Act to keep an accurate accounting of all disclosures of their employees' records to other agencies or persons, except when the disclosure was required by the Freedom of Information Act or when a disclosure was made within the agency on a need-to-know basis. With the exception of disclosures requested by law enforcement agencies, a list of all recipients of an employee's records must be given to the worker upon request.

Under the Privacy Act, federal employees may sue an agency for refusing to release or amend their records. Employees also may sue if they are adversely affected by an agency's failure to comply with any of the other provisions of the Act. Employees may be able to obtain money damages in certain circumstances if they can prove, among other things, that they have been adversely affected as a result of the agency's intentional and willful disregard of the Act's provisions. Court costs and attorney fees may be awarded.

The Act provides criminal penalties for the knowing and willful disclosure of records to those not entitled to receive them, willfully maintaining a record that is not in accordance with the Privacy Act, and knowing and willful attempt to gain access to an individual's records under false pretenses.

Currently employed workers who desire access to or amendment of their personnel records should contact their personnel office or their agency's designated Privacy Act officer if they need assistance in processing their request. Usually, the request will have to be made to the employing agency. Requests from former federal employees regarding their Official Personnel Folders should be directed to Workforce Information, Office of Personnel Management, 1900 E St., N.W., Washington, DC 20415.

When making a Privacy Act request, employees should be sure to provide enough identifying information to enable the agency to find their records, and assure the agency of their identity. Generally, this means that employees should provide their full name, date of birth, and Social Security number to facilitate this process.

Religious Freedom Guidelines

Employees' religious practices ranging from keeping a Bible or Koran on a desk to participating in prayer sessions during breaks and wearing religious medallions and symbols must be tolerated and protected by federal supervisors and other agency officials, under religious freedom guidelines announced by President Clinton on August 14, 1997. While the "Guidelines on Religious Exercise and Religious Expression in the Federal Workplace" do not create any new legal rights or substantive procedures, they do spell out what all federal agencies must do to protect government workers' rights to practice, pursue, or express their religious beliefs on the job.

The guidelines generally instruct the heads of all executive departments and agencies to permit and protect employees' exercise of religious freedom rights in the workplace. They include a number of specific examples designed to demonstrate how and what supervisors and managers must allow (or refrain from) in carrying out this general religious freedom mandate. However, while casting a protective mantle over most forms of workplace religious expression, the guidelines also warn that under the First Amendment "supervisors and employees must not engage in activities or expressions that a reasonable observer would interpret as government endorsement or denigration of religion or a particular religion."

Main points of the guidelines include:

• Federal employees' religious expression rights—The guidelines stress that a federal worker generally has the right to express personal religious convictions on the job "except where the employee's interest in the expression is outweighed by the government's interest in the efficient provision of public services or where the expression intrudes upon the legitimate rights of other employees or creates the appearance, to a reasonable observer, of an official endorsement of religion." These protections extend to employees' religious expressions in private work areas, religious discussions with co-workers, and display of religious mes-

sages or symbols on personal attire. Generally, these practices must be permitted as long as they do not interfere with workplace efficiency or convey any official government endorsement of religion. Similarly, even workplace "proselytizing"— i.e., employees' efforts to "spread the faith" or "persuade fellow employees of the correctness of their religious views"—is protected "to the same extent as those employees may engage in comparable speech not involving religion," according to the guidelines. However, workers must refrain from proselytizing, the guidelines add, "when a fellow employee asks that it stop or otherwise demonstrates that it is unwelcome."

• A ban on any employment-based religious discrimination by supervisors or managers—This prohibition covers discrimination in employment terms and conditions (i.e., hiring, firing, promotions, pay, etc.). It also extends to religious harassment that creates a hostile environment (e.g., an employee's repeated derogatory remarks to co-workers "about their faith or lack of faith"), as well as coercive actions that encourage or discourage employee participation in religious activities (e.g., supervisors may invite co-workers to family religious celebrations or ceremonies, but may not indicate they "expect to see" employees in church or at a religiously oriented meeting).

• Management's religious accommodation obligation—Under federal law, the guidelines stress, an agency must accommodate workers' religious beliefs and practices "unless such accommodation would impose an undue hardship on the conduct of the agency's operations." Additionally, an agency cannot deny a worker's religious accommodation request if it "regularly permits similar accommodations for non-religious purposes." This means that managers must make accommodations—like work schedule adjustments and tolerance of religious attire at work—as long as these accommodations do not result in a real (rather than "speculative") undue hardship that affects the agency's ability to conduct business or carry out its mission.

Association Rights

The 1996 Federal Employee Representation Improvement Act (P.L. 104-177) restored the right of employee associations to represent the views of their members before higher management without fear of prosecution. The law overrode a 1994 Department of Justice advisory opinion that compromised the ability of management associations to deal with top agency officials by holding that employees could be subject to criminal prosecution for expressing the views of an organization when that group may have a different interest than that of the agency on an issue affecting its members.

The Office of Personnel Management issued regulations on June 26, 1996, which, for the first time, required agencies to consult with employee associations. Previously such consultative relationships by agencies with management associations were discretionary. The regulations reinstituted and revised chapters 251 and 252 of the former Federal Personnel Manual (FPM), which OPM had eliminated on December 31, 1994.

The rules govern agency relations with managerial, supervisory, professional and other organizations that are not labor unions. The OPM rules:

• Require agencies to establish and maintain systems for intra-management communication and consultation with their supervisors and managers, and establish consultative relationships with associations whose membership is primarily composed of federal supervisory and/or managerial personnel.

• Authorize agencies to provide support services to organizations representing federal employees, and their members, when such action would benefit the agency's programs or be warranted as a service to employees. This includes space for meeting purposes, excused absence for training, internal agency mail and e-mail and other support.

• Reaffirm the eligibility of members of managerial and other federal employee organizations to make an allotment for dues withholding from their paychecks.

Agencies have broad discretion in implementing these requirements. They can, for example, retain the systems they had in place while FPM Chapter 251 was in effect, or they can modify aspects of those systems, such as membership requirements, in light of their experiences under the FPM program.

While agencies are required to commu-nicate and consult with associations of supervisors and managers, dealings with other non-labor organizations representing federal employees are discretionary, because, among other things, of the likelihood that members of such organizations will also be members of bargaining units for which labor organizations hold exclusive recognition regarding their conditions of employment.

Benefits Upon Death in Service

The following summarizes policies governing benefits for employees who die in service—that is, while actively employed. These benefits differ in some ways from those governing benefits upon the death of a retiree; for information about benefits after the death of a retiree, see Chapter 4. For further details on each of these benefits, see the pertinent material in each applicable section of this *Almanac*.

Unpaid Compensation—This includes the unpaid hours worked, and the unused hours of annual leave accrued as of the date of death. This amount is distributed in a lump sum payment to the employee's beneficiary or by order of precedence established by federal statute.

Health Insurance—If the employee was enrolled in self and family under the Federal Employees Health Benefits program at the date of death and there is a survivor annuity payable to a spouse and/or children, the survivor may continue health insurance coverage. Premiums will be deducted from the survivor annuity. If the employee was enrolled in self and family coverage at the date of death, but there is no survivor annuity payable, the enrollment terminates with the survivors having the right to convert to a private policy within 30 days. Exception: If covered under the Federal Employees Retirement System and the deceased federal employee has at least 18 months of service, the survivor may keep the health benefits coverage, but will be required to make direct premium payments to the Office of Personnel Management. If the employee was enrolled in self-only coverage at the date of death, the enrollment terminates at death with no right to enroll or convert for the survivors.

Life Insurance—Any Federal Employees

Group Life Insurance benefits payable will be paid in the order of precedence established by federal statute, unless the employee has a SF 2823, Beneficiary Form, on file. However, a valid court order filed with the employing agency after October 1998, but before the employee's death will take precedence over a written designation of beneficiary.

Long Term Care Insurance—If a spouse or other eligible family member is enrolled in the Federal Long-Term Care Insurance Program upon the employee's death, that coverage continues as long as the enrollee continues to pay the premiums. However, eligibility to first enroll would end unless the individual is otherwise eligible.

Thrift Savings Plan—All money in the employee's TSP account is payable in the order of precedence established by federal statute, unless the employee has a TSP-3, Beneficiary Election form on file.

Death Gratuity Payment—If an employee's death results from an injury sustained in the line of duty, a death gratuity payment may be paid to the personal representative of the employee. The amount payable is up to $10,000 minus the amount payable by Office of Workers' Compensation Programs (OWCP) under 5 U.S.C. 8331 (f), usually $200 and 8134 (a), usually $800.

Survivor Annuity, General—The surviving spouse and/or children may be eligible for a survivor annuity under the Civil Service Retirement System (CSRS) or Federal Employees Retirement System (FERS) dependent upon the employee's retirement system. If the spouse and/or children are not eligible for a survivor annuity or there is no surviving spouse or children, the retirement contributions will be paid to the employee's designated beneficiary or, in the absence of a designated beneficiary, in the order of precedence established under statute.

For survivor benefits to be payable upon death in service, the employee must have 18 months of creditable civilian service and be covered by the applicable retirement system at the date of death. The surviving spouse must have been married to the employee for at least nine months at the time of death or be a parent of a child of the marriage. The length of marriage requirement is deemed satisfied in cases involving accidental death. Children must be unmarried, under the age

of 18 (or 22 if attending school) or any age if disabled before age 18. If the employee has less than 18 months of civilian service or no eligible survivor annuitant at the date of death, a lump-sum payment of his/her retirement contributions is payable to the employee's designated beneficiary in the order of precedence established under federal statue.

The Office of Personnel Management authorizes payment and the Treasury Department prepares and mails the check or transfers the payment via direct deposit. OPM will send the survivor a statement indicating when to expect their first regular monthly payment shortly after OPM authorizes it. After that, the annuity payment is payable on the first business day of the month.

In addition to any spousal benefits payable, eligible children receive benefits in a set dollar amount established by law. For 2003, the children's rate when there is a surviving parent is $383 per month per eligible child or $1,150 per month divided by the number of eligible children (if four or more). If there is no surviving parent the rate is $459 per month per eligible child or $1,359 per month divided by the number of eligible children (if four or more). The amount payable is not reduced by any Social Security survivor benefits payable to the children. A child annuity is paid to his or her legal guardian if one has been appointed. If there is no legal guardian, OPM will make the payment (at its discretion) to the person who is responsible for the child.

Benefits may also be payable to a former spouse in accordance with a court order. The amount awarded by the court to a former spouse reduces the amount payable to any surviving spouse.

Annuity payments are taxable.

Survivor Annuity, CSRS—A spousal annuity is 55 percent of an annuity computed as if the employee had retired on a disability retirement as of the date of death. Spouses receive 55 percent of the higher of:

• an annuity computed under the general formula based on the deceased employee's high-3 average salary and length of service to date of death, including credit for unused sick leave; or

• a "guaranteed minimum" which is the lesser of 40 percent of the deceased employee's high-3 average salary; or the regular annuity obtained after increasing the deceased employee's length of service by the period of time between the date of death and the date he or she would have been age 60.

Survivor annuity, FERS—If the employee has at least 18 months of civilian service, the surviving spouse will receive:
• a lump sum ($24,330.97 in 2003, indexed each year), plus
• a lump sum of the higher of 50 percent

of annual basic pay at time of death or 50 percent of high-3 average salary, plus
• any Social Security benefits payable.

In addition, if the employee had more than 10 years of service and died while subject to FERS deductions, the surviving spouse will receive an annuity equal to 50 percent of the employee's basic annuity as of date of death. This earned annuity is computed in the same manner as if the employee retired, but without any reduction for age.

Section 5—Separation Before Retirement Eligibility

The following summarizes policies governing benefits for employees who separate before retirement eligibility. These benefits differ in some ways from benefits upon retirement (see Chapter 4). For further details on each of these benefits, including the rules on retirement eligibility, see the pertinent material in each applicable section of this *Almanac*.

Thrift Savings Plan

Upon separation before retirement eligibility, you have the same options for withdrawing your TSP account that apply to retirees. You may leave your money in TSP; transfer all or part of your TSP balance into an Individual Retirement Account (IRA) or other eligible retirement plan; receive your TSP account balance in a lump sum payment; receive your TSP account balance in equal monthly installments; purchase a life annuity through TSP if you have at least $3,500 in your account; or use a combination of those choices.

If you also have a uniformed services TSP account, you may transfer your civilian TSP account into the uniformed services account. Complete Form TSP-65 and submit to the TSP Service Office. Form TSP-65 may be obtained from the TSP web site at www.tsp.gov or from the TSP Service Office at (504) 255-6000.

If you separate before the year in which you reach age 55 and withdraw your account balance in a single payment or series of equal monthly payments, you will be subject to a 10 percent penalty as well as income tax on all amounts you receive before age 59 1/2. The penalty does not apply to money drawn out as an annuity or

to a series of monthly payments based on life expectancy.

If you separate during or after the year in which you reach age 55, you will only be subject to income tax and not the 10 percent penalty on the withdrawal regardless of how you receive the money.

If you have an outstanding TSP loan you must repay the loan in full, including interest, on the outstanding balance to the date of repayment. Delay in repaying your loan may affect the processing of your withdrawal. If you do not repay the loan within the required timeframe specified by TSP, a taxable distribution will be declared to the IRS in the amount of the unpaid loan balance and any unpaid interest. The distribution will be subject to income tax and a 10 percent penalty as described above.

Your personnel office will either provide you with the TSP Withdrawal Package or refer you to the TSP web site at *http://www.tsp.gov/forms*. The withdrawal package consists of the booklets "Withdrawing Your TSP Account After Leaving Federal Service" and "Thrift Savings Plan Annuities"; forms TSP-70, Withdrawal Request, TSP-70-T, Transfer Information, TSP-3, Designation of Beneficiary, TSP-16, Exception to Spousal Requirements, TSP-9, Change of Address for Separated Participants; and the notice "Important Tax Information About Payments From Your TSP Account."

Federal Employees Group Life Insurance

Your life insurance automatically terminates effective with your separation from federal employment. You then have a 31-day extension of coverage during which coverage will continue at no cost to you. During the 31-day period, you may apply for conversion to an individual policy.

You may convert all or any part of your Basic and Optional insurance to an individual policy (porting Option B coverage is no longer an available alternative). However, if you assigned your insurance, only your assignee may apply for conversion. Also, you may not convert the family option if you no longer have any eligible family members.

The purchase of a policy is a private business transaction between you and the insurance company. The cost is determined by the insurance company and is based on your age and class of risk.

Your personnel office will provide you with SF 2819 (Notice of Conversion Privilege). The SF 2819 represents notice of your loss of group life insurance coverage and the right to convert. In addition, you will need a form SF 2821 (Agency Certification of Insurance Status). After reading Part B, complete Part C and forward the SF 2819 to OFEGLI at P.O. Box 2627, Jersey City NJ 07303-2627. Be sure to attach the original (Part 1) SF 2821 to the SF 2819 when mailing to OFEGLI. However, if you have not received SF 2821 when you are ready to mail the SF 2819, do not delay—send it anyway while you await the SF 2821.

Your request for conversion must be postmarked within 31 days after the date of your separation or within 31 days of receipt of the SF 2819, whichever is later. If you do not receive SF 2819 on time or you are unable to request conversion on time due to reasons beyond your control, you can request a belated conversion by writing to OFEGLI at the above address. The request for belated conversion must be mailed within six months after the date you first became eligible to convert and must show that you were not notified of the loss of coverage and the right to convert and were not otherwise aware of it, or you weren't able to convert because of reasons beyond your control. If six months or more have passed since the date you first became eligible to convert, OFEGLI cannot accept a request for conversion.

If you do not wish to convert Option C coverage, your family members covered under Option C are eligible to convert their coverage to an individual policy. If this is the case, and you are separating from employment, you should ask your personnel office to provide each eligible family member an SF 2819. Family members may apply for conversion by sending the completed SF 2819 to OFEGLI at the above address.

Note: You cannot reinstate your life insurance coverage if you receive a deferred annuity.

Further information is available online at www.opm.gov/insure/life.

Federal Long-Term Care Insurance Program

Coverage under the FLTCIP is fully portable. As long as you continue paying premiums, your insurance coverage will continue. If you were paying premiums by payroll deduction and you leave the government, you'll have to make arrangements with the insurance carrier, LTC Partners, to start paying premiums directly or by automatic debit from your bank account. But you get to keep the insurance at the same premiums as if you never left the eligible group.

Certain relatives are qualified relatives as long as you are in one of the groups eligible to apply for this insurance. If they enrolled while you were eligible (whether you enrolled or not), they will keep the coverage even if you leave the eligible group. However, once you leave an eligible group, they can no longer apply for the insurance.

Federal Employees Health Benefits Program

Enrollment in the Federal Employees Health Benefits (FEHB) program terminates on the last day of the pay period during which you separate. You then have a 31-day free extension of coverage. During the 31-day period, you may apply to convert to a non-group contract or apply for temporary continuation of coverage (TCC).

Temporary Continuation of Coverage— When you separate from service, you may choose to continue FEHB coverage for a period of 18 months after your separation. TCC allows you to continue the same level of health benefits coverage enjoyed while employed. The TCC family enrollment covers the same family members as were covered under your plan while employed.

If you take advantage of the TCC option,

you must pay both the employee and the employer share of the health benefits premium plus an administrative charge of 2 percent of the premium. You can choose to enroll in the same plan you had at separation or any other plan, option, or type of enrollment for which you are eligible. (DoD employees should check with their personnel department concerning payment of premiums.)

TCC begins as soon as the 31-day free extension of coverage ends regardless of when you elect it. Your agency is required to notify you about your eligibility for temporary continuation of coverage within 60 days after you separate. You have 60 days after receiving the notice to enroll. If you enroll after the 31-day free extension expires, your enrollment will be retroactive to the expiration of the 31-day free extension and you will be billed for the retroactive coverage.

You are not entitled to TCC if your separation from service is involuntary due to gross misconduct. Also, cancellation of coverage prior to expiration at 18 months results in a loss of conversion privilege.

You may get additional information about TCC from the pamphlet RI 79-27, Temporary Continuation of Coverage (TCC) under the Federal Employees Health Benefits Program, which is available through your employing office.

Conversion—If you do not want to continue your health benefits coverage under the temporary continuation provision described above, you may convert to an individual (non-group) contract. The conversion contract is available only from the carrier of the plan you are enrolled in when you separate.

If you convert to a non-group contract, you will not be able to later apply for TCC; by the time the conversion process is completed, the time limit for applying for TCC will have passed. But if you continue your coverage under the temporary continuation provision, you will have another opportunity to convert to an individual contract at the end of the 18-month period.

To convert, you must write to your health plan within 31 days of the termination of your health insurance coverage and request information on converting to a non-group contract. The plan will provide you with an application for conversion, and

information on benefits and costs. Additional information on the conversion process may be found in Part B on the reverse side of Standard Form 2810 (Notice of Change in Health Benefits).

If you do convert, you must pay the entire cost of coverage and your benefits may be less than previous coverage. However, the carrier must offer you a non-group contract regardless of any health problems you or your family members may have.

When you separate, your employing office must terminate your enrollment by completing an SF 2810 and forwarding you a copy. The SF 2810 tells about the 31-day extension of coverage and how to convert to an individual (non-group) contract and gives information about TCC. Your agency will also give you a notice about your eligibility for the TCC described above (and information about how to enroll).

You cannot reinstate your health benefits coverage if you receive a deferred annuity.

Further information is available at www.opm.gov/insure/health.

Retirement—FERS

If you separate before retirement eligibility you have two basic options regarding your retirement, a refund or a deferred annuity.

Refund—You may apply for a refund of your retirement contributions if you have been separated from federal service for at least 31 days (or have occupied a position not covered by the Federal Employees Retirement System for at least 31 days). If you have more than one year of service, interest on the contributions will be part of the refund. The form to use is SF 3106, Application for Refund of Retirement Deductions.

Before you can receive a refund, generally you must notify your spouse and any former spouse that you have filed the application. Also, you may be barred from receiving a refund if the refund would end the court-ordered right of any spouse or former spouse to future benefits based on your service.

Refunded FERS contributions cannot be redeposited and the service covered by the refund cannot be re-credited.

If you elected to transfer to FERS and qualify to have a portion of your annuity computed under CSRS rules, and later separate from federal service, you may apply for a refund of your CSRS contributions only. (You may redeposit the CSRS contributions according to CSRS deposit rules.) By leaving your FERS contributions in the retirement fund, you will retain title to a FERS deferred annuity.

> Note: If you were covered by CSRS-Offset provisions (both CSRS and Social Security) when you transferred to FERS, your Offset service is now treated as FERS service. You cannot redeposit a refund of Offset service deductions that you receive after transferring to FERS. The service covered by that refund cannot be recredited.

> Note: A refund of all deductions voids any retirement options, including survivor benefits.

Deferred Annuity—If you have at least five years of creditable civilian service for which withholdings or deposits remain in the fund, and you are not eligible for an immediate retirement benefit, you will be eligible for a deferred annuity. You may receive a deferred annuity beginning on the first day of the month after you attain age 62. Alternatively, if you have at least 10 years of creditable service, you may elect to receive a deferred annuity as early as the first day of the month after you attain your Minimum Retirement Age (MRA).

If you are eligible for a deferred annuity beginning after you attain your MRA, your deferred annuity will be reduced by $\frac{5}{12}$ percent for each month (5 percent per year) by which the commencing date of annuity precedes your 62nd birthday, unless you: have at least 30 years of service; have 20 years of service and postpone the commencing date until you are age 60; or have at least 20 years of service as an air traffic controller, firefighter, law enforcement officer, or Member of Congress.

The form to use is RI 92-19, Application for Deferred or Postponed Retirement. Call (202) 606-0500 or write to: OPM, P.O. Box 45, Boyers, PA 10617-0045. Complete the form and mail it to OPM no sooner than two months before you turn age 62. The deferred annuity begins on your 62nd birthday.

The deferred annuity is based on the length of your service and your high-3 average salary. The basic annuity computation formula is 1 percent of your high-3 average

pay times years of creditable service. If you retire at age 62 or later with at least 20 years of service, a factor of 1.1 percent is used rather than 1 percent.

If you want to make a deposit for post-1956 military service so that you can receive credit for this service in the computation of your deferred annuity, you must pay the deposit to your employing agency before you separate from federal employment. OPM cannot accept your payment.

If you die before applying for a deferred annuity and you have less than 10 years of creditable service or no eligible survivor, any contributions remaining in the retirement fund are paid in a lump sum (with interest) to your designated beneficiary or person in the order of precedence set by law.

If you die before applying for a deferred annuity, your surviving spouse is entitled to a survivor annuity if:

• you have at least 10 years of creditable service for which withholdings or deposits remain in the fund (five years of which is creditable civilian service); and

• your spouse was married to you at the time of your separation from federal service.

• Your surviving spouse may elect to receive a lump-sum payment of your retirement contributions in lieu of the survivor annuity.

Retirement—CSRS

If you separate before retirement eligibility you have two basic options regarding your retirement, a refund or a deferred annuity.

Refund—You may apply for a refund of your retirement contributions if you have been separated from federal service for at least 31 days or have occupied a position not covered by the Civil Service Retirement System or Federal Employees Retirement System for at least 31 days. The form to use is SF2802, Application for Refund of Retirement Deductions.

If you take a refund of your retirement contributions at separation, you can redeposit the refund (with interest) only if you return to federal service under CSRS or FERS.

Before you can receive a refund, you generally must notify your spouse and any former spouse that you have filed the application. Also, you may be barred from receiving a refund if the refund would end the court-ordered right of any spouse or former spouse to future benefits based on your service.

Note: A refund of all deductions voids any retirement options, including survivor benefits, until the refund is re-deposited .

Deferred Annuity—If you have at least five years of creditable civilian service, do not receive a refund of all retirement contributions, and are not eligible for an immediate retirement benefit, you may be eligible for a deferred annuity at age 62. The form to use is Form 1496A, Application for Deferred Retirement. Call (202) 606-0500 or write to: OPM, P.O. Box 45, Boyers PA 16017-0045. Complete the form and mail it to OPM no sooner than two months before you turn age 62. The deferred annuity begins on your 62nd birthday.

The general formula for computing annuities can be expressed as a percentage of your "high-3" average salary. Your high-3 average salary is the highest three years of base pay or salary you earned in any consecutive three-year period (usually your last three years). The percentage is determined by a three-part formula based on your length of creditable service:

• 1.50 percent per year for the first five years (7.50 percent) plus
• 1.75 percent per year for the next five years (8.75 percent) plus
• 2.00 percent per year for service over 10 years.

If you want to make a deposit for post-1956 military service so that you can receive credit for this service in the computation of your deferred annuity, you must pay the deposit to your employing agency before you separate from federal employment. OPM cannot accept your payment.

Section 6—Labor-Management Relations

Title VII of the Civil Service Reform Act of 1978 (CSRA), established into law a system for federal employees to form, join, or assist any labor organization, or to refrain from any such activity, freely and without fear of penalty or reprisal. Once formed, these labor organizations exclusively represent the bargaining unit employees in all matters affecting their working conditions. This portion of the CSRA U.S. Code (Chapter 71 of Title 5 of the U.S. Code) is referred to as the Federal Service Labor-Management Relations Statute (the Statute.)

On an exclusive-recognition basis, labor organizations represent more than half of the non-postal federal work force. Negotiated agreements, which cover nine-tenths percent of the employees represented, increasingly determine personnel policies and practices.

Although most local unions are nationally affiliated, local officers and stewards are members of the installation's workforce and have been elected or appointed to office by the local union membership. Management is not involved in this selection process.

The Statute requires supervisors to deal exclusively with the certified labor union on establishing or modifying conditions of employment affecting bargaining unit employees. This means that supervisors and management officials cannot negotiate over personnel policies, practices, or working conditions directly with bargaining unit employees. Rather, these dealings must be solely with the union officials representing them. Failure to adhere to this requirement (known as bypassing the union) may result in an unfair labor practice with management's actions being reversed until the requirement to negotiate with the union, if requested, has been satisfied.

Key elements of the labor-management program are:

• Federal employees have the right to join or not to join any labor organization. Unions with exclusive recognition have the right and the obligation to represent all employees in an exclusive unit. Third-party procedures are provided for resolving labor-management disputes.

• An independent Federal Labor Relations Authority of three members who serve five-year terms, subject to removal only for cause, and a general counsel who investigates and prosecutes complaints of unfair labor practices. The FLRA generally is responsible for administering the federal government's labor relations program. As a result of the enactment of The Foreign Service Act of 1980 (Public Law 96-465 of October 17, 1980), there is within the Federal Labor Relations Authority a three member Foreign Service Labor Relations Board. The chairman of the

FLRA serves as the chairman of the FSLRB. The function of the board in the foreign service is similar to that performed by the FLRA in the civil service.

• The scope of matters subject to negotiated grievance and arbitration procedures includes such adverse actions as discharge, demotion, and long-term suspensions. The negotiated procedures do not cover prohibited political activities, retirement, life insurance or health insurance, suspension or removal for national security, examination, certification or appointment, position classification which does not result in loss of grade or pay or any matter the union and agency agree to exclude. Concerning matters covered by the negotiated grievance procedure with binding arbitration is the sole procedure available to bargaining unit employees—except that in adverse actions, unacceptable performance and EEO discrimination cases the employee may use either the negotiated procedure or the statutory appeals procedure (but not both).

• Departments and agencies such as OPM and GSA, which issue government-wide regulations, are required to consult over substantive changes in any condition of employment with labor organizations representing a substantial number of employees.

• The Act clarifies "management rights," reserving to agency officials the authority to make decisions and take actions which are not subject to the collective bargaining process, and excludes bargaining on federal pay and benefits or non-voluntary payments to unions by employees. In the management rights area, the Act: (1) prohibits agencies from bargaining on mission, budget, organization, number of employees or internal security; and (2) permits, but does not require, them to negotiate over the methods, means and technology of conducting agency operations. Management's right to select or non-select from a promotion certificate or to fill a position from any appropriate source (internally or externally) is specifically stated. The Act contains the basic rights of federal employees to form, join and assist labor organizations or to refrain from these activities. It also contains prohibitions against strikes and slowdowns, as well as picketing which interferes with government operations.

Other key features and provisions of the federal government's labor relations program include:

• A special expedited procedure for most negotiability disputes, i.e., to determine whether a particular matter falls within the obligation to bargain.

• FLRA decisions and orders are subject to court enforcement, including judicial review in unfair labor practice and negotiability cases.

• Authority to make an employee whole in an unjustified or unwarranted personnel action—including back pay plus attorney fees.

• Dues withholding—based on voluntary allotments by employees—is allowed at the exclusive union's request. Allotments are irrevocable for one year, and the withholding service is at no charge to the employee or labor organization. Dues withholding also is authorized for unions with 10 percent or more membership in appropriate bargaining units where there is no exclusive union.

• Official time for employees representing the union in negotiations during regular working hours (including attendance at impasse settlement proceedings), but the number of employees on official time shall not exceed the number of management officials representing the agency.

To assist in resolving negotiation impasses, the mediation services of the Federal Mediation and Conciliation Service are available, and unresolved negotiation impasses may be referred to the Federal Service Impasses Panel, an entity within the FLRA.

Supervisors and managers are excluded from coverage under the program. They cannot be represented in dealings with management by unions that represent rank-and-file employees. (They may be covered instead by agency systems for intra-management communication and consultation under Office of Personnel Management guidelines.)

Union Organizing

The Federal Service Labor-Management Relations Statute provides that an agency shall recognize a labor organization as the exclusive representative of employees in a bargaining unit, if that organization has been selected as the representative by a majority of the unit's employees who voted in a secret ballot election.

For a union to represent employees, it

must first file a petition with the Federal Labor Relations Authority. That petition must establish that at least 30 percent of the employees in the proposed unit wish to be represented by the union as evidenced by their signatures and that the unit is appropriate. To be appropriate, a unit must insure a clear and identifiable community of interest among unit employees, promote effective dealings with the agency, and promote the efficiency of agency operations

Employees already represented by a union may petition the FLRA to be represented by another union or to be unrepresented. A petition must be filed with signatures of at least 30 percent of the employees in the unit asserting that the exclusive representative is no longer the representative of a majority of unit employees. Provided at least one year has elapsed since a representation election was conducted, the FLRA will hold an election and representation (or lack thereof) will be determined by a majority of the ballots cast. A negotiated agreement between labor and management bars another union from seeking to represent the bargaining unit until shortly before the expiration of the existing negotiated agreement. At that time (not more than 105 or less than 60 days prior to the expiration of an agreement of three years or less), the FLRA will consider timely a petition filed by a rival union.

In addition to determining questions of representation, petitions may be filed to amend or clarify the description of a bargaining unit, and to consolidate two or more bargaining units. It is strongly recommended that activities file these later types of petition upon any organizational changes which impact on the bargaining unit's definition.

Bargaining Units

The bargaining unit is a group of employees with common interests who are represented by a labor union in their dealings with agency management.

Bargaining unit status (that is, whether the position is in or out of the unit) pertains solely to the employee's position in the agency—it does not take into consideration whether the employee is a dues paying union member. As such, these are two distinct groups. Bargaining unit members are employees whose positions are included in the defined

bargaining unit while union members are employees who pay dues to the labor organization. Bargaining unit employees may elect to join the local union and pay dues either through direct payment to the union or through automatic dues withholding, or they may decide not to join the union.

Once a union has been certified as the exclusive representative, though, it must represent all bargaining unit members equally, regardless of their union membership. As such, when the union and management negotiate a collective bargaining agreement, its terms and conditions cover all employees in the bargaining unit irrespective of their union membership.

There are, however, limited situations where the union can favor union members over non-members by offering certain services to only dues paying members. In these instances, though, the services are not related to the employee's conditions of employment. For example, a union can offer the services of a tax attorney to only dues paying union members.

The Federal Service Labor-Management Relations Statute specifically excludes certain positions from bargaining unit coverage. Individuals employed as supervisors, management officials and employees engaged in personnel work in other than a purely clerical capacity cannot be included in a bargaining unit. These individuals cannot be represented by unions and their conditions of employment can be unilaterally set by management.

Negotiations

The Federal Service Labor-Management Relations Statute outlines the broad topics that must be negotiated with a labor union, those that are reserved to management and those that may be negotiated at management's election (see Management Rights, below). The obligation to negotiate requires discussion and consideration of the other side's proposals—it does not compel either side to agree to a proposal or to make a concession.

Negotiations occur at various times and for different reasons. The most prominent is the formal negotiations for a collective bargaining agreement. These are full scope negotiations. This process results in a written collective bargaining agreement signed by both management and the union establishing various personnel policies, practices, and conditions of employment. The agreement is normally distributed to everyone at the installation affected by its application. The document may be referred to as the contract, the collective bargaining agreement or the labor-management negotiated agreement. It is normally subject to renegotiations every three years but is frequently automatically renewed (rolled over) from year to year.

At times, negotiations arise as a result of management proposed changes to bargaining unit employees' conditions of employment (e.g., an agency reorganization, the introduction of new equipment, changes in regulations of outside authorities, etc.), which are not addressed in the parties' negotiated agreement or where there is no current agreement. In these cases, when an agency decides to make changes to conditions of employment during the life of an agreement—sometimes called midterm bargaining—or when there is no agreement, two types of negotiations may result:

• negotiations on the decision itself (substance bargaining); and/or

• negotiations on the effects of the proposed change—normally referred to as impact and implementation bargaining.

Management Rights

Management rights is a term which defines those areas over which management exercises exclusive decision-making authority. These rights are spelled out in section 7106 of the Federal Service Labor-Management Relations Statute. There are two categories of management rights, "mandatory" or reserved rights, and "permissive" rights.

Rights reserved to management under Section 7106(a)(1) governing general management practices include the authority to determine the agency's mission, budget, organization, number of employees, and internal security practices. Reserved rights under Section 7106(a)(2) governing employment practices include the authority to: hire, assign, direct, lay off, retain, suspend, remove, reduce in grade or pay, or take other disciplinary action against employees, assign work, make determinations with regard to contracting out, deter-

mine the personnel by which agency functions will be performed, make selections from among properly ranked and certified candidates for promotion or any other appropriate source; and take whatever action may be necessary to carry out the agency mission during emergencies.

Permissive rights under Section 7106(b)(1) are those rights that management may bargain, but is not statutorily required to do so. These include the numbers, types, and grades of employee's or positions assigned to any organizational subdivision, work project, or tour of duty and the technology, methods, and means of performing work. (Note: Clinton administration orders to require agencies to bargain over permissive rights—Executive Orders 12871, 12983 and 13156—were overturned by a Bush administration order, Executive Order 13203 of February 17, 2001.)

Even with respect to nonnegotiable "mandatory" management rights, management must bargain, upon request, over the procedures it will use in exercising these rights and on appropriate arrangements for employees adversely affected by the exercise of such rights. For example, in a reduction-in-force, the decision to RIF is a management right, but how that RIF is conducted and outplacement or other assistance for displaced employees are negotiable issues.

When there is a question whether a proposal is outside the duty to bargain because it involves a management right or is subject to bargaining as a condition of employment, the matter may be raised as a negotiability appeal to the Federal Labor Relations Authority. Negotiability decisions of the FLRA can be challenged in federal court.

A union may propose measures whose purpose is to alleviate the adverse impact on unit employees of a management action. If, however, the union's proposal seriously interferes with the exercise of a management right, the FLRA will apply the "excessive interference" test. That test provides that a union proposal whose purpose is to ameliorate the adverse affects of a management decision is negotiable unless it impinges upon a management right to an excessive degree.

Even where a proposal would violate management rights, management is encouraged to discuss these proposals with the union and attempt to resolve the union's concerns while preserving management's rights.

Employees' Rights

Employees have the right to form, join or assist a union or to refrain from doing so. Employees are free to exercise this right without fear of penalty or reprisal and shall be protected in exercising this right.

Employees have the right to:
• act as a union representative, and in that capacity, to present union views to agency management, the Congress or other authorities; and
• negotiate over conditions of employment through their chosen representative.

While typically an employee has no control over whether he or she is in a bargaining unit, it is the employee's decision whether to be a union member, and if a union member, how actively engaged. Additionally, management does not have a say in which bargaining unit employee serves as a union official.

Union Rights

Representational Rights—Several provisions of the Federal Service Labor-Management Relations Statute address the opportunities unions have in representing the bargaining unit employees' interests. For example, the union is able to:
• negotiate with management in good faith concerning conditions of employment for bargaining unit members;
• obtain data normally maintained by management that are reasonably available and necessary to the union for full and proper discussion, understanding, and negotiation of subjects within the scope of collective bargaining;
• present its views to heads of agencies and other officials of the executive branch of the government, the Congress, or other appropriate authorities;
• have employees representing the union on official time when negotiating agreements with management; and
• be represented at certain discussions management may have with bargaining unit employees.

Formal Discussions—Management has an obligation to invite the union to attend any formal discussion between one or more representatives of the agency and one or more employees in the unit or their representatives concerning any grievance or any personnel policy or practices or other general condition of employment.

For a meeting to be considered a formal discussion, it must include:
• one or more representatives of the agency (e.g., supervisor(s), management official(s), personnelist(s), or attorney(s)); and
• one or more employees in the bargaining unit or their representative(s).

A meeting does not become a formal discussion unless the subject concerns an individual's grievance or general conditions of employment.

A discussion between management and a grievant relating to a grievance is a formal discussion. The union must be invited to attend even if the employee is representing him or herself in the negotiated grievance proceeding.

Discussions with bargaining unit members about general conditions of employment or personnel policies and practices. Normal shop talk is not a formal discussion.

If the meeting meets the definition of a formal discussion, the supervisor must invite the union to attend. Having a shop steward who works in the office at the meeting in his or her role as an employee does not meet this obligation. Rather, the supervisor must invite the union to the meeting with the union being free to designate whom it wants to act as its representative.

Finally, the union is allowed to participate in these meetings by raising questions/comments/concerns, but it cannot disrupt them.

Examination of Employees ('Weingarten' Meetings)—The union is entitled to represent bargaining unit employees' at meetings in connection with an investigation. This provision is often referred to as employees' "Weingarten" rights, based on a Supreme Court decision. The Federal Service Labor-Management Relations Statute establishes three conditions for a "Weingarten" meeting:
• one or more agency representatives are examining (questioning) a bargaining unit employee in connection with an investigation;
• the employee reasonably believes that the examination may result in disciplinary

action against the employee; and
• the employee requests union representation.

Once all three conditions have been met, supervisors may generally not continue the examination without allowing the employee his or her requested representation. Specifically, the supervisor's options under these circumstances are:
• grant the request and notify the union that a meeting to examine a bargaining unit employee is going to take place and that the employee has requested union representation. If the union attends the meeting, it must be allowed to make relevant comments but cannot disrupt the meeting nor can it answer the questions posed to the employee;
• discontinue the interview and rely on evidence already available or information obtained from other sources; or
• offer the employee a clear choice to continue the interview without representation, or have no interview.

"Weingarten" rights are not applicable when management issues a disciplinary action since management is not asking any questions. Additionally, the "Weingarten" right does not come into play when engaging in performance counseling as this does not concern disciplinary matters but, rather, performance issues.

Finally, management, usually the installation labor relations specialist, is responsible for annually notifying employees of their "Weingarten" rights.

Negotiated Grievance Procedures

The Federal Service Labor-Management Relations Statute defines a negotiated grievance as any complaint by any employee concerning any matter relating to the employment of the employee, by any labor organization concerning any matter relating to the employment of any employee or by any employee labor organization, or agency concerning:
• the effect or interpretation, or a claim of breach, of a collective bargaining agreement; or
• any claimed violation, misinterpretation or misapplication of any law, rule, or regulation affecting conditions of employment.

Every negotiated agreement contains a negotiated grievance procedure. This is the exclusive procedure for resolving bargaining unit employees' grievances that fall within its coverage; the union is the exclusive representative under this procedure. Note: Negotiated grievance procedures do not apply to employees serving probationary periods.

The negotiated grievance system is a full-scope procedure. That is, it covers all matters falling within the definition that are not specifically excluded by the Statute. (For example, the negotiated grievance system cannot include grievances concerning retirement, life insurance or health insurance, or the classification of any position which does not result in the reduction in grade or pay of an employee.) Management and the union can, through collective bargaining, exclude any additional subject from coverage of the negotiated procedure. For example, if the parties agree that grievances over performance appraisals are to be excluded from the negotiated procedure, these types of grievances would then have to be raised under the administrative grievance procedure or some alternative system developed by the parties.

Employees filing grievances under the negotiated procedure can elect to have the union represent them or they can represent themselves. They cannot hire their own representatives unless the union states that the private representative is acting for the union. Even if the employee represents him or herself, the union must be invited to attend any grievance meetings as these are considered formal discussions.

The negotiated grievance procedure usually begins with the grievant or his or her representative presenting an informal grievance to the first-line supervisor. If not resolved, the grievant can raise the matter up through the chain of command. (Each negotiated agreement details the administrative steps of the grievance process.) Once the final decision has been issued, the matter can be raised to final and binding arbitration by the union—an employee cannot raise a matter to arbitration.

A recent development concerning negotiated grievances is the advent of alternative dispute resolution (ADR) procedures. Under an ADR program, alternate means are introduced to resolve employee complaints before a grievance reaches the final stage. Some ADR processes include mediation, peer-panel reviews, facilitation, etc. The goal of ADR is to provide an informal, local method for amicably resolving disputes at the lowest possible level without the need for invoking third party arbitration. For more information on the Federal Labor Relations Authority's role in grievance procedures and for further information on ADR, see Chapter 9.

Unfair Labor Practices

An unfair labor practice (ULP) is normally a violation of the Federal Service Labor-Management Relations Statute. Anyone can file a ULP charge—an individual, an employee, the union or management. The respondent to the charges, though, will always be either management or the union. The vast majority of ULP charges are filed by the union against management. The reason for this is that management is usually the party which takes the actions.

Unfair labor practice charges are filed with the General Counsel of the Federal Labor Relations Authority. The General Counsel investigates the charge to determine if there is sufficient evidence to warrant issuing a complaint. If a complaint is issued, a hearing is set and the parties go before an adminstrative law judge (ALJ) with the General Counsel prosecuting. The administrative law judge will issue a decision either finding that a ULP was committed or dismissing the complaint. If either party is dissatisfied with the ALJ's decision, the case can be appealed to the Authority.

If the agency is found to have committed a ULP, various remedies can be assigned. The most common is a posting stating that the agency committed a ULP and won't do it again. Another remedy issued by the Authority is a reversal of the management action that caused the ULP. For example, if management realigns an office without giving the union an opportunity to bargain, a ULP remedy may be to reverse the realignment and to require management to bargain with the union. This is called a status quo ante remedy. Tied into the status quo ante remedy can be a make whole order with back pay. If the realignment discussed above resulted in employees losing pay or allowances (e.g. differentials or consistent overtime opportu-

nities), the ULP remedy may include back pay for these employees.

Management Unfair Labor Practices— Section 7116(a) of the Federal Service Labor-Management Relations Statute (see Title 5 of the US Code) provides that it is an unfair labor practice for management to:

• interfere with, restrain, or coerce employees in the exercise by the employee of any right under the Statute;

• encourage or discourage membership in any labor organization by discrimination in connection with hiring, tenure, promotion, or other conditions of employment;

• sponsor, control or otherwise assist any labor organization, other than to furnish, upon request, customary, and routine services and facilities if the services and facilities are also furnished on an impartial basis to other labor organizations having equivalent status;

• discipline or otherwise discriminate against an employee because the employee has filed a grievance, complaint, affidavit, or petition or has given any information or testimony;

• refuse to consult or negotiate in good faith with a labor organization;

• fail or refuse to cooperate in impasse procedures and impasse decisions;

• enforce any rule or regulation (other than a rule or regulation addressing prohibited personnel practices) which is in conflict with any applicable collective bargaining agreement if the agreement was in effect before the date the rule or regulations was prescribed; or

otherwise fail or refuse to comply with any provision of the Statute.

Union Unfair Labor Practices—Section 7116(b) of the Federal Service Labor-Management Relations Statute defines those actions which, if taken by the union, would result in a ULP. The statute provides that it is an unfair labor practice for the union to:

• interfere with, restrain, or coerce any employee in the exercise by the employee of any right under the Statute;

• cause or attempt to cause an agency to discriminate against any employee in the exercise by the employee of any right;

• coerce, discipline, fine, or attempt to coerce a member of the labor organization as punishment, reprisal, or for the purpose of hindering or impeding the member's work performance or productivity as an employee or the discharge of the members duties as an employee;

• discriminate against an employee with regard to the terms of conditions of membership in the labor organization on the basis of race, color, creed, national origin, sex, age, preferential or nonpreferential civil service status, political affiliation, marital status, or handicapping condition;

• refuse to consult or negotiate in good faith with a labor organization;

• fail or refuse to cooperate in impasse procedures and impasse decisions;

• to call, or participate in, a strike, work stoppage, or slowdown, or picketing of an agency in a labor-management dispute if such picketing interferes with an agency's operations, or

• otherwise fail or refuse to comply with any provision of the Statute.

Official Time

Official time is the time granted to an employee by the agency to perform representational functions on behalf of the union. Official time is granted without charge to leave or loss of pay and is authorized only when the employee would otherwise be in a duty status. Official time is considered hours of work.

Official time must be granted to employees representing a labor organization when engaged in collective bargaining, to include attendance at impasse proceedings. The number of employees for whom official time is authorized may not exceed the number of individuals designated as representing the agency in the negotiations. (Although the union can bargain for additional union negotiators to be on official time.)

Official time cannot be granted for internal union business.

The Federal Labor Relations Authority can authorize official time for employees representing the union in any phase of proceedings before the Authority. This would include unfair labor practice proceedings, bargaining unit representation proceedings, etc.

Official time for representing bargaining unit employees on matters covered by the Statute may be granted in any amount the agency and the union involved agree to be reasonable, necessary and in the public interest. The amount and use of official time for representational purposes is fully negotiable. The amount of official time authorized to union representatives at the installation is detailed in the parties' negotiated agreement or is set through past practice.

Strikes

Individuals who participate in a strike against the government of the United States or the government of the District of Columbia may not accept or hold a position in the government of the United States (5 USC 7311). Such individuals are also not considered employees within the meaning of the Act, 5 USC 7103(a)(2)(B)(v).

It is an unfair labor practice for a labor organization to "call, or participate in, a strike, work stoppage, or slowdown, or picketing of an agency in a labor-management dispute if such picketing interferes with an agency's operations" or "to condone any activity described (above) by failing to take action to prevent or stop such activity," (5 USC 7116(b)(7)(A) and (B)). Further, the Act by definition excludes labor organizations that engage in such activity from coverage and thus from acting as the exclusive representative of employees, (5 USC 7103(a)(4) (D)).

The FLRA is given the power when it finds a labor organization that has either by omission or commission willfully and intentionally violated section 7116(b)(7) of the Act to "revoke the exclusive recognition status of the labor organization . . ." or "take any other appropriate disciplinary action," (5 USC 7120(f)).

A strike by employees against the government of the United States or the government of the District of Columbia also constitutes a criminal violation (18 USC 1918). Any person found guilty of violating this section of the law is subject to a fine of not more than $1,000 or imprisonment of not more than a year and a day, or both.

Labor-Management Partnerships

Executive Order 13203 of February 17, 2001 revoked Clinton administration Executive Orders 12871, 12983 and 13156, which were designed to foster a partnership arrangement between federal unions and management and which established the National Partnership Council, made up of top agency officials and presidents of federal unions, to oversee and promote partnership.

The 2001 order dissolved the Council and ordered the Office of Personnel Management and heads of federal agencies to rescind any orders, rules, guidelines or other policies implementing the partnership program, "to the extent consistent with law" and with any collective bargaining agreements in effect at the time.

Later OPM guidance stated that the 2001 order "does not prescribe any particular approach to labor-management rela-

tions" and that it gave agencies "discretion to adopt a labor relations strategy best suited to their own needs." Such strategies can include partnership arrangements, although the prior mandate to use them no longer exists. OPM said, however, that agencies are "strongly encouraged to establish cooperative labor-management relationships."

The order also had the effect of revoking Clinton administration initiatives to require agencies to bargain on subjects that are negotiable at an individual agency's discretion under federal labor law (see above).

Section 7—Alternative Personnel Practices

Overview

While there always have been exceptions to the civil service rules and procedures, the exceptions recently have been growing in number and scope, especially because federal agencies, managers, and individual employees have been expressing increased frustration about the government's policies on hiring, evaluating, promoting, rewarding, and compensating employees under the government's general rules, which may not always apply well to specialized situations.

Alternative personnel systems fall into several categories. The best known is the demonstration project. However, many agencies, or parts of them, have received alternative personnel authority through other legislation apart from demonstration project authority. These include changes in basic policies regarding position classification, compensation, performance evaluations, reduction-in-force protections, and other rules and procedures.

From time to time, pressures raised by the public, by private-sector companies doing business with agencies, and by other interested parties have spurred legislative changes in the way certain agencies are structured and in how they conduct themselves. The two most recent examples of this involve the Federal Aviation Administration and the Internal Revenue Service. In both cases, personnel and organizational reforms at the agencies have been viewed as potential test cases, not only for what might happen with other agencies that encounter difficulties functioning under standard personnel

rules, but also as a precedent for broader civil service reforms.

Meanwhile, some agencies and quasi-agencies have been outside the structure of Title 5 of the U.S. Code, the body of law generally governing federal employment programs, for many years. Their experiences are being examined as possible models for creating further exceptions from Title 5 for other agencies.

In addition to such formalized exceptions to the rule are the numerous flexibilities that have grown up over the years—especially so within the last decade—to give agencies more discretion in staffing, work arrangements, compensation, classification, performance management, and dispute resolution. A parallel development has been the deregulation and delegation of federal personnel management.

Further, performance-based organizations with alternative personnel systems have been established at the Patent and Trademark Office, an agency of the Commerce Department, in the student financial assistance program of the Education Department, and in certain air traffic functions of the Federal Aviation Administration.

While certain areas have been roped off from reform initiatives, at least for now, the past decade has shown that virtually everything else is subject to change. With continuing interest in further change arising from within agencies, as well as from OPM and on Capitol Hill, the evolution of the federal personnel system is continuing.

Government-Wide Personnel Flexibilities

Largely in reaction to complaints that government-wide personnel rules created recruiting and retention problems and did not always mesh well with agency missions, numerous special authorities have been authorized in recent years giving individual agencies—and even individual hiring officials, managers and supervisors—far greater discretion over personnel decisions on a localized basis than was true in the past. However, some of these authorities have existed for many years and have been widely applied across the government. These flexibilities include:

Hiring—Agencies have the authority to: conduct competitive examining for all positions (except administrative law judges); use commercial recruiting firms and nonprofit employment services to recruit for vacancies; waive the 40 hours per week limitation on basic pay to one position and recruit current federal employees for second jobs when "required services cannot be readily obtained otherwise" and "under emergency conditions relating to health, safety, protection of life or property, or national emergency;" allow a detail within a Department of its employees for up to 120 days, plus extensions in 120-day increments (intra-agency details in increments of 120 days are allowed when approved by the head of the Department); use commercial temporary help services for brief periods (120 days, with extension of additional 120 days) for short-term situations; use temporary appointments for short term needs that are not expected to last longer than one year. Veterans Readjustment Appointments give veterans appointments up through the GS-11 or equivalent grade level, and the streamlined student employment program for meeting future workforce needs; use term appointments for one to four years when the need for the employee's services is not permanent; employ experts or consultants for temporary or intermittent employment; and give a noncompetitive temporary appointment of more than 60 days or a term appointment to any veteran retired from active military service with a disability rating of 30 percent or more or rated by the Department of Veterans Affairs (VA) within the preceding year as having a compensable service-connected disability of 30 percent or more.

Alternative Staffing Options—Agencies have the authority to: use the Federal Career Intern Program to recruit and attract exceptional individuals into a variety of occupations; allow eligible veterans to apply for positions announced under merit promotion procedures when the agency is recruiting from outside its own workforce; use the Presidential Management Intern Program to attract outstanding graduate students (masters and doctoral-level) from a wide variety of academic disciplines; appoint veterans in the excepted service under the Veterans Readjustment Appointment, under which agencies can appoint an eligible veteran up through the GS-11 or equivalent grade level without competition; and appoint graduate and undergraduate students in the excepted service under the Student Educational Employment Program, which provides special authorities under which agencies can appoint students who are enrolled or have been accepted for enrollment in at least a part-time schedule at an accredited institution.

Compensation—Agencies have considerable discretionary authority to provide additional direct compensation in certain circumstances to support their recruitment, relocation, and retention efforts. Some of these are at the agency's sole discretion while others require approval by the Office of Management and Budget and/or the Office of Personnel Management. See Pay Flexibilities in Chapter 1 for details.

Lateral and Upward Movement—Agencies may determine the knowledge, skills, and abilities and define the specialized experience required to perform each job. They may use training agreements under which employees may receive accelerated training or on-the-job experience to gain new skills more rapidly. Agencies may design merit promotion plans. Agencies also may establish career ladders that allow noncompetitive promotion based on performance and acquisition of appropriate knowledge and skills.

Student Loan Repayment—Using this authority, agencies may repay federally insured student loans as a recruitment or retention incentive for candidates or current employees. The program implements 5 U.S.C. 5379, which authorizes agencies to set up their own loan repayment programs to attract or retain highly qualified employees. Individuals interested in student loan repayment opportunities must contact agencies directly.

Hours of Work and Scheduling Flexibilities—Agencies have the discretionary authority to determine the hours of work for their employees to help agencies meet organizational goals and employees balance personal needs. Agencies may establish: full-time, part-time, intermittent, and seasonal work schedules; hours of work for employees, including traditional day shifts, night and weekend duty, rotating shifts, and "first-40" schedules; paid and unpaid breaks in the workday; alternative work schedules to replace traditional schedules (i.e., eight hours per day/40 hours per week, with fixed starting and stopping times); adjusted work schedules for religious observances for employees whose personal religious beliefs require abstaining from work at certain times of the workday or workweek; and the use of job sharing arrangements.

Telecommuting—Telecommuting allows employees to work at home or at another approved location away from the regular office. A telecenter is a multi-agency facility that provides a geographically convenient office setting as an alternative to the employee's main office. A telecenter can also serve as an administrative support center for employees working at home.

Leave Flexibilities—Under expanded sick leave policies, employees may use up to 12 weeks of paid sick leave each year to care for a family member with a serious health condition. In addition, an employee may use limited amounts of sick leave each year to care for a family member who is incapacitated by illness or injury, accompany family members to routine health care appointments, arrange for or attend the funeral of a family member, and for absences related to adopting a child. Leave sharing programs allow an employee who has a personal or family medical emergency and who has exhausted his or her own leave to receive donated annual leave from other employees through the voluntary leave transfer or leave bank programs.

Federal agencies can support employees' commitment to community service by ensuring that all employees are aware of the various flexibilities available to them to participate in volunteer activities. Agencies may permit employees to make maximum use of existing flexibilities such as alternative work schedules, annual leave, leave without pay, credit hours under flexible work schedules, compensatory time off, and excused absence (administrative leave), where appropriate, to perform community service.

Classification—Although there is a single statutory classification system for general schedule employees (as well as for prevailing rate system employees), various administrative flexibilities are available for use in responding to organizational changes and workload shifts. Agencies may: use generic or job family standards for General Schedule positions that use a broader approach to job evaluation by consolidating an entire family of work into one position classification standard, with one set of job family grading criteria; redesign the duties of positions by eliminating a higher level skill so that more candidates may qualify for the position or by adding higher level skills and restructuring the position so that they may offer higher starting salaries; redesign jobs to make them more appealing to candidates by adding desirable duties and eliminating undesirable duties; structure new and vacant positions to allow entry at lower levels from the current workforce thereby encouraging high performance and rewarding excellence with greater opportunity; use team leaders rather than supervisors when practical to facilitate work; and plan positions so that there are logical entrance levels, and logical career patterns for progression to more skilled and higher-grade positions as employees gain skill and ability to assume greater responsibility.

Performance Management—Within a broad framework, the performance management regulations give agencies the freedom to choose the design of their appraisal systems and programs. An agency can establish an overarching performance appraisal system that allows its components to design a variety of appraisal programs, or requires one program for all its employees, or is some variation of these options.

Appraisal programs can use as few as two and as many as five summary rating levels in official ratings of record.

OPM's regulations require that each employee's performance plan include at least one critical element, which, by definition, measures individual performance and establishes individual accountability. However, appraisal programs can also include non-critical and additional performance elements, which can measure individual, group, or organizational performance.

Agencies can take group and organizational performance into account when assigning ratings of record above Unacceptable.

Incentive Awards and Recognition— Agencies have authority to design extensive awards programs that include cash awards, honorary awards, informal recognition awards, and time-off awards. Agencies can give these awards to employees to recognize employee and group performance, and can design incentive programs with awards granted because an individual or a group achieved pre-established goals. OPM award regulations allow: referral bonuses to provide incentives or recognition to employees who bring new talent into the agency; rating-based cash awards of up to 10 percent of salary, or up to 20 percent for exceptional performance; individual or group cash awards in recognition of accomplishments that contribute to the efficiency, economy, or other improvement of government operations of up to $10,000 without external approval, up to $25,000 with OPM approval, and in excess of $25,000 with Presidential approval; quality step increases to employees who have received the highest rating of record available under the applicable performance appraisal program; honorary and informal recognition programs that use recognition items as awards to recognize individual and group performance; and time off from duty without charge to leave or loss of pay as an award to individuals or groups of employees. For details, see Chapter 1.

Title 5 Exemptions

One way the government-wide trend toward flexibility has manifested itself is in the number of agencies exempted fully or partially from the requirements of Title 5, which governs federal personnel rules in general. Agencies such as the Tennessee Valley Authority, the Veterans Health Administration (i.e., many of its medical-related positions, which account for the majority of the agency's work force), and the Federal Reserve Board have been outside Title 5 for decades. The U.S. Postal Service constitutes the majority of the Title 5-exempt work force.

The scope of Title 5 exemptions includes government corporations, independent establishments, executive branch agencies with legislative approval to create alternative personnel systems, and other legal entities. Some of these are quasi-governmental entities because they have some type of corporate or other self-funding aspects, while others are in security or other highly specialized fields. Examples include the Central Intelligence Agency, the National Security Agency, "Sallie Mae," the Metropolitan Washington Airport Authority, the Peace Corps, the Office of Federal Housing Enterprise Oversight, the Federal Deposit Insurance Corporation, and non-appropriated fund entities of the Defense Department. Legislative agencies such as the Library of Congress and General Accounting Office also have Title 5 exemptions.

The scope of Title 5 coverage actually is more like a continuum, with totally Title 5-covered agencies on the one end, totally non-Title 5 on the other, and many gradations in between. For example, organizations such as the TVA and USPS have extensive exemptions from Title 5, while other organizations, such as the Nuclear Regulatory Commission and the Office of Federal Housing Enterprise Oversight, are only partially exempt. Such agencies may be exempt only for classification and compensation purposes, but must adhere to all other provisions of Title 5, such as staffing, performance management, and adverse action rules.

In addition, there are some organizations where only certain classes or portions of employees are exempt from Title 5, while the remainder of the organization is covered.

Examples include the Department of State, where only foreign-service employees are outside of Title 5, and the Smithsonian Institution, where approximately one-third of the work force is funded and operates under a trust fund, with the remainder covered under the Title 5 system.

While some agencies are formally exempt

from certain provisions of Title 5, they may follow them as a matter of policy nevertheless. For example, many exempt agencies are not covered by the merit system principles, but still employ them, or similar merit-based organizational values, such as equity, fairness, and open competition, in their personnel systems. And they typically provide for some form of rating and ranking, classification and compensation systems based on rank or position, and formal due process procedures that mirror Title 5 in many ways. However, this does not mean that they necessarily interpret and implement Title 5's merit system principles or merit processes the same way as covered agencies.

Similarly, all these organizations are covered by the civil rights laws and, in many cases, by collective bargaining agreements similar to those in effect at other agencies. The USPS, for example, is a highly unionized environment in which the unions play a stronger role than they do at other agencies.

Demonstration Projects

Demonstration projects, sometimes called "Chapter 47" projects for the chapter of Title 5 authorizing them, may run for no more than five years, with some extension permitted, and may involve no more than 5,000 employees. There may be no more than 10 active demonstration projects at one time. Since the 1978 Civil Service Reform Act created the authority, nine demonstration projects have been authorized, with two currently under way and the others now made permanent or deemed completed.

In addition to the two current demonstration projects under Chapter 47, several other demonstration projects are operating under separate legislation. These include the FBI and certain units of the Treasury Department testing alternative hiring, classification, and compensation systems for certain scientific employees, and a Bureau of Indian Affairs test of alternative personnel practices at certain universities it operates.

In a demonstration project, an agency obtains authorization from OPM to be exempt from Title 5's regulations and to propose, develop, test, and evaluate changes in its own human resources management system. Examples of allowable changes in these projects include:

• qualification requirements, recruitment,

and appointment to positions;
• classification and compensation;
• assignment, reassignment, or promotions;
• disciplinary actions;
• providing incentives;
• establishing hours of work;
• involving employees and labor organizations in personnel decisions; and
• reducing overall agency staff and grade levels.

No waivers are permitted in areas of employee leave, employee benefits, equal employment opportunity, political activity, merit system principles, or prohibited personnel practices. Consultation and negotiation with affected employees and unions are required.

Many demonstration projects have studied ideas that later worked their way into government-wide policy, such as enhanced recruiting and retention payments, and greater flexibility in hiring. Other ideas studied include the concept of "broadbanding"—i.e., replacing traditional grade and step schedules with broad pay bands in which agencies have greater flexibility in setting employee pay rates. Broadbanding removes the pay barriers between GS grades that are placed in the same band, which can allow high-performing employees to earn higher salaries than they would under the current system. For example, banding of grades GS-7 and GS-8 allows employees who would have reached the top of the GS-7 grade to have access to the GS-8 pay range.

Another common theme of demonstration projects is linking performance evaluations more closely to promotions, merit-based pay increases, and downsizing protections. Also common are tests of alternative employee evaluation methods, including specific requirements for achievements related to overall agency goals.

However, some ideas tested in demonstration projects have been less successful or were addressed to a specific need without the potential for wider application.

The ongoing demonstration projects currently operating under Chapter 47 and their key features are:

Department of Defense Acquisition Work Force—This is the first demonstration project to cover an occupational workforce rather than an organizational entity. All the military services participate, with some 5,000 employees in numerous facilities nationwide affected. While operating under Chapter 47 rules for other purposes, because of separate legislation the test is not subject to the 5,000-employee limit, and thus it eventually could involve some 50,000 employees. Key features include: hiring based on scholastic achievement in a field of study specified for an occupation with a positive education requirement, with veterans' preference continuing to apply but the "rule of three" eliminated; occupations with similar characteristics grouped together into three career paths with broadbands; and a contribution-based compensation and appraisal system.

Department of Commerce—This project involves about 2,600 employees of six Commerce sub-agencies at two dozen sites and builds on certain elements of the former demonstration project, now made permanent, at Commerce's National Institute of Standards and Technology. Key features include: pay-for-performance in a broadbanding framework, supervisory performance pay and pay differentials, extended probationary periods for research scientists, delegated examining authority, supplemental hiring tools such as flexible entry salaries, more flexible promotion pay increases, and a two-level rating system (eligible or unsatisfactory).

Defense Department Research Laboratory Projects

Separate from the "Chapter 47" demonstration project authority is authority for the Defense Department to conduct similar types of tests at its research laboratories. These projects mirror in many ways the tests under Chapter 47, including OPM guidance and review. However, the DoD laboratory projects are exempt from two of Chapter 47's restrictions, the time limit and the cap on the number of affected employees. And unlike Chapter 47 projects, those demonstrations could be made permanent without the need for further legislation.

Typical features of these projects include broadbanding, a pay-for-performance management system, special hiring and appointment authorities, employee development emphasis, and revised reduction-in-force procedures. Current projects are:

Air Force Research Laboratory—This project involves about 2,800 scientific and engineering employees at 20 locations.

Army Aviation Research, Development and Engineering Center—This project involves about 800 employees in five locations.

Army Engineer Research and Development Center—This project involves about 1,400 employees at Vicksburg, Miss., and 16 other locations.

Army Missile Research, Development and Engineering Center—This project involves about 2,000 employees at 12 sites, primarily at Redstone Arsenal, Ala.

Army Research Laboratory—This project involves about 2,600 employees at Adelphi and Aberdeen Proving Ground, Md, and 39 other locations.

Naval Sea Systems Command Warfare Centers—This project is the largest of the DoD laboratory projects. It provides an umbrella structure within which each of the seven Centers' divisions can frame its own operating procedures within the project plan specifications. It involves about 24,000 laboratory employees, excluding senior executives and wage grade employees, at 14 major sites and numerous smaller sites.

Army Medical Research and Materiel Command—This project involves about 1,200 employees at Fort Detrick, Md., and 17 other sites.

Naval Research Laboratory—This project involves about 3,000 employees in Washington, D.C., and six other locations.

Permanent Demonstration Projects

Three of the tested demonstration projects have now been made permanent, most notably the "China Lake" project that represented the first extensive test of broadbanding. The three are:

The Navy Demonstration Project—Commonly known as "China Lake," this was the first personnel demonstration project under Chapter 47 and put the word "broadbanding" in the federal personnel vocabulary. The project draws its commonly used name from the location of one of the Navy facilities where it was tested, the Naval Air Warfare Center, Weapons Division at China Lake, Calif. It involved more than 12,000 employees, including scientists, engineers, technicians, administrative, technical specialists and clerical staff there and at the Naval Command, Control and Ocean Surveillance Center in San Diego. It began in 1980 and was made permanent in 1994.

Key features include: a broadbanding system that employs five career paths or occupational groupings; a "rank-in-person system that allows employees moving from one position to another in the same pay band to retain their "rank" or pay; a performance-based compensation system that allows employees who exceed performance expectations to get incentive pay increases substantially exceeding government-wide pay increases, while those who fully meet expectations get at least the government-wide increases; performance evaluation procedures that call for employees to get an annual performance plan, containing specific details about what is expected during the performance year; and RIF retention procedures that base employee rankings within each competitive level primarily on performance, and allows for retention of outstanding performers at all levels, with secondary factors consisting of such elements as tenure, veterans' preference, and length of service.

National Institute of Standards and Technology—This authority involves about 3,100 employees, including scientists, engineers, technicians, clerks, and administrative staff at Gaithersburg, Md., and Boulder, Colo. The project began in 1988, was extended several times, and was made permanent in 1997.

Key features include: broadbanding; pay for performance for all white-collar employees; supervisory pay differentials; recruitment and retention bonuses; expanded hiring authority and flexibility in setting starting salaries; expanded hiring authorities for professional and support occupations; agency-based hiring for the administrative and technical occupations; and flexible probationary periods.

Department of Agriculture—This program for new hires involves more than 200 sites of the Forest Service and Agricultural Research Service. This was the first demonstration project testing a comprehensive simplification of the hiring system for both white- and blue-collar federal employees. The project began in 1990 and was made permanent in 1998.

Key features include: decentralized determination of shortage categories; streamlined examining process using quality groupings in place of numerical ratings and "rule of three;" recruitment incentives, including bonuses and relocation expenses; and extended probationary periods for research scientists.

Other Major Alternative Personnel Authorities

A law (P.L 107-296). enacted in 2002 creating a Department of Homeland Security (DHS) contains several provisions exempting that department from standard civil service rules. Two other significant recent legislative changes creating alternative personnel systems focused on the Federal Aviation Administration under P.L. 104-50 of 1996 and the Internal Revenue Service under P.L. 105-206 of 1998.

DHS—The enabling legislation for DHS requires that the agency operate a "flexible" and "contemporary" personnel system to be crafted by the DHS secretary in conjunction with the Office of Personnel Management. This system could include alternative practices in areas such as pay setting, performance evaluation, hiring, job classification, and discipline. However, basic employee protections in areas such as merit principles, veterans preference and anti-discrimination law remain unchanged.

The law also specifies that any changes in personnel policies are to be written in collaboration with employee representatives, who are to receive 30 days of notice and an opportunity to review and make recommendations on any proposal. The department is to give those recommendations "full and fair consideration." Regarding any recommendations the department does not accept, it must notify Congress regarding those parts and meet and confer for at least 30 calendar days with employee representatives in order to attempt to reach agreement.

At the department's option, or at the request of the majority of employee representatives who have made recommendations, the Federal Mediation and Conciliation Service may be brought in. However, if the department determines that further consultation and mediation is unlikely to produce agreement, it may implement its plans at its discretion.

The law further specifies that any alternative appeals procedures the department may create must provide fair treatment and the protections of due process.

Regarding union rights, the law generally requires that any bargaining units existing before creation of the department continue to be recognized unless the mission and responsibilities of the agency or subdivision materially change and most of the employees have as their primary duty intelligence, counterintelligence or investigative work directly related to terrorism investigation.

The President may revoke union representation by issuing a determination that continued representation would have a "substantial adverse impact on the ability of the department to protect homeland security." Any such action would have to be delayed until at least 10 days after Congress is notified of the President's intent.

FAA—Among other things, Section 347 of the 1996 legislative change freed FAA from many standard government procedures, including many federal personnel rules to provide more flexibility in hiring, training, compensating, and deploying personnel. While FAA was exempted from most Title 5 requirements, including the merit system principles, the agency declared that its system would be consistent with those principles and would provide a balance between fairness and the flexibility to achieve organizational results. Key elements of the revised FAA system include:

• A centralized applicant pool system that provides automatic consideration for applicants and the opportunity for managers to hire without announcing a vacancy, on-the-spot hires for special program needs and hard-to-fill positions, elimination of time-in-grade, use of the Internet for job applications, non-competitive conversion from temporary to permanent status if competition is held initially for the temporary position, standardized position descriptions, and reduction in the number of hiring authorities to three (permanent, temporary with time limit, and temporary without time limit).

• Decentralized and deregulated training funding and decision making. Each organizational "line of business" identifies its needs and develops a training plan. Line of business units have more flexibility to make decisions

about employee training, including support for employees pursuing degree programs that address the organization's mission.

• A personnel appeals process, called Guaranteed Fair Treatment, designed to replace the Merit Systems Protection Board appeal process and reduce time frames for resolving disputes. It consists of a three-member panel made up of one advocate chosen by each side in a dispute and a neutral arbitrator resolves appealed actions. The panel issues a decision within 10 days of the hearing. In 2000, Congress enacted a provision as part of a later FAA reform law giving FAA employees the choice of using that system or pursuing traditional MSPB appeal rights.

• Pay bargaining with unions. The most notable result was a 1998 contract with the National Air Traffic Controllers Association in which the agency agreed to provide pay raises of up to 30 percent for specified air traffic controllers by the year 2003.

IRS—Title I, Subtitle C of the IRS Restructuring Act of 1998 created an alternative personnel system at the agency whose features include: critical pay to attract senior managers; streamlined authority to conduct demonstration projects of alternative personnel systems; rewards to senior executives for meeting IRS goals and objectives; requirements to terminate employees for certain specified types of misconduct; a new performance appraisal system to set retention standards for employees that could be used to deny pay increases, promotions, transfers, reassignments or other actions to resolve performance problems; freer use of relocation, recruitment and retention payments; an end to the use of enforcement statistics in employee evaluations; and a training program that emphasizes customer service.

Also authorized was a new awards program that provides incentives and recognition for individual achievements as well as group or organizational accomplishments. The IRS is required to operate these new personnel flexibilities "consistent with" merit systems principles.

Key features of the personnel reforms include:

• Revised performance standards to permit evaluation of each employee's performance on the basis of the individual and organizational performance requirements, taking into account individual contributions toward the attainment of any goals or objectives.

• Authority to conduct demonstration projects to: improve personnel management; provide increased individual accountability; eliminate obstacles to the removal of or imposing any disciplinary action with respect to poor performers, subject to the requirements of due process; expedite appeals from adverse actions or performance-based actions; and promote pay based on performance. Such projects will not be subject to the OPM approval processes generally applicable.

• Authority to establish one or more broad-banded pay systems to replace the general schedule structure and give it flexibility in setting salaries. Using this provision, the agency has begun carrying out plans to combine former GS-14 and GS-15 managers to reduce staffing imbalances.

• Mandatory firing of employees for offenses including: willful understatement of tax liability, willful failure to file returns on time, making false statements under oath, falsifying or destroying documents to conceal mistakes, and using tax laws to harass or retaliate against taxpayers or for personal gain.

Performance-Based Organizations

A performance-based organization (PBO) is a government program, office, or other discrete management unit with strong incentives to manage for results. The organization commits to specific measurable goals with targets for improved performance. In exchange, the PBO is allowed more flexibility to manage its personnel, procurement, and other services.

The concept of PBOs was launched in 1996. The goal is to set forth clear measures of performance, hold the head of the organization clearly accountable for achieving results, and grant the head of the organization authority to deviate from government-wide rules if needed to achieve agreed-upon results.

PBOs are characterized by:

• separating service operations from their policy components and placing them in separate organizations reporting to the agency or department head;

• negotiating a three- to five-year framework document between the PBO and the departmental secretary to set out the explicit goals, measures, relationships, flexibilities, and limitations for the organization; and,

• creating the position of chief operating officer to head the service operation functions, where the chief operating officer is appointed or hired on contract through a competitive search for a fixed term, with a clear agreement on services to be delivered and productivity goals to be achieved.

While there have been many proposals to turn a number of federal functions into PBOs, only three have been approved.

Student Financial Assistance—Turning the delivery of federal student financial assistance at the Education Department into a PBO was authorized by P.L. 105-244. The PBO is responsible for all aspects of managing the data and information systems that support the student financial assistance programs. The PBO has increased flexibility in procurement, with an emphasis on performance-based contracting. It also has new flexibility in personnel management, including hiring and evaluating senior managers and recruiting technical personnel. The chief operating officer and employees of the PBO have specific, measurable performance goals aimed at ensuring accountability for defined results.

Patent and Trademark Office—The United States Patent and Trademark Office became a PBO under P.L. 106-113, which reformed the U.S. patent and trademark systems in a number of ways, including changes designed to allow the agency to operate more like a business. The primary changes involve greater flexibilities in procurement, an important issue to a technology-heavy agency that must continually upgrade and replace electronic equipment. The new authority is intended to shorten the procurement cycle. In the personnel arena, PBO changes at the agency include the right to negotiate on pay in certain circumstances, greater flexibility in telecommuting arrangements and performance awards, including the potential for year-end bonuses based on individual performance and achievement of agency goals. Other steps include the elimination of sign-in sheets for employees and extension of flexitime policies. The agency also has more leeway regarding the assignment of senior executives and greater autonomy over its budget and hiring procedures.

Air Traffic Organization—Executive Order 13180 of December 7, 2000 created the Air Traffic Organization (ATO), a PBO entity within the Federal Aviation Administration consisting of FAA's Air Traffic Services and Research and Acquisition organizations that direct connection and give sup-port to the provision of day-to-day operational air traffic services. The order directed the chief operating officer of the air traffic control system to develop a five-year strategic plan, including objectives for the system's safety, efficiency and productivity. The ATO is to optimize use of management flexibilities and authorities, establish strong incentives to managers for achieving results and make fuller use of FAA's unique procurement and personnel authorities.

Section 8—Veterans' Employment Benefits

General Preference Policy

Under certain circumstances, preferential treatment in federal employment situations is granted to those who have served in the armed forces and been honorably discharged. That preference gives veterans (including certain spouses, widows, widowers, and mothers of veterans) a leg up in hiring for government jobs and protects them in reductions-in-force (RIFs). Eligibility for veterans' preference is determined by the time period in which an individual performed military service and the length of that service. Additional credits may be granted to those veterans who are disabled.

The principle of veterans' preference was written into law over a century ago when, in 1865, Congress gave preference to veterans with service-incurred disabilities. Since then the national policy has been broadened and strengthened by law, executive order, and regulation. In 1944, the various statutes, White House directives and civil service regulations were unified into a single law, known as the Veterans' Preference Act.

Veterans' Hiring Preference

In public civil service examinations, individuals who are veterans get five points added to their earned ratings if they were: honorably discharged from service between December 7, 1941, and July 1, 1955; honorably discharged after more than 180 consecutive days of active duty (other than for training), any part of which occurred after January 31, 1955, and before October 15, 1976; or honorably discharged after having served in a declared war or after receiving campaign or expeditionary medals for service in a combat zone. In addition, a two-year minimum active service condition applies to those qualified veterans who entered military service after September 7, 1980. (Reserve and National Guard members need not have served two years, provided they served the full period called or were ordered to active duty by the United States.) This condition does not apply to disabled veterans.

Persons who retired from the military with the rank of major and higher (or its equivalent) are not entitled to veterans' preference, except in cases of service-connected disability.

The following persons are eligible to receive ten points in addition to their earned ratings: a disabled veteran, the spouse of a veteran who suffered a service-connected disability and is too disabled to work, the unmarried widow or widower of a campaign veteran or one who served between December 7, 1941, and July 1, 1955, and in some cases the mother of a dead or totally and permanently disabled veteran.

Preference points are added only after a passing rating is obtained.

In jobs where experience is necessary, the veteran gets full credit for military service. It is counted as additional experience in a pre-service job or as experience gained in the service depending on which type of credit is more beneficial to the veteran.

Veteran candidates for jobs generally are listed on civil service registers in order of the examination ratings they have earned plus their preference points. However, one exception provides that disabled veterans who have compensable service-connected disabilities of ten percent or more are placed at the top of the register. (This exception does not apply to professional or scientific jobs in grade GS-9 or higher.) Those veterans who have gone to the top of the register because of a compensable disability are listed in order of their earned ratings plus ten points.

Under the rule of three, an agency is permitted to hire any one of the top three available persons on a register, except that it must give reasons to the OPM for passing over a veteran to select a non-veteran. An agency can not pass over a veteran and select a lower ranking non-veteran without sufficient reason agreed to by OPM.

Some federal examinations are reserved for veterans entitled to preference as long as they are available. These include guards, elevator operators, messengers, and custodians.

Noncompetitive Appointments

Veterans who served on active duty for more than 180 days, all or any part of which occurred after August 4, 1964, (February 28, 1961, for those who actually served in Vietnam), and received other than a dishonorable discharge, are eligible for a Veterans Readjustment Appointment (VRA), up to grade GS-11 or equivalent. Veterans with a service-connected disability are exempt from the 180-day service requirement.

Eligible Vietnam-era veterans qualify for ten years after their last discharge or separation from active duty. Eligible post-Vietnam veterans (i.e., who first began service after May 7, 1975) qualify for ten years after the date of their last discharge or release from active duty, or until December 31, 1999, whichever is later.

Veterans seeking VRA appointments should apply directly to the agency where they wish to work, not OPM. You must meet prescribed qualification requirements for the position, except that any written test requirements may be waived. Agencies have the right to select or not select qualified candidates.

The VRA is an excepted two-year appointment that combines employment with on-the-job training and development. After two years of satisfactory service, and completion of the agreed training (not required for veterans with 15 or more years of education), the veteran acquires competitive status and a permanent appointment.

Veterans who are 30 percent disabled

or more may be hired directly by agencies under a statutory authority for appointment without competitive examination.

Veterans Employment Opportunities Act of 1998

Some significant changes were made to veterans preferences in employment with the Veterans Employment Opportunities Act of 1998 (P.L. 105-339.) The law:

• Allows preference eligibles or veterans who are honorably discharged from the armed forces after three or more years of active service to compete for vacant positions, if the hiring agency is accepting applications from individuals outside its own workforce under merit promotion procedures. All merit promotion announcements open to applicants outside the hiring agency's workforce are required to indicate that these veterans and preference eligibles may apply.

• Establishes a new redress system for veterans, modeled after the one in the Uniformed Services Employment and Reemployment Rights Act of 1994 (see Part 353 of OPM's regulations).

• Makes it a prohibited personnel practice to knowingly take or fail to take a personnel action if that action or failure to act would violate a statutory or regulatory veterans' preference requirement.

• Expands certain provisions of Titles 31 and 38 relating to employment of veterans by federal contractors.

• Requires FAA to apply veterans' preference in reductions-in-force, as it already is required to do in hiring.

• Extends veterans' preference to certain White House, legislative and judicial branch positions.

Veterans' Rights in RIF Situations

In government layoff programs brought about by economic or other factors, Congress has given certain veterans in the federal service job priority rights over certain non-veterans.

Generally, employees with career civil service tenure who are eligible for veterans' preference in a reduction in force (except for certain "20-year military retirees") will be given job retention rights over other federal workers in the same competitive level and, if qualified, in other jobs in the same competitive area.

Although military retirees are preference-eligibles for purposes of examinations and appointments, the retention rights of "20-year military retirees" are reduced. Most of these retirees are not entitled to veterans' preference for reduction-in-force. For reduction-in-force purposes, they will receive credit for periods of military service during a war, or in any campaign or expedition for which a campaign badge is authorized. Retention rights remain unchanged for military personnel retired on the basis of combat disability, as well as those retired or disabled veterans who were employed on November 30, 1964, in federal civilian positions to which the laws on veterans preference apply, and who have not had a break in service of more than 30 days thereafter (5 USC 3501).

Veterans with career-conditional tenure do not have job retention rights over non-veterans who have career civil service tenure. However, they do have retention rights over non-veteran career-conditional or term workers. Veterans who are rated 30 percent disabled or more have higher standing over other preference-eligibles in reduction-in-force.

No job retention rights are given to employees—veterans or non-veterans—who have temporary appointments with definite time limitations.

Having veterans' preference in a reduction-in-force does not mean that the employee won't be separated. In many large-scale reductions, there are not enough jobs to go around and even veterans may be separated.

Disabled Veterans Affirmative Action Program

Federal departments and agencies, including the U.S. Postal Service and Postal Rate Commission, are required to have an affirmative action plan for the recruitment, employment, and advancement of disabled veterans, under Section 4214, Title 38, U.S. Code and Part 720 of Title 5 of the Code of Federal Regulations.

To be considered a disabled veteran, the individual must meet the requirements set forth in Section 4211(3), Title 38, U.S. Code. Generally, a disabled veteran must have a compensable disability.

The Office of Personnel Management annually asks agencies to submit their Disabled Veterans Affirmative Action Program (DVAAP) accomplishment reports and plan certifications. OPM then reviews each agency's submission to determine if it is consistent with law and regulation.

Minimum DVAAP plan requirements are outlined in Section 720.304(e) of Part 720 of 5 CFR. Such plans typically include:
• an assessment of the current status of disabled veteran employment within the agency;
• a description of recruitment methods used to seek out disabled veteran applicants, including 30 percent or more disabled veterans;
• a description of internal advancement opportunities for disabled veterans; and
• a description of how the agency will monitor, review, and evaluate its planned efforts during the period covered by the plan.

OPM's oversight responsibility for government-wide DVAAP consists of monitoring agencies' plans, evaluating agencies' program effectiveness, providing technical assistance and guidance and reporting annually to Congress. OPM does not entertain or prosecute specific individual complaints of unfair treatment of disabled veterans, nor does it have the authority to adjudicate individual discrimination complaints. Individuals should pursue resolutions of these problems through the avenues available to them at the agency in question.

Employment Rights of Those on Military Duty

Civilian federal employees who are members of the Armed Forces Reserve and who are called to duty are entitled to federal job rights and protections that are guaranteed by Public Law 103-353 of October 13, 1994. The rights and benefits of such individuals include:

Pay—Federal workers performing active military duty will be placed in a leave without pay (LWOP) status during their military tour of duty, but will receive compensation from the Armed Forces in accordance with the terms and conditions of their military appointment. They will not receive any compensation from their civilian employing agency unless they elect to use military leave or annual leave. Agencies should continue the payment of annual premium pay for administratively uncontrollable overtime work or regularly scheduled standby duty during periods of military leave or annual leave.

Military Leave—Employees who perform active military duty or training, as specified in 5 U.S.C. 6323(a), may request the use of paid military leave. Under the law, an eligible full-time employee accrues 15 calendar days of military leave each fiscal year, and any unused military leave at the beginning of the succeeding fiscal year (up to 15 calendar days) is carried forward for use in addition to the 15 days credited at the beginning of that fiscal year. Part-time employees accrue military leave on a prorated basis.

Annual Leave—Employees who perform active military duty may request the use of accrued annual leave to their credit. The Office of Personnel Management encourages agencies to grant such requests to the extent that they do not involve the use of annual leave that has not yet been earned as of the date the employee is placed in a LWOP status (after exhausting any available military leave or annual leave). As in the case of military leave, employees who elect to use annual leave will receive full compensation from their civilian position throughout the period charged to annual leave in addition to their military pay for the same period. Employees do not earn sick or annual leave while in a nonpay status.

Health Benefits—Individuals performing active military duty are provided medical and dental services, and their dependents are automatically covered by the Civilian Health and Medical Program of the Uniformed Services (CHAMPUS). If employees covered by the Federal Employees Health Benefits Program (FEHBP) are placed in a LWOP status, their health benefits enrollment continues for up to 12 months unless they elect in writing to have their enrollment terminated. If their FEHBP enrollment continues, such employees normally would be responsible for paying their share of the premium.

Section 519 of Public Law 107-107 amended subsection (e) of Section 8906 of Title 5, United States Code, to provide agencies with discretionary authority to pay both the employee and government health benefit contributions (and any additional adminis-trative expenses related to health care coverage) for certain employees called to active duty and their families for a period not to exceed 18 months. The employee must:

- be enrolled in an approved health benefits plan;
- be a member of a reserve component of the armed forces;
- be called or ordered to active duty in support of a contingency operation;
- be placed on leave without pay or separated from service to perform active duty; and serve on active duty for a period of more than 30 consecutive days.

This authority applies to employees called to active duty on or after December 8, 1995. Agencies may make retroactive payments to covered employees for premiums paid on or after that date.

Life Insurance—Employees placed in a LWOP status while performing active military duty are entitled to have their life insurance (both basic and all forms of optional coverage) continue for up to 12 months at no cost. If the life insurance coverage is terminated after 12 months in a non-pay status, the employee has a 31-day temporary extension of coverage for conversion to a nongroup policy.

Retirement—Employees who are placed in a LWOP status while performing active military duty continue to be covered by the federal civil service retirement system. Upon eventual retirement from civilian service, the period of military service is creditable under either CSRS or FERS, subject to the normal rules for crediting military service.

Return to Civilian Duty—Any federal employee, permanent or temporary, in an executive agency other than an intelligence agency, but including the U.S. Postal Service, Postal Rate Commission, and non-appropriated fund activity, who performs duty with a uniformed service (including active duty, active duty for training, or inactive duty training), whether voluntary or involuntary, is entitled to be restored to the position he or she would have attained had the employee not entered the uniformed service, provided the employee: gave the agency advance notice of departure except where prevented by military circumstances; was released from uniformed service under honorable conditions; served no more than a cumulative total of five years (exceptions are allowed for training and involuntary active duty extensions, and to complete an initial service obligation of more than five years); and applies for restoration within the appropriate time limits.

Employees in the intelligence agencies have substantially the same rights, but are covered under agency regulations rather than the Office of Personnel Management's and have different appeal rights.

While on duty with the uniformed services, the agency carries the employee on leave without pay unless the employee requests separation. A separation under these circumstances does not affect restoration rights.

Employees who served in the uniformed services:

• Less than 31 days (or who leave to take a fitness exam for service) must report back to work at the beginning of the next regularly scheduled work day following their completion of service and the expiration of eight hours after a time for safe transportation back to the employee's residence.

• More than 30 but less than 181 days must apply for reemployment no later than 14 days after completion of service.

• More than 180 days have 90 days after completion of service to apply for restoration.

Employees who fail to meet these time limits are subject to disciplinary action.

Agencies must reemploy as soon as practicable, but no later than 30 days after receiving the application. Agencies have the right to ask for documentation showing the length and character of the employee's service and the timeliness of the application.

Employees who served less than 91 days must be placed in the position for which qualified that they would have attained had their employment not been interrupted. If not qualified for such position after reasonable efforts by the agency to qualify the person, the employee is entitled to be placed in the position he or she left.

Employees who served more than 90 days have essentially the same rights as described above except that the agency has the option of placing the employee in a position for which qualified of like seniority, status, and pay.

Employees with service-connected disabilities who are not qualified for the above must be reemployed in a position that most closely approximates the position they would have been entitled to, consistent with the circumstances in each case.

Employees who were under time-limited appointments finish the unexpired portion of their appointments upon their return.

OPM Job Placement—If the employing agency is unable to reemploy an individual returning from duty with a uniformed service, OPM will order placement in another agency when:

• OPM determines that it is impossible or unreasonable for an agency in the executive branch (other than an intelligence agency) to reemploy the person;

• an intelligence agency or an agency in the legislative or judicial branch notifies OPM that it is impossible or unreasonable to reemploy the person, and the person applies to OPM for placement assistance; or

• a noncareer National Guard technician who is not eligible for continued membership in the Guard for reasons beyond his or her control applies to OPM for placement assistance.

Service Credit—Upon restoration, employees are generally treated as though they had never left. This means that time spent in the uniformed services counts for seniority, within-grade increases, completion of probation, career tenure, retirement, and leave rate accrual. (Employees do not earn sick or annual leave while off the rolls or in a nonpay status.)

To receive civil service retirement credit for military service, a deposit to the retirement fund is usually required to cover the period of military service. Only active, honorable military service is creditable for retirement purposes. If the employee is under the Civil Service Retirement System, a deposit of 7 percent of military basic pay (plus interest under certain conditions) is required. The deposit is 3 percent if the employee is under the Federal Employees Retirement System. However, these amounts may be different if: the employee's creditable civilian service was interrupted by military duty; and reemployment occurred pursuant to 38 U.S.C. Chapter 43 on or after August 1, 1990. In such a situation, the contribution is either the above-prescribed amount or the amount of civilian retirement deductions which would have been withheld had the individual not entered uniformed service if this amount is less than the normal deposit for military service.

Thrift Savings Plan—Employees who perform uniformed service may make up any contributions to the Thrift Savings Plan they missed because of such service. In addition, members of the Ready Reserve or National Guard serving on active duty and in any military pay status can contribute to the TSP through a uniformed services TSP account. See Chapter 6.

Section 9—Senior Executive Service

General Rules and Procedures

The Senior Executive Service covers most managerial, supervisory, and policy positions in the executive branch above grade GS-15, except those that require Senate confirmation. The SES is a system in which salary and career status are personal rather than dependent on the position occupied. Although both career and noncareer executives are SES members, the number of noncareer executives is limited by law to ten percent of the total SES allocation.

SES members oversee most federal activities in over 70 agencies. By law, however, certain agencies are excluded from SES provisions. These include the Foreign Service, FAA, FBI, DEA, CIA, DIA, NSA, and the National Imagery and Mapping Agency, some government corporations, such as TVA, certain financial regulatory agencies, and positions such as administrative law judges.

While there are no grades in the SES, there are six pay levels, the rates for which are determined annually by the President. By law the minimum rate of pay may not be less than 120 percent of GS-15, step 1 and the maximum may not exceed the rate for Executive Level IV. (However, the SES pay cap for base pay plus locality adjustment is Executive Level III.)

For the latest information on federal pay, go to OPM's website at www.opm.gov. Click on Pay and Leave, then click on Salaries and Wages.

Pay rates for individuals may only be changed once a year. While SES members may receive raises that boost them any number of rates (e.g., from an ES-3 to ES-5), their pay may be lowered only one rate per year. A career SES member must be given 15 days notice of a pay reduction.

Under special conditions, agencies may make recruitment, relocation, and retention payments to SES members of up to 25 percent of basic pay.

There are two types of SES positions, career-reserved (which must be filled by career appointees) and general (which may be filled by career or noncareer appointees, or by limited-term or limited emergency appointees).

Agencies develop their own performance rating systems to evaluate the performance of SES members, in accordance with Office of Personnel Management regulations and guidelines. By law, agency performance evaluation system must have at least three rating levels: fully successful, minimally satisfactory and unsatisfactory. Agencies may add up to two additional levels above fully successful.

Career SES members whose annual performance rating is fully successful or better may receive a performance award of a lump sum of between five and 20 percent of base pay. Agencies also may nominate career SES members whose performance is exceptional for at least three years for one of two rank awards conferred by the President: Distinguished Executive (a lump-sum payment of 35 percent of base pay) or Meritorious Executive (20 percent of base pay). However, an SES member's total compensation may not exceed Executive Level I during a calendar year. (Any excess will be paid as a lump sum at the next calendar year.)

Agency heads may grant sabbaticals to SES career members for three to 11 months during any ten year period to encourage study or uncompensated work experience that will contribute to the individual's development and effectiveness. While on sabbatical, SES members continue to receive salary and leave benefits, and agencies may authorize travel and living expenses.

SES members earn annual and sick leave at the same rates as other federal employees. However, as of October 1994, the amount of annual leave that can be carried over to a new leave year is limited to 90 days, or 720 hours. SES members with more than 720 hours of annual leave on the effective date of the change had that leave "grandfathered" as a personal leave ceiling. See Chapter 5, Section 1.

How to Apply for SES Positions

OPM does not maintain registers of eligible candidates for the SES. Instead, agencies oversee the merit staffing process required for career entry. They determine position qualification requirements, advertise career vacancies at least throughout the government, and make selections for their SES positions. However, before an initial career appointment to the SES can be made, the candidate's executive qualifications must be approved by an independent Qualifications Review Board (QRB).

There are two methods for entry into the career SES; application for a specific agency position and application to a specific agency for inclusion in its SES candidate development program. Following satisfactory completion of such a program and QRB certification of their executive qualifications, graduates are eligible for career appointment to the SES without further competition. However, an appointment is not guaranteed.

Agencies and individuals may access information about SES vacancies from USA JOBS on the Internet at www.USAjobs.

opm.gov; a phone system (912-757-3000); and Federal Job Information Touch Screen kiosks located at OPM offices and in certain federal buildings throughout the country. SES vacancy information also is available at state employment offices.

Executive Development

Agencies are required to establish development programs for executives, managers, and supervisors, as well as candidates for those positions. These executive development programs must be designed in accordance with an agency's strategic plan, foster a corporate perspective of government, and provide for initial training, continuing learning experiences, and systematic development of candidates for advancement to higher-level management positions.

There are many ways to provide developmental opportunities, such as formal and informal training experiences, seminars, forums, participation on task forces, interagency details, and mobility assignments. The goal is to develop executives, managers, and supervisors prepared to lead and manage the continuing transformation of government.

SES Candidate Development Programs have to include a formal training experience that addresses the executive core qualifications and provides interactions with a wide mix of employees outside the agency. They also have to provide participants with mentoring by a current SES member, as well as developmental assignments of at least four months duration that are outside the candidate's position of record. The purpose is to broaden the experience of candidates and prepare them for a range of executive positions.

Section 10—Reductions-in-Force and Furloughs

General Rules and Procedures

An agency is required to use RIF procedures when an employee is faced with separation or downgrading for a reason such as reorganization, lack of work, shortage of funds, insufficient personnel ceiling, or the exercise of certain reemployment or restoration rights. If an agency is going to RIF employees, it must follow specific procedures to determine which employees will

be affected by the RIF. Employees compete for retention on the basis of four factors:

• type of appointment (tenure),
• veterans' preference,
• total length of civilian and creditable military service, and
• performance ratings.

The agency decides whether a RIF is necessary, when it will take place, and what jobs are abolished. However, the abolishment of a position does not always require the use of RIF procedures. The agency may reassign an employee without regard to RIF procedures to a vacant position at the same grade and pay, regardless of where the position is located.

Competitive Areas and Levels

First, the agency defines the competitive areas that will be used as the geographical and organizational limits within which employees compete for retention. A competitive area may consist of all or part of an agency. The minimum competitive area is a subdivision of the agency within a local commuting area. If a competitive area will be in effect less than 90 days prior to the effective date of a reduction-in-force, it has to be approved by the Office of Personnel Management in advance of the RIF.

Next, the agency groups interchangeable positions into competitive levels based upon similarity of grade, series, qualifications, duties, and working conditions. For example, GS-2 typists are listed with GS-2 typists performing similar duties, and GS-9 accountants are listed with other GS-9 accountants performing similar duties.

Retention Registers, Competitive Service

A formula combining the four factors mandated by law (tenure, veterans' preference, length of service, and performance) is used to rank employees. Each competitive level becomes a retention register that lists employees in order of their standing.

Tenure—Employees are ranked on a retention register in three groups according to their types of appointment. Group I are career employees who are not serving a probationary period. Group II are career employees who are serving a probationary period and career-conditional employees. Group III are term employees, status quo employees, and employees serving under temporary appointments pending establishment of registers (temporary employees in the competitive service are not competing employees for RIF purposes and are not listed on the retention register).

Each of the tenure groups is divided into three subgroups reflecting entitlement to veterans preference. A retired member of the armed forces is considered to be a vet-

eran for RIF purposes only if the armed forces retired pay is directly based upon a combat-incurred disability or injury or for members retired below the rank of major (or equivalent) who are not disabled veterans if the retirement is based upon less than 20 years of active service, or if the employee has been working for the government since November 30, 1964, without a break of service of more than 30 days. Subgroup AD includes eligible veterans with a compensable service-connected disability of 30 percent or more. Subgroup A includes eligible veterans not included in Subgroup AD. Subgroup B includes non-veterans and veterans not eligible for preference.

Length of Service—Employees are ranked by their service dates within each subgroup. Their service dates reflect total federal service, civilian and creditable military service, and additional service credit for certain performance ratings. Retired military members can receive credit only for service performed during a war or during a campaign or expedition for which a campaign badge or expeditionary medal has been awarded, unless the retired pay was based on a combat-incurred disability or injury based on less than 20 years active service, or the retired member has been employed in the civilian service without a break in service of more than 30 days. Additionally, an employee may not receive dual retention service credit for service performed on active duty in the armed forces that was performed during concurrent civilian employment as a federal employee.

Note: The Defense Authorization Act of 1996 allows credit of non-appropriated fund (NAF) service from January 1, 1966, to the present, if the employee moved, without a break in service of more than three calendar days, from a NAF position to an appropriated fund (AF) position within the Department of Defense.

Performance—Employees may receive additional service credit for performance based on the average of their last three actual performance ratings or record received during the four-year period prior to the date the agency issues RIF notices. The four-year period is the earlier of the date the agency issues RIF notices, or the date the agency freezes ratings before issuing RIF notices.

An employee is given additional service credit based on the mathematical average (rounded in the case of a fraction to the next whole number) of the value of the employee's last three annual ratings. If an employee received more than three annual ratings during the four-year period, the three most recent annual ratings are used. If an employee received fewer than three annual ratings during the four-year period, the actual ratings received are averaged and rounded up to a whole number. Employees who have received no ratings of record are given performance credit based on the most frequently assigned performance rating in their agency or organization.

When all employees in the competitive area have ratings earned under the same type of performance rating pattern, then the standard formula for assigning performance credit is:

• 20 additional years for an Outstanding rating;

• 16 additional years for an Exceeds Fully Successful rating; and

• 12 additional years for a Fully Successful rating.

For rating received on or after October 1, 1997, agencies may (under certain circumstances) use a different formula to assign years of credit to ratings at or above the Fully Successful level. In these cases, they must still use a whole number between 12 and 20 years, but they are not required to use the standard values.

For example, if an employee with two years of federal service has one annual rating of Outstanding (20) and one of Exceeds Fully Successful (16), the employee would receive additional RIF credit on those two ratings: 20+16=36, divided by 2=18 years of RIF credit for performance. This additional credit is added to the employee's other service for RIF purposes.

Excepted Service (Schedules A and B)

Excepted service employees are those who are working under Schedule A or B appointments. Schedule A positions are those for which it is not practical to apply the qualification standards and requirements, and which are not of a confidential or policy-determining character. Schedule B positions are those for which it is not

practical to hold open competitive examinations, and which are not of a confidential or policy-determining character.

For RIF purposes, these employees are listed on the register according to the same criteria used in the competitive service, but separately from competitive service employees.

SES RIF Procedures

Before an agency conducts a reduction in force that will affect SES members, it must have a plan that explains how its RIF procedures work and how the agency will determine who is affected. Removal of career executives in a RIF must be preceded by a specific written notice and must follow competitive procedures, which give primary emphasis to performance. Veterans preference does not apply. An executive may appeal to MSPB whether the RIF complies with competitive procedures. Note: Non-career and limited-term appointees may be removed at the pleasure of the agency head.

SES career members who are affected by a RIF and have completed probation are entitled to placement in any vacant SES position in their agency for which they are qualified. If no such vacancy exists, OPM has 45 days in which to try to place the individual in an SES position in another agency.

If SES placement is not possible, the individual has fallback rights to a GS-15 position, and still retains his or her former SES basic salary. SES members who meet the age and service requirements may elect discontinued service retirement in lieu of a GS-15 position.

RIF Notices

An agency must give each non-SES employee at least 60 days specific written notice before he or she is released for a RIF action. In unforeseeable circumstances, an agency may, with OPM approval, give an employee 30 rather than 60 days specific written notice of a RIF action.

In the RIF notice, the agency must include the employee's competitive area, competitive level, subgroup, service date, and last three annual performance ratings of record received during the last four years; the place where the employee may inspect the regulations and records; the reasons for proceeding out of order in retaining a lower-standing employee in the same competitive level; information on career transition and placement programs; a severance pay estimate; information on unemployment benefits and dislocated worker programs; the option to authorize release of employment information to potential employers; and the employee's right to grieve or appeal the agency's decision.

Employee Release Order

Employees are released from a competitive level in the inverse order of their retention standing, beginning with the employee with the lowest standing on the retention register. In other words, all employees in Group III are released before employees in Group II, and all employees in Group II are released before employees in Group I. Within the subgroups, all employees in Subgroup B are released before those in Subgroup A, and all workers in Subgroup A are released before those in Subgroup AD.

However, an agency may not release a competing employee from a competitive level while retaining in that level an employee with a specific limited appointment, specifically limited temporary or term promotion, or an employee who has received a written decision that removes or demotes the employee from the competitive level.

Access to RIF Records

Employing agencies are required to provide employees and their designated representatives with access to retention records showing how the employee was selected for release. By regulation, an agency can no longer meet its obligation to provide this information by giving the employee a sanitized retention record with all the pertinent information blocked out. In addition, employees are entitled to see any agency records that detail their bump-and-retreat rights in a RIF situation (see below). Also, agencies must keep all records relating to a RIF for at least one year after the date the agency issues RIF notices.

Rights to Other Positions

Competitive service employees in Groups I and II who are released from their competitive level and have current performance ratings of at least "minimally suc-cessful" are entitled to an offer of assignment, if they have "bumping" or "retreating" rights to an available position in the same competitive area. The position must last at least three months, be one for which the released employee is qualified, have a pay rate no higher than the employee's present position, have the same type of work schedule, and be within three grades of the employee's present position. Employees in Group III (term employees and status quo employees) have no rights to another job.

Bumping—"Bumping" means displacing an employee in a lower tenure group, or in a lower subgroup within the released employee's own tenure group. Although the released employee must be qualified for the job, it may be a job he or she never held. In addition, it can be no more than three grades (or appropriate intervals) below the position from which the employee was released.

Retreating—"Retreating" means displacing an employee with less service within the released employee's own tenure group and subgroup. The position must also be the same position or essentially identical to a position held by the released employee in a federal agency on a permanent basis. An employee with a current annual performance rating of "minimally successful" only has retreat rights to positions held by employees with the same or lower rating. Also, the position can be no more than three grades (or appropriate grade intervals) below the position from which the employee was released. The exception is for those in subgroup AD (veterans with a compensable service-connected disability of 30 percent or more). Their limit is five grades (or appropriate grade intervals).

Grade Intervals—The grade limits of an employee's assignment rights are determined by the grade progression of the position from which the employee is released. The difference between successive grades in a one-grade occupation is a grade difference, and the difference between successive grades in a multi-grade occupation is a grade-interval difference. For example, an employee released from a GS-11 position that progresses GS-5-7-9-11 has bump and retreat rights to positions no lower than GS-5. An employee released from a GS-9 position that progresses

GS-6-7-8-9 has bump/retreat rights to positions no lower than GS-6.

Use of Vacant Positions

An agency is not required to offer vacant positions in a RIF, but may choose to fill all, some, or none of them. When an agency chooses to fill a vacancy with an employee reached for a RIF action, it must follow subgroup retention standing. A RIF offer of assignment to a vacant position can only be in the same competitive area, and must be within three grades (or grade-intervals) of the employee's present position. At its discretion, the agency may offer employees reassignments or voluntary changes to lower-graded positions in other competitive areas in lieu of RIF.

RIF Appeals and Grievances

An employee who has been separated, downgraded, or furloughed for more than 30 days by RIF has the right to appeal in writing to the Merit Systems Protection Board (MSPB), if the employee believes the agency did not properly follow the RIF regulations. The appeal must be filed during the 30-day period beginning the day after the effective date of the RIF action. MSPB's review of agency action is limited to the written record unless MSPB determines that there are facts in dispute. If MSPB rules in favor of the employee, the agency must restore the employee to the job that the employee was separated from or should have been assigned. The agency is usually required to give back pay to the affected employee.

An employee in a bargaining unit covered by a negotiated grievance procedure that does not exclude RIF actions must use the negotiated grievance procedure. The employee may not appeal to the MSPB unless the employee alleges the action was based upon discrimination. The time limits for filing a grievance are set forth in the collective bargaining agreement.

Transfer of Function

A transfer of function takes place when a function ceases in one competitive area and moves to other competitive areas which do not perform the function at the time of transfer. The gaining competitive area may be in the same or different agency. An employee who is identified with the transferring function has the right to transfer only if faced with separation or downgrading in the competitive area that is losing the function. The losing competitive area may use adverse action procedures to separate any employee who chooses not to transfer with his or her function. If the transfer of function results in a surplus of employees in the gaining competitive area, all employees who elected to transfer with the function compete under RIF regulations for positions in the gaining organization. (See "Career Transition Assistance" section.)

RIF-Related Benefits

Grade Retention—Employees who are placed in a lower graded position in their agency as a result of RIF procedures are eligible to retain the same grade for two years. The employee must have completed at least 52 consecutive weeks at a higher grade than that of the position to which he or she was demoted. The employee's retained grade is considered for most purposes (including pay and pay administration, retirement, life insurance, eligibility for training, promotions, and within-grade increases) as the grade of the position the employee holds after downgrading because of RIF. However, in any subsequent RIF the employee competes for retention based on the lower grade. For example, an employee who holds a GS-12 position and is downgraded because of a RIF to a GS-9 position is still considered a GS-12 for most purposes, but for a subsequent RIF, would compete as a GS-9.

Pay Retention—Employees eligible for grade retention keep their pay for the same two-year period. At the end of the two-year period, the grade of such workers is lowered. Should their pay at that time exceed the maximum rate of their new grade, they will retain their current rate of pay at the time (the exception being that the retained rate may not exceed 150 percent of the top rate of the grade to which it was reduced). Such employees will receive only 50 percent of the annual comparability pay increases. If or when their pay is lower than or equal to the maximum rate of the new grade, it will be placed at the maximum rate and the worker will then receive full comparability pay increases.

Re-promotion Priority—Agencies can give priority consideration to the re-promotion of employees who have been downgraded involuntarily to positions up to their former grade level.

Severance Pay—Severance pay is available to most individuals who have served at least 12 months continuously and are separated by a RIF, provided that such employees have not refused to accept a position within two grades of their current level in the same commuting area, are not eligible for an immediate annuity for either federal or armed forces service, and are not receiving any type of injury compensation benefits.

The severance benefit is computed at the rate of one week's pay for each year of service prior to separation. After ten years of service, an employee receives two weeks of pay for each additional year. For each year the employee is over age 40, an additional ten percent of severance pay is received. The maximum is one year's salary. Severance benefits are paid out at regular pay intervals.

Unemployment Compensation—The unemployment insurance program for federal employees is administered by the Department of Labor through state governments. Separated employees should file a claim for benefits at their state employment service office or their unemployment insurance claims office, where they also can register for work. Employees must bring their Social Security card, official notice of separation or non-pay status (Standard Form 50), and notice about unemployment insurance (Standard Form 8).

Unused Leave—All civilian employees eligible for annual leave, upon separation from the federal service, are entitled to receive a lump-sum payment for accumulated and accrued annual leave. There is no payment for unused sick leave. However, employees who are separated from the federal government are entitled to have their sick leave recredited if they are reemployed in the federal service. Unused sick leave is added to the total service of an employee who is eligible for annuity benefits under the Civil Service Retirement System (CSRS). However, unused sick leave cannot be credited for purposes of annuity computations under the Federal Employees Retirement System (FERS).

Health Insurance in RIFs

After separation, employees not eligible for an immediate annuity continue to be covered by their Federal Employees Health Benefits insurance for 31 days at no charge.

They can enroll for an additional 18 months as long as they pay both the employee and employer share of the premiums, plus two percent for administrative costs. Department of Defense employees can continue their Federal Employees' Health Benefits insurance for 18 months on the same terms as if they were still employed following RIF separation.

Employees who are eligible for an immediate annuity may continue their enrollment in the FEHB, if the retiree has been continuously enrolled or covered as a family member for the five years of service immediately preceding the commencing date of annuity payments, or for all service since the first opportunity to enroll. After retirement, the government continues to pay the same contribution that is paid for active employees.

Life Insurance in RIFs

Separated employees are covered free by FEGLI for 31 days. Employees who are separated and are not eligible for an immediate annuity may convert all or part of their life insurance to an individual policy without having to take a medical examination. The individual policy may be purchased from any eligible insurance company selected by the employee as a private transaction between the employee and the company. The employee pays the entire cost of the conversion policy. The conversion must be made within 31 days after the effective date of the RIF or within 30 days after receiving the notice from the employing office about the right to convert, whichever is later.

Employees who retire on an immediate annuity are eligible to continue their basic life insurance as well as all three types of optional insurance. At retirement, employees can elect a percentage of basic coverage they wish to retain after age 65. Retirees must have been insured for the basic coverage during the entire period the coverage was available or for the last five years of service immediately preceding the starting date of annuity payments.

Retirement Benefits in RIFs

Discontinued Service Retirement—An employee facing reduction-in-force who meets normal age and service requirements for retirement may choose to retire at any point in the process. Both the CSRS and

FERS systems also provide for immediate retirement with reduced age and service requirements for employees who are involuntarily separated (other than for cause on charges of misconduct or delinquency) who have not declined a reasonable job offer.

Once employees receive official notice that they will be involuntarily separated, they may then retire, and are not required to wait until the action has been taken. However, if the notice is rescinded prior to the employee's retirement, the right to retire also terminates.

To be eligible for a discontinued service retirement, an employee must be at least age 50 with 20 years of creditable service, or be any age with 25 years of service. Under CSRS, the annuity is reduced by two percent for each year the individual is under age 55. There is no age reduction under FERS, but the employee is not eligible for the Annuity Supplement (payable under FERS until age 62 in lieu of Social Security benefits) until attainment of the Minimum Retirement Age (55 to 57, depending upon year of birth).

Early Voluntary Retirement—If OPM, responding to the request of an agency head, determines that an agency is undergoing a major RIF or reorganization that will result in a significant number of employees losing their jobs or having their pay reduced, it may authorize early retirement for employees during a limited period. The eligibility and computation factors are the same as those discussed in the above section on Discontinued Service Retirement.

Deferred Annuity—Under both FERS and CSRS, separating employees who do not meet the requirements for an immediate annuity but who have at least five years of creditable civilian service are entitled to a deferred annuity. Under both systems, this deferred annuity can commence at age 62. The annuity is computed under the law in effect on the date of the employee's separation.

Under FERS only, employees who have at least ten years of creditable service may elect a reduced deferred annuity commencing at any time from Minimum Retirement Age until age 62. The reduction is five percent for each year the employee is under 62 when the annuity commences.

Voluntary RIFS

The fiscal year 1996 Defense Department authorization act (P.L. 104-106) created a "voluntary RIF" authority at DoD that was extended through fiscal 2005 by the 2001 Defense Authorization Act (P.L. 106-398). The program allows the release of an employee who volunteers for separation in a reduction in force even though the employee would not otherwise be subject to separation. The provision is designed to help minimize the impact of downsizing by encouraging employees to volunteer to be separated in lieu of another employee who is slated to be separated.

The authority gives component heads the discretion to allow RIF volunteers under these circumstances:

• Voluntary separation will be allowed only during a formal RIF, that is, where official RIF notices will be issued.

• Both the separation volunteer and the person to be "saved" must be in the same competitive area.

• Matches of separation volunteers with those affected by the formal RIF will be based on the similarity of their positions. Any position affected by the RIF can be identified for the placement of a RIF separation volunteer, if separation of the RIF volunteer would result in the cancellation of a RIF separation action, and the subsequent placement of a RIF-affected employee. The placement cannot result in promotion.

Where there are more volunteers than needed and all are equally good matches, activities will process voluntary RIF applicants in order of seniority. Where there are fewer volunteers than needed and there are equally good matches for placement, activities will select RIF-affected employees for placement in order of RIF retention standing.

If, at any point in the RIF process, it is determined that the voluntary separation would not result in saving a RIF-affected employee, the voluntary separation will be canceled. Volunteering for separation under the provisions of the policy does not confer RIF assignment rights.

Only U.S. citizen civilian employees of the Department of Defense serving under an appointment without time limitation, are not reemployed annuitants, and do not have a pending or approved application for disability retirement may be RIF volunteers.

Generally, employees occupying critical or hard-to-fill positions, or with critical knowledge and skills, will not be allowed to participate except with the approval of the commanding officer or activity head. Employee participation in the program is not an entitlement and is subject to the discretion of the military departments, defense agencies, and their activities and installations.

Separation volunteers will be issued RIF separation notices effective on the RIF effective date. The notice will advise them of their entitlements under the RIF. Volunteers must sign a statement that they realize the action is irrevocable once they have been issued a RIF separation notice. However, activities may cancel the action if necessary.

Separation volunteers are treated as involuntary RIF separations and are eligible for most of the benefits accrued to those involuntarily separated, such as severance pay (except for retirement eligibles) and temporary continuation of federal health insurance coverage. However, they are ineligible for registration in the priority placement program, non-federal hiring incentives and voluntary separation incentive payments (buyouts). Separation volunteers who are reemployed by the federal government are subject to the rules governing repayment of severance pay.

Furloughs

Most agency furlough actions consist of (non-pay) furloughs of employees for a period lasting 30 days or less. Furloughs for more than 30 days are handled under regular reduction-in-force rules. Furloughs of 30 days or less are covered by adverse action procedures. In cases of a 30-day-or-less furlough, agencies have the right to take such action. However, there are rules they must follow.

Employees must be given at least 30 days advance written notice of 30-day-or-less furloughs, except in the case of "unforeseeable circumstances." Employees are entitled to appeal the action to the Merit Systems Protection Board, or grieve under an applicable negotiated grievance procedure.

The total number of days that any employees may be furloughed under the adverse action procedures may not exceed 30 calendar days (if consecutive) or 22 work days (i.e., discontinuous furloughs in which employees are furloughed, for example, one day a week for a specified number of weeks).

Retirement coverage continues without cost to the employees on consecutive furloughs of 30 days or less. On discontinuous furloughs, the coverage continues but contributions by the employee are adjusted in proportion to the basic salary received during each pay period.

Life insurance coverage continues during both consecutive and discontinuous furloughs. There is no cost to the employee during consecutive furloughs, but employees on discontinuous furloughs are assessed premiums if the salary during the pay period is sufficient to cover deductions.

Health insurance coverage continues during consecutive furloughs with the employee and agency paying their respective FEHB shares for each pay period in which coverage continues. The employee may either continue paying the premium while on non-pay status or resume making payments after returning to duty and pay status.

Those on discontinuous furloughs would make contributions if the salary in the pay period is sufficient to cover the cost of full deductions.

Regarding use-it-or-lose-it annual leave, such leave can be protected from forfeiture if a request for such leave has been made in writing well in advance of the furlough and for use at some period or periods before the end of the leave year.

Employees may be eligible for unemployment compensation during furloughs, depending on the laws of a particular state.

For more information on your rights in a furlough, obtain a copy of FEND's *Your Furlough Guide*. To get your copy, use the ordering information included in this *Almanac*, or call 1-800-989-3363.

Section 11—Career Transition Assistance

Range of Help Available

Federal agencies are required to establish career transition assistance programs to help surplus and displaced workers find other jobs as the government downsizes and restructures, according to the terms of a September 12, 1995, presidential memo entitled "Career Transition Assistance for

Federal Employees." These career-transition assistance programs are to be developed in partnership with labor and management, in accordance with guidance and regulations provided by the Office of Personnel Management.

OPM issued regulations on December 29, 1995, which provided the framework for implementing the directive.

Under these regulations, agencies are required to implement a Career Transition Assistance Plan (CTAP) to provide career transition services to their surplus and displaced employees, and give special selection priority to these workers. These regulations set minimum standards for these plans, which can be supplemented at the agency's discretion.

OPM also suspended the former Interagency Placement Program, replacing it with the Interagency Career Transition Assistance Program (ICTAP). Instead of placing surplus workers in new jobs from a centralized inventory, the traditional federal model for assisting displaced civil servants, the ICTAP program gives individual workers the responsibility and tools to find, apply for, and exercise priority rights for specific vacancies in which they are interested.

Transition assistance consists of four components:

• Programs to provide career transition services to the agency's surplus and displaced employees;

• Policies for retraining displaced employees for new career opportunities;

• Policies requiring the selection of a well qualified surplus or displaced internal agency employee who applies for a vacant position in the commuting area, before any other candidate is selected from within or outside the agency; and

• Policies requiring the selection of a well qualified displaced employee from another agency who applies for a vacant position in the commuting area before any other candidate is selected from outside the agency.

Because the Department of Defense manages a separate program that provides selection priority to surplus and displaced employees within DoD—the Priority Placement Program (see below)—it is exempt from the special selection requirement affecting its own employees under the CTAP. However, DoD is subject to other

elements of the regulations, and its employees are eligible for the benefits provided by the ICTAP.

Detailed information about these programs is available through agency personnel offices and through OPM's Career Transition Hotline at (202) 606-2425.

Two Internet sites have been set up to assist surplus and displaced employees in finding other employment. OPM's USAJOBS Internet site *(http://www.usajobs.opm.gov)* provides information on employment and complete vacancy listings, which are updated daily. A joint site operated by the Department of Labor and OPM (http://safetynet.doleta.gov) titled "Planning Your Future: A Federal Employee's Survival Guide" provides information to employees affected by downsizing who are attempting to make career transitions, especially to private-sector occupations. Additional information on these sites and other career transition resources is available from OPM's Workforce Restructuring Office at (202) 606- 0960; fax (202) 606-2329.

Comprehensive information about worldwide federal job opportunities also is available from OPM by phone (912-757-3000; 912-744-2299 for TDD), electronic bulletin board (912-757-3100), and touch-screen computer kiosks in federal buildings nationwide.

Reinstatement Rights—Former career or career-conditional federal employees may be reinstated to positions in the federal service "non-competitively"—i.e., without getting on a civil service list of eligibles again—within the following time limits after separation:

• Those former employees who are not entitled to veterans' preference and who had not completed the service requirement for career tenure. This time limit, however, may be extended by certain intervening service.

• Those former employees who are entitled to veterans' preference, or who had completed the service requirement for career tenure.

For details, see Section 1 of this chapter.

General Eligibility Rules

Under the executive order, an eligible "displaced" employee is:

• a current career or career conditional

competitive service employee in tenure group 1 or 2, at grade levels GS-15 or equivalent and below, who has received a specific reduction-in-force separation notice or notice of proposed removal for declining a directed reassignment or transfer of function outside of the local commuting area; or

• a current employee in the excepted service, serving on an appointment without time limit, at grade levels GS-15 or equivalent and below, who has been given noncompetitive appointment eligibility and selection priority by statute for positions in the competitive service, and who is in receipt of a RIF separation notice or notice of proposed removal for declining a transfer of function or directed reassignment outside of the local commuting area.

An eligible "surplus" employee is:

• a current employee serving under an appointment in the competitive service, in tenure group 1 or 2, at grade levels GS-15 or equivalent and below, who has received a certificate of expected separation or other official certification issued by the agency indicating that the position is surplus (for example, a notice of position abolishment, or a notice stating that the employee is eligible for discontinued service retirement);

• a current employee serving an excepted service appointment without time limit, at grade levels GS-15 or equivalent and below, who has been issued a certificate of expected separation or other official agency certification indicating that his or her position is surplus (for example, a notice of position abolishment, or a notice stating that the employee is eligible for discontinued service retirement), and who has been conferred noncompetitive appointment eligibility and special selection priority by statute for positions in the competitive service;

• at an agency's discretion, an employee: serving a Schedule A or B excepted appointment without time limit, at grade levels GS-15 or equivalent and below, who is in receipt of a certificate of expected separation or other official agency certification indicating that his or her job is surplus (for example, a notice of position abolishment, or an official notice stating that the employee is eligible for discontinued service retirement); or an employee who has received a RIF notice of separation, or a notice of proposed removal

for declining a transfer of function or directed reassignment outside of the local commuting area. Such employees may exercise selection priority for permanent excepted service positions within the agency's local commuting area, provided the position to which they are appointed has the same appointing authority, i.e., Schedule A or B, as the position from which being separated.

An employee "well qualified" for placement is one who possesses the knowledge, skills, and abilities that clearly exceed the position's minimum qualification requirements. Agencies must ensure that a documented, independent second review is conducted whenever an otherwise eligible employee is found to be not well qualified. The applicant must be advised in writing of the results of the second review. An example of a second independent reviewer might be a supervisor in the human resources office, an equal employment opportunity official, or a subject matter specialist who was not involved in the original rating process.

Except as noted above, generally the regulations do not provide selection priority to employees separated from excepted service positions in the same way as for employees separated from the competitive service. The reason is that such employees do not have the same kind of eligibility to be appointed on an interchangeable basis as employees in the competitive civil service. Excepted service employees are eligible to receive all the other career transition services (e.g., career counseling, attendance at workshops, access to career transition centers and their resources, etc.) as competitive service employees.

Career Transition Assistance Plans

Each agency must establish a Career Transition Assistance Plan (CTAP) to actively assist its surplus and displaced employees. The plan must include policies to provide career transition services to all surplus and displaced agency employees affected by downsizing or restructuring, including employees in the excepted service and the Senior Executive Service. The plan also must include policies to provide special selection priority to well qualified surplus or displaced agency employees who apply for agency vacancies in the local commuting area, before selecting any other candidate from either within or outside the agency, as well as agency procedures for reviewing qualification issues, and operation of the agency's Reemployment Priority List.

Special selection priority is available for an individual who:

• is a surplus or displaced employee (still on the agency rolls);

• has a current performance rating of record of at least fully successful or equivalent;

• applies for a vacancy that is at or below the grade level from which the employee is being separated and that does not have a greater promotion potential than the position from which the worker is being separated;

• occupies a position in the same local commuting area of the vacancy or, at the agency's discretion, occupies a position beyond the local commuting area;

• files an application for a specific vacancy within the time frames established by the agency; and

• is determined by the agency to be well qualified for the specific vacancy.

Agencies have discretion to offer selection priority under CTAP to excepted service employees who were hired into appointments without time limit under Schedule A or B appointing authorities. If permanent Schedule A or B excepted service employees are being separated through RIF, or because they declined a transfer of function or directed reassignment outside of the local commuting area, at the agency's discretion, they may be given selection priority for other similar permanent excepted service Schedule A or B vacancies within the local commuting area.

Eligibility for special selection priority begins on the date the agency issues the employee a RIF separation notice, certificate of expected separation, notice of proposed separation for declining a directed reassignment or transfer of function outside of the local commuting area, or other official agency certification identifying the employee as being in a surplus organization or occupation.

Eligibility expires on the earliest of:

• the RIF separation date, the date of the employee's resignation from the agency, or the date of separation under adverse action procedures for declining a directed reassignment or transfer of function to another local commuting area;

• cancellation of the RIF separation notice, certificate of expected separation, notice of proposed removal for declining a directed reassignment or transfer of function outside of the commuting area, or other official agency certification identifying the employee as surplus;

• when an eligible employee receives a career, career-conditional, or excepted appointment without time limit in any agency at any grade level; or

• within an agency, and at the agency's discretion, when an eligible employee declines a career, career conditional, or excepted appointment (without time limit), for which the employee has applied and been rated well qualified.

CTAP: Order of Selection

An agency, when filling a vacancy, must select an eligible employee under its Career Transition Assistance Plan before selecting any other internal or external candidate, unless the agency can show that another employee would otherwise be separated by a RIF. Agencies may not procure temporary help services in lieu of appointing a surplus or displaced employee.

Once the agency has met its obligation to select employees eligible under its CTAP, it is free to select any other competitive service tenure group 1 or 2 candidate from its workforce, following the appropriate procedures. An agency may provide selection priority to surplus and displaced agency employees from another commuting area after it has discharged its obligation to eligible surplus and displaced agency employees from the local commuting area.

When an agency has met its CTAP obligations and elects to fill a position from outside its workforce, it must first select agency employees who have been separated through RIF and are eligible under its Reemployment Priority List (RPL); then, federal employees who are displaced from other agencies and who apply for positions in the local commuting area and are eligible under the Interagency Career Transition Assistance Plan (ICTAP).

Exceptions—Numerous actions are not covered by these requirements, including: reassignments, changes to lower grade, or promotions, when no eligible employees apply; reemployment of a former agency employee exercising regulatory or statutory reemployment rights, including the reemployment of injured workers who have either been restored to earning capacity by the Office of Workers' Compensation Programs or who have received a notice that their compensation benefits will cease because of recovery from the disabling injury or illness; position changes resulting from disciplinary actions; temporary appointments of under 121 days (including all extensions); exchange of positions between or among agency employees, when the actions involve no increase in grade or promotion potential, i.e., job swaps; non-competitive placement of an employee into a different position as a result of a formal reorganization, when the former position ceases to exist, and no actual vacancy results; assignments made under the Intergovernmental Personnel Act; the filling of a position through an excepted appointment; details; and time-limited promotions of under 121 days, including all extensions.

At the time it issues a specific RIF separation notice, certificate of expected separation, or other official agency certification, an agency must give eligible employees information in writing about the CTAP special selection priority available to them. Such information must contain guidance to the employee on how to apply for vacancies under the CTAP, and the documentation generally required as proof of eligibility. Agencies must take reasonable steps to ensure eligible employees are notified of all vacancies the agency is filling and what is required to be determined well qualified for the vacancies. Vacancy announcements within an agency must contain information on how eligible employees within the agency can apply, what proof of eligibility is required, and the agency's definition of "well qualified."

Each agency is required to advise, in writing, their surplus and displaced employees who apply for specific vacancies within its local commuting area of the results of their application, and whether they were found well qualified. If they are not found well qualified, such notice must include information on the results of an independent, second review conducted by the agency. If an applicant is found well qualified, and another well qualified surplus or displaced candidate is selected, the applicant must be so advised.

To receive this special selection priority, an eligible employee must apply for a specific agency vacancy in the same local commuting area as the position the employee occupies within the prescribed time frames, attach the appropriate proof of eligibility, and be determined well qualified by the agency for the specific vacancy.

An agency may decide the specific order of selection of its eligible employees (e.g., the agency may decide to select displaced employees before surplus employees or may select surplus and/or displaced employees from within a particular component of the agency before selecting surplus and/or displaced employees from another component of the agency). An agency cannot select any other candidate from within or outside the agency if eligible employees are available for the vacancy or vacancies. If two or more eligible employees apply for a vacancy and are determined to be well qualified, any of these eligible employees may be selected. If no eligible employees apply or none is deemed well qualified, the agency may select another agency employee without regard to this subpart.

Reemployment Priority Lists

In addition to affording eligible current employees special selection priority for internal vacancies through the CTAP as described above, agencies also maintain Reemployment Priority Lists (RPL) to give rehiring priority to employees who have RIF separation notices and those who have been separated from competitive service positions by RIF.

To be eligible to register for an RPL, an employee must:
• be in the competitive service in tenure group I or II;
• have received a performance rating above unacceptable as the last annual performance rating of record;
• have received a specific RIF notice of separation or a Certification of Expected Separation; and
• have not declined a job offer.

Employees must register within 30 days after the separation date. An RPL registrant with career status is retained on the list for two years from the date of separation. Those who have career-conditional status are retained on the list for one year.

To be entered on the RPL, an individual must submit a current SF 171, an OF-612, or a resume to the personnel office within 30 calendar days of the RIF separation date. Agency application forms may specify types of positions the employee will accept and other conditions. Registrants will be deleted from the list: upon the individual's written request, when they accept full-time non-temporary federal employment, if they resign or retire before the RIF separation, when they decline employment at a grade level equivalent to the one from which separated or scheduled to be separated, or under certain other conditions an agency may set.

RPLs give employees hiring preference only within the employee's own agency and in the local commuting area and only for positions at or below the grade level of the position from which they are being (or may be) separated, and that have no higher promotion potential. Registrants will be given priority consideration in filling vacancies for which they qualify within the commuting area as long as they are on the RPL. Registrants get priority consideration when the agency fills competitive service vacancies from outside the agency. If a registrant is available, an agency may not fill a permanent or time-limited competitive service position by a new appointment (unless the individual appointed is a 10-point veteran) or by transfer or reemployment (unless the individual appointed is exercising restoration or reemployment rights).

However, an RPL candidate does not necessarily get priority if:
• the agency is filling positions from within the current work force.
• no qualified RPL registrants are available, they decline the position, or they fail to respond to an agency inquiry of interest;
• a current, qualified agency employee is available through detail, noncompetitive conversion to the competitive service; reappointment without a break in service; or extension of a temporary appointment;
• the position is being filled by a 30-day "special needs" or "700 hour" appointment for persons with disabilities; or
• the job is being filled at a grade level different from that for which the candidates have registered, or has greater promotion potential than the last position held.

Those who believe that their reemployment priority rights under the program have been violated may appeal to the Merit Systems Protection Board.

Interagency Career Transition Assistance Plans

ICTAP provides priority consideration and selection in other federal agencies for displaced employees. The vacancy must be in the same commuting area as the location where they were or are being separated. If an individual meets the eligibility requirements, the agency must select that person before hiring outside the agency. The program requires publication of job information on all federal vacancies for this purpose.

Eligibility for ICTAP begins on the date the agency issues a specific RIF separation notice, and ends one year from the separation date. The application must comply with all job announcement instructions and a copy of the RIF separation notice must be attached.

To be eligible for the special selection priority, an individual must:
• be a displaced employee;
• have a current (or a last) performance rating of record of at least fully successful or equivalent;
• apply for a vacancy at or below the grade level from which the employee has been or is being separated and that does not have a greater promotion potential than the position from which the employee has been or is being separated;
• occupy, or have been displaced from, a position in the same local commuting area of the vacancy;
• file an application for a specific vacancy within the time frames established by the agency (and provide proof of eligibility required); and
• be determined by the agency to be well qualified for the specific position.

Eligibility for special selection priority begins: on the date the agency issues the RIF separation notice; on the date an agency certifies that it cannot place an employee eligible; on the date an employee is notified that his or her disability annuity has been or is being terminated; on the date the agency issues a formal notice of proposed separation to an employee for declining a transfer of function or directed reassignment outside the local commuting area; or on the date the National Guard

Bureau or Military Department certifies that an employee under §330.703(b)(6) has retired under 5 U.S.C. 8337(h) or 8456.

Eligibility expires:

• one year after separation, except for those employees separated on or after September 12, 1995, and prior to February 29, 1996 (for these employees, eligibility expired February 28, 1997);

• one year after an agency certifies that an individual cannot be placed;

• one year after individuals receive notification that their disability annuity has been or will be terminated;

• when an employee receives a career, career-conditional, or excepted appointment without time limit in any agency at any grade level;

• when the employee no longer meets the initial eligibility requirements (e.g., the worker is no longer being separated by RIF or under adverse action procedures for declining a transfer of function or directed reassignment outside the local commuting area, or an employee separates by resignation or non-discontinued service retirement prior to the RIF effective date); or

• at an agency's discretion, when an eligible employee declines a career, career conditional, or excepted appointment without time limit, for which the worker has applied and been rated well qualified, or upon an applicant's failure to respond within a reasonable period of time to an offer or official inquiry of availability.

Generally, when filling a vacancy from outside the agency's work force, an agency must select: current or former agency employees eligible under the agency's Reemployment Priority List described above; then at the agency's option, any other former employee displaced from the agency (under appropriate selection procedures); followed by current or former federal employees displaced from other agencies eligible under this program, and then any other candidate under appropriate selection procedures.

At the time it issues a specific RIF separation notice or notice of proposed removal for declining a directed reassignment or transfer of function outside of the local commuting area, an agency must give each of its eligible employees information in writing about the special selection priority available to them under the Interagency Career Transition Assistance Plan. Such information must contain guidance to the employee on how to apply for vacancies under the ICTAP, and what documentation is generally required as proof of eligibility.

Agencies must take reasonable steps to ensure eligible employees are notified of all vacancies the agency is filling and what is required for them to be determined well qualified for the vacancies. Each agency is required to advise, in writing, ICTAP candidates who apply for specific vacancies within its local commuting area of the results of their application, and whether or not they were found well qualified. If they are not found well qualified, such notice must include information on the results of an independent, second review conducted by the agency. If an applicant is found well qualified, and another well qualified surplus or displaced candidate is selected, the applicant must be so advised.

To receive this special selection priority, eligible employees must apply directly to agencies for specific vacancies in the local commuting area within the prescribed time frames, attach the appropriate proof of eligibility, and be determined well qualified by the agency for the specific position.

In making selections, an agency must adhere to the overall order of selection set forth above. An agency cannot select another candidate from outside the agency if eligible employees are available for the vacancy or vacancies. If two or more eligible employees apply for a vacancy and are determined to be well qualified, any of these eligible employees may be selected. If no eligible employees apply or none is deemed well qualified, the agency may select another candidate. This flexibility does not apply to selections made from the agency's Reemployment Priority List.

An agency may select a candidate from its Career Transition Assistance Plan or Reemployment Priority List, or another current agency employee (if no eligible employees are available through its CTAP) at any time.

Department of Defense RIF and Placement Benefits

The Defense Department has several career transition assistance authorities unique to that agency, largely arising out of the significant job reductions occurring there over the last decade, linked both to base closings and to changes in DoD's mission and structure.

Priority Placement Program—The PPP, sometimes referred to as "Program A" is an automated referral program for those facing involuntarily separation, downgrade, or transfer of function, which is designed to assist DoD employees in locating positions within the agency. If eligible, individuals may register voluntarily in the PPP to seek employment at other DoD installations. Those scheduled to receive severance pay benefits must register for installations within their commuting areas.

Current competitive service employees on an appointment without time limitation who have career or career-conditional status or those in the excepted service with or without personal competitive status may register in the PPP if they are scheduled for displacement. The employee's performance and conduct must be fully satisfactory.

Unless early registration is authorized, employees become eligible to register when they: receive a specific RIF notice of separation or demotion, decline in writing an official RIF reassignment or demotion out of the commuting area, decline in writing a transfer of function or a covered management-directed reassignment out of the commuting area, or receive a notice of furlough for six months or more. Employees entitled to severance pay are mandatorily registered.

Employees must register for their current skill and may register for a total of five skills, provided they are well qualified. Mandatory registrants must be registered for all skills for which they are well qualified, including appropriate special skill identifiers.

Employees must register while still employed. The employee must fill out registration forms, which are available through DoD civilian personnel offices. DoD sends personnel specialists to bases identified for closure to assist employees registering in the PPP. Unless registration is mandatory, individuals can select locations and grade levels for which they wish to be considered within program guidelines.

Competitive service employees may register no higher than current permanent

grade or retained grade. If registering for other pay systems, registration is restricted to the grade having the representative rate equal or below the rep rate of the registrant's current permanent or retained grade. If registering from GS to other pay systems, the individual may register for the highest grade for which well qualified; the potential gaining activity makes the determination as to whether an offer should be made based on their local pay scale.

Generally, employees may register down to and including three GS grades or equivalent below their current permanent grade. Employees facing separation are registered for the minimum number of activities nearest their duty station likely to provide a reasonable opportunity for placement. They may not skip over DoD activities or states to register for more distant locations. Activities in an adjoining zone that are no more distant from the employee's duty station than the furthermost activity selected in the zone may be included in the initial area of referral.

Registration does not, in and of itself, guarantee an offer of continued employment. Placement can only occur when a vacancy matching the skills is being filled and the applicant is deemed well qualified.

PPP uses a computerized system that continually matches the skills of displaced employees with vacant DoD positions. If an employee meets the skills and grade level of a vacant position, that opening must be offered to the employee. Use of an automated "stopper" and referral system ensures consideration within DoD.

Employees are referred using a numeric priority (1 through 3). The priority assigned is based on the severity of the employee's proposed personnel action. For example, an employee facing RIF separation with no offer of continued employment is assigned a Priority 1, while an employee with a RIF offer of a change to a grade one grade below their current grade held is assigned Priority 3. Priority 1 employees must be considered for placement before priority 2 and 3 employees. Additionally, the priority assigned determines which recruitment actions are "stopped" when a match occurs.

Generally, individuals can remain in the program for the duration of the notice period and for 12 months after separation.

During this period, placement in an appropriate position, declination of a valid offer, optional retirement, or a personal request can terminate registration.

Only one valid offer will be made. If that offer is declined, the employee is removed from the program. If an individual accepts a PPP offer, the government will pay related travel and transportation costs to the new location under the Department of Defense Joint Travel Regulations. Registrants in the continental U.S. (CONUS) must accept or decline offers from CONUS activities within two calendar days, and registrants outside CONUS must respond within three calendar days.

Retained Grade Placement Program— Employees on a competitive and/or excepted appointment and serving under grade retention as a result of a RIF or job reclassification are required to register in this program, sometimes known as "Program R." Employees with grade retention in the excepted service (excluding National Guard technicians) who do not have personal competitive status are eligible for excepted positions only.

Registration is mandatory for all DoD employees receiving retained grade. Affected employees must register for the retained grade position and all other skills in the same pay group for which the registrant is well qualified.

Normally, the area of referral for the duration of the retained grade period must include all DoD installations in the commuting area. However, for those who relocate to the current DoD activity at government expense, registration is restricted to the new installation for one year. If an offer is made through this program, the individual must accept the written offer or lose retained grade entitlement.

Registrants are assigned a "2" when demoted two or more GS grades or the equivalent and a "3" when demoted less than two GS grades or the equivalent. If a Priority "2" accepts or declines an offer at an intervening grade, the priority must be reviewed to determine if it is still appropriate. Valid and reasonable offers must be made in writing. Registrants must accept or decline offers within two calendar days. "R" program registrants are ineligible for temporary or term positions.

Defense Outplacement Referral Sys- **tem—**DORS is an automated referral system operated through a cooperative effort between DoD and OPM. The purpose of DORS is to provide placement opportunity for current DoD civilian personnel and their spouses through referral to other DoD activities, non-DoD agencies, state and local governments, and the private sector. Registration and placement through DORS is voluntary for both employees and participating employers. Local personnel offices have information on the program and can assist employees and their spouses in registering. Qualifications are determined based on education and experience. Only the first three different series appearing on the registration will be used for referral to private sector. Special skill identifiers will only be used for referrals within DoD.

Current employees on permanent appointments may register no higher than their current permanent grade. Employees on temporary appointments with prior federal service or spouses with prior federal service may register at the last permanent grade held. Registrants without status or with no prior federal service may register for the highest grade for which eligible based on the qualification standards. Registrants may register no more than three grades below the high grade for which registered. If registering for different pay plans, each pay plan is treated separately. An employee may register for any location in the U.S. and/or overseas, but the spouse's area of referral must be the same as the sponsor's. Relocation expenses cannot be authorized for spouses and are not guaranteed for DoD employees.

Local Placement Programs—Contacts with local, federal, state, and private employers are made by the installation in an effort to locate acceptable employment opportunities for those who wish to remain in the local area. Additionally, those who have not previously declined a reasonable offer may be given mandatory employment consideration through the Interagency Career Transition Assistance Plan.

Training and Retraining—The Department of Labor, in coordination with local downsizing activities and installations, manages training and retraining programs authorized by the Workforce Investment Act of 1998 the respective state employment security agency. This training normally is targeted to a specific and known employment opportunity. Closing or downsizing activities create employee assistance/transition centers to provide career transition instruction, including resume preparation, interview and job search techniques, financial planning, and other services. Similarly, instruction in skills such as written communication is provided through the installation's transition assistance center.

Relocation Entitlements—Generally, when relocation is in the best interest of the government, relocation expenses are paid to move the individual from one duty station to another at a different geographical location. Relocation services, also known as permanent change of station (PCS) benefits, are provided to defray the costs of transporting employees, their families, and households to new locations. The supporting personnel and transportation offices provide counseling on these benefits. Rules and regulations governing PCS benefits can be found in Chapter 4 of the DoD Joint Travel Regulations, Volume 2.

Relocation expenses usually reimbursed include:

• transportation, packing, crating, and temporary storage of household goods and personal effects up to 18,000 pounds;

• per diem and transportation for the employee and spouse when seeking permanent housing at the new duty location;

• temporary quarters subsistence expense payments for up to 60 days when warranted, which can be extended 60 days based on exceptional circumstances;

• specified expenses, when authorized, when the employee sells a residence or settles an unexpired lease at the old duty station or when buying a residence at the new duty location;

• payment of miscellaneous moving expenses of up to two weeks' pay or $700 for those who are married, and one week of pay or $350 if single (whichever is less in both cases); and

• permanent storage of household goods and personal effects when the assignment is to an isolated area where living quarters are not available.

Homeowner's Assistance Program—Under this program, a career employee who is separated from a base that is being closed (in whole or in part), where the real estate market is severely affected by the clo-

sure, may be eligible to receive assistance.

This assistance may take the form of: case-by-case payments by the government to cover part of the losses resulting from sale of the home, sale of the residence to the government, or reimbursement of losses as a result of mortgage foreclosure. Those serving under a time-limited appointment are not eligible.

The Department of Army's Corps of Engineers administers the program. There are a number of requirements that must be met before assistance can be paid. For the benefit to be authorized, there has to be an announcement of a base closing or realignment action that affects your community. Second, a determination must be made that real estate values have dropped as a result of the base closing or realignment. Many other local factors may affect the price of the real estate, but these two conditions determine whether a community is eligible for the Homeowners Assistance Program.

The basic application is made on DD Form 1607, Application for Homeowners Assistance Program. Part III of the form must be completed by a personnel officer. In addition, applicants must submit ENG Form 4161-R and a variety of documents to show evidence of ownership of the property, occupancy dates, assignment orders, efforts to sell the home (whether it was sold), and mortgage details. A complete application package can be obtained from either the housing office or the personnel office on a base.

Voluntary Early Retirement Authority (VERA)—OPM delegates this authority to agencies to help them reduce staff by allowing employees to retire under reduced age and service requirements (i.e., age 50 with 20 years of service, any age with 25 years of service). The retirement annuity is reduced by two percent per year for each year the employee is under age 55. This is also referred to as early retirement or "early out."

Buyouts—See next section.

Non-Federal Hiring Incentive—Congress approved this program as part of the National Defense Authorization for fiscal year 1995. Under it, DoD has established a pilot program at closing installations to reimburse non-federal employers for training expenses when they hire DoD employees facing separation. DoD will also pay expenses for employees to relocate to take a non-federal job. Payments are limited to $10,000 per employee.

Employee Assistance After Separation—Most employees separated by RIFs are entitled to payment for unused annual leave, severance pay (based on salary, years of service, and age), and unemployment compensation. If these employees elect to continue their health insurance for up to 18 months, DoD will pay the employer portion of the premium and any administrative fees. In addition, separated employees may remain in the priority placement program for up to one year after separation.

Section 12—Buyouts
(Voluntary Separation Incentive Payments)

General Rules and Procedures

Buyouts in the executive branch started in 1993 in the Defense Department under Public Law 102-484, and have been extended to other agencies for varying periods under several other laws. The Federal Workforce Restructuring Act of 1994 provided a government-wide buyout program to executive branch agencies from March 30, 1994, through March 31, 1995, under P.L. 103-226. Another government-wide program was authorized between September 30, 1996, and December 30, 1997, under P.L. 104-208, and permanent government-wide authority was granted by P.O. 107-296.

Agencies with separate buyout authority are the Department of Defense (until September 30, 2003), the Department of Energy (until September 30, 2003), the National Security Agency (indefinitely), the General Accounting Office (until December 31, 2003), and the Government Printing Office (until September 30, 2004).

Under Section 1151 of P.L. 106-398, DoD is authorized to pay buyouts in lump sums or in installments. There are two installment options: biweekly payments at a rate selected by the employee until the full amount of the buyout is paid, up to one year, or in two equal payments, one following separation and the other half six months later.

Under buyouts, also called voluntary separation incentive payments, incentives generally have been offered to encourage eligible employees to separate voluntarily through resignation, early retirement, or regular retirement. The goal is to minimize the need for layoffs as agencies downsize and restructure. Thus, the incentives are offered most commonly in offices and program functions that are scheduled for a personnel cut. However, separation payments sometimes will be offered at other sites where the acceptance of an incentive will, through subsequent placements or job abolishment, avoid the need for an involuntary separation. One full-time equivalent employee usually was cut for each buyout separation.

However, the authority under P.L. 107-296 allows use of buyouts for workplace restructuring aimed at improving the agency's skills mix; the agency is not required to eliminate a position for each buyout paid.

The buyout is a lump sum incentive equivalent to an employee's severance pay entitlement up to a maximum of $25,000. Buyout payments are fully taxable for purposes of federal withholding, Medicare, applicable state and local taxes, and Social Security for those covered by that system. Such payments are not counted as basic pay for purposes of calculating benefits such as retirement annuities.

The incentives often are offered in conjunction with an agency's use of voluntary early retirement authority, which allows retirement for those age 50 or older with at least 20 years of service, or at any age with at least 25 years of service (with applicable reductions in a retiree's annuity). Employees who take the incentives into early or optional retirement must meet the age and service requirements for retirement eligibility by the effective date of their retirement.

Buyout Eligibility and Conditions

A buyout may not be paid if the employee: is a reemployed annuitant; has a disability on the basis of which the employee is or would be eligible for a disability retirement, or is serving under an appointment with a time limitation. DoD and the CIA further bar buyouts to those who have not been on-board with the agency without a break in service for 12 continuous months, while the requirement at Energy is three continuous years of service.

Generally, agencies authorized to use the payments may offer buyouts at their discretion.

The agencies may define buyout eligibility according to agency component, job classification, grade level, geographic location, and similar considerations. They also may distinguish according to work schedule (e.g., making offers only to full-time employees) and type of appointment (e.g., excluding political appointees). They also can, in effect, choose by retirement-eligibility status by giving first priority to applicants who would retire over those who would resign. They may not, however, select among individuals within the same category.

Employees who accept separation pay lose their eligibility for benefits that would have applied if they had been laid off in a reduction in force. These include the full amount of the severance pay entitlement (which usually is larger than the buyout maximum of $25,000), discontinued service retirement (if otherwise eligible), selection priority under the Career Transition Assistance Program (CTAP), and Inter-Agency Career Transition Assistance Program (ICTAP), and job search assistance. In addition, most states consider buyout-takers ineligible for the unemployment compensation benefits that are available to laid-off workers.

Employees accepting the incentives must agree not to return to another federal job within five years or to repay the full (pre-tax) amount of their payments if they are reemployed, often prior to their first day at the new government job. This applies to any appointment, of any duration, full or part time, temporary or permanent, in the postal service as well as other branches of the federal government. The general rule is that the restriction covers any position in which the salary is paid by the government. In some cases, the reemployment ban also applies to working for an agency under a "personal services contract," the definition of which covers most consulting type arrangements. (At the Defense Department and CIA, the ban on returning under personal services contracts applies for only one year; however, the CIA has a more expansive list of restrictions, including bans against acting as agents or attorneys of other parties before the agency and against participating in contract decisions involving the agency for the year.) Simply working as an employee of a company under contract to the government may not protect an employee from falling under the definition of a "personal services contract." Employees who have received buyouts are urged to check with the legal counsel at the agency that paid the buyout before returning to work under any contracting arrangement to ensure that it is not personal services in nature.

Some agencies may waive the repayment requirement where the buyout taker is the only applicant uniquely qualified for the position. (This generally requires OPM approval.)

Those accepting buyout offers must promise to separate on an agreed-upon date. They generally may withdraw their acceptance up to that date, except when the agency can show a valid reason why allowing them to change their minds would cause a hardship to the agency. Such reasons may include that the person's position already has been abolished, the agency does not have enough other takers to avoid a reduction in force, and another employee whose job had been saved by the separation agreement would be adversely affected.

Where the number of employees applying for a buyout exceeds the number of offers available, the agency must choose who gets the payments based on "fair and objective" criteria. These standards are not defined by law. However, commonly used criteria include order of separation date, order of receipt of completed application, or seniority.

Employees leaving with a buyout have the same options to continue federally-sponsored health and life insurance as do similarly situated workers retiring or resigning without an incentive payment. However, a special provision for buyout takers who retire allows them to carry their health insurance into retirement as long as they were enrolled as of October 1, 1996. This constitutes a waiver of the general rule requiring enrollment for the five previous years or the entire time eligible to be enrolled.

For more information on general rules governing buyout offers and how they can help you to decide if a buyout is right for you, obtain FEND's book *Your Buyout Offer*. To get your copy, use the ordering information included in this *Almanac*, or call 1-800-989-3363.

Section 13—Federal Employment Information Resources

USAJOBS: An Overview

USAJOBS is the government-wide automated employment information system. All of the components of the system are updated with the Federal Jobs Database of more than 12,000 worldwide job opportunities every business day. The system is available in a variety of formats to provide easy and convenient access to all job seekers through telephone or computer. USAJOBS allows the public to go to one place for information about most job opportunities within the federal government, many state and local governments, and private sector jobs listings as well. The system is available 24 hours a day, seven days a week. USAJOBS consists of:

World Wide Web—The United States government's official website for jobs and employment information, may be accessed at www.usajobs.opm.gov. On the Web site, job-seekers can access current job vacancies, review Federal Employment Information Fact Sheets, and apply for some jobs online. Complete job announcements are attached to job listings and can be printed or saved from the screen. The website is available 7 days a week, 24 hours a day. The USAJOBS website (USAJOBS.opm.gov) has a new USAJOBS by e-mail service to assist with job searches. Users are notified by e-mail of new job listings posted to the site that meet their specified search criteria. Users can create and store up to three searches with this service.

Studentjobs.gov—USAJOBS also has a new website designed specifically for students. This site provides a one-stop Internet gateway for students seeking federal employment opportunities. It provides links to a student job search, a resume service, and offers additional employment information targeted to students.

Nationwide Automated Telephone System—This telephone-based automated employment information system provides instant access to information on current job vacancies, student employment programs, and many other employment information topics. General vacancy information is available and application packages can often be sent out to the users. Telephone (478) 757-3000, seven days a week, 24 hours a day. A telephone device for the deaf (TDD) is also available at (478) 744-2299.

Federal Employment Information Fact Sheets—The Office of Personnel Management prepares and issues a series of Federal Employment Information Fact Sheets. These are nationwide employment information handouts that provide quick, standard responses to inquiries on a variety of subjects related to federal employment. They are available through all of the USAJOBS components.

At any given time, there may be as many as 12,000 or more federal vacancy listings publicized on USAJOBS. Over half of these opportunities may be open to the public at large. Opportunities ranging in responsibility from entry level to senior executive are often available to all. Many special outreach programs exist for minorities, students, the disabled, and veterans. The federal government is leading the way as an equal opportunity employer, and all selections are based on individual merit.

Other Types of Assistance

Telephone Application Processing System—In some cases applying for a federal job may be as simple as making a telephone call. For example, hundreds of professional nurse and border patrol agent positions have been filled in this way through OPM's telephone application processing system. Although OPM's telephone application processing system is currently limited to a few occupations, the agency plans to expand this highly successful and easily accessible application process to include a greater number of jobs in the near future.

Career Transition Information—Career transition information can be obtained from OPM's website at www.opm.gov under the general heading "career transition." OPM's Workforce Restructuring Hotline is (202) 606-2425.

State Employment Service Offices—Each state employment office has a list of current open federal examination and vacancy announcements. The list may be on a printed report on microfiche, or on computer. Most state employment service offices can access the systems on the Federal Employment Information Highway.

Automated Telephone System Numbers

This automated phone system provides 24-hours-a-day, 7-days-a-week information about current employment opportunities (nationwide and worldwide), special programs for students, veterans, and people with disabilities, the Presidential Management Intern Program, salaries and benefits, and application request services. To access USAJOBS by phone, call (478) 757-3000. Nationwide TDD service can be reached at (478) 744-2299.

Chapter 9
Agency Roles and Responsibilities

Section 1—Office of Personnel Management

General Responsibilities and Procedures

The Office of Personnel Management is the federal government's human resources agency. The address and main phone number of OPM are: 1900 E St., N.W., Washington, DC 20415; phone: (202) 606-1800. OPM's Web site is *www.opm.gov*.

Specifically, the Office of Personnel Management:

• provides leadership to strengthen the government's human resources management;

• protects the merit system and veterans' rights through oversight;

• supports agencies in merit-based candidate assessment and hiring;

• supports agencies in workforce restructuring;

• ensures the suitability of federal employees and provides for personnel investigations;

• promotes executive leadership for a results-oriented government;

• provides government-wide human resources development leadership and policy;

• delivers executive and management development and training;

• operates the federal employees' retirement program;

• manages the federal employees' health and life insurance programs;

• administers the system for setting federal compensation and benefits;

• provides tools for effective employee performance management;

• promotes effective labor-management and employee relations;

• enhances the ability of federal employees to balance work and personal responsibilities;

• administers the government's family-friendly leave programs; and

• manages a comprehensive workforce information system.

OPM is the primary agent for helping the president carry out his responsibilities for positive management of the federal workforce. Both its director and deputy director are appointed by the president and confirmed by the Senate. They serve at the pleasure of the president. Organizationally, OPM is an independent agency within the executive branch of government.

OPM develops personnel policies governing civilian employment in executive branch agencies and in certain agencies of the legislative and judicial branches. It provides leadership and assistance to federal agencies in carrying out these policies.

Its responsibilities also include central staffing operations, program evaluation, executive development, and training policy. OPM administers federal employee retirement and insurance programs, and exercises management leadership in labor relations, affirmative action, and employee utilization.

When agencies have the competence and it is cost efficient, OPM will delegate authority and functions to the heads of federal agencies, under enforceable performance agreements.

Compensation and Leave Claims

Under Public Law 104-53, most of the claims settlement functions formerly performed by the General Accounting Office were transferred to the Office of Management and Budget, which in turn delegated to the Office of Personnel Management the authority to settle claims involving federal employees' compensation and leave, deceased employees' compensation, and proceeds of canceled checks for veterans' benefits payable to deceased beneficiaries.

A claim must be submitted by the claimant in writing and must be signed by the claimant or by the claimant's representative. While no specific form is required, the request should describe the basis for the claim and state the amount sought. The claim should also include: the name, address, telephone number, and facsimile machine number (if available) of the claimant; the name, address, telephone number, and facsimile machine number (if available) of the agency employee who denied the claim; a copy of the denial of the claim, issued by the employing agency; and any other information which the claimant believes OPM should consider.

At the discretion of the agency, the agency may forward the claim to OPM on the claimant's behalf. The claimant is responsible for ensuring that OPM receives all the information requested.

OPM may request the agency to provide an administrative report. This report should include: the agency's factual findings; the agency's conclusions of law with relevant citations; the agency's recommendation for disposition of the claim; a complete copy of any regulation, instruction, memorandum, or policy relied upon by the agency in making its determination; a statement that the claimant is or is not a member of a collective bargaining unit, and if so, a statement that the claim is or is not covered by a negotiated grievance procedure that specifically excludes the claim from coverage; and any other information that the agency believes OPM should consider.

Claims should be sent to the Program Manager, Room 7671, Office of Merit Systems Oversight and Effectiveness, Office of Personnel Management, 1900 E Street NW, Washington, DC 20415-6000, phone (202) 606-7948.

Position Classification Appeals

The Office of Personnel Management decides classification appeals from current federal employees or their designated representatives. Regulations for classification appeals for general schedule employees are in Subpart F of Part 511 of Title 5, Code of Federal Regulations. Regulations for job grading appeals for federal wage system employees are in Subpart G of Part 532 of Title 5, Code of Federal Regulations.

What May Be Appealed—Employees may seek a change in the grade, occupational series, and sometimes the title of a position, and may seek to have a general schedule position changed to the federal wage system or vice-versa.

Employees may not appeal the content or accuracy of an official position description, the accuracy of a classification standard, an agency's proposed classification decision, the classification of positions to which the employee is not officially assigned, or the classification of positions to which detailed or temporarily promoted for a period of less than two years.

Before submitting an appeal, employees should make sure that the position description identifies the major duties assigned and being performed. OPM will usually not accept an appeal until the agency has fulfilled this responsibility.

Appeal Choices—Employees may appeal the classification of a position to the employing agency at any time.

General schedule (GS) employees may appeal to the employing agency or directly to OPM. However, they may not appeal to the agency and OPM at the same time. GS employees also may make a classification appeal to OPM through the employing agency. The agency must act on the appeal within 60 days or forward it to OPM for action.

OPM recommends that GS employees first seek an appeal decision from the employing agency, since if the agency decision is unfavorable, they can still appeal to OPM. Those who appeal first to OPM and receive an unfavorable decision cannot then appeal to the employing agency.

Federal wage system employees must first appeal to the employing agency. If dissatisfied, they may appeal to OPM. The appeal to OPM must be filed within 15 calendar days of the date the employee receives the agency's decision. OPM may extend the time limit in certain circumstances.

Appealing to the Employing Agency— Appeals of position or job classification to the employing agency generally start with the human resources office, which can explain the agency's appeal procedures.

Appealing to OPM—Appeals to OPM should contain the following information in writing: name, mailing address, and commercial office telephone number; present classification of your position and the requested classification; name of the department or agency and the office; city and the installation's mailing address; a copy of the official position description and either a statement affirming that it is accurate or a detailed explanation of the inaccuracies and an explanation of the efforts made to correct the position description; any additional information about the position that will aid in understanding it; and arguments supporting the requested classification by referencing the appropriate classification standards.

Employees may have a representative (designated in writing) help prepare and present an appeal, but the representative cannot be someone with management or classification authority over the position. Appeals must be sent to the OPM oversight division serving the geographic area where the position is located. (See the OPM Oversight Divisions list.)

OPM's appeal decision is based on information supplied by the employee and the agency. If additional information is needed, it can be obtained through correspondence, telephone call, or on-site visit. OPM does not conduct appeal hearings. OPM bases decisions on the work assigned, the qualifications required to perform that work, and the classification standards. The position will not be compared to other positions. OPM does not consider such factors as employee qualifications that are not required for the work, quality of performance, or volume of work assigned to the position.

OPM decisions take about four months on average. OPM will notify both the employee and agency in writing of its decision. The effective date of any change in grade, occupational series, or title will be stated in the decision. OPM's appeal decision is binding on the agency and on all administrative, certifying, payroll, disbursing, and accounting officials. OPM may raise or lower the grade of a position as the facts warrant. The employing agency still keeps full control over the assignment of duties to a position and who performs those duties.

Reconsideration of OPM Appeal Decision—There is no automatic right to a review of an OPM appeal decision. However, OPM may, at its discretion, reconsider the decision when either the employee or agency submits written evidence or arguments that establish a reasonable doubt as to the technical accuracy of the decision, or presents new, relevant, and substantive information that was not considered in the original decision.

The Director of OPM has discretion to reconsider any decision when written evi-

dence or argument is submitted which tends to establish that the decision is erroneous in its interpretation of statute, regulation, or current policy. The Director may also reconsider a decision that involves a new or unreviewed policy consideration, which may have effects beyond the case at hand, or when the case is so exceptional that it warrants the Director's personal attention.

The deadline for submitting a request for reconsideration is 45 calendar days after the date of the decision.

Retroactivity—The effective date of a classification appeal decision can be retroactive only if it corrects a classification action that resulted in an actual decrease in pay. In order for the decision to be made retroactive, the employee must appeal the classification to either the agency or OPM, but not both at the same time, within 15 calendar days after the effective date of the reclassification action.

Retroactivity may be based only on duties and responsibilities existing at the time of demotion and cannot be based on duties and responsibilities assigned later.

OPM Oversight Divisions

The following OPM offices accept appeals of classification decisions.

Atlanta Oversight Division
(404) 331-3451
75 Spring Street, SW., Suite 1018
Atlanta, GA 30303-3109
Alabama, Florida, Georgia, Mississippi, North Carolina, South Carolina, Tennessee, Virginia (except as noted under the Washington, DC Oversight Division)

Chicago Oversight Division
(312) 353-0387
230 S. Dearborn Street, DPN 30-6
Chicago, IL 60604-1687
Illinois, Indiana, Iowa, Kansas, Kentucky, Michigan, Minnesota, Missouri, Nebraska, North Dakota, Ohio, South Dakota, West Virginia, Wisconsin

Dallas Oversight Division
(214) 767-0561
1100 Commerce Street, Room 4C22
Dallas, TX 75242-9968
Arizona, Arkansas, Colorado, Louisiana, Montana, New Mexico, Oklahoma, Texas, Utah, Wyoming

Philadelphia Oversight Division
(215) 861-3102
600 Arch Street, Room 3400
Philadelphia, PA 19106-1596
Connecticut, Delaware, Maine,
Maryland (except as noted below
under the Washington, DC Oversight
Division), Massachusetts, New
Hampshire, New Jersey, New York,
Pennsylvania, Rhode Island, Vermont,
Puerto Rico, Virgin Islands

San Francisco Oversight Division
(415) 281-7050
120 Howard Street, Room 760
San Francisco, CA 94105-0001
Alaska, California, Hawaii, Idaho,
Nevada, Oregon, Washington, Pacific
Ocean Area

Washington, DC Oversight Division
(202) 606-2990
1900 E Street, NW., Room 7675
Washington, DC 20415-6000
The District of Columbia; in Maryland:
the counties of Charles, Montgomery,
and Prince George's; in Virginia: the
counties of Arlington, Fairfax, King
George, Loudoun, Prince William, and
Stafford; the cities of Alexandria,
Fairfax, Falls Church, Manassas, and
Manassas Park; and any overseas area
not included above.

Fair Labor Standards Act Claims

Employees may file a Fair Labor
Standards Act (overtime) claim with either
the employing agency or with OPM, but
cannot pursue the same claim with both the
agency and OPM at the same time. OPM
encourages employees to get a decision on
the claim from the agency before filing at
OPM. However, this is not a requirement.

Employees who get an unfavorable
decision on an administrative FLSA claim
from the agency may still file the claim with
OPM. However, the reverse is not true.

An FLSA pay claim is subject to a two-
year statute of limitations, except in cases of
a willful violation, where the statute of limitations is three years.

Filing with the Employing Agency—
Employees filing an FLSA claim with an
agency should follow that agency's procedures. At the employee's request, the

agency may send the claim to OPM.

Filing at OPM—Claims filed at OPM
should be sent to the Program Manager,
Room 7671, Office of Merit Systems
Oversight and Effectiveness, 1900 E Street,
NW., Washington, DC 20415-6000, phone
(202) 606-2990. FLSA claims may not be
filed electronically. Claims should contain the
following information in writing: name; the
employing agency during the claim period;
the position (job title, pay plan, series, and
grade) occupied during the claim period; current mailing address, commercial telephone
number, and facsimile machine number (if
available); and if one is designated, the representative's mailing address, commercial
telephone number, and facsimile machine
number (if available); a description of the
nature of the claim and the specific issues or
incidents giving rise to the claim, including
the time period covered; a description of
actions taken to resolve the claim within the
agency and the results of any actions taken; a
copy of any relevant decision or written
response by the agency; evidence which supports the claim, including the identity, commercial telephone number, and location of
other individuals who may be able to provide
information relating to the claim; the remedy
being sought; evidence, if available, that the
claim period was preserved in accordance
with the time limits in 5 CFR 551.702 (the
date the agency or OPM received the claim,
whichever is earlier, becomes the date the
claim period is preserved); a statement that
the employee was or was not a member of a
collective bargaining unit at any time during
the claim period; for those who were members of a bargaining unit, a statement that
they were or were not covered by a negotiated grievance procedure at any time during
the claim period, and if covered, whether
that procedure specifically excluded the
claim from the scope of the negotiated grievance procedure; a statement that the
employee has or has not filed an action in an
appropriate United States court; and any
other information the employee believes
OPM should consider.

Other Challenges—An OPM decision on
a claim is final and is not subject to further administrative review. Nothing limits the employee's right to bring an action in an appropriate United States court. Filing a claim with
a federal agency or with OPM does not stop

the statute of limitations from running. OPM will not decide a claim that is in litigation.

Key OPM Officials

Kay Coles James, Director,
(202) 606-1000

Dan G. Blair, Deputy Director,
(202) 606-1000

Mark A. Robbins, General Counsel,
(202) 606-1700

Richard A. Whitford, Acting Associate Director, Employment Service, (202) 606-6500

Kathy Dillaman, Acting Associate Director, Investigations Service, (202) 606-2020

Doris Hausser, Acting Associate Director, Workforce Compensation, (202) 606-

Nancy E. Randa, Acting Associate Director, Office of Merit Systems Oversight,
(202) 606-1575

Steve Benowiz, Associate Director, Retirement and Insurance Service,
(202) 606-0600

Sandra S. Payne, Acting Director, Office of Human Resources and EEO,
(202) 606-2440

Teresa Jenkins, Director, Office of Workforce Relations, (202) 606-1918

Clarence C. Crawford, Director, Office of Executive Resources Management,
(202) 606-1610

Janet L. Barnes, Chief Information Officer, Office of Chief Information Officer,
(202) 606-2150

Steven Van Rees, Director, Office of Contracting and Administrative Services,
(202) 606-2200

John Gartland, Director, Office of Congressional Relations, (202) 606-1300

Scott Hatch, Director, Office of Communications, (202) 606-2402

Kolo Babagana, Director,
Office of the Chief Financial Officer,
(202) 606-1101

Mary Rose, Chair, Federal Prevailing Rate Advisory Committee, (202) 606-1500

Patrick E. McFarland, Inspector General,
(202) 606-1200

Section 2—Equal Employment Opportunity Commission

General Responsibilities and Procedures

The U.S. Equal Employment Opportunity Commission (EEOC) was established by Title VII of the Civil Rights Act of 1964. EEOC enforces the principal federal statutes prohibiting employment discrimination, including Title VII of the 1964 Civil Rights Act, the Age Discrimination in Employment Act of 1967, the Equal Pay Act of 1963, and Section 501 of the Rehabilitation Act of 1973. EEOC, through its Office of Federal Operations (OFO), provides oversight for the federal government's EEO complaint adjudication and affirmative employment functions and also is responsible for the federal government's EEO appellate function. The address and main telephone number of EEOC are: 1801 L St., N.W., Washington, DC 20507; phone (202) 663-4900, online *www.eeoc.gov*.

The head of each federal executive department and agency is charged by Title VII of the Civil Rights Act of 1964, as amended by the Equal Employment Opportunity Act of 1972, the Rehabilitation Act of 1973, as amended, and by Executive Order 11478, with establishing and maintaining an affirmative employment program of equal opportunity within each federal agency. The Rehabilitation Act also includes affirmative action obligations to individuals with disabilities. Guidance, leadership, and enforcement responsibility for the government-wide program is assigned to EEOC.

Long-standing government policy prohibits discrimination based on race, color, religion, sex, national origin, disability, or age. The laws, the Executive Order, and implementing regulations and instructions call for the application of this policy as an integral part of personnel policy and practice in the employment, development, advancement, and treatment of civilian employees of the federal government. As part of its leadership responsibility for the federal personnel system, the Office of Personnel Management provides guidance to agencies on career advancement programs. Also, EEOC is required by Executive Order 12067 to consult with federal agencies on appropriate standards for a continuing review and evaluation of agency equal employment opportunity activities.

Information on all EEOC-enforced laws may be obtained by calling toll free, 1-800-669-4000. EEOC's toll-free TDD number is 1-800-669-6820. For TDD calls from the Washington, D.C., metropolitan area, call (202) 663-4494.

Federal Employees News Digest, Inc. has published a comprehensive guide to employee complaint and appeal processes called *Federal Job Dispute Procedures*. See publication-ordering information in this *Almanac*.

Title VII of the Civil Rights Act

Race/Color Discrimination—Title VII of the Civil Rights Act of 1964 makes it unlawful to discriminate against any employee or applicant for employment because of his or her race or color in regard to hiring, termination, promotion, compensation, job training, or any other term, condition, or privilege of employment. Title VII also prohibits employment decisions based on stereotypes and assumptions about abilities, traits, or the performance of individuals of certain racial groups. Title VII prohibits both intentional discrimination and neutral job policies that disproportionately exclude minorities and that are not job related.

Equal employment opportunity cannot be denied because of: marriage to or association with an individual of a different race; membership in or association with ethnic based organizations or groups; or attendance or participation in schools or places of worship generally associated with certain minority groups.

Discrimination on the basis of an immutable characteristic associated with race, such as skin color, hair texture, or certain facial features violates Title VII, even though not all members of the race share the same characteristic.

Title VII also prohibits discrimination on the basis of a condition that predominantly affects one race unless the practice is job related and consistent with business necessity.

Racial Harassment—Harassment on the basis of race and/or color also violates Title VII. Ethnic slurs, racial jokes, offensive or derogatory comments, or other verbal or physical conduct based on an individual's race/color constitutes unlawful harassment if the conduct creates an intimidating, hostile, or offensive working environment, or interferes with the individual's work performance.

National Origin Discrimination—Under Title VII it is unlawful to discriminate against any employee or applicant because of the individual's national origin. No one can be denied equal employment opportunity because of birthplace, ancestry, culture, or linguistic characteristics common to a specific ethnic group.

Equal employment opportunity cannot be denied because of: marriage or association with persons of a national origin group; membership or association with specific ethnic promotion groups; attendance or participation in schools, churches, temples or mosques generally associated with a national origin group; or a surname associated with a national origin group.

Religious Discrimination—The Civil Rights Act prohibits agencies from discriminating against individuals in hiring, firing, and other terms and conditions of employment because of their religion. The Act also requires agencies to reasonably accommodate the religious practices of an employee or prospective employee, unless to do so would create an undue hardship upon the agency. Flexible scheduling, voluntary substitutions or swaps, job reassignments and lateral transfers are examples of accommodating an employee's religious beliefs.

Agencies cannot: schedule examinations or other selection activities that conflict with a current or prospective employee's religious needs; inquire about an applicant's future availability at certain times; maintain a restrictive dress code; or refuse to allow observance of a Sabbath or religious holiday, unless the agency can prove that not doing so would cause an undue hardship.

Sex-Based Discrimination—Under the Civil Rights Act, it is illegal to classify a job as "male" or "female" or to maintain separate lines of progression or seniority lists based on sex where this would adversely affect any employee unless sex is a bona fide occupational qualification for that job. This prohibition covers designating certain jobs as "light" or "heavy" since that could be a disguised form of classification by sex.

Nor may job vacancies restrict applications by gender unless there is a bona fide occupational qualifications requirement. Any preemployment inquiry that expresses any limitation, specification or discrimination as to sex is illegal unless it is based on such an occupational qualifications requirement.

Sex as a bona fide occupational qualification must be justified in terms of the requirements of the particular job and not on the basis of a general principle, such as an assumption that the turnover rate is higher among women than among men, or that men are less capable of handling certain types of work. The preference of coworkers, the employer or clients generally is not to be deemed a bona fide occupational qualifications requirement.

An employer may not discriminate between men and women with regard to benefits.

Sexual Harassment—Sexual harassment is a violation of Sec. 703 of Title VII of the Civil Rights Act. Unwelcome sexual advances, requests for sexual favors, and other verbal or physical conduct of a sexual nature constitute sexual harassment when (1) submission to such conduct is made either explicitly or implicitly a term or condition of an individual's employment, (2) submission to or rejection of such conduct by an individual is used as the basis for employment decisions affecting such individual, or (3) such conduct has the purpose or effect of unreasonably interfering with an individual's work performance or creating an intimidating, hostile, or offensive working environment.

In determining whether alleged conduct constitutes sexual harassment, the record as a whole and the circumstances, such as the nature of the sexual advances and the context in which the alleged incidents occurred, will be looked at. The determination of the legality of a particular action will be made from the facts on a case-by-case basis.

An employer is responsible for its acts of harassment and may be liable for those of its agents and supervisory employees. With respect to conduct between fellow employees, an employer is responsible for acts of sexual harassment in the workplace where the employer (or its agents or supervisory employees) knows or should have known of the conduct, unless it can show that it took immediate and appropriate corrective action.

An employer may also be responsible for acts of non-employees, with respect to sexual harassment of employees in the workplace, where the employer (or its agents or supervisory employees) knows or should have known of the conduct and fails to take immediate and appropriate corrective action. In reviewing these cases, the extent of the employer's control and any other legal responsibility that the employer may have with respect to the conduct of such non-employees will be considered.

Equal Pay Act

The Equal Pay Act prohibits sex discrimination in the salaries or wages paid to men and women who are employed in the same establishment and perform jobs requiring equal skill, effort, and responsibility under similar working conditions, except where the payment is made under a seniority system, a merit system, a system that measures earnings by quantity or quality of production, or a differential based on any factor other than sex.

To establish a *prima facie* case under this law, a plaintiff must show that the employer pays different wages to employees of the opposite sex even though the employees perform equal work on jobs requiring equal skill, effort and responsibility under similar working conditions. Once a prima facie case is made, the burden shifts to the defendant to show that the pay differential is justified by one of the statute's enumerated defenses.

Complaints of discrimination by federal employees under the Equal Pay Act can be filed under 29 CFR 1614, but unlike Title VII, the filing of an administrative complaint is not required before filing a lawsuit.

Further, a remedy for sex bias in wages may also be pursued under Title VII.

Rehabilitation Act

The Rehabilitation Act of 1973 requires agencies to develop and carry out plans for the hiring, placement, promotion and retention of persons with disabilities (many similar provisions were applied to private sector employers and state and local governments under the 1990 Americans With Disabilities Act; see below). The Rehabilitation Act protects persons who have a physical or mental impairment that substantially limits one or more of such person's major life activities, who has a record of such an impairment, or is regarded as having such an impairment.

Physical or mental impairment means: certain defined physiological disorders or conditions, cosmetic disfigurement, or anatomical loss or a mental or psychological disorder, such as mental retardation, organic brain syndrome, emotional or mental illness, and specific learning disabilities. Major life activities are functions such as caring for one's self, performing manual tasks, walking, seeing, hearing, speaking, breathing, learning, and working.

An agency must make reasonable accommodation to the known physical or mental limitations of an applicant or employee who is a qualified individual with a disability unless the agency can demonstrate that the accommodation would impose an undue hardship on the operations of its program. Reasonable accommodation may include making facilities more accessible, job restructuring, part-time or modified work schedules, acquisition or modification of equipment or devices, adjustment or modification of examinations, the provision of readers and interpreters, and other similar actions.

In determining whether an accommodation would impose an undue hardship on the agency, factors to be considered include the overall size of the agency's program with respect to the number of employees, number and type of facilities and size of budget, the type of agency operation, including the composition and structure of the agency's work force, and the nature and the cost of the accommodation.

Americans with Disabilities Act

EEOC on May 21, 2002, published rules in the Federal Register to clarify the application of the employment provisions of the Americans with Disabilities Act of 1990 (ADA) to federal government workers in relation to the Rehabilitation Act of 1973. The rules become effective on June 20, 2002, and apply to conduct occurring on or after that date. When the ADA was enacted, some of the legal requirements of the ADA differed from the Rehabilitation Act, even though the two laws shared the same purpose: ending employment discrimination based on disability. Congress subsequently amended the Rehabilitation Act, applying the ADA standards to federal employment.

The rules implemented the amendments to section 501 of the Rehabilitation Act and updated the EEOC's Rehabilitation Act regulation in 29 C.F.R. § 1614.203. They incorporated by reference the EEOC's ADA regulation, at 29 C.F.R. Part 1630. The regulatory limits on reassignment of federal employees with disabilities as a reasonable accommodation, formerly included in 29 C.F.R. § 1614.203(g), were deleted, and the ADA standard is now applied. The rules amended the federal sector disability regulation, 29 C.F.R. § 1614.203, and set forth the obligation of the federal government to be the model employer of individuals with disabilities.

The application of the ADA's nondiscrimination standards had no impact on federal affirmative action obligations or programs.

Age Discrimination in Employment Act

Pursuant to 1974 and 1978 amendments to the Age Discrimination in Employment Act of 1967, discrimination in federal employment because of age is prohibited and agencies are required to assure that all personnel actions are free from age discrimination (i.e., discrimination against persons age 40 or older). The ADEA provides the right to go to court but is not specific as to time limits or conditions for filing civil actions after a complaint has been filed under administrative procedures. In addition, the ADEA provides direct access to the courts after a 30-day notice of intent to sue is filed with the EEOC, if the notice is filed within 180 days of the discriminatory act. All regulations governing the complaint process are found in 29 CFR 1614.

Genetic Information

Executive Order 13145 of February 8, 2000, prohibited federal departments and agencies from making employment decisions based on protected genetic information, a request for genetic services, or the receipt of genetic services. The order applies to current federal employees, applicants for federal government jobs, and former federal employees.

The order defined protected genetic information as information about an individual's genetic tests or genetic tests of that individual's family members and information about the occurrence of disease, or medical condition or disorder in family members of the individual. Protected genetic information does not include current health status information about applicants and employees, such as age, sex, and physical examination results exclusive of family medical history. Departments and agencies have a limited right under the Rehabilitation Act of 1973 to acquire information about, and act on the basis of, an individual's current health status.

Federal departments and agencies may not discharge, fail or refuse to hire, or otherwise discriminate against any individual with respect to the compensation, terms, conditions, or privileges of employment because of protected genetic information or a request for, or receipt of, genetic services. Similarly, federal departments and agencies may not limit, segregate, or classify an individual or otherwise adversely affect the individual's status because of such information. They may request or require family medical history from an applicant or employee only in limited circumstances:

• First, a federal department or agency may request or require family medical history from an applicant as long as it has made a conditional offer of employment. A federal department or agency also may ask for family medical history from a current employee where the request or requirement is consistent with the Rehabilitation Act standards for seeking medical information from current employees.

• Second, departments and agencies must meet these additional prerequisites: the information may be used only to determine whether the department or agency needs to require further medical testing of the individual to assess whether the individual has a current medical condition that may affect his/her ability to perform the essential functions of the job s/he seeks or holds; and medical personnel involved in making the decision whether to require further testing will be the only persons with access to this information.

The order further permitted a department or agency to use an applicant's or employee's family medical history where the department or agency subsequently provides genetic or health care services to the individual at the individual's request.

The order also restricted the conditions in which an agency may obtain or disclose protected genetic information about an individual or information about an individual's request for genetic services. These circumstances include:

• where the department or agency provides genetic or health care services;

• where the department or agency engages in research that complies with Part 46 of Title 45, Code of Federal Regulations, which concerns the protection of human subjects of medical research;

• where the department or agency seeks to monitor the biological effects of toxic substances in the workplace;

• where the department or agency is compelled by proper authority, and

• where the genetic information is collected as a part of a lawful program, the primary purpose of which is for identification purposes.

An individual must consent to the collection and use of protected genetic information before the department or agency may obtain it for health care or monitoring purposes. Consent must be knowing and voluntary.

Protected genetic information must be kept confidential and separate from personnel files, just like other medical information.

The order does not create any legally enforceable right or benefit. Because much of what is prohibited under the order is also prohibited under Section 501 of the Rehabilitation Act of 1973, federal sector applicants and employees who believe that a department or agency has violated a provision of the order may pursue that issue under the procedure set forth at 29 C.F.R. Part 1614. Individuals should be aware, however, that not all conduct that violates the order will also constitute a violation of the Rehabilitation Act.

The 'No Fear' Act

The Notification and Federal Employee Antidiscrimination and Retaliation Act of 2002 ("No Fear" Act), P.L. 107-174 set out requirements for the written notification of federal employees and applicants of their rights and remedies under anti-discrimination and whistleblower protection laws, including by posting that information on the Internet and requirements for employee training regarding such rights and remedies.

It further required agencies to produce annual reports that include: the number and status of cases arising under such laws and the amount of money involved; the number of employees disciplined for discrimination, retaliation, or harassment; data relating to complaints filed; agency policy relating to disciplinary actions against employees who discriminated or committed another prohibited personnel practice; and an analysis including an examination of trends, causes, practical knowledge gained through experience, and actions planned or taken to improve complaint or civil rights programs of the agency.

The law also:

• required agencies to post on their websites specified summary statistical data relating to equal employment opportunity complaints filed with the agency by employees or applicants, and required the EEOC to post on its site summary statistical data relating to hearings requested on such complaints and appeals filed with it from final agency actions;

• expressed the sense of Congress that federal agencies should not retaliate for court judgments or settlements relating to discrimination and whistleblower laws by targeting the claimant or other employees with reductions in compensation, benefits, or work and that they should ensure that managers have adequate training in the management of a diverse workforce and in dispute resolution; and

• required the amount of any claim, final judgment, award, or compromise settlement paid to any current or former federal employee or applicant in connection with specified anti-discrimination and whistleblower protection complaints to be reimbursed to the Treasury out of the operating expenses of the agency to which the discriminatory conduct is attributable. Agencies are expected to reimburse the general fund of the Treasury within a reasonable time, should not use a reduction in force or furloughs as means of funding a reimbursement, but may extend reimbursement over several years to avoid reductions in force,

furloughs, reductions in compensation or benefits, or an adverse effect on the mission of the agency.

Other Forms of Discrimination

Parental Status—Executive Order 13152 of May 2, 2000 states that it is the policy of the government to prohibit discrimination in employment based on an individual's status as a parent. This applies to all policies and practices in the employment, development, advancement, and treatment of employees, to the extent permitted by law.

An individual covered as parent is someone who, with respect to an individual who is under the age of 18 or who is 18 or older but is incapable of self-care because of a physical or mental disability, is: a biological parent; an adoptive parent; a foster parent; a stepparent; a custodian of a legal ward; in loco parentis over such an individual; or actively seeking legal custody or adoption of such an individual.

Marital Status and Political Affiliation—The Civil Service Reform Act of 1978 prohibits employment discrimination in the federal government based on marital status or political affiliation.

Sexual Orientation—The CSRA prohibits discriminating against an applicant or employee on the basis of conduct which does not adversely affect the performance of the applicant or employee. The Office of Personnel Management has interpreted the prohibition of discrimination based on "conduct" to include discrimination based on sexual orientation.

Further, Executive Order 13807 of May 28, 1998 states that it is the policy of the government to prohibit discrimination in employment because of sexual orientation. This applies to all policies and practices in the employment, development, advancement, and treatment of employees, to the extent permitted by law.

Executive Order 13807 did not create any new rights. However, it did set the stage for action to make certain that the workplace is free from harassment and discrimination. Many agencies have issued policy statements prohibiting discrimination based on sexual orientation. Some have developed parallel EEO complaint procedures allowing federal employees to file

EEO complaints based on sexual orientation within their agencies.

Complaint Routes—For complaints of discrimination based on sexual orientation or status as a parent, Executive Order 13087, Executive Order 13152 and the Civil Service Reform Act provide protection. The Cabinet level agencies also have issued policy statements prohibiting discrimination based on sexual orientation. In addition, some agencies have developed parallel EEO complaint procedures allowing employees to file EEO complaints based on sexual orientation within their agencies. Employees should check with their agencies to see if processes exist to handle these complaints. In addition, employees should check their respective collective bargaining agreements and their agencies' negotiated grievance procedures to determine whether grievance procedures can be invoked to address these issues.

Whether or not an agency has internal procedures to address allegations of discrimination based on sexual orientation, employees should consult the OPM's publication, *Addressing Sexual Orientation Discrimination in Federal Civilian Employment, OWR-25 (June 1999)*, available at *www.opm.gov/ er/address2/guide01.htm*. Employees also should contact the OSC at (202) 653-7188 or at *www.osc.gov* and/or the MSPB at (202) 653-6772 or *www.mspb.gov* to determine whether they have a prohibited personnel practice complaint under 5 U.S.C. 2302(b)(10).

Complaint and Appeal Procedures

If you, as a federal employee, applicant, or former employee believe you have been subjected to discrimination because of race, color, religion, sex, national origin, disability, age or reprisal you can file an EEO complaint. There are several steps or stages of the EEO complaint and appeals process, including pre-complaint processing, the formal complaint stage, and the hearing, decision, and appeals process. These various stages of the process are described below:

• **EEO Counseling**—As a discrimination complainant, you must, as a first step, discuss the problem with an equal employment opportunity counselor—an employee of your agency—within 45 days of the alleged discriminatory act or the effective date of a personnel action. Counseling must be completed within 30 days of the date you contact the agency's EEO office with your counseling request. (As an alternative to counseling, you may be offered the chance to participate in an alternative dispute resolution program, which is described in more detail below.) If the matter is not resolved, the EEO counselor will notify you in writing of your right to file a formal discrimination complaint. The EEO counselor's responsibilities include: providing complainants with written notice of their EEO rights and obligations under federal law, including their general right (most non-postal workers) to choose between the EEOC process and the contractual grievance procedure; help complainants identify and determine the basis and issues of their claim (while avoiding "fragmentation" of the claim—see below); conducting a limited inquiry to uncover information needed, for example, to help resolve any jurisdictional questions; facilitating efforts to resolve the problem by listening to and understanding the viewpoints of both parties; holding a final interview with the complainant within 30 days, if an informal resolution is not possible and the aggrieved person has not consented to an extension (not to exceed 60 days); and notifying the employee in writing of the individual's right to file a formal complaint. At the initial counseling session or within a "reasonable time," the EEO counselor should inform employees of their right to have their charges handled through the agency's traditional counseling process or through the alternative dispute resolution procedure (see below), if the agency has opted to offer ADR.

• **Formal Complaint**—You must file a formal complaint with the agency that allegedly discriminated against you within 15 days of receiving the notice of your rights from your EEO counselor. The agency must acknowledge receipt of this formal complaint. In addition to this acknowledgment letter, the agency also should send the complainant an "acceptance letter," stating the claims asserted by the worker that will be investigated by the agency. If the agency dismisses all of the complaint, you will be notified in writing of your right to appeal to EEOC's Office of Federal Operations within

30 days of receipt of the agency's dismissal. (In such situations, the EEOC may determine that the dismissal was improper, reverse the action, and remand the matter back to the agency for completion of the investigation.) If the agency does not dismiss the complaint, it must conduct and complete an impartial and appropriate investigation within 180 days of the filing of the complaint, unless the parties agree in writing to extend the period. If you request a final decision without a hearing, the agency must take final action by issuing a decision within 60 days. (Complainants who request an agency final decision without a hearing have the right to appeal the agency's decision, including a partial dismissal, to EEOC.)

• **EEOC Hearing**—Following completion of the investigation, you have the right to request a hearing by an EEOC administrative judge. Even if the agency has not completed its investigation, you have the right to request a hearing anytime after 180 days from the date the complaint was filed. If a hearing is requested, an EEOC administrative judge must issue a decision within 180 days from the day the complaint file was received from the agency. In a major departure from its earlier procedures, EEOC's rules now stipulate that agencies can no longer reverse or overturn an EEOC AJ's decision. After the AJ issues a decision, the agency must issue a final order within 40 days, indicating whether it will "fully implement" the AJ's ruling or whether it will appeal that decision to EEOC. ("Fully implement" means that the agency agrees to adopt the AJ's decision without any modification.) If the agency does not fully implement the AJ's decision, it must file an appeal to EEOC and provide the complainant with notification of its decision and action. Complainants have 30 days from receiving notice of the agency's implementation decision to file an appeal with EEOC.

• **Complainant's Appeal Rights**—If you've requested a final agency decision without a hearing and are not satisfied with the agency's final action on your complaint, you may appeal either to the EEOC within 30 calendar days of your receipt of the final action or file a civil action in a U.S. district court within 90 calendar days of your receipt of the final action. If you appeal to the EEOC and are dissatisfied with the decision on appeal, you may file a civil action within 90 days of

your receipt of EEOC's final decision. You may also file a civil action after 180 calendar days from the date on which the complaint was filed if the agency has not taken final action on your complaint. You may also file suit after 180 days from appeal to the EEOC when no decision has been made. You have the right to be represented at any stage of the process, including the counseling stage, by your representative.

Anti-Fragmentation Rules

The EEOC rules contain a number of provisions designed to discourage or prevent fragmentation, including procedures making it easier to amend complaints to include discriminatory actions related, but subsequent, to an individual's existing claim. Similarly, new consolidation rules will permit independent claims brought by the same complaining party to be joined together for processing. The rules also include new procedures related to:

• **Partial Dismissals**—Appeal rights from partial dismissals have been eliminated. Instead, the case will continue to be processed and appeals will be preserved until the rest of the case is ready for appeal.

• **Spin-off Complaints**—The rules add a provision providing for the dismissal of spin-off complaints (i.e., complaints about the processing of an existing complaint), and specify that complaints about existing complaints should be brought up as part of the original complaint.

Class Complaints

The class complaint procedure permits employees, former employees, or applicants to file a complaint when they believe that they and other members of their class have been discriminated against by an agency personnel management policy or practice because of race, color, religion, sex, national origin, disability, or age. Prior to filing a class complaint, an aggrieved party must contact a designated EEO counselor within 45 calendar days of a specific alleged discriminatory act. If counseling is unsuccessful, after 15 days of receipt of the notice of right to file the aggrieved party may, as an agent of the class, file a complaint showing that the class is so numerous that a consolidated complaint of the members of the class is impractical, that questions of fact are common to the class, that his or her claims are typical of the claims of the class and that he or she, or representative, if any, will fairly and adequately protect the interests of the class. An initial decision is made by an EEOC administrative judge on the satisfaction of these requirements. The agency must take final action on the administrative judge's decision to accept or dismiss the class complaint within 40 days of receiving the decision.

If the complaint is accepted as a class complaint, the second phase of the procedure provides for a right to a hearing, a recommended decision by an EEOC administrative judge, and a final agency decision, which is appealable to the EEOC. In addition, an agent may file a civil action after 180 calendar days from the date in which the complaint was filed, if an appeal has not been filed and the agency has not taken final action on the class complaint. When discrimination is found, class members who believe that they are entitled to individual relief may file a written claim with the head of the agency or its EEO director within 30 days of receipt of notification by the agency of its final decision. The agency must issue a final decision on each claim within 90 days of filing. The agency's final decision is appealable to the EEOC. A claimant has the same rights to file a civil action as an agent.

Attorney's Fee Awards

Under EEOC's rules, complainants who successfully pursue discrimination charges against a federal agency may be entitled to an award of attorney's fees. The Commission's administrative judges generally are responsible for determining the amount of fees to be awarded to a prevailing complainant. An attorney's fee award also may be available for work performed during the pre-complaint process. Fees will be available for legal work done before a complaint is filed, according to the EEOC rules, in the "limited circumstances" where a complaining party prevails in a hearing, the agency chooses not to fully implement the administrative judge's decision, and the Commission subsequently finds in favor of the complaining party. Additionally, agencies and complaining parties may include attorney's fees for pre-complaint work in a settlement agreement.

However, complainants risk losing any possible entitlement to attorney's fee payments in situations where they refuse to accept an agency's "offer of resolution." Under this new procedure, which is designed to encourage settlements of EEO complaints, an agency may decide to make an offer of resolution to a complaining party. If the complainant does not accept the offer and ultimately obtains no more relief than what was offered, no attorney's fees or costs will be payable for legal work done after the offer was rejected.

Compensatory Damages

Sec. 102 of the Civil Rights Act of 1991 permits a complaining party pursuing a claim under Title VII of the Civil Rights Act of 1964, the Americans With Disabilities Act of 1990, or the Rehabilitation Act of 1973, to recover compensatory and punitive damages in the case of intentional discrimination. However, punitive damages are not available against governmental entities. In a 1999 federal-sector decision (*West v. Gibson*, 119 S.Ct. 1906, 1999), the U.S. Supreme Court upheld EEOC's right to award compensatory damages to successful EEO complainants.

The law places limits on the size of such damages awards, which can range from $50,000 to $300,000, depending on the size of the employer. In court actions, any party may demand a jury trial when a complainant is seeking either compensatory or punitive damages.

Affirmative Employment Programs

EEOC issues management directives designed to guide and instruct federal agencies on the development of affirmative employment program plans for women, minorities, and individuals with disabilities. Under these directives, agencies are to take actions to eliminate barriers to minorities, women and people with disabilities in their workforce.

EEOC has conducted on-site program reviews of affirmative employment programs at several agencies. According to EEOC, its objectives in these on-site reviews are to: (a) evaluate affirmative employment programs, (b) assess affirmative employment policies and procedures, (c) assess the implementation of affirmative employment plans, (d) identify deficiencies and recommend corrective action, and (e) provide technical assistance to assist agencies in understanding EEOC's policies and procedures in connection with affirmative employment programs.

Section 3—U.S. Merit Systems Protection Board

General Responsibilities

The Merit Systems Protection Board is an independent, quasi-judicial agency in the executive branch that serves as the guardian of federal merit systems. The Board's mission is to ensure that federal employees are protected against abuses by agency management, that executive branch agencies make employment decisions in accordance with the merit system principles, and that federal merit systems are kept free of prohibited personnel practices. MSPB's address and telephone number are: 1615 M St., N.W., Washington, DC 20419; phone (202) 653-7200, online www.mspb.gov/.

MSPB has a statutory mandate to adjudicate appeals from personnel actions for the nation's largest employer. It has worldwide jurisdiction, wherever federal civil servants are found. Additionally, under the Hatch Act, it exercises jurisdiction over state and local government employees in federally funded positions.

The bipartisan Board consists of a chairman, a vice-chairman and a member, with no more than two of its three members from the same political party. Board members are appointed by the president, confirmed by the Senate, and serve overlapping, non-renewable, seven-year terms.

The Board accomplishes its mission by:

• hearing and deciding employee appeals from certain agency personnel actions, including individual right of action appeals brought by whistleblowers who have exhausted the procedures of the Office of Special Counsel;

• hearing and deciding cases brought by the Special Counsel involving alleged abuses of the merit systems or Hatch Act violations, certain proposed actions against administrative law judges, and requests to review a regulation of the Office of Personnel Management (OPM) or implementation of an OPM regulation by an agency;

• conducting studies of the civil service and other merit systems in the executive branch to determine whether they are free of prohibited personnel practices; and

• providing oversight of the significant actions and regulations of the Office of Personnel Management to determine whether they are in accord with the merit system principles.

Federal Employees News Digest Inc. has published a comprehensive guide to employee complaint and appeal processes called *Federal Job Dispute Procedures.* See publication-ordering information in this *Almanac.*

Merit System Principles

Civil service law (5 U.S.C. 2301(b)) requires that federal personnel management be implemented consistent with the following merit system principles:

• Recruitment should be from qualified individuals from appropriate sources to achieve a work force from all segments of society, and selection and advancement should be determined solely on the basis of relative ability, knowledge, and skills, after fair and open competition which assures that all receive equal opportunity.

• All employees and applicants for employment should receive fair and equitable treatment in all aspects of personnel management without regard to political affiliation, race, color, religion, national origin, sex, marital status, age, or handicapping condition, and with proper regard for their privacy and constitutional rights.

• Equal pay should be provided for work of equal value, with appropriate consideration of both national and local rates paid by employers in the private sector, and appropriate incentives and recognition should be provided for excellence in performance.

• All employees should maintain high standards of integrity, conduct, and concern for the public interest.

• The federal work force should be used efficiently and effectively.

• Employees should be retained on the basis of the adequacy of their performance, inadequate performance should be corrected, and employees should be separated who cannot or will not improve their performance to meet required standards.

• Employees should be provided effective education and training in cases in which such education and training would result in better organizational and individual performance.

• Employees should be protected against arbitrary action, personal favoritism, or coercion for partisan political purposes, and prohibited from using their official authority or influence for the purpose of interfering with or affecting the result of an election or a nomination for election.

• Employees should be protected against reprisal for the lawful disclosure of information which the employees reasonably believe evidences a violation of any law, rule, or regulation, or mismanagement, a gross waste of funds, an abuse of authority, or a substantial and specific danger to public health or safety.

It is a prohibited personnel practice to take or fail to take any personnel action if the taking of or failure to take the action violates any law, rule or regulation implementing or directly concerning these merit system principles.

The Merit Systems Protection Board is directed by law to conduct special studies of the civil service and other federal merit systems to determine whether these statutory mandates are being met, and to report to the Congress and the President on whether the public interest in a civil service free of prohibited personnel practices is being adequately protected.

Prohibited Personnel Practices

The civil service laws (5 USC 2302(b)) also forbid personnel actions based on the following prohibited personnel practices:

• Discriminating on the basis of race, color, religion, sex, age, national origin, handicapping condition, marital status or political affiliation;

• Soliciting or considering employment recommendations not based on personal knowledge or records of the individual's work performance, ability, aptitude, general qualifications, suitability, character, or loyalty;

• Coercing the political activity of a person or taking any action as a reprisal for refusing to engage in political activity;

• Deceiving or willfully obstructing anyone from competing for employment;

• Influencing anyone to withdraw from competition for any position, whether to help or hurt anyone else's employment prospects;

• Giving unauthorized preferential treatment to any employee or applicant;

• Taking specified personnel actions based on nepotism;

• Taking or failing to take, or threatening to take or fail to take, a personnel action with respect to any employee or applicant for employment because of any legal disclosure of information evidencing specified kinds of governmental wrongdoing—that is, whistleblowing;

• Taking or failing to take, or threatening to take or fail to take, any personnel action because of exercising an appeal, complaint or grievance right; testifying or lawfully assisting any individual in the exercise of any appeal, complaint or grievance right; cooperating with or disclosing information to the Inspector General of an agency or the Special Counsel; or refusing to obey an order that would require the individual to violate a law;

• Discriminating on the basis of personal conduct that does not adversely affect the performance of any employee or applicant or the performance of others, except in case of criminal conviction for the conduct; and

• Taking or failing to take any other personnel action if that would violate any law, rule, or regulation implementing or directly concerning the merit system principles.

• In Defense Department personnel actions, violation of specified statutory provisions relating to veterans' preference.

Types of Appealable Actions

Under the Civil Service Reform Act, most federal employees are entitled to appeal to the Merit Systems Protection Board certain personnel actions taken by agencies. Certain other actions are appealable under OPM regulations.

Appealable actions include adverse actions (removals, suspensions of more than 14 days, reductions in grade or pay, and furloughs of 30 days or fewer), performance-based removals or reductions in grade, denials of within-grade increases,

Merit Systems Protection Board Regions

Offices	Geographic Jurisdiction
ATLANTA REGIONAL OFFICE 401 W. Peachtree St., N.W., Ste. 1050 Atlanta, GA 30308 (404) 730-2751, Fax (404) 730-2767 E-mail: *atlanta@mspb.gov*	Alabama, Florida, Georgia, Mississippi, South Carolina, Tennessee
BOSTON FIELD OFFICE 99 Summer St., Ste. 1810 Boston, MA 02110 (617) 424-5700, Fax (617) 424-5708 E-mail: *boston@mspb.gov*	Connecticut, Maine, Massachusetts, New Hampshire, Rhode Island, Vermont
CENTRAL REGIONAL OFFICE 230 South Dearborn St., Rm. 3100 Chicago, IL 60604 (312) 353-2923, Fax (312) 886-4231 E-mail: *chicago@mspb.gov*	Illinois, Indiana, Iowa, Kansas City (Kansas only), Kentucky, Michigan, Minnesota, Missouri, Ohio, Wisconsin
DALLAS FIELD OFFICE 1100 Commerce St., Rm. 6F20 Dallas, TX 75242 (214) 767-0555, Fax (214) 767-0102 E-mail: *dallas@mspb.gov*	Arkansas, Louisiana, Oklahoma, Texas
DENVER FIELD OFFICE 165 South Union Blvd., Ste. 318 Lakewood, CO 80228 (303) 969-5101, Fax (303) 969-5109 E-mail: *denver@mspb.gov*	Arizona, Colorado, Kansas (except Kansas City), Montana, Nebraska, New Mexico, North Dakota, South Dakota, Utah, Wyoming
NEW YORK FIELD OFFICE 26 Federal Plaza, Rm. 3137A New York, NY 10278 (212) 264-9372, Fax (212) 264-1417 E-mail: *newyork@mspb.gov*	New Jersey (counties of Bergen, Essex, Hudson, and Union), New York, Puerto Rico, Virgin Islands
NORTHEASTERN REGIONAL OFFICE U.S. Customhouse, Rm. 501 Philadelphia, PA 19106 (215) 597-9960, Fax (215) 597-3456 E-mail: *phladelphia@mspb.gov*	Delaware, Maryland (except counties of Montgomery and Prince George's), New Jersey (except counties of Bergen, Essex, Hudson, and Union), Pennsylvania, West Virginia
WESTERN REGIONAL OFFICE 250 Montgomery St., Ste. 400, 4th Floor San Francisco, CA 94104 (415) 705-2935, Fax (415) 705-2945 E-mail: *sanfrancisco@mspb.gov*	California and Nevada
SEATTLE FIELD OFFICE 915 Second Ave., Rm. 1840 Seattle, WA 98174 (206) 220-7975, Fax (206) 220-7982 E-mail: *seattle@mspb.gov*	Alaska, Hawaii, Idaho, Oregon, Washington, Pacific overseas
WASHINGTON, D.C. REGIONAL OFFICE 1800 Diagonal Rd., Ste. 205 Alexandria, VA 22304-2840 (703) 756-6250, Fax (703) 756-7112 E-mail: *washingtonregion@mspb.gov*	Washington, D.C.; Maryland (counties of Montgomery and Prince George's); North Carolina; Virginia; all overseas areas not otherwise covered

certain reduction-in-force (RIF) actions, denials of restoration to duty or reemployment rights, removals from the SES for failure to be recertified, and OPM determinations in employment suitability and retirement matters.

Under the Whistleblower Protection Act of 1989, additional personnel actions or failures by an agency to act may result in an appeal to the Board under certain circumstances. Included are such actions as appointments, promotions, details, transfers, reassignments, and decisions concerning pay, benefits and awards. Such an action may be appealed to the Board only if the appellant alleges that the action was taken because of his or her whistleblowing, and if the appellant first filed a complaint with the Special Counsel and the Special Counsel did not seek corrective action from the Board. An appeal filed with the Board by a whistleblower, after exhausting the procedures of the Office of Special Counsel, is termed an "individual right of action" (IRA) appeal.

Jurisdiction Over Individuals

For the Board to have jurisdiction over an appeal of a personnel action, it must possess jurisdiction over both the action and the individual filing the appeal. The employees and others (e.g., applicants for employment, annuitants in retirement cases) who may appeal specific actions to the Board vary in accordance with the law and regulations governing the specific action. For some actions, classes of employees, such as political appointees and employees of specific agencies, e.g., the intelligence and security agencies (FBI, CIA, etc.), are excluded.

Since the CSRA became effective, employees in the competitive service and preference-eligible employees in the excepted service have had the right to appeal adverse actions to the Board. An "employee" under the law is someone who is appointed in the competitive service and has completed a probationary or trial period, or who is preference-eligible (that is, has veterans preference rights) and has completed one year of current and continuous service. In 1987, non-preference-eligible supervisors and managers in the Postal Service gained Board appeal rights for adverse actions. Under the Civil Service Due Process Amendments, which became effective in August 1990, non-preference eligible excepted service employees who have completed two years of current and continuous service gained the right to appeal both adverse actions and performance-based actions to the Board.

Bargaining Unit Employees—There are also additional jurisdictional issues where an employee is a member of a bargaining unit that has a negotiated grievance procedure covering actions that may be appealed to the Board. In such instances, the employee normally must pursue a grievance through the negotiated grievance procedure. When a collective bargaining agreement specifically excludes from the negotiated grievance procedure actions that are appealable to the Board, such matters can be appealed to the Board.

When a negotiated grievance procedure covers adverse actions and/or performance-based actions, the employee may use the negotiated grievance procedure or may file an appeal with the Board, but may not do both. An employee also has the choice of pursuing a grievance or an appeal to the Board when the negotiated grievance procedure covers an action appealable to the Board and the employee raises an issue of prohibited discrimination in connection with that action. When an employee affected by an action appealable to the Board alleges that the action resulted from a prohibited personnel practice, the employee may use the negotiated grievance procedure, file an appeal with the Board, or seek assistance from the Special Counsel. (Under the terms of some union contracts, Postal Service employees may be able to pursue a grievance under the negotiated grievance procedure and also file an appeal with the Board.)

MSPB Appeal Procedures

Appeals to the Board must be filed in writing with the Board regional or field office having geographical jurisdiction within 30 days of the effective date of the action. Where the notice of action does not set an effective date, the appeal must be filed within 35 days of the date of the notice.

In the case of whistleblower appeals—where a complaint has first been filed with the Special Counsel—the appellant may appeal directly to the Board within 65 days after the date of a written notice from the Special Counsel stating that the office will not seek corrective action. A direct appeal to the Board is also authorized if 120 days have passed since the filing of the complaint with the Special Counsel, and the Special Counsel has not advised the appellant that the office will seek corrective action on his or her behalf.

Under the Whistleblower Protection Act, an appellant may also ask the Board to stay a personnel action allegedly based on whistleblowing. A stay request may be filed when an appellant is eligible to file a whistleblower appeal, and it may be filed before, at the same time as, or after the appeal is filed. Stay requests also are filed in writing with the Board regional or field office having geographical jurisdiction. By law, stay requests must be decided within 10 days of receipt of the request.

After an appeal has been received, the regional or field office issues an order acknowledging receipt of the appeal and raising any questions of timeliness or jurisdiction. The appeal is then assigned to an administrative judge for adjudication. The agency is required to provide its evidentiary file to the appellant and the administrative judge. The appellant and the agency then have the opportunity to present additional information for the administrative judge's consideration. Once jurisdiction and timeliness have been established, the appellant has a right to a hearing on the merits.

The agency has the burden of proving that it was justified in taking the action being appealed. If the agency meets its burden of proof, the Board must decide in favor of the agency, unless the appellant shows that there was "harmful error" in the agency's procedures, that the agency decision was based on a prohibited personnel practice, or that the decision was not in accordance with law. The appellant has the burden of proving that the appeal is within the Board's jurisdiction and that it was timely filed. The appellant has the burden of proving any affirmative defenses (e.g., discrimination or reprisal for whistleblowing) raised. The appellant also has the burden of proof in retirement cases.

Under the Whistleblower Protection Act, the Board must order corrective action if the appellant demonstrates that his or her whistleblowing was a "contributing factor" in the personnel action that was threatened, proposed, taken, or not taken. The appellant has the burden of proving by "a preponderance of the evidence" that his or her whistleblowing was a contributing factor in the personnel action. The Board will not order corrective action, however, if the agency demonstrates by "clear and convincing" evidence that it would have taken the same action in the absence of the appellant's whistleblowing.

Once the record is closed, an initial decision is issued by the administrative judge. The Board's established policy calls for the administrative judge to issue an initial decision on an appeal within 120 days from the date the appeal was filed.

When an appellant prevails in an appeal, interim relief is provided pending the outcome of any petition for review, unless the administrative judge determines that interim relief is not appropriate. An exception to interim relief is also available if the administrative judge's decision requires the return of the appellant to the workplace and the agency determines that such a return would be unduly disruptive, although the agency will still be required to provide all pay and benefits.

An administrative judge's initial decision on an appeal becomes the final decision of the Board unless a party files a petition for review with the Board within 35 days of the date of the initial decision or the Board reopens the case on its own motion. The Board may grant a petition for review when it is established that the initial decision of the administrative judge was based on an erroneous interpretation of statute or regulation, or that new and material evidence is available that, despite due diligence, was not available when the record was closed. The Board also has the discretion to reopen and consider an initial decision on its own motion.

The Board's decision on a petition for review constitutes final administrative action. Further appeal then may be available in the United States Court of Appeals for the Federal Circuit or, in cases involving allegations of discrimination, with a U.S. District Court or the Equal Employment Opportunity Commission.

The director of the Office of Personnel Management may intervene or petition the full Board for reconsideration of a final decision. The OPM Director also may seek judicial review of a final Board decision involving the interpretation of a civil service law, rule, or regulation affecting personnel management where the Board decision will have a substantial impact on a civil service law, rule, regulation, or policy.

'Mixed' Appeals That Include Discrimination Issues

A "mixed case" is a complaint based on an action that is appealable to MSPB and includes one or more allegations of discrimination. Where a discrimination issue arises in connection with an action that is not appealable to the Board, the employee may pursue a remedy through internal agency procedures and the Equal Employment Opportunity Commission's regulations.

When an appealable action has been taken against an employee and the employee raises an issue of discrimination, the employee may file a timely complaint with the agency or may file an appeal with MSPB. Employees who file a discrimination complaint with the agency then may appeal to the Board within 30 days after receipt of the agency's decision. If the employee chooses to appeal to the Board without filing a discrimination complaint with the agency, the appeal must be filed no later than 30 days after the effective date of the agency action.

Employees who have filed a grievance with the agency under a negotiated grievance procedure may request the Board to review the final decision of the arbitrator within 35 days after the date of issuance of that decision. The discrimination issue need not have been raised before the arbitrator; it can be raised first at the Board level.

An agency has 120 days to resolve a complaint of discrimination that has been timely filed. If the agency fails to meet this time limit, the employee may file an appeal with the Board at any time after the expiration of 120 days. If the agency issues a decision before the 120-day time limit expires, but the employee is dissatisfied with the decision, he or she may file an appeal with the Board not later than 30 days after receipt of the agency decision.

When discrimination is an issue in an appeal, the Board must decide both the discrimination issue and the appealable action within 120 days. If discrimination was not an issue when the appeal was filed with the Board, but became an issue after the proceedings began, the Board must decide both the issue of discrimination and the appealable action within 120 days after the issue was raised.

If an employee raises an issue of discrimination after filing an appeal with the Board, and if the parties file a written agreement with the administrative judge that the discrimination issue should be remanded to the agency, the issue will be remanded to the agency if the administrative judge determines that remand of the issue would be in the interest of justice. The remand order will specify the time within which agency action is to be completed, which can be no longer than 120 days. When an issue of discrimination has been returned to an agency for action, the Board's processing of the appeal must be completed within 120 days after the agency action is completed and the case is returned to the Board.

Following a final decision by the Board in a mixed case, the appellant may: (1) accept the decision of the Board; (2) file a civil action in the appropriate U.S. District Court within 30 days of receipt of the Board's final decision; (3) file a petition for review with the Equal Employment Opportunity Commission within 30 days of receipt of the Board's final decision; or (4) file a petition for review of the appealable action only (not the discrimination issues) with the U.S. Court of Appeals for the Federal Circuit.

If an appellant petitions the EEOC to review the Board's decision on the discrimination issue, the EEOC must determine whether it will consider the case within 30 days or the Board's decision becomes final. If the EEOC determines that it will review the decision of the Board, it must complete the process and, within 60 days, either concur in the decision of the Board or report to the Board the reasons why it disagrees with the Board's decision.

If the EEOC disagrees with the Board's decision on the discrimination issue, the Board has 30 days in which to concur in and adopt the decision of the EEOC, reaffirm its original decision, or reaffirm its original decision with whatever revisions are considered necessary. If the Board concurs in the decision of the EEOC, that decision becomes final. However, the decision may be appealed to the appropriate U.S. District Court.

If the Board does not concur in the decision of the EEOC, the matter must immediately be referred to the Special Panel. The Special Panel must issue a final decision in mixed cases no later than 45 days after the matter was referred by the Board. The decision of the Special Panel is final and may then be appealed to the appropriate U.S. District Court.

Other Complaint-Handling Processes

Prohibited Personnel Practices—If a personnel action is allegedly based on a prohibited personnel practice (including reprisal for whistleblowing), the employee may file a complaint with the Special Counsel, asking that the Special Counsel seek corrective action from the Board. If the Special Counsel does not seek corrective action from the Board, there is no further administrative recourse, except in the case of complaints alleging that the personnel action was taken because of the employee's whistleblowing.

Under the Whistleblower Protection Act of 1989, individuals who allege that a personnel action was threatened, proposed, taken, or not taken because of their whistleblowing may seek corrective action from the Board directly if the Special Counsel does not seek corrective action on their behalf.

Matters Reviewable by OPM—Certain personnel matters that are not within the jurisdiction of either MSPB or the Special Counsel may be reviewable by the Office of Personnel Management. Such matters as examination ratings, classification/job rating decisions, denial of health benefit claims by insurance carriers, and termination of retained grade or pay benefits based on refusal to accept a reasonable offer are reviewable by OPM.

Grievances—Generally, grievances involve such matters as suspensions of less than 14 days, reprimands, denial of leave requests, unhealthy or uncomfortable working conditions, etc. These matters usually are grieved with the agency involved, and there is no other avenue of redress. However, unions with exclusive recognition rights in various units can specify in their contracts with agencies that such matters are grievable and subject to arbitration.

Section 4—Office of Special Counsel

General Responsibilities and Procedures

The Office of Special Counsel (OSC) is an independent investigative and prosecutorial agency that litigates before the U.S. Merit Systems Protection Board and helps to enforce three federal statutes: the Civil Service Reform Act, the Whistleblower Protection Act, and the Hatch Act.

OSC's main responsibilities are:
• investigating alleged prohibited personnel practices;
• interpreting and enforcing Hatch Act provisions on political activity; and
• operating a whistleblower disclosure hotline for federal employees to report wrongdoing in government.

The Special Counsel heads the OSC and is appointed by the president and confirmed by the Senate. The agency is headquartered in Washington, D.C., and has field offices in Dallas and San Francisco.

During the course of an investigation the Special Counsel may issue subpoenas, order the taking of depositions and require responses to written interrogatories.

Federal Employees News Digest Inc. has published a comprehensive guide to employee complaint and appeal processes called *Federal Job Dispute Procedures*. See publication-ordering information in this *Almanac*.

Prohibited Personnel Practices

Prohibited personnel practices are those that, if committed, undermine the federal merit system. Twelve prohibited personnel practices, including reprisal for whistleblowing, are defined by law at § 2302(b) of Title 5 of the United States Code. A personnel action (such as an appointment, promotion, reassignment, or suspension) may need to be involved for a prohibited personnel practice to occur. Generally stated, § 2302(b) provides that a federal employee authorized to take, direct others to take, recommend or approve any personnel action may not:

1. discriminate against an employee or applicant based on race, color, religion, sex, national origin, age, handicapping condition, marital status, or political affiliation;

2. solicit or consider employment recommendations based on factors other than personal knowledge or records of job-related abilities or characteristics;

3. coerce the political activity of any person;

4. deceive or willfully obstruct anyone from competing for employment;

5. influence anyone to withdraw from competition for any position so as to improve or injure the employment prospects of any other person;

6. give an unauthorized preference or advantage to anyone so as to improve or injure the employment prospects of any particular employee or applicant;

7. engage in nepotism (i.e., hire, promote, or advocate the hiring or promotion of relatives);

8. engage in reprisal for whistleblowing— i.e., take, fail to take, or threaten to take or fail to take a personnel action against an employee or applicant for disclosing to the Special Counsel, or to an Inspector General or comparable agency official (or others, except when disclosure is barred by law, or by Executive Order to avoid harm to the national defense or foreign affairs), information which the employee or applicant reasonably believes evidences a violation of any law, rule or regulation; gross mismanagement; a gross waste of funds; an abuse of authority; or a substantial and specific danger to public health or safety);

9. take, fail to take, or threaten to take or fail to take a personnel action against an employee or applicant for exercising an appeal, complaint, or grievance right; testifying for or assisting another in exercising such a right; cooperating with or disclosing information to the Special Counsel or to an Inspector General; or refusing to obey an order that would require the individual to violate a law;

10. discriminate based on personal conduct which is not adverse to the on-the-job performance of an employee, applicant, or others; or

11. take or fail to take, recommend, or approve a personnel action if taking or failing to take such an action would violate a veterans' preference requirement; and

12. take or fail to take a personnel action, if taking or failing to take action would violate any law, rule or regulation implementing or directly concerning merit system principles at 5 U.S.C. § 2301.

While most federal employees and job applicants fall under OSC jurisdiction with regard to prohibited personnel practices, there are exceptions. Employees of government corporations may file whistleblower complaints with OSC, but no other prohibited personnel practice complaints. Postal Service employees may file nepotism complaints with OSC, but no other kinds of complaints. Employees of most intelligence agencies, the General Accounting Office, the Postal Rate Commission, and the Federal Bureau of Investigation are not within OSC jurisdiction.

Employees covered by a collective bargaining agreement must choose one of three avenues when pursuing a complaint of a prohibited personnel practice: an OSC complaint, an MSPB appeal, or a grievance under the collective bargaining agreement.

Complaints filed with the OSC are sent to OSC's Complaints Examining Unit for initial examination. If the examination shows a potentially valid claim, the matter will be sent to OSC's Investigation and Prosecution Division for field investigation. If a violation is found, OSC may seek a remedy. Forms of relief the OSC may take include:

• a stay of any personnel action;

• relief designed to make an employee whole (such as reinstatement and back pay); and

• disciplinary action against an employee who has committed a violation.

Disciplinary action may be taken by an employee's agency (with OSC's prior consent), or by OSC in a prosecution before the Merit Systems Protection Board.

OSC offers mediation, as an alternative to investigation, in selected prohibited personnel practice cases. Participation in the OSC Mediation Program is completely voluntary for both the complainant and the employing agency. If both parties agree to mediate their dispute, the OSC assigns a neutral third party—a mediator—to facilitate a discussion between the parties to reach a mutually agreeable resolution to the complaint.

Current or former federal employees and applicants for employment who have filed a matter with the OSC alleging actual or threatened reprisal for whistleblowing may have their allegation heard by the MSPB as an "Individual Right of Action" appeal if OSC closes the matter after investigation, or if OSC does not seek corrective action within 120 days from receiving the complaint. If such an appeal is filed, MSPB may not take into account OSC's decision to terminate an investigation of a whistleblowing complaint without seeking corrective action.

The Special Counsel may participate in most proceedings before the MSPB, but it may not intervene in certain proceedings, including Individual Right of Action cases, without the consent of the employee.

Hatch Act Enforcement

In general, employees in the executive branch of the federal government, whether in the competitive or the excepted service, employees of the District of Columbia government, and employees of the Postal Service are subject to political-activity restrictions. Part-time and temporary employees are included.

A few exemptions are made, including employees paid from the appropriation for the office of the President and officials whose position is in the United States, who determine national policy and who are appointed by the President subject to Senate confirmation. These employees may engage in political activities while on duty, while in uniform, while in a government building, or while using a government vehicle.

Employees of certain agencies (see below) are subject to more restrictive rules than the following policies, which apply to most federal and postal employees.

Permissible and Impermissible Activities—Most employees may: run as candidates for public office in nonpartisan elections; register and vote as they choose; assist in voter registration drives; express opinions about candidates and issues; contribute money to political organizations; attend polit-

ical fundraising functions; attend and be active at political rallies and meetings; join and be an active member of a political party or club; sign nominating petitions; campaign for or against referendum questions, constitutional amendments and municipal ordinances; campaign for or against candidates in partisan elections; distribute campaign literature in partisan elections, and hold office in political clubs or parties.

Under the law, employees may not: use their official authority or influence to interfere with an election; solicit, accept, or receive political contributions unless both the donor and solicitor are members of the same federal labor organization or employee organization, the one solicited is not a subordinate employee and the contribution is for the organization's multi-candidate political committee; knowingly solicit or discourage the political activity of any person who has business before the agency; engage in political activity while on duty, in any government office, while wearing an official uniform or while using a government vehicle; be candidates for public office in partisan elections.

Employees Subject to Tighter Hatch Act Restrictions

Certain federal employees, primarily in security and law enforcement agencies, are still prohibited from engaging in partisan political activity. These employees include: career senior executive service employees as well as employees of the Federal Election Commission, FBI, Secret Service, CIA, National Security Council, National Security Agency, Defense Intelligence Agency, Merit Systems Protection Board, Office of Special Counsel, Office of Criminal Investigations in the Internal Revenue Service, Central Imagery Office, the Office of Investigative Programs of the United States Customs Service, Office of Law Enforcement at the Bureau of Alcohol, Tobacco and Firearms, and Criminal Division of the Justice Department, Administrative Law Judges, and Contract Appeal Board members.

Permissible and Impermissible Activities—Under the Hatch Act's rules, employees in the agencies above may: register and vote as they choose; express opinions publicly and privately on all political subjects and candidates; display a political sign in their yard; display a partisan bumper sticker on their privately-owned vehicle (when the vehicle is regularly used for work purposes, the bumper sticker should be covered—this applies to all federal employees); make a political contribution to a candidate or political party; accept appointment to a public office; participate in a nonpartisan election either as a candidate or in support of a candidate; serve as an election official for the city or county; be politically active in connection with an issue not specifically identified with a political party; participate in the nonpartisan activities of a civic, community, social, labor, professional, or similar organization; attend a political convention, rally, fundraiser as a spectator; sign petitions; petition Congress to express a point of view on legislation.

However, under the same rules, employees may not: be candidates for public office in partisan elections; campaign for or against a candidate in a partisan election; serve as an officer of a political party; solicit, accept, or receive political contributions; sell tickets to or organize a partisan political fundraiser; take an active part in managing the political campaign of a partisan candidate for public or party office; work at the polls on behalf of a partisan candidate or political party; distribute campaign material; serve as a delegate, alternate, or proxy to a political party convention; address a convention, rally, caucus, or similar gathering of a political party in support of or in opposition to a partisan candidate for public office or political office; use a personal automobile to drive voters to the polls on behalf of a political party or partisan candidate.

OSC enforces political activity restrictions under the Hatch Act and investigates allegations of violations of the law. When it determines that a violation has occurred, OSC may file a complaint with the Merit Systems Protection Board. The penalty for violation may be removal or suspension.

In cases where a removal is ordered by the MSPB, such employees may not be reemployed in any position if paid from the same appropriation as the jobs from which they were removed.

Exemptions in Certain Communities— Special rules apply to residents of certain communities that have large numbers of federal employees. Any community in the immediate vicinity of Washington, D.C., and any municipality where the majority of voters work for the federal government, may ask the Office of Personnel Management for a partial exemption from the political activity restrictions.

This partial exemption has been granted to more than 60 communities, most of them located in the vicinity of Washington, D.C. Employees in doubt as to whether their community has been granted this partial exemption from political activity restrictions should check with the OSC.

Whistleblower Disclosure Hotline

The OSC provides a secure channel through which federal employees and former employees (and job applicants) can disclose evidence of a violation of law, rule or regulation, gross mismanagement, gross waste of funds, an abuse of authority, or a substantial and specific danger to public health or safety. Employees who want to make such disclosures can call the OSC on its whistleblower hotline at 1-800-572-2249 or (202) 653-9125. OSC guarantees confidentiality to the whistleblower.

If the OSC determines that there is a substantial likelihood of wrongdoing, the OSC can order the head of the agency concerned to conduct an investigation, and to provide a report of that investigation to the OSC. The report of investigation, with any comments by the Special Counsel and the employee whose disclosure led to the inquiry, is then sent to the President and Congress.

Other OSC Responsibilities

The Uniformed Services Employment and Reemployment Rights Act of 1994 gave OSC authority to investigate and prosecute cases involving the denial of employment or reemployment rights to veterans and reservists seeking to return to the federal workplace after active duty with the armed services. OSC can, after Labor Department review of the matter, represent a veteran or reservist before MSPB, and potentially on appeal to the U.S. Court of Appeals for the Federal Circuit.

Also, OSC is authorized to investigate: activities prohibited by any civil service law, rule or regulation; allegations of arbitrary or capricious withholding of information under the Freedom of Information Act; and involvement by any employee in any prohibited discrimination found by a court or administrative authority to have occurred in the course of a personnel action.

The Special Counsel also supports efforts to educate federal employees about their rights and remedies in connection with prohibited personnel practices, and about the rights and restrictions of the Hatch Act.

Contacting OSC

Requests for assistance in connection with allegations of prohibited personnel practices, and requests for the appropriate forms, should be directed to the Complaints Examining Unit, Office of Special Counsel, 1730 M St., N.W., Suite 201, Washington, DC 20036-4505; phone: 1-800-872-9855 (TDD-equipped) and (202) 653-7188 (TDD-equipped).

Inquiries about the Hatch Act may be made in writing or by phone: Hatch Act Unit, Office of Special Counsel, 1730 M St., N.W., Suite 201, Washington, DC 20036-4505; phone: 1-800-85-HATCH or 1-800-854-2824, (202) 653-7143. Requests for Hatch Act advisory opinions may be made by e-mail: *hatchact@osc.gov*.

Disclosures of violations of law, rule or regulation, gross mismanagement, gross waste of funds, abuse of authority, or a danger to public health or safety may be reported in confidence to (and the appropriate form requested from): Disclosure Unit, Office of Special Counsel, 1730 M St., N.W., Suite 201, Washington, DC 20036-4505; phone: 1-800-572-2249, (202) 653-9125.

Questions about the Uniformed Services Employment and Reemployment Rights (USERRA) should be directed to: USERRA Coordinator, Office of Special Counsel, 1730 M St., N.W., Suite 201, Washington, DC 20036-4505; phone: (202) 653-6005; e-mail: *userra@osc.gov*.

The San Francisco Bay Area Field Office can be reached at: 1301 Clay St., Suite 365S, Oakland, CA 94612-5217; phone: (510) 637-3460; FAX: (510) 637-3474. The Dallas Field Office can be reached at: 1100 Commerce St., Rm. 7C30, Dallas, TX 75242-1027; phone: (214) 767-8871; FAX: (214) 767-2764.

Questions from federal agencies about obtaining copies of the OSC informational program guide for federal agencies on diskette should be directed to: Office of Special Counsel, 1730 M St., N.W., Suite 201, Washington, DC 20036-4505; phone: (202) 653-9485; fax (202) 653-5161.

OSC's website is *www.osc.gov*.

Section 5—U.S. Office of Government Ethics

General Responsibilities

The Office of Government Ethics (OGE) was originally established as part of the Office of Personnel Management. OGE became a separate and distinct agency in the executive branch on October 1, 1989. The mission of OGE is to exercise leadership in the executive branch to prevent conflicts of interest on the part of government employees and to resolve conflicts that do occur. The address and phone number of OGE are: 1201 New York Ave., N.W., Suite 500, Washington, DC 20005-3917; phone (202) 208-8000 or TDD (202) 208-8025, online *www.usoge.gov*.

In partnership with executive branch agencies and departments, OGE is responsible for fostering high ethical standards for employees and strengthening the public's confidence that the government's business is conducted with impartiality and integrity.

Ethics standards are found in Executive Order 12731 of October 17, 1990, the Ethics in Government Act of 1978, and the Ethics Reform Act of 1989. In addition, the primary conflict of interest statutes that OGE provides advice on are 18 U.S.C. paragraphs 202, 203, 205, 207-209. These establish requirements for executive agency employees and officers on such matters as gift acceptance, prevention of misuse of government position for private gain, outside activities and income, preferential treatment and conflicting financial interests, travel reimbursement, proper use of government assets and information, and post-government employment restrictions.

The agency's specific responsibilities fall into six general areas:

Regulatory Authority—OGE develops, promulgates, and reviews rules and regulations pertaining to employee conflicts of interest, post-employment restrictions, standards of ethical conduct, and public and confidential financial disclosure reports in the executive branch.

Financial Disclosure—OGE reviews executive branch public financial disclosure statements of presidential nominees subject to Senate confirmation to identify and help resolve all possible conflicts of interest under applicable laws and regulations. It also oversees the administration of executive branch blind trusts and issues certificates of divestiture.

Education and Training—OGE provides information on and promotes understanding of ethical standards in executive agencies. It provides ethics training on the standards of conduct, the conflict of interest laws, executive orders, and regulations to executive branch ethics officials.

Guidance and Interpretation—OGE prepares formal advisory opinions, informal letter advice, and policy memoranda on how to interpret and comply with conflict of interest, post-employment, standards of conduct and financial disclosure requirements in the executive branch. It consults with agency ethics officials in individual cases.

Monitoring and Enforcement—OGE monitors and reviews executive agency ethics programs, including financial disclosure systems, refers possible violations of conflict of interest laws to the Department of Justice, and advises on prosecutions and appeals. It also reviews possible administrative ethics violations and orders corrective action or recommends disciplinary action as appropriate.

Evaluation—OGE comments on proposed ethics-related legislation and evaluates the effectiveness of conflict of interest regulations and policies of other executive branch agencies.

Ethical Conduct Standards

Executive Order 12674 of April 12, 1989, modified by Executive Order 12731 of October 17, 1990, sets forth fundamental principles of ethical conduct for all executive branch employees. As directed by the order, the Office of Government Ethics (OGE) published in the Federal Register of August 7, 1992, final rules on standards of ethical conduct for executive branch employees and officers. These rules took effect February 3, 1993.

The main areas of coverage in these ethical conduct standards include gifts from outside sources, gifts between employees, conflicting financial interests, impartiality in performing official duties, seeking other employment, misuse of position, and outside activities. Agencies may still issue supplemental regulations, which first require OGE approval. After being reviewed and approved by OGE, these supplemental agency regulations also must appear in the Federal Register. Many agencies have now issued such supplemental regulations.

Starting January 1, 1991, all executive branch employees (other than special government employees and enlisted personnel) were prohibited by Title VI of the Ethics Reform Act of 1989 from accepting an honorarium for any speech, article, or appearance. This provision of the 1989 Act was challenged in court and eventually found by the Supreme Court to be an unconstitutional infringement of the First Amendment. Subsequently, the Department of Justice said that the law was "effectively eviscerated" by the Supreme Court's decision and that there were no remaining applications of the law. Executive branch employees are therefore no longer subject to this prohibition on the acceptance of honoraria. Any employee who had kept honoraria in an escrow account during the litigation was authorized to receive those funds.

However, employees remain subject to pre-existing standards that preclude the acceptance of compensation for teaching, speaking, or writing on subject matter that relates to the employee's official duties. Title VI imposes additional restrictions, applicable only to senior non-career employees, that prohibit the acceptance of compensation for engaging in specified outside activities. The same non-career employees are subject to a cap on the annual amount of outside income they may earn. (See 5 CFR Part 2636, Subpart C.)

Ethical Principles for Federal Employees

Executive branch employees must adhere to the general principles of ethical conduct as well as specific ethical standards. The following is a list of the 14 general principles that broadly define the obligations of public service. By observing these principles, employees

Ethical Conduct Rules for Executive Branch Employees

Gifts from outside sources	**Guidance:** Prohibits soliciting or accepting gifts from prohibited sources or gifts given because of official position. A "prohibited source" includes anyone seeking business with or official action by his or her agency and anyone "substantially affected" by performance of worker's official duties. A "gift" is anything of monetary value, except publicly available discounts and commercial loans, and such items as coffee, donuts, greeting cards and certificates. Includes rules on how to return prohibited gifts. **Exceptions:** Unsolicited gifts with market value of $20 or less per source per occasion with a cap of $50 in a year from any single source; gifts from family or friends; free attendance at certain "widely attended" conferences and receptions when cost is borne by sponsor (or if from a nonsponsor when more than 100 persons are expected to attend the event and the gift of free attendance has a market value of $250 or less); food, refreshments and entertainment at certain events while on duty in foreign countries. Certain gifts provided in connection with participation in political management or political campaigns.
Gifts between employees	**Guidance:** Prohibits giving or soliciting for a gift to an official superior or accepting a gift from lower-paid employee unless the two workers are personal friends who are not in a superior-subordinate relationship. **Exceptions:** Employees occasionally may give and accept items totaling $10 or less per occasion, food and refreshments shared in the office and personal hospitality at a residence. Covers birthdays and traditional gift-giving holidays. For "infrequent" occasions of personal significance such as marriage and retirement, soliciting "nominal" amounts from co-workers is allowed.
Conflicting financial interests	**Guidance:** (1) Prohibits an employee from participating in government capacity in matter where he or she has a financial interest or in which spouse, minor child, employer or any one of several other specified persons have a financial interest. (2) Agencies may prohibit employees from acquiring or retaining certain financial interests. **Exceptions:** Employees who have to sell interests may be eligible to defer the tax consequences of the divestiture. Certain interests arising from the ownership of mutual funds, unit investment trusts, and employee benefit plans as well as the ownership of certain interests in securities are exempted. Also, there are miscellaneous exemptions applicable only in specific situations or only to employees of certain agencies. Instances where a waiver is granted by government.
Impartiality	**Guidance:** Employees should get specific permission before participating in certain government matters where their impartiality is likely to be questioned, such as contracts, grants and investigations that might affect members of their own households or where persons are involved with whom the employees have or are seeking a business relationship. Prohibits for two years employees who receive an "extraordinary payment" of more than $10,000, except for routine severance pay, from previous employer from handling particular government matters involving that employer. **Exceptions:** Instances where government would benefit.
Seeking other employment	**Guidance:** Prohibits employees from personally and substantially participating in their official capacities in particular matters that have a "direct and predictable" effect on the financial interests of persons with whom they are "seeking employment or with whom they have an arrangement concerning future employment." **Exceptions:** Sending unsolicited resume, for example, to someone only affected by the employee's work on general rule-making; requesting job application or rejecting an unsolicited employment overture. Instances where a waiver is granted by government.
Misuse of position	**Guidance:** Prohibits employees from using public office for own private gain, or that of friends, relatives or persons with whom they are affiliated in a nongovernment capacity, or for the endorsement of any product, service or enterprise; engaging in financial transactions using nonpublic information or allowing improper use of nonpublic information to further private interests; must conserve government property and make sure it's used only for authorized purposes; and generally prohibits using official time "other than in an honest effort to perform official duties" or encouraging subordinates to perform unauthorized activities. **Exceptions:** None.
Outside activities	**Guidance:** Prohibits employees from engaging in outside activities that conflict with their official duties; gives agencies right to require, by supplemental regulation, clearance before employees can perform certain outside employment or activities; limits outside employment or earned income applicable to certain presidential appointees and certain noncareer employees; except as authorized by the agency, prohibits employees serving as expert witnesses, other than on behalf of the United States, in certain proceedings in which the United States is a party or has a "direct and substantial interest"; generally prohibits receiving compensation for teaching, speaking or writing related to their official duties, limits fundraising in an official or personal capacity; and requires that employees satisfy their just financial obligations. **Exceptions:** An employee may receive compensation for teaching certain courses, notwithstanding that the subject matter relates to his official duties; an agency ethics official may authorize an employee to provide expert witness services in certain circumstances. Employees who are not "covered noncareer employees" as defined in 5 C.F.R. paragraph 2636.303(a) may accept travel expenses incurred in connection with teaching, speaking, or writing activities related to their official duties.

help to ensure that citizens have complete confidence in the integrity of government operations and programs.

• Public service is a public trust, requiring employees to place loyalty to the Constitution, the laws, and ethical principles above private gain.

• Employees shall not hold financial interests that conflict with the conscientious performance of duty.

• Employees shall not engage in financial transactions using nonpublic government information or allow the improper use of such information to further any private interest.

• An employee shall not, except pursuant to such reasonable exceptions as are provided by regulation, solicit or accept any gift or other item of monetary value from any person or entity seeking official action from, doing business with, or conducting activities regulated by the employee's agency, or whose interests may be substantially affected by the performance or nonperformance of the employee's duties.

• Employees shall put forth honest effort in the performance of their duties.

• Employees shall make no unauthorized commitments or promises of any kind purporting to bind the government.

• Employees shall not use public office for private gain.

• Employees shall act impartially and not give preferential treatment to any private organization or individual.

• Employees shall protect and conserve federal property and shall not use it for other than authorized activities.

• Employees shall not engage in outside employment or activities, including seeking or negotiating for employment, that conflict with official government duties and responsibilities.

• Employees shall disclose waste, fraud, abuse, and corruption to appropriate authorities.

• Employees shall satisfy in good faith their obligations as citizens, including all just financial obligations, especially those— such as federal, state or local taxes—that are imposed by law.

• Employees shall adhere to all laws and regulations that provide equal opportunity for all Americans regardless of race, color, religion, sex, national origin, age, or handicap.

• Employees shall endeavor to avoid any actions creating the appearance that they are violating the law or the standards of ethical conduct.

Conflicts of Interest

In addition to complying with the regulatory standards of conduct and Title VI of the Ethics Reform Act of 1989, employees must avoid violation of several criminal conflict of interest statutes. Sections 203, 205, 208, and 209 of Title 18, United States Code, prohibit employees from engaging in certain representational activities before agencies and courts of the federal government, from acting officially on matters on which they, certain family members, or certain others have a financial interest, and from receiving compensation from non-government sources for the performance of their official duties. Employees are also prohibited from acting personally and substantially on particular matters affecting the financial interests of prospective employers with whom they are negotiating for or have an arrangement concerning future employment.

Certain of these statutory restrictions are relaxed or do not apply at all in the case of special government employees and enlisted military members. In addition to the statutes found in Title 18, employees of several executive branch agencies are subject to additional agency-specific statutes that impose restrictions relating to their conduct.

Financial Disclosure Requirements

As a means of identifying and preventing violations of these ethics laws and regulations, many employees are required to file financial disclosure statements. Since passage of the Ethics in Government Act of 1978, all top government officials, including senior career employees, have been required to file detailed, publicly available financial disclosure reports. (See 5 CFR Part 2634 and 5 U.S.C. Appendix 4.)

The public financial disclosure reporting requirements have been revised since the Ethics in Government Act of 1978 was passed. Most recently, P.L. 104-65 amended the Ethics in Government Act of 1978 to require additional information for certain assets, income, or liabilities. The March 2000 edition of the public financial disclosure report form (SF 278) reflects all of these reporting changes. Other employees may be required by their agencies to file confidential statements of employment and financial interests if, for example, their duties are determined to have an impact on the interests of a non-federal entity. The confidential financial disclosure report (OGE Form 450) covers some of the same areas as the public report form, except that the confidential form is shorter, requires less detail, and is not available for public inspection.

Recently, the threshold for reporting gifts, reimbursements and travel expenses for both the public and confidential financial disclosure reports was increased, retroactive to January 1, 2002. The new value threshold for reportable items is more than $285 for both reports. Additionally, in meeting this threshold, a public or confidential filer may disregard gifts and travel reimbursements received from any one source during the reporting period that total $114 or less. These reporting changes will be reflected in the new edition of the SF 278 that is due for renewal in 2003. The new 2002 edition of the OGE Form 450 (replacing the April 1999 edition) reflects these changes. In addition, some agencies require that departing or former employees file reports concerning private-sector employment.

Post-Employment Restrictions

Employees terminating government service on or after January 1, 1991, are subject to the post-employment restrictions of 18 U.S.C. § 207 as amended by the Ethics Reform Act of 1989. Provisions of Section 207, as amended, restrict former employees of the executive branch from making any communication to or appearance before an employee of the United States on behalf of any other person concerning a particular matter involving specific parties, for example, a particular contract, that was either under the former employee's official responsibility (two-year bar) or one in which the former employee had participated personally and substantially (lifetime bar).

Another of Section 207's provisions applies only to certain former senior employees and precludes most communications with the individual's former agency concerning official matters for a period of one year.

See 5 CFR Part 2637 and 5 CFR Part 2641. In general, Section 207 does not prohibit behind the scenes assistance to a new non-government employer, although former employees who participated in trade or treaty negotiations or who now seek to represent "foreign entities" face restrictions in this regard. Employees must be aware that other statutes impose post-employment restrictions in addition to those of Section 207. Former employees who were involved in government procurement must be especially mindful of these additional restrictions. For example, the "procurement integrity" provisions of 41 U.S.C. 423 (implemented in the Federal Acquisition Regulation) contain additional post-employment restrictions for certain former government officials. These provisions also prohibit the release of contractor bid or proposal information and source selection information. In addition, there are a number of agency-specific statutes that restrict the post-employment activities of former employees. Executive Order 12834 of January 20, 1993—which required "senior appointees" and "trade negotiators" to sign contractual pledges agreeing to certain further post-government employment restrictions—was revoked on December 28, 2000, and is no longer in effect.

Additional Information

Each agency is required to appoint a Designated Agency Ethics Official to coordinate and manage the agency's ethics program. Employees should first contact their agency ethics official with questions concerning the standards of conduct, conflicts of interest, financial disclosure, or agency-specific requirements, or to obtain copies of relevant laws. They may also seek advice by calling or writing to the Office of Government Ethics at Suite 500, 1201 New York Avenue, N.W., Washington, DC 20005-3917. The phone number is (202) 208-8000. In addition, OGE's website at *www.usoge.gov* contains various executive orders, statutes, and regulations that form the basis for the executive branch ethics program, as well as ethics advisory opinions and letters that interpret these ethics materials. OGE has recently redesigned its Web site to make site navigation easier. OGE has also made electronically-fillable versions of the SF 278 and OGE Form 450 available on its Web site.

Section 6—Federal Labor Relations Authority

General Responsibilities

The Federal Labor Relations Authority (FLRA) administers the federal labor relations program, performing the "third party" functions as an independent and neutral body. It interprets and enforces the Federal Service Labor-Management Relations Statute (Chapter 71, Title 5, U.S. Code), which protects the rights of employees of the federal government to organize, bargain collectively, and participate through labor organizations of their own choosing in decisions which affect them. The Authority also ensures compliance with the statutory rights

FLRA Regional Offices

FLRA OFFICES	GEOGRAPHIC JURISDICTION
ATLANTA REGION Marquis Two Tower, Ste. 701 285 Peachtree Center Ave. Atlanta, GA 30303-1270 Phone: (404) 331-5212 FAX: (404) 331-5280	Alabama, Florida, Georgia, Mississippi, South Carolina, Virgin Islands
BOSTON REGION 99 Summer St., Ste. 1500 MA 02110-1200 Phone: (617) 424-5731 FAX: (617) 424 5743	Connecticut, Maine, Massachusetts, New Hampshire, New Jersey, New York, Pennsylvania, Rhode Island, Boston, Vermont, Puerto Rico
CHICAGO REGION 55 W. Monroe, Ste. 1150 Chicago, IL 60603-9729 Phone: (312) 886-3465 FAX: (312) 886-5977	Illinois, Indiana, Iowa, Kentucky, Michigan, Minnesota, North Dakota, Ohio, Tennessee, Wisconsin
DALLAS REGION 525 Griffin St., Dallas, TX 75202-1906 Phone: (214) 767-6266 FAX: (214) 767-0156	Arkansas, Louisiana, New Mexico, Oklahoma, Texas, Panama (limited FLRA jurisdiction)
DENVER REGION 1244 Speer Blvd., Ste. 100 Denver, CO 80204-3581 Phone: (303) 844-5226 FAX: (303) 844-2774	Arizona, Colorado, Kansas, Missouri, Montana, Nebraska, South Dakota, Utah, Wyoming
SAN FRANCISCO REGION 901 Market St., Ste. 220 San Francisco, CA 94103-1791 Phone: (415) 356-5002 FAX: (415) 356-5017	Alaska, California, Hawaii, Idaho, Nevada, Oregon, Washington, and all land and water areas West of the continents of North and South America (except coastal islands) to longitude 90° E
WASHINGTON, D.C. REGION Tech World, 800 K St., N.W., Ste. 910 Washington, DC 20001-1206 Phone: (202) 482-6702 FAX: (202) 482-6724	Delaware; District of Columbia; Maryland; Virginia; West Virginia; North Carolina; and all land and water areas East of the continents of North and South America to longitude 90° E, except the Virgin Islands, Panama, Puerto Rico, and coastal islands.

and obligations of federal employees and the labor organizations that represent them in their dealings with federal agencies. The FLRA's address and phone number are: 607 14th St., N.W., Washington, DC 20424; phone: (202) 482-6500, online *www.flra.gov*.

Federal Employees News Digest, Inc. has published a comprehensive guide to employee complaint and appeal processes called *Federal Job Dispute Procedures*. See publication-ordering information in this *Almanac*.

Labor Relations Role

The Authority provides leadership in establishing policies and guidance relating to the federal service labor-management relations program. In addition, FLRA:

• determines the appropriateness of bargaining units;

• supervises or conducts representation elections;

• prescribes criteria and resolves issues relating to the granting of consultation rights to labor organizations with respect to internal agency policies and government-wide rules and regulations;

• resolves negotiability disputes, unfair labor practice complaints, and exceptions to arbitration awards; and

• takes such other actions as are necessary and appropriate to effectively administer the provisions of the statute.

The jurisdiction of the FLRA extends to executive branch agencies as well as the Library of Congress, the Government Printing Office, both legislative branch agencies, and to U.S. citizens and foreign nationals in that area of the Republic of Panama which is formerly known as the Canal Zone. Agencies not within FLRA jurisdiction are the General Accounting Office, the Postal Service, the Tennessee Valley Authority, the National Security Agency, the Federal Bureau of Investigation, and the Central Intelligence Agency.

For information on labor policies, see the Labor-Management Relations section in Chapter 8.

Organization and Structure

The Authority is composed of three members who are appointed by the President, with the advice and consent of the Senate,

for a five-year term. One member is designated by the President as the chairman and serves as the chief executive and administrative officer of the Authority. The general counsel of the Authority is appointed by the President with the advice and consent of the Senate for a five-year term. As established by the Foreign Service Act of 1980, the chairman and the general counsel of the Authority also serve as the chairman and general counsel to the Foreign Service Labor Relations Board, which administers a separate labor-management relations program for foreign service personnel.

Office of Administrative Law Judges— The Administrative Law Judges (ALJ's) hear unfair labor practice complaints and issue decisions which are reviewed by the Authority members who can affirm, modify, or reverse the ALJ's recommendation. Almost all unfair labor practice complaints moving from the regional office to the adjudicative process are initially heard by the Office of the Administrative Law Judges. A small number of cases come as stipulated records, directly to the authority without ALJ involvement.

Office of the Solicitor—The FLRA may seek enforcement of its decisions and orders in a U.S. Circuit Court of Appeals. Any person aggrieved by a final order of the FLRA can institute an action for judicial review in the Court of Appeals, requiring the FLRA to defend its final order in court. The Office of the Solicitor is responsible for this representation. Additionally, the solicitor's office advises the authority on: (1) legal questions presented by major case decisions and policy statements, and (2) the impact of statutes, executive orders, and regulations on case processing.

Collaboration and Alternative Dispute Resolution—The Collaboration and Alternative Dispute Resolution program (CADR) of the Federal Labor Relations Authority integrates alternative dispute resolution (ADR) into all of FLRA's case processes, that is, negotiability, arbitration, representation, unfair labor practice, and impasse bargaining processes. CADR provides prevention and intervention, ADR design, and facilitation and training services to parties on a joint and voluntary basis in pending cases and case-related matters.

Office of the General Counsel—The Office of the General Counsel is responsible for investigating alleged unfair labor practices, filing and prosecuting unfair labor practice complaints, and processing representation petitions, including representation elections to determine whether employees wish to be represented by a labor organization. The general counsel's decision to sustain a regional director's dismissal of an unfair labor practice charge is final.

The general counsel has authority over and is responsible for employees in the regional offices and for the effective and efficient operation and administration of the Authority's seven regional offices and four sub-regional offices.

The general counsel and his/her executive staff provide advice, assistance, and review of all phases of field office operations to ensure policy and procedure conformance.

Regional Offices—The FLRA has established seven regional offices in the following locations: Boston, Washington, D.C., Atlanta, Chicago, Dallas, Denver, and San Francisco. The regional offices are responsible for initially investigating and processing all representation and unfair labor practice cases.

For further information, visit *www.flra.gov* or contact the Assistant to the Executive Director, 607 14th St., N.W., Washington, DC 20424-0001; phone (202) 482-6550.

The Federal Service Impasses Panel

The role of the Federal Service Impasses Panel is to provide assistance to federal agencies and unions representing federal employees in resolving impasses arising from negotiations over conditions of employment. The

FSIP's address is 607 14th St., N.W., Washington, DC 20424-0001, and online at *www.flra.gov/fsip/panel.html*.

If bargaining between the parties and mediation assistance from the Federal Mediation and Conciliation Service prove unsuccessful, the panel, as an entity within the Federal Labor Relations Authority, has authority under section 7119 of the Federal Service Labor-Management Relations Statute to recommend procedures, such as arbitration, for the resolution of an impasse. It also provides direct assistance to the parties through fact-finding, written submissions, or other methods it deems appropriate.

If these efforts do not lead to a settlement, the panel may take whatever action is necessary to resolve the impasse. Such final action, typically an arbitration award or a decision and order of the panel itself, is binding on the parties during the term of their agreement unless they agree otherwise. If the parties to a negotiation impasse agree to adopt a procedure for using a private arbitrator, the procedure must be approved by the panel.

The statute also assigns special third-party functions to the Federal Mediation and Conciliation Service (FMCS) and to the Assistant Secretary of Labor for the Office of the American Workplace, an agency and entity outside the Federal Labor Relations Authority. FMCS provides services and assistance to agencies and exclusive representatives in the resolution of negotiation impasses, prior to or in conjunction with the panel. The assistant secretary enforces standards of conduct for unions governing democratic process and fiscal integrity.

Section 7—Alternative Dispute Resolution and Settlements

Each of the federal appeals agencies employs various alternative dispute resolution techniques and settlement initiatives to adjudicate matters over which it has jurisdiction, and each is engaged in substantial outreach efforts to encourage potential litigants to use their respective ADR and settlement processes. Further, individual employing agencies, in some cases at the direction of the appellate agencies, use many of the same types of techniques to resolve disputes before they turn into formal appeals.

Federal Employees News Digest, Inc. has published a comprehensive guide to employee complaint and appeal processes called *Federal Job Dispute Procedures*. See publication-ordering information in this *Almanac*.

Equal Employment Opportunity Commission

Under EEOC charge-processing rules that took effect in November 1999, federal agencies are required to establish an alternative dispute resolution program aimed at early, informal resolution of a complainant's discrimination charges. Agencies have the discretion, on a case-by-case basis, to refrain from offering ADR for certain types of "inappropriate" disputes (e.g., geographic restrictions on the availability of a pre-complaint ADR process). However, when ADR programs are offered, agencies generally must make them available during both the pre-complaint process and the formal complaint stage.

The ADR process is voluntary and the aggrieved party can withdraw at any time.

EEO counselors are required to inform aggrieved individuals of their right to choose traditional counseling or ADR participation (if offered) at the initial counseling session (or within a reasonable time thereafter). If the agency offers ADR during the pre-complaint, or informal, stage of the EEO process, the complainant may choose between participating in the ADR program or the traditional EEO counseling activities. Once the complainant elects to participate in the ADR program, all EEO counseling activities will end. Electing ADR increases the EEO pre-complaint processing period from 30 to 90 days.

Agencies are free to offer whatever ADR program is best suited to their needs, with the choices including mediation (the most frequently used), facilitation, fact-finding, early neutral evaluation, ombudsmen, settlement conferences, "minitrials," and peer review, as well as combinations of these techniques. Whatever technique is offered, agencies must take steps to ensure the fairness of the ADR initiative. Basically, this means that an agency must make sure its ADR program incorporates certain required "core principles," including voluntariness, neutrality, confidentiality, and enforceability. Complainants may not file a new complaint based on the agency's refusal to offer ADR in their particular case.

The EEOC discourages, but does not prohibit, EEO counselors from acting as neutrals in ADR programs. This is due, in part, to the EEOC's concern that a complainant may be confused as to the role being played by the counselor. If an agency chooses to have its EEO counselors serve as neutrals, EEOC has stated that the EEO counselors may not serve as neutrals in a dispute for which they have provided counseling.

The terms of any resolution achieved through the ADR process must be set forth in writing and signed by both parties.

If the time limit expires or the ADR process fails to produce a satisfactory resolution, the aggrieved person is entitled to a final interview with the EEO counselor and has the right to file a formal complaint.

If the complainant files a complaint, the agency may also choose to offer ADR during the formal complaint stage. The 180-day processing period for the formal complaint stage may be increased by an additional 90 days to conduct ADR, if the parties agree to do so in writing.

Postal Mediation Program—EEOC and the U.S. Postal Service in 2002 began a joint ADR program to improve the processing of discrimination complaints by postal workers. Under the initiative, virtually all requests for hearings before EEOC administrative judges involving bias cases against the USPS first go through mediation.

EEOC administrative judges issue a mediation order to the parties and provide a copy to the local USPS ADR coordinator. USPS provides an external mediator to conduct the mediation session, which typically is completed within 90 days of issuance of the order.

Reaching an agreement is strictly voluntary on the part of participants. The mediator has no authority to mandate a resolution of the case and will inform the EEOC administrative judge of the outcome within 10 days of the mediation, as well as provide a copy of any resulting settlement agreement. If a mediated resolution is not reached, an EEOC administrative judge proceeds to process the complaint in accordance with the federal sector regulations (29 C.F.R. Part 1614).

Cases excluded from the program include class and systemic complaints, those involving Equal Pay Act claims, and cases involving conduct by the complainant of a criminal nature. In addition, in rare circumstances, EEOC administrative judges may determine that good cause exists for not requiring the parties to participate in mediation.

Merit Systems Protection Board

MSPB operates settlement initiatives both at the administrative judge and Board levels. Overall, more than half of the appeals filed with the Board are settled.

Administrative judges at the regional level may initiate attempts to settle the appeal informally at any time, beginning in some cases with the initial filing of the appeal. The administrative judge may conduct prehearing conferences to help achieve resolution of an appeal, or another judge may be assigned to act as a settlement judge. In most cases, settlement agreements are entered into the record, with the Board retaining enforcement authority.

On January 28, 2002, MSPB issued interim rules stating that a case may be suspended for up to 60 days to permit the parties to pursue discovery or settlement. The parties may submit a joint request for additional time. Upon receipt of such a request, the judge will suspend processing of the case for up to 30 days. The judge will grant an extension of the suspension period for up to an additional 30 days upon a joint request from the parties for additional time. Either party may submit a unilateral request for additional time to pursue discovery. Unilateral requests for additional time may be granted at the discretion of the judge. The suspension period may be terminated prior to the end of the agreed upon period if the parties request the judge's assistance relative to discovery or settlement during the suspension period and the judge's involvement under that request is likely to be extensive.

At the Board level, officials select cases that appear to have the most potential for settlement. Board settlement attorneys contact the parties in the case to initiate the resolution process and may in some cases use the services of an outside neutral to facilitate settlement.

MSPB provides an automatic extension of the regulatory time limit for filing an appeal with MSPB where an appellant and agency mutually agree, prior to the timely filing of an appeal, to attempt to resolve their dispute through an ADR process. It also has developed a program of instruction for dispute prevention specialists who can help intercept and resolve cases prior to adjudication by MSPB. The goals of the program are to help agencies anticipate, manage and reduce workplace conflict and tension while reducing costs directly and indirectly related to workplace conflicts.

MSPB also conducts an outreach program to help educate those who might be involved in Board matters, making administrative judges and other agency officials available to speak in various forums, and providing opportunities for practitioners before the Board to participate in skills-building training sessions which may include exercises in settling appeals as an alternative to formal litigation.

Federal Labor Relations Authority

FLRA's Collaboration and Alternative Dispute Resolution (CADR) program integrates ADR into all of the case processes used by the various FLRA components. The services focus on alternatives to traditional case processing and formal dispute resolution.

The CADR program assists the parties both in preventing disputes before they become cases and in finding ways to informally resolve disputes in pending cases. This includes interest-based conflict resolution and intervention services in pending unfair labor practice cases, representation cases, negotiability appeals and impasse bargaining disputes. The CADR program also provides facilitation, training and education to help labor and management develop collaborative relationships. The program is voluntary.

FLRA regulations for negotiability, unfair labor practice, and representation cases ensure that parties have the opportunity to use ADR to resolve their cases. For example, in negotiability cases, during the post-petition conference, if the parties express interest in using ADR services, the case will be put on hold to give the parties time to get help from the CADR office. In unfair labor practice cases, an ADR process is available that allows the parties to resolve the underlying dispute by facilitating a problem-solving approach, rather than having the regional office investigate the facts and determine the merits of the charge.

For cases on their way to hearing, an administrative law judge settlement program is available for one more attempt at informal resolution.

ADR services are also available in some circumstances for parties who do not have a case filed, but would like assistance with disputes or relationship issues.

The FLRA office of the general counsel

ADR services program provides dispute resolution services to resolve parties' labor-management disputes and to assist parties in developing the type of labor-management relationship that is best suited to their own needs. The office will work with the parties to customize a program that assists them. It provides services including facilitation, intervention, training and education.

Federal Service Impasses Panel

Once it decides to assert jurisdiction in a dispute, the FSIP may recommend or direct the use of procedures for resolving an impasse through any method it deems appropriate. If the procedure selected does not result in a settlement, the panel may then take whatever final action is necessary to resolve the dispute, including the issuance of a decision and order. The order is binding during the term of the parties' collective bargaining agreement unless the parties agree otherwise.

Where circumstances warrant, the Panel will select the procedure most likely to lead to a voluntary settlement. The Panel encourages the parties to continue efforts to resolve the issues voluntarily at every stage of case processing.

To maximize the parties' opportunity to reach a voluntary resolution of the dispute, a Panel-appointed representative (usually a Panel or staff member) explores settlement possibilities with the parties in a face-to-face setting. Should such efforts prove unsuccessful, the representative reports to the full Panel, which then takes final action on the matter.

To provide the parties with a final opportunity to resolve the dispute themselves at the late stage of the negotiation process, a Panel-appointed mediator-arbitrator explores possible areas of agreement. If a voluntary agreement does not occur during the mediation phase, an arbitration hearing then immediately follows. The arbitrator ultimately has the authority to render a binding arbitration decision on those issues not resolved during the mediation portion of the procedure.

The law also authorizes the parties to voluntarily submit a dispute to a private mediator-arbitrator with Panel approval. Further, the Panel may direct an expedited arbitration procedure.

Office of Special Counsel

OSC offers ADR to resolve selected prohibited personnel practice complaints. The Office primarily uses mediation to provide parties the opportunity to resolve an OSC complaint without the need for an investigation or litigation.

Participation in the OSC Mediation Program is voluntary. In selected cases that are slated for referral to OSC's Investigation and Prosecution Division, the OSC ADR specialist contacts the complainant and the employing agency to invite them to participate in the mediation program. The factors considered include the nature of the case, the relationship of the parties, the complexity of the case, and the relief sought by the complainant. Allegations that do not warrant referral to the Investigation and Prosecution Division are not eligible for mediation.

If both parties agree, OSC schedules a mediation session. OSC mediators conduct a mediation session at a mutually convenient time and location. If mediation results in resolution, the agreement is put into writing and becomes binding on both parties.

The complainant and a representative from the employing agency attend the mediation. While it is not necessary to have an attorney or other representative attend the session, either party may choose to do so. The individuals attending the mediation session must have the authority necessary to resolve the dispute.

If one party declines OSC's invitation to mediate, or decides to terminate mediation before resolution of the complaint, the complaint will be assigned to the Investigation and Prosecution Division, as it would have been had mediation not been offered to the parties. Similarly, if mediation is held and resolution is not achieved, the complaint is assigned to the Investigation and Prosecution Division, as it would have been had the parties not tried mediation.

Mediation may be available as an option at the investigation and prosecution stages at the discretion of OSC.

For further information, contact the Alternative Dispute Resolution Unit, 1730 M Street, N.W., Suite 201, Washington, D.C. 20036-4505, phone (800) 872-9855 or (202) 653-2253, ext. 4625, email:adr @osc.gov.

Employing Agencies

Like the appeals agencies, individual employing agencies have increasingly used alternative dispute resolution techniques and settlement initiatives in an attempt to resolve disputes before they reach the formal appeals stage. A presidential memorandum of May 1, 1998, directed all federal agencies to promote greater use of ADR.

Techniques agencies employ include: binding arbitration, involving the presentation of a dispute to an impartial or neutral individual (arbitrator) or panel (arbitration panel) for issuance of a binding decision; conciliation, involving building a positive relationship between the parties to a dispute; cooperative problem-solving, most commonly used when a conflict is not highly polarized and prior to the parties forming hard line positions; dispute panels, which use one or more neutral or impartial individuals to clarify misperceptions, fill in information gaps, or resolve differences over data or facts; early neutral evaluation, which uses an impartial third party to provide a non-binding evaluation that gives the parties to a dispute an objective perspective on the strengths and weaknesses of their cases; facilitation, which involves techniques to improve the flow of information in a meeting between parties to a dispute; fact finding, an impartial expert (or group) selected by the parties, an agency, or by an individual with the authority to appoint a fact finder; interest-based problem-solving, which aims to effect solutions while improving the relationship between the parties; mediated arbitration, in which an impartial or neutral third party is authorized by the disputing parties to mediate their dispute until such time as they reach an impasse; mediation, the intervention into a dispute or negotiation of an acceptable, impartial and neutral third party who has no decision-making authority; mini-trials, a structured settlement process in which each side to a dispute presents abbreviated summaries of its cases before the major decision makers for the parties, who have authority to settle the dispute; non-binding arbitration, which involves presenting a dispute to an impartial or neutral individual (arbitrator) or panel (arbitration panel) for issuance of an advisory or non-binding decision; ombudsmen, individuals who rely on techniques including counseling, mediating, conciliating, and fact finding; and peer review, a problem-solving process where an employee takes a dispute to a group or panel of fellow employees and managers for a decision.

Availability of such channels varies among agencies and among sites within agencies. For bargaining unit employees, certain options and procedures might be required by labor-management contracts.

Chapter 10
Taxes

Section 1—Main New Income Tax Provisions Affecting Taxpayers

Summary of Tax Legislation

The most significant tax legislation of 2002, the Job Creation and Worker Assistance Act, created a number of incentives designed to help the economy recover from the devastation of the September 11, 2001, tragedy. Most of the provisions are of particular interest to businesses. Several provisions do effect individuals. For the first time, eligible teachers will be able to take a $250 deduction, above the line, for qualified classroom expenses. For all taxpayers in business, any new equipment purchased prior to September 11, 2004, is allowed an additional 30 percent depreciation allowance in the tax period of acquisition.

The Economic Growth and Tax Relief Reconciliation Act of 2001 was the largest tax cut of the past 20 years, with the total reduction in the nation's taxes conservatively forecast at $1.35 trillion dollars.

Beginning January 1, 2002, all bracketed rates except the 15 percent rates dropped by one percent. When the rate reductions in this bill are fully phased in, the tax brackets will be 10, 15, 25, 28, 33 and 35 percent.

Starting in 2002, there is a new deduction for college tuition costs. The deduction is dollar for dollar up to $3,000, which will increase to $4,000 in 2004. The provision expires after 2005. The deduction is not available if adjusted gross income (AGI) exceeds $65,000 for single and $130,000 for joint returns.

A major change in the education IRA rules increases the amount that individuals may contribute and allows distributions for elementary and secondary education. The nature and fundamental purpose of education IRAs would suggest a need for families to analyze the merits of utilizing the funds prior to college.

Many changes have occurred affecting IRAs. Contribution limits for IRAs and Roth IRAs increased to $3,000 in 2002, and will increase again to $4,000 in 2005 and $5,000 in 2008. The AGI limits have not changed. Starting in 2002, "older Americans" reaching 50 by the end of 2002 could make catch-up contributions of $500 ($1,000 in 2006) in addition to the normal limitations.

Deferrals for 401(k) and 403(b) plans increased to $11,000 in 2002 and will increase an additional $1,000 per year through 2006. "Older Americans" could make catch-up contributions of $1,000 starting in 2002, a figure which will increase by $1,000 each year through 2006.

Changes due to recent legislation in the retirement and estate tax arena are significant. It is imperative that individuals review their retirement and estate plans to ensure that they are still suitable and optimal. Individuals may wish to consult tax professionals to determine the effect of these and other new provisions.

As this volume goes to press, there are several other bills before Congress containing tax legislation. For the latest updates, visit *www.FederalDaily.com*.

Section 2—Individual Income Tax Rates

Personal Exemptions

When a taxpayer's adjusted gross income (AGI) exceeds a threshold amount, personal exemptions are reduced by two percent for each $2,500 or fraction thereof by which the taxpayer's AGI exceeds the threshold amount. In order to eliminate any advantage gained by filing "married filing separately," personal exemptions are reduced by two percent for each $1,250 by which the taxpayer's AGI exceeds the threshold amount.

Married Filing Jointly and
   Surviving Spouse $206,000
Married Filing Separately $103,000
Single $137,300
Head of Household $171,650
Because personal exemptions are reduced

by two percent for each $2,500 or fraction thereof in excess of the threshold amount, the personal exemptions allowed are completely phased out when the taxpayer's AGI exceeds the threshold amount by more than $122,500 (or $61,250 if married filing separately).

The personal exemption amount for 2002, as indexed for inflation, is $3,000. A personal exemption amount may not be claimed for a full-time student after the child reaches the age of 24 unless the child's gross income does not exceed the exemption amount.

Standard Deduction Amounts

The basic standard deduction amounts for 2002 and 2003 as adjusted for inflation are:

	2002	2003
Married Filing Jointly and Surviving Spouse	$7,850	$7,950
Married Filing Separately	$3,925	$3,975
Single	$4,700	$4,750
Head of Household	$6,900	$7,000

The additional standard deduction amount for married taxpayers 65 or older or blind are $900 for 2002 and $950 for 2003. For a single taxpayer or head of household, the additional standard deduction amount is $1,150 for 2002 and $1,150 for 2003. For an individual who can be claimed as a dependent on another's return, the basic standard deduction is $750 for 2002 and $750 for 2003. The standard deduction for a taxpayer who can be claimed as a dependent on another's return is the lesser of: (1) the standard deduction for single taxpayers or (2) the greater of: (a) the basic standard deduction ($750 for 2002), or (b) the individual's earned income plus $250.

Itemized Deductions

Taxpayers whose AGI exceeds a threshold amount must reduce their itemized deductions allowed (other than medical expenses, investment interest, casualty losses, and wagering losses to the extent of wagering

gains) by three percent of the excess of their AGI over the threshold amount.

The threshold amounts for 2002 are as follows:

Married Filing Jointly and Surviving Spouse	$137,300
Married Filing Separately	$68,650
Single	$137,300
Head of Household	$137,300

The total reduction, however, may not exceed 80 percent of the taxpayer's otherwise allowable itemized deductions.

Alternative Minimum Tax Rates

Individual taxpayers are subject to a two-tier graduated tax rate schedule for computing their alternative minimum tax liabilities.

The graduated tax rate schedule for 2002 is as follows:

• 26 percent rate applies to the first $175,000 of the taxpayer's alternative minimum taxable income ($87,500 for married individuals filing separately) in excess of the applicable exemption amount.

• 28 percent rate applies to the taxpayer's alternative minimum taxable income that is greater than $175,000 ($87,500 for married individuals filing separately) in excess of the applicable exemption amount.

The exemption amounts for alternative minimum tax purposes for 2002 are as follows:

Married Filing Jointly and Surviving Spouse	$49,000
Married Filing Separately	$24,500
Single	$35,750
Head of Household	$35,750

2003 Auto Standard Mileage Rates (Cents per Mile)

Business Mileage Rate	36 cents
Charitable Mileage Rate	14 cents
Medical Mileage Rate	12 cents
Moving Mileage Rate	12 cents

Section 3—Taxation of Federal Payments and Benefits

Contribution Refunds Upon Leaving Government Service

An employee leaving government service prior to retirement can choose to receive a refund of the money credited to his civil serv-

ice retirement fund. If only the refund of the contribution is received, no part of the refund is taxable. If a refund is received that exceeds the total contributions to the fund, the excess is interest and is taxable in the year it is received. All or part of the interest may be rolled over into a qualified plan. A rollover is a tax-free withdrawal of assets from one plan and its reinvestment in another plan. It is important that the rollover be made directly from one plan to another without the employee actually receiving any portion of the amount being rolled over. Otherwise, the Office of Personnel Management is required to withhold federal income tax of 20 percent on the interest portion of the refund received.

An employee who transferred from the CSRS to the FERS with less than five years of service under the CSRS may have received a refund of the additional money paid for the CSRS service plus interest. The interest received on this type of refund is taxable and cannot be rolled over.

Taxability of Annuities

Each of a federal retiree's monthly annuity payments is comprised of two parts:
- A tax-free portion that represents a return of cost.
- The taxable balance.

Taxpayers must use the General Rule or, if they qualify, the Simplified General Rule to compute the taxable portion of their annuity payments.

General Rule: In order to determine the tax-free portion of each full monthly payment under the General Rule, an exclusion percentage must be calculated as of the annuity starting date (commencing date). To determine the exclusion percentage, divide the adjusted investment in the contract by the expected return. The Office of Personnel Man-

Income Tax Rates, Thresholds, Statutory Amounts for 2001
Individual Income Tax Rates

Married Filing Jointly and Surviving Spouses

If Taxable Income is: Over -	But Not Over -	The Tax is:	Of the Amount Over -
$ 0	$12,000	10.0%	$0
$12,000	$46,700	$1,200 + 15.0%	$12,000
$46,700	$112,850	$6,405 + 27.0%	$46,700
$112,850	$171,950	$24,266 + 36.0%	$112,850
$171,950	$307,050	$41,996 + 35.0%	$171,950
$307,050		$89,281 + 38.6%	$307,050

Married Filing Separately

If Taxable Income is: Over -	But Not Over -	The Tax is:	Of the Amount Over -
$0	$6,000	10.0%	$0
$6,000	$23,350	$600 + 15.0%	$6,000
$23,350	$56,425	$3,203 + 27.0%	$23,350
$56,425	$85,975	$12,133 + 30.0%	$56,425
$85,975	$153,525	$20,998 + 35.0%	$85,975
$153,525		$44,640 + 38.6%	$153,525

Single

If Taxable Income is: Over -	But Not Over -	The Tax is:	Of the Amount Over -
$0	$6,000	10.0%	$0
$6,000	$27,950	$600 + 15.0%	$6,000
$27,950	$67,700	$3,983 + 27.0%	$27,950
$67,700	$141,250	$14,625 + 30.0%	$67,700
$141,250	$307,050	$36,690 + 38.6%	$141,250
$307,050			$307,050

Head of Household

If Taxable Income is: Over -	But Not Over -	The Tax is:	Of the Amount Over -
$0	$10,000	10.0%	$0
$10,000	$37,450	$1,000 + 15.0%	$10,000
$37,450	$96,700	$5,118 + 27.0%	$37,450
$96,700	$156,600	$ 21,115 + 30.0%	$96,700
$156,600	$307,050	$ 39,085 + 35.0%	$156,600
$307,050		$ 91,743 + 38.6%	$307,050

agement will provide the unadjusted investment in the contract. In order to determine the adjusted investment in the contract, a reduction of the value of the refund feature is made from the total contributions. The expected return is based upon the rate in effect at the annuity starting date under the appropriate actuarial table for the retiree's life expectancy. The annuity tables and examples are provided in Internal Revenue Service Publication 939.

Simplified General Rule: This simplified rule may be used by taxpayers if:

• Their annuity starting date is after July 1, 1986.

• Their annuity payments are for either the life of the retired employee or the survivor receiving a survivor annuity, or the retired employee/survivor's life and that of the beneficiary.

Under the Simplified General Rule, the tax-free portion of each monthly payment is determined by dividing the taxpayer's cost in the plan by a certain number of months based on the taxpayer's age.

The taxpayer's cost in the plan includes any "deemed deposit" or "deemed redeposit." "Deemed deposits" (including interest) are deposits deemed to be made for federal employment during which time no retirement contributions were withheld from the employee's pay. "Deemed redeposits" (including interest) are for any refunds of retirement contributions that were received but have not yet been repaid. If the retired employee/survivor received a lump-sum payment under an alternative annuity option, the lump sum does not reduce the cost in the plan.

A table detailing the number of months to be utilized in the calculation and examples are provided in Internal Revenue Service Publication 721.

Taxpayers with an annuity starting date after July 1, 1986, can change the method of computing the tax-free portion of their annuity from the General Rule to the Simplified General Rule, or vice versa, by filing amended tax returns for all tax years beginning with the year in which they received their first annuity payment. Due to the statute of limitations on filing amended tax returns, taxpayers can only change methods within three years from the due date of the tax return for the year in which

the taxpayer received the first annuity payment or, if later, within two years from the date the tax for that tax year was paid.

Regardless of whether the General Rule or the Simplified General Rule is used, if the annuity starting date is after July 1, 1986, and the retiree (or last annuitant) dies prior to recovering the entire annuity cost, the unrecovered annuity cost is allowed as a miscellaneous itemized deduction not subject to the two percent of adjusted gross income limitation in the taxpayer's last tax year.

Thrift Savings Plan-For information on the taxability of contributions, investments, withdrawals, and tax considerations of the TSP, please refer to the "Thrift Savings Plan" section.

Lump-Sum Benefit Payment

Certain individuals who retire under either CSRS or FERS may elect to receive a lump-sum benefit payment equal to their total contributions to the retirement plan. The option is only available to employees retiring with certain life-threatening illnesses. The monthly annuity is reduced by about 5 to 15 percent to adjust for this payment. Usually, 85 to 95 percent of the lump-sum benefit is taxable income. For federal income tax purposes, the lump-sum payment will include:

• All deemed deposits for federal employment during which no retirement contributions were withheld from pay (plus interest).

• Any deemed redeposits for any refunds of retirement contributions that have been received but not repaid (plus interest).

An employee can roll over the taxable portion of the payment to an IRA or a qualified plan. The Office of Personnel Management is required to withhold income tax of 20 percent on the taxable portion of the payment, unless the employee requests that OPM transfer that portion of the payment directly to an IRA or a qualified retirement plan.

Taxability of Federal Life Insurance Benefits

Death benefit payments made under the Federal Employees Group Life Insurance to a designated beneficiary are not taxable as income to the beneficiary. As with any life insurance policy in which the decedent had maintained incidents of ownership (the right to change the beneficiary), the proceeds are includible in the insured's

2003 Federal Employees Almanac

estate and may be subject to estate tax to the extent the estate is taxable.

Living benefits paid by FEGLI and benefits paid by a qualified settlement provider (a person or firm which regularly purchases or takes assignment of life insurance contracts on the lives of the terminally ill) to terminally ill insureds are excludable from taxable income. In addition, chronically ill individuals who are not also terminally ill may exclude up to $180 per day of accelerated benefits received from life insurance contracts.

Government-Provided Business Reimbursements

Reimbursed Employee Business Expenses—If an employee does not receive a per diem or the fixed allowance, reimbursed employee business expenses will not be deductible from adjusted gross income unless the following conditions are met:

• The employee must substantiate the expenses covered by the reimbursement arrangement to the employer.

• The employee must return any reimbursement in excess of the substantiated expenses.

If these requirements are not met, all reimbursements must be included in income, and expenses may be deducted only as a miscellaneous itemized deduction subject to the two percent of adjusted gross income limitation. Meals and entertainment expenses are subject to a 50 percent limitation prior to applying the two percent limitation.

Transportation and per diem allowances received by a federal employee are deemed substantiated. Therefore, there is no excess retained by the employee from the fixed allowance. But if expenses exceed the fixed allowance, a deduction is allowed as a miscellaneous itemized deduction subject to the 2 percent of adjusted gross income floor. In order to claim a deduction for unreimbursed employee business expenses, Form 2106, Employee Business Expenses, must be completed by the taxpayer and attached to his tax return. Detailed records and substantiation are required by the Internal Revenue Service to ensure compliance with the law.

Mileage Reimbursements—The federal government's reimbursement rate for business automobile mileage in 2002 was 36.5 cents a mile, and decreased to 36.0 cents per mile on January 1, 2003. For income tax purposes, actual expenses or the "optional mileage" method may be used for computing business deductions. If actual expenses are claimed, the business percentage is based on business miles relative to total miles driven during the calendar year. In this situation, the amount reimbursed offsets the expenses claimed and the excess is reported as a miscellaneous itemized deduction, subject to the two percent of adjusted gross income floor.

Rural Mail Carriers—A rural mail carrier who receives a qualified reimbursement of expenses incurred for the use of his vehicle for performing the collection and delivery of mail on a rural route is allowed a deduction for an amount equal to the qualified reimbursement received. The reimbursement is treated as being paid under an accountable plan and is excluded from gross income. The special standard mileage rate and provisions related to its use by rural mail carriers have been repealed.

Federal Employees Engaged in Criminal Investigations—The travel expenses incurred by a federal employee engaged in a criminal investigation away from home are fully deductible regardless of the length of time spent away from home. In order to qualify under this special provision, the employee must be certified by the Attorney General or her delegate as traveling on behalf of the United States on temporary duty status to investigate or provide support services for the investigation of a federal crime.

Military Pay and Benefits

Generally, members of the U.S. Armed Forces include the same items in income as do civilians. However, certain pay and benefits resulting from service in the Armed Forces are exempt, as follows:

Armed Forces Benefits—Retirement pay received from the government by Armed Service members is not exempt from income tax. Disability retirement pay that is computed on the basis of the percentage of disability is fully excludable from gross income, but disability retirement pay that is computed by reference to years of service is excludable only to the extent allowed under the percentage-of-disability method. Any pension, annuity, or similar payment for personal injury or sickness that resulted from combat-related service in the armed forces of any country or in the Coast and Geodetic Survey or the Public Health Service of the United States is exempt from tax.

Veterans' benefits under any law administered by the Veterans Administration are not includible in income. This includes amounts paid to veterans or their families as educational, training, or subsistence allowances, grants for homes with wheelchair access, and grants for vehicles for veterans who lost their sight or use of their limbs.

Dividends and proceeds from maturing government endowment insurance contracts under all acts relating to veterans are exempt. Interest on dividends left on deposit with the Veterans Administration is also exempt.

Armed Forces Allowances—Allowances for subsistence, quarters, travel, and moving paid to any member of the Armed Forces, Coast and Geodetic Survey, or Public Health Service, are excludable from income. These include housing and cost-of-living allowances to cover the excess cost of quarters and subsistence while on permanent duty at a post outside the United States, as well as family separation allowances received on account of overseas assignment.

Combat Zone Compensation—Compensation received by an enlisted member of the armed forces of the United States is excluded from the taxpayer's gross income for any month during which the taxpayer served in a combat zone or was hospitalized as a result of wounds, disease, or injury incurred while serving in a combat zone. The exclusion for months of hospitalization does not apply for any month beginning more than two years after the termination of combatant activities in the zone. For a commissioned officer of the armed forces, the exclusion is limited to "the maximum enlisted amount." This amount is the highest basic pay rate at the highest pay grade that enlisted personnel may receive plus the amount of hostile fire/imminent danger pay that the officer receives.

Compensation other than basic military pay that is excludable includes such items as:

• compensation for annual leave earned by an enlisted member of the armed forces while serving in a combat zone, though no services are performed by the member of the armed forces in a combat zone in the year of payment;

• a cash award received by an enlisted member of the armed forces for an employee suggestion that he submitted while serving in a combat zone, even though the award was granted and received outside of the combat zone;

• an enlisted member's bonus for reenlisting while serving in a combat zone, even though the reenlistment bonus was received outside of the combat zone.

Generally, the time and place that the military compensation was earned determines excludability, not the time and place of payment.

Taxes Due from Member of Armed Forces Upon Death—If a member of the Armed Forces dies while serving in a combat zone or as a result of wounds, disease, or injury while so serving, the income tax for the year of death and any prior year ending on or after the first day served in a combat zone is canceled. Any unpaid taxes of such individual that relate to tax years prior to service in a combat zone may also be abated. A similar rule applies to U.S. military and civilian employees who die as a result of wounds or injury occurring outside the United States in a terrorist or military action against the United States or any of its allies.

Extensions of Time to File Taxes—All U.S. citizens living outside the U.S. and Puerto Rico are granted an automatic extension up to and including the 15th day of the 6th month following the close of their tax year for filing a return if a statement is attached to the return showing they are entitled to the extension. In addition, Armed Forces members and civilians serving in support of them in a designated combat zone or hospitalized outside the U.S. as a result of an injury received while serving in a combat zone qualify for an extension for filing returns and paying tax. The extension is granted for the period of combat service or hospitalization plus 180 days.

Section 4—State Tax Treatment of Civil Service Annuities

State Provisions and Exemptions

The following states have no personal income tax laws: Alaska, Florida, Nevada, New Hampshire*, South Dakota, Tennessee*, Texas, Washington, Wyoming. (*Tax is imposed on interest and dividend income in these states.)

The following states exempt the total amount of the taxable portion of civil service annuities: Alabama, Hawaii, Illinois, Kansas, Louisiana, Massachusetts**, Michigan, Mississippi, New York, Pennsylvania. Wisconsin does not tax annuities of federal employees who were retired before January 1, 1964, or who were employed by the government and covered by one of the retirement systems as of December 31, 1963, and retired at a later date. North Carolina has not taxed annuities since 1998 if an individual has five years of government service as of Aug 12, 1989. (**Totally exempt if the plan is contributory.)

The following states allow partial tax exemptions, based either on a taxpayer's attainment of a specified age (e.g., age 62) or on a specified nontaxable portion of a civil service annuity: Arizona, Arkansas, Colorado, Delaware, District of Columbia, Georgia, Idaho, Indiana, Iowa, Kentucky, Maryland, Missouri, Montana, New Jersey, North Carolina, North Dakota, Ohio, Oklahoma, Oregon, South Carolina, Utah, and West Virginia. For information about the specific portion of an annuity that may be taxable in a particular state, contact the state's Department of Revenue.

The following states levy tax on the taxable portion of civil service annuities: California, Connecticut, Maine, Minnesota, Nebraska, New Mexico, Rhode Island, Vermont, Virginia.

States not listed have no special tax provisions affecting civil service annuities. Also, states have varying exemptions from income for persons 62+ or 65+ and minimum income levels subject to tax that have not been listed here.

Note: A certain number of states now have withholding agreements with the federal government whereby residents who commute to and work in another state may request a voluntary payroll deduction to apply to their state-of-residence income tax obligation.

Note: In addition to the state tax laws and regulations, many cities have their own income tax regulations. Check with your local municipal offices for current regulations.

Limitations on State Taxation of Pensions

All states and their subdivisions, the District of Columbia, and the possessions of the United States are prohibited from imposing income tax on any retirement income of any individual who is not a resident of or domiciled in the state.

While states may no longer impose these "source" taxes, retirement income remains taxable within the state in which the taxpayer resides. Taxpayers who have excluded retirement income from resident state taxation because it was taxable in another state or who have received a credit against resident state income tax because of taxes paid on retirement income to another state are no longer entitled to the exclusion or the credit.

Section 5—Other Tax Provisions of Interest to Federal Employees

Sale of Principal Residence

If a taxpayer sold a principal residence in 2002, up to $500,000 of the gain can be excluded from taxable income if filing a joint return ($250,000 if filing single), as long as certain conditions are met. Generally, the taxpayer must have owned and occupied the home as a principal residence for at least two of the five years preceding the sale. However, if the current residence was acquired in a qualified rollover of gain on the previous residence, the taxpayer can include the holding period of the previous residence for purposes of the "two out of five years" rule.

The exclusion may be claimed no more frequently than once every two years. If, because of health reasons, job relocation, or other unforeseen circumstances, a taxpayer fails to meet the "2 out of 5 years" rule or the "once in two years sale" rule he is entitled to a prorated amount of the exclusion.

The generous exclusion amounts might reduce the need for most taxpayers to keep tedious records of improvements made on a principal residence; however, we would encourage keeping the records just the same because rules change. It will still be necessary to keep records of the original cost of the home.

IRA Provisions

Generally, a taxpayer who is not an active participant in an employer maintained retirement plan may make deductible contributions to an Individual Retirement Account to the extent of the lesser of (1) $3,000 or (2) the individual's compensation included in gross income for the year. For a married couple filing a joint return (neither of whom are active participants in employer sponsored plans), the deductible contributions may be $6,000, as long as includible compensation is at least that amount.

Participation in an employer sponsored retirement plan does not preclude contributing to an IRA. A taxpayer may make fully or partially deductible or nondeductible contributions as long as certain conditions are met.

Deductible Contributions—A married couple filing a joint return, who are both participants in employer sponsored retirement plans, may make deductible contributions of up to $6,000 ($3,000 for a single filer) to traditional IRAs if adjusted gross income (AGI) for 2002 is less than $54,000 ($34,000 for a single filer). The deductible amount is phased out between $54,000 and $64,000 ($32,000 and $44,000 for a single filer).

A non-participating spouse of an active participant may make deductible contributions of up to $3,000 (even if the non-participating spouse has no compensation) as long as a joint return is filed, total compensation for the couple equals or exceeds IRA contributions, and AGI is less than $150,000. The deductible amount is phased out between $150,000 and $160,000.

Nondeductible Contributions—Any taxpayer may make nondeductible contributions of up to $6,000 for a married couple filing jointly ($3,000 for a single filer) as long as compensation for the year equals or exceeds the amount of the contributions. Earnings on nondeductible contributions are tax deferred until distributed. Older Americans (those who turn 50 by December 31) are eligible to make an additional $500 contribution (1,000 in 2006).

Nondeductible contributions must be reported on Form 8606, which is attached to Form 1040 or Form 1040A.

Contributions to a Roth IRA—A taxpayer may make an annual contribution of up to $3,000 to a tax-exempt Roth IRA. A married couple may contribute $3,000 for each spouse, provided combined compensation is at least equal to the contributed amount. Contributions to a Roth IRA are nondeductible for income tax purposes, and the maximum $3,000 contribution will be phased out if adjusted gross income is between $150,000 and $160,000 on a joint return (between $95,000 and $110,000 if single). Generally, after five tax years, distributions from a Roth IRA are tax-free (not tax-deferred) if made in any of the following circumstances:

- after the individual reaches age 59 1/2;
- to a beneficiary after the individual's death;
- after the individual becomes disabled; or
- for qualified first-time homebuyer expenses of the individual or the individual's spouse, children, grandchildren, or ancestors.

Taxpayers with adjusted gross income of less than $100,000 can convert traditional IRAs to Roth IRAs without paying the ten percent penalty on early withdrawals. The deemed distribution in the conversion will be included in income. Married couples who file separately cannot take advantage of this rollover provision.

A taxpayer that converts a regular IRA to a Roth IRA and then determines that AGI for the year of conversion exceeds the $100,000 limitation may reconvert the Roth IRA to a regular IRA without penalty. The reconversion must be accomplished in a trustee-to-trustee transfer by the due date of the taxpayer's return (including extensions) for the year of conversion.

Limit on Contributions—A taxpayer may make any combination of deductible, nondeductible, and Roth IRA contributions in the same year to the extent that total contributions do not exceed the lesser of (1) $3,000 or (2) compensation included in gross income for the year. IRA contributions must be made by the due date of the taxpayer's tax return, excluding extensions.

Distributions from IRAs—Generally, distributions from traditional IRAs are taxed as ordinary income unless a portion of the IRA account represents nondeductible contributions. When there are nondeductible contributions, a portion of each distribution is exempt from tax until the participant's nondeductible investment in the account has been recovered. Distributions prior to age 59½ are subject to a 10 percent penalty tax unless a specific exemption applies. Distributions from Roth IRAs within the first five years of establishing the IRA are treated as distributions from a regular nondeductible IRA.

Taxable distributions from traditional IRAs will not be subject to the 10 percent penalty (on distributions made prior to age 59½) if the distributions are:

1) due to death or disability of the participant;

2) made as a series of substantially equal periodic payments;

3) made to cover deductible medical expenses;

4) made to pay health insurance premiums for a participant who is collecting unemployment;

5) used to pay for qualified acquisition costs of a first home for the participant, spouse, child, grandchild or ancestor of the participant or spouse;

6) used to pay qualified higher education expenses.

Coverdell education IRA: A taxpayer may make nondeductible contributions of up to $2,000 annually for each beneficiary of an Education IRA to help fund the beneficiary's future education expenses. All earnings held in an Education IRA will be tax exempt. Distributions from the IRA will be tax-free to the extent they do not exceed the beneficiary's qualified education expenses, including room and board. Eligible expenses now include tuition (public, private or religious) for Kindergarten through 12th grade. If a beneficiary chooses not to use the IRA assets for qualified education expenses, distributions will be taxable to the beneficiary to the extent of the income portion of the distributions. Such distributions also would be subject to the 10 percent penalty for early withdrawal.

The $2,000 contribution limit is subject to a phase-out limit of $190,000-$220,000 for joint returns ($95,000-$110,000 for single returns).

Contributions to Education IRAs are not included in the maximum of $2,000 allowed for contributions to all other IRAs.

This area had many other changes in the 2001 tax act. Please consult your tax advisor for more details.

Interest on Student Loans

For interest due and paid after December 31, 2001, taxpayers will be able to deduct annually, whether or not they itemize deductions, up to $2,500 of interest on student loans. The phase out ranges in 2002 have been increased to $100,000 to $130,000 on a joint return and $50,000 to $65,000 on a single return.

Itemized Deductions

Medical Expenses—Medical expenses are generally deductible to the extent that they exceed 7.5 percent of a taxpayer's adjusted gross income. For purposes of the alternative minimum tax, medical expenses that exceed ten percent of adjusted gross income are deductible. Medical expenses include amounts paid for the diagnosis, cure, mitigation, or prevention of disease; transportation essential to medical care; and insurance (including long-term care insurance, within certain limits). This includes hospital and physician costs, laboratory tests, prescription drugs, birth control pills, and lodging (but not meals) while away from home if essential for medical care, etc.

Expenses incurred for "unnecessary" cosmetic surgery are not deductible medical expenses. Cosmetic surgery will continue to be allowed in the case of deformity related to a congenital abnormality, personal injury from an accident or trauma, or a disfiguring disease.

State Taxes—State and local income taxes withheld or paid within the tax year may be deducted. In addition, real estate taxes and personal property taxes are also deductible. Generally, automobile registration is not considered a tax for this purpose.

Interest Expense—Generally, home mortgage interest or "qualified residential interest" is fully deductible by a taxpayer. Interest on debt that is secured by a primary and/or second home is deductible to the extent of (1) debt that is not more than $1 million, provided that the proceeds are used by the taxpayer to buy, build, or substantially improve the home, and (2) up to $100,000 of a home equity loan. Thus, interest on total debt of $1.1 million would be deductible. However, if a mortgage is refinanced, only the interest on the amount of the new mortgage applicable to the original purchase is deductible for purposes of the alternative minimum tax.

An individual may claim an immediate deduction for points paid in connection with the purchase of a principal residence, regardless of whether the points are paid by the buyer or the seller, if the following requirements are met:

• The points must be designated as points on the settlement sheet, and shown as paid from either the borrower or seller at settlement.

Note: Amounts designated as points include such items as loan origination fees, loan discounts, and discount points.

• The points must be computed as a percentage of the stated principal amount of debt.

• The points must be paid in connection with a loan secured by the individual's principal residence.

• The points must be paid directly by the individual. Points are considered to be paid directly by the individual if he pays as part of the overall transaction an amount at least equal to the amount required to be applied as points at closing. The individual must pay such amount from funds that have not been borrowed for such purpose.

Points paid in the acquisition of a principal residence are not fully deductible to the extent that the amount is allocable to a principal loan amount in excess of the $1 million limitation.

In computing the basis of the new residence purchased, the buyer must subtract the amount of any seller-paid points from the purchase price of the residence.

An individual may not claim an immediate deduction for points paid upon refinancing a principal residence. The individual is required to capitalize such points and amortize them over the life of the loan. Any points paid in connection with the old loan that have not yet been deducted may be deducted in full in the year in which the refinancing is completed.

Individuals are permitted to deduct, in full in the year paid, points paid on debt incurred for improvement of the principal residence provided that:

The debt is secured by the principal residence.

It is an established business practice to pay points in the area in which the debt is incurred.

The amount paid as points does not exceed the amount generally charged in the area.

In order to ensure a deduction for points paid in connection with home improvement indebtedness, taxpayers are advised to pay for the points at closing with a separate check.

Taxpayers are no longer allowed an interest deduction for personal interest. Investment interest can be deducted on 2002 tax returns up to the amount of net investment income, which includes interest, dividends, and long-term gain (requires election on tax return) from the sale of investments.

The deduction for interest expense can be very complex if passive losses are reported. Internal Revenue Service publications should be referred to for details.

Charitable Contributions—A taxpayer who makes a charitable contribution of $250 or more must obtain written substantiation from the charity acknowledging the donation in order to claim a charitable contribution deduction. The acknowledgment must be obtained on or before the earlier of (1) the date the taxpayer files a tax return for the year in which the contribution was made, or (2) the due date, including extensions, for filing the tax return.

The written substantiation from the charity must contain the following information:

• The amount of cash contributed, and a description of any property other than cash contributed.

• Whether the donee organization provided any goods or services in consideration, in whole or in part, for any property contributed.

• Description and good faith estimate of the value of goods or services contributed or, if the contributed goods and services consist solely of intangible religious benefits, a statement to that effect.

A contribution made by means of withholding from a taxpayer's wages and paid by the taxpayer's employer to a donee organization may be substantiated by:

A pay stub, Form W-2, or other document furnished by the employer that evidences the amount withheld from the employee's wages for the purpose of payment to a donee organization, and a pledge card or other document prepared by the donee organization that includes a statement that the organization does not provide goods or services as whole or partial consideration for any contributions made to the organization by means of payroll deductions. The regulations indicate that the amount withheld from each payment of wages to an employee is to be treated as a separate contribution in determining whether the taxpayer must obtain written substantiation.

Miscellaneous Itemized Deductions— There are two categories of miscellaneous itemized deductions: (1) those expenses that are deductible only to the extent that they exceed 2 percent of adjusted gross income; and (2) those expenses that are not limited. Some examples of expenses that are limited by the two percent floor include tax preparation fees, employee business expenses that are not reimbursed by the employer, investment advice, job-related education, professional fees and publications, and membership dues in unions and professional or trade organizations.

Other miscellaneous itemized deductions not subject to the 2 percent floor include casualty and theft losses, gambling losses to the extent of gambling winnings, and expenses of a handicapped individual for attendant care services at his place of employment, plus other expenses in connection with his place of employment which are necessary for the individual to be able to work.

Travel expenses incurred in attending professional, union, and business meetings or conventions continue to be deductible by federal employees only if attendance at the meeting benefits the employee's job. Examples include: attendance at meetings and conventions of medical societies and associations (doctors), meetings of local or national associations (attorneys and accountants), meetings of scientific associations (engineers and scientists), etc., and delegates to union conventions. If the employee attends the meeting for the primary purpose of obtaining a business benefit, then the cost of transportation, meals (subject to the 50 percent limitation), and lodging is deductible.

If the expenses are incurred primarily for business, but the employee also combines the trip with a vacation, those costs attributable to personal expenses will not be allowed. The cost of transportation to and from the destination and meals and lodging while attending the business meeting or convention are deductible. Personal expenses such as meals and lodging after the business is concluded, sightseeing expenses, and expenses related to the rest of the family are not deductible.

Unreimbursed employee business expenses must be taken as an itemized deduction subject to the two percent of adjusted gross income limitation. Business meals are subject to the limitation (refer to meal and entertainment expenses below). Business meals at conventions and seminars must be separately stated and are subject to the same limitation. Supporting documentation should be kept to substantiate these deductions.

Travel expenses incurred for a spouse, dependent, or other individual who accompanies a taxpayer on a business trip are not deductible unless:

• the spouse, dependent, or other individual is an employee of the person or corporation paying the expenses, and

• the travel of the spouse, dependent, or other individual is for a bona fide business purpose, and

• the expenses of the spouse, dependent, or other individual would otherwise be deductible.

Tax Credits

New Tax Credits—Three relatively new tax credits, which may be of use to a broad range of taxpayers, have been available since 1998:

• *Child Tax Credit:* A nonrefundable tax credit of $600 is available for each qualifying child under age 17. Qualifying children include the taxpayer's offspring, stepchild, grandchild, or eligible foster child that the taxpayer claims as a dependent. The credit is phased out at a rate of $50 for each $1,000 (or fraction thereof) by which the taxpayer's adjusted gross income exceeds $110,000 ($75,000 for singles and heads of household; $55,000 for those married filing separately). If a taxpayer qualifies for the Earned Income Credit or has three or more children, a portion of the child credit may be refundable. Complex criteria and calculations exist for determining this amount.

• *Hope Tuition Tax Credit:* A taxpayer who

incurs post secondary education expenses for himself, a spouse, or a dependent child may be entitled to a tax credit of up to $1,500 per student per year. This "Hope Tuition Tax Credit" applies only to tuition and fees paid during the first two years of post secondary education in a degree or certificate program. The credit is for 100% of the first $1,000 and 50% of the second $1,000 of expenses paid. No credit is allowed for expenses for room and board. The Hope credit phases out if adjusted gross income is between $82,000 and $102,000 ($41,000 and $51,000 for singles).

 • *Lifetime Learning Credit:* A taxpayer may be entitled to up to $1,000 per return for qualified post-secondary education tuition and fees. This "Lifetime Learning Credit" differs from the Hope Tuition credit in that the Lifetime Learning credit is for an unlimited number of years, can be used for graduate or professional degrees as well as undergraduate degrees, and the student can be enrolled less than half time. Also, while the Hope Tuition credit is a per student per year credit, the Lifetime Learning credit consists of a maximum of 20% of the first $5,000 ($10,000 in 2003) paid for qualified education expenses. A Lifetime Learning credit may not be taken for expenses paid for a student for whom a Hope Tuition credit has been claimed in the same year. The Lifetime Learning Credit phases out if adjusted gross income is between $82,000 and $102,000 ($41,000 and $51,000 for singles).

Neither the Hope credit nor the Lifetime Learning credit may be taken for the same beneficiary in a year in which the beneficiary has received qualified distributions from an Education IRA.

Credit for Elderly or Disabled—An individual may be able to claim a credit for the elderly or disabled if either of the following applies:

 • the individual is 65 years of age or older at the close of the tax year; or

 • the individual is under the age of 65 at the close of the tax year and is permanently and totally disabled, received disability income during the tax year and did not reach mandatory retirement age before the beginning of the tax year.

Most federal employees do not have a mandatory retirement age. However, some federal employees such as air traffic controllers, firefighters employed by the U.S. government, and law enforcement officers employed by the U.S. government have a mandatory retirement age.

An individual who is permanently or totally disabled must have his doctor complete the physician's statement in Schedule R and attach the schedule to the individual's Form 1040 that is filed with the Internal Revenue Service.

Adoption Credit—Taxpayers may claim a nonrefundable credit of up to $10,000 for qualified adoption expenses paid for each eligible child. The credit is phased out for taxpayers with adjusted gross incomes between $150,000 and 230,000. Starting in 2003, the credit is available without regard to actually incurring the expenses for a special needs child.

The 'Nanny Tax'

Individuals who are considered to be the "employer" of a domestic worker are required to withhold FICA taxes from the wages of their domestic employees who are paid more than $1,100 in a calendar year for domestic services. The employer is also required to make payment for an equal amount of FICA tax.

The Internal Revenue Service has developed a 20-factor test to determine whether a worker should be classified as an employee or an independent contractor. With respect to domestic workers, the following factors should be emphasized:

 • Does the employer have the right to discharge the worker?

 • Does the employer provide the worker with tools and a place to work?

Personal Injury, Sickness, and Punitive Damages

Exclusion from gross income is limited to damages for physical injury or physical sickness only. Emotional distress is not considered a physical injury or sickness unless it is attributable to physical injury or sickness.

All punitive damages are fully includible in the income of the recipient, regardless of whether the damages are paid in connection with personal injury or sickness, unless received under any written binding agreement, court decree, or mediation award in effect or issued on or before September 13, 1995.

Five-Year Averaging

Five-year averaging for lump-sum distributions has been repealed for distributions after December 31, 1999.

State Tuition Plans for College Savings (Section 529 Plans)

A number of states have created tax-exempt qualified state tuition programs under which persons may (1) purchase tuition credits or certificates for higher education for a designated beneficiary or (2) make contributions to an account that is established for the sole purpose of meeting qualified higher education expenses of the beneficiary. This has been changed in 2002 to include private colleges and universities. The income earned by such programs will not be currently taxable to the persons purchasing certificates or credits or contributing to the account. Upon distribution of funds for qualified higher education expenses, the portion of distributions which is attributable to earnings is includible in the income of the beneficiary, who may be able to use the Hope and lifetime Learning credits to reduce tax.

Starting in 2002, contributions to both an Education IRA and a state-sponsored prepaid tuition plan in the same year for the same beneficiary are now allowed, even if the contributions are made by different people.

Moving Expenses

A taxpayer may only deduct as moving expenses the reasonable costs of moving household goods and traveling, including lodging during the period of travel (from the taxpayer's former residence to the new residence). A taxpayer may no longer deduct the cost of meals consumed while traveling and while living in temporary quarters near the new workplace. A taxpayer may not deduct as moving expenses the costs of selling or settling an unexpired lease on the former residence or the cost of buying a new residence. The allowable deduction for moving expenses is to be treated as an above-the-line deduction subtracted from gross income in arriving at adjusted gross income, rather than being treated as an itemized deduction not subject to the two percent floor.

To qualify for the moving expense deduction, the taxpayer's new place of work must be at least 50 miles (increased from 35) farther from his former residence than his prior place of employment. In addition, during the 12-month period immediately following arrival at the new job location, the taxpayer must have full-time employment for at least 39 weeks.

Qualified moving expenses reimbursed by an employer are excluded from the employee's gross income as a qualified fringe benefit to the extent that the expenses would be deductible as moving expenses if directly paid or incurred by the employee.

Military moving allowances provided by the Department of Defense in connection with the transfer of military personnel to a new permanent duty station may still be excluded from gross income. However, no deduction is allowed for expenses incurred in connection with the transfer of military personnel to a new permanent duty station to the extent that the expenses are reimbursed by such an allowance.

Social Security Benefits

Taxpayers whose provisional income (adjusted gross income excluding Social Security plus tax exempt interest plus one half of Social Security benefits received) exceeds $32,000 if married filing jointly or $25,000 if single may be taxed on up to 85 percent of their Social Security benefits received. The instructions for Form 1040 include a worksheet that should be used to determine the taxable amount of benefits received.

Rental Real Estate and Passive Activities

If an individual actively participates in the rental activity, up to $25,000 of losses and equivalent credits are allowed each year to offset other income. The $25,000 allowance is phased out for taxpayers with adjusted gross income between $100,000 and $150,000. Any losses in excess of this amount are treated as passive losses and are carried forward to be used in later years.

Individual taxpayers or their spouses who materially participate in rental real estate activities may be able to treat the rental real estate activities as active rather than passive activities. An individual taxpayer is deemed to materially participate in rental real estate activities when:

• More than 50 percent of the taxpayer's personal services during the tax year are performed in real property trades or businesses in which the individual materially participates.

• The taxpayer performs more than 750 hours of service in the real property trades or businesses in which the taxpayer materially participates.

In applying these tests, the personal services of an employee are not treated as being performed in a real property trade or business unless the employee is a five percent owner. Generally, limited partners are not considered to materially participate in the activity of the limited partnership. The 750 hour test applies to each rental property, unless the taxpayer makes an election to aggregate the properties for this purpose.

Losses (and credits) from passive activities are only available to offset income from other passive activities. Therefore, such losses may not be used to offset income from salaries, active business income, interest, dividends, royalties, etc. Losses (and credits) that are not currently deductible can be carried forward to offset future passive income, and any remaining suspended losses and credits may be claimed in full upon the sale or disposition of the entire activity.

Passive investments include all rental activities (except as discussed above) and limited partnership interests.

Savings Bond Redemption for College Education Costs

Amounts received on the redemption of U.S. savings bonds are exempt from tax to the extent that the taxpayer makes payments for educational costs to a college, university, or a vocational education school to finance tuition and fees required for the enrollment or attendance of the taxpayer, or his or her spouse or dependents. In 2002, the benefits of this provision start to phase out when the taxpayer's modified adjusted gross income exceeds $57,600 for single taxpayers and $86,400 for married individuals filing jointly.

Series E and EE Bonds

Series E bonds that were issued before December, 1965, reach their maturity 40 years after their issue date. Series E bonds issued after November, 1965, and all Series EE bonds reach their maturity 30 years after their issue dates.

In general, the increase in value of Series E and EE bonds is deferred until the bonds either reach maturity or are disposed of or redeemed. However, an election may be made to report the interest as it accrues. This election will apply to all Series E and EE bonds owned currently or acquired in the future. Once made, the election can be changed only with Internal Revenue Service permission. An election must be attached to a timely filed return.

Taxpayers who hold Series E bonds maturing in 2002 should consider exchanging them for Series HH bonds. Interest on the Series HH bonds is paid semiannually and is currently taxable, but any accrued interest on the surrendered Series E bonds continues to be deferred.

Disaster Loss Relief for Residence Damage

Insurance proceeds received for a principal residence or any of its contents destroyed in a presidentially-declared disaster area will generally be tax-free. The proceeds are taxable at the taxpayer's election, only to the extent that they are received for a qualifying principal residence or any of its contents, and not reinvested within four years to acquire similar property. This provision applies to renters to the extent that the residence would constitute their principal residence if they owned it.

Unearned Income of a Minor Child

In 2002, net unearned income of a child under the age of 14 that exceeds $1,500 is taxed at the parents' highest marginal rate. The first $750 of the child's unearned income is offset with a $750 standard deduction and there is no tax effect. The second $750 is taxed at the child's tax rate. In effect, the child can have at least $1,500 of unearned income that is not taxed at the parents' rate. Form 8615 is used to compute the child's tax.

Children age 14 and older are taxed at their own rates on earned as well as unearned income.

An election is available for a parent to report the unearned income of a minor child (under the age of 14) on the parent's tax return if the following requirements are met:

• The child's only income is from interest, capital gain distributions and dividends.

• The child's income from interest and dividends exceeds $750 but not $7,500.

• No estimated tax payments have been made using the Social Security number of the child.

• The child is not subject to backup withholding.

If this election is made, the child is not required to file a tax return. Parents wishing to make this election should use Form 8814.

Reimbursements for Daily Transportation Expenses

Reimbursements for nondeductible commuting expenses are taxable. Examples of such taxable reimbursements include:

• Reimbursements for commuting on a daily basis to a temporary work site located within the metropolitan area where the taxpayer lives and normally works unless the travel is irregular or short-term.

• Reimbursements for commuting from an employee's residence to temporary work sites outside the metropolitan area where the taxpayer lives and normally works, if the temporary assignment is for more than one year.

The General Accounting Office has revised its policy regarding local travel reimbursement. It has announced that reimbursement for transportation expenses from an employee's residence to a temporary work site located within the metropolitan area where the taxpayer lives and normally works will be based on the lesser of the following two computations:

• The difference between actual transportation expenses incurred and the employee's normal commuting cost.

• The difference between the employee's round-trip mileage cost from the employee's home to the work location; and the round-trip mileage cost from the employee's home to his regular place of work plus parking fees and tolls.

Estimated-Tax Safe Harbors

A taxpayer can generally avoid estimated tax penalties by making current-year estimated tax payments (and withholding) equal to at least 100 percent of his prior year tax or 90 percent of his current year tax. If adjusted gross income for 2001 exceeded $150,000, the taxpayer was required to pay in at least 112.0% of the prior year's tax to avoid penalties for 2002. The annual tax threshold requiring any taxpayer to make estimated tax payments is $1,000.

Estate and Gift Tax

An individual can make annual gifts of up to $11,000 per donee without triggering gift tax. In addition, in 2002, an individual generally could give away up to $1 million (either during life or at death) without triggering a gift or estate tax. If properly planned, a married couple could transfer up to $2 million ($1 million each) without triggering estate or gift tax. This amount is called the "applicable exclusion amount" (formerly the "unified credit exclusion amount"). Beginning with gifts made in 2002, the applicable lifetime exclusion is fixed at $1 million.

The applicable exclusion amount is currently scheduled to increase as follows:

2002-2003	$1,000,000
2004-2005	$1,500,000
2006-2008	$2,000,000
2009	$3,500,000

Luxury Car Tax

For 2002, the luxury tax was 4 percent of the amount of the purchase price that exceeded $38,000. This excise tax will expire after December 31, 2002.

Chapter 11
Travel, Transportation, and Relocation

Section 1—Federal Travel and Transportation Policies

General

Federal employee travel is governed by the federal travel regulation (FTR) that is published in Chapters 300 through 304 of Title 41 of the Code of Federal Regulations. This regulation covers a wide range of subjects, and ranges from per diem rates to transportation allowances. All agencies and field activities maintain copies in their travel offices and it is available online at http://policyworks.gov/ftr.

The law (5 U.S.C. 5702) authorizes the General Services Administration to prescribe the worldwide subsistence reimbursement system in the FTR and to establish per diem and actual subsistence expenses rates for CONUS (the 48 contiguous states and the District of Columbia) travel. It also provides authority for reimbursement of certain travel expenses of employees who experience personal emergencies while on official travel and for payment of subsistence and transportation expenses for threatened law enforcement/investigative employees and their families who must occupy temporary living accommodations. The FTR establishes rules for when and how such payments should be made (subject to agency authorization and/or approval).

Employees having a question about their allowances and entitlements while on government travel should get in touch with their agency travel office. If someone in that office cannot answer the question, they may address the question to the GSA. Note: A direct call to GSA by an employee often results in only a partial answer, since agency policy often governs what an employee will receive.

Per diem rates for locations outside the CONUS are contained in the Maximum Travel Per Diem Allowances for Foreign Areas (MTPDA), published by the Department of State. These rates are updated monthly.

The Department of State has jurisdiction for foreign travel. The Department of Defense has responsibility for non-foreign travel (such as to Alaska, Hawaii and U.S. possessions and territories).

Federal Employee Charge Card—The 1998 Travel and Transportation Reform Act (P.L. 105-264) requires traveling federal workers to use government-issued cards, although agencies are allowed to exempt categories of employees and certain types of expenses from the requirement. Using the contractor-issued charge card, federal employees pay for routine travel expenses such as airplane tickets, hotels, and meals and then are billed for those expenses. Employees are reimbursed by their agencies for the allowable amounts of the charged expenses. The 1998 law places a greater burden on agencies to reimburse employees quickly but also allows agencies to obtain personal financial records and garnishee salaries when employees are late in paying the credit card bills for undisputed charges. The government's travel program—the Travel and Transportation Payment Expense control system—was developed to reduce cash accounts maintained by the agencies for travel advances. Under the charge card program, agencies also may authorize federal employee use of ATM services for cash withdrawal while traveling on official business.

Hotel and Motel Fire Safety Requirements—The Hotel and Motel Fire Safety Act of 1990 (P.L. 101-391) mandates that federal employees on travel must stay in public accommodations that adhere to certain safety requirements. The law also states that federally funded meetings and conferences cannot be held in properties that do not comply with the law. It is applicable to all places of public accommodation, and requires that such properties are equipped with:

• hard-wired, single-station smoke detectors in each guestroom in accordance with the National Fire Protection Association (NFPA) standard 72; and

• an automatic sprinkler system, with a sprinkler head in each guest room in compliance with NFPA standards 13 or 13R. Properties three stories or lower in height are exempt from the sprinkler requirement.

A listing of hotels and motels meeting those guidelines is at *http://www.usfa. fema.gov/applications/hotel*.

Military Housing—Public Law 96-527 requires Defense Department civilian employees on official travel to use "adequate" military housing for lodging whenever available. Employees who are in a travel status more than 50 percent of their time are exempted from this provision.

DoD Personnel—The Per Diem, Travel and Transportation Allowance Committee administers the Joint Travel Regulations for DoD civilian personnel, which set per diem, travel and transportation allowances, relocation allowances, and certain other allowances of DoD civilian employees. The committee's members are a Deputy Assistant Secretary for each of the DoD military departments and the Director of the National Oceanic and Atmospheric Administration Corps (NOAA), the Commandant of the Coast Guard (USCG), and the Surgeon General.

With the exception of DoD civilian employees appointed under Section 625(d) of the Foreign Assistance Act of 1961, as amended (22 U.S.C. §2385(d)), who are entitled to per diem, travel, and transportation allowances in accordance with Volume 6, State Department Foreign Affairs Manual (FAM), these regulations are the sole entitlement regulations for DoD components.

These rules, which in many ways mirror the GSA-set policies for other agencies, are online at *http://www.dtic.mil/perdiem/trvl-regs.html*.

Contact Point—GSA's travel management policy office is at 1800 F St., N.W., Washington, D.C. 20405, or get information online by visiting *www.gsa.gov* and clicking "Travel on Government Business."

Travel Costs and Allowances

It is general policy of the government that less-than-premium-class accommodations shall be used for all passenger transportation. Employees are furnished, or reimbursed for costs of transportation by trains, planes, boats, etc., in connection with official travel. This reimbursement includes authorized costs of taxis, buses, or use of privately owned automobiles, etc., to and from carrier terminals and in some circumstances round-trip mileage between residence and office on the day of departure and day of return on official travel. Agencies may authorize rail service when its use is advantageous to the government.

By Air—Employees must travel by coach-class unless their agency approves a higher class based on circumstances justifying their use. There are three classes recognized—"first-class," "premium class other than first class," and "coach."

By Train—The policy is about the same as for air travel above, except there are only three classes recognized—"coach," "business class" and "first-class."

In both air and train travel, agencies may authorize first-class travel at government expense "only when there is no reasonably available alternative, when exceptional security circumstances exist, or when the employee has a disability that makes first-class transportation accommodations necessary to accommodate the employee's disability." By ship: Travel by steamer is authorized only for the lowest class unless security reasons or disability makes a higher class necessary.

Other considerations concerning the class of travel are: (1) frequent traveler benefits gained while traveling on official business may not be used to upgrade to first-class air, although such mileage may continue to be used to upgrade to premium-class other than first-class, and (2) premium-class other than first-class may be allowed instead of a rest stop en route or a rest period at destination.

Conference Travel—Agencies must "exercise strict fiscal responsibility" when choosing a site to conduct a conference, especially if the site might be considered extravagant in the public eye. But if the agency can make the case that even though such a site may appear extravagant it still can save the government money, then they should "avail themselves of the opportunity to save costs in selecting a conference site." As provided under CFR 301-74, agencies may increase by 25 percent the per diem rate for conference travel.

Indirect Route Travel—A federal traveler must use noncontract fare service (that is, a carrier not contracted by GSA to provide discounted tickets) for that portion of travel by indirect route which is for personal convenience. And the traveler may not use either a Government Transportation Request or a contractor-issued travel charge card to procure transportation for indirect route travel, except when that indirect travel is authorized at government expense.

All agencies, except DoD, shall follow the rules established in 41 CFR Part 301-10, which require the use of contract air carriers for official air travel between certain city-pairs. DoD shall conform to the Joint Travel Regulations, Volume 2, regarding contract air carrier use.

Payment from a Non-Federal Source—As provided for in FTR Chapter 304, agencies may accept payment from a nonfederal source (or authorize an employee to accept the payment on behalf of the government) for the employee to attend a meeting or similar function which the employee has been authorized to attend in an official capacity on behalf of the employing agency. The policy extends to the employee's spouse who may accompany the employee as long as it's in the agency's interest. Rules published in the November 30, 2001, Federal Register allow reimbursement by a non-federal source for travel expenses of employees for speaking at events outside their official duties in circumstances similar to those for which reimbursement for speaking within their official duties is allowed.

Pre-employment Interview Travel—The law (5 U.S.C. 5706b), authorizes agencies to reimburse certain pre-employment interview travel expenses of interviewees. Reimbursable expenses include most of the expenses payable to a federal employee traveling on official business. Specific information is contained in Subpart C of Part 301-75 of the FTR.

Travel Expenses of Federal Employees with Disabilities—The FTR authorizes payment of certain additional travel expenses necessarily incurred by an employee as a result of the employee's disability.

Reimbursable expenses include travel and transportation of an attendant; cost of specialized transportation to, from, and/or at the temporary duty location; cost of specialized services provided by a commercial carrier; cost of baggage handling; and cost of transporting or renting a wheelchair.

Automobile Insurance in Foreign Areas—When an automobile is rented for official travel in foreign areas, employees may be reimbursed for the cost of collision damage waiver or collision damage insurance, when rental or leasing agency requirements, foreign statute, or legal procedures that could cause extreme difficulty to government employees involved in an accident make such insurance necessary.

Travel Advances

Federal employees may receive travel advances for cash transaction expenses (i.e., expenses that as a general rule cannot be charged and must be paid using cash, a personal check, or travelers check). These include:

• meals and incidental expenses covered by the per diem allowance or actual expenses allowance;

• miscellaneous transportation expenses such as local transportation system and taxi fares; parking fees; ferry fees; bridge, road, and tunnel fees; and aircraft parking, landing, and tie-down fees;

• gasoline and other variable expenses covered by the mileage allowance for advantageous use of a privately owned automobile for official business; and

• other authorized miscellaneous expenses that cannot be charged using a government contractor-issued charge card and for which a cost can be estimated.

For non-cash transaction expenses (i.e., lodging, common carrier), employees may receive advances only in the following situations:

• the government contractor-issued charge card is not expected to be accepted;

• your agency has decided not to provide you a government contractor-issued individually billed travel card;

• your agency determines that use of a government contractor-issued individually billed travel card would not be feasible incident to a transfer, particularly a transfer to another agency; or

• financial hardship would be incurred.

Frequent Traveler Benefits

Under Section 1116 of the National Defense Authorization Act for fiscal 2002 (P.L. 107-107), a federal traveler who receives a promotional item such as frequent flyer miles, upgrades, or access to carrier clubs or facilities received as a result of using travel or transportation services obtained at federal government expense, or accepted under Section 1353 of Title 31, United States Code, may retain the promotional item for personal use, if the promotional item is obtained under the same terms as those offered to the general public and at no additional cost to the federal government. This includes all benefits earned, including those earned before enactment of the act.

The act repealed Section 6008 of the Federal Acquisition Streamlining Act of 1994 (5 U.S.C. 5702 note; P.L. 103-355) that had previously prohibited personal retention of such promotional items. That policy also previously had been reflected in the Federal Travel Regulation at (41 CFR 301-53) and the Federal Property Management Regulations (41 CFR 101-25). GSA formally revised its rules in a Federal Register notice on April 12, 2002. Further information is in GSA Travel Advisory Number 5.

You may use frequent traveler benefits earned on official travel to obtain travel services for subsequent official travel assignments; however, you may also retain such benefits for your personal use, including upgrading to a higher class of service.

It is the responsibility of each traveler to communicate directly with a service provider to establish his/her frequent travel promotional benefits account. Any associated costs are to be paid by the traveler and are not a reimbursable expense.

You may not select a travel service provider based on whether it provides frequent traveler benefits. You must use the travel service provider for which your agency is a mandatory user. This includes contract passenger transportation services and travel management systems. You may not choose a travel service provider to gain frequent traveler benefits for personal use.

It is the policy of the government that employees generally must travel by coach class accommodations. However, you may upgrade your transportation class of service at your own expense. Therefore, as frequent traveler benefits may be retained for your personal use, you may use any frequent traveler benefits you have earned to upgrade your transportation class to premium service. The regulations governing upgrades to premium airline accommodations are at FTR §§ 301-10.123 and 301-10.124. Your agency cannot pay for any upgrades, unless you meet one of the exceptions in those regulations.

A denied boarding benefit (e.g., cash, free ticket coupon) is not a promotional item given by an airline.

Travelers seeking further guidance should contact their supervisor or travel-approving official.

Tax Implications—Guidance issued by the IRS following the frequent traveler change (IRS Announcement 2002-18) said that although it may deem such benefits as taxable income in the future, it currently does not do so and that any change in policy would apply only prospectively. It noted, however, that such benefits may not be used for tax avoidance purposes, such as by converting them to cash or receiving compensation in the form of travel or other promotional benefits.

Mileage Allowances

Generally, employees using privately-owned transportation when it is advantageous to the government in performing official business travel will be reimbursed as follows:

• 36.5 cents per mile for privately owned automobile;
• 97.5 cents per mile for privately owned airplane; and
• 28 cents per mile for privately owned motorcycle.

These rates typically change early in each calendar year. To check changes online, visit www.gsa.gov, click on "Travel on Government Business," then click on "Privately Owned Vehicle Reimbursement Rates."

Additionally, parking fees; road, tunnel and bridge costs; and airplane parking, landing and tie-down fees may be authorized.

Use of Government Vehicles

Federal law requires that government

motor vehicles be used only for official purposes, as defined by each agency. If a government vehicle is used for other than official purposes, both the vehicle operator and anyone who authorizes or condones such use are subject to penalties ranging from a mandatory minimum suspension of one month without pay up to and including dismissal from government service.

Home to Work Transportation—By statute, certain federal officials are authorized home-to-work transportation, as are employees who meet certain statutory criteria as determined by their agency head. The federal officials authorized by statute are the President, the Vice-President, and other principal federal officials and their designees, as provided in 31 U.S.C. 1344(b)(1) through (b)(7).

Also, employees engaged in field work or faced with a clear and present danger, an emergency, or a compelling operational consideration may be authorized home-to-work transportation as determined by their agency head. No other employees are authorized home-to-work transportation. Determinations may be made in advance when the federal agency wants to have employees ready to respond to a clear and present danger, an emergency or a compelling operational consideration.

Agencies consider the following when making a determination to authorize home-to-work transportation for field work:

• the location of the employee's home in proximity to work and to the locations where non-TDY travel is required; and

• the use of home-to-work transportation for field work should be authorized only to the extent that such transportation will substantially increase the efficiency and economy of the government.

Examples of positions that may involve field work include, but are not limited to: quality assurance inspectors; construction inspectors; dairy inspectors; mine inspectors; meat inspectors; and medical officers on outpatient service. The assignment of an employee to such a position does not, of itself, entitle an employee to receive daily home-to-work transportation.

Situations may arise where, for cost or other reasons, it is in the government's interest to base a government passenger carrier at a government facility located near the employee's home or work rather than authorize the employee home-to-work transportation.

The comfort or convenience of an employee is not considered sufficient justification to authorize home-to-work transportation. Authorized employees may not use home-to-work transportation for other than official purposes. However, if your agency has prescribed rules for the incidental use of government vehicles (as provided in 31 U.S.C. note), you may use the vehicle in accordance with those rules in connection with an existing home-to-work authorization.

An employee authorized home-to-work transportation may share space in a government passenger carrier with other individuals, provided that the passenger carrier does not travel additional distances as a result and such sharing is consistent with his/her agency's policy. When an agency establishes its space sharing policy, the agency should consider its potential liability for and to those individuals. Home-to-work transportation does not extend to the employee's spouse, other relatives, or friends unless they travel with the employee from the same point of departure to the same destination, and this use is consistent with the agency's policy.

Use of Portable Phones—General Services Administration policy states that while individual agencies may set their own policies regarding the use of portable phones while driving in government-owned or leased vehicles, in general they should:

• discourage the use of hand-held wireless phones by a driver while operating motor vehicles owned or leased by the federal government;

• provide a portable hands-free accessory or a hands-free car kit for government owned wireless phones; and

• educate employees on driving safely while using hands-free wireless phones.

Generally, federal employees are not exempt from state and local laws governing operation of a motor vehicle, including those restricting the use of wireless phones while driving.

Tobacco Use—The General Services Administration in 1993 barred the use of tobacco products in GSA fleet vehicles used by federal employees. In 2002 it issued a bulletin encouraging agencies to also prohibit the use of tobacco products in vehicles they own or lease, begin any needed discussions with employee unions and organizations to carry out such a policy and develop appropriate policy regarding disciplinary action to be taken against employees violating the prohibition. Many agencies already prohibited the use of tobacco products in their vehicles but previously there had been no government-wide guidance.

Seat Belts—Under Executive Order 13043 of April 16, 1997, each federal employee occupying any seating position of a motor vehicle on official business, whose seat is equipped with a seat belt, must have the seat belt properly fastened at all times when the vehicle is in motion.

Contact Point—GSA's federal vehicle policy division is at 1800 F St. NW, Rm. 1221, Washington, D.C. 20405-0002, phone (202) 208-7631, or get information online by visiting *www.gsa.gov* and clicking "Travel on Government Business."

Section 2—Relocation Allowances

General

An employee may be entitled to receive moving expenses when transferring from one official duty station to another permanent one, provided the transfer is in the interest of the government and the employee agrees in writing to remain in government service for 12 months after the effective date of the transfer. The authority to provide this benefit includes employees transferred from the Postal Service to a federal agency (as defined in 5 U.S.C. 5721).

Covered expenses generally include the packing and shipment of household goods (and their temporary storage), transportation of a mobile home, per diem and mileage en route, a "house-hunting" trip to the new duty station, temporary quarters (where needed), real estate and lease costs associated with the move, and certain miscellaneous expenses. In addition, there are limited allowances available for certain groups of employees, such as new appointees and retiring members of the SES.

To help their employees relocate, agencies have the authority to enter into contracts with relocation companies.

Household Goods

The maximum weight allowance is 18,000 pounds for all employees regardless of family status (with or without dependents).

Shipments of household goods are authorized under a Commuted Rate Schedule (wherein the employee handles the arrangements and pays for the move) unless there is a transportation savings of $100 or more in which case a government bill of lading may be used (wherein the government handles the arrangement and pays for the move).

When an employee handles his own move he is reimbursed according to allowances contained in commuted rate schedules that are in the Household Goods Carrier Bureau Tariff. Under this system the employee may perform the moving services utilizing commercial rental vehicles wherein he is reimbursed based on weight supported by proper weight certificates and mileage by the most direct routes.

Storage of Household Goods—Temporary storage of household goods may be allowed for a period of 90 days. However, upon an employee's request, the 90 days may be extended an additional period not to exceed 90 days, under certain circumstances. Extended storage may be allowed up to three years when an employee is transferred to an isolated duty station within the 48 contiguous states where he is unable to use his household goods. For change of duty station outside the 48 contiguous states, extended storage may be allowed for a period of time not to exceed the overseas tour of duty plus one month prior to the time the tour begins. Storage may continue beyond the tour of duty when necessary and approved by the agency.

Mobile Homes

An employee who is entitled to transportation of household goods is entitled, in lieu of such transportation, to an allowance for the transportation of a mobile home within CONUS (the 48 contiguous states and the District of Columbia), within Alaska and through Canada en route between Alaska and CONUS. Transporting the mobile home may be accomplished by use of a privately owned vehicle or a commercial carrier. Allowable costs include those associated with preparing the mobile home for transportation and for resettling the mobile home at the destination (e.g., costs of blocking and unblocking; anchoring and unanchoring; labor for removing and installing skirting; separating, preparing, and sealing each section for movement; reassembling the two halves of a double-wide mobile home; and travel lift fees). Excluded are costs of replacement parts, tire purchases, maintenance, repairs, storage, etc. If a mobile home is not relocated, certain expenses for the sale and/or purchase of a mobile home (which is used, or is to be used, as a residence) may be allowed under the real estate transaction allowances.

A boat used as a primary residence is treated as a mobile home. Overland transportation costs payable for a boat used as a primary residence shall be the same as for any other mobile home; over-water transportation costs include, among others, the costs for fuel, port or harbor fees, and commercial towing or pushing by barge.

Per Diem and Mileage En Route

Per diem allowance for lodging and meals is provided for the employee and the employee's immediate family while en route from the old to the new official station. In addition, allowances are provided for use of a privately owned automobile while en route. The mileage allowance is based on the number of travelers in the automobile and differs from the mileage allowance for temporary duty travel. In certain cases the use of more than one automobile may be authorized within CONUS.

Quarters

Seeking Residence Quarters—When deemed necessary and appropriate by the agency, one round trip by an employee and spouse to the new official station to seek residence quarters may be permitted. Transportation expenses and per diem are payable within prescribed limits. Reasonable expenses for local transportation at the new official station location are allowable; however, use of taxicabs is limited to transportation between carrier terminals and place of lodging.

Temporary Quarters—Where justification exists, subsistence expenses incident to occupying temporary quarters may be authorized for a period of not more than 60 consecutive days for all transferred employees whose new official station is located within the United States, its territories and possessions, Commonwealth of Puerto Rico and Panama. An additional period of time not to exceed 60 consecutive days may be authorized when the agency head or designee determines on a case-by-case basis that there are compelling reasons for the continued occupancy of temporary quarters. When the new official station is located in a foreign area, an employee is not eligible for temporary quarters allowances under GSA's Federal Travel Regulation. When temporary lodgings are obtained in a foreign area, or in the United States prior to transferring to a foreign area, the employee may be eligible for an allowance under regulations issued by the Department of State. Reimbursement for subsistence expenses while in temporary quarters may not exceed limitations which are based on the applicable per diem rate (i.e., the standard per diem rate within CONUS) or the maximum per diem rate prescribed by the Secretary of Defense for the locality involved when temporary quarters are located in Alaska, Hawaii, or other non-foreign areas outside CONUS.

Real Estate and Lease Transactions

Certain expenses incurred in connection with selling a residence at the old station and buying a residence at the new station are allowed. These include real estate commissions (applicable to sale only) and certain legal and miscellaneous costs subject to an overall limitation of ten percent of the actual sales price of the residence at the old official station. Reimbursement expenses shall not exceed five percent of the actual purchase price. An allowance is also provided for expenses incurred in settling a non-expired lease involving the employee's residence or a lot on which a mobile home used as the residence was located at the old official station.

Employees transferred from a foreign to a domestic post of duty also are eligible for payment of real estate expenses under certain conditions. To be eligible, employees must be transferred to a different duty station in the United States or a non-foreign area other than the one they left when transferred to the foreign post of duty.

Equitable Residence Transaction Expenses—Federal employees who have transferred in the interests of the government may be entitled to "equitable residence reimbursement."

The reimbursement is allowed under four equitable title situations: (1) when title is held in trust for the benefit of the employee, (2) when title is held in the name of a financial institution pursuant to state laws governing financing arrangements secured by real property, (3) when title is held in the name of an accommodation party, and (4) when title is held by the seller of the real property under a financial arrangement which requires fixed periodic payments and transfer of title to the employee upon completion of the payment schedule.

Note that the government can recognize other equitable title situations if the employee can provide sufficient documentation spelled out in FTR Amendment 37.

Senior Executive Service (SES) Last Move Home Allowance

Agencies are authorized to pay limited "last move home" relocation allowances to eligible SES career appointees and employees who previously were SES career appointees and who elected to retain SES retirement benefits upon their retirement. Payment is limited to travel expenses of the individual, transportation expenses of the immediate family, and transportation and temporary storage of household goods. To be eligible for this benefit, SES employees must be eligible to receive an annuity for optional retirement under section 8336(a), (b), (c), (e), (f), or (j) of Subchapter III of Chapter 83 Civil Service Retirement System; or are within five years of eligibility to receive an annuity for optional retirement; or are eligible to receive an annuity based on discontinued service retirement, or early voluntary retirement under an Office of Personnel Management authorization; or separated from federal service on or after September 22, 1988; or are eligible to receive an annuity upon separation under the provisions of Subchapter III of Chapter 83 (CSR) or Chapter 84 (FERS) of Title 5, U.S.C., including an annuity based on optional retirement, discontinued service retirement, early voluntary retirement

under OPM authorization, or disability retirement; and have not previously received or been authorized to receive "last move home" benefits upon separation from federal service for retirement.

New Appointees

First Duty Station Allowances—Public Law 101-509 authorizes payment of limited relocation allowances to any person newly appointed to government service including eligible members of a Presidential Transition Team who relocate following the most recent presidential election but before appointment to a federal position.

Relocation Expenses—Each agency establishes specific criteria for determining which new appointees qualify for payment of allowable relocation expenses. The Office of Personnel Management has issued guidelines in 5 CFR Part 572 for agencies to follow in making these personnel determinations.

Miscellaneous Expenses

A miscellaneous expenses allowance is provided to defray various costs associated with discontinuing and establishing a residence, such as cutting and fitting rugs, drapes and curtains; automobile registration; driver's license; etc. This allowance is paid without support of expenses based on:

- $500, or the equivalent of one week's basic pay, whichever is the lesser amount, for an employee without immediate family; and
- $1,000, or the equivalent of two weeks' basic pay, whichever is the lesser amount, for an employee with an immediate family.

Allowances in excess of these may be authorized if supported by evidence of the amounts claimed, provided that the aggregate amount does not exceed one week's basic pay for an employee without immediate family or two weeks' basic pay for an employee with immediate family. In no instance will the amount exceed the maximum rate of grade GS-13.

Taxes

The law (5 U.S.C. 5724b) provides policies and procedures for reimbursement of the relocation income tax (RIT) allowance. These policies and procedures are published in the Federal Travel Regulation (FTR) (41 CFR Part 302-17).

The RIT federal and state tax tables for each calendar year are issued annually and published as amendments to 41 CFR Part 302-17. The RIT allowance covers additional federal, state, Puerto Rican and local income taxes incurred as a result of relocation allowance reimbursements. Affected employees should consult with the agency official responsible for authorizing their relocation allowances for further details and pertinent agency claims procedures.

Reemployment After Separation

Former employees separated by reason of reduction-in-force or transfer of function who, within one year of the separation date, are reemployed on a permanent basis at a different permanent duty station from that where the separation occurred may be paid these expenses and other allowances if otherwise eligible.

Section 3—Travel and Relocation Payment Appeals

Under P.L. 104-316, the General Services Administration Board of Contract Appeals has authority to resolve questions involving payment of travel or relocation expenses that were formerly resolved by the Comptroller General. A disbursing or certifying official of an agency, or the head of an agency, may request from the Board a decision on a question involving a payment the disbursing official or head of agency will make, or a voucher presented to a certifying official for certification, which concerns a claim for reimbursement of expenses incurred while on official temporary duty travel or a claim for reimbursement of expenses incurred in connection with relocation to a new duty station.

A request for a decision must be in writing, but no particular form is required. The request must refer to a specific payment or voucher; it may not seek general legal advice. The request should: explain why the official is seeking a Section 3529 decision, rather than taking action on his or her own regarding the matter; state the question presented and include citations to applicable statutes, regulations, and cases; include the name, address, telephone number, and facsimile machine number (if available) of the official making the request, the name, address, telephone number, and facsimile number (if available) of the employee affected by the specific payment or voucher; and any other information which the official believes the Board should consider.

Claims must be sent to the Office of the Clerk of the Board, Room 7022, General Services Administration Building, 1800 F Street, NW, Washington, DC 20405, phone (202) 501-0116, fax (202) 501-0664. The Board's working hours are 8:00 a.m. to 4:30 p.m., Eastern Time, on business days.

A written notice of docketing will be sent to the official and the affected employee. The notice of docketing will identify the judge to whom the request has been assigned.

The official submitting a request for a decision must send to the affected employee copies of all material provided to the Board. An affected employee who wishes to submit any additional information to the Board must submit such information within 30 calendar days after receiving the copy of the request for decision and supporting material (or within 60 calendar days after receiving the copy, if the affected employee is located outside the 50 states and the District of Columbia). To expedite proceedings, if the employee does not wish to make an additional submission, the employee should so notify the Board and the agency.

The agency or the affected employee may request additional time to make any filing. The judge may hold a conference with the agency and the affected employee, at any time, for any purpose. The judge may provide the participants a memorandum reflecting the results of a conference. The judge may require the submission of additional information at any time.

The judge will issue a written decision based upon the record, which includes submissions by the agency and the affected employee, and information provided during conferences. The agency and the affected employee will each be furnished a copy of the decision by the Office of the Clerk of the Board. In addition, all Board decisions are posted on *www.gsbca.gsa.gov*.

A request for reconsideration may be made by the agency or the affected employee. Such requests must be received by the Board within 30 calendar days after the date the decision was issued (or within

60 calendar days after the date the decision was issued, if the agency or the affected employee making the request is located outside the 50 states and the District of Columbia). The request for reconsideration should state the reasons why the Board should consider the request. Mere disagreement with a decision or re-argument of points already made is not a sufficient ground for seeking reconsideration.

Section 4—Per Diem

A lodgings-plus per diem system applies worldwide. Under the lodgings-plus system, travelers are reimbursed for the actual cost of lodging within a prescribed limit (supported by receipts) plus a flat daily allowance for meals and incidental expenses (M&IE) that ranges from $30 to $50. The total of these amounts may not exceed the applicable maximum locality per diem rate. GSA prescribes maximum per diem rates for defined localities within CONUS (the 48 contiguous states and the District of Columbia). For areas not on the annual list, a standard CONUS rate of $55 for lodging and $30 for M&IE applies. The applicable per diem locality rate is determined by the location of the temporary duty assignment.

Unless otherwise specified, the per diem locality is defined as "all locations within, or entirely surrounded by, the corporate limits of the key city as well as the boundaries of the listed counties, including independent entities located within the boundaries of the key city and the listed counties." The maximum per diem rates payable for localities in a non-foreign area are prescribed by the Department of Defense. Maximum per diem rates payable for localities in a foreign area are prescribed by the Department of State.

The M&IE rate is payable without itemization of expenses or receipts and is prorated on the first and last days of travel.

For computing per diem allowances, official travel begins and ends at the time the traveler leaves and returns to home, office, or other point of departure or return.

Federal Premier Lodging Program

In the Federal Premier Lodging Program, lodgings guarantee that a certain number of rooms will be available at or below the local per diem rate. Federal employees are encouraged to use this program where it is available. Travelers may reserve a FPLP room by contacting their local travel arranger (generally a travel agent or travel management center under contract to the agency) or by contacting the FPLP property directly.

You pay the rate established by the FPLP contract with that property. If all of the contracted rooms at that property are taken for a set date, contact another FPLP property. If all FPLP properties have already committed their rooms, you may contact any other property in a location for a room.

Under FPLP, properties commit to honor reservations that are made by a set time period. At FPLP properties, travelers have to make a room reservation at least three days prior to their arrival data. For extended-stay FPLP properties, it is 10 days. If a reservation is not made before the set time period, the property has the right to make the room available to the general public.

The FPLP is not available in all locations. A listing of participating lodgings is posted at http://www.policyworks.gov/org/main/mt/homepage/mtt/perdiem/plp/plphp.html.

Value Lodging Program

The Value Lodging Program, formerly known as the "Best Available Lodging Value," is designed to provide federal travelers with increased room availability, additional complimentary amenities and rates within the per diem allowance. More than 200 hotels in more than 100 cities including hotels overseas participate. Currently participating facilities are listed at http://apps.fss.gsa.gov/tmcservices/travel/balv.htm.

To obtain the published rate federal travelers must make reservations by contacting the hotel at the telephone number listed at that site. The individual making the reservation must clearly indicate that the reservation is for a federal employee on official travel and request the "GSA/Government Rate." Travelers are encouraged to make reservations through local travel management centers.

Shared Rooms

Each federal employee, for official travel

away from the official station, is entitled to a daily payment for lodging, meals and related incidental expenses. If, for whatever circumstances, a lodging receipt shows a charge for double occupancy, such fact shall be shown on the travel voucher. If the person sharing the room is a government employee on official travel, one-half of the double occupancy charge is allowable for each employee. If the person sharing the room is not another government employee on official travel, identification of the person is not required and the employee may be allowed the single room rate.

Tips

An employee's obligation, under the prudent person rule while traveling on official business, is to exercise the same care in incurring expenses that a prudent person would exercise if traveling on personal business. All expenses may not be necessarily incurred. Tips to porters, baggage carriers, bellhops, hotel maids, stewards or stewardesses and others on vessels, and hotel servants in foreign countries are included as part of incidental expenses covered by per diem. Tips related to meals are covered as part of your per diem meals expenses. Reimbursement of tips when authorized for the use of taxicabs will be allowed, but is not included as an incidental expense.

Telephone Calls

FTR Part 301-12 allows for the reimbursement of official telephone calls while in a travel status as a miscellaneous travel expense. Agencies determine which types of calls are official. Calls to inform family members of safe arrival, change of itinerary or a daily check-in are reimbursable if your agency determines that such calls are official.

You may make as many official calls as necessary to accomplish your mission and there is no dollar limit for such calls. However, your agency may limit the number of calls and amount of reimbursement for allowable calls to your family members. Calls to family members may be charged to a government telephone charge card if permitted by your agency.

For specific policy guidelines contact your agency's travel coordinator.

Taxes

A federal employee on official travel is obligated to pay all taxes unless the state or local authority assessing the tax provides a specific exemption. The per diem rates exclude lodging taxes, but travelers must pay the taxes, when applicable, and file for reimbursement under Miscellaneous Expenses.

Actual Subsistence Expense Reimbursement

An agency may authorize necessary actual subsistence expense reimbursement not to exceed 300 percent of the applicable maximum per diem rate for travel within CONUS when special or unusual circumstances exist and the applicable per diem locality rate would clearly be insufficient to cover the necessary subsistence expenses.

The maximum daily rate for subsistence expenses shall not exceed the amount prescribed by: (a) The Department of Defense, Per Diem, Travel and Transportation Allowance Committee, for non-foreign areas, and (b) the Department of State, for foreign areas, as set forth in Section 925, a per diem supplement to the U.S. Department of State Standard Regulations.

Additionally, an agency may request, and the GSA administrator may establish, a maximum daily rate for subsistence expenses not to exceed 300 percent of the applicable maximum per diem rate prescribed for an area within CONUS where special or unusual circumstances result in an extreme increase in subsistence costs for a temporary period (for example, a disaster area declared by the president of the United States) or when these circumstances give rise to an increase over a "sustained" period.

Approval should be obtained by the employee before travel begins, but when justified, it may also be approved after completion of the travel. The FTR details the requirements for itemization, receipts, etc.

Current Rates

The Per Diem Rates table shows rates for the contiguous states and District of Columbia (CONUS) current as of fiscal 2003. Certain rates may change during a fiscal year. Updated rates for CONUS are in the FTR (41 CFR Appendix A to Chapter 301), and online at *http://www.policyworks.gov/org/main/mt/*

homepage/mtt/perdiem/download03.html. Employees should consult with their employing agencies for current rates at the time travel is performed. Employees should also check their agency regulations for locality definitions to determine the per diem rates for any cities not listed.

Federal agencies may submit a request to GSA for review of the costs covered by per diem in a particular city or area where the standard CONUS rate applies when travel to that location is repetitive or on a continuing basis and travelers' experiences indicate that the prescribed rate is inadequate. Requests for per diem rate adjustments must be submitted by the agency headquarters office to the General Services Administration, Office of Governmentwide Policy, Attn: Travel and Transportation Management Policy Division (MTT), Washington, DC 20405.

Section 5—2003 Per Diem Rates (Effective October 1, 2002)

2003 State/Key City (1)		County and/or other defined location (2, 3)	Start Season¹	End Season¹	2003 Max Lodging Rate	2003 MIE	2003 Max Per Diem
AL	Birmingham	Jefferson			$59	$42	$101
AL	Decatur	Morgan			$69	$34	$103
AL	Gulf Shores	Baldwin	5/15	9/4	$101	$38	$139
AL	Gulf Shores	Baldwin	9/5	5/14	$64	$38	$102
AL	Huntsville	Madison			$67	$38	$105
AL	Montgomery	Montgomery			$57	$42	$99
AL	Tuscaloosa	Tuscaloosa			$63	$34	$97
AZ	Casa Grande	Pinal	1/1	4/30	$80	$38	$118
AZ	Casa Grande	Pinal	5/1	12/31	$65	$38	$103
AZ	Chinle	Apache	5/1	10/31	$98	$38	$136
AZ	Chinle	Apache	11/1	4/30	$55	$38	$93
AZ	Flagstaff	All points in Coconino County not covered under Grand Canyon per diem area	5/1	10/31	$67	$38	$105
AZ	Flagstaff	All points in Coconino County not covered under Grand Canyon per diem area	11/1	4/30	$55	$38	$93
AZ	Grand Canyon	All points in the Grand Canyon National Park and Kaibab National Forest within Coconino County	5/1	10/21	$106	$46	$152
AZ	Grand Canyon	All points in the Grand Canyon National Park and Kaibab National Forest within Coconino County	10/22	4/30	$94	$46	$140
AZ	Kayenta	Navajo	4/15	10/15	$98	$34	$132
AZ	Kayenta	Navajo	10/16	4/14	$65	$34	$99
AZ	Phoenix/Scottsdale	Maricopa	1/1	4/15	$107	$46	$153
AZ	Phoenix/Scottsdale	Maricopa	4/16	5/31	$79	$46	$125
AZ	Phoenix/Scottsdale	Maricopa	6/1	8/31	$59	$46	$105
AZ	Phoenix/Scottsdale	Maricopa	9/1	12/31	$90	$46	$136
AZ	Tucson	Pima County; Davis-Monthan AFB	1/1	4/15	$85	$42	$127
AZ	Tucson	Pima County; Davis-Monthan AFB	4/16	12/31	$58	$42	$100
AZ	Yuma	Yuma			$68	$38	$106
AR	Hot Springs	Garland			$60	$34	$94
AR	Little Rock	Pulaski			$72	$38	$110
CA	Clearlake	Lake	5/5	9/30	$85	$34	$119
CA	Clearlake	Lake	10/1	5/4	$69	$34	$103
CA	Contra Costa County	Contra Costa			$108	$46	$154
CA	Death Valley	Inyo			$60	$46	$106
CA	Fresno	Fresno			$73	$34	$107
CA	Kern County	Kern County			$68	$42	$110
CA	Los Angeles	Los Angeles; Orange and Ventura Counties; Edwards AFB; Naval Weapons Center and Ordinance Test Station, China Lake (see Santa Monica)			$99	$50	$149
CA	Mammoth Lakes	Mono			$70	$46	$116
CA	Marin County	Marin			$108	$46	$154
CA	Merced	Merced			$62	$34	$96
CA	Modesto	Stanislaus			$60	$38	$98
CA	Monterey	Monterey	5/1	10/31	$94	$46	$140
CA	Monterey	Monterey	11/1	4/30	$75	$46	$121
CA	Napa	Napa	4/1	11/15	$125	$46	$171
CA	Napa	Napa	11/16	3/31	$110	$46	$156
CA	Oakhurst	Madera	5/1	9/30	$79	$42	$121

2003 State/Key City (1)	County and/or other defined location (2, 3)	Start Season¹	End Season¹	2003 Max Lodging Rate	2003 MIE	2003 Max Per Diem
CA Oakhurst	Madera	10/1	4/30	$55	$42	$97
CA Oakland	Alameda			$118	$42	$160
CA Ontario/Barstow/ Victorville	San Bernardino			$84	$42	$126
CA Palm Springs	Riverside	1/1	5/31	$129	$46	$175
CA Palm Springs	Riverside	6/1	12/31	$84	$46	$130
CA Point Arena/ Gualala	Mendocino			$109	$42	$151
CA Redding	Shasta			$78	$34	$112
CA Sacramento	Sacramento			$79	$46	$125
CA San Diego	San Diego			$99	$50	$149
CA San Francisco	San Francisco			$159	$50	$209
CA San Luis Obispo	San Luis Obispo			$79	$42	$121
CA San Mateo/ Redwood City	San Mateo			$134	$46	$180
CA Santa Barbara	Santa Barbara			$114	$42	$156
CA Santa Cruz	Santa Cruz			$108	$46	$154
CA Santa Monica	City limits of Santa Monica (see Los Angeles)	6/1	9/30	$125	$42	$167
CA Santa Monica	City limits of Santa Monica (see Los Angeles)	10/1	5/31	$109	$42	$151
CA Santa Rosa	Sonoma			$89	$46	$135
CA Solano County	Solano; Travis Air Force Base			$79	$46	$125
CA South Lake Tahoe	El Dorado (see also Stateline, NV)	6/1	8/31	$97	$46	$143
CA South Lake Tahoe	El Dorado (see also Stateline, NV)	9/1	5/31	$84	$46	$130
CA Sunnyvale/ Palo Alto/ San Jose	Santa Clara			$150	$50	$200
CA Tahoe City	Placer			$145	$46	$191
CA Truckee	Nevada	6/15	9/30	$81	$46	$127
CA Truckee	Nevada	10/1	6/14	$63	$46	$109
CA Visalia	Tulare			$69	$42	$111
CA West Sacramento	Yolo			$69	$34	$103
CA Yosemite National Park	Mariposa	5/1	9/30	$114	$46	$160
CA Yosemite National Park	Mariposa	10/1	4/30	$82	$46	$128
CO Aspen	Pitkin	1/1	4/30	$145	$46	$191
CO Aspen	Pitkin	5/1	12/31	$89	$46	$135
CO Boulder	Boulder			$93	$46	$139
CO Colorado Springs	El Paso	5/15	9/15	$73	$42	$115
CO Colorado Springs	El Paso	9/16	5/14	$59	$42	$101
CO Cortez	Montezuma			$69	$34	$103
CO Crested Butte	City limits of Crested Butte (see Gunnison County)	11/15	4/15	$97	$46	$143
CO Crested Butte	City limits of Crested Butte (see Gunnison County)	4/16	6/15	$58	$46	$104
CO Crested Butte	City limits of Crested Butte (see Gunnison County)	6/16	11/14	$71	$46	$117
CO Denver	Denver, Adams, and Arapahoe Counties, that portion of Westminster ocated in Jefferson County, and Lone Tree in Douglas County			$112	$46	$158
CO Durango	La Plata	5/15	9/30	$99	$42	$141
CO Durango	La Plata	10/1	5/14	$70	$42	$112
CO Fort Collins	Larimer (except Loveland)			$76	$38	$114
CO Glenwood Springs	Garfield	5/15	10/15	$95	$34	$129

2003 State/Key City (1)		County and/or other defined location (2, 3)	Start Season¹	End Season¹	2003 Max Lodging Rate	2003 MIE	2003 Max Per Diem
CO	Glenwood Springs	Garfield	10/16	5/14	$55	$34	$89
CO	Grand Junction	Mesa			$64	$34	$98
CO	Gunnison	Gunnison (except Crested Butte)	5/15	9/30	$70	$38	$108
CO	Gunnison	Gunnison (except Crested Butte)	10/1	5/14	$55	$38	$93
CO	Jefferson County	Jefferson			$94	$38	$132
CO	Loveland	City limits of Loveland (see Larimer County)			$69	$34	$103
CO	Montrose	Montrose			$69	$38	$107
CO	Pueblo	Pueblo	6/1	9/30	$72	$38	$110
CO	Pueblo	Pueblo	10/1	5/31	$58	$38	$96
CO	Silverthorne/ Keystone	Summit			$170	$42	$212
CO	Steamboat Springs	Routt			$59	$42	$101
CO	Telluride	San Miguel	12/20	9/30	$147	$46	$193
CO	Telluride	San Miguel	10/1	12/19	$85	$46	$131
CO	Trinidad	Las Animas			$62	$34	$96
CO	Vail	Eagle	12/1	3/31	$200	$46	$246
CO	Vail	Eagle	4/1	11/30	$105	$46	$151
CT	Bridgeport/Danbury	Fairfield			$109	$42	$151
CT	Hartford	Hartford			$120	$42	$162
CT	Lakeville/Salisbury	Litchfield			$95	$42	$137
CT	Middlesex County	Middlesex			$78	$34	$112
CT	New Haven	New Haven			$87	$38	$125
CT	New London/Groton	New London	5/1	10/31	$107	$38	$145
CT	New London/Groton	New London	11/1	4/30	$79	$38	$117
CT	Putnam/Danielson	Windham			$56	$34	$90
CT	Storrs/Mansfield	Tolland			$70	$34	$104
DE	Dover	Kent	5/25	9/4	$75	$38	$113
DE	Dover	Kent	9/5	5/24	$64	$38	$102
DE	Lewes	Sussex			$120	$42	$162
DE	Wilmington	New Castle	4/1	9/30	$109	$38	$147
DE	Wilmington	New Castle	10/1	3/31	$99	$38	$137
DC	Washington, DC	(also the cities of Alexandria, Falls Church, and Fairfax, and the counties of Arlington, Loudoun, and Fairfax, in Virginia; and the counties of Montgomery and Prince George's in Maryland). (See also Maryland and Virginia.)"			$150	$50	$200
FL	Altamonte Springs	Seminole			$71	$42	$113
FL	Bradenton	Manatee	1/1	4/30	$65	$34	$99
FL	Bradenton	Manatee	5/1	12/31	$55	$34	$89
FL	Cocoa Beach	Brevard			$105	$38	$143
FL	Daytona Beach	Volusia	2/1	8/31	$90	$42	$132
FL	Daytona Beach	Volusia	9/1	1/31	$69	$42	$111
FL	Fort Lauderdale	Broward	12/15	4/30	$100	$46	$146
FL	Fort Lauderdale	Broward	5/1	12/14	$69	$46	$115
FL	Fort Myers	Lee	1/15	4/15	$70	$46	$116
FL	Fort Myers	Lee	4/16	1/14	$55	$46	$101
FL	Fort Pierce	Saint Lucie	12/15	4/30	$70	$42	$112
FL	Fort Pierce	Saint Lucie	5/1	12/14	$55	$42	$97
FL	Fort Walton Beach	Okaloosa	5/1	10/31	$110	$42	$152
FL	Fort Walton Beach	Okaloosa	11/1	4/30	$80	$42	$122
FL	Gainesville	Alachua			$61	$38	$99
FL	Gulf Breeze	Santa Rosa	5/1	9/30	$115	$42	$157
FL	Gulf Breeze	Santa Rosa	10/1	4/30	$59	$42	$101
FL	Jacksonville/ Mayport	Duval; Mayport Naval Station			$81	$38	$119

2003 State/Key City (1)	County and/or other defined location (2, 3)	Start Season[1]	End Season[1]	2003 Max Lodging Rate	2003 MIE	2003 Max Per Diem
FL Key West	Monroe	1/1	4/30	$180	$46	$226
FL Key West	Monroe	5/1	12/31	$109	$46	$155
FL Kissimmee	Osceola	2/1	4/30	$77	$38	$115
FL Kissimmee	Osceola	5/1	1/31	$64	$38	$102
FL Lakeland	Polk			$71	$38	$109
FL Leesburg	Lake	11/1	4/15	$68	$34	$102
FL Leesburg	Lake	4/16	10/31	$55	$34	$89
FL Miami	Dade			$98	$46	$144
FL Naples	Collier	12/16	4/15	$109	$42	$151
FL Naples	Collier	4/16	12/15	$69	$42	$111
FL Ocala	Marion			$59	$34	$93
FL Orlando	Orange			$95	$46	$141
FL Palm Beach	Palm Beach			$98	$46	$144
FL Panama City	Bay			$74	$42	$116
FL Pensacola	Escambia			$85	$34	$119
FL Punta Gorda	Charlotte	12/15	4/15	$75	$38	$113
FL Punta Gorda	Charlotte	4/16	12/14	$55	$38	$93
FL Sarasota	Sarasota	1/1	4/30	$80	$42	$122
FL Sarasota	Sarasota	5/1	12/31	$70	$42	$112
FL Sebring	Highlands			$64	$34	$98
FL St. Augustine	St. Johns			$65	$42	$107
FL Stuart	Martin			$57	$42	$99
FL Tallahassee	Leon			$65	$38	$103
FL Tampa/ St. Petersburg	Pinellas and Hillsborough			$93	$42	$135
FL Vero Beach	Indian River	12/15	4/15	$99	$34	$133
FL Vero Beach	Indian River	4/16	12/14	$59	$34	$93
GA Albany	Dougherty			$57	$38	$95
GA Athens	Clarke			$69	$38	$107
GA Atlanta	Fulton			$112	$42	$154
GA Clayton County	Clayton			$89	$34	$123
GA Cobb County	Cobb			$112	$42	$154
GA Columbus	Muscogee			$63	$38	$101
GA Conyers	Rockdale			$69	$38	$107
GA DeKalb County	DeKalb			$112	$42	$154
GA Dublin	Laurens			$57	$34	$91
GA Gwinnett County	Gwinnett			$69	$42	$111
GA Savannah	Chatham			$89	$42	$131
ID Boise	Ada			$61	$42	$103
ID Coeur d'Alene	Kootenai			$56	$38	$94
ID Ketchum	Blaine (except Sun Valley)	5/1	11/30	$84	$42	$126
ID Ketchum	Blaine (except Sun Valley)	12/1	4/30	$74	$42	$116
ID McCall	Valley			$62	$42	$104
ID Sun Valley	City limits of Sun Valley (see Blaine County)			$149	$42	$191
IL Aurora	Kane (except Elgin)			$66	$34	$100
IL Chicago	Cook and Lake			$155	$50	$205
IL Du Page County	Du Page			$89	$42	$131
IL Elgin	City limits of Elgin (see Kane County)			$60	$34	$94
IL Rockford	Winnebago			$60	$34	$94
IN Carmel	Hamilton			$65	$42	$107
IN Ft. Wayne	Allen			$58	$34	$92
IN Indianapolis	Marion County; Fort Benjamin Harrison			$70	$46	$116
IN Indianapolis	Marion County; Fort Benjamin Harrison			$83	$46	$129
IN Lafayette	Tippecanoe			$59	$34	$93
IN Michigan City	La Porte			$65	$38	$103
IN Nashville	Brown	4/1	11/15	$75	$42	$117
IN Nashville	Brown	11/16	3/31	$59	$42	$101

2003 State/Key City (1)	County and/or other defined location (2, 3)	Start Season[1]	End Season[1]	2003 Max Lodging Rate	2003 MIE	2003 Max Per Diem
MA Andover	Essex			$109	$42	$151
MA Boston	Suffolk			$159	$50	$209
MA Cambridge	Middlesex (except Lowell)			$159	$50	$209
MA Falmouth	City limits of Falmouth	6/1	9/30	$105	$38	$143
MA Falmouth	City limits of Falmouth	10/1	5/31	$70	$38	$108
MA Hyannis	Barnstable			$94	$42	$136
MA Lowell	City limits of Lowell (except Cambridge) (see Middlesex County)			$99	$38	$137
MA Martha's Vineyard	Dukes	6/1	10/15	$150	$46	$196
MA Martha's Vineyard	Dukes	10/16	5/31	$85	$46	$131
MA Nantucket	Nantucket	6/15	10/15	$150	$46	$196
MA Nantucket	Nantucket	10/16	6/14	$75	$46	$121
MA New Bedford	City limits of New Bedford (see Bristol County)	5/15	10/15	$75	$38	$113
MA New Bedford	City limits of New Bedford (see Bristol County)	10/16	5/14	$65	$38	$103
MA Northampton	Hampshire			$72	$38	$110
MA Pittsfield	Berkshire			$65	$42	$107
MA Plymouth	Plymouth	6/15	10/15	$119	$38	$157
MA Plymouth	Plymouth	10/16	6/14	$99	$38	$137
MA Quincy	Norfolk			$74	$42	$116
MA Springfield	Hampden			$99	$38	$137
MA Taunton	Bristol (except New Bedford)			$74	$34	$108
MA Worcester	Worcester			$79	$38	$117
MI Ann Arbor	Washtenaw			$75	$42	$117
MI Berrien County	Berrien			$59	$34	$93
MI Charlevoix	Charlevoix	6/1	8/31	$105	$42	$147
MI Charlevoix	Charlevoix	9/1	5/31	$59	$42	$101
MI Detroit	Wayne			$109	$50	$159
MI East Lansing/Lansing	Ingham			$65	$42	$107
MI Frankenmuth	Saginaw			$69	$34	$103
MI Frankfort	Benzie			$62	$34	$96
MI Gaylord	Otsego			$65	$38	$103
MI Grand Rapids	Kent			$62	$38	$100
MI Holland	Ottawa			$60	$38	$98
MI Leland	Leelanau			$75	$38	$113
MI Mackinac Island	Mackinac			$165	$46	$211
MI Midland	Midland			$72	$38	$110
MI Mount Pleasant	Isabella			$65	$38	$103
MI Muskegon	Muskegon	5/1	8/31	$79	$34	$113
MI Muskegon	Muskegon	9/1	4/30	$59	$34	$93
MI Ontonagon	Ontonagon			$65	$34	$99
MI Petoskey	Emmet	6/1	10/31	$65	$42	$107
MI Petoskey	Emmet	11/1	5/31	$55	$42	$97
MI Pontiac/Troy/Auburn Hills	Oakland			$94	$42	$136
MI Sault Ste Marie	Chippewa	5/15	10/15	$63	$38	$101
MI Sault Ste Marie	Chippewa	10/16	5/14	$55	$38	$93
MI South Haven	Van Buren			$76	$38	$114
MI Traverse City	Grand Traverse			$125	$46	$171
MI Warren	Macomb			$79	$38	$117
MN Anoka County	Anoka			$65	$38	$103
MN Dakota County	Dakota			$80	$38	$118
MN Duluth	St. Louis	6/1	10/31	$85	$42	$127
MN Duluth	St. Louis	11/1	5/31	$56	$42	$98
MN Minneapolis/St. Paul	Hennepin County and Fort Snelling Military Reservation and Navy Astronautics Group (Detachment BRAVO), and Ramsey County			$95	$50	$145

2003 State/Key City (1)		County and/or other defined location (2, 3)	Start Season[1]	End Season[1]	2003 Max Lodging Rate	2003 MIE	2003 Max Per Diem
MN	Minneapolis/St. Paul	Hennepin County and Fort Snelling Military Reservation and Navy Astronautics Group (Detachment BRAVO), and Rosemount; Ramsey County			$110	$50	$160
MN	Rochester	Olmsted			$73	$38	$111
MS	Bay St. Louis	Hancock	4/1	10/31	$69	$38	$107
MS	Bay St. Louis	Hancock	11/1	3/31	$55	$38	$93
MS	Biloxi/Gulfport	Harrison			$61	$42	$103
MS	Robinsonville	Tunica			$59	$34	$93
MO	Branson	Taney	4/1	12/31	$62	$38	$100
MO	Branson	Taney	1/1	3/31	$55	$38	$93
MO	Hannibal	Marion			$57	$34	$91
MO	Jefferson City	Cole			$60	$34	$94
MO	Kansas City	Jackson, Clay and Kansas City International Airport			$85	$46	$131
MO	Kansas City	Jackson, Clay and Kansas City International Airport			$84	$46	$130
MO	Osage Beach	Camden			$89	$34	$123
MO	Platte	Platte (except Kansas City International Airport)			$61	$38	$99
MO	Platte	Platte (except Kansas City International Airport)			$84	$38	$122
MO	Springfield	Greene			$63	$34	$97
MO	St. Louis	St. Louis and St. Charles			$90	$50	$140
MO	St. Robert/ Ft. Leonardwood	Pulaski			$74	$34	$108
MT	Big Sky	Gallatin (except West Yellowstone)			$125	$46	$171
MT	Polson/Kalispell	Lake and Flathead	6/1	9/15	$64	$34	$98
MT	Polson/Kalispell	Lake and Flathead	9/16	5/31	$55	$34	$89
MT	West Yellowstone	City limits of West Yellowstone (see Gallatin County)	6/1	9/30	$92	$38	$130
MT	West Yellowstone	City limits of West Yellowstone (see Gallatin County)	10/1	5/31	$55	$38	$93
NE	Omaha	Douglas		.	$63	$42	$105
NV	Incline Village/ Crystal Bay	City limits of Incline Village and Crystal Bay	5/15	9/15	$99	$42	$141
NV	Incline Village/ Crystal Bay	City limits of Incline Village and Crystal Bay	9/16	5/14	$79	$42	$121
NV	Las Vegas	Clark County; Nellis AFB			$79	$42	$121
NV	Stateline	Douglas (see also South Lake Tahoe, CA)			$129	$46	$175
NH	Concord	Merrimack	5/1	10/31	$68	$38	$106
NH	Concord	Merrimack	11/1	4/30	$58	$38	$96
NH	Conway	Carroll			$89	$42	$131
NH	Durham	Strafford			$89	$34	$123
NH	Hanover/ Sullivan County	Grafton and Sullivan			$95	$38	$133
NH	Laconia	Belknap			$73	$38	$111
NH	Manchester	Hillsborough			$89	$38	$127
NH	Newington	Rockingham County; Pease AFB (except Portsmouth)	7/1	10/31	$81	$38	$119
NH	Newington	Rockingham County; Pease AFB (except Portsmouth)	11/1	6/30	$65	$38	$103

2003 State/Key City (1)	County and/or other defined location (2, 3)	Start Season¹	End Season¹	2003 Max Lodging Rate	2003 MIE	2003 Max Per Diem
NH Portsmouth	City limits of Portsmouth (see Rockingham County)	1/1	10/15	$85	$42	$127
NH Portsmouth	City limits of Portsmouth (see Rockingham County)	10/16	12/31	$69	$42	$111
NJ Atlantic City	Atlantic	6/1	11/30	$149	$46	$195
NJ Atlantic City	Atlantic	12/1	5/31	$109	$46	$155
NJ Cape May	Cape May (except Ocean City)	6/1	11/30	$155	$46	$201
NJ Cape May	Cape May (except Ocean City)	12/1	5/31	$95	$46	$141
NJ Cherry Hill/ Camden/ Moorestown	Camden and Burlington			$74	$46	$120
NJ Eatontown	Monmouth County; Fort Monmouth; (except Freehold)			$84	$42	$126
NJ Edison	Middlesex (except Piscataway)			$169	$34	$203
NJ Flemington	Hunterdon			$80	$38	$118
NJ Freehold	City limits of Freehold (see Monmouth County)			$85	$38	$123
NJ Millville	Cumberland			$58	$34	$92
NJ Newark	Essex, Bergen, Hudson and Passaic			$125	$46	$171
NJ Ocean City	City limits of Ocean City (see Cape May County)	6/15	9/15	$215	$42	$257
NJ Ocean City	City limits of Ocean City (see Cape May County)	9/16	6/14	$80	$42	$122
NJ Parsippany/ Picatinney Arsenal/ Dover	Morris			$114	$42	$156
NJ Piscataway/ Belle Mead	Somerset; and City limits of Piscataway			$144	$42	$186
NJ Princeton/Trenton	Mercer			$139	$46	$185
NJ Tom's River	Ocean	5/15	9/15	$89	$42	$131
NJ Tom's River	Ocean	9/16	5/14	$79	$42	$121
NJ Union County	Union			$107	$42	$149
NM Albuquerque	Bernalillo			$65	$42	$107
NM Cloudcroft	Otero	6/1	10/31	$74	$34	$108
NM Cloudcroft	Otero	11/1	5/31	$65	$34	$99
NM Las Cruces	Dona/Ana			$60	$34	$94
NM Los Alamos	Los Alamos			$71	$38	$109
NM Santa Fe	Santa Fe			$99	$46	$145
NM Taos	Taos			$75	$38	$113
NY Albany	Albany			$96	$46	$142
NY The Bronx/ Brooklyn/Queens	The boroughs of The Bronx, Brooklyn and Queens			$168	$46	$214
NY Buffalo	Erie			$78	$42	$120
NY Glens Falls	Warren	6/1	9/30	$74	$38	$112
NY Glens Falls	Warren	10/1	5/31	$55	$38	$93
NY Ithaca	Tompkins			$69	$38	$107
NY Kingston	Ulster			$79	$42	$121
NY Lake Placid	Essex	6/15	10/15	$86	$42	$128
NY Lake Placid	Essex	10/16	6/14	$59	$42	$101
NY Manhattan	The borough of Manhattan			$208	$50	$258
NY Nassau County/ Great Neck	Nassau			$190	$46	$236
NY Niagara Falls	Niagara	5/1	10/31	$89	$38	$127

2003 State/Key City (1)	County and/or other defined location (2, 3)	Start Season¹	End Season¹	2003 Max Lodging Rate	2003 MIE	2003 Max Per Diem
IN South Bend	St. Joseph			$61	$38	$99
IN Valparaiso/ Burlington Beach	Porter			$89	$38	$127
IA Cedar Rapids	Linn			$60	$30	$90
IA Des Moines	Polk			$67	$34	$101
KS Kansas City/ Overland Park	Wyandotte and Johnson			$85	$42	$127
KS Kansas City/ Overland Park	Wyandotte and Johnson			$84	$42	$126
KS Wichita	Sedgwick			$59	$42	$101
KY Covington	Kenton			$80	$42	$122
KY Lexington	Fayette			$65	$34	$99
KY Louisville	Jefferson			$69	$42	$111
KY Newport	Campbell			$74	$34	$108
LA Baton Rouge	East Baton Rouge Parish			$78	$42	$120
LA Gonzales	Ascension Parish			$59	$38	$97
LA Lake Charles	Calcasieu Parish			$70	$38	$108
LA New Orleans/ St. Bernard	Orleans, St. Bernard, Plaquemine and Jefferson Parishes	1/1	5/31	$139	$46	$185
LA New Orleans/ St. Bernard	Orleans, St. Bernard, Plaquemine and Jefferson Parishes	6/1	12/31	$89	$46	$135
LA Shreveport/ Bossier City	Caddo			$60	$42	$102
LA Slidell	St. Tammany			$65	$34	$99
LA St. Francisville	West Feliciana			$75	$42	$117
ME Bar Harbor	Hancock	6/15	10/15	$110	$42	$152
ME Bar Harbor	Hancock	10/16	6/14	$89	$42	$131
ME Bath	Sagadahoc	5/1	10/31	$61	$38	$99
ME Bath	Sagadahoc	11/1	4/30	$55	$38	$93
ME Kennebunk/ Kittery/Sanford	York	6/15	10/31	$129	$42	$171
ME Kennebunk/ Kittery/Sanford	York	11/1	6/14	$69	$42	$111
ME Portland	Cumberland	7/1	10/31	$119	$42	$161
ME Portland	Cumberland	11/1	6/30	$79	$42	$121
ME Rockport	Knox	7/1	8/26	$87	$46	$133
ME Rockport	Knox	8/27	6/30	$55	$46	$101
ME Wiscasset	Lincoln	7/1	10/31	$99	$42	$141
ME Wiscasset	Lincoln	11/1	6/30	$72	$42	$114
MD For the counties of Montgomery and Prince George's, see District of Columbia.				$150	$50	$200
MD Annapolis	Anne Arundel			$90	$46	$136
MD Baltimore	Baltimore			$137	$46	$183
MD Cambridge	Dorchester			$70	$34	$104
MD Columbia	Howard			$110	$46	$156
MD Frederick	Frederick			$65	$34	$99
MD Grasonville	Queen Annes			$75	$42	$117
MD Harford County	Harford County			$104	$42	$146
MD Lexington Park/ Leonardtown/ Lusby	St. Mary's and Calvert			$75	$38	$113
MD Ocean City	Worcester	6/15	10/31	$144	$46	$190
MD Ocean City	Worcester	11/1	6/14	$59	$46	$105
MD St. Michaels	Talbot			$100	$46	$146

2003 State/Key City (1)		County and/or other defined location (2, 3)	Start Season[1]	End Season[1]	2003 Max Lodging Rate	2003 MIE	2003 Max Per Diem
NY	Niagara Falls	Niagara	11/1	4/30	$55	$38	$93
NY	Nyack/Palisades	Rockland	4/1	9/30	$67	$42	$109
NY	Nyack/Palisades	Rockland	10/1	3/31	$57	$42	$99
NY	Owego	Tioga			$73	$34	$107
NY	Poughkeepsie	Dutchess			$74	$42	$116
NY	Rochester	Monroe			$83	$46	$129
NY	Saratoga Springs	Saratoga	7/1	10/31	$95	$42	$137
NY	Saratoga Springs	Saratoga	11/1	6/30	$75	$42	$117
NY	Staten Island	Richmond			$120	$46	$166
NY	Suffolk County	Suffolk			$149	$42	$191
NY	Syracuse	Onondaga			$70	$38	$108
NY	Tarrytown	Westchester (except White Plains)			$114	$46	$160
NY	Waterloo/Romulus	Seneca	6/15	9/15	$89	$34	$123
NY	Waterloo/Romulus	Seneca	9/16	6/14	$69	$34	$103
NY	Watkins Glen	Schuyler			$59	$38	$97
NY	West Point	Orange			$121	$38	$159
NY	White Plains	City limits of White Plains (see Westchester County)			$165	$46	$211
NC	Atlantic Beach	Carteret	6/1	8/31	$64	$34	$98
NC	Atlantic Beach	Carteret	9/1	5/31	$55	$34	$89
NC	Chapel Hill	Orange			$80	$42	$122
NC	Charlotte	Mecklenburg			$71	$42	$113
NC	Cherokee	Swain	4/1	10/31	$62	$34	$96
NC	Cherokee	Swain	11/1	3/31	$55	$34	$89
NC	Fayetteville	Cumberland			$63	$38	$101
NC	Greensboro	Guilford			$87	$42	$129
NC	Greenville	Pitt			$64	$34	$98
NC	Kill Devil	Dare	5/1	9/30	$114	$42	$156
NC	Kill Devil	Dare	10/1	2/28	$75	$42	$117
NC	Kill Devil	Dare	3/1	4/30	$55	$42	$97
NC	New Bern/ Havelock	Craven			$62	$38	$100
NC	Raleigh	Wake			$74	$42	$116
NC	Research Triangle Park/Durham	Durham			$85	$46	$131
NC	Wilmington	New Hanover	4/1	9/15	$65	$38	$103
NC	Wilmington	New Hanover	9/16	3/31	$58	$38	$96
NC	Winston-Salem	Forsyth			$64	$42	$106
OH	Akron	Summit			$72	$42	$114
OH	Bellevue	Huron			$72	$34	$106
OH	Cambridge	Guernsey			$60	$34	$94
OH	Cincinnati	Hamilton and Warren			$69	$50	$119
OH	Cleveland	Cuyahoga			$86	$46	$132
OH	Columbus	Franklin			$75	$42	$117
OH	Dayton	Montgomery, Wright-Patterson AFB"			$65	$34	$99
OH	Fairborn	Greene			$66	$38	$104
OH	Geneva	Ashtabula			$59	$38	$97
OH	Hamilton	Butler			$59	$38	$97
OH	Lancaster	Fairfield			$66	$34	$100
OH	Port Clinton/ Oak Harbor	Ottawa	6/1	9/5	$95	$38	$133
OH	Port Clinton/ Oak Harbor	Ottawa	9/6	5/31	$69	$38	$107
OH	Sandusky	Erie	5/1	9/5	$85	$42	$127
OH	Sandusky	Erie	9/6	4/30	$55	$42	$97
OH	Toledo	Lucas			$69	$34	$103
OK	Oklahoma City	Oklahoma			$65	$42	$107
OR	Ashland	Jackson			$59	$46	$105

2003 State/Key City (1)	County and/or other defined location (2, 3)	Start Season[1]	End Season[1]	2003 Max Lodging Rate	2003 MIE	2003 Max Per Diem
OR Beaverton	Washington			$59	$42	$101
OR Bend	Deschutes	6/1	9/30	$69	$42	$111
OR Bend	Deschutes	10/1	5/31	$59	$42	$101
OR Clackamas	Clackamas			$66	$38	$104
OR Crater Lake	Klamath			$74	$34	$108
OR Eugene	Lane (except Florence)			$62	$42	$104
OR Florence	City limits of Florence (see Lane County)			$80	$38	$118
OR Gold Beach	Curry			$58	$34	$92
OR Lincoln City/ Newport	Lincoln			$65	$38	$103
OR Portland	Multnomah			$91	$42	$133
OR Seaside	Clatsop	7/1	8/31	$79	$38	$117
OR Seaside	Clatsop	9/1	6/30	$59	$38	$97
PA Allentown	Lehigh			$62	$34	$96
PA Chester/Radnor/ Essington	Delaware (except Wayne)			$75	$38	$113
PA Easton	Northampton			$69	$34	$103
PA Erie	Erie			$65	$34	$99
PA Gettysburg	Adams	5/1	10/31	$82	$38	$120
PA Gettysburg	Adams	11/1	4/30	$55	$38	$93
PA Harrisburg	Dauphin (except Hershey)			$79	$46	$125
PA Hershey	City limits of Hershey (see Dauphin County)	6/1	9/15	$125	$42	$167
PA Hershey	City limits of Hershey (see Dauphin County)	9/16	5/31	$55	$42	$97
PA King of Prussia/ Ft. Washington/ Bala Cynwyd	Montgomery	4/1	11/30	$119	$46	$165
PA King of Prussia/ Ft. Washington/ Bala Cynwyd	Montgomery	12/1	3/31	$99	$46	$145
PA King of Prussia/ Ft. Washington/ Bala Cynwyd	Montgomery			$124	$46	$170
PA Lancaster	Lancaster	5/1	10/31	$70	$42	$112
PA Lancaster	Lancaster	11/1	4/30	$60	$42	$102
PA Malvern/ Downington/ Valley Forge	Chester			$83	$42	$125
PA Mechanicsburg	Cumberland			$74	$34	$108
PA Philadelphia	Philadelphia			$118	$50	$168
PA Philadelphia	Philadelphia			$124	$50	$174
PA Pittsburgh	Allegheny			$79	$46	$125
PA Reading	Berks			$75	$42	$117
PA Scranton	Lackawanna			$60	$34	$94
PA Warminster	Bucks County; Naval Air Development Center			$75	$38	$113
PA Wayne	City limits of Wayne (see Delaware County)			$100	$46	$146
RI East Greenwich	Kent County; Naval Construction Battalion Center, Davisville			$79	$42	$121
RI Newport	Newport	4/1	12/31	$111	$46	$157
RI Newport	Newport	1/1	3/31	$79	$46	$125
RI North Kingstown	Washington			$89	$30	$119
RI Providence	Providence			$89	$46	$135
SC Aiken	Aiken			$65	$34	$99
SC Charleston/ Berkeley County	Charleston and Berkeley			$106	$42	$148
SC Columbia	Richland			$65	$34	$99

2003 State/Key City (1)	County and/or other defined location (2, 3)	Start Season¹	End Season¹	2003 Max Lodging Rate	2003 MIE	2003 Max Per Diem
SC Greenville	Greenville			$65	$42	$107
SC Hilton Head	Beaufort	3/15	9/30	$95	$46	$141
SC Hilton Head	Beaufort	10/1	3/14	$75	$46	$121
SC Myrtle Beach	Horry County; Myrtle Beach AFB	3/1	11/30	$99	$46	$145
SC Myrtle Beach	Horry County; Myrtle Beach AFB	12/1	2/28	$59	$46	$105
SD Custer	Custer	6/15	8/19	$70	$34	$104
SD Custer	Custer	8/20	6/14	$55	$34	$89
SD Hot Springs	Fall River	6/15	10/15	$108	$34	$142
SD Hot Springs	Fall River	10/16	6/14	$79	$34	$113
SD Rapid City	Pennington	5/15	9/30	$99	$34	$133
SD Rapid City	Pennington	10/1	5/14	$55	$34	$89
SD Sturgis	Meade	6/15	8/15	$79	$30	$109
SD Sturgis	Meade	8/16	6/14	$55	$30	$85
TN Alcoa/Townsend	Blount			$63	$34	$97
TN Gatlinburg	Sevier	5/1	10/31	$78	$42	$120
TN Gatlinburg	Sevier	11/1	4/30	$70	$42	$112
TN Memphis	Shelby			$75	$42	$117
TN Murfreesboro	Rutherford			$57	$34	$91
TN Nashville	Davidson			$82	$46	$128
TN Williamson County	Willamson			$60	$34	$94
TX Amarillo	Potter			$57	$34	$91
TX Arlington/Grapevine	Tarrant			$77	$38	$115
TX Austin	Travis			$80	$42	$122
TX Bryan	Brazos (except College Station)			$60	$34	$94
TX College Station	City limits of College Station (see Brazos County)			$69	$38	$107
TX Corpus Christi	Nueces			$59	$42	$101
TX Dallas	Dallas			$89	$46	$135
TX El Paso	El Paso			$78	$34	$112
TX Fort Davis	Jeff Davis			$68	$34	$102
TX Fort Worth	City limits of Fort Worth			$94	$42	$136
TX Galveston	Galveston			$76	$46	$122
TX Granbury	Hood			$60	$30	$90
TX Houston	Harris County; L.B. Johnson Space Center and Ellington AFB			$73	$46	$119
TX Killeen	Bell			$59	$34	$93
TX Laredo	Webb			$70	$34	$104
TX McAllen	Hidalgo			$70	$38	$108
TX Plano	Collin			$70	$38	$108
TX San Antonio	Bexar			$91	$46	$137
TX South Padre Island	Cameron	3/1	8/15	$91	$38	$129
TX South Padre Island	Cameron	8/16	2/28	$70	$38	$108
TX Waco	McLennan			$57	$34	$91
UT Bullfrog	Garfield			$73	$34	$107
UT Cedar City	Iron			$59	$38	$97
UT Moab	Grand	3/15	10/31	$90	$38	$128
UT Moab	Grand	11/1	3/14	$55	$38	$93
UT Ogden/Layton/ Davis County	Weber and Davis	1/15	2/28	$169	$38	$207
UT Ogden/Layton/ Davis County	Weber and Davis	3/1	1/14	$69	$38	$107
UT Park City	Summit	12/15	3/31	$169	$46	$215
UT Park City	Summit	4/1	12/14	$79	$46	$125
UT Provo	Utah	1/15	2/28	$169	$42	$211
UT Provo	Utah	3/1	10/31	$69	$42	$111
UT Provo	Utah	11/1	1/14	$60	$42	$102

2003 State/Key City (1)	County and/or other defined location (2, 3)	Start Season[1]	End Season[1]	2003 Max Lodging Rate	2003 MIE	2003 Max Per Diem
UT Salt Lake City	Salt Lake and Dugway Proving Ground and Tooele Army Depot	1/15	2/28	$169	$38	$207
UT Salt Lake City	Salt Lake and Dugway Proving Ground and Tooele Army Depot	3/1	1/14	$75	$38	$113
VT Burlington/ St. Albans	Chittenden and Franklin			$89	$38	$127
VT Manchester	Bennington			$68	$46	$114
VT Middlebury	Addison			$68	$42	$110
VT Montpelier	Washington			$62	$34	$96
VT White River Junction	Windsor	9/15	10/31	$90	$34	$124
VT White River Junction	Windsor	11/1	9/14	$55	$34	$89
VA For the cities of Alexandria, Fairfax, and Falls Church, and the counties of Arlington, Fairfax, and Loudoun, see District of Columbia				$150	$50	$200
VA Charlottesville				$60	$46	$106
VA Colonial Heights				$77	$34	$111
VA Dinwiddie County	Dinwiddie			$77	$34	$111
VA Fredricksburg	Spotsylvania and Stafford			$72	$30	$102
VA Hopewell				$77	$34	$111
VA Lynchburg				$64	$42	$106
VA Manassas/ Woodbridge	Prince William			$84	$38	$122
VA Petersburg				$77	$34	$111
VA Prince George County	Prince George			$77	$34	$111
VA Richmond	Chesterfield and Henrico Counties, also Defense Supply Center			$77	$42	$119
VA Roanoke				$59	$38	$97
VA Virginia Beach	Virginia Beach (also Norfolk, Portsmouth and Chesapeake)	4/1	10/31	$109	$42	$151
VA Virginia Beach	Virginia Beach (also Norfolk, Portsmouth and Chesapeake)	11/1	3/31	$55	$42	$97
VA Wallops Island	Accomack	6/1	9/5	$89	$38	$127
VA Wallops Island	Accomack	9/6	5/31	$69	$38	$107
VA Williamsburg	Williamsburg (also Hampton, Newport News, York County, Naval Weapons Station, Yorktown)	4/1	10/31	$99	$42	$141
VA Williamsburg	Williamsburg (also Hampton, Newport News, York County, Naval Weapons Station, Yorktown)	11/1	3/31	$59	$42	$101
VA Wintergreen	Nelson			$125	$46	$171
WA Anacortes	Skagit and Island			$64	$42	$106
WA Bremerton	Kitsap			$61	$38	$99
WA Everett	Snohomish (except Lynnwood)			$59	$42	$101
WA Friday Harbor	San Juan	5/1	9/30	$95	$46	$141
WA Friday Harbor	San Juan 1	0/1	4/30	$65	$46	$111

2003 State/Key City (1)	County and/or other defined location (2, 3)	Start Season[1]	End Season[1]	2003 Max Lodging Rate	2003 MIE	2003 Max Per Diem
WA Lynnwood	City limits of Lynnwood (see Snohomish County)			$89	$38	$127
WA Ocean Shores	Grays Harbor	4/1	9/30	$82	$42	$124
WA Ocean Shores	Grays Harbor	10/1	3/31	$55	$42	$97
WA Olympia/Tumwater	Thurston			$58	$42	$100
WA Port Angeles	City limits of Port Angeles (see Clallam County)			$65	$42	$107
WA Port Townsend	Jefferson			$79	$38	$117
WA Seattle	King			$143	$50	$193
WA Sequim	Clallam (except Port Angeles)	6/29	9/1	$62	$38	$100
WA Sequim	Clallam (except Port Angeles)	9/2	6/28	$55	$38	$93
WA Spokane	Spokane			$63	$42	$105
WA Tacoma	Pierce			$79	$34	$113
WV Berkeley Springs	Morgan			$69	$38	$107
WV Charleston	Kanawha			$78	$42	$120
WV Martinsburg/ Hedgesville	Berkeley			$59	$34	$93
WV Morgantown	Monongalia			$66	$38	$104
WV Shepherdstown	Jefferson			$79	$38	$117
WV Wheeling	Ohio			$71	$38	$109
WI Brookfield	Waukesha			$66	$42	$108
WI Green Bay	Brown			$59	$38	$97
WI Lake Geneva	Walworth	6/1	9/4	$85	$42	$127
WI Lake Geneva	Walworth	9/5	5/31	$66	$42	$108
WI Madison	Dane			$62	$42	$104
WI Milwaukee	Milwaukee			$95	$46	$141
WI Racine	Racine			$80	$34	$114
WI Sheboygan	Sheboygan			$59	$34	$93
WI Sturgeon Bay	Door	5/15	10/15	$81	$38	$119
WI Sturgeon Bay	Door	10/16	5/14	$56	$38	$94
WI Wisconsin Dells	Columbia	6/1	9/30	$85	$42	$127
WI Wisconsin Dells	Columbia	10/1	5/31	$55	$42	$97
WY Cody	Park	5/15	10/15	$98	$34	$132
WY Cody	Park	10/16	5/14	$55	$34	$89
WY Jackson	Teton	11/1	9/15	$115	$46	$161
WY Jackson	Teton	9/16	10/31	$69	$46	$115

Chapter 12
Postal Service

Section 1—Postal Organization

The Postal Service is the largest civilian organization in the United States. With more than 800,000 full-time career employees and 100,000 part-time employees and an annual budget of more than $60 billion, the Postal Service delivers over 200 billion pieces of mail every year.

USPS has headquarters in Washington, D.C., but maintains postal facilities throughout the United States, including nearly 38,000 post offices. The Postal Service is governed by a nine-member Board of Governors, whose members are appointed by the President with Senate confirmation. The nine Governors then select a Postmaster General, who becomes a member of the Board. Those ten select a Deputy Postmaster General, who also serves on the Board.

The nine Governors of the Postal Service are appointed for staggered nine-year terms and can be removed only for cause. In addition, no more than five Governors may belong to the same political party. The Postmaster General serves at the pleasure of the Governors for an indefinite period and is the Chief Executive Officer of the Postal Service. The Deputy Postmaster General serves at the pleasure of the Postmaster General and the Board.

The Board directs the exercise of the powers of the Postal Service, directs and controls its expenditures, reviews its practices, conducts long-range planning, and sets policies on all postal matters. The Board takes up matters such as service standards, capital investments and facilities projects exceeding $10 million. It also approves officer compensation.

Following are the current members of the Board of Governors:

Robert F. Rider .... Chair
S. David Fineman .... Vice Chair
Ernesta Ballard .... Member
LeGree S. Daniels .... Member
Albert V. Casey .... Member
James Miller .... Member
Alan C. Kessler .... Member
Ned R. McWherter .... Member
John F. Walsh .... Member
John Nolan .... Deputy DPMG

John E. "Jack" Potter .... PMG & CEO

There are two general divisions within the Postal Service, each headed by a vice president. One division is composed of processing and distribution sites, such as bulk mail centers and the second is composed of 90 customer service districts managing all the post offices.

Finances

The Postal Service announced in November 2002 that it had been overfunding its Civil Service Retirement System (CSRS) account for 30 years and owed $5 billion, instead of $32 billion, to the fund. If Congress approves a change in the Postal Service's funding payment schedule, it will have to pay $2.9 billion less into the CSRS fund for 2002 and $2.6 billion less for the next several years than it thought it would. The post office's financing formula includes 30-year and 15-year amortization schedules aimed at covering retirement costs linked to postal employee pay raises and cost-of-living adjustments (COLAs). Postmaster General John E. Potter said the reduction in pension contributions would be used to pay down the debt and keep postal rates steady until 2006.

A review team led by the Office of Personnel Management (OPM) discovered that the USPS had been overpaying the billions of dollars. It found the statutory formula that sets the rate for pension payments was out of whack, in part because of higher-than-anticipated yields on pension investments. The Postal Service paid $152.1 billion into CSRS to cover annuities for postal workers and was due to pay $91.5 billion more in future payments, under the formula. That figure, it turned out, was $71 billion higher than the amount needed to cover the cost of future postal retirements, officials said.

The Postal Service subsequently announced that it had a surplus of $27 billion. Potter stressed that the agency would continue to cut costs, consolidate mail-handling plants and urge Congress to permit more flexibility in the processing and pricing of mail.

Section 2—Labor Unions and Employee Organizations

An overwhelming majority of postal employees belong to either labor unions or one of the management or supervisory organizations. The 1970 Postal Reorganization Act authorized collective bargaining on wages and working conditions under laws applying to the private sector and provided for binding arbitration if an impasse persists 180 days after the start of bargaining. The ability of many postal employees to bargain over their pay rates is a right that is not enjoyed by other federal employees, although postal workers, like other federal employees, are still barred from striking.

Four large postal unions represent most postal workers and negotiate for them during collective bargaining. They are:

• The American Postal Workers Union, AFL-CIO, representing 366,000 union members.

• The National Association of Letter Carriers, AFL-CIO, representing 315,000 postal workers.

• The National Rural Letter Carriers Association, representing 96,000 postal workers.

• The National Postal Mail Handlers Union, representing 50,000 postal workers.

In addition to the four major unions, there are smaller unions representing postal inspectors and postal nurses.

Three management associations represent postal supervisors and postmasters. These associations cannot bargain over pay issues like the unions but they do negotiate over other working conditions. The associations are:

• The National Association of Postal Supervisors. NAPS represents 35,000 active and retired supervisors and managers.

• The National Association of Postmasters of the United States. NAPUS represents 40,000 active and retired postmasters.

• The National League of Postmasters. The League represents 27,000 active and retired postmasters.

Section 3—Postal Pay

General Salary Structures

There are two general types of salary structures used by the postal service, as well as a specialized structure for rural letter carriers.

The two general salary structures are:

• PS-Postal Service salary structure. Applicable to bargaining unit personnel (clerks, carriers, etc.) except rural letter carriers, mailhandlers, nurses, and postal police officers.

• EAS-Executive and Administrative Salary structure. Applicable to executives, professionals, supervisors, postmasters, and technical, administrative and clerical non-bargaining employees. Salary grades in the schedule range from EAS-1 through EAS-26. Postmasters whose offices are open less than 40 hours per week are on a separate schedule.

The pay period for all employees begins on Saturday and covers a 2-week period ending on Friday. Employees are paid every 2 weeks following the end of the pay period.

The schedules covering the various categories of postal employees appear at the end of this section.

Computing Postal Pay

A summary of the formula and pertinent detail employed in the computation of postal pay schedules follows.

Full-Time Employees—Annual salary is divided by 26. The pay for anything less than a full biweekly pay period (80 hours), or specifically the hourly rate, is computed by dividing the annual salary by 2,080 hours. Net pay before taxes takes into account deductions for civil service retirement, and net take-home pay includes the further deduction of the required withholding based on the number of exemptions claimed. Eligible employees on the PS schedule and eligible employees through EAS Schedule grade 18 may get time-and-one-half overtime pay.

Part-Time, Regular Schedule Employees—The appropriate equivalent annual salary rate for these employees can be computed by multiplying the hourly rate by 2,080 (the number of pay hours in the calendar year for this category of employees). They are entitled to holiday pay if they are scheduled for a minimum of five days in a service week or are scheduled to work on a holiday, and they receive overtime pay for all work in excess of eight hours in one day at a time-and-one-half rate. Insurance entitlement must be determined in each individual case based upon the specified number of hours of annual employment.

Part-Time, Flexible Schedule Employees—The appropriate equivalent annual salary rate for these employees can be computed by multiplying the hourly rate by 2,000, the number of working hours in 52 weeks less holidays. Insurance deduction is predicated on the equivalent annual rate.

Additionally, there are other items that are not reflected in the Postal Service pay schedules and that should be considered on an individual basis to determine net pay. For example:

• State and territory income tax withholding (some states now have withholding agreements with the federal government whereby their residents commuting and working in another state may request a voluntary payroll deduction to apply to state-of-residence income tax obligation);

• Postal employee unions' dues checkoff arrangements stemming from a voluntary withholding request by the individual; and

• Deductions for items like savings bonds, charitable contributions, and voluntary retirement Thrift Savings Plan contributions, none of which are reflected in the pay schedules presented in this chapter.

Overtime and Premium Pay

Overtime and extra compensation and night differential pay to employees in the PS schedule and eligible employees in the EAS schedule is paid as follows:

• Time-and-one-half rates for work in excess of regular work schedule pertain to full-time employees.

• The time-and-one-half rate, computed on the basis of the base hourly rate, is applicable to part-time, regular schedule employees for work in excess of eight hours in one day or 40 hours in one week and to part-time, flexible schedule employees in the bargaining unit for work in excess of eight hours of duty in a service day or 40 hours in one service week.

• For work on holidays, except Christmas Day, full-time employees must be paid extra at the rate of their hourly base compensation for the time worked; extra compen-

sation at the time-and-one-half rate must be paid for work on Christmas Day. Part-time, flexible schedule employees receive extra compensation at the rate of 50 percent for work on Christmas Day.

• Employees whose normal schedule includes work on Sunday are entitled to a Sunday premium of 25 percent of their hourly straight time rate for each hour of work up to 8 hours. Sunday premium is not paid for leave time.

• All employees except postmasters, postal inspectors, and certain top administrative officials are paid a night differential for work performed between 6:00 p.m. and 6:00 a.m. Bargaining unit employees receive a fixed dollar amount specified in the applicable bargaining agreement. Nonbargaining employees receive an amount equal to 9 percent of their straight-time hourly rate.

• No full-time regular employee will be required to work overtime on more than five consecutive days in a week.

• Penalty overtime is paid at the rate of two times the base hourly straight-time rate if an employee is required to work overtime on more than four of the employee's five scheduled days in a service week; over ten hours on a regularly scheduled work day; over eight hours on a non-scheduled day; or over six days in a service week.

Pay Step Increases

Employees in the Postal Service schedule, salary level 10 and below, who have not reached the maximum step for their position (aside from other limitations), shall be advanced to the next step at the beginning of the first pay period following the completion of the required period of satisfactory service, if no equivalent increase was received during the period.

Cost-of-Living Adjustments

The base salary schedule for employees in the EAS and PS schedules is increased one cent per hour for each full 0.4 of a point increase in the Consumer Price Index above the base index, according to schedules set by contract or management benefit packages.

Consumer Price Index refers to the National Consumer Price Index for Urban Wage Earners and Clerical Workers, published by the Bureau of Labor Statistics, U.S. Department of Labor (1967 = 100) and is referred to as the Index. The base index refers to the Consumer Price Index month from which all future calculations are made.

The cost-of-living adjustment is taken into account only in computing base rates, overtime and shift premiums, and in determining call-in pay, leave pay and holiday pay. It does not immediately become a fixed part of the EAS or PS basic salary schedules.

However, letter carriers who retired on disability and the survivors of those who died while still working were not eligible for compensatory payments for lost annuity and life insurance resulting from delayed COLAs. Because of this situation, COLA pay was rolled in automatically so the carriers can start earning retirement credit on COLA increases as soon as they are paid.

Pay Upon Promotions

A bargaining unit employee promoted to an EAS position receives an adjustment to base salary equal to five percent of the employee's base salary in the former grade. If the new salary falls between two salary steps of the new grade, the worker's pay is advanced to the higher step.

A non-bargaining employee promoted within the EAS schedule receives up to an eight percent increase in basic pay for a one-grade promotion. If the new salary falls between steps of the new grade, the employee's pay is advanced to the next higher step.

Merit Pay and Economic Value-Added Programs

Executive, administrative, and supervisory employees (EAS schedule) are eligible for annual merit increases and economic value added (EVA) payments.

Merit increases are based on individual accomplishment. For example, if a postmas-

ter accomplishes her agreed-to goals and objectives, she receives an amount based on a percentage of her income throughout the year. This is added to her pay for the following year. The percentage level of the merit increases varies depending on the individual rating and the location of the employee on the salary schedule.

The EVA awards are team-based and dependent on the performance of a district. These lump-sum payments are primarily determined by the amount of money a district makes in a year and are calculated at the end of the Postal Service's fiscal year. The following positions are eligible for EVA payments: senior officer; PCES employees; EAS-Exempt employees (these workers get half of what the PCES employees get); and EAS-Non-Exempt employees (receive half of what the EAS-Exempt worker receive). Postmasters and supervisors at level 13 are not eligible for EVA awards.

Severance Pay

Any career postal worker who is involuntarily separated and who has been employed continuously by the Postal Service for at least 12 consecutive months (without a break in service of three or more consecutive days) immediately prior to the separation is eligible for severance pay, with a few exceptions. Employees will not receive severance pay if they can retire on an immediate annuity, are receiving workers' compensation, or declined a similar position in the Postal Service or another federal agency in the same commuting area.

Employees receive one week of basic compensation for each year of creditable service up to 10 years. Employees receive two weeks of basic compensation for each year of creditable service after 10 years.

Section 4—Postal Employee Benefits

Postal employees generally receive the same benefits as other federal employees with a few exceptions.

Retirement—Postal Service career employees, like federal career employees, are covered by one of three retirement systems administered by OPM: the Federal Employees Retirement System (FERS), the Civil Service Retirement System (CSRS) and by CSRS Offset. FERS is a retirement system with both defined benefit and defined contri-

bution components. Under FERS, employees receive retirement benefits from a federal retirement annuity, Social Security, and the Thrift Savings Plan. The FERS annuity benefit, while also based on an employee's high-three average salary and years of service, produces a smaller benefit than CSRS does. CSRS is a defined benefit retirement system. Annuity benefits are based on an employee's high-three average salary and years of service. CSRS Offset is similar to CSRS but requires

Social Security contributions. Upon Social Security eligibility, the CSRS annuity is reduced by any Social Security benefit resulting from periods of CSRS Offset service, to produce a benefit equivalent to what would have been received under CSRS.

Health Insurance—The Postal Service participates in the Federal Employees Health Benefits Program and all postal employees can receive health insurance coverage through that plan with the cost split between the Postal Service and the worker. For most federal employees the split is determined by Congress. However, postal unions negotiate the actual split as part of the collective bargaining agreements, so postal workers often pay a different amount than other federal workers, and postal workers from different unions may pay different amounts. Postal employees should review the health benefits section of the Almanac for complete information on how the FEHBP works, premium amounts and plan contact information.

Life Insurance—The Postal Service offers life insurance coverage through the Federal Employees Life Insurance Program. However, while other federal employees must pay part of the cost of the basic coverage, the Postal Service pays the entire premium amount for its active employees. There are additional options for purchasing more insurance through the FEGLI program. Postal employees should review the life insurance section in the Almanac for more details.

Flexible Spending Accounts—Employees can use Flexible Spending Accounts (FSAs) to pay for certain health care and dependent care expenses with contributions made through pretax payroll deductions. FSAs were first offered in 1992 to certain non-bargaining unit employees and now include all employees. Employees experience tax savings as well, which vary according to the individual's contribution amounts and marginal tax rates.

Thrift Savings Plan—Postal employees may participate in the Thrift Savings Plan (TSP), which is administered by the Federal Retirement Thrift Investment Board. The rules for

TSP participation differ depending on the employee's retirement system. For FERS employees, the Postal Service contributes one percent of basic pay to TSP, fully matches employee contributions up to 3 percent of basic pay, and matches one-half of employee contributions from 3 to 5 percent of basic pay. The Postal Service does not match CSRS or CSRS-Offset employee contributions to the TSP.

Leave—Postal Service employees are provided both sick and annual leave at the same rate as other federal sector employees. However, postal employees have a higher annual leave carryover limit than their federal sector counterparts. Earned annual leave may be donated to other career or transitional Postal Service employees who have exhausted their own leave and have a serious health problem. The Postal Service allows the use of 80 hours of accrued sick leave for dependent care under a policy available to all career employees.

Family and Medical Leave—Postal employees are covered by the 1993 Family and Medical Leave Act, which provides time off for employees who are dealing with serious health conditions. The law provides that eligible employees can take up to 12 workweeks of leave within a Postal Service leave year for the following: birth or adoption of a child, taking in a child for foster care, caring for a family member with a serious health condition, or dealing with the employee's own serious health condition. Time taken for family and medical leave can be taken as annual leave, sick leave, leave without pay or a combination of those.

Holidays—The Postal Service observes the 10 designated federal holidays each year. They are: New Year's Day, January 1; Martin Luther King Jr.'s Birthday, third Monday in January; Presidents' Day, third Monday in February; Memorial Day, last Monday in May; Independence Day, July 4; Labor Day, first Monday in September; Columbus Day, second Monday in October; Veterans Day, November 11; Thanksgiving Day, fourth Thursday in November; Christmas Day, December 25.

Section 5—Workplace Policies

Debt Collection

For non-bargaining unit employees who owe money to USPS, the Postal Service generally may withhold a maximum of 15 per-

cent of an employee's disposable pay each pay period, after providing the employee with certain due process rights. If, however, a federal court has granted judgment upholding the debt, up to 25 percent of the employee's current pay may be withheld each pay period.

For bargaining unit employees who owe money to the USPS, generally up to 15 percent of an employee's disposable pay may be deducted in monthly installments or at "officially established pay intervals." A greater percentage may be deducted with the written consent of the worker. Bargaining unit employees can initiate a grievance concerning a debt.

Employee Claims

It is Postal Service policy to reimburse employees for loss or damage to personal property when the property is damaged in their employment while they are on duty or on postal property. Nonbargaining unit employees should file Form 2146, *Employee's Claim for Personal Property*, within 90 days of the loss. The Postal Service also will accept any written documentation within the prescribed time limit if it contains substantiating information.

Depending on where employees work, the claim should be filed at the field office, area office, headquarters or with the deputy chief inspector of administration for inspection service personnel. If the claim is denied it can be appealed.

Bargaining unit employees are covered by their collective bargaining agreement.

Workers' Compensation

Postal employees are covered by the Federal Employees' Compensation Act if they are injured on the job or develop a job-related disease. FECA payments are generally calculated at two-thirds of the employee's monthly rate if the worker has no dependents, or three-fourths of the pay rate if married or with one or more dependents.

In addition to monetary compensation, FECA also provides medical care benefits including treatment for the effects of the injury, vocational rehabilitation, and allowances in the case of severe injuries.

Workers' compensation was included in the Transformation Plan, which the Postal Service announced in April 2002, to reduce costs to the agency for injuries that are sustained on the job. The Transformation Plan noted that there are specific issues under

FECA that are contributing to escalating compensation costs:

1. The Postal Service's inability to contact the employee's medical provider by phone.

2. The fact that there is no waiting period before wage-loss compensation is paid for traumatic injuries.

3. They believe that compensation rates are too generous.

4. The Postal Service contends that compensation should not be a lifetime benefit. At retirement age, compensation should be adjusted to a tax-free amount equal to what a retiree would receive.

5. Medical costs are not adequately controlled by fee schedule.

The Postal Service is proposing five strategies to achieve these goals:

1. Expanding the Preferred Provider Organization Program with First Health and the Office of Workers' Compensation Programs (OWCP). First Health pays medical providers at agreed upon rates that are usually substantially lower than what OWCP would allow through its bill payment system.

2. Move all Federal Employees' Compensation Act recipients to FECA annuity at age 65. The Postal Service is proposing a FECA managed retirement program that would calculate benefits similar to those of a normal retirement for all present and former employees over age 65 on the compensation rolls of OWCP. What this means is that once an injured worker reaches age 65, his/her compensation benefits would be recalculated from the 66 2/3 percent or 75 percent level to a figure that would more closely mirror their earned retirement benefits.

3. Encourage OWCP to revise current regulations to allow for direct contact with the treating physician by the employing agency. In January 1999, OWCP amended their regulations to prevent agency personnel from contacting an employee's treating physician directly (by phone and/or in person). The Postal Service is looking to regain that right in order to explain limited duty assignments and offer options to accommodate employees. The agency believes that changing this regulation would ensure that postal managers initiated close monitoring of employees' physical condition and it would allow early worker's compensation program specialists' intervention to assist the employee in a prompt return to work.

4. Private sector outplacement of Injured Postal Service employees and the creation of new internal positions to accommodate injured workers. The goals of this strategy are to successfully implement, with OWCP, an accelerated private sector placement program that reduces the amount of time necessary for an outplacement from up to two years to less than one year, and to reduce the number of postal employees in non-productive rehabilitation assignments by placing them in private sector employment.

5. Interagency work cooperation to attain organizational objectives. The Postal Service believes that cooperation must exist between it and OWCP, especially as it relates to the timely processing of compensation claims and medical bills. The Postal Service wants to work with OWCP in developing joint strategies to achieve both agencies objectives. The goal is to have all claims paid in a timely manner, while performing quality checks to prevent the duplicate payment of medical bills.

Training Centers

The Postal Service operates several training and development centers. Following are the locations and phone numbers of the main USPS training facilities:

Management & Employee Development
W.A. Stefl, Manager
475 L'Enfant Plaza, S.W., Rm. 9600
Washington, DC 20260-4215
(202) 268-5624
Fax: (202) 268-2531

William F. Bolger Center
for Leadership Development
Suzanne Henry, Manager
9600 Newbridge Dr.
Potomac, MD 20854-4436
(301) 983-7001
Fax: (301) 983-7149

National Center for
Employee Development
Steve Mosier, Acting Manager
2701 E. Imhoff Rd.

Norman, OK 73071-1198
(405) 366-4301
Fax: (405) 366-4309

Adverse Action and EEO Complaints

Postal employees who are represented by a union generally are entitled to file a grievance over adverse management decisions or actions under the grievance-arbitration procedure specified in their collective bargaining agreement.

Certain postal employees may have additional (or alternative) rights to file an appeal with the Merit Systems Protection Board if they are affected by adverse personnel decisions or actions, such as a removal or suspension that exceeds 14 days. To be eligible for MSPB appeal rights, postal workers generally must have served with USPS for at least one year and fall into one of three categories: (1) managers and supervisors, (2) employees engaged in personnel work (except those in non-confidential clerical positions), or (3) employees with veterans' preference eligibility. Bargaining unit workers who have MSPB appeal rights generally either must choose between the Board's process and the contractual grievance procedure; in some cases, they have the right to submit their dispute to both channels.

Postal employees with MSPB appeal rights can refer to the MSPB section in this *Almanac* for a complete description of the Board's jurisdiction and appeal processes.

All postal employees are covered by the EEO complaint processes established under the rules of the Equal Employment Opportunity Commission. Bargaining unit employees are entitled to pursue their discrimination complaints through the EEOC process, as well as the contractual grievance procedure, although action on the EEO complaint may be deferred pending resolution of the grievance process. Postal workers with EEO concerns should refer to the EEOC section in this *Almanac* for complete information.

Section 6—Union Bargaining

Postal unions have been bargaining with USPS over pay and other working conditions since the passage of the Postal Reorganization Act (P.L. 91-375) in 1970. The bargaining has not always resulted in a negotiated agreement and, at various times, the two parties have had to move into binding arbitration. Collective bargaining rights are protected by the National Labor Relations Board. Below is the current status of the labor agreements between the various unions and the Postal Service, by union.

American Postal Workers Union. APWU and the Postal Service agreed on a two-year extension of the current three-year labor agreement that would otherwise have expired Nov. 20, 2003. The extension for approximately 340,000 postal clerks, maintenance employees, and motor vehicle operators represented by APWU would provide a 1.3 percent pay hike for each of the next two years. The first increase would take effect Nov. 15, 2003, and the second on Nov. 27, 2004. Both increases would be based on wages in effect as of Sept. 6, 2003. An agreement to extend the existing contract two years instead of negotiating a new one precludes the possibility of an early retirement package and a freeze on plant closings, which could result in workers being relocated. The contract extension additionally calls for a cost-of-living increase. The extension, which would expire Nov. 20, 2005, also calls for cost-of-living increases in March and September 2004, and in March and September 2005.

National Association of Letter Carriers. In May 2002, the 307,000-member NALC and the Postal Service agreed to a five-year contract calling for general wage increases of 7.1 percent for city letter carriers that will remain in force until Nov. 20, 2006. Under the pact, carriers will pay raises of 1.8 percent, retroactive to Nov. 20, 2001; 1.5 percent, effective Nov. 20, 2002; 1.2 percent, effective Nov. 20, 2003; 1.3 percent, effective Nov. 20, 2004; and 1.3 percent, effective Nov. 20, 2005.

National Postal Mail Handlers Union. The union representing some 61,000 mail handlers reached a four-year agreement providing 6 percent in general wage increases, including two retroactive increases, over a term extending from Nov. 20, 2000, to Nov. 20, 2004.

National Rural Letter Carriers Association. An arbitration panel resolved a dispute between the rural letter carriers organization, which represents about 118,000 workers, issued a contract running through Nov. 20, 2004, with pay increases totaling 5.6 percent.

Executive Pay and Benefits

Due to the limit imposed on Executive Schedule I salaries by the Postal Reorganization Act, pay and benefits for Postal Service officers and some key executives do not meet private sector comparability standards. During 2002, the average salary for Postal Service officers was $141,593. The average executive salary was $105,494.

To focus on continuous improvements and long-term results, the 2002 payments consisted of a percentage of prior year's reserve account and the current year's earned credit. In 2002, award payouts averaged $2,270 for exempt non-bargaining EAS employees, $876 for nonexempt non-bargaining employees, and $8,858 for executives. While the program was designed to recognize team performance, provisions were made to exclude individual employees who did not contribute to the performance of the organization.

Section 7—Postal Pay Tables

On the following pages are pay tables covering most postal employees.

Schedule One (P1)

Postal Service Schedule (PS) Full-Time Annual Rates
Effective November 16, 2002

	GRADES					
STEPS	2	3	4	5	6	7
D	37,172	37,772	38,423	39,129	39,889	40,714
E	37,420	38,039	38,712	39,441	40,228	41,079
F	37,667	38,312	39,006	39,754	40,570	41,443
G	37,915	38,576	39,295	40,063	40,905	41,808
H	38,168	38,846	39,582	40,378	41,247	42,176

Schedule One (P1)

Postal Service Schedule (PS)
Part-Time Flexible Employees—Hourly Rates
Effective November 16, 2002

	GRADES					
STEPS	2	3	4	5	6	7
D	18.59	18.89	19.21	19.56	19.94	20.36
E	18.71	19.02	19.36	19.72	20.11	20.54
F	18.83	19.16	19.50	19.88	20.29	20.72
G	18.96	19.29	19.65	20.03	20.45	20.90
H	19.08	19.42	19.79	20.19	20.62	21.09

Schedule One (P1)

Postal Service Schedule (PS)
Part-Time Regular Employees—Hourly Rates
Effective November 16, 2002

	GRADES					
STEPS	2	3	4	5	6	7
D	17.87	18.16	18.47	18.81	19.18	19.57
E	17.99	18.29	18.61	18.96	19.34	19.75
F	18.11	18.42	18.75	19.11	19.50	19.92
G	18.23	18.55	18.89	19.26	19.67	20.10
H	18.35	18.68	19.03	19.41	19.83	20.28

Schedule Two (P2)
Postal Service Schedule (PS) Full-Time Annual Rates
Effective November 16, 2002

					GRADES						
STEPS	1	2	3	4	5	6	7	8	9	10	11
BB	23,864	24,948	26,026								
AA	24,802	25,876	26,945								
A	25,740	26,804	27,864	29,508	31,106	32,805	33,590				
B	26,678	27,732	28,783	30,373	31,924	33,577	34,386				
C	27,616	28,660	29,702	31,238	32,742	34,349	35,182				
D	28,554	29,588	30,621	32,103	33,560	35,121	35,978	39,414	40,342	41,319	42,350
E	29,492	30,516	31,540	32,968	34,378	35,893	36,774	40,009	40,971	41,987	43,058
F	30,430	31,444	32,459	33,833	35,196	36,665	37,570	40,604	41,600	42,655	43,766
G	31,368	32,372	33,378	34,698	36,014	37,437	38,366	41,199	42,229	43,323	44,474
H	32,306	33,300	34,297	35,563	36,832	38,209	39,162	41,794	42,858	43,991	45,182
I	33,244	34,228	35,216	36,428	37,650	38,981	39,958	42,389	43,487	44,659	45,890
J	34,182	35,156	36,135	37,293	38,468	39,753	40,754	42,984	44,116	45,327	46,598
K	35,120	36,084	37,054	38,158	39,286	40,525	41,550	43,579	44,745	45,995	47,306
L	36,058	37,012	37,973	39,023	40,104	41,297	42,346	44,174	45,374	46,663	48,014
M	36,996	37,940	38,892	39,888	40,922	42,069	43,142	44,769	46,003	47,331	48,722
N	37,934	38,868	39,811	40,753	41,740	42,841	43,938	45,364	46,632	47,999	49,430
O	39,141	39,905	40,730	41,618	42,558	43,613	44,734	45,959	47,261	48,667	50,138
P								46,554	47,890	49,335	50,846
RC	40,079	40,833	41,649	42,483	43,376	44,400	45,530	47,149	48,519	50,003	51,554

Schedule Two (P2)
Postal Service Schedule (PS)
Part-Time Flexible Employees—Hourly Rates
Effective November 16, 2002

					GRADES						
STEPS	1	2	3	4	5	6	7	8	9	10	11
BB	11.93	12.47	13.01								
AA	12.40	12.94	13.47								
A	12.87	13.40	13.93	14.75	15.55	16.40	16.80				
B	13.34	13.87	14.39	15.19	15.96	16.79	17.19				
C	13.81	14.33	14.85	15.62	16.37	17.17	17.59				
D	14.28	14.79	15.31	16.05	16.78	17.56	17.99	19.71	20.17	20.66	21.18
E	14.75	15.26	15.77	16.48	17.19	17.95	18.39	20.00	20.49	20.99	21.53
F	15.22	15.72	16.23	16.92	17.60	18.33	18.79	20.30	20.80	21.33	21.88
G	15.68	16.19	16.69	17.35	18.01	18.72	19.18	20.60	21.11	21.66	22.24
H	16.15	16.65	17.15	17.78	18.42	19.10	19.58	20.90	21.43	22.00	22.59
I	16.62	17.11	17.61	18.21	18.83	19.49	19.98	21.19	21.74	22.33	22.95
J	17.09	17.58	18.07	18.65	19.23	19.88	20.38	21.49	22.06	22.66	23.30
K	17.56	18.04	18.53	19.08	19.64	20.26	20.78	21.79	22.37	23.00	23.65
L	18.03	18.51	18.99	19.51	20.05	20.65	21.17	22.09	22.69	23.33	24.01
M	18.50	18.97	19.45	19.94	20.46	21.03	21.57	22.38	23.00	23.67	24.36
N	18.97	19.43	19.91	20.38	20.87	21.42	21.97	22.68	23.32	24.00	24.72
O	19.57	19.95	20.37	20.81	21.28	21.81	22.37	22.98	23.63	24.33	25.07
P								23.28	23.95	24.67	25.42
RC	20.04	20.42	20.82	21.24	21.69	22.20	22.77	23.57	24.26	25.00	25.78

Schedule Two (P2)
Postal Service Schedule (PS)
Part-Time Regular Employees—Hourly Rates
Effective November 16, 2002

GRADES

STEPS	1	2	3	4	5	6	7	8	9	10	11
BB	11.47	11.99	12.51								
AA	11.92	12.44	12.95								
A	12.38	12.89	13.40	14.19	14.95	15.77	16.15				
B	12.83	13.33	13.84	14.60	15.35	16.14	16.53				
C	13.28	13.78	14.28	15.02	15.74	16.51	16.91				
D	13.73	14.23	14.72	15.43	16.13	16.89	17.30	18.95	19.40	19.86	20.36
E	14.18	14.67	15.16	15.85	16.53	17.26	17.68	19.24	19.70	20.19	20.70
F	14.63	15.12	15.61	16.27	16.92	17.63	18.06	19.52	20.00	20.51	21.04
G	15.08	15.56	16.05	16.68	17.31	18.00	18.45	19.81	20.30	20.83	21.38
H	15.53	16.01	16.49	17.10	17.71	18.37	18.83	20.09	20.60	21.15	21.72
I	15.98	16.46	16.93	17.51	18.10	18.74	19.21	20.38	20.91	21.47	22.06
J	16.43	16.90	17.37	17.93	18.49	19.11	19.59	20.67	21.21	21.79	22.40
K	16.88	17.35	17.81	18.35	18.89	19.48	19.98	20.95	21.51	22.11	22.74
L	17.34	17.79	18.26	18.76	19.28	19.85	20.36	21.24	21.81	22.43	23.08
M	17.79	18.24	18.70	19.18	19.67	20.23	20.74	21.52	22.12	22.76	23.42
N	18.24	18.69	19.14	19.59	20.07	20.60	21.12	21.81	22.42	23.08	23.76
O	18.82	19.19	19.58	20.01	20.46	20.97	21.51	22.10	22.72	23.40	24.10
P								22.38	23.02	23.72	24.45
RC	19.27	19.63	20.02	20.42	20.85	21.35	21.89	22.67	23.33	24.04	24.79

City Carriers' (CC) Schedule

Full-Time Annual Basic Rates
Effective November 16, 2002

CC							STEPS							
Grade A	B	C	D	E	F	G	H	I	J	K	L	M	N	O
1 33,217	36,544	37,834	40,306	40,646	40,988	41,324	41,665	42,005	42,341	42,683	43,022	43,362	43,704	44,042
2 34,918	38,455	38,536	41,067	41,436	41,804	42,167	42,534	42,903	43,261	43,631	43,999	44,363	44,736	45,101

Part-Time Regular Employees—Hourly Basic Rates
Effective November 16, 2002

CC							STEPS							
Grade A	B	C	D	E	F	G	H	I	J	K	L	M	N	O
1 16.28	17.91	18.55	19.76	19.92	20.09	20.26	20.42	20.59	20.76	20.92	21.09	21.26	21.42	21.59
2 17.12	18.85	18.89	20.13	20.31	20.49	20.67	20.85	21.03	21.21	21.39	21.57	21.75	21.93	22.11

Part-Time Flexible Employees—Hourly Basic Rates
Effective November 16, 2002

CC							STEPS							
Grade A	B	C	D	E	F	G	H	I	J	K	L	M	N	O
1 16.61	18.27	18.92	20.15	20.32	20.49	20.66	20.83	21.00	21.17	21.34	21.51	21.68	21.85	22.02
2 17.46	19.23	19.27	20.53	20.72	20.90	21.08	21.27	21.45	21.63	21.82	22.00	22.18	22.37	22.55

Mail Handlers' Schedule Effective November 16, 2002

Step	FULL-TIME ANNUAL RATES		PART-TIME EMPLOYEES REGULAR HOURLY RATE	PART-TIME EMPOYEES FLEXIBLE HOURLY RATE
	Grade 4	Grade 6	Grade 4	Grade 4
A	26,967	28,364	12.96	13.48
B	31,932	33,669	15.35	15.97
C	34,278	36,080	16.48	17.14
D	37,733	38,415	18.14	18.87
E	38,011	38,715	18.27	19.01
F	38,294	39,020	18.41	19.15
G	38,572	39,317	18.54	19.29
H	38,852	39,620	18.68	19.43
I	39,132	39,925	18.81	19.57
J	39,416	40,223	18.95	19.71
K	39,695	40,526	19.08	19.85
L	39,975	40,823	19.22	19.99
M	40,255	41,128	19.35	20.13
N	40,535	41,429	19.49	20.27
O	40,814	41,730	19.62	20.41

Postal Career Executive Service (PCES-I) Salary Structure

PCES-I	Authorized Minimum	Authorized Maximum
	$68,000	$135,800

Postal Career Executive Service (PCES-II) Salary Structure

PCES-II	Authorized Minimum	Authorized Maximum
Officers	$93,000	$161,200

This applies to Chief Executive Officer and Postmaster General; Deputy Postmaster General; Chief Operating Officer and Executive Vice President; Consumer Advocate; Chief Inspector; General Counsel; Judicial Officer; Chief Financial Officer, Finance and Planning Vice President; and all Vice Presidents.

Executive and Administrative Schedule (EAS)
Full-Time Annual Rates

Grade	Effective December 28, 2002			Effective December 27, 2003		
	Minimum	Mid-Point	Maximum	Minimum	Mid-Point	Maximum
A-E	10.81	13.02	15.22	11.31	13.52	15.72
1	20,875	23,693	26,511	20,875	23,693	26,511
2	21,559	24,470	27,380	21,559	24,470	27,380
3	22,269	25,275	28,281	22,269	25,275	28,281
4	23,167	26,295	29,422	23,167	26,295	29,422
5	23,939	27,171	30,402	23,939	27,171	30,402
6	24,802	28,150	31,498	24,802	28,150	31,498
7	25,818	29,304	32,789	25,818	29,304	32,789
8	26,853	30,478	34,103	26,853	30,478	34,103
9	27,902	31,669	35,435	27,902	31,669	35,435
10	28,931	32,837	36,742	28,931	32,837	36,742
11	30,340	36,478	42,615	30,492	37,193	43,893
12	31,796	38,229	44,661	31,955	38,978	46,001
13	33,280	40,012	46,744	33,446	40,796	48,146
14	35,017	42,101	49,185	35,192	42,927	50,661
15	36,935	44,407	51,878	37,120	45,277	53,434
16	38,246	47,783	57,320	38,437	48,882	59,326
17	39,942	49,902	59,86	40,142	51,049	61,956
18	41,697	52,094	62,491	41,905	53,292	64,678
19	43,673	54,563	65,452	43,891	55,817	67,743
20	46,042	57,523	69,003	46,272	58,845	71,418
21	48,279	60,317	72,355	48,520	61,704	74,887
22	51,149	64,407	77,664	51,405	66,088	80,771
23	53,937	67,917	81,897	54,207	69,690	85,173
24	56,606	71,278	85,950	56,889	73,139	89,388
25	59,422	74,824	90,225	59,719	76,777	93,834
26	62,386	78,556	94,725	62,698	80,606	98,514

Chapter 13
Legal Trends and Rulings
Section 1—U.S. Supreme Court Roundup

The U.S. Supreme Court decided on three significant private-sector cases in 2002 dealing with employment issues under the Americans with Disabilities Act (ADA) of 1990. The rulings in these cases could affect how similar situations are decided regarding federal employees.

Accommodating Workers

A case brought against an airline involved the issue of reasonable workplace accommodation juxtaposed with the seniority systems—and which one takes precedence when someone with a disability requests a job that is usually based on seniority. Robert Barnett worked for US Airways as a cargo handler when he injured his back in 1990. Because of the injury he transferred to a mailroom position that was less physically demanding. Two years after the transfer his position opened up to be filled on a seniority basis. Barnett learned that two employees senior to him were applying and requested that the airline allow him to remain in the position in order to accommodate his disability.

US Airways denied his request and Barnett lost his job. He filed suit claiming the airline had violated the ADA by discriminating against him and not accommodating his needs. Under the ADA, employers cannot discriminate against workers who can perform jobs if given "reasonable accommodation." The only way employers can be exempt from that requirement is if they can prove that it would impose undue hardship on the operation. In this case US Airways argued that altering its seniority system would constitute an undue hardship to the airline and its non-disabled employees.

A district court ruled in favor of US Airways but Barnett appealed and the U.S. 9th Circuit Court of Appeals reversed the lower court's decision, saying each case must be analyzed individually to determine whether seniority or disability should prevail. Because the courts reached different conclusions, the U.S. Supreme Court agreed to address the legal significance of a seniority system. The high court rejected both the US Airways position that any accommodation that infringed on a seniority system was not reasonable and Barnett's contention that a seniority system would never justify denying a disabled person reasonable accommodation.

"A demand for . . . accommodation could prove unreasonable because of its impact . . . on fellow employees—say because it will lead to dismissals, relocations or modification of employee benefits," said the high court. An accommodation is usually not reasonable if it conflicts with seniority rules, the court added. Employers are not required to prove that seniority should take precedence over making accommodations for disabled employees every time the issue comes up.

The Supreme Court ruled that even though seniority systems generally take precedence, the plaintiff is free to prove special circumstances to justify accommodation (for example, if the employer frequently changes the seniority system and already makes so many exceptions that one more would not matter). (Barnett v. US Airways, Supreme Court, No. 00-1250, 4/29/02)

Defining Disability

A district court and an appellate court differed on whether Ella Williams had a defined disability. This case came to the Supreme Court to clarify how a disability in performing manual tasks is determined. Williams began working for Toyota on an automobile assembly line in 1990 and shortly thereafter developed carpel tunnel syndrome and tendonitis. Her doctor placed her on work restrictions and she worked on modified jobs for several years. She wished for more accommodations in her work restrictions and eventually was placed on a Quality Control Inspections Operation team.

Williams worked in two areas that

required virtually no manual work. She had no problems until Toyota said all members of the inspections teams would be required to perform four specific tasks, one of which was physical and caused her more pain and physical impairments such as tendon inflammation and nerve compression. Williams asked if she could perform only the two tasks she had been doing but Toyota did not change her responsibilities and she missed many days of work.

By her last day of work, she was on no-work-of-any-kind restrictions. The following month Williams received a letter stating she was being terminated for poor attendance. She filed suit against Toyota with the U.S. District Court for the Eastern District of Kentucky, claiming she was disabled and Toyota had violated the ADA by not giving her reasonable accommodation.

The District Court rejected her claims, saying she did not have a disability as defined by the ADA because she had no impairment that "substantially limited" any "major life activity," such as walking, seeing and hearing. When the court granted Toyota summary judgment, Williams appealed to U.S. 6th Circuit Court of Appeals, which reversed the District Court's decision, finding that Williams was indeed disabled because her ability to perform manual tasks associated with the assembly line job was very limited. She could not perform jobs that required gripping tools or repetitive work with her hands or arms extended at or above shoulder level for extended periods.

Toyota asked that the Supreme Court determine standards for whether an individual has a manual task disability. Williams had sought a ruling that if an employee who can do some aspects can still be categorized as disabled and entitled to accommodation. The high court said that by not examining her limitations closely enough, according to the ADA's definition of disability, the appellate court erred in determining Williams was disabled. It failed to evaluate whether she was incapable of "tasks that are of central importance to most people's daily lives," such as bathing, brushing teeth and doing chores, which is the standard for disability under the Act. The appeals court instead focused on tasks associated with her job.

Since repetitive work with her hands and arms extended at shoulder level are not important to most people's daily lives, Williams' inability to do such work did not qualify her as disabled. The high court found she did not have a disability based on the ADA definition. (*Williams v. Toyota, Supreme Court, No. 00-1089, 1/8/02*)

Potential Hiring Risks

When Chevron declined to hire Mario Echazabal, the Supreme Court agreed to decide whether an Equal Employment Opportunity Commission (EEOC) regulation is valid justification for this action under the ADA. Chevron cited the EEOC regulation as a defense, stating that Echazabal's disability would pose a threat to his own health on the job. Echazabal argued that the EEOC regulation was not lawful, thus Chevron's refusal to hire him because of his disability was illegal.

Echazabal worked for a contractor at one of Chevron's oil refineries and applied twice for a job. Both times Chevron made offers with the stipulation that he must pass the company's physical fitness examination. The exam revealed liver damage or an abnormality, and the job offers were withdrawn because Chevron's doctors said the toxins at the refinery would worsen Echazabal's liver condition.

Following the second time that liver problems showed up, Chevron asked the contractor who employed Echazabal to reassign him where he would not be exposed to harmful chemicals or to remove him from the refinery. The contractor then fired him. Echazabal filed a suit claiming that Chevron violated the ADA by refusing to hire him or allow him to continue working based on his disability.

In its defense, Chevron used the EEOC regulation that states that an employer can refuse to hire someone if hiring him/her would cause a safety or health threat. Chevron found the regulation reasonable because employers forced to hire people at risk could be subject to litigation under law and loss of time for sick leave, and could be liable for violating the Occupational Safety and Health Act (OSHA), which requires that every worker has safe and healthy working conditions.

The District Court granted Chevron

summary judgment against Echazabal but on appeal the U.S. 9th Circuit Court reversed the lower court's decision saying that the EEOC regulation was not permissible under the ADA. The law includes some instances in which employers may deny disabled persons advancement, but only if employers can meet qualification standards that are "job-related…and…consistent with business necessity." The ADA says that employers cannot hire someone who would pose a threat to the health or safety of co-workers. The EEOC regulation extends this defense by saying employers can refuse to hire someone with a disability that would jeopardize his or her health or

safety on the job.

Echazabal argued that the ADA does not mention threats to the disabled person— only to others—and the EEOC regulation is not lawful under it. The Supreme Court found that the "threat to others" mentioned in the ADA is only one example of a justifiable reason for not hiring someone with a disability. The threat-to-self reasoning falls within general "job related" and "business necessity" standards. The high court reversed the 9th Circuit's decision, finding the EEOC regulation is lawful. *(Echazabal v. Chevron, Supreme Court, No. 00-1406, 6/10/02)*

Section 2—Lower Court Cases

Special Back Pay Suit

After nearly 20 years, a class-action suit was finally settled in 2002 brought on behalf of all federal employees who received special pay rates but were denied annual pay adjustments between 1982 and 1988. The 212,000 affected employees or their heirs will learn during 2003 how to claim the money they are owed. In November 2002, the U.S. Court of Federal Claims conducted a fairness hearing on the proposed settlement, whereby the government would pay $173.5 million to those individuals represented in the class.

The National Treasury Employees Union (NTEU) initiated the suit in 1983 after the Office of Personnel Management (OPM) instituted a regulation the previous year that denied employees who received special rates from also getting annual pay adjustments—and therefore denied them increases. In 1987, the U.S. District Court for the District of Columbia found the regulation illegal and since then NTEU and OPM had debated the details of awarding the appropriate back pay. *(NTEU v. U.S., No. 02-128)*

Reductions In Force

The Federal Service Impasses Panel (FSIP) found that the Defense Commissary

Agency was not obliged to move senior employees in order to save them from losing their jobs during a reduction in force (RIF). When the union representing the commissary employees learned of upcoming RIFs in three commissaries, it proposed to move the least senior employees to the location that would suffer the biggest RIF and the most senior to the commissary that would suffer the least. The FSIP found in favor of the Defense Department agency and agreed that too much time and work would have to go in to shuffling workers between locations to justify protecting a few senior employees.

Discrimination In Promotions

NASA's Goddard Space Flight Center agreed to pay black employees to settle a class-action suit outside of court. In this case, 120 black scientist and engineers at the Wallops Island Flight Center in Virginia claimed they were denied promotions to GS-14 and 15 positions from 1991 to 2002. NASA agreed to pay them $3.75 million, hire an independent firm to revise the promotion system and monitor statistics to ensure there is no further disparity between black and white scientists and engineers in those job levels.

Denial Of Career Advancement

In a similar case, African-American male employees of the Social Security Administration (SSA) filed a complaint with the Equal Employment Opportunity Commission (EEOC) alleging they, as class of 2,200 people, had been denied career opportunities since 1987. Specifically they claimed they had not been promoted and had been treated unfairly regarding performance appraisals, awards and bonuses and disciplinary actions. The SSA settled without going to court and agreed to pay $7.75 million to black male employees making the claim, but admitted no guilt. The EEOC believes this case could set a precedent for resolving discrimination cases outside of court. *(Burden et al. v. SSA, EEOC Case Nos. 120-99-6378X, 6379X, 6380X)*

Whistleblower Protection

The issues of whistleblower protection came up in several forms last year, especially in light of the terrorist attacks of Sept. 11, 2001. Federal employees alleged that their agencies could have acted differently to thwart the attacks.

James P. Hopkins of the Federal Aviation Administration (FAA) alerted the FAA of a possible link between one of the Sept. 11 hijackers and someone who trained at the FAA Academy. He was subsequently fired and the Office of Special Counsel (OSC) investigated and reported that the FAA appeared to violate the Whistleblower Protection Act by terminating him.

Hopkins read a news article after the attacks and learned that two of the hijackers had gone through U.S. flight training. He searched for their names and nationalities in the FAA International Training Program database and found a match for one of the hijackers mentioned in the news article.

When his supervisor refused to give him permission to share the information with the FAA, he did so anyway and later contacted FBI investigators as well. After the investigation into his termination, the OSC asked the FAA to reinstate Hopkins, which the FAA originally refused to do. Hopkins received reassignment to a position at the same grade and pay as the one he previously held. He also received full relief, including back pay, benefits and attorney fees.

In another case, the OSC found the Immigration and Naturalization Service (INS) violated the Whistleblower Protection Act when it proposed to suspend and demote two Border Patrol agents in Michigan for talking to the media about security lapses on U.S. borders. Both had reported that only 324 agents served the entire U.S.-Canadian border, 28 agents were assigned to protect 804 miles of waterway and shoreline, and the equipment was sparse and in bad condition.

Border Patrol officials felt the agents had been disloyal and suspended them for 90 days and demoted them for one year. However, the OSC ordered the INS to grant them full back pay and cancel their suspensions and demotions.

Refusing Anthrax Vaccine

Two civilian employees of the Navy Department were dismissed for refusing to take anthrax vaccine. They were given the order because the ship on which they worked was bound for Korea, which was considered a high-risk area. A judge denied their appeal that the vaccine order was unauthorized and the penalty of being fired was excessive. Both claimed they had medical waivers to excuse them, but the Navy did not find they were entitled to an exemption. A judge found that because the employees violated a legal order, the Navy had the right to terminate them. *(Mazares and Testman v. Dept. of Navy, U.S. Ct. of Appeals for Fed. Cir., Nos. 01-3337, 3338, 9/11/02)*

Section 3—Legislation

Homeland Security Bill

With the creation of the new Transportation Security Administration (TSA) in 2002, there was debate over whistleblower protection for new TSA employees from retaliation if they reported any crime, fraud, waste, mismanagement or abuse. Originally they had limited protection rights.

Ultimately, TSA employees gained full protection under the Whistleblower Protection Act in the bill the President signed in November to create the Department of Homeland Security (H.R. 5005).

After a year of input from the administration, agencies, unions and management experts, Sen. Geroge Voinovich, R-Ohio, authored legislation to reform workforce policies in preparation of agency needs that will result from the wave of federal employee retirements coming in the near future. He pushed hiring, training, incentive payment and other personnel management reforms in the new homeland security act.

Under the new homeland bill, the federal hiring system will be changed from "rule of three" to "category ranking," allowing managers to make hiring selections from a larger number of candidates than a list of three.

New legislation for workforce restructuring: The homeland bill includes a provision that creates a permanent government-wide authority to offer voluntary separation incentive payments (buyouts) of up to $25,000 and there is also a government-wide voluntary early retirement authority.

The new bill instructs most agencies to create a Chief Human Capital Officer to align agencies' personnel policies with their strategic goals and to set development strategies for the workforce.

Under the new bill the president can exempt employees from collective bargaining rights for national security reasons. Federal employee unions can appeal new personnel rules, but can not ultimately block them as the president has the final word.

No FEAR Act

President Bush signed the Notification and Federal Employee Anti-discrimination and Retaliation Act (No FEAR) into law in May 2002. The Act's purpose is to make federal agencies more accountable for discrimination violations and enforcing whistleblower protection laws. In addition, agencies that lose discrimination and whistleblower cases are now required to reimburse those pay-

ments that go to employees for claims, final judgments, awards or settlements. Previously, a Justice Department fund paid those costs instead of the agency itself. Agencies too must provide employees with written notification of their rights and protections, which is to be posted on agencies' Web sites along with the number of EEO complaints filed.

Within 180 days of the end of each fiscal year, agencies must submit reports that include the status of cases, the amount of money paid, the number of employees disciplined for discrimination, retaliation or harassment, descriptions of disciplinary policies and any actions planned or taken to improve complaint or civil rights programs.

Congress anticipates that by notifying employees of their rights in this regard, more agencies will comply with the law. By requiring annual reports of the numbers of discrimination and whistleblower cases brought against each agency, Congress expects to improve its oversight of agencies.

Dismissal For Late Filings

IRS employees can still be fired for late filing of their federal income tax returns. The IRS Restructuring and Reform Act of 1998 lists offenses for which IRS employees can be dismissed at once (known as the 10 Deadly Sins), including filing their own taxes late, even if they are due a refund. There was pressure during the year to persuade Congress to alter the law's list of offenses. In March 2002, the House Ways and Means Committee moved to bar late filings from the list of offenses for IRS employees.

The National Treasury Employees Union (NTEU) and Bush administration supported the change in law, contending the change would improve morale at the agency. However, the House failed to pass the Taxpayer Protection and IRS Accountability Act of 2002, which would have modified the 1998 law and reduced penalties for several of the offenses, including late filing.

Chapter 14
Resources and References

Section 1—U.S. Office of
Personnel Management (OPM)

Phone Numbers and E-mail

For general information, OPM's phone number is (202) 606-1800. (202 is the area code for all numbers below unless otherwise noted.) Send inquiries, via e-mail, to question@opm.gov unless a different address is listed.

Adoption *(workandfamily@opm.gov)*	606-1166
Alcohol and Drug Abuse	606-2920
Appeals: *(fedclass_appeals@opm.gov)*	
Adverse Actions	606-2920
Classification of Position	606-2990
Grade and Pay Retention	606-2858
Disability Retirement	606-0555
Regular Retirement	606-0299
Awards Program	606-2720
Buyouts *(eswebmaster@opm.gov)*	606-0960
Classification of Position:	
Policy (GS/GM and FWS only)	606-2950
Senior Executive Service *(ses@opm.gov)*	606-2246
Combined Federal Campaign *(cfc@opm.gov)*	606-2564
Communications	606-1800
Dual Compensation Waivers:	
GS/GM-15 and below	606-0830
Above GS/GM-15	606-2246
Early Retirement	606-0960
Employee Assistance Programs	606-1269
Employment Services	606-0900
Examining and Applications Information	606-2700
Excepted Positions (General Information, Schedules A, B, and C of the Civil Service Rules at GS-15 and below)	606-0830
Fair Labor Standards Act (FLSA):	
Hours of work and pay computations	606-2858
Coverage and Compliance	606-2290
Fare Subsidy Program (Public Transit Subsidies)	606-2220
Federal Prevailing Rate Advisory Committee	606-1500
Flexiplace	606-0830
Flexitime	606-2858
Furloughs	606-2920
Grievances:	
Administrative Grievance Procedures	606-2920
Negotiated Grievance Procedures	606-2930
Holidays	606-2858
Incentive Awards Program	606-2720
Insurance, Health: *(fehb@opm.gov)*	
Retirees/Survivors	1-888-767-6738
Insurance, Life: *(fegli@opm.gov)*	
Retirees/Survivors	1-888-767-6738

Veterans:

Section 2—General Government Information

Top Government Officials

Executive Branch

President: George. W. Bush
Vice President: Richard B. Cheney
Secretary of State: Colin L. Powell
Secretary of Treasury: John Snow (nominee)
Secretary of Defense: Donald H. Rumsfeld
Secretary of Army: Thomas E. White
Secretary of Navy: Gordon R. England
Secretary of Air Force: Dr. James G. Roche
Attorney General: John Ashcroft
Secretary of Interior: Gail A. Norton
Secretary of Commerce: Donald Evans
Secretary of Energy: Spencer Abraham
Secretary of Labor: Elaine L. Chao
Secretary of Agriculture: Ann M. Veneman
Secretary of Health and Human Services:
Tommy G. Thompson
Secretary of Education: Rod Paige
Secretary of Transportation:
Norman Y. Mineta
**Secretary of Housing and Urban
Development:** Mel Martinez
Secretary of Veterans Affairs:
Anthony Principi
Postmaster General: John E. Potter
**Director, Office of Management and
Budget:** Mitchell E. Daniels, Jr.
**Director, Office of Personnel
Management:** Kay Cole James
Director, Central Intelligence Agency:
George Tenet
**Chairman of the Board of Governors for
the Federal Reserve:**
Alan Greenspan
**Commissioner, Social Security
Administration:** JoAnne Barnhart
**Administrator, General Services
Administration:** Stephen A. Perry
Representative to the United Nations:

John Negroponte
**Administrator, Environmental Protection
Agency:** Christine Todd Whitman
**Comptroller General, General
Accounting Office:** David M. Walker
Office of Homeland Security: Tom Ridge
President's Chief of Staff:
Andrew H. Card, Jr.
National Security Advisor:
Condoleezza Rice

The Congress

Senate Majority Leader:
Sen. Bill Frist, R-TN
Asst. Senate Majority Leader and Whip:
Sen. Mitch McConnell, R-KY
Senate Minority Leader:
Sen. Tom Daschle, D-SD
Asst. Senate Minority Leader and Whip:
Sen. Harry Reid, D-NV
Speaker of the House:
Dennis J. Hastert, R-IL
House Majority Leader:
Rep. Tom DeLay, R-TX
House Minority Leader:
Rep. Nancy Pelosi, D-CA

Congressional Committees

The House Government Reform and Oversight Committee and the Senate Governmental Affairs Committee are the key committees in Congress as far as federal and postal employee legislation is concerned. The House and Senate Appropriations and Budget Committees are also important to government workers since they control the purse strings of the various governmental departments and agencies and hence the number of civilian jobs as well as promotion opportunities and other employment factors dependent on the amount of money that an agency gets each year from Congress.

The Senate Finance Committee and the House Ways and Means Committee are vital for government workers because they handle all Social Security legislation.

Members of Congress and Congressional Committees may be addressed at The Capitol, Washington, DC. The House ZIP code is 20515. The Senate ZIP code is 20510. The phone number for Congress is (202) 224-3121.

House Committee on Government Reform: Rm. 2157, Rayburn House Office Building, phone: (202) 225-5074; *www.house.gov/reform*

House Civil Service Subcommittee (of the House Committee on Government Reform): Rm. B371C, Rayburn House Office Building, phone: (202) 225-6427

Senate Governmental Affairs Committee: Rm. 340, Dirksen Senate Office Building, phone: (202) 224-2627; *www.senate.gov/~gov_affairs*

Senate Budget Committee: Rm. 624, Dirksen Office Building, phone: (202) 224-0642; *budget.senate.gov*

House Budget Committee: Rm. 309, Cannon House Office Building, phone: (202) 226-7270; *www.budget.house.gov*

Senate Finance Committee: Rm. 219, Dirksen Office Building, phone: (202) 224-4515; *finance.senate.gov*

House Ways and Means Committee: Rm. 1102, Longworth House Office Building, phone: (202) 225-3625; *waysandmeans.house.gov*

Senate Appropriations Committee: Rm. S-128, The Capitol Building, phone: (202) 224-3471; *appropriations.senate.gov*

House Appropriations Committee: Rm. H-218, The Capitol Building, phone (202) 225-2771; *www.house.gov/appropriations*

Legislative Information

Legislative Status Office: Information on status of legislation in either House or Senate, whether committee hearings have been held, the numbers of committee reports, etc. (202) 225-1772.

Senate Document Room: Information on availability and copies of bills, reports, and public laws from the Senate can be obtained by calling (202) 224-7701, by faxing (202) 228-2815, or by writing to the Senate Document Rm., B-04 Hart Bldg., Washington, DC 20510.

House Legislative Resource Center: Information on availability and copies of bills, reports, and public laws from the House can be obtained by calling (202) 226-5200 or by writing the House Legislative Research Center, B-106, Cannon Building, Washington, DC 20515.

White House Executive Clerk's Office: Information on when a bill was signed or vetoed: (202) 456-2226.

The office of any member of Congress, Committee, and Subcommittee may be reached by calling (202) 224-3121.

Legislative information and bill status is also available on the Library of Congress' website at *www.loc.gov*.

How to Get General Accounting Office Reports

The General Accounting Office, the investigative and auditing branch of the Congress, issues numerous reports on government personnel policies and practices, employee benefits and entitlements, etc. We cover highlights of these in our weekly Federal Employees News Digest.

GAO reports are available on the agency's website at www.gao.gov. You can also request written copies of GAO materials by mailing your request to: U.S. General Accounting Office, 441 G Street NW, Room LM, Washington, DC 20548. You also can call GAO at (202) 512-6000, or Fax: (202) 512-6061.

The first copy of individual reports is free of charge. Additional copies of bound audit reports are $2.00 each. Additional copies of unbound reports (i.e., letter reports) and most other publications are $2.00 each. Sales orders must be prepaid on a cash, check, or money-order basis.

Checks or money orders should be made out to the "Superintendent of Documents." Visa, MasterCard, Discover and American Express also are accepted.

How to Get the
Federal Register

The *Federal Register*, published on business days by the Government Printing Office, contains proposed and final rules from agencies, notices of meetings of government boards and commissions, executive orders, proclamations, and other presidential documents. An index is published monthly and is cumulated for 12 months. Also, a "unified agenda" is published in March and October of the rules each agency is rewriting or expects to review in the following six months.

The *Federal Register* is available free on the Government Printing Office's website at *www.gpo.gov*. Print subscriptions are available for $764 for one year. Single copies are $10. Call (202) 512-1800 for current prices and availability.

Subscriptions are available from the Superintendent of Documents, PO Box 371954, Pittsburgh, PA 15250-7954. Single issues can be ordered from that address, or call (202) 512-1800. Payment by check, money order, GPO deposit account, Visa, MasterCard, Discover and American Express is accepted.

How to Get the
Congressional Record

The *Congressional Record*, the journal of the public proceedings of the House and Senate, is published daily by the Government Printing Office when one or both houses are in session. It contains speeches and debates made on the floor of each chamber, bills introduced and passed, committee actions, hearing schedules, communications from the White House to Capitol Hill and extraneous material inserted by members of Congress. The Record does not contain transcripts of hearings; those are published by individual committees.

The *Congressional Record* is available free on the Government Printing Office's website at *www.gpo.gov*. A one-year print subscription is available from the Superintendent of Documents, PO Box 371954, Pittsburgh, PA 15250-7954 for $393. Call (202) 512-1800 for current prices and availability. Single issues are $4 each and can be ordered from that address, or call (202) 512-1800. Payment by check, money order, GPO deposit account, credit cards accepted.

How to Get MSPB, EEOC, FLRA, and FSIP Decisions

Federal employees can obtain individual copies of rulings on employment disputes by contacting the deciding agencies and providing the case title and number. The decisions generally are provided free of charge by the agencies unless a large number of copies is being requested. The agencies do not provide copies of court rulings on their decisions, however. Those must be obtained from the individual courts.

Final decisions of the Merit Systems Protection Board or its regional hearing officials can be obtained from MSPB's Office of the Clerk, 1615 M St., N.W., Washington, DC 20419, phone: (202) 653-7200. Copies of MSPB reports can be obtained from the Office of Policy and Evaluation, same address as above, phone: (202) 653-8900.

For decisions of the Federal Labor Relations Authority and the Federal Service Impasses Panel, an arm of FLRA, contact FLRA's Office of Information Resources and Research Services, 607 14th St., N.W., Washington, DC 20424, phone: (202) 482-6550 (FLRA) or (202) 482-6670 (FSIP).

For a copy of an EEOC decision contact Personnet at 1-800-320-4555 or visit Personnet's website at *www.personnet. com*.

The Federal Information Center Program

The Federal Information Center program (FIC) is a one-stop source of help for questions or problems related to the government.

Questions routinely concern veterans' benefits, Social Security, immigration and naturalization, patents, copyrights, tax assistance, wage-and-hour laws, Medicare, and federal job information. The FIC also answers many other types of questions concerning the laws and regulations affecting all American citizens.

The FIC is managed by the General Services Administration and was created to reduce the countless phone calls to government offices, with the inevitable transfers and referrals that are expensive, time-consuming, and frustrating.

Call 1-800-688-9889, a toll-free number for most major metropolitan areas.

Users of text telephones (TTY/TDD) may reach the FIC toll-free from anywhere in the United States by dialing 1-800-326-2996.

Section 3—Union, Trade, and Professional Groups

Federal Employee Unions

American Federation of Government Employees. AFL-CIO. 80 F St., N.W., Washington, DC 20001. Bobby L. Harnage, Sr., Nat. Pres. Phone: (202) 737-8700. Fax: (202) 639-6442. *www.afge.org*

National Air Traffic Controllers Association. AFL-CIO. 1325 Massachusetts Ave., N.W., Washington, DC 20005. John Carr, Pres. Phone: (202) 628-5451. Fax: (202) 628-5767. *www.natca.org*

National Association of Government Employees. 159 Burgin Parkway, Quincy, MA 02169. David Holway, Pres. Phone: (617) 376-0220. Fax: (617) 984-5695. *www.nage.org*

National Federation of Federal Employees. IAMAW. 1016 16th St., N.W., Washington, DC 20036. Richard N. Brown, Pres. Phone: (202) 862-4471. Fax: (202) 862-4432. *www.nffe.org*

National Treasury Employees Union. 901 E St., N.W., Suite 600, Washington, DC 20004. Colleen Kelley, Nat. Pres.; Frank Ferris, Nat. Exec. Vice Pres. Phone: (202) 783-4444. Fax: (202) 783-4085. *www.nteu.org*

National Weather Service Employees Organization. 601 Pennsylvania Ave. Suite 900, Washington D.C. 20004. Phone: (703) 293-9651. Fax: (703) 293-9653. *www.nwseo.org*

Professional Airways Systems Specialists. AFL-CIO. 1150 17th st., Suite 702, Washington, DC 20036. Michael D. Fanfalone, Pres. Phone: (202) 293-7277. Fax: (202) 293-7727. *www.pass-national.org*

Postal Employee Unions and Professional Groups

American Postal Workers Union. AFL-CIO. 1300 L St., N.W., Washington D.C. 20005. William Burrus, Pres.; Cliff Guffey, Vice-pres.; Robert Tunstall, Sec. Treas.; Roy Braunstein, Legis. Dir.; Greg Bell, Dir. of Industrial Relations; Frank A. Romero, Dir. of Org.; Jim McCarthy, Clerk Director; Steven G. Raymer, Maintenance Director; Robert Pritchard, MVS Director. Phone: (202) 842-4200. Fax: (202) 842-4297. *www.apwu.org*

National Alliance of Postal and Federal Employees. 1628 11th St., N.W., Washington, DC 20001. James McGee, Pres.; Wilbur L. Duncan, Sec. Phone: (202) 939-6325. Fax: (202) 939-6389. E-mail: *napfe@patriot.net* *www.napfe.com*

National Association of Letter Carriers. AFL-CIO. 100 Indiana Ave., N.W., Washington, DC 20001. William H. Young, Jr., Pres.; Jim Williams, Exec. Vice-Pres.; Jane Broendel, Sec.-Treas. Phone: (202) 393-4695. Fax: (202) 737-1540. *www.nalc.org*

National Association of Postal Supervisors. 1727 King St., Suite 400, Alexandria, VA 22314-2753. Vince Palladino, Pres.; Ted Keating, Exec. Vice-pres.; Louis M. Atkins, Sec.-Treas. Phone: (703) 836-9660. Fax: (703) 836-9665. *www.naps.org*

National Association of Postmasters. 8 Herbert St., Alexandria, VA 22305-2600. Walter Olihovik, Nat. Pres.; Charles Moser, Exec. Dir. Phone: (703) 683-9027. Fax: (703) 683-6820. *www.napus.org*

National Postal Mail Handlers Union. AFL-CIO. 1101 Connecticut Ave., Suite 500, Washington, DC 20036. John F. Hegarty, Pres.; Mark Gardner, Sec./Treas. Phone: (202) 833-9095. Fax: (202) 833-0008. *www.npmhu.org*

National League of Postmasters. 1023 North Royal St., Alexandria, VA 22314-1569. Steve D. LeNoir, Pres. Phone: (703) 548-5922. Fax: (703) 836-8937. *www.postmasters.org*

National Rural Letter Carriers' Association. 1630 Duke St., 4th Floor, Alexandria, VA 22314-3465. Gus Baffa, Pres.; Dale A. Holton, Vice Pres. Phone: (703) 684-5545. Fax: (703) 548-8735. *www.nrlca.org*

Skilled Trade, Professional, Retirement, and Miscellaneous Groups

AFL-CIO Metal Trades Department. 888 16th St., N.W., Suite 690, Washington,

DC 20006. Ron Ault, Pres. Phone: (202) 974-8030. Fax: (202) 974-8035. *www.metaltrades.org*

Air Traffic Control Association. Inc. 2300 Clarendon Boulevard, Suite 711, Arlington, VA 22201. Gabriel A. Hartl, Pres.; Carol Newmaster, Sr. V-Pres. Phone: (703) 522-5717. Fax: (703) 527-7251. *www.atca.org*

Alliance of Government Managers. 5098 Foothills Blvd., Suite 3-254, Roseville, CA 95747-6526. John M. Ellis, Pres.; John Bartoli, Exec. Dir. Phone: (916) 788-1513. Fax: (916) 788-1513. *canvex@jps.net*

American Federation of State, County, and Municipal Employees. 1625 L St., N.W., Washington, DC 20036. Gerald W. McEntee, Pres.; William Lucy, Sec-Treas. Phone: (202) 429-1000. Fax: (202) 429-1293. *www.afscme.org*

American Federation of Teachers, AFL-CIO. 555 New Jersey Ave., N.W., Washington, D. C. 20001. Sandra Feldman, Pres.; Nat LaCour, Exec. Vice-pres.; Edward J. McElroy, Sec.-Treas.; Ron Krouse, Chief of Staff. Phone: (202) 879-4415. Fax: (202) 393-7479. *www.aft.org*

American Foreign Service Association. 2101 E. St., N.W., Washington, DC 20037. John Naland, Pres. Phone: (202) 338-4045. Fax: (202) 338-6820. *www.afsa.org*

American Nurses Association. 600 Maryland Ave., S.W., #100W, Washington, DC 20024-2571. Linda Stierle, Exec. Dir. Phone: 800-274-4262. Fax: (202) 651-7001. *www.nursingworld.org*

American Society for Public Administration. Mary R. Hamilton, Ph.D., Exec. Dir., Suite 700, 1120 G St., N.W., Washington, DC 20005-3885. Phone: (202) 393-7878. Fax: (202) 638-4952. *www.aspanet.org*

Association of Civilian Technicians. 12510-B Lake Ridge Dr., Lake Ridge, VA 22192. Thomas G. Bastas, Pres./CEO. Phone: (703) 494-4845. Fax: (703) 494-0961. *www.actnat.com*

Association of Government Accountants. 2208 Mount Vernon Ave., Alexandria, VA 22301. Charles W. Culkin, Exec. Dir. Phone: (703) 684-6931. Fax: (703)

548-9367. *www.agacgfm.org*

Blacks in Government. 1820 11th St., N.W., Washington, DC 20001-5015. Gregg Reeves, Nat. Pres. Phone: (202) 667-3280. Fax: (202) 667-3705. *www.bignet.org*

The Federal Bar Association. 2215 M St., N.W., Washington, DC 20037. Kent Hofmeister, Pres.; Jack Lockridge, Exec. Dir. Phone: (202) 785-1614. Fax: (202) 785-1568. *www.fedbar.org*

Federal Bureau of Investigation Agents Association. P.O. Box 250, New Rochelle, NY 10801. Nancy L. Savage, Pres.; Frederick Bragg, Vice-pres. Phone: (914) 235-7580. *www.fbiaa.org*

Federal Criminal Investigators Association. P.O. Box 23400, Washington, DC 20026-3400. James Grimes, Natl. Pres. Phone: (800) 961-7753. Fax: (703) 426-8400. *www.fedcia.org*

Federal Education Association. 1201 16th St., N.W., Suite 117, Washington, DC 20036. Sheridan Pearce, Pres. Phone: (202) 822-7850. Fax: (202) 822-7867. *www.feaonline.org*

Federal Law Enforcement Officers Association. P.O. Box 326, Lewisberry, PA 17339. Richard Gallo, Nat. Pres. Phone: (717) 938-2300. Fax: (717 932-2262. *www.fleoa.org*

Federal Managers Association. 1641 Prince St., Alexandria, VA 22314, Michael B. Styles, Nat. Pres. Phone: (703) 683-8700. Fax: (703) 683-8707. *www.fedmanagers.org*

Federal Physicians Association. 9001 Braddock Rd., #380, Springfield, VA 22151, Dennis W. Boyd, Exec. Dir. Phone: (703) 323-9888. Fax: 800-528-3492. *www.fedphy.org*

Federally Employed Women. 1666 K Street, N.W., Suite 440, Washington, DC 20006. Patricia M. Wolf, Pres. Phone: (202) 898-0994. Fax: (240) 266-3232. *www.few.org*

Forum of United States Administrative Law Judges. P.O. Box 14076, Washington, DC 20044-4076. Charles Bullock, Pres. Phone: (202) 205-3320. Fax: (202) 205-1852.

Government Accountability Project. 1511 Third Ave., Suite 321, Seattle, WA 98101. Phone: (206) 292-2850 or in

Washington, D.C. (202) 408-0034. Fax: (206) 292-0610. *www.whistle-blower.org*

Graphic Communications International Union. 1900 L St., N.W., Washington, DC 20036. George Tedeschi, Pres. Phone: (202) 462-1400. Fax: (202) 721-0600. *www.gciu.org*

International Association of Fire Fighters. 1750 New York Ave., N.W., Washington, DC 20006. Harold A. Schaitberger, General Pres.; Vincent J. Bollon, General Sec-Treas. Phone: (202) 737-8484. Fax: (202) 737-8418. *www.iaff.org*

International Association of Machinists and Aerospace Workers. 9000 Machinists Place, Upper Marlboro, MD 20772-2687. R. Thomas Buffenbarger, Nat. Pres. Phone: (301) 967-4500. Fax: (301) 967-4586. Internet: *www.iamaw.org*

International Brotherhood of Boilermakers, Iron Ship Builders, Blacksmiths, Forgers and Helpers. 753 State Ave., Kansas City, KS 66101. Charles W. Jones, Int. Pres. Phone: (913) 371-2640. Fax: (913) 281-8105. *www.boilermakers.org*

International Brotherhood of Electrical Workers. 1125 15th St., N.W., Washington, DC 20005. Phone: (202) 833-7000. Fax: (202) 467-6316. *www.ibew.org*

International Brotherhood of Teamsters. 25 Louisiana Ave., N.W., Washington, D.C, 20001. James P. Hoffa, General Pres. Phone: (202) 624-6800. Fax: (202) 624-6918. *www.teamsters.org*

International Federation of Professional and Technical Engineers. 8630 Fenton St., Suite 400, Silver Spring, MD 20910. Gregory J. Junemann, Pres. Phone: (301) 565-9016. Fax: (301) 565-0018. *www.ifpte.org*

International Personnel Management Association. 1617 Duke St., Alexandria, VA. 22314. Neil Reichenberg, Exec. Dir. Phone: (703) 549-7100. Fax: (703) 684-0948. *www.ipma-hr.org*

International Union of Operating Engineers. 1125 17th St., N.W., Washington, DC 20036. Frank Hanley, Gen. Pres. Phone: (202) 429-9100.

Fax: (202) 778-2688. *www.iuoe.org*

Marine Engineers' Beneficial Association, AFL-CIO. 444 North Capitol St., N.W., Suite 800, Washington, DC 20001. Ron Davis, Natl. Pres. Phone: (202) 638-5355. Fax (202) 638-5369. *www.d1meba.org*

National Association of Air Traffic Specialists. 11303 Amherst Ave., Suite 4, Wheaton, MD 20902. Walter W. Pike, Pres. Phone: (301) 933-6228. Fax: (301) 933-3902. *www.naats.org*

National Association of Federal Injured Workers. 2701 Coed Place, Grants Pass, OR 97527. Wil Clow, Exec. Dir. Phone: (541) 472-8940 Fax: (541) 472-9101. *la.znet.com/~bluegoose/nafiw.htm*

National Association of Federal Veterinarians. 1101 Vermont Ave., N.W., Suite 710, Washington, DC 20005. Dr. Joe O. Yearous, Pres.; Dr. Dale D. Boyle, Exec. Vice Pres. Phone: (202) 289-6334. Fax: (202) 842-4360. *www.erols.com/nafv*

National Association of Immigration Judges. 550 Kearny Street, Suite 800, San Francisco, CA 94108. Hon. Dana Marks Keener, Pres. Phone: (415) 705-4415, ext. 262. Fax: (415) 705-4418. E-mail: *Dana.Keener@usdoj.gov*

National Association of Retired Federal Employees. 606 N. Washington St., Alexandria, VA 22314-1943. Charles Fallis, Pres. Phone: (703) 838-7760. Fax: (703) 838-7785. *www.narfe.org.*

National Conference of Shomrim Societies, Inc. 45 E. 33rd St., Suite 601, New York, NY 10016. Phone: (212) 689-2015. Fax: (212) 447-1633.

National Society of Professional Engineers. 1420 King St., Alexandria, VA 22314-2794. Albert C. Gray, Ph.D., P.E., CAE. Phone: (703) 684-2800. Fax: (703) 836-4875. *www.nspe.org*

Organization of Professional Employees of the U.S. Department of Agriculture. P.O. Box 381, Washington, DC 20044. Phone: (202) 720-4898. Fax: (202) 720-6692. *www.usda.gov/opeda*

Overseas Federation of Teachers, AFT, AFL/CIO. Dr. Marie Sainz-Funaro, Pres., Unit 31301, Box 65, APO AE 09613. Phone: 39-0586-503418 (Italy). Steve Osborne, European Dir., PSC

808, Box 15, FPO AE 09618, Phone: 39-081-575-3710 (Italy). Margie Lally, Vice Pres., PSC 808, Box 39, FPO AE 09618, Phone: 39-081-866-1253 (Italy). *www.oftonline.org*

Patent Office Professional Association. P.O. Box 2745, Arlington, VA 22202. Ronald J. Stern, Pres. Phone: (703) 308-0818.

Police Emerald Society of the Washington D.C. Area. 6006 Greenbelt Road, Suite 320, Greenbelt, MD 20770. Brian Manion, Pres., Patrick F. O'Brien, Treas. Phone: (301) 858-0972. Fax: (301) 858-0974. E-mail: *peswashdc@aol.com*

Professional Engineers in Government (PEG), a division of NSPE. 1420 King St., Alexandria, VA 22314. Chris Hanson, Dir., Practice Divisions; Erin Garcia, Mgr., Practice Divisions. Phone: (703) 684-2884 Fax: (703) 836-4875. www.nspe.org E-mail: *egarcia@ nspe.org*

Public Employees Roundtable. P.O. Box 75248, Washington, DC 20013-5248. Phone: (202) 927-4926. Fax: (202) 927-4920. *www.theroundtable.org*

Public Employees for Environmental Responsibility. 2001 S St., N.W., Suite 570, Washington DC 20009. Jeff Ruch, Exec. Dir. Phone: (202) 265-7337. Fax: (202) 265-4192. *www.peer.org*

Senior Executives Association. P.O. Box 44808, Washington, DC 20026-4808. Carol A. Bonosaro, Pres. Phone: (202) 927-7000. *www.seniorexecs.com*

Service Employees International Union (AFL-CIO-CLC). 1313 L St., N.W., Washington, DC 20005. Andrew Stern, Pres. Phone: (202) 898-3200. *www.seiu.org*

Society of Federal Labor and Employee Relations Professionals. P.O. Box 25112, Arlington, VA 22202. Paco Martinez-Alvarez, Exec. Dir. Phone: (703) 685-4130. Fax: (703) 685-1144. *www.sflerp.org*

Uniformed Services Benefit Association. P.O. Box 418258, Kansas City, MO 64141. Larry G. Vogt, Rear Admiral, USN (Ret.), Pres. Phone: (800) 821-7912. Fax: (800) 368-7030. *www.usba.com*

Veterans Groups

American Ex-Prisoners of War. National Headquarters: 3201 E. Pioneer Parkway, Suite 40, Arlington, TX 76010-5396. Clydie J. Morgan, Nat. Adjutant. Phone: (817) 649-2979. Fax: (817) 649-0109. *www.axpow.org*

American Legion, National Economic Commission. 1608 K St., N.W., Washington, DC 20006. Phone: (202) 861-2700. Fax: (202) 833-4452. *www.legion.org*

AMVETS. National Headquarters: 4647 Forbes Boulevard, Lanham, MD 20706-4380. James B. King, PNC, Natl. Exec. Dir. Phone: (301) 459-9600. Fax: (301) 459-7924. *www.amvets. org*

Blinded Veterans Association. 477 H St., N.W., Washington, DC 20001. Thomas Miller, Exec. Dir. Phone: (800) 669-7079 or (202) 371-8880. E-mail: *bva@bva.org*

Catholic War Veterans, USA, Inc. 441 North Lee St., Alexandria, VA 22314. Phone: (703) 549-3622. Fax: (703) 684-5196. E-mail: *cwvlmt@aol.com*. *www.cwv.org*

Disabled American Veterans. National Service & Legislative Headquarters, 807 Maine Ave., S.W., Washington, DC 20024. Arthur H. Wilson, Natl. Adjt. Phone: (202) 554-3501. *www.dav.org*

Jewish War Veterans of the USA. 1811 R St., N.W., Washington, DC 20009. Dan Weiss, Nat. Commander. Phone: (202) 265-6780. *www.jwv.org*

Military Order of the Purple Heart. 5413-B Backlick Rd., Springfield, VA 22151. Phone: (703) 642-5360. Fax: (703) 642-2054. *www.purpleheart.org*

National Association for Uniformed Services/Society of Military Widows. 5535 Hempstead Way, Springfield, VA 22151. Maj. Gen. Richard D. Murray, USAF (Ret.), Pres. Phone: (703) 750-1342. Fax: (703) 354-4380. *www.naus.org*

Paralyzed Veterans of America. 801 18th St., N.W., Washington, DC 20006. Joseph L. Fox, Sr., Natl. Pres. Phone: (800) 424-8200. *www.pva.org*

U.S. Navy Cruiser Sailors Association. 55 Donna Terrace, Taunton, MA 02780. Ronald J. Maciejowski, (U.S.S. Worcester CL-144), Sec. Phone: (508)

824-0789. Fax: (508) 824-0789. E-mail: *clcanavy@aol.com*. *www.navy-cruisers.org*

Veterans of Foreign Wars. 406 West 34th St., Kansas City, MO 64111. John J. Senk, Jr., Adj. Gen. Phone: (816) 756-3390. Fax: (816) 968-1149. *www.vfw.org*

Editor's note: The above list is as inclusive and factual as possible. If any organization has been omitted or any change of officers or address has occurred, please contact Federal Employees News Digest, Inc.

Federal Employee Education and Assistance Fund

The Federal Employee Education and Assistance Fund (FEEA) is directed by Steve Bauer, and is located at Suite 200, 8441 W. Bowles, Ave., Littleton, CO 80123. It provides college scholarships, student loans, and emergency loans and grants to eligible federal and postal employees and their dependents. FEEA also administers the OK Fund; the fund established for federal employees and their families who were victims of the April 1995 federal building bombing in Oklahoma City.

FEEA, which receives no government funds, is a Combined Federal Campaign charity founded in 1986 that manages its programs through a network of more than 5,000 volunteers nationwide. Its services are:

Emergency Assistance—Financial assistance is available for hardship and need. Homelessness, utility shutoff, eviction threats, and the loss of a family member are some examples where assistance is provided to federal families. FEEA also helps federal families affected by natural disasters.

Oklahoma City—FEEA established the OK Fund to provide assistance to federal employees and their families who were victims of the bombing in Oklahoma City, as well as educational assistance to children who lost a federal employee parent in the building. President Clinton asked FEEA to establish the President's OKC Fund to guarantee a post-secondary education to every child who lost or had a parent severely disabled. Donations are still being accepted and can be sent to the address above.

Scholarships and Educational Loans—FEEA scholarships range from $500 to $1,700 per school year. Minimum requirements are at least three years of federal service and a 3.0 grade point average on the 4.0 scale. Applications are available January through April of each year. FEEA student loans include the government-backed Stafford and PLUS loans as well as two privately backed loans with no income limitations and higher lending limits than federal loans. FEEA has awarded nearly $1.5 million in scholarships to federal employees and their dependent family members.

To apply for FEEA assistance, call 1-800-323-4140 or (303) 933-7580. For information and applications on scholarships or student loans, send a self-addressed, stamped business-size envelope to FEEA, Suite 200, 8441 W. Bowles Ave., Littleton, CO 80123.

FEEA World Trade Center/Pentagon Fund—Following the tragic events of Sept. 11, 2001, the Federal Employee Education & Assistance Fund established a FEEA World Trade Center/Pentagon Fund to assist affected civilian federal employees and their families. In the first month after the terrorist attacks, the Fund provided more than $150,000 in assistance to everyone involved, including those affected by the Pennsylvania tragedy.

FEEA also is designed to ensure that the minor children of those killed or permanently injured in the attacks will be financially able to attend the college of their choice. Families may register children for the program by calling FEEA at 1-800-323-4140 and providing the following information: Employee's name and agency/department; Child's name, date of birth, and year in school; and the name, address and phone number of the child's guardian.

Families seeking assistance can call FEEA at 1-800-323-4140 or 303-933-7580. To download the emergency assistance application, go to: *www.feea.org/wtc_pentagon_app.pdf*

Donations to the Fund may be made by sending a check to: FEEA World Trade Center/Pentagon Fund, 8441 W. Bowles Ave., Suite 200, Littleton, CO 80123-9501, or via MasterCard or Visa cards by calling FEEA at 303-933-7580.

2003

JANUARY
s	m	t	w	t	f	s
			1	2	3	4
5	6	7	8	9	10	11
12	13	14	15	16	17	18
19	20	21	22	23	24	25
26	27	28	29	30	31	·

FEBRUARY
s	m	t	w	t	f	s
·	·	·	·	·	·	1
2	3	4	5	6	7	8
9	10	11	12	13	14	15
16	17	18	19	20	21	22
23	24	25	26	27	28	·

MARCH
s	m	t	w	t	f	s
·	·	·	·	·	·	1
2	3	4	5	6	7	8
9	10	11	12	13	14	15
16	17	18	19	20	21	22
23/30	24/31	25	26	27	28	29

APRIL
s	m	t	w	t	f	s
·	·	1	2	3	4	5
6	7	8	9	10	11	12
13	14	15	16	17	18	19
20	21	22	23	24	25	26
27	28	29	30	·	·	·

MAY
s	m	t	w	t	f	s
·	·	·	·	1	2	3
4	5	6	7	8	9	10
11	12	13	14	15	16	17
18	19	20	21	22	23	24
25	26	27	28	29	30	31

JUNE
s	m	t	w	t	f	s
1	2	3	4	5	6	7
8	9	10	11	12	13	14
15	16	17	18	19	20	21
22	23	24	25	26	27	28
29	30	·	·	·	·	·

JULY
s	m	t	w	t	f	s
·	·	1	2	3	4	5
6	7	8	9	10	11	12
13	14	15	16	17	18	19
20	21	22	23	24	25	26
27	28	29	30	31	·	·

AUGUST
s	m	t	w	t	f	s
·	·	·	·	·	1	2
3	4	5	6	7	8	9
10	11	12	13	14	15	16
17	18	19	20	21	22	23
24/31	25	26	27	28	29	30

SEPTEMBER
s	m	t	w	t	f	s
·	1	2	3	4	5	6
7	8	9	10	11	12	13
14	15	16	17	18	19	20
21	22	23	24	25	26	27
28	29	30	·	·	·	·

OCTOBER
s	m	t	w	t	f	s
·	·	·	1	2	3	4
5	6	7	8	9	10	11
12	13	14	15	16	17	18
19	20	21	22	23	24	25
26	27	28	29	30	31	·

NOVEMBER
s	m	t	w	t	f	s
·	·	·	·	·	·	1
2	3	4	5	6	7	8
9	10	11	12	13	14	15
16	17	18	19	20	21	22
23/30	24	25	26	27	28	29

DECEMBER
s	m	t	w	t	f	s
·	1	2	3	4	5	6
7	8	9	10	11	12	13
14	15	16	17	18	19	20
21	22	23	24	25	26	27
28	29	30	31	·	·	·

☐ = FEDERAL HOLIDAYS

New Year's Day
Wednesday, January 1

Birthday of Martin Luther King, Jr.
Monday, January 20

Washington's Birthday
Monday, February 17

Memorial Day
Monday, May 26

Independence Day
Friday, July 4

Labor Day
Monday, September 1

Columbus Day
Monday, October 13

Veterans Day
Tuesday, November 11

Thanksgiving Day
Thursday, November 27

Christmas Day
Thursday, December 25

Index

A

Administrative grievances, 273
Administrative law judges, 2, 9, 48, 233, 296, 309, 344, 352, 360, 430
Administrative appeals judges, 2
Administratively uncontrollable overtime, 171, 307
Affirmative employment programs, 343-344
Age discrimination, 249, 335, 338
AIDS in the workplace, 272
Air traffic controllers, 31, 114, 138, 143, 163, 302, 377, 429
Alimony, 17-18, 31, 119, 203, 211, 213, 219, 223, 229-232
Alternative dispute resolution and settlements, 361
Alternative form of annuity. See retirement
Alternative personnel practices
    agency-specific policies: DHS, FAA, IRS, 301-303
    demonstration projects, 233, 299
    government-wide authorities, 296-298
    performance-based organizations, 295
Title 5 exemptions, 298
Alternative work schedules, 251, 258-260, 297
Annual leave, 8, 26, 69, 117, 121, 126, 165, 169-178, 181, 191, 238, 240, 242-243, 254, 260-261, 272, 281, 297, 306-308, 310, 315, 317, 327, 371, 410
Appeals. See MSPB, EEOC, FLRA, grievances
Association rights, 280-281
Associations and other employee groups, 280-281, 429-433
Availability pay, 23, 27-28, 171

B

Bonuses
    recruitment, 19, 21, 301, 425
    referral, 19, 135, 298
    relocation, 19, 21, 301, 425
Buyouts
    eligibility and conditions, 328
    general rules, 327

C

Call-back pay, 29
Career *intern* program, 238, 296
Career transition

career transition assistance plans, 319, 322
    DoD RIF and placement benefits, 323-327
    interagency career transition assistance plans, 322
    reemployment priority lists, 321-322
Civil Rights Act, 249, 272, 335-337, 343
Civil Service Retirement System. See retirement
Child care, 259, 274-275
Child support, 17-18, 119, 203, 211, 213, 216, 219, 223, 229-232
Combined Federal Campaign, 35, 424, 433, 277
Claims
    compensation and leave, 331
    Fair Labor Standards Act (overtime), 334
    travel and relocation payments, 389-390
Compensatory damages, 343
Compensatory time, 24-25, 29, 178-180, 243, 251-255, 260, 297
Competitive service, 15, 235-238, 245-247, 268, 275, 311-313, 319-322, 324, 347
Conflicts of interest, 354-355, 357-358
Congressional Record, 143, 428
Cost-of-living adjustments (retirees), 162-163
Cost-of-living allowances (geographic), 6-12, 37-47
Court rulings, 419-422, 428
CSRS-Offset. See retirement

D

Death benefits after retirement. See retirement
Death benefits before retirement, 97-98
Decisions. See legal rulings
Deferred retirement. See retirement
Demonstration projects, 233, 299-300, 302-303
Disability retirement. See retirement
Disabled, employment of, 238-239
Discontinued service retirement. See retirement
Discrimination. See Equal Employment Opportunity Commission
Divorce
    basic effects, 219
    garnishment, 223, 229-232

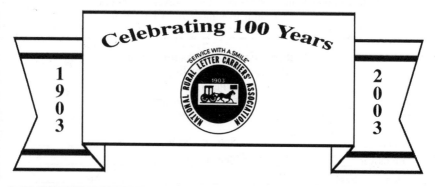